(Continued on back endsheets)

British Prose Writers of the Early Seventeenth Century

Dictionary of Literary Biography® • Volume One Hundred Fifty-One

British Prose Writers of the Early Seventeenth Century

Edited by
Clayton D. Lein
Purdue University

A Bruccoli Clark Layman Book
Gale Research Inc.
Detroit, Washington, D.C., London

Printed in the United States of America

Published simultaneously in the United Kingdom
by Gale Research International Limited
(An affiliated company of Gale Research Inc.)

The paper used in this publication meets the minimum requirements
of American National Standard for Information Sciences—Permanence
Paper for Printed Library Materials, ANSI Z39.48-1984. ∞ ™

Library of Congress Cataloging-in-Publication Data
British prose writers of the early seventeenth century / edited by Clayton D. Lein.
     p. cm. – (Dictionary of literary biography; v. 151)
"A Bruccoli Clark Layman book."
Includes bibliographical references and index.
ISBN 0-8103-5712-7 (alk. paper)
     1. English prose literature – Early modern, 1500–1700 – Bio-bibliography. 2. Authors, English –
Early modern, 1500–1700 – Biography – Dictionaries. 3. English prose literature – Early modern,
1500–1700 – Dictionaries. I. Lein, Clayton D. II. Series.
PR769.B75   1995
828'.30809 – dc20   95–5786
[B]   CIP

10 9 8 7 6 5 4 3 2 1

Contents

Plan of the Series

. . . Almost the most prodigious asset of a country, and perhaps its most precious possession, is its native literary product – when that product is fine and noble and enduring.

Mark Twain*

The advisory board, the editors, and the publisher of the *Dictionary of Literary Biography* are joined in endorsing Mark Twain's declaration. The literature of a nation provides an inexhaustible resource of permanent worth. We intend to make literature and its creators better understood and more accessible to students and the reading public, while satisfying the standards of teachers and scholars.

To meet these requirements, *literary biography* has been construed in terms of the author's achievement. The most important thing about a writer is his writing. Accordingly, the entries in *DLB* are career biographies, tracing the development of the author's canon and the evolution of his reputation.

The purpose of *DLB* is not only to provide reliable information in a convenient format but also to place the figures in the larger perspective of literary history and to offer appraisals of their accomplishments by qualified scholars.

The publication plan for *DLB* resulted from two years of preparation. The project was proposed to Bruccoli Clark by Frederick C. Ruffner, president of the Gale Research Company, in November 1975. After specimen entries were prepared and typeset, an advisory board was formed to refine the entry format and develop the series rationale. In meetings held during 1976, the publisher, series editors, and advisory board approved the scheme for a comprehensive biographical dictionary of persons who contributed to North American literature. Editorial work on the first volume began in January 1977, and it was published in 1978. In order to make *DLB* more than a reference tool and to compile volumes that individually have claim to status as literary history, it was decided to organize vol-

*From an unpublished section of Mark Twain's autobiography, copyright by the Mark Twain Company

umes by topic, period, or genre. Each of these free-standing volumes provides a biographical-bibliographical guide and overview for a particular area of literature. We are convinced that this organization – as opposed to a single alphabet method – constitutes a valuable innovation in the presentation of reference material. The volume plan necessarily requires many decisions for the placement and treatment of authors who might properly be included in two or three volumes. In some instances a major figure will be included in separate volumes, but with different entries emphasizing the aspect of his career appropriate to each volume. Ernest Hemingway, for example, is represented in *American Writers in Paris, 1920–1939* by an entry focusing on his expatriate apprenticeship; he is also in *American Novelists, 1910–1945* with an entry surveying his entire career. Each volume includes a cumulative index of the subject authors and articles. Comprehensive indexes to the entire series are planned.

With volume ten in 1982 it was decided to enlarge the scope of *DLB*. By the end of 1986 twenty-one volumes treating British literature had been published, and volumes for Commonwealth and Modern European literature were in progress. The series has been further augmented by the *DLB Yearbooks* (since 1981) which update published entries and add new entries to keep the *DLB* current with contemporary activity. There have also been *DLB Documentary Series* volumes which provide biographical and critical source materials for figures whose work is judged to have particular interest for students. One of these companion volumes is entirely devoted to Tennessee Williams.

We define literature as the *intellectual commerce of a nation*: not merely as belles lettres but as that ample and complex process by which ideas are generated, shaped, and transmitted. *DLB* entries are not limited to "creative writers" but extend to other figures who in their time and in their way influenced the mind of a people. Thus the series encompasses historians, journalists, publishers, and screenwriters. By this means readers of *DLB* may be aided to perceive literature not as cult scripture in the keeping of intellectual high priests but firmly positioned at the center of a nation's life.

DLB includes the major writers appropriate to each volume and those standing in the ranks immediately behind them. Scholarly and critical counsel has been sought in deciding which minor figures to include and how full their entries should be. Wherever possible, useful references are made to figures who do not warrant separate entries.

Each *DLB* volume has a volume editor responsible for planning the volume, selecting the figures for inclusion, and assigning the entries. Volume editors are also responsible for preparing, where appropriate, appendices surveying the major periodicals and literary and intellectual movements for their volumes, as well as lists of further readings. Work on the series as a whole is coordinated at the Bruccoli Clark Layman editorial center in Columbia, South Carolina, where the editorial staff is responsible for accuracy of the published volumes.

One feature that distinguishes *DLB* is the illustration policy – its concern with the iconography of literature. Just as an author is influenced by his surroundings, so is the reader's understanding of the author enhanced by a knowledge of his environment. Therefore *DLB* volumes include not only drawings, paintings, and photographs of authors, often depicting them at various stages in their careers, but also illustrations of their families and places where they lived. Title pages are regularly reproduced in facsimile along with dust jackets for modern authors. The dust jackets are a special feature of *DLB* because they often document better than anything else the way in which an author's work was perceived in its own time. Specimens of the writers' manuscripts are included when feasible.

Samuel Johnson rightly decreed that "The chief glory of every people arises from its authors." The purpose of the *Dictionary of Literary Biography* is to compile literary history in the surest way available to us – by accurate and comprehensive treatment of the lives and work of those who contributed to it.

The *DLB* Advisory Board

Introduction

British prose of the early seventeenth century emanates from an exceedingly contentious and eventful period full of the gravest intellectual, religious, and political tensions. It is prose to which eminent writers and thinkers have returned again and again to refresh their spirits. Samuel Taylor Coleridge read works by Francis Bacon, John Milton, Jeremy Taylor, John Donne, and Thomas Fuller with enormous delight, making acute observations on their habits of mind and style. Emily Dickinson cherished the works of Sir Thomas Browne; Henry David Thoreau enjoyed those of Browne and Izaak Walton. T. S. Eliot found the prose of Lancelot Andrewes exceptionally enlightening, preferring it to that of Donne. The finest works of the period – Bacon's *Essays* (1597), Donne's *Devotions upon Emergent Occasions* (1624), Browne's *Hydriotaphia* (1658), and Milton's *Areopagitica* (1644) – have the power to seize the imaginations of readers today as much as in their own time. The great writers confront their experience and the tensions of their times in such a bold and alert manner that they render classic statements of the human condition.

This prose is the product of a literary revolution that took shape during the final years of Queen Elizabeth and carried over into the reigns of King James and his son, Charles I. By and large, the revolution was fomented by an exceptional generation of young men who had come to London fresh from the universities, frequently to continue their education at the Inns of Court, the "third university" of the land. They belonged to a restless generation, zealous for something new – at times, at any cost – and they perfected a restless prose (deemed by some "baroque prose"), welding a stylistic rebellion to a brilliant generic revolution.

Customary treatments of this prose have been rhetorical, focusing on the period's stylistic rebellion against the effusive and elaborate styles favored by the Elizabethans. This emphasis has led to a focus on manifestations of a "Senecan" style. Seneca was certainly in the minds of these writers: "I respect matter, not words," writes Robert Burton, "remembering that of Cardan, *verba propter res, non res propter verba* [words for matter, not matter for

words], and seeking with Seneca, *quid scribam, non quemadmodum,* rather what then how to write." Joseph Hall, one of the most determined of these innovators, became so identified (by choice) with the new style that he became known as "our English Seneca." As we shall see, focus on Senecan style, while possessing considerable value, does not shed sufficient light on the experience of encountering the forms and reading the masterpieces of this period. An understanding of certain features of the prose does, however, promote understanding of its character and artistry.

One may start with some typical sentences from representative works of the early years of the century:

> Correction is never vain. Vice is a miry deepness; if thou strivest to help one out and dost not, thy stirring him sinks him in the further. (Owen Felltham)

> Cast in he was, and the storme ceased streight, the ship came safe home. And the Evening and the morning were the first day. (Andrewes)

> But when we do it, we must be allowed leisure. Ever *veniemus,* never *venimus;* ever coming, never come. We love to make no very great haste. To other things perhaps; not to *adorare,* the place of the worship of God. Why should we? Christ is no wild-cat. (Andrewes)

To compare these passages with equally representative ones by major prose writers of the previous generation, such as Sir Philip Sidney, John Lyly, and Richard Hooker, is to perceive the difference immediately. What distinguishes early-seventeenth-century prose is concision and compaction. The prose is driven by bursts of short phrases, often militantly monosyllabic. Such prose packs power and arrests attention by virtue of style alone. The writers seem determined to practice Mark Twain's celebrated advice: "Eschew surplusage." The mind is further engaged by an aphoristic content wedded to the style: "correction is never vain"; "we love to make no very great haste." Behind the emergent style is a clear dislike and distrust of the rhetorically ornate prose from the earlier era. Fewer words, more matter is the agenda of the day, and the reaction is expressed at every level of discursive practice. The stylistic revolution is carried out, however, in a highly technical fashion, one rhetorical style being canceled out by another sanctioned style.

Writers in this period enjoyed a highly focused rhetorical education that began at the grammar schools, which were attended by virtually every male writer included in their volume (those who were privately tutored generally received a similar education). This humanist education revolved around Latin, learned initially through rote repetition, and it placed intense emphasis on mastery of the theory and practice of Latin composition, stressing knowledge of rhetorical forms and figures and placing great value on the ability to move swiftly between Latin and English. Latin verse and prose selections were analyzed exhaustively, until students became astute critics of Latin style.

Becoming a critic of Latin prose style meant mastering the artful construction of the periodic sentence; students were generally educated in more than one form of sentence structure, although primary emphasis was placed on fluency in analyzing and generating the exceptionally elaborate periodic structures of Cicero. Students trained in this fashion became alert to every element of sentence construction — relationships between clauses, repetitive patterns of words, euphonious relationships within phrasings.

What distinguishes Ciceronian sentences is harmony, balance, and poise in the service of an idea, maintained over considerable space. Each of the major writers of the period learned how to construct such sentences, but it was not the form they preferred. They gave their allegiance instead to forms of sentence structure that emphasized ellipsis, imbalance, and asymmetry. These maneuvers were identified with the styles of Tacitus and Seneca, who became the preferred stylistic models. Senecan style, moreover, flowered in two contrasting modes: the *stile coupé* (curt style) and a so-called loose Senecan style. The sentences offered at the opening of this discussion represent the curt style, the more rebellious one. Members in the sentence are exceedingly short; syntactic ligatures are almost ruthlessly suppressed, making movement between members generally abrupt; imagery is infrequent (though what imagery appears is arguably more forceful and memorable by its general absence); and the prose is heavily aphoristic. Bacon, the young Donne, and Hall all joined forces with this style (deployed within the new forms), and it became the dominant style in the prose character, the early essay, and the resolve, where it received steady support from Felltham. It reached greatness in Bacon's *Essayes*.

The asymmetry among members was central to the attractiveness of the style to the rebels. Morris W. Croll, who spent much time analyzing the style, viewed its accomplishment as the attainment of a "hovering imaginative order." The asymmetrical syntax (a violent rejection of the excessively parallel syntax of the euphuistic style of the previous generation, which measured parallel members in terms of the exact number of syllables) announced an apparent spontaneity, a flow of uncalculated thought on its way to an as-yet-unknown truth.

This terse style was mastered by the majority of the writers of the period, and most of them deploy such sentences regularly in their compositions. Here is an example from Donne: "Here we are but *Viatores,* Passengers, way-faring men; This life is but the high-way, and thou canst not build thy hopes here; Nay, to be buried in the high way is no good marke; and therefore bury not thy selfe, thy labours, thy affections upon this world."

With the notable exceptions of Hall, Bacon, and Felltham, however, most of the major writers of the period preferred the "loose" Senecan form, a more relaxed version of Senecan style. It, too, favored asymmetrical syntax but placed heavy emphasis on ligatures between members, favoring connectives such as *and, but, for, where, whereas, yet,* and *though* — connectives that provided for loose relationships without insisting on strict grammatical dependency. The style is also characterized by certain marks of its own: it features members built on the absolute participle; it favors parenthesis; and, although its members are generally short (in comparison with members within full-fledged Ciceronian periods), it allows for members of greater length than are found in the curt style. Where the Ciceronian construction attains a point of balance at or near the center of the periodic movement, moreover, the loose Senecan sentence tends to drive forward, pushing progressively to the end, toward new or more complicated moral, imaginative, and spiritual perceptions. The style is overwhelmingly associative, commonly digressive, and, like the curt style, gives the impression of a mind in motion. (Croll and his follower George Williamson have been sharply challenged by later critics, however, for not recognizing that the Ciceronian sentence can also embody the mind in motion; hence, some generalizations forged earlier in the twentieth century have been abandoned). Behind both styles is a reaction against the hyperorganization of Ciceronian prose, and it seems reasonably clear that the spirits of the new generation regarded it initially as a more experimental, flexible, unofficial mode of expression. Its angularity embodied their disgust with the repetitive character of Elizabethan expression, permitting more individual variation (in the same way that the variegated structures of Donne's amorous lyrics allow for diverse representation of mental states). In the hands of the prose masters of this period such sentences were capable of fine effects, as can be seen in this passage from Browne: "Wee are not onley ignorant in Antipathies and occult qualities, our ends are as obscure as our beginnings, the line of our dayes is drawne by night, and the various effects therein by a pencill that is invisible; wherein though wee confesse our ignorance, I am sure we doe not erre, if wee say, it is the hand of God."

If on the level of style one finds the new writers rejecting Ciceronian periods, on the level of form one finds them refusing to create the elaborate fictional narratives characteristic of Elizabethan prose (Lyly's *Euphues* [1578] and Sidney's *Arcadia* [1590], for example), introducing in their place an array of new, compact, nonfictional forms of discourse — essays, paradoxes, problems, letters, characters, resolves, "conceited news." Some of these forms (and other, lengthier forms that rose to prominence during the period) continue to define discourse; to this extent, it is possible to see the period as early modern. These forms are analytic. They exhibit pointed wit. They value elaboration of learning less than its distillation, encyclopedic fullness of vision less than keenness of perception. Brief in compass, they paradoxically provide more space for the individual voice trying to define its own discursive habits.

To discuss the revolution simply in terms of prose, however, is to take too restricted a view. An aesthetic revolution was being promulgated throughout every literary domain simultaneously — drama, poetry, and prose — and the ringleaders in one territory are often influential in another. Donne and Ben Jonson are clearly at the heart of things. Jonson's movement into the comedy of humors in the same period is obviously a related revolutionary development, and it hardly seems accidental that his new comedy overlaps with the development of the prose character. Jonson's experiments in prose within his dramas likewise participate in the larger stylistic revolution and advance it. Donne is in the midst of all the revolutions, pursuing new forms in prose (the paradox and the problem) as well as in poetry.

Indeed, the revolutions fomented by Donne and Jonson in poetry bear strong resemblances to the larger patterns of the revolutions in style and form in prose writing. Both men reject the sonnet as firmly as the leading prose writers reject the prose romance, and the forms they substitute for the sonnet bear a family likeness to the forms emerging in prose. Both writers sponsor classical forms such as the epigram, the classical satire, and the letter in verse. In prose and in poetry they turn to the classical tradition for inspiration. (The classical influence can be seen to be broader when we recognize cross-generic influences: the letters of Seneca and Cicero inform the practice of the emerging essay). Similarly, Donne and Jonson fashion and promulgate styles of diamondlike brilliance: the language of poetry is brought to heel as firmly as is the language of prose, as in Donne's "I wonder by my troth, what thou, and I / Did, till we lov'd?" Discipline reigns.

The result, in both mediums, is a gain in what a contemporary termed "masculine expression." The shared stylistic premises are nowhere more apparent than in the opening gestures in all the new forms. The bold, witty openings of an essay or a finely wrought character — "He that hath wife and children hath given hostages to fortune" (Bacon); "Surely he was a little wanton with his leisure that first invented poetry" (Felltham); "An Idle Gallant Is one that was born and shaped for his clothes: and if Adam had not fallen, had lived to no purpose" (John Earle); and "A Fine Gentleman Is the cinnamon tree, whose bark is more worth than his body" (Sir Thomas Overbury) — resembles nothing so much as the brash openings of a Donne poem: "Goe, and catche a falling starre." The intention on all fronts is to snag the mind's attention at once through witty, decisive speech. The mode of utterance, in the end, is more important than the generic means of expression.

Other features come to mind. The sonnet sequence may be taken as a guide. If one places Donne's *Songs and Sonets* (originally published, without this title, in his *Poems* [1633]; the title was added in the second edition [1635]) side by side with sonnet sequences by Samuel Daniel and Michael Drayton, for instance, one quickly perceives further dimensions of the rebellion. Part of the extraordinary creative enterprise within the sonnet sequence was the attempt to render (or discover) a coherent self under pressure of passion that threatens to destroy that self. Stability of that nature is nowhere to be found within the bounds of *Songs and Sonets*: within Donne's enterprise one glimpses chaos. No stance carries through to the adjacent poem. No single constructed self, no master narrative emerges. Instead, the reader confronts a miscellany of experiences, each set forth compellingly. The perceptions of one poem jostle uncomfortably with the verities of another. A similar experience emerges in reading the early collections of prose from this period. The formal authority of the sonnet sequence carries over in some respects – Felltham, Hall, and Fuller, for example, compose "centuries" of prose compositions as the sonneteers composed "centuries" of sonnets. But within the bounds of the prose collections, whether essays or characters or resolves, one encounters a heterogeneity of experience not unlike the mode of experience charted by Donne in *Songs and Sonets,* by Andrew Marvell in his collected poems, or by George Herbert in *The Temple* (1633). They all avoid the excessively programmatic tendencies of Elizabethan literature. As Walton confesses with refreshing honesty at the outset of *The Compleat Angler* (1653), "I have not observed a method." Instead, the reader is led to enjoy untrammeled discursivity. Jolts in orientation are to be expected. Promethean dimensions of mentality and experience become featured because they best seem to represent the human condition. Burton asks: "*Fleat Heraclitus, an rideat Democritus?* in attempting to speak of these symptoms, shall I laugh with Democritus, or weep with Heraclitus? they are so ridiculous and absurd on the one side, so lamentable and tragical on the other: a mixed scene offers itself, so full of errors and a promiscuous variety of objects, that I know not in what strain to represent it." Only a discourse infinitely subtle and flexible could hope to capture the "promiscuous variety" of mind and matter. The sheer exuberance of roving mentality reaches its apogee in Burton's polyphonous discourse, but in one sense Burton simply takes to an extreme the favored form of mental action. Michel de Montaigne, whom Burton advances as a model for his own style, found ready admirers and imitators throughout the period, and the alliance of these discursive habits with ironic and satiric habits of mind and temperament should not go unremarked.

Binding Montaigne's form of prose and the prose of this period is not simply associative discursivity but what Ralph Waldo Emerson called Montaigne's "most uncanonical levity." Wit drives all activity in this period: life is lived and prose is written (as are poems and plays) in expectation to be adjudged witty: that is the affirmation of its success. (One recalls here Donne's flamboyant parody of the liturgy in his personal portrait as a melancholic lover and Fuller's recollection of the battles of wit between Jonson and William Shakespeare as the truly memorable feature of their lives to be preserved.) To his friend Henry King, Donne was a "Rich soule of wit, and language," and Thomas

Carew's tribute to Donne has become immortal: "*Here lies a King, that rul'd as hee thought fit / The universall Monarchy of wit.*" "Witty" was Sir Kenelm Digby's instant reaction on reading Browne's *Religio Medici* (1642) – he was also considerably flustered by some of its thinking; Samuel Pepys, decades later, concurred in that judgment, averring that Browne's book was one of the three "most esteemed and generally cried up for wit in the world."

The wit of seventeenth-century prose has many dimensions. One of the most attractive dimensions is the fashion by which it is universally applied to promote shrewd social and psychological observation, as in Earle's "A Plain Country Fellow Is one that manures his ground well, but lets himself lie fallow and untilled" or in Fuller's "Almost twenty years since I heard a profane jest, and still remember it. How many pious passages of far later date have I forgotten. It seems my soul is like a filthy pond, wherein fish die soon, and frogs live long." Little prose of distinction exists in this period apart from a certain ironic detachment – a detachment that can, when necessary, burst into biting satiric commentary. Seventeenth-century wit manifests itself perpetually, too, in what Thomas Corns, in his study of Milton's language, calls "ludic lexis," the sportive use of language. Writers are disposed to explore and indulge in the ambiguities and playful dimensions of language. (In no period is the pun more pervasive in the common style of expression.) Donne's paradox, "That Nature is our worst Guide," is wholly representative, centering its witty maneuvers on the slippery connotations of the word *nature* itself.

More important, wit is repeatedly used to breach generic decorum – Montaigne's "uncanonical levity" – thereby creating prose of multitudinous tonalities. The most serious discussion will be leavened by flashes of humor and flights of irreverent observation. In this respect Walton reflects his age when he announces to the reader that for his work not to read "*dull,* and *tediously,* I have in severall places mixt some innocent Mirth." Even a fishing tract needs leavening. And he excludes the overly sober reader: "if thou be a severe, sowr complexioned man, then I here disallow thee to be a competent Judg." When Walton goes further and declares that the resulting texture is justified because "the whole discourse is a kind of picture of my owne disposition," he comes closer to the character of the age. Behind the prose of the seventeenth century lie minds determined to represent themselves and to incorporate reaches of the mind unavailable to sobriety, imaginations disposed to associative habits of mentality.

The period is distinguished by an autobiographical impulse. It can hardly be claimed that interest in the self suddenly appeared in the early seventeenth century; the autobiography of Margery Kempe (written circa 1432–1436) would explode any such notion. Clearly, medieval men and women had a sense of self that was capable of rendition. Nonetheless, it appears that some special combination of cultural forces intersected in the late sixteenth century to encourage and advance self-expression, and self-representation is a crucial and distinctive feature of the literature of the English Renaissance and the early seventeenth century.

The formal sign of such interest is the explosion of intimate forms — the diary, the epistle, and, of course, the fully developed autobiography. It is in these forms that the woman's voice — those of Lady Margaret Hoby and Lady Anne Clifford, for example — begins to emerge with a special pungency. Donne wrote so many letters revealing his mental states that his biographer R. C. Bald affirmed that he is the first poet in the language of whom a sufficient biography could be written; Edmund Spenser or Shakespeare cannot be recaptured in the same fashion. And the early seventeenth century produced several memorable self-portraits, particularly those by Edward, Lord Herbert of Cherbury; Browne; and Donne.

More remarkable, however, is what may be termed autobiographical penetration. Interest in the self is such a dominant force in the discourse of the period that it is rare to find writing that lacks autobiographical touches. It is in the writings of the early seventeenth century that one is able to assemble a reasonable number of glimpses into childhood experience in the early modern world: Donne, Burton, Felltham, Browne, Richard Brathwaite, and Henry Peacham all left records of that experience.

More important, it is in the early seventeenth century that men and women become motivated not simply to chronicle their activities but also to express their self-perceived individuality. Walton's remark, cited earlier, is representative: even a fishing tract may be bent to the purpose of delineating a specific way of living in the world, and ranging through the various attempts of men and women in this epoch to provide such a delineation is one of the pleasures presented by seventeenth-century prose. To watch Browne sift through his idiosyncrasies, Donne describe and analyze specific reac-

tions to experience, or Burton struggle to come to grips with the winsome vagaries of his mind is to meet intelligences of the past in a way generally unavailable before this period, and the riches of autobiographical expression are extraordinary. The writers are sufficiently self-conscious, moreover, to probe the issues of selfhood in ways verging on the modern: they attempt to determine the shape of the self, to establish its relation to received conditions (social and hereditary), and to recover the most important experiences underlying the formation of their sensibilities (hence their need for the recovery of childhood experience). It is but a step from these private operations to full-scale biographical enterprise, which, not surprisingly, also emerges powerfully in this period. (Joan Webber contends, furthermore, that various ideological conditions produced distinct forms of self-realization throughout the period).

Equally characteristic of the best writing of the early seventeenth century is a certain spaciousness manifest at every level of structure, content, and style. Titles alone reveal something of the unusual space constructed in the works; Francis Osborne's *A Miscellany of Sundry Essays, Paradoxes, and Problematicall Discourses, Letters, and Characters* (1659) is a delightful example. Genres bleed into and influence other genres with such consistency that it must be granted that writers in this period rarely bound themselves to a strict sense of genre in the neoclassical sense. One has, accordingly, Nicholas Breton's *Characters upon Essais Morall, and Divine* (1615), Sir William Cornwallis's *Essayes Or Rather Encomions* (1616) and *Essayes of Certain Paradoxes* (1616), and Geffray Mynshul's *Essayes and Characters of a Prison and Prisoners* (1618).

All of the major forms of the period, in fact, become accretive, incorporating and subsuming lesser forms. In Burton's and Browne's works, medical treatise and scientific tract embrace elements of the personal essay. In the works of Thomas Adams the sermon absorbs the prose character; in Walton's hands the character is absorbed into the larger discursive form of biography. In Donne's writings the sermon incorporates the resources of the formal meditation; and in his *Devotions upon Emergent Occasions* Donne fuses formal meditation with spiritual autobiography. In *Religio Medici,* on the other hand, Browne joins autobiography and essay.

A surprising number of prose works from this period are, thus, generically disruptive. What is one to make of Burton's *The Anatomy of Melancholy* (1621), which combines within its vast boundaries generic elements drawn from the anatomy, the medical treatise, the book of casuistry, the essay, the *consolatio philosophiae,* the sermon, the satire, the utopia, the imaginary voyage, the treatise on education, the conduct book, the love dialogue, the paradox, and the picaresque novel, as well as features from Desiderius Erasmus's *Moriae encomium* (1511; translated as *The Praise of Folie,* 1549)? Walton's *Compleat Angler* interweaves the elements of a manual of instruction with elements drawn from georgic and pastoral traditions, treatises of moral philosophy, and tracts for the times and offers along the way a small verse anthology. Critics are repeatedly compelled to discuss the lasting productions of the period as idiosyncratic creations. The texts openly rehearse the interpenetration of forms and discourse modern critics attempt to discuss as constitutive features of all writing.

Seventeenth-century prose presents some peculiar complications in terms of modern knowledge and tastes. It may never be possible to recover fully the linguistic dexterity enjoyed by men trained so intensely through exercises that moved seamlessly between English and Latin. Their linguistic flexibility was extraordinary, their range of expression boundlessly inventive. Hence, another quality of seventeenth-century prose is its lexical range. Words from the Anglo-Saxon heritage jingle ceaselessly with terms drawn from Latin, Greek, and a host of Continental languages. It is easy to mistake the precise meanings of many terms; the prose demands of the modern reader, in consequence, a certain adroitness and rather constant recourse to the dictionary. One of the supreme pleasures shared by writers in this period, moreover, was a zest for neologism, an aspect of witty literary creativity as apparent in Donne and Browne and Milton in the early seventeenth century as it is in James Joyce in the twentieth. Here, as in few other ways, we experience the writers as makers.

In poetry and prose the leading writers are virtuoso wordsmiths, forging vocabulary wholesale for the necessary expressive tasks. They make no concessions to the reader. In *Pseudo-Martyr* (1610) Donne engages the reader with such words as *insimulates, grassation, deprehend, illations,* and *tetrical.* Burton experiments less in this fashion, but he nonetheless coins *jument, diverb, perstringe, immund,* and *collogue.* Samuel Johnson reproached Browne, in particular, for "this encroaching licence," accusing him of having poured into the language "a multitude of exotick words." It is true that in one extended passage alone Browne challenges the reader with such

concoctions as *decussation, forcipal, impulsor, hypomochlion* (borrowed by Coleridge), and *fulciment.* But his orientation does not differ from that of his contemporaries. The wit and expressive feats of seventeenth-century prose in part depend on such lexical expansiveness.

Analysis of the specific verbal texture of each writer frequently seems more rewarding than a concentration on variations within categories of Senecan prose. Donne, Burton, Bacon, and Browne, for example, all qualify as Senecan stylists, but that label helps not at all in determining the quality of one's experience as one reads them (reading Burton can be like taking a roller-coaster ride; Browne at times makes one want to banish polysyllables forever; Donne's tortuous sentences make one sprint for aspirin). Each writer creates a characteristic verbal fabric, one uniquely tailored to the movements of his mind and to interests and demands of the task at hand. Thus the understandings supplied by an awareness of Senecan style need supplementation.

Appreciation of many remarkable effects obtained by these writers in their finest moments, for example, demands that attention be paid to every feature of their finely honed utterances. Seventeenth-century prose makes regular use of the full range of resources one expects to find in poetry — intricate structures of rhythm and sound, imagery used both for local and structural effects (in Browne's and Donne's works certain patterns of imagery attain symbolic status) — all supporting developing patterns of meaning. Every feature of the language, not simply the structure of the sentences, requires investigation if one is to grasp the craft involved. In the rhythmic and sonorous prose of Donne and Milton and Browne, in particular — although their writing is not alike in most respects — one encounters some of the most subtle and harmonious prose composed by writers in the English tradition.

Discussions of Senecan prose also generally fail to recognize other resources of sentence construction that are equally prominent in the period's prose. Brian Vickers contends that one of the factors underlying the exceptional excellence of prose in this period is a mastery of syntactical symmetry. The artistry here involves consummate planning, particularly in the careful construction of the internal units of the sentence. One might consider the opening sentences of Donne's final sermon, presented schematically:

Buildings stand by the benefit
    of their foundations

```
            that sustain and support them,
    and of their buttresses
            that comprehend and embrace them,
    and of their contignations
            that knit and unite them.
The foundations
            suffer them not to sink,
the buttresses
            suffer them not to swerve,
and the contignation and knitting
        suffers them not to cleave.
```

These sentences have been meticulously crafted to clarify the salient ideas and to deliver the greatest impact, and considerable resources have been brought to bear in their construction. In addition to the parallel structures, we may note the extensive alliteration (*buildings, benefit, buttresses, embrace; foundations, suffer; contignation, knit, unite; suffer, swerve*). There are more-precise technical operations that would be apparent to people trained as Donne was: symmetry of length (isocolon), careful correspondence in respective parts of successive clauses (parison), and the same word (*them*) ending consecutive phrases (epistrophe). These are rhetorical resources to which writers of the seventeenth century return insistently, as in a sample from Bacon's *Essays:*

```
A man cannot speak to his son but as a father;
            to his wife but as a husband;
            to his enemy but upon terms;
whereas a friend can speak as the case requires;
            and not as it sorteth with the person.
```

Symmetrical structure can be used to many expressive ends, commonly to give greater power to a delayed observation, as in Bacon's essay "Of Friendship":

```
For a crowd is not company;
    and faces are but a gallery of pictures;
    and talk      but a tinkling cymbal,
            where there is no love.
```

Here is Felltham:

```
I never yet knew any man so bad
            but some have thought him honest,
                        and afforded him
love.
Nor ever any              so good,
            but some have thought him vile,
                        and hated him. . . .
And few again are         so just
            as that they seem not to some unequal;
either the ignorance,
        the envy,
        the partiality of those that judge
```

```
do constitute a various man.
                    (italics added)
```

This passage is a thoughtful observation, presented deftly. Felltham was advanced initially to define the revolutionary "Senecan" style. It is clear from the second example, however, that multiple forces operate within his prose and that a mastery of symmetrical syntax can be one of the most important. Even those involved in the anti-Ciceronian reaction (Donne, Bacon, and Felltham among them) shape their discourse artfully and expressively by exploiting syntactic symmetry at crucial moments in their writing. The example from Felltham is especially elegant, for symmetrical structure is felt strongly even while the author artfully varies the length and arrangement of each of the individual units. An understanding of the full rhetorical resources available thus leads to continually deepening appreciation of the wit and artistry of early-seventeenth-century prose.

The rhetorical and dialectical training shared by writers in the early seventeenth century similarly attuned them to the larger structures of discourse — to the partition and division of material — and some of the literary wit in the period manifests itself through patterns of organization. The reader is meant to be attentive to patterning and to pursue the implications of the patterns presented, whether it be the divisions of the text of a sermon or partitions within larger works of poetry and prose. Browne's yoking of *Hydriotaphia* to *The Garden of Cyrus,* thereby forming a dual structure, is as significant as Donne's republication of his *An Anatomy of the World* (1611), under the title *The First Anniuersarie,* in the same volume as *The Second Anniuersarie* (1612) or Milton's division of *De Doctrina Christiana* (1825) into two parts: the divisions clarify meanings. Rhetorical training disposed the writers, moreover, to a predilection for superimposed rather than organic form, and special knowledge is, on occasion, required to unlock structures and meanings. Jonson's manipulation in *The Alchemist* (1612) of ideas and elements drawn from alchemy is a case in point. Throughout the Renaissance, writers were much concerned with what Browne termed the "more curious Mathematicks" of the universe, the Art of Nature. Writers frequently reflect what they take to be the divine numbered structure of the world by replicating those patterns in their art. Among the major works of the seventeenth century, numerological structures appear in Bacon's *New Atlantis* (1626), Donne's *Devotions upon Emergent Occasions,* and the works of Browne, as well as in Milton's *Paradise Lost* (1667). Behind the creation of "centuries" of aesthetic objects, likewise, lies the notion of 100 as a perfect, divine number. The same logic applies to Donne's decision to organize his reflections in the *Devotions upon Emergent Occasions* into tripartite units. Just as writers imposed form on the sentence, so, too, the great writers of the period – Bacon, Donne, Milton, Burton, and Browne – produce intricately patterned larger forms.

The general love of contrariety and antithesis and the deep-rooted devotion to paradox in the writings of this period can likewise be traced to rhetorical training – in particular, to training in the practice of Ciceronian *controversia* – that was intensified in many cases by legal studies. Much of the wit of the period involves play with surface, rhetorical paradox, but the disposition of the age is to pursue that interest to more profound levels of philosophical and religious paradox. Again and again Donne turns to paradox to express the strange states of being in which he or his imagined lovers appear to find themselves, whether the terrifying paradox of loving ("Wee can dye by it, if not live by love") or the paradoxical spiritual condition imposed on him by divinity ("That I may rise, and stand, o'erthrow mee"). His sermons and *Devotions upon Emergent Occasions* drive to similar revelations. In the seventeenth century, moreover, the paradox, explored as a brief, minor form much like the essay earlier in the century, is raised by the major writers to new formal heights: Donne's *Biathanatos* (1647), Burton's *The Anatomy of Melancholy,* and Browne's *Religio Medici* are all extended formal paradoxes (to maintain that doctors – universally suspected of being atheists – could have a religion was to maintain a paradox indeed).

This disposition of mind produced realizations of stunning pungency. It leads Donne to notice that there is "scarce any *happines,* that hath not in it so much of the *nature* of false and base money, as that the *Allay* is more then the *Mettall.* Nay is it not so . . . even in the exercise of *Vertues?*" Browne stumbles to the insight that "we are what we all abhorre, *Anthropophagi* and Cannibals, devourers not onley of men, but of ourselves . . . we have devoured our selves." A like refusal to simplify and equal willingness to recognize antithetical relations leads Burton, in the greatest work of paradoxy from the period, to the realization that melancholy is simultaneously cause and effect, disease and symptom. To be human, he discovers, is to live paradox, for "Melancholy in this sense is the character of mortality." (Frank L. Huntley has rightly described *Religio Medici* as "the paradox of one man's mind.")

At stake in such prose is the nature of one's understanding of the world. When writers from this period move beyond flashy rhetorical paradoxes to paradoxes of a more serious variety, they challenge the reader's understanding. The reader is brought to distrust conventional wisdom and ordinary lazy ways of thought, frequently by way of struggling toward a deeper understanding of a vaster (frequently divine) form of truth. Early-seventeenth-century wit, in this regard, is honed to sort through the odd data of reality for evidence of a reality beyond that taught by custom and beyond a reality given authority by the senses. There is a tendency in this wit, moreover, to modulate to wonder, a feature allying it to medieval habits of mind. When one moves to the prose of the end of the century, one experiences a profound sense of loss. The prose remains self-advertisingly witty, but its range is constricted. In the age of John Dryden, wit has shriveled into raillery and urbanity.

All this said, however, it must be stressed that too much can be made of rhetorical matters. In truth, many prose styles were practiced in the early seventeenth century. Various versions of the plain style were overwhelmingly dominant, and the racy, colloquial style of "Martin Marprelate," the pseudonymous author of the *Marprelate Tracts* (1588–1589), found imitators throughout the period, first in the drama, then in the fiercely contentious religious and political writings that erupted in the middle of the century. Although a more learned style does characterize more of the great prose from this period than not, one finds enormous stylistic diversity in writings from the early seventeenth century – divergences in style as great as the divisions in political and religious opinion.

The more experienced writers, moreover, exhibit an unusual self-consciousness which leads them to be more than casually interested in the nature of their own textuality. The narratives they fashion possess peculiar dimensions that they advertise by means of shared central metaphors. Many of them, deeply read in travel literature, conceive of their narratives as voyages of discovery, with the final result unknown: "I will adventure," declares Burton, comparing himself thereby to the great discoverers and merchant adventurers of his time. Gale H. Carruthers, Jr., has pointed out how many of Donne's sermons revolve around the trope of a journey, and *The Compleat Angler* delivers its instruction by means of a journey. (Rosalie L. Colie notes that the trope of the anatomy, given great popularity through the work of Vesalius, is likewise a metaphor for all kinds of "discoveries.") In *Hydriotaphia* Browne deploys the trope with an archaeological twist, commencing the work with the idea of discovery that the work will pursue: "In the deep discovery of the Subterranean world, a shallow part would satisfie some enquirers." He is aroused by the rare and arbitrary operation of time, which has made new knowledge possible: "Time hath endlesse rarities, and shows of all varieties; which reveals old things in heaven, makes new discoveries in earth, and even earth it self a discovery." Note his assumption that the full resources of intelligence are needed to decode deeper layers of reality. Equally dominant is the trope of the labyrinth. For Donne its use is necessary to describe the soul: "Poore intricated soule! Riddling, perplexed, labyrinthicall soule!" Browne, Burton, Bacon, and Donne all use this figure to describe the tortuous turnings of their narratives and thoughts. For Walton the trope expresses the difficulty facing Donne's biographer – "And now, having brought him through the many labyrinths and perplexities of a various life: even to the gates of death and the grave; my desire is, he may rest." Much of the extraordinary narrative energy of texts from this period arises from jostlings between labyrinthine textual maneuvers and intellectual frames imposed on the material. The texts become sites of unusual intellectual, emotional, and organizational strain. Of Donne, Alastair Fowler ventures to say that "No prose more dynamic had been achieved in English."

The struggle with labyrinth and order highlights central features of the period's prose: the search for the organizing principles of the world, for the shape of truth itself. As Donne wrote to a friend, "Our soul is not sent hither, only to go back again: we have some errand to do here." The greater writers of the early seventeenth century are engaged in ruthless, honest, passionate quests for truth, quests that often bring them into conflict with received opinion and, on occasion, with political authorities. The truths they provisionally perceive about their world and themselves are truths that arbiters of public opinion find unsettling. But Donne's immortal challenge in *Satyre 3* (1633) rings through the century: "Keepe the'truth which thou hast found." Burton will not yield his melancholic insights; Browne will not retract his genial heresies, nor Milton his notions on divorce; Donne will not burn his heretical manuscript on suicide.

And what earns continuing respect, as it gained the respect of Coleridge, Emerson, Yeats, Thoreau, Dickinson, and Eliot, is the ability of these writers to reach explosive moments of revelation. Their unique capacities in learning and acumen, wedded to awesome fluencies in modes of expression, in confrontation with the enormous pressures and perplexities of life, lead to stunning disclosures that transfix readers' minds as powerfully today as they did then. Discourse leading to such moments as Donne's realization that "No man is an island entire of itself; every man is a piece of the continent, a part of the main"; Browne's rapturous insight that "Life is a pure flame, and we live by an invisible Sun within us"; or Milton's conviction that "as good almost kill a man as kill a good book: who kills a man kills a reasonable creature, God's image; but he who destroys a good book, kills reason itself, kills the image of God, as it were, in the eye," leading to the impassioned cry, "Give me the liberty to know, to utter, and to argue freely according to conscience, above all liberties" is writing to be cherished. Hints of these and many other treasures to be discovered in the artful prose of this period can be discerned in the entries that follow.

– *Clayton D. Lein*

Acknowledgments

This book was produced by Bruccoli Clark Layman, Inc. Karen L. Rood is the senior editor for the *Dictionary of Literary Biography* series. Philip B. Dematteis was the in-house editor.

Production coordinator is James W. Hipp. Photography editor is Bruce Andrew Bowlin. Photographic copy work was performed by Joseph M. Bruccoli. Layout and graphics supervisor is Penney L. Haughton. Copyediting supervisor is Denise W. Edwards. Typesetting supervisor is Kathleen M. Flanagan. Systems manager is George F. Dodge. Julie E. Frick and Laura S. Pleicones are editorial associates. The production staff includes Phyllis A. Avant, Ann M. Cheschi, Melody W. Clegg, Patricia Coate, Joyce Fowler, Laurel M. Gladden, Stephanie C. Hatchell, Rebecca Mayo, Kathy Lawler Merlette, Jeff Miller, Pamela D. Norton, Delores I. Plastow, Patricia F. Salisbury, Emily Sharpe, William L. Thomas, Jr., and Robert Trogden.

Walter W. Ross and Robert S. McConnell did library research. They were assisted by the following librarians at the Thomas Cooper Library of the University of South Carolina: Linda Holderfield and the interlibrary-loan staff; reference-department head Virginia Weathers; reference librarians Marilee Birchfield, Stefanie Buck, Cathy Eckman, Rebecca Feind, Jill Holman, Karen Joseph, Jean Rhyne, Kwamine Washington, and Connie Widney; circulation-department head Caroline Taylor; and acquisitions-searching supervisor David Haggard.

British Prose Writers of the Early Seventeenth Century

Thomas Adams

(1582 or 1583 – circa 26 November 1652)

Moira P. Baker
Radford University

BOOKS: *The Gallants Burden: A Sermon Preached at Pavles Crosse, the Twentie Nine of March, Being the Fift Sunday in Lent* (London: Printed by W. White for Clement Knight, 1612);

Heaven and Earth Reconcil'd: A Sermon Preached at Saint Paules Church in Bedford, October 3, 1612 (London: Printed by W. White for Clement Knight, 1613);

The White Devil Or The Hypocrite Vncased: Jn a Sermon Preached at Pavls Crosse, March 7. 1612 (London: Printed by Melchisedech Bradwood for Ralph Mab, 1613);

The Deuills Banket: Described in Foure Sermons. 1. The Banket Propounded; Begunne. 2. The Seasoned Seruice. 3. The Breaking vp of the Feast. 4. The Shot or Reckoning. The Sinners Passing-Bell. Together with Physicke from Heauen (London: Printed by Thomas Snodham for Ralph Mab, 1614);

The Divells Banket: Described in Six Sermons (London: Printed by Thomas Snodham for Ralph Mab & John Budge, 1614);

Englands Sicknes, Comparatively Conferred with Israels: Diuided into Two Sermons (London: Printed by Edward Griffin for John Budge & Ralph Mab, 1615);

The Blacke Deuill or The Apostate: Together with The Wolfe Worrying the Lambes. And The Spirituall Navigator, Bound for the Holy Land. In Three Sermons (London: Printed by William Jaggard, 1615);

Mystical Bedlam: Or, the World of Mad-Men (London: Printed by George Purslowe for Clement Knight, 1615);

Diseases of the Sovle: A Discourse Divine, Morall, and Physicall (London: Printed by George Purslowe for John Budge, 1616);

A Divine Herball: Together with A Forrest of Thornes. In Five Sermons. 1. The Garden of Graces. 2. The Prayse of Fertilitie. 3. The Contemplation of the Herbes. 4. The Forrest of Thornes. 5. The End of Thornes (London: Printed by George Purslowe for John Budge, 1616);

The Sacrifice of Thankefulnesse: A Sermon Preached at Paules Crosse, the Third of December Being the First Adventuall Sunday, Anno 1615. Whereunto Are Annexed Fiue Other of His Sermons Preached in London, and Else-where; Neuer before Printed (London: Printed by Thomas Purfoot for Clement Knight, 1616);

The Sovldiers Honovr. Wherin by Diuers Inferences and Gradations It Is Euinced, That the Professions Is Iust, Necessarie, and Honourable; to Be Practiced of Some Men, Praised of All Men. Together with a Short Admonition Concerning Munition, to thir Honour'd Citie. Preached to the Worthy Companie of Gentlemen, That Exercise in the Artillerie Garden: And Now on Their Second Request, Published to Further Vse (London: Printed by Adam Islip & Edward Blount, 1617);

The Happines of the Church. Or, A Description of Those Spirituall Prerogatives wherewith Christ Hath Endowed Her. Considered in Some Contemplations vpon Part of the 12. Chapter of Hebrewes. Together with Certain Other Meditations and Discourses vpon Other Portions of Holy Scriptures . . . Being the Summe of Diuerse Sermons Preached in S. Gregories London (London: Printed by George Purslowe for John Grismand, 1618);

Eirenopolis: The Citie of Peace (London: Printed by Augustine Matthewes for John Grismand, 1622);

The Barren Tree: A Sermon Preached at Pavls Crosse October 26. 1623. (London: Printed by Augustine Mathewes for John Grismand, 1623);

The Temple: A Sermon Preached at Pauls Crosse the Fifth of August. 1624. (London: Printed by Augustine Mathewes for John Grismand, 1624);

Three Sermons Preached 1. In Whitehall, March 29. Being the First Tuesday after the Departure of King Iames into Blessednesse. 2. In Christs Church, at the Trienniall Visitation of the Right Reverend Father in God, the Lord Bishop of London. 3. In the Chappell by Guildhall, at the Solemne Election of the Right Honourable the Lord Maior of London (London: Printed by Augustine Matthewes & John Norton, 1625);

Five Sermons Preached vpon Sundry Especiall Occasions. Viz. 1 The Sinners Mourning Habit: In Whitehall, March 29. Being the First Tuesday after the Departure of King Iames into Blessednesse. 2 A Visitation Sermon: In Christs Church, at the Trienniall Visitation of the Right Reverend Father in God the Lord Bishop of London. 3 The Holy Choice: In the Chappell by Guildhall, at the Solemne Selection of the Right Honorable the Lord Maior of London. 4 The Barren Tree: At Pauls Cross Octob. 26. 5 The Temple: At Pauls-Crosse. August 5. (London: Printed by Augustine Mathewes & John Norton for John Grismand, 1626);

The Workes of Tho: Adams: Being The Svmme Of His Sermons, Meditations, And Other Divine And Morall Discovrses. Collected and Published in one intire Volume. With Additions of Some New, and Emendations of the Old (London: Printed by Thomas Harper & Augustine Mathewes for John Grismand, 1629);

A Commentary or, Exposition upon the Divine Second, Epistle Generall, Written by the Blessed Apostle St. Peter, 2 volumes (London: Printed by R. Badger & F. Kyngston for Jacob Bloome, 1633);

Gods Anger and Mans Comfort: Two Sermons (London: Printed by Thomas Maxey for Samuel Man, 1652).

Editions: *An Exposition upon the Second Epistle General of St. Peter,* edited by James Sherman (London: Samuel Holdsworth, 1839);

The Three Divine Sisters, Faith Hope and Charity, edited by W. H. Stowell (London: Nelson, 1847; New York: Carter, 1847);

The Works of Thomas Adams: Being the Sum of His Sermons, Meditations, and other Divine and Moral Discourses, 3 volumes, edited by Thomas Smith (Edinburgh: Nichol, 1861–1862);

The Sermons of Thomas Adams, the Shakespeare of Puritan Theologians: A Selection, edited by John Brown (London: Cambridge University Press, 1909).

Vilified by John Vicars in a 1647 Puritan tract as "a known profane pot-companion . . . and otherwise a loose-liver, a temporizing Ceremony monger, and malignant against the parliament," Thomas Adams was acclaimed in the nineteenth century as the "prose Shakespeare of Puritan theologians." His condemnation for presumed anti-Puritan leanings and his rehabilitation as an eminent Puritan divine suggest the ironies of politics and literary history. Like his better-known contemporary Bishop Joseph Hall, Adams, though Calvinist in his theology, cannot be called a Puritan in any strict use of that vexed term. He maintained a moderate position within the Church of England, suffering persecution for this stance amid the political and ecclesiastical controversies that racked England during the first half of the seventeenth century. And like Hall, whose works he admired and imitated, Adams could appease neither High Church Laudians nor Puritans during those crucial years that hurtled England toward civil war. One of the most popular preachers in London during the first quarter of the seventeenth century, Adams fell into disrepute during the sequestrations of the 1640s. Yet the eclipse of his reputation belies the achievement of his earlier career and his enduring stature as a gifted preacher. In his study of Puritan preaching, John Brown ranks Adams above the silver-tongued Henry Smith; Morris W. Croll finds him to be an important transitional figure in the development of English prose style; William Fraser Mitchell calls him the "greatest of all early Puritan divines"; and Douglas Bush singles out the writings of Adams, Lancelot Andrewes, John Donne, and Jeremy Taylor as exemplars of seventeenth-century religious prose at its finest.

Born in 1582 or 1583, Adams was educated at Cambridge, where he took his B.A. in 1601 and his M.A. in 1606. Following his ordination in 1604 Adams served in several scantily paid rural posts. In 1605 he was licensed to the curacy of Northill in Bedfordshire, but he was dismissed when Northill College Manor was sold. His dismissal marked the beginning of a lifelong struggle to maintain himself and his family; the first of his three children, Ann, was born in January 1609 (neither the date of Adams's marriage, nor his wife's name, are known). His experience of financial difficulty must have made him keenly aware of the exploitation of the poor that attended the social and economic changes of his time, for he preached a gospel of social justice: resounding with the voice of prophetic utterance, his sermons excoriated abuses that wrung profit from the weak during the profound dislocations that shaped early modern England.

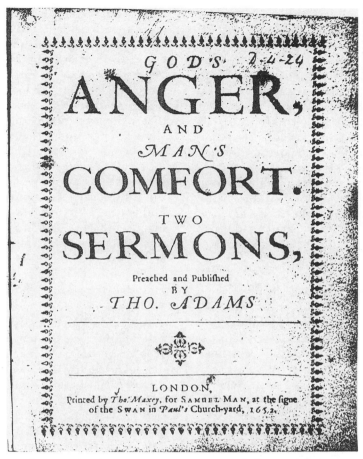

*Title page for Thomas Adams's final publication (Union Theological
Seminary Library, New York)*

By 1611 Adams had assumed the vicariate of Willington, where he preached and prepared his sermons for publication and where his wife bore their other two children: Jane in April 1612 and Edward in January 1613. While at Willington, Adams also began to distinguish himself as an occasional preacher, appearing twice at Paul's Cross in London and once before the clergy at Bedford for the visitation of the archdeacon. His first Paul's Cross sermon, *The Gallants Burden* (1612), fared respectably in print, going through three printings by 1616. Preached at Paul's Cross in 1613 and published the same year, *The White Devil,* his most popular sermon, reached five editions by 1621. During his time at Willington, Adams also completed his first of several sermon suites, *The Devills Banket* (1614), which went into two editions.

The sermons Adams published during the early years of his ministry sound the theme that was to run throughout his career, reveal the rich literary traditions that inform his prose, and demonstrate his consummate skill in accommodating literary forms to his homiletic purposes. In the preface to *The Devills Banket* Adams announces: "The main intents of all preachers and the contents of all sermons aim to beat down sin and convert sinners." Conventional as this concern seems, Adams, like the other great preachers of his day, drew on a wealth of rhetorical, devotional, and literary traditions to forge a distinctive idiom and individualized style. In his preface to the 1615 edition of *The White Devil* he discloses the literary tradition that exerted the greatest influence on his idiom and style: "It is excepted that I am too merry in describing some vice. Indeed, such is their ridiculous nature, that their best conviction is derision. . . . Others say, I am otherwhere too satirically bitter. It is partly confessed." Through his manipulation of satiric conventions Adams urges his auditors to recognize the absurdity of vice, repudiate their own sins, and seek forgiveness and comfort in the grace of God.

One of the most striking literary features of Adams's sermons is his ubiquitous use of the satiric prose character, a form introduced into English prose by Joseph Hall's *Characters of Vertues and Vices* in 1608. Hall's collection ushered in a vogue that extended through the enormously popular "characters" that Thomas Overbury appended to his poem *A Wife, Nowe a Widowe* (1614) — producing a collection marked by extravagant fancy, pungent wit, and flippant mockery of social folly — and John Earle's *Microcosmographie* (1628). Drawing on earlier homiletic traditions, as well as the contemporary literary practices of Hall and the Overburians, Adams fashions characters appropriate to his preaching of conversion. In *The Gallants Burden,* for example, he includes generalized sketches, in the tradition of the medieval *descriptio,* of four "scorners" that destroy the commonwealth: atheists, epicures, libertines, and "common profane" clergy. *The White Devill* presents a series of twelve characters modeled after those of Hall, whom he calls "our worthy Divine and best Characterer." Unjust magistrates, deceitful lawyers, bribe takers, greedy merchants, impropriators (those who seize or occupy church lands), unjust landlords, grain engrossers, enclosers of common lands, debauched taverners, flattering counselors, extortionary brokers, and usurers appear as they truly are — thieves who prey upon the poor. The flatterer, for example, "eate[s] like a Moth into liberall mens coates. . . . Doth his Lord want money? he puts into his head such fines to be levied, such grounds inclosed, such rentes improved: . . . Sinne hath not a more impudent bawd, nor his master a more impious theefe, nor the commonwealthe a more sucking horse-leech." The four sermons of *The Devills Banket,* a tour de force in which Adams integrated into the older "figure" sermon form a series of satiric characters, use the metaphoric framework of a feast complete with a host, inviters, food, guests, a banquet house, and the inevitable "shot" (bill) to analyze specific sins and their consequences.

In 1614 Adams accepted an appointment as vicar of Wingrave. While there he undertook a lectureship at St. Gregory's, in the shadow of St. Paul's Cathedral in London. During Adams's years at Wingrave several collections of his sermons were published, and he was even more in demand as a popular city preacher. The publication of Overbury's collection, which reached its fifth impression and grew to eighty-two characters in 1615, spurred Adams to charge his characters with flippant wit and edge them with caustic irony. In *The Mysticall Bedlam* (1615), one of his most imaginative figure sermons, Adams uses the frame of a morris of bedlamites to expose the sins of the world in a series of

twenty characters. Introducing dramatic dialogue into the form, Adams shapes highly theatrical characters such as the Epicure: "Can you tend it, Belly-God? The first question of my Catechisme shall be, *What is your name? Epicure. Epicure? What's that?* . . . One that would make my belly my executour. . . . Rehearse the Articles of your beleefe. . . . I beleeve that midnight revels, perfumed chambers, soft beds, close curtains, and a Dalilah in mine arms, are very comfortable." In the treatise *Diseases of the Soule* (1616) he uses his most complex metaphoric schema for organizing a collection of characters. Examining the nature, cause, symptoms, and cure of nineteen bodily diseases, Adams analyzes the vices that plague the soul. In "A Forrest of Thornes," first published with "A Divine Herball" in 1616, Adams couches his characters of common social abuses in the metaphor of thorns, briars, and brambles that rend the flesh of the commonwealth.

As the provocative titles of Adams's sermons suggest, he appealed to the popular taste for the sensational that was evident in the drama of his time. In *Mysticall Bedlam* he marshals grotesque images of death and bodily decay with as chilling an effect as the bitter musings of Vindice on his dead mistress's beauty in Cyril Tourneur's *The Revenger's Tragedy* (1608). Drawing on the memento mori tradition that informs Tourneur's play, Adams warns: "Know that the earth shall one day set her foot on your neckes, and the slime of it shall defile your sulphered beauties: . . . be not proud, be not madde: you must die." The macabre array of dancing madmen in the same sermon evokes not only the social practice of exhibiting inmates of Bethlehem Hospital but also the morris of bedlamites cavorting in the lurid half-light of John Webster's *The Duchess of Malfi,* which was performed sometime before December 1614. In *The Devills Banket* Adams exploits the affective force of lurid images to initiate a process of meditation in his auditors. Likening hell to a fetid charnel house, he asks his listeners to imagine a "deepe Lake, full of pestilent dampes and rotten vapours; . . . some corpses standing upright in their knotted winding-sheetes; others rotted in their Coffins: . . . The sight is afflicted with darknes and ugly devils; . . . the smelling with noysome stenches: . . . the feeling with intolerable, yet unquenchable fire." Obviously aware of the market in which his sermons competed for a readership, Adams skillfully integrated popular satiric forms or theatrical conventions with devotional practices to preach conversion effectively both in the pulpit and in print.

In 1618 Adams published *The Happines of the Church,* a collection of twenty-seven sermons gathered for the press during a period of illness. He was appointed rector of St. Bennet's, near Paul's Wharf, London, in 1619; he would reside there until the end of his life, earning an unpredictable living that was largely dependent on funds available to St. Paul's Cathedral. In December 1619 Adams's wife died, leaving their two daughters and son in his care. During a subsequent period of illness Adams wrote *Eirenopolis* (1622), an eloquent treatise in which he allegorizes the four gates of London in an appeal for peace amid the growing factionalism of James's reign. Still much in demand in other pulpits, he preached *The Barren Tree* at Paul's Cross in 1623, dedicating it to his friend and patron Donne, Dean of St. Paul's. Returning to Paul's Cross in 1624 for his final appearance, Adams preached *The Temple* in commemoration of King James's deliverance from the Gunpowder Plot. Adams concluded his sermon by calling James "The Defender of the Faith" who had insured "that our Temples be not profaned with Idols, nor the Service of God blended with superstitious devices." The appearance of *Three Sermons* (1625) suggests Adams's continuing prominence, since it includes sermons preached for important civil, ecclesiastical, and court occasions: for the lord mayor's election, for the triennial visitation of the bishop of London, and for the bereaved audience at Whitehall two days after James's death. Culminating his publication of sermons, *The Workes of Tho: Adams,* comprising sixty-three sermons and three treatises, appeared in 1629.

No further sermons by Adams were published until the final two appeared as *Gods Anger and Mans Comfort* in 1652. His only intervening work was *A Commentary or, Exposition upon the Divine Second, Epistle Generall, Written by the Blessed Apostle St. Peter* (1633), two massive folio volumes totaling 1,634 pages, on which he worked between 1620 and 1633. The learned and elegant capstone to his career, the commentary reaches a more sophisticated level of scriptural exegesis and theological analysis than is possible in the sermon form. As in his sermons, he uses both the older euphuistic style, with its sound devices or schemata, and the newer Senecan style, with its emphasis on brevity and point.

It is difficult to explain Adams's abrupt disappearance from public view. Much about his ministry would have been distasteful to William Laud, who had become bishop of London in 1628 and archbishop of Canterbury in 1633 and whose increasingly repressive episcopacy silenced many suspected of Puritan leanings. Adams's staunch defense of the monarchy and ecclesiastical hierarchy notwithstanding, his strongly Calvinist doctrines,

his bitter antipapal sentiments, his wish that matters of ceremony be left "indifferent" rather than enforced, his criticism of the popish "idolatry" that threatened to creep into the Church of England, and his popularity as a lecturer may have raised suspicions about his conformity.

Ironically, Adams fared little better at the hands of nonconforming Puritans. His loyalty to the king, his tolerance of ceremony, and his support of an Episcopalian form of church government would have made him objectionable to the more radical Puritans who were gaining ascendancy in Parliament. Unable to escape the political vicissitudes of his times, Adams was sequestered, as were many other clergymen unsympathetic to the Parliamentarians' cause. By 1642 he was no longer rector of St. Bennet's, although he was allowed to remain in residence in the parish house until his death. During the final months of his life Adams relied on the charity of his former parishioners; in the dedicatory epistle to *Gods Anger and Mans Comfort* Adams thanks them for their support in his "necessitous and decrepit old age." Referring, no doubt, to the political and religious upheavals of his own day, Adams claims in "Gods Anger": "David's pestilence of three dayes was a storm soon blown over: . . . Gods displeasure hath dwelt longer upon us." Yet in his final sermon, speaking as one who has experienced the anguish of personal loss and the contradictions of a world "all in pieces," Adams urges his auditors to repent and seek solace in "the God of all comfort." The exact date of Adams's death is unknown; he was buried on 26 November 1652.

Recognized today as a noteworthy preacher in an age characterized by dazzling pulpit oratory, Adams developed a highly flexible and distinctive homiletic style. Throughout his career he skillfully drew on the full range of prose styles available to him, blending the old and the new, the euphuistic and the Senecan, the ornate and the emerging essay styles to create subtle rhythmic effects in his preaching of conversion. Responding to changing literary tastes and developments in genre, Adams modified popular satiric and dramatic conventions to shape sermons that are at times astonishing in their vitality, wit, and affective force. A resourceful writer and learned theologian who called himself simply a "preacher of God's word," Thomas Adams need not be compared to William Shakespeare: his prose can stand on its own.

References:
Moira P. Baker, " 'The Dichotomiz'd Carriage of All Our Sermons': Satiric Structure in the Ser-

mons of Thomas Adams," *English Renaissance Prose,* 3 (October 1989): 1–17;

Baker, "The Homiletic Satires of Thomas Adams," Ph.D. dissertation, University of Notre Dame, 1982;

Benjamin Boyce, *The Theophrastan Character in England to 1642* (Cambridge, Mass.: Harvard University Press, 1947);

John Brown, *Puritan Preaching in England* (London: Hodder & Stoughton, 1900);

Douglas Bush, *English Literature in the Earlier Seventeenth Century* (Oxford: Oxford University Press, 1962);

Morris W. Croll, "The Sources of the Euphuistic Rhetoric," in John Lyly, *Euphues: The Anatomy of Wit; Euphues & His England,* edited by Croll and Harry Clemons (London: Routledge / New York: Dutton, 1916; reprinted, New York: Russell & Russell, 1964), pp. xv–lxiv;

Edgar F. Daniels, "Thomas Adams and 'Darkness Visible' (*Paradise Lost,* I, 62–3)," *Notes and Queries,* 204 (October 1959): 369–370;

Cabell V. Flanagan, "Robert Southey on Thomas Adams," *Notes and Queries,* 197 (20 December 1952): 554–555;

Flanagan, "A Survey of the Life and Works of Thomas Adams," Ph.D. dissertation, University of Pennsylvania, 1954;

William Haller, *The Rise of Puritanism* (New York: Columbia University Press, 1928);

David Mills Harralson, "The Sermons of Thomas Adams," Ph.D. dissertation, Kent State University, 1969;

Laurence Hedges, "Thomas Adams and the Ministry of Moderation," Ph.D. dissertation, University of California, Riverside, 1974;

Millar Maclure, *The Pauls Cross Sermons: 1543–1642,* University of Toronto Department of English Studies and Texts, no. 6 (Toronto: University of Toronto Press, 1958);

William Fraser Mitchell, *English Pulpit Oratory from Andrewes to Tillotson: A Study of its Literary Aspects* (New York & Toronto: Macmillan, 1932; reprinted, New York: Russell & Russell, 1962);

William Mulder, "Style and the Man: Thomas Adams, Prose Shakespeare of Puritan Divines," *Harvard Theological Review,* 48 (April 1955): 129–152;

W. J. Paylor, *The Overburian Characters* (Oxford: Blackwell, 1936);

Francis Xavier Prior, "Animal Analogy in the Writings of Thomas Adams," Ph.D. dissertation, Saint John's University, 1969;

John Vicars, *A Just Correction and Inlargement of a Scandalous Bill of the Mortality of the Malignant Clergie of London, and other Parts of the Kingdome, Which Have Been Justly Sequestred from Their Pastorall-Charges, and since that (some of them) Defunct, by Reason of the Contageous Infection of the Prelaticall Pride and Malignancie of their Owne Spirits; since the Yeare 1641. to this Present Yeare, 1647* (London, 1647).

Lancelot Andrewes

(25 September? 1555 – 25 September 1626)

Trevor A. Owen
Potomac State College of West Virginia University

BOOKS: *The Wonderfull Combate (for Gods glorie and Mans saluation) betweene Christ and Satan: Opened in seuen most excelent, learned and zealous Sermons, vpon the Temptations of Christ, in the wildernes, &c.* (London: Printed by John Charlwood for Richard Smith, 1592);

The Copie of the Sermon preached on good Friday last before the Kings Maiestie (London: Printed by Robert Barker, 1604);

A Sermon Preached before the Kings Maiestie, at Hampton Court, Concerning the Right and Power of Calling Assemblies. On Sunday the 28. of September, Anno 1606 (London: Printed by Robert Barker, 1606);

Tortura Torti: Sive, Ad Matthaei Torti librum responsio, qui nuper editus contra apologiam serenissimi potemtissimique principis, Iacobi, Dei gratia, Magnae Britanniae, Franciae, & Hiberniae regis, pro ivramento fidelitatis, anonymous (London: Printed by Robert Barker, 1609);

Responsio ad Apologiam Cardinalis Bellarmini; quam nuper edidit contra Praefationem Montioriam. Serenissimi ac Potentissimi Principis Iacobi, Dei Gratia Magnae Britanniae, Franciae, & Hiberniae Regis, Fidei Defensionis, Omnibvs Christianis Monarchis, Principibus atque Ordinibus inscriptam (London: Printed by Robert Barker, 1610);

A Sermon Preached before His Maiesty, On Sunday the fifth of August last, at Holdenbie (London: Printed by Robert Barker, 1610);

A Sermon Preached before the Kings Maiestie at White-Hall, On Munday the 25. of December, Being Christmas day, Anno 1609 (London: Printed by Robert Barker, 1610);

A Sermon Preached before His Maiestie at White-Hall, on Tuesday the 25. of December being Christmas Day. By the Bishop of Elie His Maiesties Almoner. Anno 1610 (London: Printed by Robert Barker, 1611?);

A Sermon Preached before His Maiestie at White-Hall: On the 24. of March last, being Easter Day, and being also the day of the Beginning of His Maiesties most Gracious Reigne (London: Printed by Robert Barker, 1611);

Scala coeli: Nineteene Sermons Concerning Prayer. The First Sixe Guiding to the True Doore: The Residue Teaching How so to Knocke Thereat That Wee May Enter. The Former Part Containing a Preparation to Prayer, the Latter an Exposition upon the Seuerall Petitions of the Lords Prayer (London: Printed by N. Okes for F. Burton, 1611);

A Sermon Preached before His Maiestie, At Whitehall, on Easter day last, 1614 (London: Printed by Robert Barker, 1614);

A Sermon Preached before His Maiestie, At Whitehall the fift of Nouember last, 1617 (London: Printed by John Bill, 1618);

A Sermon Preached before His Maiestie At Whitehall, on Easter day last, 1618 (London: Printed by John Bill, 1618);

Sermons (London: Printed by Robert Barker, 1618);

A Sermon Preached at White-Hall, on Easter Day the 16. of April, 1620 (London: Printed by Robert Barker & John Bill, 1620);

XCVI. Sermons by the Right Honorable and Reverend Father in God, Lancelot Andrewes, late Lord Bishop of Winchester. Published by His Majesties speciall Command, edited by William Laud and John Buckeridge (London: Printed by George Miller for Richard Badger, 1629);

Reverendi in Christo Patris, Lanceloti, Episcopi Wintoniensis, Opvscvla Quaedam Posthvma, edited by Laud and Buckeridge (London: Printed by Felix Kyngston for Richard Badger & Andrew Hebb, 1629);

Stricturae; or, A Briefe Answer to the XVIII. Chapter of the First Booke of Cardinall Perron's Reply Written in French, to King James — His Answer Written by Mr. Casaubon in Latine (London: Printed by Felix Kyngston for Richard Badger & Andrew Hebb, 1629);

Two Answers to Cardinall Perron, and Two Speeches in the Starr-Chamber (London: Printed by Felix

Lancelot Andrewes; portrait by an unknown artist (Jesus College, Oxford)

Kyngston for Richard Badger & Andrew Hebb, 1629);

Institutiones Piae or Directions to Pray, Also A short exposition of the Lords Prayer, the Creed, the tenne Commandements, Seven Penitential Psalmes, and seaven Psalmes of Thanksgiving paraphrased, edited by Henry Isaacson (London: Printed for H. Seile, 1630);

A Patterne of Catechisticall Doctrine: Wherein many profitable questions touching Christian Religion are handled. And the whole Decalogue succinctly and judiciously expounded (London: Printed for William Garrett, 1630);

A Manuall of Directions for the Visitations of the Sicke, with Sweete Meditations and Prayers to Be Used in Time of Sicknesse (London: Printed by R. Cotes for S. Cartwright, 1642);

The Morall Law Expovnded, 1. Largely, 2. Learnedly, 3. Orthodoxly: That Is, the Long-Expected, and Much-Desired Worke of Bishop Andrewes, upon the Ten Commandments: Being His Lectures Many Yeares since in Pembroch-Hall Chappell, in Cambridge . . . Never before This, Published in Print. Whereunto Is Annexed Nineteene Sermons of His, upon Prayer in Generall, and upon the Lords Prayer, in Particular. Also seven Sermons upon Our Saviours Tentations, in the Wildernesse, edited by John Jackson (London: Printed for Michael Sparke, Robert Milbourne, Richard Cotes & Andrew Crooke, 1642);

Sacrilege a Snare: A Sermon Preached, Ad Clerum, In the Vniversity of Cambridg, by the R. Reverend Father in God Lancelot Andrews: Late L. Bishop of Winchester. When he proceeded Doctor in Divinity. Translated for the benefit of the Publike (London: Printed by T. B. for Andrew Hebb, 1646);

Of Episcopacy: Three Epistles of Peter Moulin Doctor and Professor of Divinity. Answered By the Right Reverend Father in God Lancelot Andrews, Late Lord Bishop of Winchester. Translated for the benefit of the Publike (N.p., 1647);

Of the Right of Tithes: A Divinity Determination in the Publike Divinity Schools of the University of Cambridg. Translated for the Benefit of the Publike (London: Printed for Andrew Hebb, 1647);

The Private Devotions of the Right Reverend Father in God Lancelot Andrewes. Late Bishop of Winchester (London: Printed for Humphrey Moseley, 1647); Greek and Latin version published as *Rev. patris Lanc. Andrews episc. Winton: Preces private graecè & latinè,* edited by John Lamphire (Oxford: Sheldonian Theatre, 1675);

A Manual of Directions for the Sick: With Many Sweet Meditations and Devotions of the Right Reverend Father in God, Lancelot Andrews, Late L. Bishop of Winchester. To Which Are Added Praiers for the Morning, Evening, and H. Communion. Translated out of a Greeke ms. of His Private Devotions, translated by Richard Drake (London: Printed for Humphrey Moseley, 1648);

A Manual of the Private Devotions and Meditations of the Right Reverend Father in God Lancelot Andrews, Late L. Bishop of Winchester: Translated out of a fair Greek Ms. of his Amanuensis, translated by Drake (London: Printed by W. D. for Humphrey Moseley, 1648);

A Learned Discourse of Ceremonies Retained and Used in Christian Churches, edited by Edward Leigh (London: Printed for Charles Adams, 1653);

Ἀποσπασματια *sacra; or, A Collection of Posthumous and Orphan Lectures: Delieved at St. Pauls and St. Giles His Church by the Right Honourable and Reverend Father in God, Lancelot Andrews, Lord Bishop of Winchester. Never Before Extant* (London: Printed by R. Hodgkinsonne for Humphrey Moseley, Andrew Crooke, D. Pakeman, L. Fawne, R. Royston & N. Elkins, 1657);

The Forme of Consecration of a Church or Chappel: And of the Place of Christian Buriall. Exemplified by the R.R.F. in God Lancelot Andrewes, late Lord-Bishop of Winchester, in the consecration of the Chappel of Jesus in the foresaid diocess (London: Sold by T. Garthwait, 1659).

Editions and collections: *The Works of Lancelot Andrewes, Sometime Bishop of Winchester,* 11 volumes, edited by J. P. Wilson and James Bliss (Oxford: Parker, 1841–1854);

The Preces privatae of Lancelot Andrewes, Bishop of Winchester, translated by Frank Edward Brightman (London: Methuen, 1903; New York: Living Age, 1961);

Sermons, edited by G. M. Story (Oxford: Clarendon Press, 1967).

In his own age Lancelot Andrewes was well known as a churchman, a controversialist, and, above all, an extraordinary preacher at the courts of Queen Elizabeth and King James I. With Richard Hooker he was the architect of the Church of England, steering a middle course between Roman Catholicism and Puritanism, and he defended the position of his church and monarch in his works of controversy. He was esteemed by his contemporaries as *Stella Praedicantium* (the star of preachers), but after his death his style of preaching was rejected as extravagant and old-fashioned. In the twentieth century Andrewes would have been forgotten if T. S. Eliot had not paid him tribute in his essay "Lancelot Andrewes" (1932) and had not quoted from Andrewes's second Wise Men sermon in the first five lines of his poem "The Journey of the Magi" (1927). Although Andrewes's works of controversy have long been forgotten, he is still revered as a saint in the Anglican church. Passages from his sermons retain their interest for the modern reader because of their exciting prose style, created in the most glorious period of English prose: the age of the King James Bible, which Andrewes helped to translate.

Andrewes was born in London in 1555. The exact date of his birth is uncertain – he says that he was born on a Thursday but does not give the month – but one tradition places it on 25 September, the same date as his death. His mother's name, apparently, was Joan; his father was Thomas Andrewes, a descendant of an old Suffolk family, a mariner, and in his later years one of the masters of Trinity House, a fraternity of seamen. The eldest of thirteen children, at about the age of eight Andrewes was sent to Cooper's Free School in Radcliffe, where the master, a Mr. Ward, recognizing the boy's abilities, persuaded his parents that he should not be apprenticed to a trade. Andrewes was sent to the Merchant Taylors' School in London, perhaps attending at the same time as the future poet Edmund Spenser. The school's headmaster was the noted educator Richard Mulcaster, and under his supervision the boys learned Latin and, perhaps, Greek and Hebrew. Andrewes's scholarly abilities were as quickly recognized by Mulcaster as they had been by Ward, and the boy's devotion to scholarship would be vividly described by John Buckeridge in his sermon at Andrewes's funeral: " 'he accounted all that time lost that he spent not in his studies,' wherein in learning he outstripped all his equals, and his indefatigable industry had almost outstripped himself. He studied so hard when others played, that if his parents and masters had

Pembroke College, Cambridge University, where Andrewes was a student throughout the 1570s

not forced him to play with them also, all the play had been marred." He would study late into the night and rise at four in the morning to resume his work.

In September 1571 Andrewes entered Pembroke College, Cambridge, under one of the new Greek scholarships established by Dr. Thomas Watts, archdeacon of Middlesex. He was also named scholar of Jesus College, Oxford, although he did not take up residence there. During Andrewes's early years at Pembroke College, Spenser was also enrolled as a student. In 1575 Andrewes received the bachelor of arts degree, and in 1576, having defeated a fellow student, Thomas Dove, in a scholastic trial, he was appointed a fellow of Pembroke Hall. In 1578 he was granted the master of arts and was appointed catechist of Pembroke College. In 1580 he was ordained deacon and made junior treasurer of the college; in 1581 he was made senior treasurer of Pembroke and incorporated master of arts at Jesus College, Oxford; and in 1585 he took the bachelor of divinity degree at Cambridge. Andrewes's devotion to scholarship at Cambridge is related by Henry Isaacson, his first biographer, who declares that in a few years Andrewes "had laid the foundations of all arts and sciences, and had gotten skill in most of the modern languages." Andrewes's appetite for scholarship was so keen that during his Easter vacation visits to his parents' home he directed his father to find someone who could guide him in attaining some new language or art. Isaacson also vividly describes Andrewes's love for the beauties of nature, an enthusiasm he would later reveal in some of the best passages of his sermons: "his ordinary exercise and recreation was walking either alone by himself, or with some other selected companion, with whom he might confer and argue, and recount their studies; and he would often profess that to observe the grass, herbs, corn, trees, cattle, earth, waters, heavens, any of the creatures, and to contemplate their natures, orders, qualities, virtues, uses, &c, was ever to him the greatest mirth, content, and recreation that could be: and this he held to his dying day."

In 1578, as catechist of Pembroke College, Andrewes delivered a series of lectures on the Ten

Commandments that were so popular that they attracted students from other colleges and people from the surrounding countryside. His popularity as a lecturer is confirmed by John Jackson, an early editor of the lectures, who declares that "he was scarce reputed a pretender to learning and piety then at Cambridge, who made not himself a disciple of Mr. Andrewes by diligent resorting to his Lectures." The lectures were published under the titles *A Patterne of Catechisticall Doctrine* (1630) and *The Morall Law Expounded* (1642). In the preface to the former work Andrewes presents a justification of the Christian faith in general and the position of the Church of England in particular, and the lectures that follow could be described as a handbook of Christian morality. In his lecture on the fourth commandment, his insistence that the keeping of the Sabbath is a moral law that the Christian must obey represents the same position as that of the Puritans. In its themes and style, *A Patterne of Catechisticall Doctrine* provides a good introduction to the sermons Andrewes would later preach; thus, it is an important work of apprenticeship.

Andrewes's reputation soon brought him to the attention of the nobility. In 1586 he was made chaplain to Henry Hastings, third Earl of Huntingdon and president of the Council of the North (the northern counties of England), who was sympathetic to Puritanism. Andrewes accompanied the earl to the north where, Isaacson declares, "God so blessed his painful preachings, and moderate private conference, that he converted recusants, priests, and others to the Protestant religion." Andrewes also came to the attention of Sir Francis Walsingham, secretary of state to Queen Elizabeth. While Andrewes was at Cambridge, Walsingham had hoped to make him reader of controversies so that he could maintain certain points of the Puritans, with whom Walsingham was sympathetic. Andrewes had not accepted this position, but through Walsingham he was made vicar of St. Giles, Cripplegate; prebendary of the Collegiate Church of Southwell; and prebendary of St. Pancras, in St. Paul's, London, all in 1589. Andrewes expressed his gratitude and sense of responsibility to Walsingham in a letter of 24 May 1589: "My prayer to God is, that I may not live unworthy of these so honourable dealings, but that in some sort, as His holy wisdom shall appoint, I may prove serviceable to your honour, and to your honour's chief care, this Church of ours."

As vicar of St. Giles, Andrewes was engaged in visiting the sick, and it is probable that he used his own *Manuall of Directions for the Visitations of the Sicke* (1642) in his ministry. The work is a collection of scriptural meditations and devotions appropriate for the sick Christian in various stages of spiritual enlightenment; the scriptural passages are interspersed with probing questions from the minister and recommended responses for the sick person. It is designed mainly for Christians who are grievously ill or dying; and the sense of human mortality that hovers over the work is nicely captured in the first sentence, an ominous scriptural command: "Set thine house in order, for thou shalt die."

In 1590 Andrewes and forty-one other preachers were appointed by the bishop of London to visit imprisoned sectaries and try to persuade them to renounce their unorthodox beliefs. Andrewes visited the Separatist Henry Barrow and the Puritan John Udal, but both refused to recant. At the opening of the Convocation of Canterbury on 20 February 1593 Andrewes preached a powerful sermon in Latin attacking the abuses of the Church of England. He preached frequently at the court of Queen Elizabeth, and in March 1597 she appointed him prebend of the eleventh stall of Westminster Abbey. He was elected treasurer of the chapter on 5 December 1597, and in July 1601 he was nominated by Sir Robert Cecil as dean of the Collegiate Church of St. Peter, Westminster Abbey. Andrewes developed a warm relationship with the boys at Westminster School that was described in later years by Bishop John Hacket, one of his former students. Hacket relates that Andrewes "never walked to Chiswick for his recreation without a brace of this young fry, and in that wayfaring leisure had a singular dexterity to fill those narrow vessels with a funnel. And . . . he sent for the uppermost scholars to his lodgings at night, and kept them with him from eight till eleven, unfolding to them the best rudiments of the Greek tongue, and the elements of the Hebrew grammar."

Queen Elizabeth died on 24 March 1603, but Andrewes's fortunes continued to rise under King James I. Invited to attend the Hampton Court Conference from 14 to 16 January 1604, where a new English translation of the Bible was commissioned, Andrewes was chosen chairman of the Westminster Company, whose task was to translate the books of Genesis through 2 Kings. The Authorized or King James Version of the Bible was published in 1611 and remains a monument of English prose.

It was under James, too, that Andrewes received his highest ecclesiastical positions, being appointed bishop of Chichester in 1605, bishop of Ely in 1609, and bishop of Winchester in 1618. James also appointed him privy councillor of England on

29 September 1616 and dean of the Chapels Royal on 1 January 1619. Andrewes accompanied the king on his progress to Scotland in 1617, was present at Queen Anne's funeral in 1619, and in 1621 was appointed by the king to the bribery trial of Francis Bacon and to the commission investigating the charge of "casual homicide" against the archbishop of Canterbury, George Abbott, who had accidentally shot a groom during a hunting party.

It was under James that Andrewes somewhat reluctantly took on the task of controversialist. His two longest works of controversy grew indirectly out of the Gunpowder Plot, a conspiracy by certain Catholics to blow up the king and members of Parliament on 5 November 1605. As a newly elected bishop, Andrewes attended Parliament that day and might have been injured or killed had the plot been successful. The threat to King James led to the institution of an oath of allegiance to the king, but in 1606 and again in 1607 Pope Paul V ordered English Catholics to abstain from taking the oath. The controversialist Cardinal Robert Bellarmine defended the pope's position, and Andrewes, commissioned by the king to respond to the cardinal, did so in his *Tortura Torti,* published in June 1609. In this Latin work of 496 pages Andrewes attacks what he considers the excessive powers of the papacy and affirms the duty of all subjects to obey their monarch. In answer to Bellarmine's accusation of novelty in the English church, Andrewes declares: "Nec innovamus quicquam; renovamus forte, quae apud veteres illos fuerent, et apud vos jam in *novitates* abierunt" (We do not innovate; it may be we renovate what was customary with those same ancients, but with you has disappeared in *novelties*). Bellarmine responded to Andrewes's work with a treatise; Andrewes replied in turn with his longest work, the 500-page *Responsio ad Apologiam Cardinalis Bellarmini* (1610). He again defends the Church of England, proudly proclaiming it "Catholic" and asserting that it was closer to the spirit of the primitive church than is the Roman church. Andrewes's labors on behalf of the Church of England were much appreciated by the king, who, according to Isaacson, selected Andrewes "as his choicest piece, to vindicate his regality against his foulmouthed adversaries."

Andrewes apparently found the public role of controversialist uncongenial, but he enthusiastically embraced the private life of devotion that is revealed in his *Private Devotions* (1647). Buckeridge called Andrewes's life a life of prayer, declaring that he spent about five hours a day in meditation. It was in these solitary times of prayer, as well as in his hours of private study, that he received the in-

spiration for his sermons, and it was in the pulpit that Andrewes achieved his greatest triumphs as court preacher to Queen Elizabeth and King James.

Andrewes was well aware of the popularity of sermons during his age. In a sermon preached before King James in 1607 he observes, "now is the world of sermons," and in one of his last sermons, preached before James on Ash Wednesday 1623, he compares the many sermons pouring from the presses to measures of seed thrown on the ground. For Andrewes both the content and the style of a sermon were important. In the Ash Wednesday sermon he declares that "The only true praise of a sermon is, some evil left, or some good done upon the hearing of it." In his catechism he had advised Cambridge students that the minister's task was to seek new ways of expressing "old matters."

Andrewes's sermons are enriched by the Bible, classical literature, and the writings of the church fathers. Especially evident in Andrewes's style is a love of words that is revealed in the thoroughness with which he examines each word of the biblical texts of his sermons. In a Nativity sermon preached in 1614, for example, he playfully dissects the word *Immanuel* into three parts, which he calls "a second kind of Trinity": *Im* is Christ, *anu* is we (humanity), and *El* is God. Andrewes is sensitive to the sounds of words; he frequently uses rhyme, as in his paraphrase of the angel's reassuring words to the frightened shepherds: "your terror groweth out of error." He brings together words of similar sounds to emphasize differences, as in his contrast of Christ's appearance during his earthly life and at the Second Coming: "He that cometh here in clouts, He will come in the clouds one day." In common with many in his age, he delights in punning, as in his description of the abasement of Christ: "He that sits on the throne thus be thrown in a manger." And he creates new words, coining *Immanu-hell* and *Immanu-all,* calling Christ's death a "satis-passion" and describing Christ as being "minorated" and "minimated" when he left heaven for earth.

Andrewes favors simple, often monosyllabic words and short, pithy sentences, a preference he expresses in a passage from his sermon on the text "Remember Lot's Wife": "it fareth with sentences as with coins: in coins, they that in smallest compass contain greatest value are best esteemed: and in sentences those that in fewest words comprise most matter, are most praised." The short sentences and phrases that make up Andrewes's paragraphs provide fine examples of the Senecan prose style favored by English writers of the early seventeenth century.

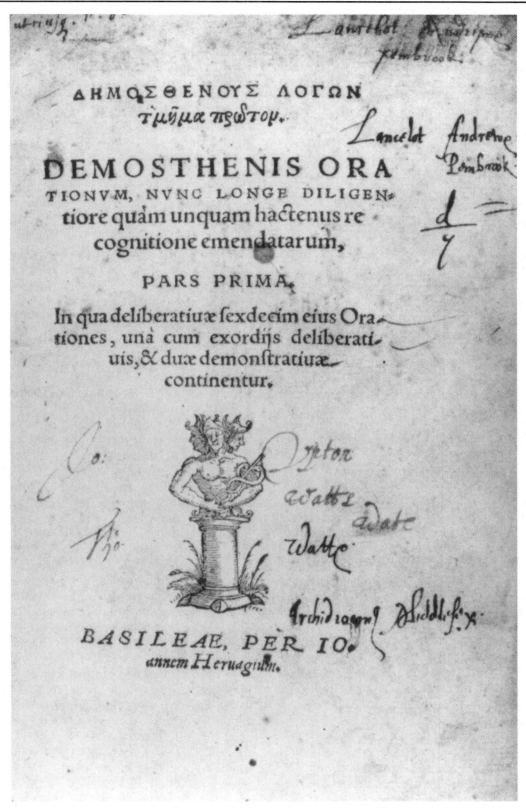

Andrewes's signature on the title page of a copy of Demosthenes' orations (Pembroke College Library, Cambridge University)

Andrewes's prose is enhanced by the power and richness of his imagery. Many of his images, such as maps, perspective glasses, and those derived from medicine and law, are common to his age; especially prominent in his work are images from the theater and from nature. Andrewes has been taken to task by later critics for his more far-fetched images, which have been labeled metaphysical. Some of Andrewes's metaphysical imagery was borrowed from the church fathers, but some was, apparently, original. A characteristic example is his question about the Holy Ghost and Christ in his 1611 Pentecost sermon: "Are they like two buckets? one cannot go down, unless the other go up?" The effect of this grotesque kind of imagery is surprise; its extravagance indelibly impresses the point being illustrated on the minds of the congregation or readers.

Perhaps the aspect of Andrewes's style that is most jarring to the sensibilities of the modern reader is his practice of weaving Latin – and occasionally Greek and Hebrew – into the fabric of his English prose. Andrewes's congregations at court, however, were as familiar with Latin as with English, and they probably enjoyed hearing the text expounded in two languages. Since Andrewes almost always follows a Latin quotation with an English translation, he achieves both richness and emphasis. In his first Nativity sermon, preached in 1605, for example, the suggestiveness of the Latin words and the repetition of the idea in English blend to create a vivid picture of the miserable abode of humanity: "*inter pulices, et culices, tineas, aracneas et vermes;* our place is here 'among fleas and flies, moths and spiders, and crawling worms.' There is our place of dwelling."

Andrewes's sermons are carefully structured, single-mindedly and thoroughly developing the sermon text word by word. In constructing his sermons he closely followed the traditional pattern inherited from the Middle Ages, a structure that is as formal as that of a symphony. It consists of the introduction or exordium, which includes the division of the text, the exposition of the text, and the conclusion. In a typical Andrewes sermon the introduction discusses the significance of the day on which the sermon is delivered and the appropriateness of the text for the day. The division breaks the text into sections and subsections and serves as a convenient outline of the rest of the sermon. The exposition, the longest part of the sermon, is a thorough analysis of the text, and the conclusion is an application of the exposition to the congregation.

Andrewes's themes are those that are basic to Christianity: humanity's fall and its redemption through the birth, sacrificial death, and Resurrection of Jesus Christ, presented against the vivid background of the holy days of the church. Andrewes celebrates the paradox of the Incarnation, the sacrifice and triumph of the Passion, the glory of the Resurrection, and the bounty of Pentecost. In emphasizing the basic themes of Christianity, Andrewes avoids controversial doctrines; his sermons are devoted not to disputed points but to what he considered the "necessary" and "plain" truths of Christianity.

The first collected edition of Andrewes's sermons was published by his friends Buckeridge and William Laud at the command of King Charles I in 1629, three years after Andrewes's death. The ninety-six sermons are divided, except for eleven miscellaneous ones, according to the holy days of the church: there are seventeen Nativity sermons, six delivered during Lent, eight for Ash Wednesday, three on the Passion, eighteen on the Resurrection, and fifteen on the sending of the Holy Ghost at Pentecost. There are also eight sermons celebrating King James's deliverance from the Gowrie Conspiracy and ten preached on the anniversary of his escape from the Gunpowder Plot; these days of deliverance were also observed in England as holy days.

"Sermon Preached at the Spittle" (in Andrewes's time *spital* was spelled *spittal* and *spittle*) is the earliest and longest of Andrewes's surviving sermons. It was preached in the yard of St. Mary's Hospital, London, on 10 April 1588 to a congregation of lawyers, merchants, and businessmen. The text – "Charge them that are rich in this world, that they be not high-minded" (1 Tim. 6:17–18) – Andrewes calls "the rich man's Scripture," and the whole sermon reveals his ability to adapt his style and message to his audience. Much of the style is highly colloquial, as in the reference to the Pharisees who jest and scoff at Christ's charge "and wash it down with a cup of sack." The tone shifts frequently, adapting itself to the requirements of the message. At times Andrewes addresses his congregation in a directly personal way, as in his informal comment on the progress of the sermon: "I shall never get out of this point if I break not from it." And he gives voice to thoughts that may lurk in the minds of some members of the congregation, as when he takes on the voice of the high-minded man scorning the preacher: "Tush, he doth prate, these things shall not come upon me, though I walk still according to the stubbornness of mine own heart." The sermon reaches an emotional climax near the

Engraving of Cardinal Robert Bellarmine, who carried on a controversy with Andrewes over the oath of allegiance to the king that was instituted after the Gunpowder Plot

end as it vividly glimpses Judgment Day: "It will not come yet it is true, it will be long in coming, but when it comes, it will never have an end." Andrewes's "Sermon Preached at the Spittle" provides a good introduction to his later sermons; the style, the dramatic tone, the thorough development of each section of the text, and the careful organization of the work are characteristics that Andrewes displays throughout his preaching career.

Andrewes's greatest sermons are those that celebrate the holy days of the Christian church: Christmas, Ash Wednesday, Good Friday, Easter, and Pentecost. In all these sermons Andrewes reveals a sensitivity to the special significance of each day that is equal to his reverence for the text; for him the day represents a memorial of a sacred event. The ideal of recurring days of commemoration is most beautifully expressed in one of Andrewes's secular sermons, his first Gunpowder Plot sermon, delivered in 1606: "Of keeping in remembrance, many ways there be: among the rest this is one, of making days, set solemn days, to preserve memorable acts, that they be not eaten out by them, but even revived with the return of the year, and kept still fresh in continual memory."

Of all Andrewes's sermons, the Nativity group is the most familiar to the modern reader — especially the second sermon on the Wise Men, preached in 1622, which inspired Eliot's "The Journey of the Magi." On seventeen Christmas days between 1605 and 1624 Andrewes preached before King James in the royal chapel at Whitehall. In the collected edition of his sermons this group is given prominence by appearing first. In these sermons his imagination ranges throughout time and space. Contrasts are proclaimed between the high and the low, the great and the little, the divine and the human, heaven and earth, the Divine Son and the Human Child, the Word and the flesh, the message of the angel and the sign of the manger, birth and death. Indeed, death is as prominent as birth in the Nativity sermons, which contain some of Andrewes's most powerful passages on Christ's Passion. In no other group of sermons is Andrewes's enthusiasm for antithetical constructions so appropriate to his message as it is in these, which present the great paradox of God becoming man. Andrewes's favorite image for presenting this paradox is "the *Verbum infans,* the Word without a word; the eternal Word not able to speak a word," a figure he borrowed from Saint Bernard and develops four times in the course of these sermons. In his sermon preached in 1611, on the text "and the Word was made flesh," Andrewes pays high tribute to the human word: "For there is not in all the world a more pure, simple, inconcrete procreation than that whereby the mind conceiveth the word within it, by *dixit in corde* [said in the heart]." The paradox of the Word becoming flesh provided Andrewes with his greatest opportunity to display his affection for the word. The Nativity group reaches its climax with the two pairs of sermons on the shepherds and the wise men, preached in 1618, 1619, 1620, and 1622. The second Wise Men sermon is Andrewes's best-known work, especially the *Venimus* (coming) section, from which Eliot quoted: "A cold coming they had of it at this time of the year, just the worst time of the year to take a journey, and specially a long journey in. The ways the deep, the weather sharp, the days short, the sun farthest off, *in solstitio brumali,* the very dead of winter."

Andrewes wrote eight "Sermons of Repentance and Fasting" to be preached on Ash Wednesdays: three preached before Queen Elizabeth, four before King James, and one never delivered. The 1621 sermon on fasting – a practice that must have encountered opposition since Andrewes declares that he chose the text "to stop the mouths of them that malign it" – provides a glimpse of Andrewes's own spiritual life, which is most clearly revealed in his *Private Devotions.* The chief beauty of these sermons is to be found in those passages that describe the beauties of the natural world. Because the beginning of spring coincides with the beginning of Lent, Andrewes frequently develops the parallel between nature and the Christian life. In his last surviving sermon preached to Queen Elizabeth, in 1602, less than a year before her death, Andrewes's words are prophetic as he commemorates the season: "now do these fowls return. Who knoweth whether he shall live to see them return any more? It may be the last spring, the last swallow-time, the last Wednesday of this name or nature we shall ever live to hear this point preached."

The three surviving Passion sermons are all early works, but in no other group of sermons does

Andrewes re-create a scene with such intensity. In the first sermon, preached at the Elizabethan court in 1597, Andrewes not only encourages the members of the congregation to observe the Crucifixion in their imaginations but makes them participants in it: "So that it was the sin of our polluted hands that pierced His hands, the swiftness of our feet to do evil that nailed His feet, the wicked devices of our heads that gored His head, and wretched desires of our heart that pierced His heart." The imagery Andrewes uses in depicting this spectacle is traditional. Christ is associated with Old Testament themes: the offering of Isaac in sacrifice, the selling of Joseph, the deliverance of Israel from Egypt, the death of Josias, and Zerubbabel's building of the temple. The most frequent image is of Christ as Moses' brazen serpent, lifted up in the wilderness. Christ is also compared to the Passover lamb, the leafless vine, the treader in the winepress, and the lodestone of love. Two unusual images are Christ as the Morning Hart, "stricken and pierced," and as the Book of Love, in which the stripes of the lash are lowercase letters and the nails are capitals. Christ's Passion, like his Nativity, presents a paradox, because while it was seemingly a degradation it was in reality an exaltation. In the final Passion sermon Andrewes declares that the Savior "went to His Passion with Psalms, and with such triumph and solemnity, as He never admitted all His life before."

Eighteen of Andrewes's Resurrection sermons – more than of any other group – survive. Three of these sermons, on Mary Magdalen, were preached before King James on Easter Sundays in 1620, 1621, and 1622. Mary attracted the attention of the age, and the three sermons on her meeting with Jesus bring the Resurrection group to a climax as the Wise Men sermons crown the Nativity group. The 1620 sermon is one of Andrewes's greatest achievements, its chief virtue lying in the single-mindedness with which he penetrates to the humanity of Mary's character. Andrewes applies the image of a garden to Mary: "The gardener had done His part, made her all green on the sudden." The sermon preached in 1623 is Andrewes's most powerful Resurrection sermon: Christ is compared to a lion "imbrued with blood, the blood of His enemies," triumphantly bearing the banner of his victory over death in the manner of a Roman conqueror.

The fifteen Pentecost sermons, preached before King James on Pentecost Sundays between 1606 and 1621, present Andrewes's most complete definition of the Trinity. The group varies in quality, and at times Andrewes appears to be straining to say something significant about a subject he has already presented adequately. The greatest of the Pentecost sermons, preached in 1614 on the text "Thou are gone up on high" (Psalm 68:18), however, ranks with Andrewes's best work. In the discussion of the words "Thou hast led captivity captive" Andrewes vigorously depicts Christ rising as a lion, a champion overcoming his enemies in battle and leading them in triumph: "so He . . . 'broke up the gates of death,' and made the gates of brass fly in sunder; trod on the serpent's head and all to bruised it; 'came up on him, took from him his armour wherein he trusted, and divided his spoils.' "

Andrewes's secular sermons were preached before James on the anniversaries of the king's deliverance from the Gowrie Conspiracy on 5 August 1600 and from the Gunpowder Plot on 5 November 1605. The eight Gowrie sermons lack interest for the modern reader, but the ten sermons on the Gunpowder Plot reveal the same variety and range of vision that bring distinction to the Nativity group. Much of the strength of these sermons lies in the vivid contrast between the horror of what might have happened and the glory of deliverance. In the introductory sermon, preached on the first anniversary of the plot, Andrewes concisely re-creates the horror of the intended destruction in striking hyperbole: "wherein [were] so much blood as would have made it rain blood, so many caskets of heads, so many pieces of rent bodies cast up and down, and scattered all over the face of the earth." As the sermon progresses the mood shifts to a spirit of exaltation, reaching a climax in an elaborate proclamation of joy. In the most magnificent sermon in the group, preached on the tenth anniversary of the plot, Andrewes's imagination ranges widely through time and space, as it does in the Nativity group; God's boundless mercies are revealed in the creation of the Earth, the creation of man, and Christ's birth in the manger and death on the cross. Although the Gunpowder Plot sermons have been neglected by scholars, they include some of Andrewes's most excellent work.

Andrewes's last surviving sermon, for Christmas Day 1624, is in the nature of a valediction. Taking as his text "I will preach the law" (Psalm 2:7), he emphasizes, perhaps for the last time, the profound responsibilities of both preacher and congregation. The remaining two years of his life were plagued with sickness. In his funeral sermon Buckeridge says that when his "weakness grew on him, and that by infirmity of his body he grew unable to preach, he began to go little to Court, not so much for weakness as for inability to preach." When King James was dying he called for Andrewes to pray

Engraving of Andrewes

with him and to administer the Sacrament, but Andrewes was too sick with gout and kidney stones to do so. His sickness also prevented him from attending the king's funeral on 7 May 1625.

Andrewes's last days are described by Buckeridge: "And when his brother Master Nicholas Andrewes died, he took that as a certain sign and prognostic and warning of his own death, and from that time till the hour of his dissolution he spent all his time in prayer; and his prayer-book, when he was private, was seldom seen out of his hands." Andrewes died in Winchester House on 25 September 1626; he was given an elaborate funeral on 11 November and was buried in the upper aisle of the parish church of St. Saviour's in Southwark. "He is now at rest and peace in heaven," declared Buckeridge, and "follows the Lamb wheresoever He goes."

Although Lancelot Andrewes was *Stella Praedicantium* in his own age, his star has not shone so brightly in succeeding generations. His distinctive style of preaching was imitated by Laud, Hacket, Ralph Brownrig, John Cosin, and Mark Frank but was gradually abandoned during the seventeenth century. In Thomas Fuller's *The History of the Worthies of England* (1662) Andrewes's friend Nicholas Felton, bishop of Ely, commented unfavorably on Andrewes's style: "I had almost marred my own natural Trot by endeavouring to imitate his artificial Amble." At the end of the century Andrewes's method of preaching was described by John Evelyn as "full of logical divisions, in short and broken periods, and Latin sentences, now quite out of fashion in the pulpit, which is grown into a far more profitable way of plain and practical discourses" (cited by Charles Smyth in *The Art of Preaching,* 1940). In the Restoration period this newer style of preaching was exemplified in the sermons of Robert South and John Tillotson, the most popular preachers of their age. Andrewes's sermons suffered almost complete neglect in the eighteenth century, but his reputation rose again when the first complete edition of his works was published from 1841 to 1854. Twentieth-century criticism of Andrewes's sermons has been both positive and negative. The best-known and most laudatory estimation of Andrewes is that by Eliot, who accorded him "a place second to none in the history of the formation of the English Church," calling him "the first great preacher of the English Catholic Church" and ranking his sermons "with the finest English prose of their time, of any time."

Bibliography:

Elizabeth McCutcheon, "Recent Studies in Andrewes," *English Literary Renaissance,* 11 (Winter 1981): 96–108.

Biographies:

Henry Isaacson, *An Exact Narration of the Life and Death of . . . Lancelot Andrewes, Late Bishop of Winchester: Which May Serve as a Pattern of Piety and Charity to All Godly Disposed Christians* (London: Printed for John Stafford, 1650);

Arthur T. Russell, *Memoirs of the Life and Works of the Right Honorable and Right Rev. Father in God Lancelot Andrewes* (Cambridge: Palmer, 1860);

Robert L. Ottley, *Lancelot Andrewes* (London: Methuen, 1894);

Alexander Whyte, *Lancelot Andrewes and His Private Devotions,* second edition (Edinburgh & London, 1896);

Douglas Macleane, *Lancelot Andrewes and the Reaction* (London: Allen, 1910);

Florence Higham, *Lancelot Andrewes* (London: SCM Press, 1952);

Paul A. Welsby, *Lancelot Andrewes* (London: SPCK, 1958).

References:

T. S. Eliot, "Lancelot Andrewes," in his *Selected Essays* (New York: Harcourt, Brace, 1950), pp. 299–310;

John Hacket, *Scrinia reserata: A Memorial Offered to the Great Deservings of J. Williams* (London: Printed by E. Jones for S. Lowndes, 1693);

Nicholas Lossky, *Lancelot Andrewes The Preacher (1555–1626): The Origins of the Mystical Theology of the Church of England* (Oxford: Clarendon Press, 1991);

Peter E. McCullough, "Lancelot Andrewes and Language," *Anglican Theological Review,* 74 (Summer 1992): 304–316;

Elizabeth McCutcheon, "Lancelot Andrewes' *Preces Privatae*: A Journey through Time," *Studies in Philology,* 65 (April 1968): 223–241;

William Fraser Mitchell, *English Pulpit Oratory from Andrewes to Tillotson* (New York & Toronto: Macmillan, 1932);

Trevor Owen, *Lancelot Andrewes* (Boston: G. K. Hall, 1981);

Maurice F. Reidy, S.J., *Bishop Lancelot Andrewes* (Chicago: Loyola University Press, 1955);

Charles Smyth, *The Art of Preaching: A Practical Survey of Preaching in the Church of England 747–1939* (London: SPCK, 1940);

Joan Webber, "Celebration of Word and World in Lancelot Andrewes' Style," in *Seventeenth-Century Prose: Modern Essays in Criticism,* edited by Stanley E. Fish (New York: Oxford University Press, 1971), pp. 336–352;

George Williamson, "Scheme and Point in Pulpit Oratory," in his *The Senecan Amble: A Study in Prose Form from Bacon to Collier* (London: Faber & Faber, 1951; Chicago: University of Chicago Press, 1966), pp. 231–274.

Francis Bacon
(22 January 1561 – 9 April 1626)

John Channing Briggs
University of California, Riverside

BOOKS: *Essayes. Religious Meditations. Places of perswasion and disswasion. Seene and allowed* (London: Printed by Johannes Windet for Humpfrey Hooper, 1597); enlarged as *The Essaies of Sr Francis Bacon Knight, the Kings Sollictier Generall* (London: Printed by John Beale, 1612); enlarged as *The Essayes or Covnsels, Civill and Morall, of Francis Lo. Vervlam, Viscovnt S^t. Alban* (London: Printed by John Haviland for Hanna Barret & Richard Whitaker, 1625);

A Letter Written Out of England to an English Gentleman at Padua, containing a true Report of a strange Conspiracie, contriued betweene Edward Squire, lately executed for the same treason as Actor, and Richard Wallpoole a Iesuite, as Deuiser and Suborner against the person of the Queenes Maiestie (London: Printed by Deputies of C. Barker, 1599);

A Declaration of the Practises & Treasons attempted and committed by Robert late Earle of Essex and his Complices, against her Maiestie and her Kingdoms, and of the proceedings as well at the Arraignments & Convictions of the said late Earle, and his adherents, as after: Together with the very Confessions and other parts of the Euidences themselues, word for word taken out of the Originals (London: Printed by Robert Barker, 1601);

A Briefe Discourse, Tovching the Happie Vnion of the Kingdomes of England, and Scotland, anonymous (London: Printed by R. Read for Fælix Norton, sold by William Aspley, 1603);

Sir Francis Bacon His Apologie, in Certaine imputations concerning the late Earle of Essex Written to the right Honorable his very good Lord, the Earle of Deuonshire, Lord Lieutenant of Ireland (London: Printed for Felix Norton, 1604);

Certaine Considerations touching the better pacification and Edification of the Church of England, anonymous (London: Printed by T. Purfoot for Henrie Tomes, 1604);

The Twoo Bookes of Francis Bacon. Of the proficience and aduancement of Learning, diuine and humane (London: Printed by T. Purfoot for Henrie Tomes, 1605); translated and enlarged as *Opera Francisi Baronis de Vervlamio, Vice-Comitis Sancti Albani; Tomvs Primvs: Qui continet De Dignitate & Augmentis Scientiarum, Libros IX* (London: Printed by John Haviland, 1623); translated by Gilbert Watts as *Of the Advancement and Proficience of Learning or the Partitions of Sciences, IX Bookes* (Oxford: Printed by Leon Lichfield for Robert Young & Edward Forrest, 1640);

De Sapientia Veterum Liber (London: Printed by Robert Barker, 1609); translated by Arthur Gorges as *The Wisedome of the Ancients* (London: Printed by John Bill, 1619);

The Charge of Sir Francis Bacon Knight, His Maiesties Attourney generall, Touching Duells, upon an information in the Star-chamber against Priest and Wright (London: Printed by G. Eld for Robert Wilson, 1614);

Instauratio Magna [Novum Organum] (London: Printed by Bonham Norton & John Bill, 1620);

The Historie of the Raigne of King Henry the Seuenth (London: Printed by W. Stansby for Matthew Lownes & William Barret, 1622);

Historia Natvralis et Experimentalis ad Condendam Philosophiam: Sive, Phænomena Vniversi: Quæ est Instaurationis Magnæ Pars Tertia [Historia de Ventis] (London: Printed by Matthew Lownes & William Barret for John Haviland, 1622); translated by R. G. [Robert Gentili?] as *The Naturall and Experimentall History of Winds, &c.* (London: Printed for Humphrey Moseley, 1653);

Historia Vitæ & Mortis. Sive, Titvlus Secvndvs in Historiâ Naturali & Experimentali ad Condendam Philosophiam: Quæ est Instavrationis Magnæ Pars Tertia (London: Printed by Matthew Lownes for J. Haviland, 1623); translated anonymously as *The Historie of Life and Death: With Observations Naturall & Experimentall for the Prolonging of Life* (London: Printed by J. Okes for Humphrey Mosley, 1638);

Apophthegmes New and Old (London: Printed by John Haviland for Hanna Barret & Richard Whittaker, 1625 [i.e., 1624]);

Sylva Sylvarvm: or A Naturall Historie. In Ten Centuries, edited by William Rawley (London: Printed by John Haviland for William Lee, 1626) – includes "New Atlantis: A Worke vnfinished";

The Beginning of the History of the Reign of King Henry the Eighth (London, 1629) – includes "Novis Orbis Scientarum, Sive Desiderata";

Considerations Tovching a Warre with Spaine (London, 1629);

Certaine Miscellany Works of the Right Honourable, Francis Lo. Verulam, Viscount S. Alban, edited by Rawley (London: Printed by John Haviland for Humphrey Robinson, 1629) – includes "An Advertisement Touching an Holy Warre";

The Elements of the Common Lawes of England (London: Printed by the assigns of J. More, 1630);

Operum Moralium et Civilum Tomus (London: Printed by Edward Griffin, sold by Richard Whitaker, 1638);

The Confession of Faith (London, 1641);

Cases of Treason (London: Printed by the assigns of John More, sold by Matthew Walbancke & John Coke, 1641);

A Speech Delivered by Sir Francis Bacon, in the lower House of Parliament quinto Iacobi, concerning the Article of Naturalization of the Scottish Nation (London, 1641);

The Office of Constables: Being an Answer to the Questions proposed by Sir Alexander Hay, touching the Office of Constables. Declaring what power they have, and how they ought to be cherished in their Office (London: Printed for Francis Cowles, 1641);

Three Speeches of The Right Honorable, Sir Francis Bacon Knight, then his Majesties Solliciter Generall, after Lord Verulam, Viscount Saint Alban: Concerning the Post-Nati, Naturalization of the Scotch in England, Union of the Lawes of the Kingdomes of England and Scotland (London: Printed by Richard Badger for Samuel Broun, 1641);

A Wise and Moderate Discourse, Concerning Church-Affaires: As it was written, long since, by the famous Author of those Considerations, which seem to have some reference to this, Now published for the common good (London, 1641);

The Learned Reading of Sir Francis Bacon, One of her Majesties learned Counsell at Law, upon the Statute

Portrait from the studio of Paul van Somer (National Portrait Gallery, London)

of Uses: Being his double Reading to the Honourable Society of Grayes Inne (London: Printed for Mathew Walbancke & Lawrence Chapman, 1642);

Ordinances made By The Right Honourable Sir Francis Bacon Knight, Lord Verulam, and Vicount of Saint Albans, being then Lord Chancellor (London: Printed for Mathew Walbancke & Lawrence Chapman, 1642);

The Remaines of the Right Honorable Francis Lord Verulam, Viscount of St. Albans, sometimes Lord Chancellour of England: Being Essayes and severall Letters to severall great Personages, and other pieces of various and high concernment not heretofore published. A Table whereof for the Readers more ease is adjoyned (London: Printed by B. Alsop for Lawrence Chapman, 1648); published as *The Mirrour of State and Eloquence* (London: Printed for Lawrence Chapman, 1656);

The Felicity of Queen Elizabeth: And Her Times, With other Things (London: Printed by T. Newcomb for George Latham, 1651);

Scripta in Natvrali et Vniversali Philosophia, edited by Issac Gruter (Amsterdam: Printed by Ludovico Elzevir, 1653);

Resuscitatio, Or, Bringing into Publick Light Severall Pieces, of the Works, Civil, Historical, Philosophical, & Theological, Hitherto Sleeping; of the Right Honourable Francis Bacon, Baron of Verulam, Viscount Saint Alban: According to the best Corrected Coppies. Together, With his Lordships Life, edited by William Rawley (London: Printed by Sarah Griffin for William Lee, 1657);

Opuscula Varia Posthuma, Philosophica, Civilia, et Theologica, edited by Rawley (London: Printed by R. Daniels, 1658);

A Letter of Advice Written by Sr. Francis Bacon To the Duke of Buckingham, When he became Favourite to King James, Never before Printed (London: Printed for R. H. & H. B., 1661);

Opera Omnia, Quæ extant: Philosophica, Moralia, Politica, Historica, edited by Johann Baptiste Schönwetter (Frankfurt am Main: Printed by Matthaeis Kampffer, 1665);

The Second Part of the Resuscitatio or a Collection of several pieces of the Works of the Right Honourable Francis Bacon, Baron of Verulam, and Viscount of St. Albans: Some of them formerly Printed in smaller Volumes, and being almost lost, are now Collected and put into Folio, with some of his other Pieces, which never yet was published, edited by Rawley (London: Printed by S. G. & B. G. for William Lee, 1670);

Baconiana: Or Certain Genuine Remains of Sr. Francis Bacon, Baron of Verulam, and Viscount of St. Albans, edited by Thomas Tenison (London: Printed by J. D. for Richard Chiswell, 1679);

Gesta Grayorum: Or the History of the High and mighty Prince, Henry Prince of Purpoole, Arch-Duke of Stapulia and Bernardia, Duke of High and Nether Holborn, Marquis of St. Giles and Tottenham, Count Palaztine of Bloomsbury and Clerkenwell, Great Lord of the Cantons of Islington, Kentish-Town, Paddington and Knights-bridge, Knight of the most Heroical Order of the Helmet, and Sovereign of the Same; Who Reigned and Died, A.D. 1594. Together with A Masque, as it was presented (by His Highness's Command) for the Entertainment of Q. Elizabeth; who, with the Nobles of both Courts, was present thereat (London: Printed for W. Canning, 1688);

Letters and Remains of the Lord Chancellor Bacon, edited by Robert Stephens (London: Printed by W. Bowyer, 1734) – includes "Filum Labyrinthi sive Formula Inquisitionis ad filos";

The Works of Francis Bacon, 14 volumes, edited by James Spedding, Robert Leslie Ellis, and Douglas Denon Heath (London: Longman, Simpkin, Hamilton, Whittaker, J. Bain, E. Hedgson, Washbourne, Richardson Brothers, Houlston, Bickers & Bush, Willis & Sotheran, J. Cornish, L. Booth, J. Snow, Aylott, 1858–1874; New York: Garrett Press, 1968).

Editions: *Bacon's Essays and Colours of Good and Evil,* edited by Wright (Cambridge & London: Macmillan, 1862; Freeport, N.Y.: Books for Libraries Press, 1972);

The Essays or Counsels, Civil and Moral, of Francis Bacon, edited by Samuel Harvey Reynolds (Oxford: Clarendon Press, 1890);

Essays, edited by Alfred S. West (Cambridge: Cambridge University Press, 1897);

The Advancement of Learning, edited by W. Aldis Wright, fifth edition (Oxford: Clarendon Press, 1900);

A Harmony of the Essays, Etc., of Francis Bacon, edited by Edward Arber, English Reprints, no. 27 (London, 1927);

Essays, Advancement of Learning, New Atlantis, and Other Pieces, edited by Richard Foster Jones (Garden City, N.Y.: Doubleday, Doran, 1937);

Selected Essays, edited by J. Max Patrick (New York: Crofts, 1948);

Selected Writings, edited by Hugh G. Dick (New York: Modern Library, 1955);

The New Organon, and Related Writings, edited by Fulton H. Anderson (New York: Liberal Arts Press, 1960);

Francis Bacon: A Selection of His Works, edited by Sideny Warhaft (London: Macmillan, 1965);

The History of the Reign of King Henry the Seventh, edited by F. J. Levy (New York: Bobbs-Merrill, 1972);

The Essayes or Counsels, Civill and Morall, edited by Michael Kiernan (Cambridge, Mass: Harvard University Press, 1985).

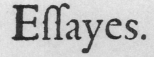

Essayes.

Religious Meditations.

Places of perswasion and dißwasion.

Scene and allowed.

At London,
Printed for Humfrey Hooper, and are
to be sold at the blacke Beare
in Chauncery Lane.
1597.

Title page for Bacon's first published book

OTHER: *The Translation of Certaine Psalmes into English Verse,* translated by Bacon (London: Printed for Hanna Barret & Richard Wittaker, 1625);

"The Use of the Law," attributed to Bacon, in John Dodderidge's *The Lawyers Light; or, A due direction for the Study of the Law* (London: Printed for Benjamin Fisher, 1629).

Francis Bacon, whom Denis Diderot's *Encyclopédie* (1751–1780) praised for glimpsing "the general principles that must serve as the foundation of the study of nature" and whom Thomas Jefferson called one of the three greatest men the world has ever known, was born at York House, London, on 22 January 1561, a few years after the young Princess Elizabeth had taken the throne of England. In that time of promise and suspense, with its guarded hope for a peace and prosperity that might follow from an English settlement of the religious controversies that had boiled out of the Reformation, Bacon was raised by powerful parents who embodied two of the dynamics of the age: courtly power and Reformist piety. Nicholas Bacon, his father, was the queen's lord keeper of the Great Seal. Ann Cooke Bacon, his mother, was the sister-in-law of William Cecil, afterward known as Lord Burghley; learned in Latin and Greek, she was an energetic and pious Reformist whose trilingual letters to Bacon and his brother, Anthony, three years his senior, show an unstinting, if meddlesome, attention to their spiritual, bodily, and political health.

Bacon had great expectations: when he was a boy, the queen enjoyed greeting him as "my little Lord Keeper." At age thirteen he entered Trinity College, Cambridge; accompanied by Anthony, he began his education in the law at Gray's Inn in June 1575. A year later he accompanied the queen's ambassador, Sir Amias Paulet, to France, where he observed the art of diplomacy in a land violently exercised by religious conflict.

By the time Bacon left for Paris he had already found the traditional learning of the universities — particularly Aristotelian logic and natural philosophy — distasteful. From an early stage he seems to have embarked on the development of a "new learning" based on empiricism and inductive experimentation, but he never clearly abandoned some assumptions and beliefs that today would be considered archaic or occult. The mixture of the old and the new in Bacon's project for the advancement of learning complicates the understanding of his achievements.

In his later writings Bacon records two intriguing events that took place during his stay in Paris — events he remembers and interprets in ways that do not adhere to the conventional picture of his contribution to modern science. The first is his invention of a double-coded diplomatic cipher, the story of which appears many years later in a detailed summary in *De Dignitate & Augmentis Scientiarum* (1623), the Latin translation and enlargement of his *Of the Proficience and Advancement of Learning* (1605). He describes his invention as an encryption device that uses randomly selected signs. In such randomness lies the power to convey the opposite of what one seems to say: in Bacon's illustration the code conveys a welcome message to naive audiences while blocking their understanding of a deeper and opposite meaning. The ignorant interpreter reads the reassuring message "Stay till I come," while the wise interpreter, who knows the cipher, discovers the warning "Fly!" The wise look for the opposite of appearances and thus save themselves from harm. In Bacon's later works a similarly arbitrary and antithetical encryption was to become a paradigm for the divine "ciphering" of the world.

The second Parisian incident is a notable example of the recrudescence or persistence of a premodern sensibility in Bacon's works. As he recollected forty-five years later in his *Sylva Sylvarum* (1626), he had a dream on the night of 17 February 1579 in which he thought he foresaw his father's death: "I myself remember, that being in Paris, and my father dying in London, two or three days before my father's death I had a dream, which I told to divers English Gentlemen, that my father's house in the country was plastered all over with black mortar." He records the event as an instance suggesting that there might be "secret passages of sympathy between persons of near blood" that the new sciences ought to study. Rather than cast doubt on the workings of the imagination (as he does in other passages) Bacon takes care in the *Sylva Sylvarum* to establish the facts and the presence of witnesses.

The account urges inquiry into "the relations touching the force of imagination and the secret instincts of nature," which "are so uncertain, as they require a great deal of examination ere we conclude upon them."

The death of Bacon's father on 20 February 1579 was, of course, more than a scientific curiosity: it was a double disaster in that it not only deprived him of a parent but also blighted his hopes for early recognition at court. On his return from Paris he found that his prospects for inheriting an estate that would support his ambitions as a courtier had disappeared because his father had not purchased the expected legacy for his youngest son.

In 1580 Bacon unsuccessfully sought a position at court. The alternative was to earn his living — at least until the queen or a high courtier elevated him — by mastering the law. He did so and was called to the bar on 27 June 1582. His disappointed expectations, in combination with an often-professed desire to retire from the world of courtly ambition and devote himself to natural philosophy, worked on him for many years and seem to have influenced the form and substance of the concept of the new sciences that emerged from his composite life.

The next decade is marked by no certain publications or writings, though he appears to have been busy. He won his first seat in the House of Commons in 1584. In 1586 he became a bencher of Gray's Inn, a position that allowed him to plead cases. Elizabeth may have solicited a few disquisitions on domestic and foreign policy from him before he was thirty; the edition of Bacon's works (1858–1874) edited by James Spedding, Robert Leslie Ellis, and Douglas Denon Heath includes several texts that Bacon might have proffered to the queen, whether she had asked for them or not. (Throughout his life Bacon wrote documents in anticipation of getting the royal ear.)

The undated "Letter of Advice to Queen Elizabeth," published in 1651 in a collection of works by various authors and wrongly attributed to Burghley, is a closely reasoned plea for moderation in governing religious nonconformity. (Spedding, the first to publish the corrected version, says that the work is "not improbably" from Bacon's hand in 1584.) Given the rising national sentiment against "Papists" who were alleged to be in league with Spanish plans to supplant Elizabeth, whom the pope had excommunicated, Bacon's argument is remarkably moderate: it advises Elizabeth to reduce the threat posed by English Catholics by preaching to them rather than persecuting them. Another manuscript, assigned to the period around 1589, when

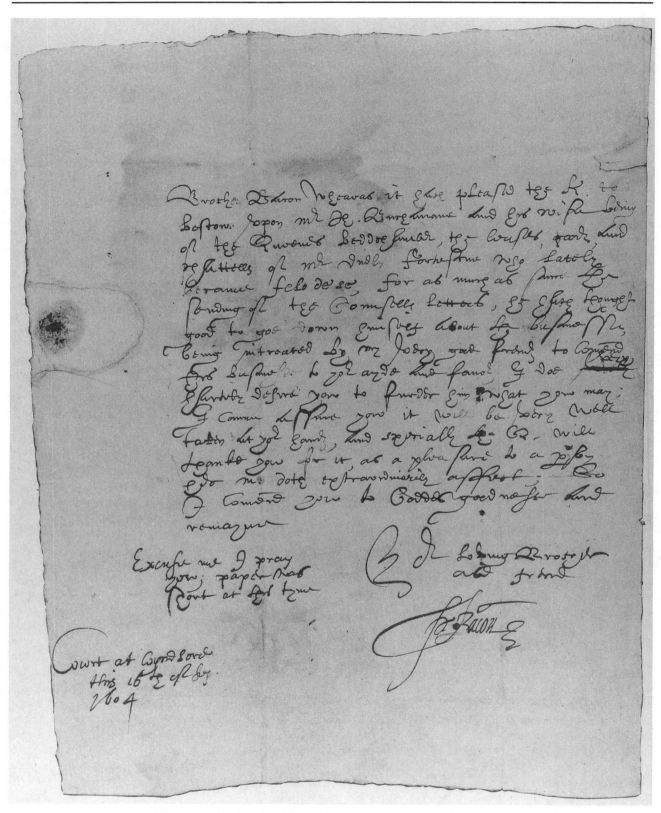

Letter from Bacon to his half brother, Sir Nicholas Bacon (Pierpont Morgan Library, MA 1215)

the Marprelate controversy pitted reformist polemicists against the established church, also urges an unusually temperate approach. It counsels the queen to be evenhanded in her criticism and protection of both the reformers and the established-church men they are attacking.

A document of certain authorship – Bacon's letter to Lord Burghley written on 6 May 1586 – gives an indication of the complexity of Bacon's role as a highly intelligent, ambitious, underemployed courtier in waiting. Accused of behaving arrogantly, Bacon replies by addressing his prospective patron in a meticulously unaffected yet fervent voice, becoming the political scientist as well as the ardent confessor of his own troubles: "Indeed I find in my simple observation that they which live as it were *in umbra* [in the shadows] and not in public or frequent action, how moderately and modestly soever they behave themselves, yet *laborant invidia* [fall victim to envy]. I find also that such persons as are of nature bashful (as myself is), whereby they want that plausible familiarity which others have, are often mistaken for proud. . . . if I think well of myself in anything it is in this that I am free from that vice." If true modesty cannot depend on an unhypocritical appearance to prove itself – if, in fact, modesty is a victim, in the envious world of appearances, of allegations that it is the opposite of itself – then an absolute, almost boastful humility is one's only defense.

In a favor-seeking letter to Burghley written around 1592 Bacon ventures another paradoxical argument. Presenting his credentials with an extreme, almost mocking rationality, he seems to forgo what he asks for. On the one hand, he asserts his interest in "vast contemplative ends" ("I have taken all knowledge to be my province") – ends that seem more important than his "moderate civil ends." On the other hand, his desire for the contemplative life is proof of his worthiness for high office. As a philosopher, he says, he would exercise the sort of ambition that would help conquer rebels, as though the decadent Aristotelians he wished to overturn were Irish insurrectionists: "This, whether it be curiosity, or vain glory, or nature, or (if one take it favourably) *philanthropia,* is so fixed in my mind as it cannot be removed."

Bacon's motive is ambition, or charity, or a fusion of both. His goal is high office or the freedom to become a scholar of all knowledge – or better, a yoking of the two: he wants higher office, he says, in order to gain "commandment of more wits than a man's own." The question whether he seeks office in order to carry out his speculative enterprise or to use his learning for the sake of courtly service is left open. The lack of clarity in such arguments, amid their lucid paradoxes, enables Bacon to disavow and pursue both ends at once.

In 1592 Bacon spoke in Parliament against the "double subsidy," an extraordinary tax the queen wished to levy for the purpose of making preparations for war against Spain. He favored a new levy, but not one so unprecedented. The speech, which exhibited remarkable independence in a man who is sometimes remembered as notoriously pliable, won Bacon the queen's lasting disfavor. Three years later, when Elizabeth was about to appoint a new solicitor general – a post Bacon had long coveted – he maintained, in a letter to Burghley written on 7 June 1595, the justice of his original arguments. When he was informed that the appointment would be given to someone else, he considered giving up his courtly ambitions altogether.

Bacon's paradoxical fusion of worldly ambition and yearning for release to contemplative ends is evident in the selection Spedding found in a copybook and published as "Mr. Bacon in Praise of Knowledge," perhaps written in the early 1590s for Robert Devereux, second Earl of Essex, as an entertainment for the queen; in the *Gesta Grayorum* (1688), a masque written around 1594; and in "Speeches of the Philosopher, the Captain, the Councillor, and the Squire" (first published by Spedding) for another royal entertainment around 1594.

Bacon's circumstances were complicated by forces beyond his ken, particularly the volatile relationship between Elizabeth and the earl of Essex, who had become Bacon's zealous champion at court. The earl's erratic, sometimes violent displays of passion, including his shows of pique at the queen's delays in showing preferment to his protégé, hurt Bacon's chances. Elizabeth, faced with the problem of determining how best to use the popular and ambitious earl without being used by him, was not inclined to elevate his man swiftly. (Essex reported to Bacon in a letter probably written in May 1594 that Elizabeth thought him learned and well-spoken in the law but not "deep" enough to be appointed as the queen's counsel.) This opinion did not, however, prevent the queen from using Bacon as an unofficial counselor.

Thomas Babington Macaulay's disparaging essay on Bacon (1837) makes the well-known charge (which was passionately countered by Spedding a generation later) that Bacon's entire life exhibited "a coldness of heart and meanness of spirit" that made him "incapable of feeling strong affection, of facing great dangers, of making great sacrifices," and it is true that Bacon benefited from his patron's troubles. In the mid 1590s he received a substantial estate from Essex in consolation for Essex's failure to secure him the attorney generalship. When the queen gave Bacon some temporary employment, he wrote to Essex (in a letter that Spedding assigns to November 1595) that he was the queen's man first and Essex's as far as the law allowed. Moreover, his warnings to the earl, counseling him to temper his ambition with "obsequious observance" rather than "violent courses," have been taken as evidence of his willingness to indulge in "petty tricks" to win the favor of authority. In the end Essex's disastrous attempt to seize power in 1600 required Bacon to choose sides, and ever after he had to face the charge that he had been disloyal to his patron. In the last months of Elizabeth's reign he rehabilitated himself (though certainly not in the eyes of some of his biographers) by becoming one of the queen's prosecutors of Essex, who was executed for treason. The case he made against Essex during the trial does not, in some biographers' eyes, reflect the complexity of Essex's motives. To such accusations Spedding responds that Bacon's authoritative testimony, which he laid out in his *Apology Concerning the Late Earl of Essex* (1604), should be believed: he put his queen above his patron when Essex pushed his demands too far.

Evidence of Bacon's philosophical preoccupations during the controversial period of Essex's rise and fall can be found in the three brief texts he presented to the queen in 1596. The first, *The Elements of the Common Laws of England,* which was not published until 1630, proposes a reduction and recodification of the common law. The existing common law is unsystematic, Bacon argues, but a careful canvass of the laws would reveal inherent organizing principles. The Baconian method of reform is twofold. One movement is to break up the law into maxims so as to "leave the wit of man more free to turn and toss, and to make use of that which is so delivered to more several purposes and applications. For we see all the ancient wisdom and science was wont to be delivered in that form; as may be seen by the parables of Solomon, and by the aphorisms of Hippocrates." The other is to provide glosses for each maxim, suggesting that the proverbs say more in juxtaposition than they do in isolation. Proverbs are "many times plain fallacies" unless they are configured to hint at a deeper meaning. Bacon's commentaries expose exceptions and contradictions that question the seeming wisdom of individual maxims, which are mere "sound in the air" unless they are incorporated into an art of application,

a process of elimination that discovers the appropriate passage for a particular case.

Maxims and interpretations appear again in "Of the Colours of Good and Evil," published in the 1597 edition of the *Essayes.* The "colors" are rhetorical commonplaces, analogous to proverbs; Bacon lists some of them, with commentaries, and he says that they are both trivial and profound. On the one hand, they merely "represent" truth to "make things appear good and evil," whereas "true and solid reasons" are those that "perform" truth by way of proofs. Since the true reasons often do not persuade, however, they are not sufficient; more-superficial principles are necessary. Indeed, neither the "colors" nor "true and solid reasons" can be used properly "but out of a very universal knowledge of the nature of things." In the hands of such universal knowledge, the insubstantial, popular colors of rhetoric not only become powerful levers to move audiences but also reveal deeper laws of influence.

Bacon's apparently conventional declaration of faith in the *Meditationes Sacrae* (Religious Meditations), also published in the first edition of the *Essayes,* elaborates on these principles. He selects and arranges Christian doctrines in ways that suggest affinities between revealed religion and the new Baconian sciences' drive toward useful and fundamental laws. Bacon takes pains to distinguish the new sciences from religion, arguing that theology is one of the few areas of learning that is not in need of fundamental reform; still, he insists that the new sciences will exhibit the Christian virtue of charity in their devotion to alleviating human suffering. He also adapts the reformers' iconoclasm, for which he finds precedent in Moses' destruction of the Golden Calf, to scientific purposes in his emphasis on the importance of destroying the "idols of the mind" that stand in the way of the progress of learning. Finally, Bacon is preoccupied with scientific "preaching," or rhetoric, whereby the new man of science will be able to communicate the revelatory insights he has won through his investigation of nature to audiences from which he might gain converts to the new outlook.

One of the meditations is devoted to describing hope as false faith, a disease of the imagination that flatters the inquirer and makes the mind "light, frothy, unequal, wandering." The only worthy hope is that which is "employed upon the life to come in heaven"; earthly hopes must be purged so as to direct the senses to "things present." This meditation reveals Bacon's doctrine of "self-denying induction" — the method of apprehending the world

*Engraving of Bacon by William Marshall, frontispiece for the 1640
edition of* The Advancement of Learning

by purging the inquirer's anticipation of answers and the comforts that might derive from those answers. Here one also encounters Bacon's condemnation of poets' offerings to the imagination of "a pleasant dream" that robs from the enterprises of the present. The eloquence of his sentences exhibits his paradoxical dependence on the "colors" of rhetoric to convey to the imagination a glimpse of the scientific prospect, even as he identifies the imagination's shortcomings.

The difference between faith and hypocrisy is evident, Bacon argues, in the disparity between private and public behavior: the hypocrite displays his piety on his sleeve but not in private; the religious man expresses it in private worship but not in public, where he acts mildly and pliably as a master

rhetorician, as "*all things to all people*" – the Apostle Paul's description of how he evangelizes among the unconverted. Paul is willing to take all shapes to convert the non-Christian; the protean preacher undergoes his transformations for the sake of transforming others. A similar principle emerges in "Of the Colours of Good and Evil," where Bacon shows the scientific rhetorician how to work on various audiences. Mastery of the laws of influence enables the speaker to seize and transmute his audience by using methods not accessible to the crowd's scrutiny. This work raises the question of how duplicity can exist in the new sciences, which supposedly dedicate themselves to reforming the fraudulent scholasticism inherited from the Middle Ages. One answer seems to lie in Bacon's likening of his cause to Paul's: if the new sciences are pious and charitable, then the powerful duplicity of the scientific inquirer and rhetorician is as forgivable as the evangelist's. And if the transformation that the new sciences effect is conformable to the divine ordering of things, then the ability of the man of science to disguise himself is even more justified.

Such notions seem to be far from the utilitarian, prudential advice that makes up the carefully phrased essays that appeared in 1597. On closer inspection, however, the counsel of "Of Studies," the first of the small volume's ten brief essays, hints at a double doctrine: there is a deeper, "wise" study that comes from experience and observation and is beyond the reach of ordinary reading. Wise study entails weighing and considering; it is an ordeal both for the student and that which is studied. Those few books that are worthy of careful study must be "chewed and digested."

The rest of the essays, such as "Of Discourse" and "Of Ceremonies and Respects," repeat traditional bits of advice but then set those elements against one another. Stanley Fish observes that if the Baconian essay is read for more than its disparate elements, it becomes a tortuously negative definition of its topic. In fact, Bacon wants the sagacious reader to winnow truth from the experience, repeated almost line by line, of giving up what was formerly embraced. Bacon's advice to use duplicitous rhetorical techniques, for example, is in competition with his prudent warnings to audiences and speakers, respectively, about the dangers of being outwitted or misunderstood. "Of Followers and Friends" is particularly revealing: it is not about friendship so much as about the dangers of affiliations, especially close ones, and the rarity – perhaps the nonexistence – of real friendship, which succumbs to vanity and the desire to gain or hold advantage.

In the later editions of the *Essayes*, friendship is Bacon's most problematic topic. A new essay on the subject appears in the 1612 edition and is rewritten in the edition of 1625. In other instances of revision Bacon almost never omits what he has written in previous versions; for him revision is typically a process of adding more maxims, illustrations, and commentary. In the 1625 edition, however, the essay on friendship has been totally recast. The essays of 1612 and 1625 praise friendship, putting it in a much more favorable light than in 1597, but the new versions also suggest that the real value of friendship might lie in sophisticated calculations of usefulness and in its reflection of a physical law: the attraction, manifested by all bodies, of like to like. What is supposed to save Baconian friendship from

becoming Machiavellianism, which he elsewhere claims to reject, is charity.

To these doctrines about friendship there was one great exception: Bacon's relationship with his brother, Anthony. The two men lodged in the same rooms at Cambridge, traveled to France together, and shared living quarters between 1591, when Anthony returned from his decade of intelligence gathering on the Continent, and 1594. Anthony was, in Bacon's published opinion, more politically astute and worthy of the queen's favor than was Bacon himself. In the dedication to the 1597 edition of the *Essayes* Bacon addresses his brother in a passage that links their relationship to Bacon's desire to advance the sciences: "I sometimes wish your infirmities translated upon myself, that her majesty might have the service of so active and able a mind and I might be with excuse confined to those contemplations and studies for which I am fittest." Anthony was lame, and lameness came to embody for Bacon the halting method of true scientific inquiry as well as the retirement from public life that made such inquiry possible. After Anthony's death in 1601, Bacon's first petition for office in the reign of James I was based not on his own qualifications but on Anthony's secret diplomatic service for James during the reign of Elizabeth, and the document granting Bacon a pension in 1604 cites Anthony's service rather than Bacon's.

The almost claustrophobic brevity of the 1597 texts gives way to the expansive *Of the Proficience and Advancement of Learning,* which Bacon dedicated to James I in late 1605. James had knighted Bacon in 1603 and had named him to the commission on the union of England and Scotland in 1604. These tentative signs of favor encouraged grander ambitions in Bacon, and the dedication urges James to support a long-range plan to master and renovate all forms of knowledge. Bacon's flattery of James is more than the conventional praise of a potential patron. James was a sort of scholar too, whose writings include a treatise on witchcraft; since virtue is without defenses unless one knows "all forms and natures of evil," James is a model of the wise researcher who can descend into corruption without being defiled.

Bacon self-consciously popularizes his ideas (he writes, he says, "not with true measure, but with popular estimates and conceit"), and almost every page contains striking illuminations of the new sciences that he will set out in much more technical detail in later works. The old learning is not, just because it is old, the fundamental enemy. In book 1 Bacon defends both the old and the new learning against the traditional objections that all learning encourages atheism and heresy. The new learning's purpose is not only to overturn traditional learning but also to resume the ancient search for a comprehensive account of the natural world. Thus the great innovator Nicolaus Copernicus, by Bacon's lights, wrongly separates astronomy from "universality or *philosophia prima*," which is that "common fountain" that men have abandoned for the sake of relatively narrow, self-serving ditherings. Divine, natural, and human philosophy "are like branches of a tree that meet in one stem."

Bacon's praise of the old learning is rich with intimations of innovation. He allows that superstitions might shadow forth something real: astrology, magic, and alchemy are commendable for their "noble" ends, though they are full of falsehoods. The stars do not determine people's actions, but they do seem to have an influence that ought to be examined. Magic suggests precedents for new and useful sciences capable of changing anything into anything else. Alchemy's dream of making gold is a scientific possibility.

Bacon warns against mixing theology and worldly learning, while hypothesizing that the new learning has power to decode God's ordinances and decrees in Genesis. On the one hand, he says that "we should not place our felicity in knowledge, as we forget our immortality"; mixtures of religion and natural philosophy produce "heretical religion" and "imaginary philosophy." On the other hand, Bacon speculates that the new discoveries will overcome "all fears together" of mortality and corruptibility. Bodies purified by the workings of worldly science, not only by the powers of the divine, "shall be advanced to immortality." In *De Dignitate & Augmentis Scientiarum* he goes so far as to claim that physicians, second only to God, can become dispensers of prolonged life, a gift *"ex terrenis quasi maximum"* (of earthly gifts perhaps the greatest).

The advancement of knowledge depends on experimentation: "trials and vexation" are necessary. In Homer's *Odyssey,* Proteus, captured and manacled by Menelaus, writhes in torment, changing into all possible shapes until his essential being emerges to tell the secrets his captor wants to know; nature, like Proteus, must be "crossed" or placed under duress until it reveals its secrets. Bacon is likening the investigation of nature to the interrogation of prisoners under torture. In the late 1590s Bacon had been employed to question prisoners in the Tower of London who were accused of plotting against Elizabeth's life: Macaulay alleges that Bacon was "among the last Englishmen who used the rack." Bacon would be present, a decade after writing *Of the Proficience and Advancement of Learning,* to witness the testimony under torture of Edmond

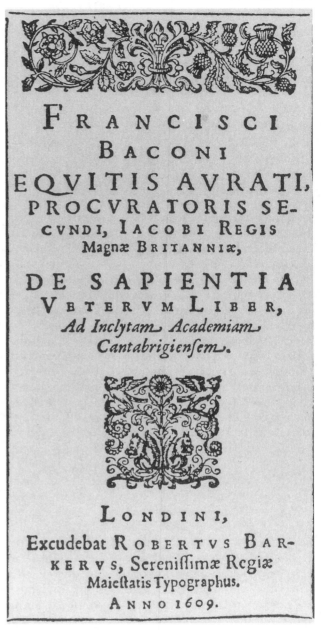

Title page for Bacon's collection of thirty-one "parables" based on ancient myths

Peacham, a clergyman accused of taking part in a conspiracy against the king.

Bacon also insists on the suffering of the experimenter: "wise and industrious suffering . . . draweth and contriveth use and advantage out of that which seemeth adverse and contrary." Wise suffering breaks the imagination's self-indulgent preference for "affirmative" instances; the imagination must be "delivered and reduced" by a "negative or privative" method until only truly useful cases — instances of the laws of nature — are left.

Bacon applies this principle of reduction to political and religious activities. The trials of public life – the ordeals of governing while being subject to dangerous circumstances – are like "strange and hard stops" to which the master politician's hands, like the lutenist's, must be broken. In religion, he notes, rituals of deprivation such as fasting are similarly effective mortifications of wayward imagination.

Bacon distinguishes between the "magistral" and the "initiative" methods of scientific investigation. The first, he says, is corrupt: the grasping, wayward imagination is all too ready to accept its high-flown, authoritative rhetoric in place of real inquiry. The initiative method, by contrast, advances learning through the rigor of an induction that is not unlike religious initiation. The initiative method delivers knowledge "as a thread to be spun on . . . *in the same method wherein it was invented.*" It subjects its user and audience to a process of purgative denial, of discovery by negation. Reducing the investigator's and audience's anticipations, the initiation enables them to capture and sift away Proteus's disguises. Hence, Bacon prefers aphoristic reports of inquiry that imitate Solomon's book of proverbs. Aphorisms require their makers and audiences to piece together natural laws by scourging their expectations. Their "broken knowledge," if it is interpreted arduously and without vain anticipation, yields a deeper knowledge.

But if the initiative method is best, how can the new learning foster hope? In fact, Bacon's project depends on a general expectation of its success and rewards, and for this reason he urges the creation of a "Georgics of the mind," which would show how hope should be cultivated without mere trickery or self-delusion. One approach would be an encyclopedic investigation of the appetites, for the sake of controlling them by means of the fundamental laws of their action. Another would be an inquiry into the workings of the imagination, though Bacon says that he steers away from an extensive, explicit analysis of the imagination because the subject is dangerous: since imagination can be the ally of religion as well as of heresy, a science that would put the imagination under human control poses a threat to faith and, hence, to charity.

The comprehensive science of influence that encourages useful hope is rhetoric, and it is no accident that Bacon is remembered as the quintessential rhetorician. (Ben Jonson said that audiences were unwilling to accept that Bacon's speeches must end.) The greatest rhetorician is God, who, without revealing the mysteries of his will, "doth grift [graft] his revelations and holy doctrine upon the notions of our reason, and applieth his inspirations to open our understanding."

Rhetoric, in Bacon's often-quoted definition, is reason applied to the imagination for the better moving of the will. Poetry is far more influential on the imagination than is reason. Used unwisely, poetry fans heresy by pandering to idolatrous passions; yet, properly understood and mastered, it resembles religion in holding out the possibility of making the imagination the servant of wisdom.

The modern belief that Bacon condemns poetry ignores his interest in poetry's intimation of deeper laws of the imagination's operations. According to *De Dignitate & Augmentis Scientiarum,* dramatic poetry is highly useful when it is employed wisely. One of nature's most important secrets is the susceptibility of people's minds when they are assembled in large audiences. Parables are more forceful than arguments and examples, and fables are the oldest writings next to sacred texts. In *The Advancement of Learning* Bacon writes that poetry not only cultivates magnanimity, morality, and delight but also has "some participation in divineness, because it doth raise and erect the mind, by submitting the shews of things to the desire of the mind: whereas reason doth buckle and bow the mind unto the nature of things." Poetry must become an instrument for enlightened manipulation, supplying accessible, effective revelations of what the new sciences hope for.

De Sapientia Veterum Liber (translated as *The Wisedome of the Ancients,* 1619) was published in 1609, three years after Bacon's marriage on 10 May 1606 to Alice Barnham and two years after his appointment as solicitor general. The work consists of thirty-one "parables" derived from ancient myths. Parables are a "method of teaching" that is "sometimes indispensable" to scientific inquiry as well as to religion. Parables are like codes: they "serve to disguise and veil the meaning, and they serve also to clear and throw light upon it." Myths are enigmas that are beyond human capacity to create; and yet, precisely because they are so strange, they are accessible to those who detect their contrariety to common sense.

The myth of Cassandra, titled "Plainness of Speech," exemplifies the failure of the truthful prophet who does not appreciate the necessity of veils and of knowing when and how to speak so that others will listen. The satyrlike Pan signifies nature, in which "all things are in truth biformed and made up of a higher species and a lower." His piping music seems ugly and inferior to Apollo's but is, in fact, the "somewhat harsh and untunable" harmony of God's government of the world, which ordinary listeners cannot appreciate. Pan is also a better investigator into nature than is Orpheus, or philosophy, because Pan relies on experience and accident rather than desire, which deprives the back-glancing Orpheus of his beloved wife, Eurydice. The single life, such as Pan's, is more arduous but more fertile with discoveries of nature's laws than is the married life. The parables of Venus, Cupid, and Dionysus show limitations of love: Venus's rule of the world by concord and consent is temporary at best; Cupid's love, which governs the motion of the atom, is beyond human comprehension; Dionysus symbolizes desire, the "appetite and aspiration for apparent good" that always results "in some unlawful wish." Theseus is the heroic decoder of the labyrinth, but superior even to Theseus in scientific acumen is Daedalus, the inventor of the labyrinth, who makes available the clue to the maze. "Filmi Labyrinthi" (The Clue to the Maze), first published in 1734, gives this role ultimately to God: "it is the glory of God to conceal, but it is the glory of man . . . to invent," the human spirit being *as the lamp of God, wherewith he searcheth every secret.*

But Daedalus is "a man of the greatest genius but of very bad character." He is a murderer and an unscrupulous technician who serves depraved lusts by making himself available to the highest bidder. How can human genius gain insight into the laws of nature and establish the empire that such laws make available, if Daedalus is the dangerous precedent?

The answer lies in the parable of Prometheus, Bacon's most elaborate story and commentary. Not only must the genius of the new sciences endure "the command of experience," not letting himself "thirst for experiments either of profit or ostentation," but he must also learn from Prometheus's example that true virtue under these circumstances is "not natural": it must come "from without." Bound to the rock for stealing fire and for assaulting the chastity of Minerva, the goddess of wisdom, Prometheus cannot be saved by his own fortitude. He needs Hercules, who releases him from his torment after traveling across the ocean in a frail vessel. Bacon observes in this myth "a wonderful correspondency with the mysteries of the Christian faith": "an image of God the Word hastening in the frail vessel of the flesh to redeem the human race." A kind of grace, not mere virtue, is required if the practice of enlightened science is to transcend criminality.

The relationship among knowledge, wisdom, and power is one of Bacon's chief subjects in the *Novum Organum,* his most elaborate treatment of the

new sciences' principles and methods. His chaplain reported having seen the treatise in a dozen drafts; Bacon chose to have it published in 1620, in the late efflorescence of his public career, having been made attorney general on 27 October 1613, privy councillor on 9 June 1616, lord keeper on 7 March 1617, lord chancellor on 7 January 1618, and Baron Verulam on 12 July 1618. The table of contents shows that the project is far from complete: the *Novum Organum* is the second part of a six-part "Great Instauration" or renovation of the sciences, which begins with the division of the sciences under the headings of memory, imagination, and reason. (A more detailed version of this division is set out in *De Dignitate & Augmentis Scientiarum* and was used by the eighteenth-century philosophes as the organizing principle of the *Encyclopédie.*)

After the division of the sciences and the introduction in the *Novum Organum* of scientific methods and principles, the third part of the "Great Instauration" is to be natural and experimental histories that collect, for the sake of further analysis, what is already known. Bacon attaches the "Parasceve ad Historium Naturalem et Experimentatum: Preparative towards a Natural and Experimental History" to the *Novum Organum* as a brief example of what he has in mind; the later *Historia Naturalis et Experimentalis* (1622), *Historia de Ventis* (1622), and *Historia Vitæ & Mortis* (1623) are meant to go into this category, as does the *Sylva Sylvarum* (1626), the "forest of forests" that displays Bacon's own researches into the commonplaces and special topics of existing natural philosophy. The fourth part is the "scale of the intellect," which derives from more-advanced research by means of the new scientific methods. (Only the brief "Filum Labyrinthi" conforms to this type.) The fifth part is what Bacon calls "Forerunners, or Anticipations of the New Philosophy," which look beyond the new methods by using the unaided understanding. Here Bacon demonstrates once again that his project involves the generation of hypotheses and rhetorical projections, not merely inductive catalogues and siftings, to garner his audience's hopes and energies for the sake of scientific advancement. The final part of the "Great Instauration" is "the New Philosophy, or Active Science." The nature of this part of the project is obscure, though its outlines are hinted at in the civil and scientific ways of life one glimpses in Bacon's "New Atlantis" (1626).

The *Novum Organum* is Bacon's attempt to replace Aristotle's *Organon,* which comprises rhetoric, dialectic, and syllogistic demonstration and which had become entwined — confused, Bacon thought —

Title page for Bacon's Novum Organum, *intended to be part of his "Great Instauration," or renovation of the sciences. The project was never completed.*

with scholastic theology. Bacon's aphoristic treatise adamantly divides divine truths from human utility, but throughout he grapples with the problem of reconciling religion and the new sciences. The paradoxical result is that he magnifies the new sciences' utility in a way that becomes indistinguishable from his emphasis on their detection of God's "stamp upon creation": "Be it known then how vast a difference there is . . . between the Idols of the human mind and the Ideas of the divine. The former are nothing more than arbitrary abstractions; the latter are the creator's own stamp upon creation, impressed and defined in matter by true and exquisite lines. Truth therefore and utility are here the very same things: and works themselves are of greater value as pledges of truth than as contributing to the comforts of life." What looks like a reduction of the scientific project to useful pursuits rather than theological speculation becomes an inquiry into "pledges of truth."

Idolatry is the worst error among those who pursue science, much as it is the greatest sin against true religion. Vulgar minds, which fail to appreciate the urgency and rigor of the quest for the divine code, worship four kinds of idols. The Idols of the Tribe, arising from weakness in human nature itself, are worshiped by those who find order prematurely or in the wrong places. They fuel their idolatry with gossipy evidence that confirms their prejudices. They believe in final causes which are beyond the reach of experiments into cause and effect. Even if it seeks isolation, the individual mind is subject to Idols of the Cave, which arise from habit and accident rather than inquiry. Those who venture into the company of others to pursue scientific inquiry almost inevitably worship Idols of the Market-Place, the most powerful of illusions because they offer a false sense of control: facility with words rather than knowledge of things. Finally, the Idols of the Theater await those benighted sophisticates who think they can pursue science merely by taking in the shows put on by academicians. In all these idolatries, self-gratification and flattery displace the ordeal of true inquiry.

In *Novum Organum* Bacon therefore returns to the question of torture. If nature is to give up her secrets she must be commanded, confined, vexed, and tormented; but to be commanded she must be obeyed. The lineaments of creation cannot be violated: "human knowledge and human Power do really meet in one" when divine laws are detected and used. Detecting and using those laws requires "religious care" and restraint amid the fruits and comforts offered by ingenious inventions. The aphorism is the sign of that restraint — it is confining, fragmenting, and self-abasing, yet it allows one to savor and project the fruits of wise contemplation.

To create aphorisms, which conceal yet suggest deeper laws, one must gather interpretations "here and there from very various and widely dispersed facts" that may deny the anticipations of the creator of the aphorisms. "Harsh and out of tune," these facts resemble "mysteries of the faith." Thus the truly revolutionary inventions of the new era (for example, the seaman's compass and the art of printing) burst upon a world that had no glimmer of their possibility. To foster more such inventions, investigators must escape the prejudice that man is the measure of all things. What counts is the "going to and from to remote and heterogenous instances, by which axioms are tried as in the fire," not by anticipation but by inductive "rejection and exclusion."

These new methods must be understood as a "true and just humiliation of the human spirit." They comprise a scourging "machine" (Bacon may have the rack in mind here) that must be experienced by each true investigator seeking to command nature's secrets by submitting to her deepest laws. Traditional inquiry and persuasion are, by comparison, useless. Bacon has no wish to found a school, for schools of philosophy attempt to proselytize and to train their members. The ancient sophists knew better than Plato and founded no schools. Their reclusive interest in the ways of power rather than the beguilements of ideas helped them break down and master the created world by working "silently and serenely and simply." Superior to the modern medical charlatan Paracelsus, such investigators are wisely laconic and do not recklessly promise to bring heaven to earth. On the other hand, the Baconian investigator can know something about the relation between divine Providence and worldly fact because he knows that Providence is a code whereby God seems to do one thing (selling Joseph into Egypt) while doing another (providing for the Hebrews' liberation from slavery).

Bacon finds the story of Oedipus to signify the solitary, purifying torment of the scientific inquisitor who detects what is real rather than what merely seems. The myth complements that of Proteus, who represents the subject of the inquirer's code-breaking torments. His feet crippled by his father after the prophecy that he will commit patricide, Oedipus is a maimed hero. In adulthood he hobbles toward his confrontation with the riddling Sphinx (Bacon's emblem, in *De Sapientia Veterum Liber,* for science), whom he masters precisely because his arduous, tortuous advance requires heroic indifference to his goal even as he pursues it. Bacon argues that without the blind haste of vainglorious ambition and idolatrous anticipation, Oedipus is capable of overcoming the monster's riddle.

The "New Atlantis," Bacon's vision of a society governed by the new learning, appeared after his death in the same volume as the *Sylva Sylvarum.* The work is unfinished; in the preface the editor, William Rawley, claims that Bacon intended to write a concluding account of Atlantis's laws but was distracted by the composition of his natural histories. The story is a merchant sea captain's recounting of his voyage to and stay on an island called Bensalem, from which he has returned to describe that enlightened society. A sustained gale propelled his ship for many days until, its provisions exhausted, it entered Bensalem's harbor.

The natives' enigmatic welcome — remote yet comforting — was a sign of things to come. The captain and crew prostrated themselves before their hosts, thanking them for what seemed "a picture of our salvation in heaven," "a happy and holy ground" after their escape from "the jaws of death"; but at every stage of their apparent assimilation the island society surrounded them with prohibitions and secrets. Visitors to Bensalem are few, and those who touch its shores almost never return to their homes; just thirteen have done so in nineteen hundred years. The attractiveness of the island made the sailors "forget all that was dear" in their own countries, ensuring that they would not return home to spread the news of Bensalem's location and riches.

The captain alone was allowed to hear of the most important Bensalemite institution, the research and development laboratories of Salomon's House, though the information he received from a "Father" of the house is a list of wonders rather than a revelation of natural laws. Salomon's House is devoted to the "enlarging of the bounds of

Human Empire, to the effecting of all things possible," including the resuscitation of what might "seem dead in appearance." Its researches focus on discovering the means of making anything into anything else, either materially or by means of illusions that are generated in "perspective houses" and "houses of deceits of the senses." Spy missions to the outside world collect additional information about scientific innovations. The Salomonic priesthood withholds some inventions from the state; those it publishes are made known "without all affectation of strangeness" so as not to "induce admiration" by making their operations "seem more miraculous." Hymns are sung daily, in prayer to God for guidance in new inquiries and applications. The priesthood's extraordinary secrecy, power to alter the world, and ability to alter perceptions of its accomplishments are mitigated — and yet concealed — by its private religiosity and the benevolent appearance of its wonders.

There are religious wonders in Bensalem, but these must be certified by the scientific priests. It was a Father of the House of Salomon who interpreted the revelation of Christianity to the Bensalemites when a column of light topped with a cross appeared in the sea near the coast. Unable to approach it nearer than sixty yards, the people were dumbfounded until a representative of Salomon's House, the institution serving as "the very eye" of the kingdom, certified the wonder as a genuine miracle. The miracle was indistinguishable from an illusion without the authoritative word of a member of the pious scientific elect. Bensalem's scientific certification of miracles demonstrates Bacon's interest in controlling religious enthusiasm so that it justifies but does not influence science and affairs of state.

When Bacon was made viscount St. Albans on 27 January 1621, he reached the apogee of his political career and of his material fortunes. His trial, conviction, fine of forty thousand pounds, and imprisonment in May 1621 for accepting bribes in the king's service are, next to his accusation of Essex, the incidents that most taint his memory. Consistent with his previous interpretation of Solomon's rule as a judicious kingship that descended into corruption without becoming tainted, Bacon admitted that the charge against him was true and yet argued that he had carried out his duties without corruption; his accusers had brought the charge after he had accepted their bribes and then ruled against them. Bacon also claimed that he had acted far more justly than his recent predecessors in office. King James released him from the Tower in Sep-

tember, pardoning him on the condition that he never again approach the court.

Bacon's industry during his retirement was prodigious. The extensive *History of the Reign of King Henry the Seventh* and the *Historia de Ventis* (History of the Winds) appeared in 1622, the *De Dignitate & Augmentis Scientiarum* and *Historia Vitæ & Mortis* (History of Life and Death) in 1623. His dialogue "An Advertisement Touching an Holy War" (1629), written around 1622 and dedicated to the churchman Lancelot Andrewes, advances ideas about managing international political and religious conflicts. *Apophthegms New and Old,* the third edition of the *Essayes,* and *Translations of Certain Psalms* were all published in 1625, and the *Sylva Sylvarum* in 1626.

In the late winter of 1626 Bacon, traveling by coach, stopped to conduct an experiment in suspending the process of decay by gathering snow to stuff a chicken's carcass. He caught a chill and retired to a nearby noble's residence, where he died on 9 April, Rawley says, "of a gentle fever, accidentally accompanied with a great cold." He was buried at St. Michael's Church, St. Albans.

Bacon was, unquestionably, ambitious. His ordeal by disappointment exhibited the methods and principles of the new sciences, and his frequent illnesses, according to his own testimony, provided him with the enforced leisure necessary for his remarkable production of literary, philosophical, and political texts. In the last months of his life he concluded that his wife had been unfaithful, and he revoked his will. But rather than embittering him, his life seems to have produced in him an almost preternatural resistance to disappointment.

What he praised in Queen Elizabeth, a few years after her death, he valued most in himself. He considered it "part of her felicity that she was raised to sovereignty from a private fortune," because "Princes who are brought up in the reigning house with assured expectation of succeeding to the throne, are commonly spoiled by the indulgence and license of their education, and so turn out less capable and less temperate. And therefore you will find that the best kings are they who have been trained in both schools of fortune; such as Henry the Seventh," who "of late years" came to the throne "from an adverse and troubled fortune." Similarly, Elizabeth "at her birth was destined to the succession, then disinherited, afterwards superseded. . . . And yet she did not pass suddenly from the prison to the throne, with a mind embittered and swelling with the sense of misfortune, but was first restored to liberty and comforted with expecta-

Title page for the volume that includes the first publication of Bacon's
utopia, "New Atlantis"

tion; and so came to her kingdom at last quietly and prosperously, without tumult or competitor."

This was precisely what Bacon's friend and patron, the earl of Essex, could not do. In the trial Bacon had charged him with presumptuous impatience under extreme adversity – a lack of faith in his severe, humiliating queen's ultimate favor: "for you, my Lord, should know that though princes give their subjects cause of discontent, though they take away the honours they have heaped upon them, though they bring them to a lower estate than they raised them from, yet ought they not to be so forgetful of their allegiance that they should enter into an undutiful act; much less upon open rebellion."

Bacon's ordeal, insofar as it culminated in his efforts to make King James into a Solomonic friend of the new sciences, ended in failure. The kingly favor Bacon lost became, in his eyes, something to be won for the world from the heavenly King – or,

at least, from an enlightened posterity that would detect and use the difficult, sometimes hidden doctrines in his works. Throughout Bacon's writings one glimpses this deeply personal attempt to win the favor of Providence by piously and arduously mastering nature. Bacon's genealogical legacy adumbrates his intellectual one: he died childless, as did the monarch, Elizabeth, whose life he described as patterning his own, and modern historians of science are divided over the degree and quality of his contribution. There was, however, no doubt in the mind of Thomas Sprat. In his *History of the Royal Society* (1667) he attributes the society's scientific accomplishments to Bacon's inspiration. The history includes a poem by Abraham Cowley that likens Bacon to the biblical lawgiver Moses.

Letters:

Letters of Sr Francis Bacon, Baron of Verulam, Viscount St. Alban, and Lord High Chancellor of England: Writ-

ten during the Reign of King James the First. Now Collected, and Augmented with Several Letters and Memoirs, Address'd by him to the King and Duke of Buckingham, which were never before Published, edited by Robert Stephens (London: Printed for Benjamin Tooke, 1702).

Bibliographies:

R. W. Gibson, *Francis Bacon: A Bibliography of His Works and of Baconiana to the Year 1750* (Oxford: Scrivener Press, 1950);

Brian Vickers, *Francis Bacon* (London: Longman, 1978).

Biographies:

A. R. Skemp, *Francis Bacon* (London: Jack / New York: Dodge, 1912);

John Aubrey, *Aubrey's Brief Lives,* edited by Oliver Lawson Dick (London: Secker & Warburg, 1949; Ann Arbor: University of Michigan Press, 1962), pp. 8–16;

Catherine Drinker Bowen, *Francis Bacon: The Temper of a Man* (Boston: Little, Brown, 1963).

References:

F. H. Anderson, *The Philosophy of Francis Bacon* (Chicago: University of Chicago Press, 1948);

Judah Bierman, "The *New Atlantis,* Bacon's Utopia of Science," *Papers on Language and Literature,* 3 (Spring 1967): 99–110;

Bierman, "Science and Utopia in the *New Atlantis* and Other Renaissance Utopias," *PMLA,* 78 (December 1963): 492–500;

John C. Briggs, *Francis Bacon and the Rhetoric of Nature* (Cambridge, Mass.: Harvard University Press, 1989);

Phyllis B. Burke, "Rhetorical Considerations of Bacon's Style," *C C C,* 18 (1967): 23–31;

Walter Davis, "The Imagery of Bacon's Late Work," *Modern Language Quarterly,* 27 (June 1966): 162–173;

Benjamin Farrington, *The Philosophy of Francis Bacon: An Essay on Its Development from 1603 to 1609, with New Translations of Fundamental Texts* (Liverpool: Liverpool University Press, 1964; Chicago: University of Chicago Press, 1966);

Stanley Fish, *Self-Consuming Artifacts* (Berkeley: University of California Press, 1972);

D. G. James, *The Dream of Learning: An Essay on "The Advancement of Learning," "Hamlet," and "King Lear"* (New York: Oxford University Press, 1951);

Lisa Jardine, *Francis Bacon: Discovery and the Art of Discourse* (Cambridge: Cambridge University Press, 1974);

Charles W. Lemmi, *The Classic Deities in Bacon* (Baltimore: Johns Hopkins University Press, 1933);

Thomas Babington Macaulay, "Lord Bacon," *Edinburgh Review,* 65 (July 1837): 1–104;

Jonathan L. Marwil, *The Trials of Counsel: Francis Bacon in 1621* (Detroit: Wayne State University Press, 1976);

Elizabeth McCutcheon, "Bacon and the Cherubim: An Iconographical Reading of the *New Atlantis,*" *English Literary Renaissance,* 2 (Autumn 1972): 334–355;

Paul Quinton, *Francis Bacon* (Oxford: Oxford University Press, 1974);

Paolo Rossi, *Francis Bacon: From Magic to Science,* translated by Sacha Rabinovitch (London: Routledge & Kegan Paul, 1968);

Robert M. Schuler, *Francis Bacon and Scientific Poetry* (Philadelphia: American Philosophical Society, 1992);

Sister M. F. Schuster, "Philosophy of Life and Prose Style in Thomas More's *Richard III* and Francis Bacon's *Henry VIII,*" *PMLA,* 70 (June 1955): 474–487;

William A. Sessions, *Francis Bacon's Legacy of Texts* (New York: AMS Press, 1990);

Sessions, ed., "The Legacy of Francis Bacon," *Studies in the Literary Imagination,* special issue 4 (April 1971);

Thomas Sprat, *History of the Royal Society of London for the Improving of Natural Knowledge* (London: Printed by T. R. for J. Martyn & J. Allestry, 1667);

James Stephens, "Bacon's Fable-Making: A Strategy of Style," *Studies in English Literature,* 14 (Winter 1974): 111–127;

Stephens, "Bacon's New English Rhetoric and the Debt to Aristotle," *Speech Monographs,* 39 (November 1972): 248–259;

Stephens, *Francis Bacon and the Style of Science* (Chicago: University of Chicago Press, 1975);

James S. Tillman, "Bacon's *Ethos:* The Modest Philosopher," *Renaissance Papers* (1976): 11–19;

Geoffrey Tillotson, "Words for Princes: Bacon's Essays," in his *Essays in Criticism and Research* (Cambridge: Cambridge University Press, 1942);

Brian Vickers, *Essential Articles for the Study of Francis Bacon* (Hamden, Conn.: Archon, 1968);

Vickers, *Francis Bacon and Renaissance Prose* (Cambridge: Cambridge University Press, 1968);

Karl Wallace, *Francis Bacon and the Nature of Man* (Carbondale: Southern Illinois University Press, 1967);

Wallace, *Francis Bacon on Communication and Rhetoric* (Chapel Hill: University of North Carolina Press, 1943);

Marjorie Walters, "The Literary Background of Francis Bacon's Essay 'Of Death,' " *Modern Language Review,* 35 (January 1940): 1–7;

Jerry Weinberger, *Science, Faith, and Politics: Francis Bacon and the Utopian Roots of the Modern Age* (Ithaca, N.Y.: Cornell University Press, 1985);

Charles Whitney, *Francis Bacon and Modernity* (New Haven: Yale University Press, 1986);

B. H. G. Wormald, *Francis Bacon: History, Politics and Science, 1561-1626* (Cambridge: Cambridge University Press, 1993);

Jacob Zeitlin, "The Development of Bacon's Essays — with Special Reference to the Question of Montaigne's Influence upon Them," *Journal of English and Germanic Philology,* 27 (1928): 496–519.

Papers:

The primary collections of Francis Bacon's manuscripts are in the British Library and the Public Record Office, London. Other significant archives are in the libraries of Cambridge University, the University of London, Alewick Castle, and Chatsworth House. Additional manuscripts and letters are in the Bibliothèque Nationale, Paris; the Bodleian Library, Oxford; and at Aberdeen University and Manhattan College, New York City. Letters are also at the Folger Shakespeare Library, Washington, D.C.; the Henry E. Huntington Library and Art Gallery, San Marino, California; the Francis Bacon Library, Claremont, California; the House of Lords Record Office; Hatfield House; and the Bibliotheca Bodmeriana, Switzerland.

Augustine Baker

(9 December 1575 – 9 August 1641)

Anthony Low

New York University

BOOKS: *Apostolatus Benedictinorum in Anglia, sive Disceptatio historica, de antiquitate Ordinis congregationisque monachorum nigrorum S. Benedicti in regno Angliae, in qua demonstratur S. Gregorius ejus nationis Apostolum, fuisse Benedictinum,* edited by David Baker, John Jones, and Clement Reyner (Douai: Printed by Lawrence Kellam, 1626);

The Holy Practices of a Divine Lover, or the Sainctly Ideots Devotions (Paris, 1657); published, with authorship erroneously assigned to Dame Gertrude More, as *The Holy Practices of a Divine Lover; or, the Saintly Idiot's Devotions,* edited by Dom H. Lane Fox (London: Sands, 1909);

Sancta Sophia. Or Directions for the Prayer of Contemplation &c. Extracted out of more then XL. Treatises written by the Late Ven. Father F. Augustin Baker A Monke of the English Congregation of the Holy Order of S. Benedict: and Methodically Digested, edited by Serenus Cressy (2 volumes, Douai: Printed by John Patté & Thomas Fievet, 1657; 1 volume, New York: Dunigan, 1857); published as *Holy Wisdom; or, Directions for the Prayer of Contemplation Extracted out of More than Forty Treatises by the Ven. Father F. Augustine Baker: Methodically Digested by R.F. Serenus Cressy and Now Edited from the Douay Edition of 1657,* edited by Norbert Sweeney (London: Burns, Oates & Washbourne / New York: Benziger, 1890?);

Life of Dame Gertrude More, edited by Henry Collins (London: T. Richardson & Sons, 1877); abridged as volume 1 of *The Inner Life and Writings of Dame Gertrude More,* edited by Dom Benedict Weld-Blundell (London: Washbourne / New York: Benziger, 1910).

Edition: *Holy Wisdom; or, Directions for the Prayer of Contemplation,* edited by Gerard Sitwell (London: Burns & Oates, 1964).

OTHER: "Fr. Baker's Autobiography," in *Memorials of Father Augustine Baker and Other Documents Relating to the English Benedictines,* edited by Dom Justin McCann and Dom Hugh Connolly, Publications of the Catholic Record Society, volume 33 (London: Privately printed for the Society by J. Whitehead & Son, 1933).

Augustine Baker was the chief exponent of British Catholic mysticism during a period when mystical and other forms of devotion were on the rise in Europe in response to the Reformation. He was also a significant actor in the history of British recusancy and exile. Although he was an important figure historically and spiritually and more is known about him than about most men and women of his time through his early biographers and disciples, Baker has been neglected by historians and critics. Post-Reformation Roman Catholic writers in England were classified under the separate — and distinctly unequal — category of "recusants" by political authorities then and are so classified by scholars now. Because the original reasons for separate treatment no longer apply, perhaps this habit of marginalization will be reconsidered.

Born in the market town of Abergavenny, Wales, on 9 December 1575 to William and Maude Lewis Baker, Baker was the youngest of thirteen children, of whom all but the first and last were girls. His given name was David, after the Welsh saint, although he is usually known by his religious name, Augustine, taken when he joined the Benedictines. His father was steward to the Neville family, who held the lordship of Abergavenny; he was also a justice of the peace and may have been sheriff of Monmouthshire. William Baker was a "Church Papist"; that is, he conformed outwardly and attended Church of England services — the minimal observances necessary to retain his employment and escape persecution — but privately preferred Catholicism. He told his son that he would have accepted exile had he not had a family to support.

Augustine Baker (from a 1634 woodcut)

Baker's uncle, David Lewis, was more prominent than his father: under Queen Elizabeth he was master of requests, master of Saint Catherine's Hospital, and sole judge of the admiralty. At his death in 1584 he left Baker a house and property that provided him an independent income for the rest of his life.

Baker began his education at the local free grammar school. When he was eleven his father sent him to Christ's Hospital school in London. On the evening of his arrival in London, 8 February 1587, he witnessed the bonfires that celebrated the execution of the Catholic Mary, Queen of Scots. Ralph Waddington, master of Christ's Hospital, was, according to Baker's autobiography, a "zealous Protestant" who made the boys read the English Bible and recite services from the Book of Common Prayer daily. On Sundays they attended church to "hear the common service both morning and evening with severall sermons at those two times, besides the singing of psalms." They were then obliged to submit written summaries of the sermons for the master's approval. In 1590 Baker entered Broadgates Hall, Oxford (later Pembroke College). His tutor was a relative, William Pritchard, another "zealous Protestant" but "anti-Puritan" and a "meetly good Ciceronian." On his own testimony Baker fell into lax company, neglected his studies, spent his funds treating his friends to feasts, and was "daily and nightly abroad." He left Oxford in May 1592 without a degree and returned to Abergavenny.

For the next four years Baker lived in his father's large house, Beili Baker, and studied law.

After two attempts to find a position for him in Abergavenny fell through, he returned to London in the fall of 1596 to continue his legal studies. After a month at Clifford's Inn he entered the Inner Temple in November. He became a competent solicitor; he was also a frequent playgoer. On 7 October 1598 his brother, Richard, died, and Baker was summoned home to take his place. He became recorder of Abergavenny and was increasingly involved in legal affairs. Meanwhile, his religious faith decayed.

The turning point in his life came about 1600 when, while riding out on business, he escaped drowning in a swollen stream by what he considered miraculous means. Other factors also drew him to Catholicism: his father's devotional practice, the beliefs of his mother and one of his sisters, and the vivid report of the debate in the Tower of London between Edmund Campion and the Protestant ministers that his brother had witnessed. He also read widely in the Catholic library of his brother-in-law Henry Pritchard, who was disbarred for recusancy. To these factors, which Baker mentions, one might add that the Welsh, like the Scots, resisted the imposition of Anglican uniformity. Baker, whose parents had thought it safest to bring their sons up in the established church to further their careers, formally converted to Catholicism in May 1603, making his profession to Father Richard Floyd.

Increasingly discontent with his career, at the beginning of 1605 he went to London, where he met the English Benedictine dom Thomas Preston. In February he and Preston took ship from Dover for Italy, where Baker was accepted into the Benedictine community of Saint Justina's in Padua on 27 May 1605. His chronically weak health was not able to tolerate a foreign diet, and after a year he was released with testimonials that would allow him to join a monastery elsewhere. He returned to Wales, where he found that his father was dying. After his father's death he returned to London to settle the estate and provide for his sisters.

In London, Baker took part in a project to keep alive the English congregation of Benedictines, nearly extinguished after the dissolution of the monasteries by Henry VIII and the collapse of the Marian revival. He was ordained a priest at Rheims about 1613. After years of being without a proper community – Benedictines take vows of stability and ordinarily spend their lives in one monastery – Baker joined the English Congregation he had helped to revive when the pope officially restored it in 1619. When its legitimacy was challenged, Baker met with many of England's most distinguished an-

tiquaries in the course of researching the defense. Anthony à Wood reports in *Athenae Oxoniensis* (1691, 1692) that Baker was aided "by the learned *Cambden* [William Camden], Sir *Rob.* [Robert] *Cotton*, Sir *Henry Spelman*, Mr. *Joh.* [John] *Selden*, and Dr. *Fr.* [Francis] *Godwin*, Bishop of *Hereford:* to all of whom he was most familiarly known." Evidently, pride in ancient traditions took precedence in the minds of these authorities over suspicion of Catholic plots. The results of Baker's research appeared as *Apostolatus Benedictinorum in Anglia* (1626), his only book to be published in his lifetime.

With the return in 1623 of Prince Charles and George Villiers, first Duke of Buckingham, from Spain, where their negotiations for the marriage of Charles and the Infanta Maria had failed because of Charles's refusal to convert to Catholicism, there was a resurgence of Protestant fervor and increased persecution of Catholics in England. Consequently, in 1624 Baker accepted an invitation from Dom Rudisind Barlow, president of the English Congregation, to return to the Continent as spiritual adviser to the English nuns at Cambrai. There he spent the most fruitful period of his life writing treatises of advice for the nuns and translating the works of the great medieval mystics Jan van Ruysbroeck, Johann Tauler, Richard Rolle, Walter Hilton, and Thomas à Kempis, and the anonymous *Cloud of Unknowing*. Again he turned to Cotton; in a letter of 3 June 1629 he begs for books for the nuns: "There were manie good English bookes in olde time, whereof thoughe they have some, yet they want manie; and thereupon I am in their behalff become an humble suitor unto you to bestowe on them such bookes as you please, either manuscript or printed. . . ." If treatises on particular points were unavailable, Baker wrote them himself, including most of the "more than forty" that Serenus Cressy would use to compile Baker's most notable posthumous book, *Sancta Sophia* (1657). Among the nuns were members of many prominent English families, including Dame Catherine Gascoigne, the abbess, and Dame Gertrude More, a notable mystic and writer who was descended from Sir Thomas More.

Baker's happy days at Cambrai ended with the arrival of another priest, Father Francis Hull. Hull favored Ignatian spiritual practices: frequent examinations of conscience, complicated meditations, conferences, and regular use of Saint Ignatius of Loyola's *Spiritual Exercises* (1548). Baker preferred less formal and restrictive methods. Factions developed among the nuns, and Hull brought charges against Baker before a general chapter. Baker was exonerated, and in 1633 both priests

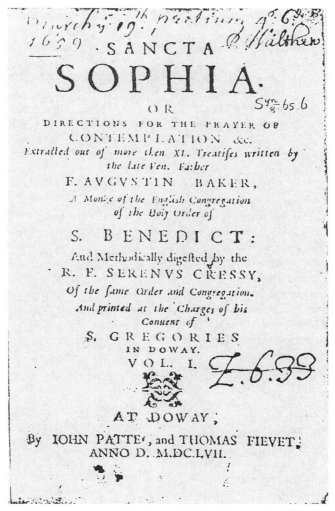

*Title page for Baker's posthumously published examination
of mysticism*

were transferred to Douai. There Baker continued to write, leaving his cell only for mass and meals. Even so, he became a magnet for visitors, including many from other orders and from the neighboring English Seminary.

Baker's growing popularity and his spiritual method, which seemed to encourage individual liberty at the expense of obedience, got him into trouble with his superiors. He may, as Frances Meredith has suggested, also have been caught in rivalries between Welsh and English monks. In important matters Baker was notably obedient, but, like many mystics, he suffered for his views at the hands of pragmatically minded superiors. The Carmelites of Antwerp and the nuns of Cambrai both asked to have Baker as their spiritual adviser, which would have resolved the growing controversy, but, under obedience, Baker declined.

In 1638 Baker's relationship with his superior, Father Barlow, deteriorated to the point where he was dismissed from the monastery and sent on "the English mission" (priests sent back to England, at risk to their lives, to provide the sacraments to English Catholics), accompanied by his friends and disciples Leander Pritchard and Cressy. Because of his age and unworldliness he was an unsuitable candidate for the mission and was more of a danger than a help to his companions. Separated from them he spent his last days moving from house to house just ahead of the pursuivants who, at the opening of the Long Parliament, were searching out and arresting Catholics. A royal proclamation banished all priests on pain of death, and in 1641 alone eighteen priests, including Saint Ambrose Barlow, were either executed or died in prison. Baker barely escaped arrest, catching a fever from which the frightened pursuivants fled. He died on 9 August 1641 and was buried at St. Andrew's, Holborn.

Baker's having escaped actual execution — although he was certainly hounded to death — may be one reason why his name was not put forward when forty English and Welsh martyrs were canonized in Rome on 25 October 1970. Instead, he is informally honored as "the late venerable Father Augustine Baker."

Baker's reputation rests on *Sancta Sophia,* which was assembled from his manuscripts after his death by his disciple Cressy. Few of Baker's original writings have seen print; the longest of those that have been published, his autobiography, is highly readable and is a notable source of information on Baker's times. It may be that Baker's writings are too specialized for general consumption or, as James Gaffney has suggested, that they are too idiosyncratic in style: Baker constantly qualifies, out of a concern to avoid misunderstanding of sometimes delicate spiritual points. Others have found him readable — certainly in comparison with other writers of the period whose works have been revived because of the light they throw on aspects of their times.

Baker's *Sancta Sophia* may be the clearest and most lucid examination ever written of the various types of mysticism and of the differences between mysticism and other forms of devotion. Baker has fresh and notable things to say about mysticism, especially about the possibility of its practice by ordinary people, not just by extraordinary saints such as Saint John of the Cross or Saint Teresa of Avila. The work is also a valuable source for the study of the varieties of spirituality and mental prayer in Baker's time, of which only meditation is known to most modern scholars. Furthermore, it is notable for its examination of religious freedom, a subject that got Baker into trouble with his superiors: he argues that people should not all be confined to the same rigid methods of devotion. The Ignatian method was immensely popular in his day; he had no quarrel with the method per se, but he felt that it was being forced indiscriminately on persons who were temperamentally unsuited for it. The work also deserves reexamination for its sympathetic treatment of women. Baker's contemporaries reported that he made many converts and had many successful disciples. Since his death many readers have made profitable use of *Sancta Sophia.*

Letters:
"Mr. Augustine Baker to Sir Robert Cotton, entreating for a present of books for the English Mon-
astery at Cambray," in *Original Letters,* edited by Henry Ellis, second series, volume 3 (London: Harding & Lepard, 1827), p. 256.

Biographies:
Dom Wilfred Reeve, "An Account of the Venerable Father Augustine Baker," *Ampleforth Journal,* 4 (1898): 59–74, 196–213;

Richard Baker Gabb, *The Families of Baker of Baily Baker and Baker Gabb, Abergavenny: A Memoir* (London, 1903);

Dom Peter Salvin and Dom Serenus Cressy, *The Confessions of Venerable Father Augustine Baker, O. S. B.,* edited by Dom Justin McCann (London: Burns, Oates & Washbourne, 1922);

McCann and Dom Hugh Connolly, eds., *Memorials of Father Augustine Baker and Other Documents Relating to the English Benedictines,* Publications of the Catholic Record Society, volume 33 (London: Privately printed for the Society by J. Whitehead & Son, 1933);

James Gaffney, "Biographical Preliminaries for a Life of Dom Augustine Baker," *American Benedictine Review,* 19 (1968): 515–535.

References:
Luke Bell, "Augustine Baker's Exposition of the Rule of St. Benedict," *Downside Review,* 107 (April 1989): 86–105;

Dom Cuthbert Butler, "Father Augustine Baker," *Downside Review,* 51 (1933): 577–595;

Dom Hugh Connolly, "The Buckley Affair," *Downside Review,* 49 (1931): 49–74;

Patrick Cowley, "Father Augustine Baker and the Sources of *Sancta Sophia,*" *Theology,* 37 (1938): 6–16;

James Gaffney, "Augustine Baker on Inspiration: A Study in English Recusant Spirituality," Ph.D. dissertation, Gregorian University, 1968;

Renée Haynes, "Augustine Baker," *Month,* 25 (March 1961): 160–172;

Bishop John Cuthbert Hedley, "Father Baker's *Sancta Sophia,*" *Dublin Review,* 79 (October 1876): 337–367;

Sister M. St. Teresa Higgins, C. S. J., "Augustine Baker," Ph.D. dissertation, University of Wisconsin, 1963;

Dom Philip Jebb, "A Hitherto Unnoticed Manuscript of the Venerable Augustine Baker," *Downside Review,* 104 (January 1986): 25–40;

David Knowles, *The English Mystical Tradition* (London: Burns & Oates / New York: Harper, 1961);

Anthony Low, *Augustine Baker* (New York: Twayne, 1970);

Frances Meredith, " 'Forced Acts': A Study of Dom Augustine Baker's Doctrine of Prayer," *Ampleforth Journal*, 76 (1971): 62–69;

Hywel Wyn Owen, "Extracts from the UpHolland Anthology: An Augustine Baker Manuscript," *Downside Review*, 108 (January 1990): 49–61;

Owen, "More Extracts from the UpHolland Anthology: An Augustine Baker Manuscript," *Downside Review*, 108 (April 1990): 131–145;

Owen and Bell, "The UpHolland Anthology: An Augustine Baker Manuscript," *Downside Review*, 107 (October 1989): 274–292;

Edward Ingram Watkins, *Poets and Mystics* (London: Sheed & Ward, 1953).

Papers:

Many of Augustine Baker's writings have never been published, and of those in print many have been cut and revised by successive editors. Manuscripts are scattered, mainly in England, Wales, and France; the most significant holdings are at Ampleforth, Colewich, and Downside abbeys and at the Bodleian Library, Oxford. The indispensable register of manuscripts is Dom Justin McCann's appendix to Dom Peter Salvin and Dom Serenus Cressy's *The Confessions of Venerable Father Augustine Baker, O. S. B.,* edited by McCann (London: Burns, Oates & Washbourne, 1922), supplemented by his "Ten More Baker MSS.," *Ampleforth Journal*, 63 (1958): 77–83.

Richard Brathwait
(circa 1588 – 4 May 1673)

Frederick Waage
East Tennessee State University

BOOKS: *The Golden Fleece. Whereto bee annexed two Elegies Entitled Narcissus Change, and Æsons Dotage* (London: Printed by W. Stansby for Christopher Pursett, 1611);

The Poets Willow: or, The Passionate Shepheard: With Sundry Delightfull, and no lesse Passionate Sonnets: describing the passions of a discontented and perplexed Lover, anonymous (London: Printed by John Beale for Samuel Rand, 1614);

The Prodigals Teares: or His fare-well to Vanity. A Treatise, of Soveraigne Cordials to the disconsolate Soule, surcharged with the heavy burthen of his sinnes: Ministering matter of remorse to the Impenitent, by the expression of Gods Judgements (London: Printed by N. Okes for T. Gubbins, 1614); enlarged as *The Prodigals Teares. With a Heavenly New Yeers Gift sent to the Soule; Contayning many most zealous and comfortable Prayers, with devout Meditations; Both worthie the acceptance of all Christians, and their expence of time to persue. By H. G. Preacher of the most Sacred Word of God* (London: Printed by B. Alsop for John Browne, 1620);

The Schollers Medley, or, An Intermixt Discourse upon Historicall and Poeticall Relations: A Subject of It Selfe Well Meriting the Approbation of the Judicious, Who Best Know How to Confirme Their Knowledge, by This Briefe Survey, or Generall Table of Mixed Discourses. And No Lesse Profitable to Such as Desire to Better Their Immaturity of Knowledge by Morall Readings. Distinguished into Severall Heads for the Direction of the Reader, to All Such Historicall Mixtures, as Be Comprehended in This Treatise. The Like Whereof for Variety of Discourse, Mixed with Profite, and Modest Delight, Hath Not Heretofore Beene Published (London: Printed by N. Okes for G. Norton, 1614); published as *A Survey of History: Or, a Nursery for Gentry: Contrived and Comprized in an Intermixt Discourse upon Historicall and Poeticall Relations* (London: Printed by John Okes for Jasper Emery, 1638);

A Strappado for the Divell: Epigrams and Satyres alluding to the time, with the divers measures of no lesse delight, anonymous (London: Printed by J. Beale for Richard Redmer, 1615) – includes "Loves Labyrinth: Or The true-Lovers Knot: Including the disastrous fals of two star-crost Lovers Pyramus and Thysbe A Subject heeretofore handled, but now with much more proprietie of passion and varietie of invention, continued";

A Solemne Joviall Disputation, Theoretike and Practicke; briefly shadowing the law of drinking; Together, with the Solemnities and Controversies Occurring; Fully and Freely Discussed according to the Civill Law. Which, by the Permission, Priviledge and Authority, of that Most Noble and Famous Order in the University of Goddesse Potina; Dionisius Bacchus Being Then President, Chiefe Gossipper, and Most Excellent Governour, Blasius Multibibus, aliàs Drinkmuch, a Singular Proficient and Most Qualifi'd in Both the Liberall Sciences of Wine and Beare; in the Colledge of Hilarity, Hath Publikely Expounded to His Most Approved and Improved Fellow-Pot-Shots; Touching the Houres before Noone and after, Usuall and Lawfull. We Are to Observe Whether This May Be, or How Much of This Is Admitted to Be in the Society of Men. . . . Faithfully rendred according to the originall Latine copie, anonymous (Oenozψthopolis [i.e., London]: At the Signe of Red-Eyes, 1617) – includes "The Smoaking Age, or, The man in the mist: With The life and death of Tobacco; dedicated To those three renowned and imparallel'd Heroes, Captaine Whiffe, Captaine Pipe, and Captaine Snuffe, to Whom the Author Wisheth as Much Content as This Smoaking Age Can Afford Them. Divided into Three Sections: 1. The Birth of Tobacco. 2. Pluto's Blessing to Tobacco. 3. Times Complaint against Tobacco";

The Good Wife: or, A rare one amongst Women. Whereto is annexed an Exquisite Discourse of Epitaphs: Including the choicest thereof, Ancient or Moderne, as Musophilus (London: Printed for Richard Redmer, 1618) – includes "Remains after Death: Including by way of introduction di-

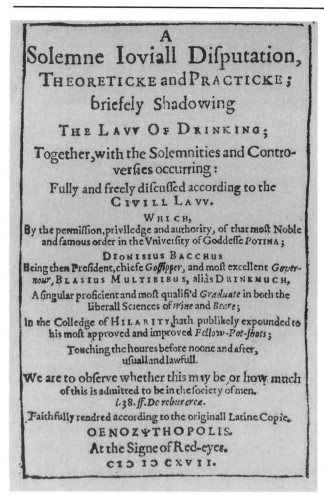

A
Solemne Ioviall Difputation,
THEORETICKE and PRACTICKE;
briefely Shadowing
THE LAVV OF DRINKING;
Together, with the Solemnities and Contro-
verfies occurring:
Fully and freely difcuffed according to the
CIVILL LAVV.
WHICH,
By the permiffion, privlledge and authority, of that moft Noble
and famous order in the Vniverfity of Goddeffe POTINA;
DIONISIUS BACCHUS
Being then Prefident, chiefe Goffipper, and moft excellent Gover-
nour, BLASIUS MULTIBIBUS, aliàs DRINKMUCH,
A fingular proficient and moft qualifi'd Graduate in both the
liberall Sciences of Wine and Beare;
In the Colledge of HILARITY, hath publikely expounded to
his moft approved and improved Fellow-Pot-fhots;
Touching the houres before noone and after,
ufuall and lawfull.
We are to obferve whether this may be, or how much
of this is admitted to be in the fociety of men.
L.38. ff. De rebus circa.
Faithfully rendred according to the originall Latine Copie.
OENOZYTHOPOLIS.
At the Signe of Red-eyes.
CIↃ IↃ CXVII.

THE
Smoaking Age,
OR,
The man in the mift:
WITH
The life and death of Tobacco.
Dedicated
To thofe three renowned and impa-
rallel'd Heroes, Captaine WHIFFE,
Captaine PIPE, and Cap-
taine SNUFFE.
To whom the Author wifheth as much content,
as this Smoaking Age can afford them.
Divided into three Sections.
1. The Birth of Tobacco.
2. PLUTO's bleffing to Tobacco.
3. TIMES complaint againft Tobacco.
Satis mihi pauci lectores, fatis eft unus, fatis eft
Nullus.
Upon TOBACCO.
This fome affirme, yet yeeld I not to that,
'Twill make a fat man leane, a leane man fat,
But this I'm fure (howfere it be they meane)
That many whiffes will make a fat man leane.
OENOZYTHOPOLIS.
At the Signe of Teare-Nofe.
CIↃ IↃ CXVII.

Title page for the volume in which Richard Brathwait's satire of the tobacco craze was included and the separate title page for the satire itself

vers memorable observances occasioned upon discourse of Epitaphs and Epycedes . . . Annexed there be divers select Epitaphs and Hearce-attending Epods";

A New Spring Shadowed in Sundry Pithie Poems, as Musophilus (London: Printed by G. Eld for Thomas Baylie, 1619);

Essaies Upon the Five Senses, with a pithie one upon Detraction. Continued With Sundry Christian Resolves, full of passion and devotion, purposely composed for the zealously-disposed (London: Printed by Edward Griffin for R. Whittaker, 1620); enlarged as *Essaies Upon the Five Senses, Revived by a new Supplement; with a pithy one upon Detraction. Continued With sundry Christian Resolves and divine Contemplations, full of passion and devotion; purposely composed for the zealously-disposed* (London: Printed by Anne Griffin for Henry Shepherd, 1635);

Times Curtaine Drawne, or The Anatomie of Vanitie. With Other Choice Poems, Entituled; Health from Helicon (London: Printed by John Dawson for John Bellamie, 1621) — includes "Panedone or Health from Helicon Containing Emblemes, Epigrams, Elegies, With other continuate poems full of all generous delight";

Natures Embassie: or, the Wilde-Mans Measures: Danced naked by twelve Satyres, Which Sundry Others Continued in the Next Section (London: Printed by R. Field for R. Whitaker, 1621) — includes "Shepherds Tales, containing Satyres Eglogues and Odes," "The Second Section of Divine and Morall Satyres: with an Adiunct upon the Precedent; whereby the Argument with the first cause of publishing these Satyres be evidently related," "The Shepheardes Tales," "Omphale, or the Inconstant Shepheardesse," "His Odes: or Philomels Teares";

The English Gentleman; Containing Sundry excellent Rules or exquisite Observations, tending to Direction of every Gentleman, of selecter ranke and qualitie; How to demeane or accomodate himselfe in the manage of publike or private affaires (London: Printed by John Haviland for Robert Bostock, 1630; enlarged, 1633);

The English Gentlewoman, drawne out to the full Body: Expressing what Habillements doe best attire her, What Ornaments doe best adorne her, What Complements doe best accomplish her (London: Printed by B. Alsop and T. Fawcet for Michael Sparke, 1631);

Whimzies: or, a New Cast of Characters, as Clitus-Alexanrinus (London: Printed by Felix Kingston for Ambrose Rithirdon, 1631) – includes "A Cater-Character, throwne out of a Boxe By an Experienc'd Gamester";

Novissima Tvba. Libellus, in sex Dialogos apprimè Christianos, digestus, as Musophilus (London: Printed by Felix Kingston for Robert Bostock, 1633); translated by John Vicars as *The Last Trumpet or, A Six-Fold Christian Dialogue* (London: Printed by Thomas Harper for Robert Bostock, 1635);

Anniversaries Upon His Panarete (London: Printed by Felix Kingston for Robert Bostock, 1634);

Anniversaries Upon His Panarete; Continued: With her Contemplations, penned in the languishing time of her Sicknesse. The second Yeeres Annivers., anonymous (London: Printed by Felix Kingston for Robert Bostock, 1635);

The Arcadian Princesse; or the Triumph of Justice: Prescribing excellent rules of Physicke, for a sicke Justice. Digested into Fowre Bookes, And Faithfully Rendered to the originall Italian Copy (London: Printed by Th. Harper for Robert Bostock, 1635);

Raglands Niobe: or, Elizas Elegie: Addressed to the unexpiring memory of the most noble Lady, Elizabeth Herbert, wife of the truly honourable, Edward Somerset, Lord Herbert (London: Printed by Felix Kingston for Robert Bostock, 1635);

The Lives of All the Roman Emperors, Being Exactly Collected, from Iulius Cæsar, unto the Now Reigning Ferdinand the Second. With Their Births, Governments, Remarkable Actions, & Deaths, anonymous (London: Printed by Nicholas & John Okes, to be sold by George Hutton, 1636);

Anniversaries Upon His Panarete: Continued. The third yeeres Annivers., anonymous (London: Printed by Felix Kingston for Robert Bostock, 1636);

Barnabæ Itinerarium, Mirtili & Faustuli nominibus insignitum (London: Printed by J. Haviland, 1636?); translated and enlarged as *Barnabees Journall, Under the Names of Mirtilus & Faustulus shadowed: for the Travellers Solace lately published, to most apt numbers reduced, and to the old Tune of Barnabe commonly chanted,* as Corymboeus (London: Printed by John Haviland, 1638);

The Psalmes of David the King and Prophet and of other holy Prophets paraphras'd in English: Conferred with the Hebrew Veritie, set forth by B. Arias Montanus, together with the Latine, Greek Septuagint, and Chaldee Paraphrase (London: Printed by Robert Young for Francis Constable, 1638);

A Spiritval Spicerie: Containing Sundrie Sweet Tractates of Devotion and Piety (London: Printed by John Haviland for George Hutton, 1638);

Ar't asleepe Husband? A Boulster Lecture; Stored With all variety of witty jeasts, merry Tales, and other pleasant passages; Extracted, From the choicest flowers of Philosophy, Poesy, antient and moderne History. Illustrated with Examples of incomparable constancy, in the excellent History of Philocles and Doraclea, as Philogenes Panedonius (London: Printed by R. Bishop for Richard Best or his Assignes, 1640);

The Two Lancashire Lovers: Or The Excellent History of Philocles and Doriclea, Expressing The faithfull constancy and mutuall fidelity of two Loyall Lovers; Stored with no lesse variety of discourse To delight the Generous then of Serious advice to instruct the Amorous, as Musaeus Palatinus (London: Printed by Edward Griffin for R. B. or his Assignes, 1640);

Astraea's Teares: An Elegie Vpon the death of that Reverend, Learned and Honest Judge, Sir Richard Hutton Knight; Lately one of his Majesties Iustices in his Highnesse Court of Common Plees at Westminster, anonymous (London: Printed by T. H. for Philip Nevil, 1641);

Mercurius Britannicus. Judicialis Censura: Vel, Curialis Curia. Febris Judicialis. Sententia navalis. Tragi-Comoedia Lutetiæ, Summo cum applausu publice acta (N.p.: N.d. [1641?]); translated as *Mercurius Britanicus, or The English Intelligencer. A Tragic-Comedy, at Paris. Acted with great Applause,* anonymous (London, 1641);

A Paraphrase upon the Lords Prayer, and the Creed, anonymous (London, 1641);

The Penitent Pilgrim: Psal. 66.16. Come and Hearken, All Yee That Feare God, and I Will Tell You What He Hath Done to My Soule, anonymous (London: Printed by John Dawson, sold by John Williams, 1641);

A Preparative to Studie: or, The Vertue of Sack (London, 1641);

The English Gentleman; and The English Gentlewoman: Both In one Volume couched, and in one Modell portrayed: to the living glory of their Sexe, the lasting story of their Worth. Being Presented to present times for ornaments; commended to posterity for Presidents. With a Ladies Love-Lecture And a Supplement lately annexed, and Entituled The Turtles Triumph (London: Printed by John Dawson, 1641) – includes "The Turtles Triumph Presented In a Supplement: Highly Conducing to an usefull Application, and gracefull Reconciliation of the two former subjects," enlarged as *Times Treasury: or, Academy for Gentry. Laying downe excellent grounds both Divine and Humane, in relation to Sexes of Both Kindes: For their accomplishment in arguments of Discourse, Habit, Fashion: and happy progresse in their Spiritual Conversation.* (London: Printed for Nathaniel Brooke, 1652);

The Devills White Boyes: Or, A mixture of malicious Malignants, with their much evill, and manifold practices against the Kingdome and Parliament. With a bottomlesse Sack-full of Knavery, Popery, Prelacy, Policy, Trechery, Malignant Trumpery, Conspiracies, and Cruelties, filled to the top by the Malignants, laid on the shoulders of Time, and now by Time emptied forth, and powred out, to shew the Truth, and shame the Devill (London: Printed for R. S., 1644);

A Mustur Roll of the evill Angels embattled against St. Michael. Being a Collection, according to the order of Time, (throughout all the Centuries) of the chiefe of the Ancient Heretikes, with their Tenets, such as were condemned by General Councels. Faithfully collected out of the most Authentike Authors, as R. B. Gent (London: Printed for William Sheers, 1655); published as *Capitall Hereticks, Or, The Evill Angels embattel'd against St. Michael* (London: Printed for William Sheers, 1659);

The Honest Ghost, Or A Voice From The Vault, as Parthenius Osiander (London: Printed by Richard Hodgkinsonne, 1658);

Lignum Vitæ. Libellus In quatuor partes distinctus: Et Ad Utilitatem Cujusque Animae in altiorem vitae perfectionem suspirantis, Nuperrimè Editus (London: Printed by John Grismond, 1658);

Panthalia: or The Royal Romance. A Discourse Stored with infinite variety in relation to State-Government And Passages of matchless affection gracefully interveined, and presented on a Theatre of Tragical and Comical State, in a successive continuation to these Times, anonymous (London: Printed by John Grismond for Anthony Williamson, 1659);

To His Majestie upon his Happy Arrivall In our late discomposed Albion (London: Printed for Henry Brome, 1660);

The Chimneys Scuffle, attributed to Brathwait (London, 1662);

The Captive-Captaine: or, the Restrain'd cavalier drawn to his full bodie, in These Characters . . . Presented and Acted to Life in a Suit of Durance, an Habit Suiting Best with His Place of Residence, as R. B. (London: Printed by John Grismond, 1665);

A Comment Upon The Two Tales Of Our Ancient, Renowned, and Ever-Living Poet Sr Jeffray Chaucer, Knight. Who, For his Rich Fancy, Pregnant Invention, and Present Composure, deserved the Countenance of a Prince, and his Laureat Honour. The Miller's Tale; And The Wife of Bath., anonymous (London: Printed by W. Godbid, sold by Robert Crofts, 1665);

Tragi-Comoedia, Cui in titulum inscribitur Regicidium, Perspicacissimis Judiciis acuratius perspecta, pensata, comprobata (London: Printed by John Grismond for Theodore Sadler, 1665); published as *Regicidium, sanguinis Scrutinium. Tragi-comoedia memoratu dignissima, cedratis tabulis meritò imprimenda* (London: Printed by John Grismond, 1665);

The History of Moderation; Or, The Life, Death, and Resurrection of Moderation: Together With Her Nativity, Country, Pedigree, Kinred, Character, Friends, and also her Enemies, as Heyschius Pamphilus (London: Printed for Thomas Parkhurst, 1669); published as *The Trimmer: or, the Life and Death, of Moderation* (London: Printed for Dorman Newman, 1683).

Editions: *Barnabæ Itinerarium: or, Barnabee's Journal. The 7th Edition: To Which Are Prefixed an Account of the Author, Now First Discovered; a Bibliographical History of the Former Editions of the Work; and Illustrative Notes,* edited by Joseph Haslewood (London: Printed for J. Harding by R. & A. Taylor, 1818); revised edition, 2 volumes, edited by W. Carew Hazlitt (London: Privately printed, 1876);

Natures Embassie: Divine and Morall Satyres: Shepheards Tales, Both Parts: Omphale: Odes, or Philomels Tears, Etc. (Boston, U.K.: Printed by Robert Roberts, 1877);

A Strappado for the Diuell, introduction by J. W. Ebsworth (Boston, U.K.: Printed by Robert Roberts, 1878);

Richard Brathwait's Comments, in 1665, upon Chaucer's Tales of the Miller and the Wife of Bath, edited by C. F. E. Spurgeon (London: Published for the Chaucer Society by Kegan Paul, Trench, Trübner, 1901);

Frontispiece, with explanation, for the second of Brathwait's courtesy books

The meaning of the *Frontispice*, wherein the *Effigies* it selfe; together with all the Emblemes, Deuices, Features, and Impre. zas thereto properly conducing, are to life described.

APPARELL.

APPARELL being by a Curtaine first discouered, where shee appeares sitting in a *Wardrobe* richly furnished, is expressed in a comely or seemely *Habit*; holding a *vaile* in her hand; poudred with teares, implying the *Necessity* of that *Liuery* to bee deriued from the losse of her *Originall purity*; as one therefore, neither impenitent for her *sinne*, nor ignorant of her *shame*, but constantly tender what may best suit or sort with her fame, shee deliuers her mind in this Mott. *Comely, not Gaudy.*

BEHAVIOVR presents her selfe in a modest *attire*; with a cheerefull and gracefull *aspect*; by those *children* shee hath about her, she expresseth what she professeth; Breeding or Education of Youth; which she performes with that modest facility, and natiue liberty, as she admits of no *forraine fashion*, tasting of *affectation*, into her Company; which she expresseth in this Mott. *Louing Modesty a Lining Beauty.*

COMPLEMENT.

COMPLEMENT is accommodated like a *Courtier*; and at first Encounter seemes accoasted by a *Phantasticke Gallant*, whose *sense* consists in *sent*; and whose *formall Congies* are his sole *Complement*; she makes knowne her neglect of him by sleighting or putting him aside by her hand; and presenting to his eye the obiect of an *Ape*, as a complete Embleme of his formality, and one vnworthy of her society, she molds her selfe in this Mot. *Ciuill Complement, my best Accomplishment.*

DECENCY.

DECENCY is portrayed in a louely but comely dresse; her *eye* modestly fixt on her glasse; *Feathers* with other like *Apish favours*, are offered her, which she reiects; Chaplets of *Flowers* are presented her, which she accepts; These she bestowes in her bosome, as Emblemes of those *flourishing vertues* which are lou'd by her, and only admitted *to lodge* with her: This she shadowes in her Mott. *Virgin-Decency is Vertues Liuery.*

ESTIMATION.

ESTIMATION is displayed, reposing her selfe in an Arbour; where shee is beleagred by two powerfull assailants; *Price* and *Prayer*, on her right hand, expressed by a *Purse* and a *Petition*; *Feare* and *Fury* on her left hand, discouered by a *Pistoll* and *Steletto*; both which she sleights with a gracefull contempt: while eying the Bird *Porphyrio* houering aboue her head, who makes her defiled bed her place of buriall; shee clozeth her resolues with this Mot. *My Prize is her owne Praise.*

FANCY.

FANCY is featured with a louely and liuely presence; fixing her eye intentiuely on a *Tablet*, presenting the portraiture of her *Louer*: Drawing aside a Curtaine, she discouers an *amorous Picture*, and compares it with her *Tablet*, which enshrines her *best feature*. In the middle of the *Picture* is engrauen a *wounded heart*, implying loues intimacy; aboue it, a *burning Lampe*, importing loues purity; below it, a paire of *Turtles* mating, inferring loues constancy. All which expressiue Emblemes of her minde, she seconds with this Mot. *My Choyce admits no Change.*

GENTILITY.

GENTILITY is deblazoned by her proper *Crest* or *Cognizance*; A Pedigree furnished with variety of choyce and ancient Coats hanging by her; vnder these, a *Deaths head*, *houre-glasse*, and *syhe*, memorials of her mortality; An aged Personage, seemingly deiected and in misery, presenting the person of *Hospitality*, shee embraceth, and offers her Precedency; A *Crowne* is presented to her by *Piety* with this Mott. *Desert Crownes Descent.*

HONOVR.

HONOVR is discouered vnder a Canopie; the *foure Corners* supported by foure *Cardinall vertues*; The *Three graces* goe before her; *Workes of Mercy* after her: *Fame* standing on a Mount aboue her; Captiues inchained and led by her; Trophies of *honour* erected for her; which shee defaceth, and tramples vnder foot, implying her noble contempt of *vaine-glory*; And standing vpon the *Globe of Earth*, shee pusheth at it, as a thing vnworthy her delight; while viewing the *Globe of heauen*, she expresseth by her eye, the obiect of her *desire*; Retiring from the Theatre of *honour*, and reposing in a securer harbour: Where she is inclosed with a flowry greue of *Osyers*, implying *privacy*; and impaled with a *Coronet of Sun-beames*, displaying her felicity, shee summes vp her content, and shewes her conceit in this Mott. *Honour is vertues harbour.*

In the middle, betwixt the Vinnets, is portrayed a modest comely personage, with a *Lilly* in her bosome, implying the odor of purity: a *Manuall* in her hand, importing the honour of piety; with this *Motto*, to conduct her to the Port of glory: *Grace my Guide, Glory my Goale.*

For other appropriates, attributes, or Compartments, whereby either the *Frontispice* might become better beautified, or the *acmiees* fuller explained, they are onely shadowed, being by the weake hand of *Art* not to be otherwise expressed.

EAch Subiect had distinguish'd beene by line,
And form'd their Modell to the first deuice,
But this choyce piece was hastened so by time,
It scarce got sight of that first Frontispice:
Yet from this shrine such natiue beames arise,
Impartiall eyes will iudge, right sure I am,
" Her grace improues the place from whence shee came:
" And well deserues an ENGLISH GENTLEMAN.

The Law of Drinking, edited by W. Brian Hooker (New Haven: Tuttle, Morehouse & Taylor, 1903).

Richard Brathwait was born of country gentry at Burneshead Hall, near Kendal, Westmoreland, probably in 1588. Many autobiographical details are scattered in his works; they give a picture of a normal yet deeply remembered rural childhood, as when he recalls in *A Spiritual Spicerie* (1638) that when in the house he always wanted to be in the fields, and when in the fields, in the house. In 1604 he was admitted as a commoner to Oriel College, Oxford; he seems to have left without a degree in 1607. Apparently, he was also associated in some capacity with Pembroke College, Cambridge, during these years. In 1609, in accord with parental wishes but strongly against his own, he entered Gray's Inn in London to study law.

Brathwait's first published writings correspond with a period of ignorance of specifics about his life, between his father's death in 1610 and his marriage in 1617, but references in them suggest an impecunious and perhaps irresponsible urban lifestyle among academic and nonacademic wits, growing local recognition as a writer, and much experience with theaters, alehouses, and brothels. His first published work, a collection of moral and amorous verse titled *The Golden Fleece,* appeared the year after his father's death and is dedicated to the uncle who helped him through this difficult period. *The Poet's Willow* (1614), a conventional pastoral dialogue in verse, may or may not reflect his actual experience as "a discontented and perplexed lover."

His first prose works, *The Schollers Medley* and *The Prodigals Teares,* also appeared in 1614. The former is a medley of knowledge acquired in college and focuses on history. Under the heads of the scope and fruits of history and the profits to be gained from family history he covers such topics as "feigned" poetic history, the morality of history, and the archaeological history of Roman Britain. The ideal definition of history, he says, is that it is a "Picture, Emblem, and Mirror of Mankind." *The Prodigals Teares* deals with immoral behavior and is addressed to other youths who "walke after the lusts of your hearts" and to himself as an exemplary "converted pervert." Intermixed with many classical and Christian accounts of repentance are a series of moral resolutions whereby the author hopes to "redeem the time."

Before actualizing these resolves by becoming a responsible husband and father, Brathwait wrote one of his best-known works in a popular genre: *A*

Strappado for the Divell (1615) is a collection of urban verse characterological satire. One piece is addressed to his godfather, Richard Hutton; another, "Frankes Anatomie," probably refers to Frances Lawson, whom he married on 7 May 1617 at Hurwurth, near Durham. "Panarete," as he would call her in future writings, would provide him with land that would allow him to maintain a prosperous life as a country squire.

The period from 1617 to 1622 saw a remarkable output of publications by Brathwait. At the beginning of the period he was living in London with his family and had no apparent income – he was once, apparently, imprisoned for debt; at the end he was master of Burneshead Hall in Westmorland, a justice of the peace, a man of prosperity and strong Royalist sentiments. His "The Smoaking Age" mingles prose and poetry to satirize, mock-heroically and mock-academically, the tobacco craze; the framing device is a semi-dramatic prose debate among several college students, some from the West Indies, on tobacco's virtues and vices. *The Good Wife* (1618), surely inspired by his wife, is a medley of short works in prose and verse linking the living wife to the anticipation and memory of death. The section on epitaphs, "Remains after Death," is presented as a bequest from his late father. Brathwait tells the reader that he delayed publication of his work so that it would not be confused with Sir Thomas Overbury's *A Wife, Now a Widowe* (1614).

Between two volumes of moral verse, *A New Spring* (1619) and *Times Curtaine Drawne* (1621), Brathwait produced a collection of essays and "resolves" (the genre popularized by Owen Felltham), *Essaies upon the Five Senses* (1620), shaped by the conceit of a court case against the senses. The first edition consists of conventional religious-moral prose, but the second (1635) presents "senses" in a more subtle way – for example, as the "sense" of others' misery – in a series of contemplations on the death of Panarete.

Brathwait's final work before a near decade of literary silence is a confusing yet characteristic medley of verse and prose, *Natures Embassie* (1621), in which he writes as the "Satyrist" directing men in the "course and progresse of vertue." The first and second main sections of the work consist of both short and extensive prose "arguments" prefacing verse satires in couplets on sins, such as Sloth and Disdain, represented in the behavior of classical figures. These satiric texts are incongruously linked to pastoral eclogues, odes, and other poems that appear under the rubric "Shepherds Tales."

During the rest of the 1620s Brathwait was absent from the literary scene, presumably consolidating his economic, social, and political position in Westmorland and raising his growing family (children were born to Frances in 1620, 1622, 1623, 1624, 1625, 1629, and 1630). A pair of substantial courtesy books, *The English Gentleman* and *The English Gentlewoman,* were published in 1630 and 1631, respectively. The former is divided into sections, called "Observations," on eight attributes of the gentleman; personified images of these attributes are depicted on the ornate title page: Youth, Recreation, Disposition, Acquaintance, Education, Vocation, Moderation, and Perfection. The advice Brathwait gives under each of these heads is clearly meant to guide the country gentleman of his own moderately high station and wealth. Under "Vocation" he criticizes at one extreme great "Men of Place" and at the other "they who beautifie themselves for the Stage"; the recreations he encourages are hawking, hunting, fishing, running, and shooting. He proclaims the house to be the husband's castle and the wife's "commonwealth," and with remarkable enlightenment he urges that a wife not be restrained "from the use of any pleasure which she affecteth." The companion volume is similarly ordered under the heads of Apparell, Behavior, Complement, Decencie, Estimation, Fancie, Gentilitie, and Honour; its epistle to the "Gentlewoman Reader" characterizes her as a sister "whose improved Education will bee no blemish but a beautie to her Nation." Matthew Wilson Black points out that, in contrast to its nearest analogue, Henry Peacham's *Compleat Gentleman* (1622), Brathwait's book views "conduct" in moral rather than merely practical terms. Also in 1631 Brathwait's *Whimzies* was published. It is a prose character-book comprising sharp observations on and gentle ridicule of such unusual types as the forester, metall-man, launderer, and under-sheriff.

Brathwait's next work was published in Latin in 1633 as *Novissima Tuba* (translated as *The Last Trumpet,* 1635). Throughout his career Brathwait's love for, and pride in his ability in, classical languages is evident; his classicism gives his works an interesting hybrid effect due to their simple, popular content. In *Novissima Tuba* he presents six moral dialogues between such speakers as God and the Soul. Almost medieval in format, the dialogues are directed toward the common literate Christian and deal intensely with issues of personal eschatology.

Frances Brathwait died on 7 March 1633. Left with eight children – the oldest of whom was sixteen – Brathwait, as a practical country gentleman, did not hesitate to marry again. By June of that year he was espoused to Mary Crofts, daughter of Roger Crofts of Kirtlington, Yorkshire, whose estate, Catterick, became his seat. His devotion to the memory of Panarete continued, however: through 1636 he published three "Anniversaries," or memorial poems. In contrast to these works of devotion came the ribald burlesque verses of *Barnabæ Itinerarium* (1636), originally published in Latin and then, in 1638, in parallel Latin and English as *Barnabees Journal,* a sexual-alcoholic tour of England claimed by the author to have been a task of the "first Spring of my minoritie." Despite its aura of undergraduate slumming, the work was much admired and often reprinted. He compensated with *A Spiritual Spicerie,* a devotional treatise that includes his spiritual autobiography, "Holy Memorials," in which he traces his own life from conception in sin to his anticipated death: in childhood he desired to "learne in jest but playe in earnest"; as a partying lawyer and aspiring writer he would hear the "Crie of the wits": "There goes an Author!"; in his youthful indulgence, "long winter nights seemed but a Midsummer nights dream." This touching material contrasts strongly to the rest of the text, an interminable sequence of devotional adaptations from works of the fathers of the church.

Brathwait's flood of publications in 1640 and 1641 seems to demonstrate an awareness that, as an unabashed Royalist in unsympathetic provinces, he would soon not have the freedom of expression (and possibly of movement) that he enjoyed under the Stuarts. *Ar't asleep Husband? A Boulster Lecture* (1640) is based on the frame situation of a wife trying to speak her mind to her husband in bed. Written in verse and prose and filled with tales, the work covers many aspects of women's lives without falling into either overpraise or mysogyny. Another substantial work on male-female relationships is his novel *The Two Lancashire Lovers* (1640). The lovers Philocles and Doriclea and the other characters bear the names and perform the stereotyped actions of Italianate romance, and the action is interrupted by soliloquies, but Brathwait creates a highly credible provincial setting. The psychological ambivalence and self-questioning of the lovers, a cherished only daughter and her tutor, are richly conveyed. They fall in with hermits and magicians, and there is the obligatory parental opposition; but eventually, through the threat of Doriclea's desperate illness, they are reconciled with her family and are able to marry.

Mercurius Britannicus (1641?), a Latin courtroom closet drama, criticizes the judges who in 1638 decided against John Hampden in his opposition to Charles I's levy of ship money; one of many such controversial works of the period, it shows Brathwait as an activist political writer. *The Penitent Pilgrim* (1641) seems to take a different tack, describing the experiences of pilgrims encountering the basic truths of Christianity, but it may also have a political subtext: the forces of "innovation" that opposed the Hampden verdict are also wandering away from the traditional premises of Christian submission.

As a vocal Royalist, Brathwait was subject to constant harassment by Commonwealth officials; many of his properties were expropriated in the 1650s, but his political voice would not be silenced. His *Mustur Roll* (1655) compares the Puritans to ancient heretics. *The Honest Ghost* (1658) is a more generalized satire of the various "Apes" found in society, and *Lignum Vitae,* of the same year, is another prose compendium of derived moral and spiritual wisdom that includes some autobiographical references. Black contends that these works originated thirty to forty years earlier, before Brathwait's country-gentleman period. Brathwait could be seen as trimming with this "safe" material, but his topical and controversial writings undermine this notion.

Panthalia (1659) also indicates Brathwait's willingness to address immediate events. Disguised as an exotic Arcadian romance, the drama is actually an allegory of English history during Brathwait's lifetime, from the later reign of Elizabeth to the abdication of Richard Cromwell as lord protector in early 1659; published in a historical limbo, with the return of the monarchy obviously foreordained but not yet proclaimed, it is a fascinating attempt to fix an unfixed moment in history.

Although Brathwait's own celebratory poem (1660) joined many others at the Restoration, the works of his last decade show a persistent social — verging on political — criticism. An exception is his delightful 1665 commentary on Geoffrey Chaucer's "Miller's Tale" and "Wife of Bath's Tale," considered by Black to be resurrected from 1617. Saying that his commentary was "importuned" by "persons of quality," Brathwait provides a line-by-line prose explication of the tales, with particular care to explain difficult words and phrases. *The Chimneys Scuffle* (1662) satirizes the condition of England, in verse, under the guise of criticism of a hearth tax;

The Captive-Captaine (1665) is another satiric medley of genres and subjects, referring to his "imprisonment" on his lands during the Commonwealth and giving much advice to his rural compatriots and to royal emissaries.

Brathwait's final known publication is *The History of Moderation* (1669), pejoratively retitled *The Trimmer* in its 1683 reprint. It takes the form of a narrative moral allegory in which moderation figures as an idealized lady, Arimathea, who, although descended from an honorable family, "hath of later days lived obscurely, as a Stranger to most Nations of the Earth." For Brathwait, obviously, the reign of Charles II did not, any more than those of Oliver and Richard Cromwell, embody moderation. Although he was conventional in much of his religion, ethics, and politics, Brathwait's work hews to the difficult path of moderation, without unquestioned allegiance to any system. This creative individualism, along with its variety, extent, and virtuosity, gives Brathwait's work a claim to substantial significance in seventeenth-century letters.

Biography:

Matthew Wilson Black, *Richard Brathwait: An Account of His Life and Works* (Philadelphia: University of Pennsylvania Press, 1928).

References:

R. H. Bowers, "Brathwait's 'Comments' upon Chaucer," *Notes and Queries,* 196 (22 December 1951): 558–559;

Benjamin Boyce, "History and Fiction in *Panthalia: or The Royal Romance,*" *Journal of English and Germanic Philology,* 57 (July 1958): 477–491;

Leo Daugherty, "A 1614 Borrowing from Shakespeare's Sonnet 13," *Notes and Queries,* 227, series 2 (April 1982): 126–127;

Jay A. Gertzman, "Changes in Dedications in Early Editions of Richard Brathwait's *The English Gentleman* and *The English Gentlewoman,*" *Analytical and Enumerative Bibliography,* 3 (Winter 1979): 39–49;

Thomas P. Haviland, "The Heroic *Panthalia,*" *University of Pennsylvania Library Chronicle,* 3 (1935): 14–15.

Sir Thomas Browne

(19 October or 19 November 1605 – 19 October 1682)

Sharon Cadman Seelig
Smith College

BOOKS: *Religio Medici* (London: Printed for Andrew Crooke, 1642) [unauthorized edition]; revised as *Religio Medici: A true and full coppy of that which was most imperfectly and Surreptitiously printed before vnder the name of: Religio Medici* (London: Printed for Andrew Crooke, 1643);

Pseudodoxia Epidemica: or, Enquiries into Very many received Tenents, And commonly presumed Truths (London: Printed by Thomas Harper for Edward Dod, 1646; revised edition, London: Printed by A. Miller for Edward Dod & Nath. Elkins, 1650; revised again, London: Printed by R. W. for Nath. Elkins, 1658; revised again, London: Printed for the assigns of Edward Dod, 1669; revised again, London: Printed by J. R. for Nath. Elkins, 1672);

Hydriotaphia, Urne-Buriall, or, A Discourse of the Sepulchrall Urnes lately found in Norfolk. Together with The Garden of Cyrus, or the Quincunciall, Lozenge, or Net-work Plantations of the Ancients, Artificially, Naturally, Mystically Considered. With Sundry Observations (London: Printed for Hen. Brome, 1658);

Certain Miscellany Tracts (London: Printed for Charles Mearn, 1683);

A Letter to a Friend, Upon occasion of the Death of His Intimate Friend (London: Printed for Charles Brome, 1690);

Posthumous Works of the Learned Sir Thomas Browne, K^t. M.D. Late of Norwich: Printed from his Original Manuscripts. Viz. I. Repertorium: Or, The Antiquities of the Cathedral Church of Norwich. II. An Account of some Urnes, &c. found at Brampton in Norfolk, Anno 1667. III. Letters between Sir William Dugdale and Sir Tho. Browne. IV. Miscellanies (London: Printed for Edmund Curll & R. Gosling, 1712);

Christian Morals (Cambridge: Printed at the University-Press for Cornelius Crownfield, sold by Mr. Knapton & Mr. Morphew, London, 1716).

Collections and editions: *The Works Of the Learned Sr Thomas Brown, Kt. Doctor of Physick, late of Norwich* (London: Printed for Tho. Basset, Ric. Chiswell, Tho. Sawbridge, Charles Mearn & Charles Brome, 1686);

Christian Morals: by Sir Thomas Browne, Of Norwich, M.D., and author of Religio Medici. The Second Edition. With a life of the author, by Samuel Johnson; and explanatory notes (London: Printed by Richard Hett for J. Payne, 1756);

Sir Thomas Browne's Works: Including His Life and Correspondence, 4 volumes, edited by Simon Wilkin (London: Pickering, 1835–1836);

Sir Thomas Browne's Religio Medici Letter to a Friend &c. and Christian Morals, edited by W. A. Greenhill (London: Macmillan, 1881; revised, 1885);

Religio Medici, edited by Jean-Jacques Denonain (Cambridge: Cambridge University Press, 1953);

The Works of Sir Thomas Browne, 4 volumes, edited by Geoffrey Keynes (London: Faber & Faber / Chicago: University of Chicago Press, 1964);

Religio Medici and Other Works, edited by L. C. Martin (Oxford: Clarendon Press, 1964);

The Prose of Sir Thomas Browne, edited by Norman J. Endicott (New York: New York University Press, 1968);

Sir Thomas Browne: The Major Works, edited by C. A. Patrides (Harmondsworth, U.K.: Penguin, 1977);

Pseudodoxia Epidemica, 2 volumes, edited by Robin Robbins (Oxford: Clarendon Press, 1981).

Sir Thomas Browne, physician, member of the Royal College of Physicians, and writer of extraordinary prose, was, to borrow William Butler Yeats's phrase, a marker of things "past, or passing, or to come," a writer who sums up more eloquently than almost anyone else of his time received notions in philosophy and religion yet gives a good deal of attention to empirical observation, to the approach to the natural world that would be so significant to later generations. In *Religio Medici* (The Religion of a Physician, 1642) Browne articulates the nature of

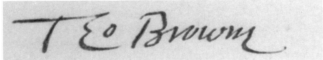

*Drawing attributed to David Loggan (National Portrait
Gallery, London)*

his faith in relation to the tradition of Anglican Christianity; in *Pseudodoxia Epidemica* (Vulgar Errors, 1646), by patient examination of authorities and of the evidence, he subjects many of the popular and learned errors of his time to withering skepticism. In the companion pieces *Hydriotaphia, Urne-Buriall, or, A Discourse of the Sepulchrall Urnes Lately Found in Norfolk* and *The Garden of Cyrus,* published together in 1658, Browne proceeds from a contemplation of physical and anthropological facts to a meditation on mortality and immortality, time and eternity. A master of Senecan prose, a style designed to reflect the mind in motion rather than to produce the cadences of oratory, Browne moves from high to low, from symmetry to asymmetry, from meditation to discovery, celebration, or affirmation, as suits his particular subject and occasion.

Browne was born in London in the autumn of 1605, a few weeks before or a few weeks after the attempt by Catholic extremists to blow up the Houses of Parliament in the Gunpowder Plot. If Browne was indeed born on 19 October, as his daughter Elizabeth asserted, his death on the same day seventy-seven years later would have "made his circle just" in a way that would have pleased him; but Browne himself, in a letter to John Aubrey written in 1672, gave his birth date as 19 November. Browne was the fourth child and only son of Thomas Browne, a successful cloth merchant from a family of minor gentry in Cheshire, and Anne Garroway Browne of Middlesex. Late in 1613 Browne's father died, leaving an estate of five thousand pounds and attendant debts to his widow and five children. Within a year Anne Browne married Sir Thomas Dutton, an army captain and courtier who was often in debt and who was quarrelsome enough to have killed a superior officer in a duel. Although Dutton has been criticized for dissipating Browne's inheritance from his father, Browne does not appear to have been in financial straits during his youth. Moreover, the two seem to have been on good terms: in later years (probably in 1629)

Browne would accompany Dutton on a tour of Ireland, where Dutton owned land and commanded an important chain of forts.

In 1616 Browne enrolled at Winchester, the oldest grammar school in England, where he learned Latin and Greek; in 1623 he proceeded to Broadgates Hall, Oxford. Although he failed in the competition for a scholarship to enter New College, Browne distinguished himself as a student, being chosen in his first year to deliver the undergraduate Latin address when Broadgates Hall became Pembroke College. Browne's studies at Oxford would have been largely traditional, based on the medieval trivium (grammar, rhetoric, and logic) and quadrivium (arithmetic, geometry, astronomy, and music). But Pembroke also showed evidence of the new directions in learning: in 1619 it acquired chairs in geometry and astronomy, and in 1624 a readership in anatomy, with provision for an annual dissection of a cadaver, was added to the established chair in medicine.

Although Browne is remembered today as a prose stylist, he was by training and by profession a member of the scientific community. After receiving his B.A in 1626 and his M.A. in 1629 Browne pursued his medical education on the Continent, where the study of the sciences was more advanced than at Oxford or Cambridge. His travels took him to the most distinguished schools of medicine in Europe – Montpellier, which combined the heritage of Arabic medical knowledge with newer scholarship in botany and surgery; Padua, where the great anatomist Andreas Vesalius had worked in the previous century and which was then the center of anatomical studies; and Leiden, well known for anatomy and therapeutic chemistry. On 21 December 1633 Browne received his M.D. from the University of Leiden and returned to Oxfordshire for his medical apprenticeship. On 10 July 1637 he was incorporated doctor of physic at Oxford.

Around 1637 or 1638 Browne settled in Norwich, a thriving city of approximately thirty thousand inhabitants in the county of Norfolk; he may have been drawn there by the presence of several friends from Oxford – Nicholas Bacon, Charles LeGros, Justinian Lewyn, and his tutor, Thomas Lushington. Browne seems to have been well liked and to have been successful as a physician, and he served as a mentor to younger practitioners. In 1641 he married Dorothy Mileham, described by John Whitefoot in "Minutes for the Life of Sir Thomas Browne" (in *Posthumous Works of the Learned Sir Thomas Browne,* 1712) as "a Lady of such a Symmetrical Proportion to her worthy Husband, both in the Graces of her Body and Mind, that they seemed to come together by a kind of Natural Magnetism." Their first child, Edward, was born in 1644, followed by another each year until 1650 and six more thereafter; but five died before the age of six, and two others by their twenty-fourth year. Edward would become a physician of considerable prominence and a member of the Royal Society. The second son, Thomas, in some ways the child most like Browne, joined the navy and died at twenty-one. A daughter, Elizabeth, would remain at home until her marriage in 1680; her commonplace book records the works she read to her father in the evenings. She would also gather his papers and in 1716, the year of her death, would authorize the publication of his *Christian Morals.*

Perhaps during his medical apprenticeship in Oxfordshire, Browne had begun writing one of his best-known and most engaging works, *Religio Medici,* an account of his own attitudes and opinions in relation to the doctrines of what he calls "the great wheele of the Church." According to the preface to the first authorized edition (1643), *Religio Medici* was written about "seven yeares past" and was not originally intended for publication, "being . . . rather a memoriall unto me then an example or rule unto any other." Although such prefatory statements are by no means unusual in works of the time, this one may be accurate: forty of the book's seventy-five sections begin either with "I" or another personal pronoun or refer explicitly to the author within the first few clauses – "Againe, I beleeve," "I am naturally bashfull," "I thanke God," "For my conversation," "It is a riddle to me," and "But to difference my self neerer," for example. *Religio Medici* may be seen as a meditation or an epistolary address; the conversational tone conveys Browne's confidence that he is writing to an approving audience of one or two friends. Or the audience may be smaller yet: one senses that *Religio Medici* is not only self-descriptive but also an encouragement to its author to continue in the behavior he describes. But Browne's account can also be seen as hortatory and prescriptive, presenting a model of Christian belief and practice to his readers and laying contrary practices open to censure.

Religio Medici is divided into two main parts, setting forth the physician's religious position under the (unannounced) headings of faith and charity. Although the third member of the Pauline trinity – hope – has been omitted, the division does treat the two directions of religious obligation: toward God and toward one's fellow human beings. The first part, which delineates the nature of belief, is by far

Browne and his wife, Dorothy Mileham Browne; painting attributed to Joan Carlile
(National Portrait Gallery, London)

the longer; Browne, clearly warming to his subject, is enthusiastic in his belief — some have found him too enthusiastic — taking as his motto the statement of the third-century church father Tertullian: "Certum est quia impossibile est" (It is certain because it is impossible). By contrast, the discussion of the virtue of charity in part 2 is largely the practical working out of the consequences of the first virtue and does not elicit from Browne the imaginative flights of part 1. At the conclusion Browne comes back to the beginning, finding the basis of charity in the love of God, the visible in the invisible.

On the subject of faith, Browne explores what he believes and what he rejects in Christian doctrine, finding his tendency to heresy mild and excusable and his capacity for belief large. He affirms that "me thinkes there be not impossibilities enough in Religion for an active faith" and reminds his reader that to credit what seems reasonable or what one has seen is not faith but sight. The ease of some of Browne's statements testifies to the predominance of theory over experience in the author's life: as he approaches his thirtieth year he finds himself less afraid of death than ashamed of it; he rejoices in his lack of pride while finding that he would have reason enough to be proud; and he wishes that "we might procreate like trees, without conjunction, or that there were any way to perpetuate the world without this triviall and vulgar way of coition,"

which Browne describes as "the foolishest act a wise man commits in all his life." While his comment "If . . . there rise any doubts in my way, I doe forget them, or at least defer them, till my better setled judgement, and more manly reason be able to resolve them" hardly does justice to the problem of doubt, it reflects his underlying confidence and his purposes: to offer a series of meditations on faith, to define and celebrate belief, and to depict himself not as an individual but as representative of humanity. In this context his statement "Now for my life, it is a miracle of thirty yeares, which to relate, were not a History, but a peece of Poetry" assumes a reverential rather than an egocentric aspect.

Although Browne takes delight in belief and in the difficulties posed by belief — he approaches the latter like an athlete trying to keep in condition — he also employs his reason. For Browne, human beings in the exercise of reason are responsive to divine initiative: "The world was made to be inhabited by beasts, but studied and contemplated by man: 'tis the debt of our reason wee owe unto God, and the homage wee pay for not being beasts." He speaks of the intellectual and rhetorical adventure on which he has embarked as a form of recreation, signifying both enjoyment and refreshment: "In my solitary and retired imaginations . . . I remember I am not alone, and therefore forget not to contemplate him and his attributes who is ever with mee, especially those two mighty ones, his wisedome and eternitie; with the one I recreate, with the other I confound my understanding." For him faith is not the abandonment of reason but the use of it to the point that it proves inadequate; its inadequacy then becomes evidence of the superiority of divine wisdom and providence. The process begins with the understanding of the beautiful ordering of nature, which Browne calls the "Art of God," and proceeds to the exploration of divine mystery: "for who can speake of eternitie without a soloecisme, or thinke thereof without an extasie? Time we may comprehend, 'tis but five dayes elder then our selves, and hath the same Horoscope with the world; but to retire so farre backe as to apprehend a beginning, to give such an infinite start forward, as to conceive an end in an essence that wee affirme hath neither the one nor the other; it puts my reason to Saint *Pauls* Sanctuary; . . . God hath not made a creature that can comprehend him, 'tis the priviledge of his owne nature." Characteristically, Browne elaborates on an idea in a series of statements that represent not so much the logical advancement of the idea as the emotional grasping of it. He begins with what seems evident and understandable: "Time we may comprehend"; but the sequence ends in a mind-boggling reversal: "to give such an infinite start forward, as to conceive an end in an essence that wee affirme hath neither the one nor the other." The effect, finally, is to make human reason surrender to divine mystery; as Browne says in one of his best-known passages: "I love to lose my selfe in a mystery, to pursue my Reason to an *o altitudo*."

In *Religio Medici* Browne gives special emphasis to the doctrine of the Incarnation: that Christ was both God and man, flesh and spirit, bound by time and eternal. Some of his most striking effects are found in his articulation of the point that all human beings share in this duality of nature: "*Before Abraham was, I am,* is the saying of Christ, yet is it true in some sense if I say it of my selfe, for I was not onely before my selfe, but *Adam,* that is, in the Idea of God, and the decree of that Synod held from all Eternity. And in this sense, I say, the world was before the Creation, and at an end before it had a beginning; and thus was I dead before I was alive." In this passage, characteristic of Browne's Senecan prose, each successive clause marks not a new beginning but an ever-more-dramatic expression of an idea, a rhetorical and emotional elaboration of it. To criticize Browne for pushing belief too far is to miss the point of the passage: "to *exercise* [his] faith in the difficultest points," to revel in the brilliant presentation of a central Christian doctrine.

Browne takes special delight in expressing such paradoxes as that of the duality of the human condition: the human being is both body and soul, both bound by time and yet related to eternity. He defines humanity as "that great and true *Amphibium,* whose nature is disposed to live not onely like other creatures in divers elements, but in divided and distinguished worlds" — the material and the spiritual — and aware, unlike other beings, of the existence of those two worlds: "for though there bee but one [world] to sense, there are two to reason; the one visible; the other invisible." So firmly does Browne the physician insist on the spiritual as well as the physical dimension of reality that he affirms, referring to the Spirit of God, that "whosoever feels not the warme gale and gentle ventilation of this Spirit, (though I feele his pulse) I dare not say he lives."

Here, as elsewhere, Browne splendidly uses the loose Senecan style to work out the consequences of an idea rather than to present a finished position. But Browne's accomplishment as a prose stylist has drawn mixed responses: while some critics find his mode essentially essayistic, a representation of the mind in the process of discovery, and meditative rather than rhetorical, others argue that his positions are fully worked out in advance and that he uses his prose to display firmly held ideas — perhaps even to dramatize them excessively, exaggerating the difficulties of belief to display his own prowess as a believer. Some have found him to be a writer who allows his readers to take serious problems less seriously than they ought (in the words of Joan Webber, he "pulls the sting from pain"), but he has also been seen as one who celebrates the joy in mysteries and paradoxes without being troubled by them.

Religio Medici is both a markedly personal and a significantly exemplary work. Written in a time of religious discord and published at the beginning of the civil war, it advocates the virtue of tolerance, to which Browne describes himself as naturally inclined: "I could never divide my selfe from any man upon the difference of an opinion, or be angry with his judgement for not agreeing with mee in that, from which perhaps within a few days I should dissent my selfe: I have no Genius to disputes in Religion, and have often thought it wisedome to decline them, especially upon a disadvantage, or when the cause of truth might suffer in the weakenesse of my patronage." But in a climate of strong disagreement over theology and church governance, not all of Browne's contemporaries welcomed exhortations to broad-mindedness or statements of belief that stretched the boundaries of the acceptable. The flamboyant Royalist, duelist, and Roman Catholic Sir Kenelm Digby sat up all night reading a copy of the original pirated version of *Religio Medici* and promptly produced some forty pages of response: while praising the work as "witty," "handsome," and "sweet," Digby took issue with Browne's questions about whether God could act inconsistently, his speculations on the mortality of the soul, and his emphasis in part 2 on charity as directed toward one's fellow human beings rather than toward God. In preparing the authorized edition for the press, Browne modified some of his phrasing in apparent response to Digby's objections. In his *Medicus Medicatus* (1645) the ardent Puritan Alexander Ross fiercely attacked *Religio Medici* as pro-Catholic; ironically, his book appeared at the same time that the Vatican placed Browne's work on its index of Prohibited Books.

These objections to *Religio Medici* from both sides show the difficulty of holding to a via media in religion or politics in a country moving rapidly toward civil war. But while *Religio Medici* was once read as a personal and slightly idiosyncratic credo, more-recent commentators have noted that the work occupies a definite political position: while affirming tolerance, Browne is explicit in his contempt for "the multitude," of which he says "it is no breach of Charity to call these fooles"; in his refusal to insist on religious uniformity; and in his rejection of the notions characteristic of the more radical religious and political groups of the mid seventeenth century.

Whereas *Religio Medici* uses reason to go beyond the bounds of reason into the realm of faith, Browne's next work, *Pseudodoxia Epidemica,* is a complementary attempt to use reason against excessive credulity. A massive undertaking in seven books, on which Browne continued to labor nearly until his death, *Pseudodoxia Epidemica* was revised and republished in 1650, 1658, 1669, and 1672. Whereas *Religio Medici* takes its origin from the author's own religious positions, *Pseudodoxia Epidemica* has its inception in beliefs that had been widely held. If the author of *Religio Medici* is a professional believer, the author of *Pseudodoxia Epidemica* is a professional skeptic, carefully examining received truth, reports of observation, popular mythology, and learned commentary in search of verifiable facts.

Many of the notions Browne takes up may hardly seem worth consideration, but the seventeenth century was a time when ideas and approaches that today appear quaint or bizarre mingled freely with new discoveries. Browne does reject as patently ridiculous and "false below confute"

– as things that "if we believe we must be apt to swallow any thing" – notions such as that "the Serpent went erect like Man, and that that Beast could speak before the Fall," that a "Nightingale hath no tongue," and that the sting of a scorpion may be alleviated by sitting "upon an Ass with one's face toward his tail"; but he patiently examines many others, such as that "a Diamond is made soft, or broke by the blood of a Goat," "that Coral is soft under water, but hardneth in the air," "that a Badger hath the Legs of one side shorter than of the other," "that a Bever to escape the Hunter bites off his testicles," and "that the Chameleon lives only by air."

Browne's undertaking in *Pseudodoxia Epidemica* bears an important if complicated relationship to one of the most significant developments of the seventeenth century: the progress of science. In a period in which discoveries regarding the circulation of the blood, magnetism, and microscopy mingled with belief in witches and planetary influence on human affairs, Browne joined with Francis Bacon, who in *The Advancement of Learning* (1605) called for a systematic and empirical approach to the development of knowledge, and with those who founded the Royal Society in 1660, who took an interest in the observations of naturalists as well as in more systematic methods of experimentation. There are strong similarities between the categories under which Browne carries out his investigation and those laid out by Bacon in *The Advancement of Learning*. Like Bacon, and like Robert Burton in *The Anatomy of Melancholy* (1621), Browne begins his work with a treatment of the origin of error; he traces it to the Fall of humanity, the source of all deception and confusion. He then moves through the "chain of being," dealing in book 2 with minerals and plants, including the properties of crystals, magnetism, and static electricity; in book 3 with animals; and in book 4 with human beings. The remaining three books treat questionable pictorial representations, both biblical and classical; "sundry common opinions Cosmographical and Historicall," that is, errors in historical accounts and common beliefs; and a diverse group of misconceptions, ranging from the view "That there was no Rain-bow before the Flood" to the proposition "That the Army of Xerxes drank whole Rivers dry." In contrast to Burton, who cites authority with enthusiasm, Browne, although he quotes learned opinion, joins Bacon in finding a source of error in too much reverence for tradition; he cautions especially against trusting writers (including the church fathers) in matters outside their areas of expertise. Other sources of error are misapprehension, false deduction, and excessive credulity.

*Engraved title page by William Marshall for the unauthorized first edition
of Browne's account of his religious beliefs (from Geoffrey Keynes, A
Bibliography of Sir Thomas Browne, 1924)*

Much of Browne's material in *Pseudodoxia Epidemica* comes from emblem books, moralized natural histories, encyclopedias, and bestiaries. In considering, for example, the question of whether the ostrich digests iron, Browne cites authorities – "Rhodiginus, Langius," and "swarms of others" – but also the usual pictorial representations of the ostrich with a horseshoe in its mouth. In this instance Browne is not able to add information of his own – "although I have had the sight of this Animal, I have not had the opportunity of its experiment"– but in other cases he did perform experiments. For example, in response to the notion that "glass is poison" he notes that, "having given unto Dogs above

a dram thereof, subtilly powdered in Butter and Paste," he detected no "visible disturbance"; he also investigated the formation of ice: "as we have made trial in glasses of water, covered an inch with oyl, which will not easily freeze in hard frosts of our climate." Browne points to many errors that arise from taking literally that which was meant metaphorically, as is the case with classical mythology and some biblical accounts. Browne demonstrates the absurdity of believing things that a moment's observation would disprove – that people cough but oxen or cows do not; that people grow gray but animals do not; that "Pellitory of the Wall" never grows in the sight of the North Star, "wherein how wide he [Leonardo Fioravanti, an Italian physician] is from truth, is easily discoverable unto every one, who hath but Astronomy enough to know that Star."

Browne's method throughout the work is to state a proposition and then consider which authorities have affirmed it, which have declared against it, and what evidence or record of observation has been offered pro or con; if the proposition is false, he asks what might have led observers to such a conclusion: for example, he explains the belief in centaurs as the result of men watering their horses while remaining on their backs and the notion that elephants have no joints as stemming from "the gross and somewhat Cylindrical composure of the legs . . . ; they appearing when he standeth, like Pillars of flesh, without any evidence of articulation." Although Browne frequently takes his propositions from ancient authors, he also cites such recent scientific observations as William Gilbert's discoveries regarding magnetism. There is also a good deal of common sense and rational deduction — applied, for example, to the notion that the badger's legs are shorter on one side.

Although Browne may be associated with Bacon as a seeker after truth, the program of *Pseudodoxia Epidemica* is not so much the ascertaining of truth as the refuting of error — a process that often leads to a profound skepticism. For example, rather than questioning the existence of the unicorn Browne, so to speak, "kills it off" with excessive belief: he finds it not only among the mammals, where he lists five ("the Indian Ox, the Indian Ass, the Rhinocerous, the Oryx, and that which is more eminently termed *Monoceros,* or *Unicornis*"), but even among fish and beetles, until that rare and mysterious creature may be found under every stone. As a matter of principle, Browne says, he prefers belief to ignorance; but, given the nature of his enterprise in this work, he far more often has to declare for disbelief. *Pseudodoxia Epidemica* is progressively inclined to skepticism as Browne discovers ever more misconceptions, myths that cannot be documented, and writings taken literally that are meant not to be so taken. Browne does not, finally, establish truth but rather seeks to dislodge error, leaving his reader disabused of false conceptions but in a state of uncertainty.

Pseudodoxia Epidemica, though it may well appear odd and antiquated to modern eyes, moves in the direction of observation and rationality. In that unusual pair of works published together in 1658 as *Hydriotaphia, Urne-Buriall, or, A Discourse of the Sepulchrall Urnes Lately Found in Norfolk. Together with The Garden of Cyrus, or the Quincunciall, Lozenge, or Net-work Plantations of the Ancients, Artificially, Naturally, Mystically Considered. With Sundry Observations* Browne moves once again, as he did in *Religio Medici,* from the physical to the metaphysical. *Hydriotaphia* has its inception in an account of an archaeological discovery, that of a group of funeral urns in a field in Norfolk; it becomes a meditation on mortality and immortality. *The Garden of Cyrus* deals with images of order in art and nature. Each work is exquisitely patterned; each consists of five chapters and proceeds from specific details and concrete images to the meanings of those details and images, from the visible to the invisible. As Browne declares in the fourth chapter of *The Garden of Cyrus:* "Light that makes things seen, makes some things invisible: were it not for darknesse and the shadow of the earth, the noblest part of the Creation had remained unseen. . . . The Sunne it self is but the dark *simulachrum,* and light but the shadow of God."

The urns found in Norfolk are the occasion for some of the most splendid and sonorous prose Browne ever wrote. In the first chapter he relies heavily on contemporary scholarship as he deals with funeral customs throughout the ancient world, from Abraham and the patriarchs through the Greeks, the Romans, European tribes, Indians, and Chaldeans; he concludes with the practices of elephants, cranes, ants, and, finally, bees, "which civill society carrieth out their dead, and hath exequies, if not interrments." The second chapter begins with an account of the discovery of the Norfolk urns: "In a Field of old *Walsingham,* not many moneths past, were digged up between fourty and fifty Urnes, deposited in a dry and sandy soile, not a yard deep, nor farre from one another: Not all strictly of one figure, but most answering these described: Some containing two pounds of bones, distinguishable in skulls, ribs, jawes, thigh-bones, and teeth, with fresh impressions of their combustion. Besides the extraneous substances, like peeces of small boxes, or combes handsomely wrought, handles of small brasse instruments, brazen nippers, and in one some kinde of *Opale.*" The curious thing about this passage is that for all its explicit detail, in which it resembles an observer's notebook, the result is finally indeterminate. The passage is heavily qualified by the use of negatives — "not many moneths past," "not a yard deep," "not all strictly of one figure" — and it concludes with the description of an object whose precise nature and function are uncertain ("some kinde of *Opale*"). Browne's original surmise, that the urns were probably of Roman origin (which was proved by later investigation to be mistaken), is even here subject to doubt: "A great obscurity herein, because no medall or Emperours Coyne enclosed, which might denote the date of their enterrments"; also, "some uncertainty there is from the period or term of burning, or the cessation of that practise." The chapter ends in complete uncertainty: "Mean while to what Nation or person belonged that large Urne found at *Ashburie*, containing mighty bones, and a Buckler; What those large Urnes found at little *Massingham*, or why the *Angelsea* Urnes are placed with their mouths downward, remains yet undiscovered."

The lack of certainty about the urns expressed in chapter 2 leads to a discourse in chapter 3 on the obscurity that surrounds death generally and in chapters 4 and 5 to a treatment of the way in which burial customs, whether pagan or Christian, imply some sense of an afterlife. In chapter 5 Browne offers ever-more-sweeping images of uncertainty, moving from an insistence on mortality to immortality itself. He says that the decline of the human race is not merely to be anticipated but is already well advanced: "The number of the dead long exceedeth all that shall live. The night of time far surpasseth the day, and who knows when was the Æquinox? Every houre addes unto that current Arithmetique, which scarce stands one moment. . . . Since the brother of death daily haunts us with dying *memento's,* and time that grows old it self, bids us hope no long duration." But no sooner has Browne declared humanity to be in the midst of darkness than he turns from the funeral pyres that created the ashes in the urns to the affirmation that "Life is a pure flame, and we live by an invisible Sun within us"; since "There is nothing strictly immortall, but immortality," all earthly life, and the remains of it, are transient. The last sentences of *Hydriotaphia* suggest, given that truth, that the whole of Browne's magnificent inquiry is irrelevant: "'Tis all one to lye in St. *Innocents* Church-yard, as in the Sands of *Ægypt:* Ready to be any thing, in the extasie of being ever, and as content with six foot as the Moles of *Adrianus*." The focus, finally, of *Hydriotaphia* is not on death but on life, and in that sense it leads naturally to its companion piece, *The Garden of Cyrus.*

For all the grand sweep of *Hydriotaphia,* with its peroration in the grand style, its prose is astonishingly rich and varied; the work contains humor, subtle modulation, and deflation of expectations. In the opening paragraph, for example, Browne leads the reader to anticipate great things and then radically narrows the perspective: "In the deep discovery of the Subterranean world, a shallow part would satisfie some enquirers; who, if two or three yards were open about the surface, would not care to rake the bowels of *Potosi* [the rich mountain of *Peru*], and regions towards the Centre. Nature hath furnished one part of the Earth, and man another. The treasures of time lie high, in Urnes, Coynes, and Monuments, scarce below the roots of some vegetables." Here Browne uses parallel sentence structure, sharply contrasting diction, alliteration, and assonance to mingle wide reference in time and space with the mundane — with the literally earthy. His balanced syntax juxtaposes human aspiration and human limitation, setting out what humanity hopes to achieve and showing how it falls short. In a dramatic preparation for a calculated anticlimax Browne appears to celebrate human remains, "the treasures of time," then deflates that expectation with associations of turnips and carrots. Even in the most factual sections, such as the opening of chapter 2, which details the find itself, or the massive assembly of authority on burial customs worldwide, one moves from the little that is known to the great deal that is not.

If *Hydriotaphia* has, at least, the occasion of an archaeological discovery to recommend it to the modern reader, *The Garden of Cyrus* might well appear totally frivolous — a work, as C. A. Patrides puts it, that constitutes "the ultimate test of one's response to Browne." The work has as its unlikely subject the discovery, in far more places than one would have deemed possible, of the quincunx, a pattern of four points in a square with a single point in the center, like the five spots on a die (*quincunx* means five-twelfths and derives from the pattern on a Roman coin). The work is dedicated to Browne's friend from Oxford days, Nicholas Bacon, a kinsman of Sir Francis Bacon. But unlike *Pseudodoxia Epidemica,* which might be seen as part of the Baconian program for the advancement of knowledge, *The Garden of Cyrus* is a work of extravagant and apparently whimsical discovery. Browne points to the connection between *Hydriotaphia* and *The Garden of Cyrus* in his letter of dedication when he says that "to flourish in the state of Glory, we must first be sown in corruption"; the suggestion is that *Hydriotaphia,* with its emphasis on death, chaos, and loss, is the inevitable precursor to the paradisiacal images of *The Garden of Cyrus.*

Browne finds a justification for his inquiry in the antiquity of his subject, turning to Genesis to determine that "Gardens were before Gardiners, and but some hours after the earth" (humanity was created on the sixth day, the earth and the vegetable world on the third). He discusses the oldest gardens —

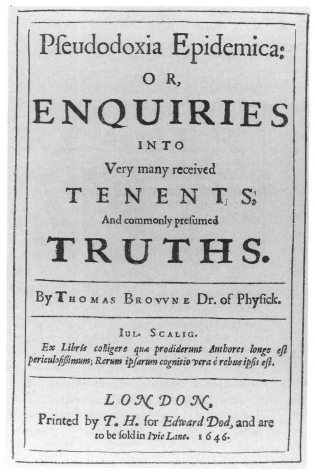

Title page for Browne's second book, in which he debunks
commonly held notions of the seventeenth century

Eden and the hanging gardens of Babylon – and gardeners: Semiramis, "the third or fourth from *Nimrod*"; Nebuchadnezzar; Cyrus the elder, "brought up in Woods and Mountains"; and the younger Cyrus, "a Lord of Gardens." The order found in gardens can be traced to its ultimate source in Eden: "since even in Paradise it self, the tree of knowledge was placed in the middle of the Garden, whatever was the ambient figure, there wanted not a centre and rule of decussation."

Having found the pattern of the quincunx in gardens, which he considered to be works of nature, Browne goes on to discover it in human artifacts, in brickwork, laurel crowns, ancient beds and windows, lapidary work, and Roman battalion formations. In chapter 3 Browne proceeds from nature as it has been ordered by humans to nature itself, to discover "how nature Geometrizeth, and observeth order in all things." He then moves in chapter 4, "The Quincunx Mistically Considered," to aesthetic considerations, to the discovery of patterns and order of all kinds, alternation of light and dark, and finally to the notion of order per se, of the invisible in the visible: "The Sunne it self is but the dark *simulachrum,* and light but the shadow of God." The work ends whimsically with the location of the quincunx in the five stars of the constellation Hyades and in a relation of night, the time of sleep, to the time of death and eternal waking.

Throughout the civil war and the Interregnum Browne flourished as a prominent and respected physician, but the Restoration of Charles II in 1660 would have been welcomed by someone of his political and religious sympathies. Browne's election as fellow of the Royal College of Physicians followed in 1664, and in 1671, on the visit of Charles to Norwich, he was knighted. Browne was never inducted into the Royal Society, the body that was so influential in the advancement of science in the later seventeenth century as well as in the shaping of a plainer, more sober English prose; but he communicated cordially with many of its members. For one of the most distinguished of them, Robert Boyle, he was "the learned Dr. Brown."

Although Browne, like his contemporaries Thomas Hobbes and John Milton, lived through the civil war, the Interregnum, and the Restoration, there is little obvious or unambiguous evidence in his writings of the effects of these events. Whether or not the T. Browne who was one of the signatories of *Vox Norwici* (1646), one of a series of pamphlets defending freedom of religious practice of the Norwich clergy, was the physician and author Thomas Browne remains uncertain. But Browne's repeated affirmations of tolerance constitute a response to the events of his time. His assertions in *Religio Medici* that religious differences are differences of opinion, not the occasion for violence, and that "every man is not a proper Champion for Truth, nor fit to take up the Gantlet in the cause of Veritie" are attempts to defuse the religious and political conflict that was then shaking England.

But there are other respects in which Browne may be seen as a man of his time, respects that have moved later admirers to apologetics. In 1664 Browne was one of twelve witnesses who gave testimony in the trial of two women who were convicted of witchcraft and hanged. Browne had affirmed his belief in witches in *Religio Medici;* although belief in witchcraft was by no means universal in the mid seventeenth century (Digby, for example, did not share it), Browne was in agreement here with some of his more notable contemporaries, including Francis Bacon, the Platonist Henry More, the prominent member of the Royal Society Joseph Glanvill, and the judge at the trial, Sir Matthew Hale. Browne's testimony that a crime had been committed was not a major factor leading to the verdict.

At his death in 1682 Browne left behind a considerable body of unpublished letters responding to inquiries on such diverse subjects as plants in Scripture, languages, hawks and falconry, and cymbals; these letters were published in 1683 as *Certain Miscellany Tracts.* There were also commonplace books and other notes and records of experiments, some of them overlapping with the materials in *Pseudodoxia Epidemica,* all testifying to Browne's lifelong curiosity and habit of observation.

Two other notable works appeared posthumously. *A Letter to a Friend* (1690) is thought to have been composed not long after December 1656 and may have originated as an account sent to Sir John Pettus of the illness and death of Browne's and Pettus's mutual friend Robert Loveday, a patient of Browne's. But Browne makes this particular death more comprehensible by placing it in a general context, that of the deaths of kings and emperors, the spread of various diseases, and the psychological effects of age and terminal illness; he considers the frequency with which death comes as a surprise, even on one's birthday (a favorite topic of his), and the appropriateness of such a death. In the last third of *A Letter to a Friend* the thought of death leads to a consideration of the moral life as preparation for it. That concluding section reappears in Browne's final work, *Christian Morals* (1716), a proverbial, sententious, and didactic treatise on such matters as avoiding pride, envy, and avarice and on the advisability of not counting on too long a life so that one may be pleasantly surprised. The manuscript for *Christian Morals,* described by Edward Browne as "a continuation of . . . my father's Religio Medici, drawn up in his elder years," was apparently left untitled and mislaid for some time among the papers of Thomas Tenison, archbishop of Canterbury. It was retrieved by Browne's daughter, Elizabeth Lyttleton, and published in 1716. While its solemnity and stylistic control moved Samuel Johnson to write a life of Browne for the second edition (1756), later readers have missed in it the variety, spontaneity, and flexibility of Browne's earlier prose.

One of the finest stylists in a period of extraordinarily rich and varied prose, Browne was an eminent writer in his own day. *Religio Medici* went through eight editions in his lifetime and, according to an opinion quoted by Samuel Pepys, was one of three books "most esteemed and generally cried up for wit in the world." *Pseudodoxia Epidemica,* the massive work that made Browne's reputation in the learned community of his time, had appeared in five editions by 1672. Despite changes in stylistic norms, Browne continued to have admirers into the eighteenth century — most notably Johnson, whose life of Browne included the first major critical evaluation of him as a writer. A favorite among the Romantics, poets and prose writers alike, Browne was also on Emily Dickinson's short list of favorite authors; his influence is deeply marked on Ralph Waldo Emerson, Herman Melville, and Henry David Thoreau; and he received extensive and admiring treatment by Walter Pater and Leslie Stephen. The first complete edition of Browne's works was that of Simon Wilkin, published in four volumes in 1835–1836; a critical edition titled *Sir Thomas Brownes' Religio Medici Letter to a Friend &c. and Christian Morals,* edited by W. A. Greenhill, appeared in 1881 and was revised in 1885.

Page from Browne's notebook with drafts of passages for chapter 5 of his Hydriotaphia *(British Library, Sloane MS 1862, f. 78ᵛ)*

Sir Thomas Browne, who characterized humankind as living "in divided and distinguished worlds," was himself "that great and true Amphibium," combining in one person seemingly incompatible traits: a delight in the paradoxes of faith and a fascination with scientific observation; a love of order and pattern and a native skepticism; a highly wrought, elaborate prose style and a curiosity about the processes of human thought; a taste for grandeur and a love of play; a sense of reverence and a sense of the absurd. As with so many of the great writers of his century, writing was not his primary occupation; but in a particularly eloquent, even extravagant, way Browne manifests the mixed attitudes toward faith and the natural world that are found also in writings of the great scientists of his time: Boyle, Gilbert, William Harvey, Johannes Kepler, and Sir Isaac Newton. He articulates for the modern reader much that is past in texts that continue to resonate.

Bibliographies:

Geoffrey Keynes, *A Bibliography of Sir Thomas Browne* (Cambridge: Cambridge University Press, 1924; revised and enlarged edition, Oxford: Clarendon Press, 1968);

Dennis Donovan, Margaretha G. Hartley Herman, and Ann E. Imbrie, *Sir Thomas Browne and Robert Burton: A Reference Guide* (Boston: G. K. Hall, 1981);

Andrea Sununu, "Recent Studies in Sir Thomas Browne (1970–1986)," *English Literary Renaissance,* 19 (Winter 1989): 118–129.

References:

Joan Bennett, *Sir Thomas Browne* (Cambridge: Cambridge University Press, 1962);

Laurence A. Breiner, "The Generation of Metaphor in Thomas Browne," *Modern Language Quarterly,* 38 (September 1977): 261–275;

William P. Dunn, *Sir Thomas Browne: A Study in Religious Philosophy,* third edition (Minneapolis: University of Minnesota Press, 1958);

Norman J. Endicott, "Some Aspects of Self-Revelation and Self-Portraiture in *Religio Medici,*" in *Essays in English Literature from the Renaissance to the Victorian Age, 1964: Presented to A. S. P. Woodhouse,* edited by Millar MacLure and F. W. Watt (Toronto: University of Toronto Press, 1964), pp. 85–102;

English Language Notes, special issue on Browne, 19 (June 1982);

Jeremiah S. Finch, *Sir Thomas Browne: A Doctor's Life of Science and Faith* (New York: Schuman, 1950);

Stanley E. Fish, "The Bad Physician: The Case of Sir Thomas Browne," in his *Self-Consuming Artifacts: The Experience of Seventeenth-Century Literature* (Berkeley: University of California Press, 1972), pp. 353–373;

Fish, ed., *Seventeenth-Century Prose* (New York: Oxford University Press, 1971);

Achsah Guibbory, " 'A Rationall of Old Rites': Sir Thomas Browne's *Urn Buriall* and the Conflict over Ceremony," *Yearbook of English Studies,* 21 (1991): 229–241;

Guibbory, "Sir Thomas Browne's *Pseudodoxia Epidemica* and the Circle of Knowledge," *Texas Studies in Literature and Language,* 18 (Fall 1976): 486–499;

Anne Drury Hall, "Epistle, Meditation, and Sir Thomas Browne's Religio Medici," *PMLA,* 94 (March 1979): 234–246;

Janet E. Halley, "Sir Thomas Browne's *The Garden of Cyrus* and the Real Character," *English Literary Renaissance,* 15 (Winter 1985): 100–121;

Frank L. Huntley, *Sir Thomas Browne: A Biographical and Critical Study* (Ann Arbor: University of Michigan Press, 1962);

Joseph A. Mazzeo, "Seventeenth-Century English Prose Style: The Quest for a Natural Style," *Mosaic,* 6 (Spring 1973): 107–144;

Egon Stephen Merton, *Science and Imagination in Sir Thomas Browne* (New York: King's Crown Press, Columbia University, 1949);

Anna K. Nardo, "Sir Thomas Browne Turning the World around for Recreation," in her *The Ludic Self in Seventeenth-Century English Literature* (Albany: State University of New York Press, 1991), pp. 159–177;

Leonard Nathanson, *The Strategy of Truth: A Study of Sir Thomas Browne* (Chicago: University of Chicago Press, 1967);

Walter Pater, "Sir Thomas Browne," in his *Appreciations, with an Essay on Style* (London & New York: Macmillan, 1889), pp. 127–166;

C. A. Patrides, ed., *Approaches to Sir Thomas Browne: The Ann Arbor Tercentenary Lectures and Essays* (Columbia: University of Missouri Press, 1982);

Jonathan F. S. Post, *Sir Thomas Browne* (Boston: G. K. Hall, 1987);

Victoria Silver, "Liberal Theology and Sir Thomas Browne's 'Soft and Flexible' Discourse," *English Literary Renaissance,* 20 (Winter 1990): 69–105;

Thomas C. Singer, "Sir Thomas Browne's 'Emphaticall decussation, or fundamentall figure': Geometrical Hieroglyphs and *The Garden of Cyrus*," *English Literary Renaissance,* 17 (Winter 1987): 85–102;

Laurence Stapleton, *The Elected Circle: Studies in the Art of Prose* (Princeton: Princeton University Press, 1973);

Leslie Stephen, "Hours in a Library: No. I. – Sir Thomas Browne," *Cornhill Magazine,* 23 (May 1871): 596–611;

Lytton Strachey, "Sir Thomas Browne," in his *Books and Characters, French and English* (New York: Harcourt, Brace, 1922), pp. 33–47;

Austin Warren, "The Style of Sir Thomas Browne," *Kenyon Review,* 13 (Autumn 1951): 674–687;

Joan Webber, *The Eloquent I: Style and Self in Seventeenth-Century Prose* (Madison: University of Wisconsin Press, 1968);

Michael Wilding, "*Religio Medici* in the English Revolution," in his *Dragon's Teeth: Literature in the English Revolution* (Oxford: Clarendon Press, 1987), pp. 89–113;

James N. Wise, *Sir Thomas Browne's Religio Medici and Two Seventeenth-Century Critics* (Columbia: University of Missouri Press, 1973).

Papers:
Major collections of Sir Thomas Browne's work, including manuscripts, are to be found in the British Museum (Lansdowne MSS); the Bodleian Library, Oxford (Rawlinson MSS); the Library of Pembroke College, Oxford; the Norwich Public Library; and the Sir William Osler Library, McGill University, Montreal.

Robert Burton
(8 February 1577 – 25 January 1640)

Barbara Hart Dixon
Purdue University

BOOKS: *The Anatomy Of Melancholy, What It Is. With All The Kindes, Cavses, Symptomes, Prognostickes, And Seuerall Cvres Of It. In Three Maine Partitions with their seuerall Sections, Members, and Svbsections. Philosophically, Medicinally, Historically, Opened And Cvt Vp. With a Satyricall Preface, conducing to the following Discourse,* as Democritus Junior (Oxford: Printed by John Lichfield & James Short for Henry Cripps, 1621; revised, 1624; revised again, 1628; revised again, 1632; revised edition, Oxford: Printed by Leonard Lichfield for Henry Cripps, 1638; revised edition, Oxford: Printed by R. W. for Henry Cripps, 1651);

Philosophaster, Comoedia, nunc primum in lucem producta. Poemata, antehac sparsim edita, nunc in unum collecta, edited by William Edward Buckley (Hertford: Printed by Stephen Austin, 1862).

Editions: *The Anatomy of Melancholy, What It Is, with All the Kinds, Causes, Symptoms, Prognostics and Several Cures of It. In Three Partitions with Their Several Sections, Members, and Subsections Philosophically, Medicinally, Historically Opened and Cut Up, by Democritus Junior. With a Satirical Preface, Conducing to the Following Discourse,* 3 volumes (London: Nimmo, 1886);

The Anatomy of Melancholy, 3 volumes, edited by the Reverend A. R. Shilleto (London & New York: Bell, 1893);

The Anatomy of Melancholy, by Robert Burton, Now for the First Time with the Latin completely Given in Translation and Embodied in an All-English Text, 2 volumes, edited by Floyd Dell and Paul Jordan-Smith (New York: Doran, 1927; London: Routledge, 1931);

Robert Burton's Philosophaster: With an English translation of the Same, Together with His Other Minor Writings in Prose and Verse, edited by Jordan-Smith (Stanford, Cal.: Stanford University Press, 1931);

The Anatomy of Melancholy, 3 volumes, introduction by Holbrook Jackson (London: Dent / New York: Dutton, 1932);

The Anatomy of Melancholy, 5 volumes projected, 2 volumes published, edited by Thomas C. Faulkner, Nicolas K. Kiessling, and Rhonda L. Blair (Oxford: Clarendon Press, 1989);

Philosophaster, edited and translated by Connie McQuillen (Binghamton, N.Y.: Medieval & Renaissance Texts and Studies, 1993).

OTHER: John Rider, *Rider's Dictionarie, Corrected, and with the Addition of above Five Hundred Words Enriched,* preface by Burton (Oxford: Printed by Joseph Barnes, 1612).

Robert Burton is known for *The Anatomy of Melancholy* (1621), a lengthy treatise on the causes and treatment of melancholy that became one of the most popular English books of the early seventeenth century. The primary source of information about Burton's life is Anthony à Wood's brief sketch in the 1721 edition of his *Athenae Oxonienses;* additional, if minimal, biographical information is supplied by *The Anatomy of Melancholy* itself, when Burton reveals details about his family and education.

The fourth of nine children, Burton was born to Ralph and Dorothy Faunt Burton at their family home, Lindley Hall, Leicestershire, on 8 February 1577. Wood characterizes the Burtons as "an ancient and genteel Family." Ralph Burton was interested in genealogy and medical remedies, and in *The Anatomy of Melancholy* Burton records that his mother had "excellent skill in Surgery, sore eyes, aches &c . . . as all the country where shee dwelt can witness." William, Burton's oldest brother, also had some literary talent: his history of the county was published in 1622.

Burton attended school at Sutton Coldfield and Nuneaton, both in Warwickshire. In *The Anatomy of Melancholy* he writes that there is "no slavery in the world . . . like to that of a Grammer Scholler."

Robert Burton in 1635; portrait by an unknown artist (Brasenose College, Oxford)

At sixteen he entered Brasenose College, Oxford, as a commoner (a student who, unlike fellows and scholars, had to pay for his own board). There, Wood reports, Burton "made considerable progress in Logic and Philosophy." In 1599 he entered Christ Church, Oxford, where he studied with Dr. John Bancroft. He took his B.A. on 30 June 1602. Nine years was a long time to pursue a degree, particularly for a student with Burton's intellect; many young men would have finished their educations before the age at which Burton started. Some scholars speculate that he was already suffering from the depression that appears to have tormented him during the better part of his life; there is a record of a Robert Burton, age twenty, who sought medical help for melancholy from Simon Forman in London in 1597, but there is no conclusive evidence that the two Burtons were one and the same. Burton's subsequent education proceeded at a more normal rate: he received his M.A. on 9 June 1605 and his B.D. in May 1614. In 1615 Burton served as a "Clerk to the Market of Oxford"; his duties included checking the accuracy of weights and measures and ensuring the freshness of the food sold in the Oxford markets.

Patronage was important in the early seventeenth century, and in *The Anatomy of Melancholy* Burton bemoans his lack of preferment. He complains that he was given false hopes by some people he believed to be his friends, but he accepted his lot "as a mired horse that struggles at first with all his might and main to get out, but when he sees no remedy, that his beating will not serve, lies still." In actuality, Burton received several preferments: in 1616 he was given the vicarage of St. Thomas Church in Oxford; from 1624 to 1631 he received income from the benefice of Walesby in Lincolnshire, although he never lived there; and in 1632 his friend George, Lord Berkeley, gave him a living as rector of Seagrave in Leicester. Berkeley was a student at Christ Church when the first edition of *The Anatomy of Melancholy* was published, and Burton may have been his tutor. The dedication to the book reads "Illustrissimo Georgio Berkleio."

Burton was conscientious about fulfilling his clerical duties; Wood reports that at St. Thomas, Burton "always gave the sacrament in Wafers." Like most of his seventeenth-century counterparts, he took religion seriously. In his writings he doggedly defends the Church of England and rails at other sects. He reflects the intolerance of his age by reserving his most bitter invective for Catholics, whom he calls "blind idiots and superstitious asses" who are "hoodwinked like hawks."

The first record of Burton's literary activities is a contribution he made to a comedy entitled *Alba,* presented before King James during a royal visitation to Oxford in August 1605. No copy of this work has survived. His next known literary effort was another comedy, *Philosophaster,* written in Latin and performed only once, on 16 February 1617; it would not be published until 1862. In *The Anatomy of Melancholy* Burton points out that he began writing the play in 1606, although it was not completed until 1615. His insistence on the early date of composition may have been to avoid accusations of having plagiarized from Ben Jonson's *Alchemist,* produced in 1610 and published two years later. Both plays feature an alchemist, and both are satiric; but there are few other similarities. Burton sets his action in the fictional Osuna, a small town in Andalusia whose inhabitants want to establish a university. This vehicle enables Burton to describe the many varieties of false learning, including magic, trickery, alchemy, and bad poetry. By the end of the play all the "damned, pseudo-Academicks" are exposed and properly punished, and the university is established on proper principles of learning. No one ventures that *Philosophaster* is a great play; it is important because it illustrates that Burton's satiric approach was already in place as early as 1606. His wit and his caustic cataloguing in *Philosophaster* expose folly in much the same way that Democritus Junior, his persona in *The Anatomy of Melancholy,* does. For example, Polumathes, one of the characters in *Philosophaster,* describes the false philosophers in a style similar to that of Democritus Junior: "They're, most part, Cuman asses, infants, outsides, phantastick shadows, barren mannikins, straw men, clods, dolts, sots, dullards, giddy-heads, lazy-bones, idiots, slaves of bed and belly, ignorant dizzards, puff'd-up clowns, mummers, babblers, whose whole equipment consisteth of venerable beards and shameless impudence."

Burton spent most of his life at Christ Church; he claims in *The Anatomy of Melancholy* that "I have liv'd a silent, sedentary, solitary, private life . . . penn'd up most part in my study." Bishop White

Kennet records: "Yet I have heard that nothing at last could make him laugh, but going down to the Bridge-foot in Oxford, and hearing the barge-men scold and storm and swear at one another, at which he would set his Hands to his sides, and laugh most profusely." According to Wood, Burton "understood the surveying of lands well," and the frontispiece of *The Anatomy of Melancholy* depicts him holding an armillary sphere and cross staff such as surveyors used.

Although Burton's tenure at Christ Church appears to have been relatively calm, there is a hint of trouble in a letter of 7 June 1630 from Burton's brother William referring to "the uncertainty of my brothers aboade in Oxford by reason of [the] troubled state of the Colledge betweene the Canons and Students." The problem seems to have been remedied by 1630, when William proposed to send his son Cassibilian to Oxford.

Burton's most significant accomplishment at Oxford was the writing and revising of *The Anatomy of Melancholy.* It is unclear when Burton began work on his masterpiece. The first edition was published in 1621, and four more editions appeared during his lifetime: in 1624, 1628, 1632, and 1638. A sixth edition, prepared from Burton's notes, was published posthumously in 1651. Burton revised each edition considerably; the second edition, for example, adds more than 70,000 words to the original text, enlarging it from 353,369 to 423,983 words. He deleted virtually nothing; although the third through sixth editions do not add as much as the second, each is longer than the previous one (the final word count is 516,384).

Burton admits that he chose melancholy as his subject because it affected him personally: "I write of Melancholy, by being busie to avoid Melancholy." He concedes that other subjects (such as divinity, the "Queene of Professions") are more worthy; nonetheless, he "was fatally driven upon this Rocke of Melancholy." Burton is, in fact, ambivalent about the condition. In the poem that prefaces the work, "The Authors Abstract of Melancholy," Burton illustrates both positive and negative aspects of the malady. Each stanza ends with a reflection on the condition of being melancholy, with adjectives alternating from positive to negative: *sweet/sad, sweet/sour, sweet/damn'd, sweet/harsh, sweet/fierce, divine/damn'd.* The word *sweet* is used more than any other to describe melancholy, yet the progression of images becomes increasingly negative until by the end of the poem the speaker is contemplating suicide as the ultimate cure. A similar ambivalence pervades Burton's entire magnum opus. This charac-

Title page for the first edition of Burton's treatise on depression

teristic is, perhaps, owing to his education: a common teaching device during the seventeenth century was to have students argue both sides of a question.

Burton's avowed goal in his masterpiece is to "anatomize" melancholy – to dissect and analyze every part of it. The anatomy was a popular genre in the sixteenth and seventeenth centuries; earlier anatomies would have led readers to expect *The Anatomy of Melancholy* to be a scientific discourse. Anatomies, moreover, were exhaustive: they sought to be the last word on their topics. Burton, accordingly, attempted to gather everything that had ever been written about the disease, but the number of sources had increased considerably during the Renaissance. Burton complains, "wee shall have a vast *Chaos* and confusion of Bookes, we are oppressed with them, our eyes ake with reading, our fingers with turning." His insistence on including everything he could find on melancholy, however, produces striking contradictions about the cause and cure of the disorder.

"The Author's Abstract of Melancholy" is followed by a "Satyricall Preface" titled "Democritus Junior to the Reader." Burton's contemporaries would have recognized the use of Democritus as a literary convention: the atomist Democritus of Abdera, who lived in the fifth century B.C., was known as the "laughing philosopher" (in contrast to Heraclitus, the "weeping philosopher"), and many authors before Burton had used Democritus to illustrate one approach to life's problems: laughing at them. Many critics claim that while the preface is satiric, the satire diminishes or disappears afterward. But Burton's choice of Democritus suggests a satiric bent to the work, and Northrop Frye has labeled *The Anatomy of Melancholy* "the greatest Menippean satire in English before Swift." Although he used a persona, Burton's identity as the author was never in question. He signed the postscript to the first edition with his real name; while the name was not included in subsequent editions, the details provided in the work about Burton's family indicate that he was making no effort to conceal his authorship. Furthermore, the third edition and all those thereafter included a picture of Burton on the title page.

Near the end of the preface appears the first published utopia originally written in English, preceding Sir Francis Bacon's *New Atlantis* (1626) by five years. (Sir Thomas More's *Utopia* [1516] had been translated from the original Latin by Ralph Robinson in 1551, and Joseph Hall's Latin *Mundus Alter et Idem* [1605] by John Healey in 1609.) Burton's utopia, which comprises only eleven and a half pages of "Democritus Junior to the Reader," satirizes seventeenth-century English politics and customs. Some of the satire may reflect Burton's disappointments; his discussion of marriage in his ideal society suggests, for example, that lack of money may have prevented Burton from marrying: "And when once they come to those yeares, poverty shall hinder no man from marriage, or any other respect, but all shall rather be enforced, then hindred." Also, that Burton may have suffered some financial disadvantages as a younger brother is indicated by a passage he added to the 1624 edition: "I will have severall orders, degrees of nobilitie, and those hereditary, not rejecting younger brothers in the meane time, for they shall be sufficiently provided for by pensions, or so qualified, brought up in some honest calling, they shall be able to live of themselves."

Creating a utopia allows an author immense artistic freedom, and Burton's creative energies are nowhere more evident than in this section of his work. He realizes, however, that his utopia is only possible in the abstract because human nature is degraded; thus, his utopia disintegrates because it must be inhabited by the very madmen he describes so vividly throughout the rest of *The Anatomy of Melancholy*. For example, Burton insists that "offensive warres, except the cause be very just, I will not allow of. . . . And in such warrs to abstaine as much as is possible from depopulations, burning of townes, massacring of Infants, &c." The qualification, "except the cause be very just," undermines his rule that there will be no offensive wars in his society; and by decreeing that his soldiers will abstain "as much as is possible" from the atrocities of war, Burton admits that they cannot abstain wholly.

The text of *The Anatomy of Melancholy* consists of three major "Partitions." The first focuses on the causes and symptoms of melancholy, the second on cures, and the third on "love-melancholy" and, to a lesser extent, religious melancholy. Each partition begins with a "Synopsis," or outline, showing the division of the partition into "Sections," "Members," and "Sub-sections." The synopses suggest that order has been imposed on chaos. Examination of the text, however, reveals considerable disorder: for example, Burton discusses the head separately from "all the body"; subjects overlap, so that a distempered liver becomes classified both as a general and a particular ailment; and when Burton wants to discuss something that does not fit into the proposed organization, he simply inserts a "digression."

One of the most remarkable qualities of *The Anatomy of Melancholy* is the erudition it displays. Burton cites more than thirteen hundred authors; he is not always exact in his quotations, does not always cite his sources, and consistently exaggerates and inflates figures. Still, compared to other works of the period the sources in *The Anatomy of Melancholy* are scrupulously documented. All of the sources appear to be genuine, even if some of the originals cannot be located.

The major appeal of Burton's work today, however, lies in the author's style. Burton describes the book as a "cento" (a work that combines quotations from many sources) and a "Maceronicon" (a document that blends two or more languages). Burton sees his role as that of a compiler: "As a good hous-wife out of divers fleeces weaves one peece of Cloath, a Bee gathers Wax and Hony out of many Flowers, and makes a new bundle of all."

Burton's style is characterized by *copia*, or fullness. A typical Burtonian sentence begins with a word or short phrase that is then played with in the rest of the sentence. Sentences can be long, the members connected only loosely by *and* or *but*. Sometimes the phrases are rhythmic and mount to a climax. The opening sentence in the "Digression of Ayre" in the second partition illustrates the tremendous stylistic control Burton employs: "As a long-winged Hawke when hee is first whistled off the fist, mounts aloft, and for his pleasure fetcheth many a circuit in the Ayre, still soaring higher and higher, till hee bee come to his full pitch; and in the end when the game is sprung, comes downe amaine, and stoopes upon a sudden: so will I, having now come at last into these ample fields of Ayre, wherein I may freely expatiate and exercise my selfe, for my recreation a while rove, wander round about the world, mount aloft to those æthereall orbes and celestiall spheres, and so descend to my former elements againe." This passage also shows his deft and powerful deployment of metaphor.

Frontispiece for the sixth edition of Burton's work, which includes his final revisions

At times "Democritus Junior" rails at the reader: "I owe thee nothing, (Reader) I looke for no favour at thy hands, I am independent, I feare not"; he also scolds, orates, cajoles, and seeks forgiveness. At times he feigns confusion:

> But where am I? Into what subject have I rushed? What have I to doe with Nunnes, Maids, Virgins, Widowes? I am a bacheler my selfe, and lead a Monasticke life in a College. . . . I will say no more.
>   And yet I must and will say something more, adde a word or two *in gratiam Virginuum & Viduarum*. . . .

That the "confusion" is deliberate is borne out by the appearance of these lines, unchanged, in all five editions published in Burton's lifetime. Such contra-dictions and digressions are typical of *The Anatomy of Melancholy*, illustrating Burton's self-professed writing style: "This roving humor (though not with like successe) I have ever had, & like a ranging spaniell, that barkes at every bird he sees, leaving his game, I have followed all. . . ."

Besides being digressive, Burton's style is exhaustive. Catalogues are common, sometimes lasting for several pages. Examples are also profuse, particularly when he rails against women: "Every lover loves his mistress, though she be . . . pimpled, pale . . . have rotten teeth, black, uneven brown teeth, beetle browed, a witch's beard, her breath stink all over the room, her nose drop winter and summer . . . pendulis massis, 'her dugs like two double jugs' or else no dugs . . . dowdy, a slut, a scold, a nasty, rank, rammy, filthy, beastly quean . . . obscene, base beggarly, rude, foolish, untaught . . . he admires her for all this. . . ."

Another stylistic characteristic of *The Anatomy of Melancholy* is profuse citation in Latin. Burton says that he originally planned to write the entire work in Latin: "It was not mine intent to prostitute my Muse in *English*." The sole reason he did not, he claims, is that the stationers "will not deal" with Latin texts. Educated seventeenth-century readers would have experienced no difficulty with Burton's abrupt switches between English and Latin; although Burton translates or paraphrases most of his quotations, many — particularly those that deal with misogyny, medical prescriptions, sex, or scatology — are left in Latin, perhaps to screen them from less educated readers.

The Anatomy of Melancholy is important as the first detailed work on psychology in English. More significantly, although it is no longer the best-seller it was in the seventeenth century, it continues to be read. In the eighteenth century James Boswell reported that it was the only book that could get Samuel Johnson out of bed "two hours sooner than he wished to rise." Its popularity waned somewhat in the nineteenth century, but A. R. Shilleto's 1893 edition helped to restore its readership. The new Oxford edition (1989–), with its planned volume that will include English translations of all the Latin, will make *The Anatomy of Melancholy* more accessible to modern readers.

Throughout his life Burton sustained an avid interest in astronomy; he records in his notebook that he viewed Jupiter's moons "by the help of a glasse 8 foot long." Astrology was considered equally scientific in the seventeenth century, and Burton was extremely interested in this field as well. His surviving notebook in the Bodleian Library at Oxford includes copious notes about astrological practice. Wood describes Burton as "an exact mathematician and a curious calculator of nativities." He calculated his own nativity charts, determining the exact time of his conception as 25 May 1576 at 9:00 P.M.; and the date he predicted for his death was so close to the actual one — 25 January 1640 — that some students speculated, according to Wood, that "rather than there should be a mistake in his calculation, he sent up his soul to heaven thro' a slip about his neck." His epitaph has generated centuries of speculation about whether he took his own life: "Paucis notus, paucioribus ignotus, hic jacet Democritus Junior, cui vitam dedit et mortem Melancholia" (Known to few, unknown

to fewer, here lies Democritus Junior, to whom Melancholy gave both life and death). Had such rumors been given credence by the authorities, however, it is probable that he would have been denied burial in Christ Church Cathedral. All that is known for certain is that Robert Burton, the studious anatomizer of melancholy whose work has cheered generations, died alone in his college rooms.

Bibliographies:

Paul Jordan-Smith, *Bibliographia Burtoniana: A Study of Robert Burton's The Anatomy of Melancholy* (Stanford, Cal.: Stanford University Press, 1931);

Dennis Donovan, *Sir Thomas Browne, 1924–1966; Robert Burton, 1924–1966* (London: Nether, 1968);

Margaretha Donovan, G. H. Herman, and Ann E. Imbri, *Sir Thomas Browne and Robert Burton: A Reference Guide* (Boston: G. K. Hall, 1981);

Joey Conn, *Robert Burton and* The Anatomy of Melancholy: *An Annotated Bibliography of Primary and Secondary Sources* (New York: Greenwood Press, 1988).

Biography:

Anthony à Wood, "Robert Burton," in his *Athenae Oxonienses,* second edition, volume 1 (London: Printed for B. Knaplock, D. Midwinter & J. Tonson, 1721).

References:

Lawrence Babb, *Sanity in Bedlam: A Study of Robert Burton's Anatomy of Melancholy* (East Lansing: Michigan State University Press, 1959);

J. B. Bamborough, "Burton and Hemingius," *Review of English Studies,* 34 (November 1983): 441–445;

Bamborough, *The Little World of Man* (London: Longmans, Green, 1952);

Bamborough, "Robert Burton's Astrological Notebook," *Review of English Studies,* 32 (August 1981): 267–285;

Rhonda L. Blair, "Robert Burton's 'Agony': A Pattern of Revision Made for the Sixth Edition of *The Anatomy of Melancholy,*" *Papers of the Bibliographical Society of America,* 78, no. 2 (1984): 215–218;

James Boswell, *The Life of Samuel Johnson, LL.D.,* 2 volumes (London: Printed by Henry Baldwin for Charles Dilly, 1791);

Anne S. Chapple, "Robert Burton's Geography of Melancholy," *Studies in English Literature,* 33 (Winter 1993): 99–130;

Rosalie Colie, *Paradoxia Epidemica: The Renaissance Tradition of Paradox* (Princeton: Princeton University Press, 1966);

W. G. Day, "Burton's *Anatomy of Melancholy*," *Notes and Queries,* 18 (February 1971): 59–60;

Nicholas Dewey, "Burton's Melancholy: A Paradox Disintered," *Modern Philology,* 68 (February 1971): 292–293;

Bergen Evans and George J. Mohr, *The Psychiatry of Robert Burton* (New York: Columbia University Press, 1944);

Stanley Fish, *Self-Consuming Artifacts: The Experience of Seventeenth-Century Literature* (Berkeley: University of California Press, 1972);

Ruth A. Fox, *The Tangled Chain: The Structure of Disorder in the Anatomy of Melancholy* (Berkeley: University of California Press, 1976);

Northrop Frye, *Anatomy of Criticism: Four Essays* (Princeton: Princeton University Press, 1957);

Martin Heusser, "Emblems in the *Anatomy of Melancholy*," *Notes and Queries,* 34 (September 1987): 298–301;

Heusser, *The Gilded Pill: A Study of the Reader-Writer Relationship in Robert Burton's* Anatomy of Melancholy (Tübingen: Stauffenburg, 1987);

Heusser, "Interpretation Analyzed and Synthesized: Robert Burton's Methods of Controlling the Reader in *The Anatomy of Melancholy*," *English Studies,* 70 (February 1989): 37–52;

Devon L. Hodges, *Renaissance Fictions of Anatomy* (Amherst: University of Massachusetts Press, 1985);

Karl-Josef Höltgen, "Literary Art and the Scientific Method in Robert Burton's *Anatomy of Melancholy*," *Explorations in Renaissance Culture,* 16 (1990): 1–36;

White Kennet, *A Register and Chronicle Ecclesiastical and Civil, Containing Matters of Fact, Delivered in the Words of the Most Authentick Books, Papers, and Records; Digested in Exact Order of Time. With Proper Notes and References towards Discovering and Connecting the True History of England from the Restauration of King Charles II* (London: Printed for R. Williamson, 1728);

Nicolas K. Kiessling, *The Legacy of Democritus Junior/ Robert Burton* (Oxford: Bodleian Library, 1990);

Kiessling, "Robert Burton's Will, Holograph Copy," *Review of English Studies,* 41 (February 1990): 94–101;

Kiessling, "Two Notes on Robert Burton's Annotations: His Date of Conception, and a Fragment of Copy for the *Anatomy of Melancholy*," *Review of English Studies,* 36 (August 1985): 375–379;

Bud Korkowski, "Genre and Satiric Strategy in Burton's *Anatomy of Melancholy*," *Genre,* 8 (March 1979): 74–87;

Bridget Gellert Lyons, *Voices of Melancholy: Studies in Literary Treatments of Melancholy in Renaissance England* (London: Routledge & Kegan Paul, 1971);

C. H. McQuillen, "On Seventeenth-Century Pedantry: A Latin Play by Robert Burton," *Selecta,* 9 (1988): 14–22;

William R. Mueller, *The Anatomy of Robert Burton's England* (Berkeley & Los Angeles: University of California Press, 1952);

Mueller, "Robert Burton's 'Satyricall Preface,' " *Modern Language Quarterly,* 15 (March 1954): 28–35;

Maurice Natanson, "From Apprehension to Decay: Robert Burton's 'Equivocations of Melancholy,' " *Gettysburg Review,* 2 (Winter 1989): 130–138;

Richard Nochimson, "Burton's *Anatomy:* The Author's Purposes and the Reader's Response," *Forum for Modern Language Studies,* 13 (July 1977): 265–284;

Michael O'Connell, *Robert Burton* (Boston: Twayne, 1986);

Sir William Osler, "Robert Burton: The Man, His Book, His Library," in *Oxford Bibliographical Society Proceedings and Papers,* edited by F. Madan (Oxford: Oxford University Press, 1927), pp. 163–190;

J. Max Patrick, "Robert Burton's Utopianism," *Philological Quarterly,* 27 (October 1948): 345–358;

David Renaker, "Robert Burton and the Ramist Method," *Renaissance Quarterly,* 24 (Summer 1971): 210–220;

Renaker, "Robert Burton's Tricks of Memory," *PMLA,* 87 (May 1972): 391–396;

Jean Robert Simon, *Robert Burton (1577–1640) et l'Anatomie de la Mélancolie* (Paris: Didier, 1964);

James S. Tillman, "The Satirist Satirized: Burton's Democritus Jr.," *Studies in the Literary Imagination,* 10 (Fall 1977): 89–96;

E. Patricia Vicari, *The View from Minerva's Tower: Learning and Imagination in* The Anatomy of Melancholy (Toronto, Buffalo & London: University of Toronto Press, 1989);

Joan Webber, *The Eloquent "I": Style and Self in Seventeenth-Century Prose* (Madison: University of Wisconsin Press, 1968).

Papers:

A few months before he died, Robert Burton added a codicil to his will instructing his executors to dispose of any books left in his library after his bequests, along with "all such Books as are written with my own hands." The Bodleian has one notebook of Burton's (4° R 9 Art.). His will is in the Public Record Office, London.

Lady Anne Clifford

(29 January 1590 – 22 March 1676)

Katherine Acheson
University of Toronto

BOOKS: *Lives of Lady Anne Clifford Countess of Dorset, Pembroke and Montgomery (1590–1676) and of Her Parents, Summarized by Herself,* edited by J. P. Gilson (London & Aylesbury: Printed for members of the Roxburghe Club, 1916);

The Diary of the Lady Anne Clifford, edited by Victoria Sackville-West (London: Heinemann, 1923; New York: Doran, 1923);

The Diaries of Anne Clifford, edited by D. J. H. Clifford (Phoenix Mill, U.K. & Wolfeboro Falls, N.H.: Sutton, 1990).

Edition: *The Diary of Anne Clifford: A Critical Edition,* edited by Katherine Acheson (New York: Garland, 1995).

OTHER: "In the yeare of oure Lorde 1603," in *Anecdotes of Some Distinguished Persons, Chiefly of the Present and Two Preceding Centuries,* volume 1, edited by William Seward (London: Cadell & Davies, 1795), pp. 141–156.

Lady Anne Clifford in 1620; portrait by an unknown artist (collection of H. Fattorini, Esq.)

Lady Anne Clifford left one of the most extensive autobiographical records of the seventeenth century, including a memoir of the year 1603; a diary for the years 1616, 1617, and 1619; an autobiography dated 1653; summary accounts of each year from 1650 to 1675; and a diary for 1676. She also dictated biographies of her ancestors from the twelfth to the sixteenth centuries. The 1603 memoir and the diary for 1616 to 1619 have attracted particular attention from historians and from literary and feminist scholars as rare examples of secular autobiographical writing from the period and are even rarer for having been written by a woman. Clifford's plain style and her lack of self-consciousness in rendering the details, both delicate and indelicate, of her personal and public life in and around the court of King James are further attractive qualities of these early works. The later works, which are both more formal and more formulaic, have been given less attention, although they, too, express a distinctive personality and are curiously unmarked by the customary declarations of insecurity found in autobiographies of her female contemporaries, such as Margaret Cavendish.

Born at Skipton Castle, Yorkshire, on 29 January 1590, Clifford was the only surviving child of George Clifford, third Earl of Cumberland, and Margaret Russell Clifford, daughter of Francis Bedford, second Earl of Bedford. Her parents and other members of her family were important courtiers during the reign of Elizabeth, and Clifford spent much of her childhood at court. The 1603 memoir records the activities of the court on the death of Elizabeth and the accession of James; she and her mother traveled with the court as the king made his entrance progress. While it provides significant his-

Clifford in 1646; portrait by an unknown artist
(National Portrait Gallery, London)

torical information, it is told from a personal point of view, opening: "In Christmas I used to go much to the Court & sometimes I did lie in my Aunt Warwick's Chamber on a Pallet, to whom I was much bound for her continual care & love of mee, inso much as if Queen Elizabeth had lived she intended to prefer me to be of the Privy Chamber for at that time there was as much hope and expectation both for my person and my fortunes as of any other young lady whatsoever."

Part of her concern with the accession involved the place her family would hold in the new court. That she and her mother found themselves somewhat less favored than before is reflected in the content and the tone of the memoir; she notes, for example, that there are lice in the chamber of one of the new king's Scottish favorites, and the memoir closes: "Now there was much talk of a Mask which the Queen had at Winchester, & how all the Ladies about the Court had gotten such ill

names that it was grown a scandalous place, & the Queen herself was much fallen from her former greatness & reputation she had in the world." Clifford probably kept retrospective records such as this one, and the summaries for 1650 to 1675, for most of her life, but only some have survived.

In 1605 Clifford's father died, leaving his estates and title to his brother Francis. For the rest of her life Clifford would contest the will on the basis that the properties and titles attached to the baronies of Clifford, Vesci, and Veteripont were, according to the deed dating to the reign of Edward II, entailed upon the "heir of the body," regardless of sex. Her suits in this regard are the principal matter of the diary of 1616 to 1619, but, like the memoir, it is a deeply personal account that also records her visits; her feelings; her tumultuous marriage to Richard Sackville, third Earl of Dorset, whom she married in 1609; the growth of their daughter Margaret, born in 1614 (of their five children only Margaret

Triptych, commissioned by Clifford in 1646 and believed to have been painted by Jan van Belcamp. The left panel depicts Clifford at age fifteen; the middle panel shows her parents, George and Margaret Russell Clifford, and her brothers Robert and Francis; the right panel is Clifford at the time the picture was commissioned (Appleby Castle, Cumbria).

and Isabella, born in 1622, survived infancy); and the shifting social alliances around her in London and at Knole House in Kent. Throughout much of the diary she is troubled and isolated; she describes her situation by borrowing from Psalm 102: "I stay'd much in the Country having many times a sorrowfull & heavy heart, and being condemn'd by most folks because I would not consent to the agreement, so as I may truly say I am like an owl in the desert." Although the king, the archbishop of Canterbury, and the major peers of the realm were ranged against her, her most intense conflict was with her husband, who wished her to accept a cash settlement and tried every means — threats of separation, refusal to sleep with her when she was fertile, social shaming, canceling of her jointure, withdrawal of her servants, and taking their child away — to persuade her. The matter was eventually heard by the king, who denied her suit, even though she declared to him, "I would not part with Westmoreland whatsoever"; it was not until 1643, when the last of the male Cliffords died, that she inherited the vast northern estates according to the reversion clause of her father's will. Only posthumously, in 1691, was she recognized as de jure Baroness Clifford, Vesci, and Veteripont.

When she inherited the property, Clifford became a woman of considerable means. Her first husband had died in 1624; in 1630 she had married

Philip Herbert, fourth Earl of Pembroke, but by 1643 she had been separated from him for several years. After the civil war she went north and established herself on her estates; she repaired the damage to her castles of Brougham, Brough, Appleby, and Skipton; she founded an almshouse for widows, which still houses a dozen women and is still funded by the countess's endowment; she organized her tenancy system, went on progresses with hundreds of retainers and important pieces of furniture, shaved her head, and smoked a pipe.

Her diary records her reading of works by Saint Augustine, Michel de Montaigne, Edmund Spenser, Sir Philip Sidney, and various works of history and theology — all in English, as her father had not permitted her to learn any other language. For this reason Virginia Woolf dubbed Clifford "the first English common reader." A more extensive catalogue of her reading is to be found in the books with which she is depicted in the *Great Picture of the Clifford Family,* believed to have been painted by Jan van Belcamp in 1647, which she commissioned. Her attitude toward her books is perhaps best illustrated by a letter she wrote in 1649 from Appleby to her secretary John Selden, as she was assessing and beginning to repair the extensive damage to her estates caused by the civil war: "if I had note exelent Chacor's booke heere to comfort mee I wer in a pitifull case, having so manny trubles as I have, butt

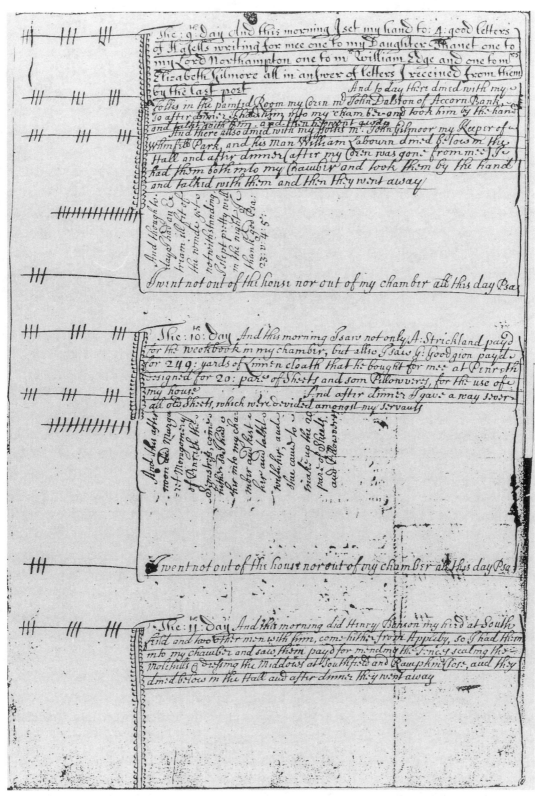

Page from Clifford's diary, with entries for 9, 10, and 11 March 1676. She died on 22 March (Collection of Mrs. W. and Mr. R. B. Hasell McCosh, Dalemain).

when I rede in thatt I scorne and make litte of tham alle, and a little partt of his devine sperett infusses itt selfe in mee."

Clifford's activities as a patron of the arts are not fully known; she appears to have continued some of the patronage initiated by her mother and to have originated some of her own. Authors who dedicated works to her include Samuel Daniel (who had been her tutor), Michael Drayton, and Aemelia Lanyer. She erected a monument in Westminster Abbey to Spenser, who was patronized by her mother, and may have helped both John Donne and George Herbert to appointments in the church. Donne enjoyed her company and, according to Edward Rainbow's funeral sermon, said of her that she could talk of matters from "slea-silk to predestination."

Clifford and her mother had collected, in aid of their legal suits, hundreds of documents pertaining to the Clifford family and the descent of the baronies within it. With the help of several secretaries Clifford assembled the discursive genealogy known as "The Great Books of the Clifford Family," which occupies three large volumes and of which she had four scribal copies made. Her autobiography and annual summaries for 1650 to 1675 are included in these volumes, and she wrote her diary for 1676 in the blank leaves of volume three of one of the scribal copies.

The autobiography is a secular version of a spiritual autobiography, with Clifford's accession to her estates taking the place of the conversion. Salted with citations from the Bible and emphasizing her deliverance from her enemies by God, it nonetheless retains her personal style. Her description of her marriages is characteristic: "the marble pillars of Knowle in Kent and Wilton in Wiltshire were to me often times but the gay arbour of anguish. Insomuch as a wise man that knew the insides of my fortune would often say that I lived in both these my lords' great familyes as the river of Roan or Rodamus runs through the lake of Geneva, without mingling any part of its streams with that lake; for I gave myself wholly to retiredness, as much as I could, in both those great families, and made good books and virtuous thoughts my companions."

The biographies of her parents, particularly that of her mother, are noteworthy for their easy style and specificity of detail and the affection shown by the author. The final diary, written when she was in her mid eighties, makes note of visits, books read, and family and local events; it also describes events that happened decades before, as

Clifford continued her habit of reading over "times past" in the "chronicles" of her life. The diary ends with 21 March 1676, the day before her death.

Biographies:

Edward Rainbow, *A Sermon Preached at the Funeral of the Right Honorable Anne, Countess of Pembroke, Dorset and Montgomery, with Some Remarks on the Life of that Lady* (London: F. Royston & H. Broom, 1677);

George C. Williamson, *Lady Anne Clifford, Countess of Dorset, Pembroke and Montgomery, 1590–1676: Her Life, Letters and Work* (Kendal: Wilson, 1923);

Martin Holmes, *Proud Northern Lady: Lady Anne Clifford, 1590–1676* (London & Chichester: Phillimore, 1975).

References:

Katherine Acheson, "The Modernity of the Early Modern: The Example of Anne Clifford," in *Discontinuities in Contemporary Renaissance Criticism,* edited by Viviana Comensoli and Paul Stevens (Toronto: University of Toronto Press, forthcoming, 1996);

Barbara Kiefer Lewalski, *Writing Women in Jacobean England* (Cambridge, Mass. & London: Harvard University Press, 1993);

Virginia Woolf, "Donne after Three Centuries," in her *Collected Essays,* volume 1, edited by Leonard Woolf (London: Hogarth Press, 1966), pp. 32–45.

Papers:

Lady Anne Clifford's 1603 memoir survives in two manuscript copies, each appended to the manuscripts of the diary for 1616 to 1619; they are Portland Papers XXIII, fols. 74–79, at Longleat House, and the Knole/Sackville Papers at the Centre for Kentish Studies in Maidstone, U269 F48/1 I, leaves 1–17. The Portland is an eighteenth-century manuscript; the Knole is dated no earlier than 1826. Three copies of the "Great Books of the Clifford Family," including the copy with the 1676 diary, are in the Hothfield Papers at the Cumbria Records Office in Kendal (WD/Hoth/10). Clifford's letters and miscellaneous papers are principally in the Sackville collection at the Centre for Kentish Studies, Maidstone, and in the Hothfield Papers at the Cumbria Records Office, Kendal; legal records survive in those collections and in the Hale manuscripts at Lincoln's Inn and the Clifford collection at Oxford.

Sir William Cornwallis the Younger

(circa 1579 – 1 July 1614)

Michael W. Price
Purdue University

BOOKS: *Essayes* (London: Printed by Simon Stafford for Edmund Mattes, 1600; revised edition, London: Printed by Joseph Harison for Edmund Mattes, 1606);

A Second Part of Essayes (London: Printed by Richard Read for Edmund Mattes, 1601); revised and enlarged as *Essayes, Newly enlarged* (London: Printed by J. Windet for John Browne, 1610) – includes *Essayes* and *Discourses upon Seneca the Tragedian*; revised as *Essayes, Newlie Corrected* (London: Printed by Thomas Harper for John Marriot, 1632);

Discovrses upon Seneca the Tragedian (London: Printed by Simon Stafford for Edmund Mattes, 1601);

The Miraculovs and Happie Vnion of England and Scotland; by how admirable meanes it is effected; how profitable to both Nations, and how free of any inconuenience either past, present, or to be discerned, anonymous (London: Printed for Edward Blount, 1604);

Essayes Or rather, Encomions, Prayses of Sadnesse: And Of the Emperovr Ivlian the Apostata (London: Printed by George Purflowe for Richard Hawkins, 1616);

Essayes of Certain Paradoxes (London: Printed for Thomas Thorp, 1616); enlarged as *Essayes of Certaine Paradoxes. The second Impression, inlarged* (London: Printed by T. Snodham for Richard Hawkins, 1617).

Editions: *Essayes by Sir William Cornwallis, the Younger,* edited by Don Cameron Allen (Baltimore: Johns Hopkins University Press, 1946);

Discourses upon Seneca the Tragedian (1601): A Facsimile Reproduction, introduction by Robert Hood Bowers (Gainesville, Fla.: Scholars' Facsimiles & Reprints, 1952);

The Encomium of Richard III by Sir William Cornwallis the Younger, edited by A. N. Kincaid (London: Turner & Devereux, 1977).

OTHER: "On the untimely Death of the incomparable Prince, Henry," in Joshua Sylvester and others, *Lachrymae Lachryma, or the Spirit of Teares distilled for the un-tymely Death of the incomparable Prince Panaretus,* third edition (London: H. Lownes, 1613), fols. E3r–Fv;

"The Encomium of Richard III," in *A Second Collection of Scarce and Valuable Tracts: Selected from an Infinite Number in Print and Manuscript, in the Royal, Cotton, Sion, and other Public, as well as Private Libraries; Particularly That of the Late Lord Sommers,* volume 1 (London: F. Cogan, 1750);

"As in tymes past the rusticke shepheards sceant," in *The Poems of John Donne,* 2 volumes, edited by Sir Herbert J. C. Grierson (London: Clarendon Press, 1912), I: 171–172;

"Four Paradoxes by Sir William Cornwallis, the Younger," edited by Roger E. Bennett, *Harvard Studies and Notes in Philology and Literature,* 13 (1931): 219–240.

Sir William Cornwallis the Younger achieved a measure of popularity in his own time; today, however, he is only occasionally remembered as one of the originators of the essay in England, one of the participants in the vogue of paradox writing at the turn of the seventeenth century, and one of the many associates of John Donne. As an essayist he is the first to register in England the influence of Michel de Montaigne, writing with something of the Frenchman's diffuse candor, while as a paradoxer he both rejuvenates hackneyed subjects and ventures dangerous ones. Informing almost the whole of Cornwallis's writings is an imperative to live a life of virtue, an imperative that manifests itself particularly in his calls to his readers to overcome adversity and resist moral corruption.

A notation in Tanner manuscript 169 in the Bodleian Library, Oxford, records that Cornwallis was twenty-two in 1600, which would place his birth around 1579. He was the firstborn son of Anne Fincham Cornwallis and Sir Charles Cornwallis of Norfolk. Virtually nothing is known of his early life or his formal education. Sir Nicholas

Title page for the final revised edition of Sir William Cornwallis's essays. First published in 1600 and 1601, the pieces have been described as the first true essays in English.

Overbury reported that his son, Sir Thomas Overbury, and Cornwallis were friends at Oxford, but this suggestion of a university education is considered to have little reliability. Others have deduced from Cornwallis's linguistic abilities – he knew Spanish and Italian but not Latin, Greek, or French – that he probably did not receive a college education but may have been trained by private tutors. Allusions in his writings demonstrate that he read widely, even if most of that reading was in translation.

On 26 August 1595 he married Katherine Parker of Erwarton, Suffolk; the couple raised eight children. Remarks by Cornwallis's father as well as confessions in Cornwallis's *Essayes* (1600) indicate that Cornwallis lived extravagantly, reducing him to a state of penury from which he was never to escape. He accompanied Robert Devereux, second Earl of Essex, on the 1599 campaign in Ireland, and on 5 August of that year he was knighted. It appears that between his return from Ireland in 1599 and his emergence at court in 1601 he retired from active life. During this retirement he wrote prolifically, generating paradoxes that he circulated in manuscript among his friends, preparing the forty-nine essays that appeared in print in 1600 and 1601, and shaping the twelve meditations on Senecan sententiae that became *Discourses upon Seneca the Tragedian* (1601).

References in Cornwallis's correspondence indicate that he wrote many paradoxes, but only four, preserved in the commonplace book of a contemporary, have survived. A minor genre today, the paradox enjoyed great popularity in England at the turn of the seventeenth century. It had flourished from time to time since the classical period in two main forms: the mock encomium and the argument against received opinion. The first is an ironic encomium, replete with burlesques of all the conventions of the formal encomium, to a person or object conspicuously unworthy of such praise; the second turns the student's mundane rhetorical exercise on its head.

The four paradoxes written around 1600 — "That a great redd nose is an ornament to the face," "That it is a happines to be in debt," "That miserie is true Faelicity," and "That Inconstancy is more commendable than Constancie" — belong to the tradition of arguing against received opinion. The first exemplifies the characteristic rhetorical strategies and wit of all four: Cornwallis successively considers the qualities of greatness and redness separately; then, to "double their excellencies," he "unites" the merits of these qualities in a conclusion. By subjecting a serious scholastic exercise to the indecorous labor of proving a ridiculous point, the paradox exploits the incongruity between structure and sense.

The *Essayes* and *A Second Part of Essayes* (1601), Cornwallis's most important works, are among the first — some argue that they are the first — essays in English. The controversy concerning their primacy stems from the elastic meaning of *essay* at the turn of the seventeenth century. The genre was just emerging and had no fixed definition; the term could, thus, encompass a wide range of discursive practices. In "Of Essaies and Bookes," in *A Second Part of Essayes,* Cornwallis notes that he has read Seneca's epistles to Lucilius, Plutarch's *Moralia,* and perhaps most important, Montaigne's *Essaies* (1580) in the translation by John Florio (Cornwallis seems to have perused Florio's manuscript prior to its publication in 1603). Montaigne originated not only the term *essay* but also the candid, diffuse, and self-referential manner of writing that influenced Cornwallis and later essayists and led Samuel Johnson to define *essay* in his dictionary (1755) as "a loose sally of the mind; an irregular indigested piece; not a regular and orderly composition."

The various pieces in *Essayes* and *A Second Part of Essayes* modulate between frivolity and gravity. On the one hand, Cornwallis toys with such trivial topics as alehouses, sleep, entertainment, jests and jesters, and fantasticalness and indulges in playful antics to amuse himself as he whiles away the time. In "Of Alehouses," in *Essayes,* for example, he admits that he is writing the essay extemporaneously as he sits in an alehouse, where, lacking the company of friends, he writes "in stead of talking to my selfe." On the other hand, the more serious essays explore ethical precepts and moral abstractions in an attempt to achieve philosophical insights that both console a man and fortify him against the ravages of earthly fortune. In such essays Cornwallis distills his observations on contemporary manners, his reflections on his studies, and (as does Montaigne) his scrutiny of himself.

But the bulk of the essays descend from such lofty heights to reflect on the quotidian world where ethical platitudes clash with human foibles and frailty. The typical Cornwallis essay capitalizes on this inevitable discrepancy, the incongruity between real and ideal providing the basis for ironic commentary. Most often Cornwallis's satire manifests itself in a good-natured lampooning of some of the social affectations Ben Jonson satirizes onstage as "humours" and Donne spoofs in his satires. In "Of Discourse," in *Essayes,* for example, he writes from the perspective of a wry observer (a frequent point of view in both *Essayes* and *A Second Part of Essayes*) who amuses himself at a pretentious social gathering by eavesdropping on the conversations of various men-about-town. First he encounters a "scholler" from the Inns of Court whose conversation is so interlarded with legal jargon that Cornwallis concludes that the inns are "places to grow fat in, not wise." Next he joins a group of university students, only to find that their "discourse is good but too finicall; you undoe them if you suffer them not to goe Methodically to worke." Finally, he notes a pretender to eloquence who "weyes every word and will be sure to turne the *verbe* behind, affects elegancy and to be thought learned." Each in his own way violates the commonsense principle that "a Gentleman should talke like a Gentleman." For his part, Cornwallis intends to abide by his own code of plain dealing: "not to loose my selfe in my tale, [but] to speak words that may be understood, and, to my power, to meane wisely rather than to speake eloquently."

Cornwallis's *Discourses upon Seneca the Tragedian* is a collection of meditative pieces on twelve passages, ranging from one to six lines, from Seneca's tragedies. The discourses do not pretend to represent dramatic criticism; instead, they treat the passages independently of the plays as occasions for moralizing on the sententiae embedded in them. For example, the ninth discourse, which comments on Nero's line in *Octavia,* "The dimwit does not know what he may do for himself," prompts a series of observations orbiting around the theme of knowledge, such as some types of self-knowledge available to a reasonable man and some practical guides to evaluating one's own character and day-to-day moral conduct. The discourses often replicate the method of the *Essayes.*

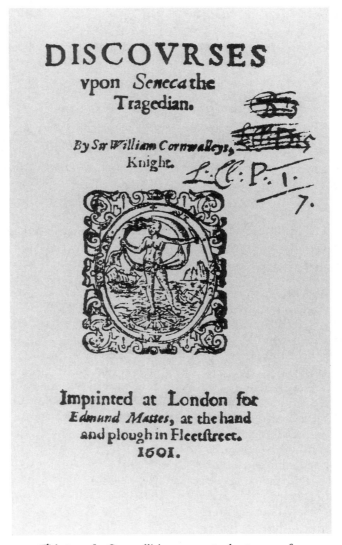

Title page for Cornwallis's essays on twelve passages from
Seneca's tragedies

Between 1601 and 1605 Cornwallis emerged from retirement to involve himself in public — especially court — life. Sir Nicholas Overbury recalled seeing Cornwallis in Scotland in 1601 or 1602, and Cornwallis's activities during the next few years seem to have centered on achieving preferment in the court of the new king. In 1603 he was sworn in as a member of James's privy chamber; in 1604 he was elected to Parliament for Orford, Suffolk. Desire for preferment may have motivated him to write a speech in favor of one of James's first major initiatives, the union of England and Scotland; the speech also flatters the king. *The Miraculous and Happie Union of England and Scotland; by how admirable meanes it is effected; how profitable to both Nations, and how free of any inconvenience either past, present, or to*

be discerned (1604) appeared without Cornwallis's name on either the title page or the dedicatory epistle; scholars have attributed the speech to him on the basis of a notation in the manuscript in the British Museum and a letter of May 1604 from an unknown correspondent (possibly Christopher Brooke) to Donne.

Most members of Parliament opposed the union — ostensibly because reconciling English and Scottish laws appeared to be a daunting task, but more significantly because English distrust of the Scots had intensified as James rewarded Scottish favorites in the English court. The speech oscillates between panegyric and polemic, at times projecting the bliss that will follow England's acceptance of the union and its proper appreciation of the new sovereign, at others invoking the deleterious consequences to England if it were to reject the union at the urging of its ill-motivated opponents. The virtues of the new king emerge as Cornwallis's trump card, nullifying all English objections to the union.

At this time Cornwallis distinguished himself both as a courier of diplomatic papers for his father, who was serving as James's ambassador to Spain, and as an intermediary in feuds between his father and his uncle, Sir William Cornwallis the Elder. Proving himself as a courtier, however, entailed more than meritorious civil service; aspiring gentlemen required lavish means to maintain themselves in a manner befitting their station. In line to receive his uncle's estate, Cornwallis lived extravagantly, exhausting his own and part of his father's fortune in the hopes of making a place for himself at court. Cornwallis failed to win preferment, however, and in 1605 he renounced the court permanently. A more devastating blow came when his uncle produced an heir, cutting Cornwallis off from his anticipated inheritance. He was elected to Parliament again in 1614 but succumbed to what appears to have been a year-long illness on 1 July, leaving his wife and eight children in poverty.

Little is known about his literary activities from 1605 until his death. A revised edition of his *Essayes* was published in 1606; three additional essays – "Of Adversitie," "Of Fortune and Her Children," and "Of the Admirable Abilities of the Mind" – appeared in *Essayes, Newly enlarged,* the revised edition of *A Second Part of Essayes,* in 1610. He also contributed an elegy, "On the untimely Death of the incomparable Prince, Henry," his only poem to be printed during his lifetime, to the third edition of Joshua Sylvester's *Lachrymae Lachryma* (1613). The dates of Cornwallis's few remaining manuscript poems – his verse letter to Donne ("As in tymes past the rusticke shepheards sceant"), "The Contrition of a Convertite," "A Heavenly Hymne," and two stanzas on "care" – are unknown, although details from the verse letter suggest a date closer to 1605 than to 1614. Addressed to his "ever to be respected friend, Mr John Done" and offering his "beast affection," it reveals that the two diverted themselves both in Cornwallis's rooms and at the theater:

What tyme thou meanst to offir Idillness
Come to my den for heer she always stayes;
If then for change of howers you seem careles
Agree with me to lose them at the playes.

Besides providing documentation for Cornwallis's friendship with Donne, these lines, if accurate, intimate something of the setting in which Cornwallis wrote his essays.

In 1616 two posthumous collections of new paradoxes attributed to Cornwallis appeared: *Essayes of Certain Paradoxes,* including "The Prayse of King Richard the Third," "The Prayse of the French Pockes," "The Prayse of Nothing," and "That it is Good to be in Debt"; and *Essayes Or rather, Encomions, Prayses of Sadnesse: And Of the Emperour Julian the Apostata.* Three of these paradoxes – the praises of indebtedness, the french pox, and nothing – resemble the four paradoxes of 1600. They are brief (four to nine pages), ironic, playful jeux d'esprit in the manner of the two prevailing modes of paradox, the mock encomium and the argument against received opinion. The praises of sadness, Julian the Apostate, and Richard III represent forays in a new mode of paradox. They are relatively long (thirty to forty pages), heavily historical discourses of manifestly serious and polemical intent. In the "Prayse of Sadness" Cornwallis defines *sadness* as a complex of behavioral characteristics – in essence, the same mixture of Christian piety and Stoic virtue he advocates in all his writings – that guides a nobleman to a lifelong, consistent pattern of impeccably idealistic behavior. "The Prayse of the Emperour Julian the Apostata" consists of a serious defense of Julian and what seem to be two appendices, "Julians Dialogue of the Caesars" and "Comparison betweene Alexander [the Great] and [Julius] Caesar," both fragmentary. In the defense of Julian, Cornwallis argues (unlike most historians) that the emperor's ultimate downfall does not disqualify his virtues.

"The Prayse of King Richard the Third," the most widely studied of the posthumously published paradoxes, is a palimpsest whose complexity continues to generate questions concerning authorship and textual transmission. One of the more compelling hypotheses is that Cornwallis wrote the encomium in response to anti-Yorkish Tudor propaganda but that once it began to circulate in manuscript an anonymous writer added sections that transform a serious defense of Richard against the prevailing view, represented by Sir Thomas More's *The History of King Richard III* (1543) and William Shakespeare's *The Tragedy of King Richard III* (1597), into a paradox (the epilogue includes the comment: "Yet for all this knowe I hold this but as a Paradoxe").

Douglas Bush writes that Cornwallis represents but one of many "porpoises" following the "whale," Francis Bacon. Bush's metaphor underscores the chief interest Cornwallis holds for scholars today – his relatively minor place in the history of the English essay – but it also minimizes Cornwallis's achievement. For Cornwallis accomplished more than merely writing some of the first English essays and participating in the vogue of paradox writing at the turn of the seventeenth century. Learning from Montaigne, he infused into English prose a spirit that was simultaneously searching yet tentative, musing yet self-reflexive, homiletic yet confessional, purposeful yet playful – in short, meditative. This meditative spirit, as Michael L. Hall has demonstrated, flowers in such later works as Donne's *Essays in Divinity* (1651), Robert Burton's *Anatomy of Melancholy* (1621), and Sir Thomas Browne's "Hydriotaphia" (1658). Critics have attributed this meditative spirit almost exclusively to Montaigne, underappreciating Cornwallis's importance as a precursor in this tradition. Cornwallis's literary experimentation in the *Essayes* constitutes a crucial advancement in English Renaissance prose, adumbrating the meditative spirit later English prose writers cultivated with so much success.

References:

Roger E. Bennett, "The Publication of Cornwallis's *Essayes* and *Paradoxes*," *Review of English Studies,* 9 (April 1933): 197–198;

Bennett, "Sir William Cornwallis' Use of Montaigne," *PMLA,* 48 (December 1933): 1080–1089;

Douglas Bush, *English Literature of the Earlier Seventeenth Century, 1600–1660,* second edition, revised (Oxford: Clarendon Press, 1962), pp. 198–200;

Rosalie Colie, *Paradoxia Epidemica: The Renaissance Tradition of Paradox* (Princeton: Princeton University Press, 1966);

V. H. Collins, *Three Centuries of English Essays: From Francis Bacon to Max Beerbohm* (Freeport, N.Y.: Libraries Press, 1967);

Conal Condren, "Cornwallis' Paradoxical Defence of Richard III: A Machiavellian Discourse on Morean Mythology?," *Moreana,* 24 (June 1987): 5–24;

Michael L. Hall, "Searching and Not Finding: The Experience of Donne's *Essays in Divinity*," *Genre,* 14 (1981): 423–440;

Sidney Lee, *The French Renaissance in England: An Account of the Literary Relations of England and France in the Sixteenth Century* (New York: Scribners, 1910), pp. 174–175;

W. L. MacDonald, *Beginnings of the English Essay* (Toronto: University of Toronto Studies, 1914);

MacDonald, "The Earliest English Essayists," *Englische Studien,* 64 (1929): 20–52;

A. E. Malloch, "The Techniques and Function of the Renaissance Paradox," *Studies in Philology,* 53 (April 1956): 191–203;

Henry Knight Miller, "The Paradoxical Encomium with Special Reference to its Vogue in England, 1600–1800," *Modern Philology,* 53 (February 1956): 145–178;

Arthur Stanley Pease, "Things without Honor," *Classical Philology,* 21 (January 1926): 27–42;

Ted-Larry Pebworth, "Not Being, But Passing: Defining the Early English Essay," *Studies in the Literary Imagination,* 10 (Fall 1977): 17–27;

M. A. Shaaber, *Seventeenth-Century English Prose* (New York: Harper, 1957), p. 25;

E. N. S. Thompson, *The Seventeenth-Century English Essay,* University of Iowa Humanistic Studies, volume 3, number 3 (Iowa City: Iowa University Press, 1926), pp. 34–37;

Alfred Upham, *The French Influence in English Literature* (New York: Octagon, 1965), pp. 266–276;

Hugh Walker, *The English Essay and Essayists* (London: Dent, 1928), p. 29;

P. B. Whitt, "New Light Upon Sir William Cornwallis, the Essayist," *Review of English Studies,* 8 (April 1932): 155–169;

W. Gordon Zeeveld, "A Tudor Defense of Richard III," *PMLA,* 55 (December 1940): 946–957.

Papers:

Transcriptions of the few known poems by Sir William Cornwallis the Younger are in the Bodleian Library in Tanner Manuscript 306. The manuscript for Cornwallis's speech in support of the union of England and Scotland is in the British Library.

Thomas Coryate

(1577? – December 1617)

Catherine C. Gannon
California State University, San Bernardino

BOOKS: *Coryats Crudities. Hastily gobled vp in five Moneths trauells in France, Sauoy, Italy, Rhetia commonly called the Grisons country, Helvetia aliàs Switzerland, some parts of high Germany, and the Netherlands; Newly digested in the hungry aire of Odcombe in the County of Somerset, & now dispersed to the nourishment of the trauelling Members of this Kingdome* (London: Printed by William Stansby, 1611);

The Odcombian Banqvet: Dished foorth by Thomas the Coriat, and Serued in by a number of Noble Wits in prayse of his Crudities and Crambe too (London: Printed for Thomas Thorpe, 1611);

Coryats Crambe, or His Colwort Twise Sodden, And Now serued in with other Macaronicke dishes, as the second course to his Crudities (London: Printed by William Stansby, 1611);

Thomas Coriate, Traueller for the English Wits: Greeting. From the Court of the Great Mogvl, Resident at the Towne of Asmere, in Easterne India (London: Printed by W. Jaggard & Henry Fetherston, 1616); republished as *Thomas Coriate, Travailer for the English wits, and the good of this Kingdome: To all his inferiour Countreymen, Greeting: Especially to the Sireniacall Gentlemen, that meet the first Friday of euerie Moneth, at the Mermaide in Breadstreet. From the Court of the great Mogor, resident at the Towne of Asmere, in the Easterne India* (London: Printed by W. Jaggard & Henry Fetherston, 1616);

Mr Thomas Coriat to his Friends in England sendeth Greeting: From Agra the Capitall City of the Dominion of the Great Mogoll in the Easterne India, the last of October, 1616 (London: Printed by John Beale, 1618).

Editions: *Coryat's Crudities; reprinted from the Edition of 1611. To which are now added, His Letters from India, &c. and extracts relating to him, from various authors: being A more particular Account of his Travels (mostly on Foot) in Different Parts of the Globe, than any hitherto published. Together with his Orations, Character, Death, &c.,* 3 volumes (London: Printed for W. Cater, Samuel Hayes, J. Wilkie / Salisbury: E. Easton, 1776);

Coryat's Crudities, 2 volumes (Glasgow: MacLehose, 1905);

Greeting from the Court of the Great Mogul, The English Experience: Its Record in Early Printed Books Published in Facsimile, volume 30 (Amsterdam: Theatrum Orbis Terrum / New York: Da Capo Press, 1968);

Coryats Crudities, edited by William M. Schutte (London: Scolar, 1978).

OTHER: "Master Thomas Coryates trauels to, and Observations in Constantinople, and other places in the way thither, and his Iourney thence to Aleppo, Damasco and Ierusalem," in *Hakluytus Posthumus or Purchas his pilgrimes,* by Samuel Purchas, 4 volumes (London: Printed by William Stansby for Henry Fetherston, 1625), I: 600–602; II: 1811–1831.

His account of his European sojourn, published as *Coryats Crudities* (1611), has earned Thomas Coryate a place in the history of English literature as an entertaining writer, a coiner of words, an eccentric wit, and an astute observer. Panegyrics contributed to the work, and Coryate's letters from abroad show that he knew many of the celebrities of his time, among them the writers Ben Jonson and John Donne, the architect Inigo Jones, and the diplomat Sir Thomas Roe. His allusions to meetings of a club at the Mermaid Tavern, the gathering place for many of the leading writers of the day, constitute the earliest indisputable contemporary evidence of the club's existence. Although an early death in India prevented him from writing a

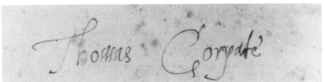

Engraving by William Hole

book about his second major journey, his surviving notes and letters project vivid pictures of Constantinople, the Levant of the Ottoman Empire, and the court of the Great Mogul.

Coryate enjoyed fabricating self-descriptions such as "The Peregrine of Odcombe" and "The Odcombian Leg-stretcher" – references to his amazing travels, which totaled more than five thousand miles, most of them on foot, and to his beloved village of Odcombe in the Somerset countryside, where he was born the only son of the Reverend George Coryate and Gertrude Coryate; his mother's maiden name may have been Williams. "Posthuma Fragmenta Poematum Georgii Coryati," some of his father's Latin verses, are included in *Coryats Crudities*.

Because relevant parish records no longer exist, the exact year of Coryate's birth is open to question. The earliest evidence appears in the records of Winchester College, to which Coryate was elected in August 1590 and which he entered eleven months later. Since pupils customarily took an oath to uphold the Statutes of Scholars soon after they came of age at fifteen, the entry for 29 September 1594 in the register of scholars implies that Coryate was born in 1579. All nine fellow scholars sworn in with Coryate on that occasion were born in that year. This record, however, does not correspond with Anthony à Wood's notation in his *Athenae Oxonienses* (1691–1692) that in early 1596 Coryate became a commoner of Gloucester Hall, Oxford, at age nineteen, which would place his birth in 1577. Two references in *Coryats Crudities* also point to 1577 as his birth year: his "Epistle to the Reader" claims, referring to a journey begun early in 1608, "I reaped more entire and sweet comfort in five

Title page for Coryate's account of his European travels

months' travels . . . than I did in all the days of my life before in England, which contained two and thirty years"; and the text surrounding Coryate's title-page portrait indicates that the author was thirty-five when *Coryats Crudities* was published.

Coryate did not take a degree at Oxford, but he distinguished himself in Greek and in humane learning. It is clear from his subsequent career that Coryate had a remarkable penchant for languages. His training in rhetoric predisposed him to compose ornate and hyperbolic orations, of which the earliest one he preserved documents his presence in Odcombe in 1606: in his second book, *Coryats Crambe* (1611), he describes a "church-ale," a fundraiser he organized; for the mock military skirmishes performed at the event Coryate cast himself as a captain on a milk-white steed and delivered an oration, resplendent with classical allusions.

Coryate's father died in March 1607; about that time Coryate left Odcombe for London. Coryate was named for his godfather, Thomas Phelips, Squire of Montacute, whose son Edward

built a splendid mansion that is said in *Coryats Crudities* to be more magnificent than the Piazza San Marco in Venice or the palace of the Archbishop of Cologne in Bonn. Edward and his son, Robert, had been knighted in 1603 after the accession of James I, and probably through their influence Coryate was received into the household of Prince Henry, James I's elder son. Since he does not appear in the 1603 or 1610 lists of the prince's household, however, he had no assigned position; he seems to have served as an unofficial court jester. Not having wealth or appointment, Coryate apparently exploited his witty tongue, euphuistic excesses, and retentive memory for the role. In the prince's household Coryate was exposed to diplomats and travelers who probably whetted his interest in a European adventure as a means of securing fortune, attention, and fame.

In May 1608 he sailed from Dover to Calais. According to *Coryats Crudities,* Coryate spent most of the voyage on deck, where he "varnished the exterior parts of the ship with the excremental ebul-

Illustration for Coryats Crudities *depicting Coryate with a Venetian courtesan (engraving by William Hole)*

litions of my tumultuous stomach, as desiring to satiate the gormandizing paunches of the hungry Haddocks." He tallies the distance he covered – 1,975 miles, "the total of my whole journey forth and back" – and the places he has been: "the cities that I saw in the space of these five months, are five and forty. Whereof in France five. In Savoy one. In Italy thirteen. In Rhetia one. In Helvetia three. In some parts of high Germany fifteen. In the Netherlands seven."

In writing his book Coryate supplemented his observations by borrowing from Franciscus Schott's *Itinerarii Italiæ* (1600) for information about Italy, from Sebastian Münster's *Cosmographia* (1544) for Switzerland and Germany, and from Lodovico Guicciardini's *Descrittione di Tutti i Paesi Bassi* (1567) for the Netherlands. The notes are expanded methodically, his account of each city typically opening with the Italian scholar Julius Caesar Scaliger's verses followed by a history of the city and then a general description, usually based on his own obser-

vations. He provides detailed accounts of the appearance and histories of the main buildings; he liberally transcribes epitaphs and inscriptions; sometimes he inserts biographies of prominent inhabitants or mentions the battles associated with the city. He only occasionally alludes to governments and other institutions, but he is fascinated by religious practices and relics, methods and places of execution and punishment, objects of record dimensions, and local customs. His descriptions of Venetian courtesans or the Italian custom of eating with forks (Coryate may have introduced the fork into England; he was certainly the first to publish a description of the utensil) or monstrous candles or "baptism" by wine are one inducement to read *Coryats Crudities;* his accounts of his ingenuity and verve – for instance, impersonating a beggar to thwart would-be robbers – are another.

The book displays two distinct styles: a straightforward, vigorous narrative prose and an or-

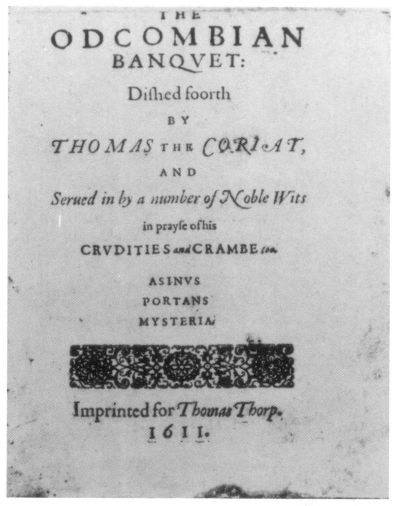

THE
ODCOMBIAN
BANQVET:

Difhed foorth

BY

THOMAS the *CORIAT,*

AND

Serued in by a number of Noble Wits

in prayfe of his

CRVDITIES *and* CRAMBE *too*

ASINVS

PORTANS

MYSTERIA

Imprinted for *Thomas Thorp.*
1611.

Title page for the pirated volume that includes the mock-panegyric verses written for
Coryats Crudities *by authors such as Ben Jonson, John Donne, and*
Michael Drayton

nate, extravagant style that was probably shaped by Coryate's admiration for classical models and by his rhetorical training. At times *Coryats Crudities* features exaggerated rhetorical tricks and extreme euphuism, including alliteration, antithesis, and masses of similes drawn from natural history. Coryate's orations also contain wonderfully far-fetched flourishes. This style, according to Michael Strachan's *The Life and Adventures of Thomas Coryate* (1962), was cultivated deliberately as a "personal badge, as a vehicle to show off his wit, and as a means of self advertisement; sometimes it was intended to amuse, more often to impress." In "The Character of the Famous Odcombian," published in *Coryats Crudities,* Jonson characterizes his acquaintance as "a great and bold Carpenter of words." Coryate introduced the word *umbrella* into English and helped to popularize words coined by others,

such as *charlatan* and *tatterdemalion*. Paradoxically, he often evaluates with pedestrian adjectives; something is "the fairest" or "the greatest" or "the most wondrous . . . that ever I saw in my life." Though the two-hundred-thousand-word book includes extraneous material, including correspondence and Coryate's translations of two Latin orations by Hermann Kirchner, professor of history and poetry at Marburg University, the work has an assured place among the best travel literature because of its reliability, its scope, and most of all its entertainment value.

None of the eleven known likenesses of Coryate corroborates Thomas Fuller's description in his *The History of the Worthies of England* (1662): "The shape of his head had no promising form, being like a sugar loaf." More-reliable and more-contemporary sources of information about Coryate are Jonson's "The Character of the Famous

THOMAS CORIATE
Traueller for the English
VVits : Greeting.

From the Court of the Great MOGVL, Resident at the Towne of ASMERE, in
Easterne INDIA.

Printed by W. Iaggard, and Henry Fetherston.
1616.

Title page for the collection of four of Coryate's letters describing
his travels in India

Odcombian" and the anecdotes recollected by the Reverend Edward Terry (1655), who met Coryate a few weeks before the traveler died.

Coryate invited some of his contemporaries to write eulogistic verses for *Coryats Crudities,* apparently touching off a mock-panegyric frenzy. More than fifty contributors, including Sir Robert Phelips, Donne, Jones, Thomas Campion, and Michael Drayton, joined Jonson in composing prefatory matter. Of these individuals about a third were either courtiers or were responsible for royal entertainments; there were also members of the Inns of Court and members of Parliament. Others had ties to Oxford and to the world of letters.

In the church in Odcombe Coryate thanked God for his safe return. Coryate gained the rector's permission to hang the shoes he had worn on his 1,975 miles of European travel as a memorial. The honor is illustrated on the title page of *Coryats Crudities* and was relished by its contributors — among them Jonson, who wrote in Coryate's next book, *Coryates Crambe* (1611):

How well and how often his shoes too were mended,
That sacred to Odcombe are now there suspended,
I mean that one pair, wherewith he so hobbled
From Venice to Flushing, were not they well cobbled?

Prior to his departure on his European tour Coryate had placed a bet of forty pounds, at three-to-one odds, with the Yeovil linen draper Joseph Starre that he would return home safely; there may also have been commercial dealings involved in the transaction. On Coryate's return there was a prolonged lawsuit over payment. If he collected the money the chancery court awarded him, Coryate apparently spent all of it on the printing of *Coryats Crudities.* Loading customized copies of his work into a box carried by a donkey, Coryate personally distributed his book to members of the royal family; he included his orations to the recipients in *Coryats Crambe.* This book is a generic hodgepodge, comprising additional verses on *Coryats Crudities* as well as verses composed especially for the new work, Coryate's petition to Prince Henry for assistance in

Sir Thomas Roe, ambassador to the Mogul Empire, with whom Coryate stayed during his final journey; painting by an unknown artist (National Portrait Gallery, London)

procuring a license for *Coryats Crudities,* the orations Coryate made to the royal family in presenting them with the earlier work, a May 1611 oration congratulating the Duke of York on his installation into the Order of the Garter, Coryate's answer to Starre's chancery bill, and descriptions of the church ales at Yeovil and Odcombe in 1606.

Shortly before *Coryats Crambe* was published there appeared *The Odcombian Banquet* (1611), a pirated volume that reprinted virtually all of the "panegyric verses" from *Coryats Crudities* with two cynical additions: first, the phrase *Asinus Portans Mysteria* (the ass carrying the mysteries) was appended to the title page, effectively transferring to the author himself the motto of the donkey Coryate had used in delivering *Coryats Crudities;* furthermore, *The Odcombian Banquet* denigrated the omitted Coryate-authored portion of *Coryats Crudities.* The prefatory

sections of *Coryats Crudities* — the talk of the court and literary London and the book's chief commercial attraction — could now be purchased at a fraction of the cost of the whole work, and Coryate's literary reputation was sullied. In an addendum to *Coryats Crambe* he concedes that *Coryats Crudities* may be overly long and padded: "Of the six hundred fifty and four pages," he says, the reader "shall find at least five hundred worthy the reading."

Strachan's view is that Thomas Thorpe, a publisher with a reputation for obtaining "neglected copy," was the pirate, probably in collusion with another member of the Stationers' Company, Edward Blount; but speculation about the culprit's identity has included John Taylor, the "Water Poet," who heaped abusive ridicule on Coryate in a tone similar to that in *The Odcombian Banquet* in *The Sculler, Rowing from Tiber to Thames* (1612). Among its sometimes obscene or bawdy epigrams are lines addressed to "Tom Coriat" that mock his linguistic talents, his court foolery, and his idle brain. Subsequent pamphlets by Taylor – *Laugh and Be Fat* (1612?), *Odcombs Complaint* (1613), and *The Eighth Wonder of the World* (1613) – furthered the satire by parodying Coryate's adventures, lampooning his copiousness, and building on his allegedly furious reactions. These and other contemporary references to Coryate suggest that he continued to feed court gossip during his absence from England on his second series of travels.

In October 1612 Coryate set forth on a journey to Constantinople, the cities of ancient Greece, and the Holy Land. *Thomas Coriate, Traveller for the English Wits* (1616) includes passages signed "R. R." that give a secondhand account of the sea voyage, but the book's core consists of Coryate's letters "from the Court of the great Mogul." One of the letters, addressed "to the High Seneschal of the right Worshipful Fraternity of Sireniacal Gentlemen, that meet the first Friday of every Month, at the sign of the Mermaid in Bread-street in London," is the earliest known allusion to periodic meetings at the tavern. The regular meetings he mentions must have taken place before his departure on his second journey – in 1612 or earlier. He calls Laurence Whitaker the club's "quondem Seneschal," but the holder of that title in 1615, when Coryate's letter was written, is not named. He mentions that before he left for Constantinople the club presented him with a witty "safe-conduct." What appears to be text of the safe-conduct was discovered in the 1960s, written on the end paper of a copy of the 1611 edition of *Coryats Crudities* in the Bainbrigg Library of Appleby Grammar School, Westmorland; it provides the detail that Coryate was the group's "beadle."

Coryate left the notes from the first leg of his second journey at Aleppo, Syria, in 1614 before leaving for India. Eventually, they reached Samuel Purchas, who condensed Coryate's material to exclude topics covered by other travelers and published it in part 2 of his *Hakluytus Posthumus or Purchas his pilgrimes* (1625). The preoccupations of *Coryats Crudities* recur here: there are details about local customs, such as women in Zante riding astride donkeys; about religious ceremonies, including proxy flagellants and circumcisions in Constantinople; and about natural history, with word portraits of fireflies and pelicans. The Purchas excerpt also includes observations of the ruins of "Troy" – actually Alexandria Troas, then believed

to be Troy – where Coryate was playfully dubbed "the first English knight of Troy" by one of his companions.

Purchas cuts off the account of Coryate's Middle Eastern travels at Damascus in 1614, but some details of his journey to Jerusalem and other holy places can be reconstructed from letters and from the recollections of the Reverend Edward Terry, the chaplain to Roe, who was then serving as ambassador to the Mogul Empire. Terry included his memories of Coryate in his *A Voyage to India* (1655). Information about Coryate's last monumental journey, in which he walked from Aleppo, Syria, to India, has survived only in letters, in the Terry account, and in notes given to Purchas by Roe. Coryate estimated the distance from Jerusalem into India at twenty-seven hundred miles, but the actual distance is more than three thousand miles – most of it in territory hostile to the survival of an unarmed, impecunious, outspoken Protestant with crosses tattooed on both wrists as mementos of his Holy Land excursion. Among the surviving anecdotes is Coryate's fulfilled ambition of riding on an elephant, his silencing of a scolding laundress by haranguing her in Hindustani, and his oration to the Great Mogul in Persian, acquired while he was adding Turkish and Arabic to his store of languages. His plans included a discourse with the king of Persia in the latter's own tongue, but Coryate's health began to falter at Mandu, where he was staying with Roe. He set out alone to Surat, carrying a letter from Roe that he had insisted be rewritten to eliminate the description of him as "a very honest poor wretch." Accepting hospitality on his arrival, Coryate, according to Terry, drank sack "moderately (for he was a very temperate man)," which "increased his flux to the point where he overtook Death in the month of December, 1617." Terry's impressions of Coryate are mixed: "As he was very particular, so was he without question a very faithful, relator of things he saw"; at the same time, "his knowledge and high attainments in several languages made him not a little ignorant of himself; he being so covetous, so ambitious of praise that he would hear and endure more of it than he could in any measure deserve."

Thomas Coryate established his literary reputation with *Coryats Crudities,* an entertaining yet reliable work that adds to modern knowledge of early-seventeenth-century Europe. His letters show that he had a large network of literary and social connections. Beyond these literary accomplishments and associations he deserves recognition as the first traveler from his nation to take a scholarly interest in the Trojan Plain, the first Englishman to visit India purely out of curiosity, and the first European to walk from the eastern shores of the Mediterranean through Persia and Afghanistan into the Mogul Empire. It is regrettable that he did not live to complete the sequel to *Coryats Crudities*.

Biography:

Michael Strachan, *The Life and Adventures of Thomas Coryate* (London: Oxford University Press, 1962).

References:

Edgar Hinchcliffe, "Thomae Coriati Testimonium," *Notes and Queries,* 15 (October 1968): 370–375;

David Riggs, *Ben Jonson: A Life* (Cambridge, Mass.: Harvard University Press, 1989), pp. 192–193;

I. A. Shapiro, "The 'Mermaid Club,' " *Modern Language Review,* 45 (January 1950): 6–17;

Michael Strachan, "The Mermaid Tavern Club: A New Discovery," *History Today,* 17 (August 1967): 533–538;

Edward Terry, *A Voyage to East-India* (London: Printed by T. W. for J. Martin & J. Allestry, 1655), pp. 57–78.

Papers:

Prince Henry's presentation copy of *Coryats Crudities,* with colored plates and bound in red velvet, is in the British Museum; it includes the only known example of Thomas Coryate's handwriting and signature, a letter to Sir Michael Hicks inserted into the back. The Bodleian Library, Oxford, holds sets of verses on Coryate and his travels and a transcription from Coryate's writings by the antiquary Thomas Hearne.

John Cosin

(30 November 1595 – 15 January 1672)

P. G. Stanwood
University of British Columbia

BOOKS: *A Collection of Private Devotions: In The Practise Of The Ancient Church, Called the Hovres of Prayer. As they were after this maner published by Authoritie of Q. Eliz. 1560. Taken Out of the Holy Scriptures, the Ancient Fathers, and the diuine Seruice of our own Church,* anonymous (London: Printed by R. Young, 1627);

A Scholastical History of the Canon of the Holy Scripture; or, The Certaine and Indubitate Books thereof, as they are received in the Church of England (London: Printed by R. Norton for T. Garthwait, 1657);

Historia Transubstantiationis Papalis. Cui præmittitur, atque opponitur, tùm S. Scripturæ, tùm veterum Patrum, & Reformatarum Ecclesiarum Doctrina Catholica, de sacris symbolis, & præsentiâ Christi in Sacramento Eucharistiae. Hanc autem disquisitionem historicam ante annos XIX scribebat, & demùm instanti multorum rogatu excudi permisit paulo ante obitum Joh. Episcopus Dunelmensis (London: Printed by Thomas Roycroft for Henry Brome, 1675); translated by Luke de Beaulieu as *The History of Popish Transubstantiation. To which Is Premised and Opposed, The Catholick Doctrin of the Holy Scripture, The Ancient Fathers and the Reformed Churches, About the Sacred Elements, and Presence of Christ in the Blessed Sacrament of the Eucharist. Written Nineteen Years Ago in Latine, by John, Late Lord Bishop of Durham, And Allowed by him to be published a little before his Death, at the earnest request of his Friends* (London: Printed by Andrew Clark for Henry Brome, 1676);

The Works of the Right Reverend Father in God John Cosin, Lord Bishop of Durham: Now First Collected, 5 volumes, edited by J. Sansom, The Library of Anglo-Catholic Theology (Oxford: Parker, 1843–1855).

Edition: *A Collection of Private Devotions,* edited by P. G. Stanwood and Daniel O'Connor (Oxford: Clarendon Press, 1967).

OTHER: "Regni Angliæ Religio Catholica," edited by Thomas Smith, in his *Vitæ quorundam Eruditissimorum et Illustrium Virorum* (London: Printed by David Mortier, 1707).

In a long career that extended across much of the seventeenth century, John Cosin was distinguished as an author of important liturgical, polemical, and homiletic works; as a remarkable churchman in an age noted for distinguished clerics; and as an ingenious and gifted ecclesiastical architect and designer. These general areas of interest often intersect, but Cosin's achievements may be conveniently assigned to three periods of his life: at Cambridge — interrupted by periods in London and Durham — before the civil war; in Paris during the Interregnum; and in Durham in the early years of the Restoration.

Cosin was born on 30 November 1595 in Norwich to settled and prosperous parents, Giles and Elizabeth Remington Cosin. Educated at the grammar school in Norwich, Cosin was selected to receive one of the scholarships to Caius College, Cambridge, that were reserved for students at the Norwich school. He took his B.A. in 1614 and his M.A. in 1617; he would not receive his D.D. until 1630. Cosin evidently showed remarkable ability at Caius, since in 1616 he attracted the attention of two eminent churchmen: both Lancelot Andrewes, bishop of Ely, and John Overall, bishop of Lichfield, offered him positions as episcopal librarian and secretary. Cosin decided in favor of Overall and remained in his service until May 1619, when Overall died at Norwich, the see to which he had been translated a few months previously. This pe-

John Cosin; engraving by W. Dolle

riod probably marked the beginning of Cosin's association with the Arminians, the party in the Church of England that is usually presumed to have most vigorously opposed the Puritans and to have taken control of ecclesiastical functions throughout Charles I's "Personal Rule." Whatever influence Overall had on Cosin — and it was likely considerable — there can be no doubt of Cosin's lasting fondness for his memory. He described Overall as his "lord and master," and in 1669 he would erect a handsome memorial to him in the cathedral church of Norwich.

After another four years at Caius as a junior fellow, during which he was rhetoric prelector in 1620–1621 and university preacher in 1622, Cosin was called by Richard Neile, bishop of Durham, to be one of his domestic chaplains. Soon after his arrival in the diocese Cosin was installed in the rectory of Elwick, with a prebendal stall in Durham Cathedral. He was made archdeacon of the East Riding of Yorkshire in 1625 and in the following year rector of Brancepeth, a living he seems to have particularly enjoyed and often occupied. Also in 1626 Cosin married Frances

Blakiston, the daughter of a canon of Durham; the couple would have a son and a daughter. Cosin must have spent much time with Bishop Neile at Durham House in London, which had become a center for discussion of theology and the current problems of the church. They were often joined there by many of the most important churchmen of the day, including William Laud, Francis White, John Buckeridge, and Richard Mountague.

These meetings of church leaders at Durham House may have provided inspiration for Mountague's *Appello Caesarem* (1625), one of the most important controversial books of the time. Although he was much older than Cosin, Mountague came to trust in the younger man's judgment; he even submitted his manuscript to Cosin and instructed him to alter it in any way that he saw fit. *Appello Caesarem,* which sets out the Arminian position that the Church of Rome is a true church though in error, brought down a storm of abuse from the Puritans in the House of Commons as soon as it appeared, for it substantiated their worst fears of the leadership of the Church of England. A conference was held at York House in London at which arguments for and against Mountague's theology were heard, with Cosin acting as secretary and speaking in Mountague's defense.

Cosin defended Mountague (and had, perhaps, indeed written some of *Appello Caesarem*) because he believed that the Anglican tradition was best expressed as a way of finding the mean between the "excesses" of Geneva and Rome while retaining Catholicity, with "Antiquity [as] the best Expositor of Faith." In a sermon preached at Durham House on 3 December 1626 at the consecration of Francis White as the bishop of Carlisle, Cosin, like Richard Hooker before him, appeals to the authority of the church fathers and the first general councils to vindicate the reformed English church, "which ever held firm (and we are able to make it good) in a continued line of succession from former known bishops, and so from this very mission of the Apostles." This sermon, on John 20:21–22, "As [*sicut*] My Father sent Me, even so send I you," expresses a theme that runs throughout Cosin's work: "We demand . . . How was Christ sent? And He was sent for two ends. The first, to be the Redeemer of our souls, and to reconcile God unto men, which He did by His death; the second, to be the Bishop of our souls, and to reconcile men unto God, which He did by leaving us a Gospel, His life and doctrine, in a Church behind Him. In the first sense the Apostles were not sent, they were to be no redeemers nor mediators neither. For it cost more to redeem men's souls, and both they and their successors must let that *sicut* alone for ever. And yet there is a *sicut similitudinis* [*as* of resemblance] in it for all that, though there be no *sicut æqualitatis* [*as* of equality], there is some likeness in their sendings this way. He, sent by His Father to be a Mediator for mankind, and to reconcile the world by His death and sacrifice upon the cross. They, sent by Him, to mediate and to pray for the people, to be ministers of the reconciliation, as St. Paul speaks, and in a manner, to be sacrificers too, representers at the Altar here, and appliers of the Sacrifice once made for all; without which last act, the first will do us no good." Cosin's determined upholding of these principles led to the request, probably from the king himself, that he undertake the compilation of a book of hours appropriate for members of the court but also suitable for general use.

A Collection of Private Devotions, Cosin's first and best-known publication, appeared in 1627. The little book aroused immediate opposition, for it seemed to emphasize the High Churchmanship of the king's party. Charles's opponents, of whom

there was an increasing number in Parliament, seized the chance to condemn the king and his advisers for their supposed "popery." Although the Arminian position espoused by Charles and his ecclesiastical advisers, including the young Cosin, was improperly confused with Romish tendencies, many persons, mainly with Puritan inclinations, suspected a plot to introduce the customs and forms of the hated Church of Rome.

Meanwhile, Cosin had upset Peter Smart, a fellow prebendary at Durham. On 27 July 1628 Smart preached an abusive sermon in the cathedral that was directed principally against Cosin; it was published that year as *The Vanitie & Downe-fall of Superstitious Popish Ceremonies*. In keeping with the High Churchmen's desire to enrich the liturgy by adding splendid ceremonial, Cosin had supported the reform of services at Durham Cathedral – though it is likely that the services had been "reformed" even before his arrival. Smart's attack reflects many Puritan dislikes: music in the church, the wearing of copes, the placing of the altar in the east end of the church with the font at the west entrance, bowing to the altar, and the use of candles. What troubled the Puritans was the theological implications of these external signs.

On 4 February 1629, soon after the opening of the next Parliament, a petition was preferred against Cosin, "with articles annexed thereunto, tending to the introduction of Popish doctrine and Popish ceremonies." Cosin was also ordered to answer to the Commons on 23 February. On 24 February the celebrated "Head and Articles Agreed upon by the House" was put forward, and Cosin was named in it. Religion, it declared, struggled sadly in a troubled state, for not only did books supporting Arminianism flourish, but services were also being established full of "popish" imitation. Cosin was guilty on both counts. It was recommended that the books of Mountague and Cosin be burned, and "that such as have been authors or abettors of those Popish and Arminian innovations in doctrine may be condignly punished." Only the royal adjournment and dissolution of Parliament saved Cosin from the implementation of these proposals. The "Personal Rule" of the eleven years that followed gave him respite from the attacks of the Puritans.

In 1634 Bishop White, who had recently been translated from Carlisle to Ely, chose Cosin from among those nominated by the fellows to fill the vacant mastership of Peterhouse, Cambridge, over which White exercised visitorial rights. Cosin retained his Durham appointments and the post of chaplain-in-ordinary to the king, which he had been

Cosin's library in Durham

given in 1627. Cosin set out to reinforce the High Church attitudes he found at Peterhouse; the college was known for the High Churchmanship of the two previous masters, Leonard Mawe and Matthew Wren. He enriched the chapel, begun under Wren, with lavish decorations and introduced an elaborate ritual that included incense and possibly the use of the canonical hours from *A Collection of Private Devotions*. He enforced an exacting discipline on the scholars, requiring fines for absence from prayers.

Cosin was named vice-chancellor of the university in 1639, and at the end of 1640 the king appointed him dean of Peterborough. As vice-chancellor Cosin instituted at the university church of Great Saint Mary's "innovations" that recalled his activities at Peterhouse and the ceremonies Smart had criticized at Durham. Such practices could not be tolerated by the House of Commons; on 21 November 1640 it declared Cosin a "Delinquent," and on the following 11 March he was held unfit to hold any office. It is not certain just when he left Cambridge, but he had surely set off well before Edward Montagu, second Earl of Manchester, arrived in March 1644 with an order from the Long Parliament to "regulate the Universities."

Before leaving England, Cosin may have hidden with friends to avoid Parliamentary arrest. By 1645 he was in Paris; he served as chaplain to the little group of Anglican Royalists there, conducting English services at Faubourg Saint Germain and writing defenses of the English church and its doctrines: "Regni Angliæ Religio Catholica" was written in 1652 but not published until 1707, while *Historia Transubstantiationis Papalis* (translated as *History of Popish Transubstantiation,* 1676) was written in 1655 and published in 1675. Living on gifts from friends and a small pension from the French government, Cosin was, according to Thomas Fuller in *The Worthies of England* (1662), "the *Atlas* of the *Protestant Religion,* supporting the same with his Piety and Learning, confirming the wavering therein, yea dayly adding *Proselytes . . .* thereunto."

After the Restoration, Cosin returned to the mastership of Peterhouse; he also resumed services at Peterborough. In October 1660 he was elected to the see of Durham, and he was consecrated on 2 December. Until his death on 15 January 1672 he was an energetic bishop, improving and enriching the diocese with lavish building and gifts. He played an important role at the 1661 Savoy Conference and the convocation to revise the Book of Common Prayer.

Cosin's last will and testament reveals a firm and unequivocal devotion to the English church and great love for liturgical order and beauty: "I do profess, with holy asseveration and from my very heart, that I am now, and have ever been from my youth, altogether free and averse from the corruptions and impertinent new-fangled or papistical (so commonly called) superstitions and doctrines, and new superadditions to the ancient and primitive religion and Faith of the most commended, so orthodox, and Catholic Church, long since introduced, contrary to the Holy Scripture and the rules and customs of the ancient Fathers."

Cosin had established many contacts with the Continental reformed churches during his exile in Paris, but they left him convinced of their inferiority to the Church of England, which he saw as, "both for doctrine and discipline, the most eminent, and the most pure, the most agreeable to Scripture and antiquity of all others." Yet in his will he rises above the divisive issues of the day: "I take it to be my duty, and of all my brethren, especially the Bishops and ministers of the Church of God, to do our utmost endeavours, according to the measure of grace which is given to every one of us, that at last an end may be put to the differences of religion, or at least that they may be lessened, and that we may follow 'peace with all men, and holiness.'"

Cosin confessed himself "addicted to the symbols, synods, and confessions of the Church of England, or rather the Catholic Church," and as testament to that love he left not only his often eloquent writings – especially *A Collection of Private Devotions* and the sermons – but also a remarkable legacy of church architecture and decoration.

Many of Cosin's splendid architectural contributions may be seen in County Durham, especially in Saint Brandon's Church, Brancepeth, where he was rector from 1626 until 1640; in the Bishop's Palace, including its chapel, Bishop Auckland; and in the cathedral itself. The parish church of Brancepeth contains unusually fine woodwork in what Nikolaus Pevsner calls "the Cosin style with its fully conscious Gothic Revival in the midst of contemporary seventeenth-century elements" and "one of the most remarkable contributions of the county to the history of architecture and decoration in England." Cosin's work, which combines the Jacobean and Gothic styles, is represented by the font cover, rood screen, and choir stalls. The overall effect is one of extraordinary consistency and harmony. Cosin rebuilt and decorated the Bishop's Palace, in-

troducing sumptuous woodwork carved according to his characteristic mixed Gothic and Jacobean style, especially in the chancel screens of the chapel. This chapel, where Cosin is buried, is a splendid monument to its greatest benefactor, as are the fine choir stalls of Durham Cathedral. There, also, Cosin's font canopy, perhaps the most gorgeous of all his work, stands forty feet high and about nine feet across at the base. On Palace Green, next to the cathedral, is the library Cosin founded and built, principally to house his enormous collection of valuable books. This building, too, shows the unmistakable taste of its designer.

Although Cosin was well known as a controversialist in his own time, only *A Collection of Private Devotions* and his sermons give him an important place in English literary history. The first is his principal pre–civil war writing, the second, collectively, his work of the Interregnum (though some of the sermons were preached much earlier). After the Restoration Cosin seems to have been principally occupied with letter writing and with the administration of his great diocese.

A Collection of Private Devotions: In the Practise Of the Ancient Church, Called the Hovres of Prayer is properly described as a primer and belongs, therefore, to an old tradition of Christian devotion, while the provision it makes for the observance of the canonical hours of prayer associates it with an even older and more universal tradition. The observance of the canonical hours can be traced back to the early fathers: Clement of Alexandria, Origen, Tertullian, and Cyprian; at that time it was a matter of purely private devotion. By the sixth century in the West, however, as the *Regula* of Saint Bernard implies, the daily offices at the canonical hours had become public services for the laypeople and secular clergy as well as the ascetics. Bernard's elaboration of the existing Roman scheme provides for a daily recitation of matins and lauds, prime, terce, sext, none, vespers, and compline. This scheme of public observances constituted the Divine Office, which, in various forms, was used throughout the West for many centuries.

Such devotions formed the basis of the book known as the primer, which is first found toward the end of the thirteenth century. During the upheavals of the sixteenth century the primer enjoyed an extensive popularity: more than 180 editions appeared during the crucial years from 1525 to 1560, most of them in English. Several of these editions were authorized by Henry VIII, Edward VI, Mary, and Elizabeth, each of whom clearly intended to use them to help establish and protect current theological positions. They reveal the shifting theological emphases of the Reformation; by the time of the Elizabethan primers, for example, the office is simpler. It is the 1560 primer that Cosin notes on his title page and obviously used as a model. This book provides for the observance of the seven canonical hours, drawing material from the breviary and the Book of Common Prayer as well as from the earlier primers. Cosin's further source is the primer authorized by Elizabeth in 1564, *Preces Privatae,* which appeared again in 1568 and, with revisions and additions, in 1573.

The growing ascendancy of the Book of Common Prayer during this period, with the accompanying development of private devotions of a more informal, nonliturgical type, helps to explain the virtual disappearance of the primer after 1564; the few that appeared were based on the *Preces Privatae* and the other Elizabethan primers. Cosin's *A Collection of Private Devotions* represents the classical Anglican version of the primer and of the canonical hours of prayer. *A Collection of Private Devotions,* however, must be seen not only in the tradition of Elizabethan primers but also against the background of Laudian churchmanship that Cosin supported. In its most characteristic form, Laudian devotion paid little attention to contemporary Rome. Deriving to a large extent from Hooker, with Andrewes and Overall as the "fathers" of the movement, typical Laudian churchmanship sought to express, in worship, prayer, and liturgy, the essentially reformed Catholicism that many persons increasingly recognized as the distinctive development of the English church. A wide and profound acquaintance with the early fathers, an intense sacramentalism, and a stress on the liturgy provided in the Book of Common Prayer were marks of Laudian devotion. Within this ethos Andrewes and Donne preached their sermons, the former framed his *Private Devotions* (1647), George Herbert wrote *The Temple* (1633) and *The Country Parson* (1652), Nicholas Ferrar evolved the community at Little Gidding, and Laud sought in *A Relation of the Conference between William Laud . . . and Mr. Fisher, the Jesuit* (1639) to establish "decency and an orderly settlement of the external worship of God in the Church."

One finds in *A Collection of Private Devotions* many of the most characteristic attitudes of the seventeenth-century High Churchmen. Cosin reveals, for example, a wide and sympathetic knowledge of the teaching and practice of the primitive church "before Popery." Besides adducing the testi-

Cosin in his bishop's robes. This portrait by an unknown artist hangs in Cosin's library in Durham.

mony of Scripture on many points, he refers with great frequency to the early fathers and councils and to "the ancient Discipline and religious custome of the Church." He also draws on the formularies of the reformed Church of England, which, he maintains, is a true and sound branch of "*Christs Catholicke Church.*" He understands the Reformation in England as wise and moderate, and he disapproves both of the unseemliness of Puritan worship and of the corruptions of the Church of Rome. For Cosin, Hooker, Andrewes, and Laud, as for most of the sixteenth-century reformers, the English church's "middle way" is a return to a primitive and Catholic Christianity.

Cosin's emphasis on "the blessings of Heaven above, and the blessings of the earth beneath" indicates the cheerful character of his faith. The care with which he quotes so many authorities — and, in controversial matters, specifically Anglican ones — shows the importance he attached to orthodoxy. An analysis of his prayers reveals a variety of structure, rhythm, and language similar to that found in the Book of Common Prayer, and frequent scriptural allusions provide an additional richness. From the brief "At the washing of our hands," "For the health of our Bodies," and "In the time of Advent" to the long and splendid "Prayer and Thanksgiving for the Whole Estate of Christs Catholike Church," Cosin manifests notable skill as a composer and reviser of prayers. His many introductory and explanatory passages form a distinguished series of lucid expositions in a prose at once concise, dignified, and pleasing. Many of the earlier primers were untidily put together, often containing matter of little relevance to normal devotional requirements; but *A Collection of Private Devotions*, with its few precise and useful rubrical directions, its neatness of arrangement, and its comparative economy of content, is an encouragement to an ordered and unburdened devotional life and reveals an orderly and practical mind in its compiler.

Originally composed for the court, the work was published in a small first edition of, perhaps, between 150 and 250 copies; the second and third editions, also published in 1627, have been estimated at 1,000 to 1,500 copies each. Five more editions appeared in Cosin's lifetime. After the twelfth edition in 1719 no further edition was published until 1838. This renewed interest is to be attributed to the Tractarians' intention of reviving the churchmanship of the Caroline divines; to this aspect of the Anglican revival in the nineteenth century may be attributed the publication of a further four editions up to that of 1867 — the seventeenth, and the last before the Oxford edition of 1967.

Most of Cosin's other writings were confined to contemporary editions. But his sermons, which rank with *A Collection of Private Devotions* as the most appealing of his compositions, remained in manuscript until their publication in 1843 as volume one of *The Works of the Right Reverend Father in God John Cosin, Lord Bishop of Durham* (1843–1855) in The Library of Anglo-Catholic Theology series. The sermons reveal great learning; Cosin often quotes or alludes to the writings of the church fathers. Like Andrewes, Cosin delights in exploring the paradoxes of the faith, especially the Incarnation — an impulse apparent in many preachers of the earlier seventeenth century.

The twenty-two extant sermons fall into two groups: the thirteen preached before the civil war, chiefly at Brancepeth, from 1621 to 1633; and those preached during the Paris exile — the first of this second group is dated 1650 and the last 1655. There appears to be no change in the sermons, either rhetorically or doctrinally, from first to last.

Several of the sermons were given on special occasions, such as the consecration of the bishop of Carlise, the marriage of an eminent couple, and the funeral of Bishop Neile's sister; and there are sermons for the great festivals of the Nativity, the Epiphany, and the Ascension. There is also a series of five sermons on two of the Ten Commandments, "Thou shalt have no other Gods before My face . . . " and "Remember that thou keep holy the Sabbath Day. . . . "

It is in the two sermons preached on the Nativity that Cosin best employs the rhetorical analysis and wit characteristic of his style. The first, on John 1:9–10, "He was that light . . . ," preached in Paris on Christmas Day 1651, is much indebted in style and structure to Donne's sermon on the same text, preached at Saint Paul's on Christmas Day 1621 and included in Donne's *Fifty Sermons* (1649); Cosin owned the book and evidently had it at hand during his years in Paris. The Caroline divines borrowed easily from each other, adapting texts and ideas to new audiences or different circumstances. Cosin follows Donne closely in this sermon, being similarly eager to study the character of the "true light" and to demonstrate the subordination of reason to faith. The theme touched Cosin deeply, and he returned to it in the second sermon on the Nativity, preached in 1655 — the latest of the extant sermons. The text is from 1 Tim. 3:16, "Great is the mystery of godliness, God manifest in the flesh," a text that affords Cosin an excellent opportunity for pursuing a fundamental paradox. The Incarnation is, he says, a mystery that is not contrary to reason but beyond its comprehension. The outward reasonable man believes "natural and moral things," the inward man "the mystery of the kingdom of heaven," which exalts "our rational apprehensions . . . to a higher level than they were before." Above all, Cosin remarks, "we call it not faith, that is not grounded upon reason; and we ground our strongest reason upon the word of God Himself, That never spake other."

One may regret that Cosin did not preserve more of his sermons; yet his position as one of the most learned of the "witty" preachers in the generation following Andrewes and Donne is secure. He is remembered not only as a homilist but also as a liturgist and a sturdy upholder of the church as he understood it – apostolic, catholic, reformed, and English. As an architect he loved and contributed to "the beauty of holiness" and fit places of worship. Cosin was, furthermore, one of the great book collectors of his age. Among the monuments he left behind are the library in Durham that bears his name (now part of the university) and a perpetual endowment to Peterhouse, where he was a remarkable and strong-minded master in a difficult time. The gift provides for an annual feast, where the fellows and their guests ever offer a formal toast "in piam memoriam Joannis Cosini."

Letters:

The Correspondence of John Cosin, D.D., Lord Bishop of Durham: Together with Other Papers Illustrative of His Life and Times, 2 volumes, edited by George Ornsby (Durham, U.K.: Published for the Surtees Society, 1869, 1872);

P. G. Stanwood and A. I. Doyle, "Cosin's Correspondence," *Transactions of the Cambridge Bibliographical Society,* 5, part 1 (1969): 74–78.

Bibliography:

L. W. Hanson, "John Cosin's *Collection of Private Devotions, 1627*," *Library,* 13 (December 1958): 282–287.

Biographies:

Isaac Basire, *The Dead Mans Real Speech* (London: Printed by E. T. & R. H. for James Collins, 1673);

Thomas Smith, "Vita Joannis Cosini," in his *Vitae Quorundam Eruditissimorum et Illustrium Virorum* (London: D. Mortier, 1707);

P. H. Osmond, *A Life of John Cosin* (London: Mowbray, 1913).

References:

Robert S. Bosher, *The Making of the Restoration Settlement: The Influence of the Laudians 1649–1662* (London: Dacre, 1951);

John Cornforth, "Auckland Castle, Co. Durham," *Country Life,* 27 (26 January 1972): 198–202; (3 February 1972): 266–270; (10 February 1972): 334–337;

G. J. Cuming, *A History of Anglican Liturgy* (London: Macmillan, 1969);

Cuming, ed., *The Durham Book* (London: Oxford University Press, 1961);

A. I. Doyle, "John Cosin (1595–1672) as a Library Maker," *Book Collector,* 40 (Autumn 1991): 335–357;

John G. Hoffman, "The Arminian and the Iconoclast: The Dispute between John Cosin and Peter Smart," *Historical Magazine of the Protestant Episcopal Church,* 48 (September 1979): 279–301;

Janel M. Mueller, "A Borrowing of Donne's Christmas Sermon of 1621," *Huntington Library Quarterly,* 30 (May 1967): 207–216;

David Pearson, "Marginalia Dunelmensia: Durham Cathedral Library, Cosin and Clarendon," *Durham University Journal,* 83 (1991): 91–92;

Nikolaus Pevsner, *The Buildings of England: County Durham,* revised by Elizabeth Williamson (Harmondsworth, U.K.: Penguin, 1953, 1983);

H. Boone Porter, Jr., "Cosin's Hours of Prayer: A Liturgical Review," *Theology,* 56 (1953): 54–58;

P. G. Stanwood, "John Cosin as Homilist 1595–1671/72," *Anglican Theological Review,* 47 (1965): 276–289.

Papers:

John Cosin's autograph sermons are in the Dean and Chapter Library of Durham Cathedral (class mark A.IV.31); much of his correspondence, as well as his notes and annotations on the Book of Common Prayer, are in the Cosin's Library, University of Durham.

Abraham Cowley

(1618– 28 July 1667)

Raymond A. Anselment
University of Connecticut

See also the Cowley entry in *DLB 131: Seventeenth-Century British Nondramatic Poets, Third Series.*

BOOKS: *Poetical Blossomes* (London: Printed by Bernard Alsop & Thomas Fawcett for Henry Seile, 1633); enlarged as *Poeticall Blossomes* (London: Printed by Elizabeth Purslowe for Henry Seile, 1636; enlarged again, 1637);

Loves Riddle. A Pastorall Comædie; Written, at the Time of His Being Kings Scholler in Westminster Schoole by A. Cowley (London: Printed by John Dawson for Henry Seile, 1638); adapted by Daniel Bellamy as *The Rival Nymphs, or, The Merry Swain* (London: Printed by E. Say for the author, 1723);

Navfragivm Ioculare, Comædia: Publicè coram Academicis Acta, in Collegio SS. et Individuæ Trinitatis. 4° Nonas Feb. An. Dom. 1638 (London: Printed for Henry Seile, 1638); translated by Charles Johnson as *Fortune In Her Wits: A Comedy* (London: Printed for Bernard Lintott, 1705); adapted by Daniel Bellamy, Jr., and Daniel Bellamy as *The Perjur'd Devotee: or, The Force of Love. A Comedy* (London, 1741);

The Prologve And Epilogve To A Comedie, Presented, At the Entertainment of the Prince, His Highnesse, by the Schollers of Trinity Colledge in Cambridge, in March last, 1641, as Francis Cole (London: Printed by Francis Cole for James Calvin, 1642);

A Satyre Against Seperatists, as A. C. Generosus (London: Printed for A. C., 1642);

A Satyre. The Puritan and the Papist. By A Scholler in Oxford, as A. C. (Oxford: Henry Hall, 1643);

The Mistresse (London: Printed by William Wilson for Humphrey Moseley, 1647);

The Guardian. A Comedie. Acted before Prince Charls His Highness at Trinity College in Cambridge, upon the Twelfth of March, 1641 (London: Printed by Thomas Newcomb for John Holden, 1650); revised as *Cutter of Coleman-Street. A Comedy.*

The Scene London, in the Year 1658 (London: Printed for Henry Herringman, 1663);

Poems (London: Printed by Thomas Newcomb for Humphrey Moseley, 1656);

Ode, Upon the Blessed Restoration and Returne of His Sacred Majestie, Charls the Second (London: Printed for Henry Herringman, 1660);

The Visions and Prophecies Concerning England, Scotland, and Ireland, of Ezekiel Grebner, Son of Obadiah Grebner, Son of Paul Grebner, Who Presented the Famous Book of Prophecies to Queen Elisabeth, anonymous (London: Printed for Henry Herringman, 1661); republished as *A Vision, Concerning his late Pretended Highnesse Cromwell, the Wicked,* anonymous (London: Printed for Henry Herringman, 1661);

A Proposition for the Advancement of Learning (London: Printed by J. M. for Henry Herringman, 1661); revised as *A Proposition for the Advancement of Experimental Philosophy* (London: Printed by J. M. for Henry Herringman, 1661);

A. Covleii Plantarum Libri Duo (London: Printed by J. Flesher & for Nath. Brooks, 1662);

Verses, Written Upon Several Occasions (London: Printed for Henry Herringman, 1663); republished as *Verses, Lately Written Upon Several Occasions* (London: Printed for Henry Herringman, 1663); enlarged as *Verses, Lately Written Upon Several Occasions . . . To Which is Added A Proposition for the Advancement of Experimental Philosophy* (London: Printed for Henry Herringman, 1663);

Abraham Couleij Angli, Poemata Latina. In Quibus Continentur, Sex Libri Plantarum, Viz. Duo Herbarum. Florum. Sylvarum. Et Unus Miscellaneorum (London: Printed by T. Roycroft, for Jo. Martyn, 1668); excerpt translated anonymously as *A Translation of the Sixth Book of Mr. Cowley's Plantarum. Being a Poem upon the late Rebellion, the Happy Restoration of His Sacred Majesty, and the Dutch War Ensuing* (London: Printed for Samuel Walsall, 1680); translation republished as

Abraham Cowley; portrait by Sir Peter Lely, circa 1667 (National Portrait Gallery, London)

An Heroick Poem. Upon the Late Horrid Rebellion (London: Printed for T. D., 1683); *Plantarum* translated in its entirety by J. O., C. Cleve, Nahum Tate, and Aphra Behn as *The Third Part of the Works of Mr. Abraham Cowley, Being His Six Books of Plants, Never Before Printed in English: Viz. The First and Second of Herbs. The Third and Fourth of Flowers. The Fifth and Sixth of Trees. Now Made English by Several Hands. With a Necessary Index* (London: Printed for Charles Harper, 1689);

The Works of Mr. Abraham Cowley. Consisting of Those Which Were Formerly Printed: And Those Which He Designed for the Press, Now Published out of the Authors Original Copies, edited by Thomas Sprat (London: Printed by John Macocke for Henry Herringman, 1668);

A Poem of the Late Civil War (London: Printed for Langly Curtis, 1679).

Editions: *The Second Part of the Works of Mr. Abraham Cowley* (London: Printed by Mary Clark for Charles Harper & Jacob Tonson, 1681);

Select Works of Mr. A. Cowley, 2 volumes, edited by Richard Hurd (London: Printed by W. Boyer & J. Nichols for T. Cadell, 1772);

The Poetical Works of Abraham Cowley, 4 volumes, edited by John Bell, Poets of Great Britain Complete from Chaucer to Churchill, volumes 36–39 (Edinburgh: Printed at the Apollo Press by the Martins, 1777);

Prose Works of Abraham Cowley, Esq. Including His Essays in Verse and Prose (London: Pickering, 1826);

The Complete Works in Verse and Prose of Abraham Cowley, 2 volumes, edited by Alexander B. Grosart (Edinburgh: Constable, 1881);

Cowley's Prose Works, edited by J. Rawson Lumby (Cambridge: University Press, 1887); revised by Arthur Tilley as *Cowley's Essays* (Cambridge: University Press, 1923);

The English Writings of Abraham Cowley, 2 volumes, edited by A. R. Waller (Cambridge: University Press, 1905, 1906);

Essays and Selected Verse of Abraham Cowley, edited by John Max Attenborough (London & New York: Walter Scott, 1915);

The Essays and Other Prose Writings, edited by Alfred B. Gough (Oxford: Clarendon Press, 1915);

The Mistress with Other Select Poems, edited by John Sparrow (London: Nonesuch, 1926);

Poetry & Prose, edited by L. C. Martin (Oxford: Clarendon Press, 1949);

The Civil War, edited by Allan Pritchard (Toronto: University of Toronto Press, 1973);

The Collected Works of Abraham Cowley, edited by Thomas O. Calhoun, Laurence Heyworth, Pritchard, and others (Newark: University of Delaware Press / London: Associated University Press, 1989–   ).

PLAY PRODUCTIONS: *Naufragium Joculare,* Cambridge, Trinity College, 2 February 1638;

The Guardian, Cambridge, Trinity College, 12 March 1642;

Cutter of Coleman Street, Lincoln's Inn Fields, Duke's Theatre, 16 December 1661.

Abraham Cowley resolved, in a long prose preface to the significant 1656 volume of his poems, to write no more poetry. The tumultuous and tragic years of civil war had, he was certain, proved inimical to the poetic muse, and his own ill-fated service to a defeated cause had strengthened a desire to seek calm in some remote American settlement. Though Cowley neither abandoned poetry nor retired to the New World, he did turn increasingly to prose. The prose works move from pressing political, literary, and scientific issues toward a preoccupation with the fulfillment to be found in rural solitude. The essays written in the Kentish countryside near the end of his life and intended, according to his friend and first biographer Thomas Sprat, "as a real Character of his own thoughts upon the point of his Retirement," became especially attractive to later readers; but Cowley is not only admired, along with Michel de Montaigne, as a familiar essayist. *Naturalness, ease,* and *familiarity* are bywords among the many assessments of a writer ranked with John Dryden as an important figure in the development of English prose. Together with the poetry, the prose published in the first years of the Restoration and in the posthumous 1668 edition of his collected works complements and completes an artistic development that reveals, in its classical, almost archetypal pattern, a unique and unified design.

The 1668 edition includes the autobiographical "Of My self," the last of the eleven pieces in "Several Discourses by Way of Essays, in Verse and Prose"; perhaps Cowley's final work, it clearly establishes the continuity of the author's life. Recalling childhood days spent wandering in the fields with no other companion than a book, Cowley contends that "I was then of the same mind as I am now (which I confess, I wonder at my self.)." Three stanzas from an ode he wrote at the age of thirteen affirm the desire for a moderate life of bookish retirement, a desire inspired by Horace and "the Poets" the schoolboy immaturely and immoderately loved. Delightful hours in the family parlor reading the poetry of Edmund Spenser made him by the age of twelve, in the essay's curious phrase, "a Poet as immediately as a Child is made an Eunuch"; and only the outbreak of civil war interrupted the love of letters that flourished in his university years. Swept by the storms of dissension into the service of a great but unnamed family and exposed to the grandeur of the English and French courts, the young man Cowley remembers never lost his early aversion to the vanity of power. Later, when the misfortunes of defeat turned into the promise of the Restoration, his only desire, he writes, remained a country retreat where the Muses, his studies, and repose could be found once again. The biographical details missing from the brief apologia reinforce the impression of a lifelong preoccupation with the freedom and fulfillment only possible, if at all, in the enclosed garden.

Cowley was the seventh child of Thomas Cowley, a London stationer who died before his son was born sometime in 1618. The family's middle-class means enabled his mother, Thomasine, to raise her children in a household where the poems of Spenser might be found in the parlor; and before she sent her youngest son to Westminster School as a King's Scholar, the precocious boy had begun to write poetry. By the time Cowley matriculated in 1636 at Trinity College, Cambridge, the first and the enlarged editions of his *Poetical Blossomes* (1633, 1636) and the composition of his play *Loves Riddle* (published in 1638) had confirmed the unusual promise of a child said by Samuel Johnson "to lisp in numbers." While at Cambridge, Cowley continued to develop his interest in poetry, composing several miscellaneous and occasional pieces; in addition to writing *The Guardian* (1650), a comedy performed for the 1642 visit of Prince Charles, he also may have begun his unfinished Old Testament epic *Davideis* (published in his *Poems*, 1656). The outbreak of the civil war, however, led him, in the words of his autobiographical essay, "in wayes most contrary to the Original design of my life." Probably by the spring of 1643, before a Parliamentary commission took away the fellowship he had held after he received his B.A. in 1639, Cowley joined supporters of the Royalist cause gathered at Oxford, where he wrote his unfinished heroic narrative *The Civil War*. Perhaps in 1644 Cowley followed the exiled court of Henrietta Maria to France; for the next decade, he recalled, "I was in business of great and honourable trust." Much of his time was spent deciphering and conveying Royalist correspondence, but he did not neglect his early love of poetry. Besides finishing the collection of love poems *The Mistresse* (1647), Cowley wrote a series of Pindaric odes and probably worked on *Davideis*. These works, and the miscellaneous poems he had continued to write, were published in the 1656 collection *Poems*, which he compiled after being arrested in London as a Royalist agent on 12 April 1655. The preface to this volume, his first significant piece of prose, marks another turning point in the original design of Cowley's life.

The preface not only expresses the author's decision to forsake the poetic muse but also suggests — in a passage deleted from all subsequent seventeenth- and eighteenth-century editions — his apparent abandonment of the Royalist cause. The appearance of apostasy arises in part from his concession, "yet when the event of battel, and the unaccountable *Will* of *God* has determined the controversie, and that we have submitted to the conditions of the *Conqueror,* we must lay down our *Pens* as well as *Arms,* we must *march* out of our *Cause* it self, and *dismantle* that, as well as our *Towns* and *Castles,* of all the *Works* and *Fortifications* of *Wit* and *Reason* by which we defended it." Other Royalists during this bleak period sought their own accommodation with Oliver Cromwell, and modern historians of the Interregnum see nothing wrong with Cowley's willingness to temporize; but not all of his contemporaries accepted his realistic decision to lay down his pen. Sensitive to the criticism of Cowley's decision, criticism that persisted into the Restoration, Sprat dismisses "the errour of one Paragraph and a single Metaphor," arguing at length in his 1668 biography for the loyalty of the poet and the wisdom of accommodation. A letter Cowley wrote in December 1659 to James Butler, Lord Ormonde, also seems defensive. Although he is willing to "acknowledge and repent them as an Errour," he nonetheless insists "I am fully satisfyed in conscience of the uprightnes of my own sence in those [two] or three Lines." Both

writers imply that it was an error in judgment rather than an act of disloyalty to publish lines that later threatened Cowley's chances for the rewards due conscientious service to king and country. Cowley's understanding of their meaning is, however, paradoxically complicated and is clarified in his next prose work, *The Visions and Prophecies concerning England, Scotland, and Ireland, of Ezekiel Grebner, Son of Obadiah Grebner, Son of Paul Grebner, Who Presented the Famous Book of Prophecies to Queen Elisabeth* (1661).

This critical, often satiric assessment of Cromwell's rule purports to have been written in the months following Cromwell's death on 3 September 1658, "the time of the late Protector *Richard the Little*." Cowley had retired to the countryside of Kent soon after his release from prison near the end of 1655 and immersed himself in the studies that led to the medical degree "Doctor of Physick" from Oxford on 2 December 1657 and to the first books of an ambitious Latin poem on botany. His renewed interest in matters of state suggests, however, that he had not become indifferent to the political forces that shaped both personal and national destiny. The scrutiny of Cromwell, probably completed before Cowley returned sometime in 1659 to France and the service of Lord Jermyn, was part of a larger vision never realized. The initial printing of the pamphlet, entered in the Stationers' Register on 29 October 1660 under the author's name but published pseudonymously in 1661, claims to be the first of three works found among Grebner's papers. The second edition of the work, published the same year, includes a new advertisement explaining that the work was written during the protectorate of Cromwell's son Richard and that the "suddain Restoration of Reason, and Right, and Happinesse" obviated the need to write the second and third parts, which would have related the suffering of the kingdom and prophesied future misfortunes. The change brought about by the Restoration is also apparent in Cowley's decision to publish the second edition anonymously under the title *A Vision, concerning His Late Pretended Highnesse Cromwell, the Wicked*. Its advertisement reinforces the desire to dispel any doubts about the "wickedness" in Oliver Cromwell's heart, but the vision is by no means an opportunistic vilification intended solely to reaffirm its author's loyalty to the restored monarchy.

The long and thoughtful piece — retitled in the posthumous 1668 collected edition as "A Discourse by Way of Vision Concerning the Government of Oliver Cromwell" — is not, as it is sometimes seen, a Royalist expression of hatred or fanaticism; Cowley confronts, openly and responsibly, issues of providential and human authority central both to his poetry and to the decades of revolutionary unrest. The speaker, who had fallen into an agitated sleep on the day of Cromwell's funeral, sees in a dream a vision of England that prompts a poetic complaint about a lost world of plenty. Nostalgic longing changes to "holy fury" in a second poem, which curses the tyrant who had plagued the country more sorely than the Old Testament visitations of suffering. The mythic and biblical dimensions of the poems are common to Royalist recollections of the Caroline prosperity and the Commonwealth years of pestilence, but as discourse displaces vision the cadences of the prose syntax and the mounting intensity of the arguments add force to the feeling of loss and the struggle to understand. The masquelike appearance of a gigantic figure painted with images of civil war battles and carrying a sword and book identified with Cromwell sets the stage for a rhetorical confrontation between this guardian spirit of the Commonwealth and Cowley's speaker. At issue is the lawful authority of Cromwell's rule. Like the contemporary "de facto" theorists who argued on behalf of the Engagement Oath and the acceptance of an established rule, Cowley is sensitive both to the Pauline warning in Rom. 12:1–2 against defying power ordained by God and to the traditional rights of rulership through conquest. Cowley's speaker can only deny that Cromwell's power flows from the right hand of God's goodness and quibble that the rights of conquest are neither germane in a civil war nor, in Cromwell's instance, validated by succeeding generations of rule. Though the discourse concedes the ruler's "extraordinary Diligence," it stresses the "infinite Dissimulation" that enabled Cromwell to rise "partly by his own Faults, but chiefly for Ours." Scornfully, the speaker characterizes him as a "Jack of the Clock-house," a wooden figure that moves to strike the hour through invisible means. God allowed him to raise the hand and strike, the argument contends, as a "temporary chastisement" of the nation and its sins; Cromwell's nature, indeed, proves that he was not an extraordinary man destined to affect extraordinary changes. Before the image of his true weakness emerges in a zealous and distorted indictment of a government ruled by avarice and prodigality, the work promises that the usurpation will not endure and the rightful heirs will be restored. But as he had in *Davideis* and in the Pindaric poem "Brutus," Cowley says that the course ordained by divine Providence and historical destiny must be accepted with patient fortitude. While "A Discourse by Way of Vision" intends primarily to see the tyranny of Cromwell anew, the perspective helps explain the "unaccountable *Will* of *God*" and the "conditions of the *Conqueror*" that led Cowley to temporize in his preface.

Self-perspective also contributes significantly to an understanding of his response to Cromwell. At times in the discourse Cowley sees himself, as well as Cromwell, ambivalently, even ironically. The guardian spirit's initial praise of Cromwell's greatness — in effect, an unintended mock encomium — nevertheless leaves some uncertainty about Cowley's own attitudes toward the Commonwealth leader. The derisive portrait of Cromwell that dominates the last part of the work concedes the courage, valor, and indefatigable energy that characterized Cromwell's rise to prominence. Cowley tacitly includes himself among the deluded who were unable to anticipate ends "no humane reason could foresee"; he is vulnerable to the guardian spirit's indictment of the speaker as someone "proud and insolent against those dead men to whom he had been humble and obedient whilst they lived." Similar self-awareness qualifies the final, impassioned view of Cromwell, a view scorned by the guardian spirit as the attitude of a cynic or an Epicurean, a pedant, and a utopian dreamer whose "Lethargical Morals" and "Golden Mediocrities" have no place in the Machiavellian world of practical politics. Though the concluding words of Cromwell's defender, a poem exalting godlike greatness, are undercut by their unintentional irony, the criticism of idealism is unanswered. All semblance of discourse disappears in the final poem with the appearance of a comely youth who bursts from a cloud as the embodiment of British monarchy and an image of Charles II. Reasoned discourse at least momentarily gives way to faith in a vision of triumph that recalls the Banqueting House masques and the portraits of an earlier era.

Soon after the publication of "A Discourse by Way of Vision," a shorter prose piece appeared in two printings under the alternative titles *A Proposition for the Advancement of Learning* and *A Proposition for the Advancement of Experimental Philosophy* reaffirmed Cowley's faith in the advent of a new order. The preface offers the newly restored king, his Parliament, and his privy council a plan to implement a society of scholarship envisioned by the proponents of science and learning. The ideal community outlined by Francis Bacon in his unfinished "New Atlantis" (1626) and described by Samuel Hartlib and his circle in the imaginary realms of Marcaria, Antilia, and Atlantis had been more concretely advanced with the founding of the Royal Society for "the promoting of experimental philosophy." Cowley was one of forty men invited to join the society, which had begun meeting formally at Gresham College on 28 November 1660. While he was apparently not an active member after his election in early March 1661, according to Sprat's *History of the Royal Society* (1667) "a Proposal by Master *Cowley,* of erecting a Philosophical Colledge" was influential in the formation of the society's aims. Cowley may have been familiar at Oxford with some of the founding members, who had met for several years in Wadham College, and conceivably the new society discussed Cowley's proposal before it was entered in the Stationers' Register on 13 February 1661. The dedication to the Royal Society by an unknown "P. P." in *A Proposition for the Advancement of Experimental Philosophy* notes that the author authorized the publication "since his going into *France.*" The discovery of several letters by Cowley indicating he left again for France late in 1660 suggests that the work may not have been written, as commonly thought, at the time of the Cromwell piece but could have been written after his friend John Evelyn disclosed his own plans for an institution for the "promotion of experimental knowledge" in a 3 September 1659 letter to Robert Boyle. Cowley's proposal, in any case, is both closer to the Baconian spirit and more comprehensive in its vision than those by Evelyn or by the proponents of reform William Petty and Bengt Skytte.

The "Philosophical Colledge" Cowley proposed to erect near London is described as an institution of research and a school for "real and useful Learning." Some of its details – such as the gallery of inventions, towers for astronomy, and vaults for experimentation – are taken from Solomon's House in "New Atlantis"; but Cowley pointedly differentiates his college from Bacon's imaginary society. Like Evelyn's plan for experimental knowledge, which even includes scale drawings, Cowley's proposal spells out in considerable detail the membership, expenses, and physical setting of the scholarly community. His interest is not limited, however, to realistic issues of organization and administration; within the cloister of learning and its ample gardens, resident professors and scholars would tend the "neglected Garden" of experimental philosophy through private experiments, public lectures, and publications. In drawing from the "Fountains of Nature" rather than the "Cisterns of men," the college would also nurture the young minds of two hundred boys taught through example and encouragement to be useful to the nation's well-being. This humanistic ideal is reminiscent of that in John Milton's treatise *Of Education* (1644); the means are the pleasurable understanding of authors who have addressed "some parts of Nature." Rich and poor students alike would form part of a larger community that would encourage, through the free and open exchange of ideas, the Baconian desire "to weigh, examine, and prove all things of Nature." Toward that end Cowley proposes in direct, unrhetorical prose to reexamine traditional views of nature and to develop the potential of science. Though he concedes that the necessary yearly expenses of four thousand pounds may not be forthcoming in an uncharitable age, pessimism does not diminish his hope of repairing the ruins of the original garden in the newly envisioned gardens of nature and learning.

Meanwhile, Cowley's hope for a new halcyon era, expressed in his May 1660 publication *Ode, Upon the Blessed Restoration and Returne of His Sacred Majestie, Charls the Second,* was largely disappointed as far as his own fortunes were concerned. Early in 1661 the king restored the Cambridge fellowship Cowley had lost in the civil war but failed to give him the promised mastership of the Savoy. The next year Henrietta Maria conveyed to Cowley lands in Kent, and sometime during this period he acquired from William Davenant a share in the Duke's Theatre in London; still, he was apparently not at ease in the Restoration world. Questions about the portrait of Royalists in the revised version of *The Guardian,* performed on 16 December 1661 as *Cutter of Coleman Street,* prompted Cowley in the preface to the published version (1663) to protest his service and loyalty to the monarchy. His concern about the onerous lot of authors who are often misunderstood and seldom appreciated is more openly and personally developed in "The Complaint," published in 1663 in a collection of his occasional verse. Though Cowley attempts to keep his disillusionment and frustration in perspective, his patient fortitude is hard-won, even forced. By the time "The Complaint" appeared in print Cowley had retired to the Surrey estate of Barn Elms. In the spring of 1665 he moved some twenty miles up the Thames to Porch House in Chertsey. There he worked on his Latin poem and wrote most of his essays.

"Several Discourses by Way of Essays, in Verse and Prose" represents, in Sprat's opinion, the "scarce finish't" design of Cowley's contemplation upon retirement. The casually developed pieces form no carefully patterned whole but appear to follow the "Pindarique way" Cowley describes in one of them: "The Matter shall be Grave, the Numbers

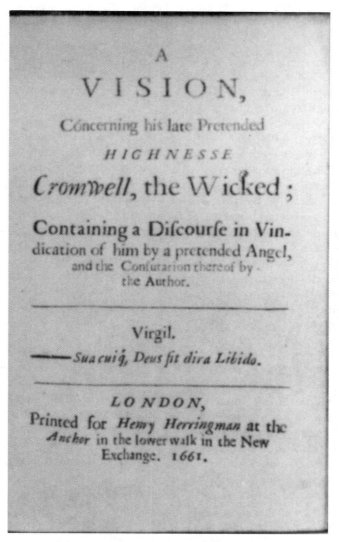

A
VISION,
Concerning his late Pretended
HIGHNESSE
Cromwell, the Wicked;

Containing a Difcourfe in Vindication of him by a pretended Angel,
and the Confutation thereof by
the Author.

Virgil.
——— *Sua cuiq, Deus fit dira Libido.*

LONDON,
Printed for *Henry Herringman* at the
Anchor in the lower walk in the New
Exchange. 1661.

Title page for Cowley's criticism of Oliver Cromwell

loose and free." Extensive passages of verse alternate with a graceful, unforced, and deceptively simple prose. At times the essays engage the audience in a conversation, creating the illusion of dialogue through their direct address and familiar voice; they are discourses, however, in the seventeenth-century sense of turning ideas in the mind, ruminating on them. Continually the essays return to the subject of the initial discourse, "Of Liberty," meditating on the nature of the estate most conducive to freedom; ultimately, they recognize in the "Pindarique way" that the sought-for looseness and freedom depend paradoxically on restraint.

The essays seek in the solitude of rural retirement the happiness their author believes cannot be found among the great and ambitious; they celebrate the unencumbered life freed from the bonds of fortune, responsibility, and ambition that shackle a Catiline, Senecio, or Cromwell. One essay locates the possibility of liberty in a position somewhere between that of a high constable and a justice of the peace, another in the rural household of five hundred pounds per annum; the "moderate plenty" central to all of them reflects the essays' indebtedness to classical tradition. Cowley values the pleasure Epicurus found in his garden and the happiness Martial enjoyed in his simple retreat, and he returns continually to a Virgilian and Horatian understanding of *Beatus ille* (the happy man). Aside from "Of Agriculture," which anticipates in its proposal for an agricultural college the eighteenth-century commitment to farming, the discourses are less interested in the georgic plow than in the untroubled country life described by Virgil and Horace. An adequate or "convenient" house and garden, good books, and a few friends are sufficient to realize the leisure with dignity praised in long passages of verse freely translated from the works of those Roman poets. The happiness bound within the laws and gardens of nature reflects the Horatian understanding that liberation comes from containment.

Though Cowley may not emphasize the centripetal direction others have seen in Horace's epistles – the capacity to free himself from time and place by turning inward – his essays are testimony to the creative freedom possible in country leisure. Unlike the ambitious career shackled by the limitless fancies of greatness, the restricted life of rural retirement offers unlimited recreation and re-creation: in the garden world of Chertsey, Cowley re-creates in his own translations and adaptations the spirit and values of the classical past. His persona as the rural philosopher nevertheless remains distinctly personal despite the conventionality of his views. The autobiographical details in "Of My self" and the occasional admission elsewhere of unspecified vanities and misfortunes are not alone the source of the intimacy, familiarity, and charm often noted in the essays. The author who confesses, with ironic obtuseness, that he did not find in the country the Arcadian simplicity and inhabitants of the "old Poetical Golden Age" can be delightfully playful. Cowley understands as well as Andrew Marvell that innocence and happiness may not exist even in the gardens of a fallen world, and his urbane, lightly mocking tone similarly qualifies his seriousness. Though some defensiveness appears in the last and most personal essay, for the most part Cowley, at the end of his life, embraces without apology the demiparadise of the enclosed garden. The Latin lines of a poem he wrote for himself, "An Epitaph on a Living Author," conclude the final essay with the assurance that "Non Indecorâ pauperie *Nitens,* / *Et Non* inerti *nobilis* otio" (Splendid in honorable poverty, he nobly employed a leisure free from sloth).

Cowley died in Chertsey on 28 July 1667 and was buried with great honor in Westminster Abbey, next to Spenser and Geoffrey Chaucer; a year later Sprat's edition of the collected works, including his biography of Cowley, provided a greater memorial. The twelve editions published by 1721 confirmed the preeminence proclaimed on the marble monument in the abbey. Several selections from his prose portrait of Cromwell were also printed during this period, but initially Cowley was remembered primarily as one of the nation's foremost poets; by 1772, when Richard Hurd edited the next signifi-

cant edition, the prose had become a more enduring monument. Alexander Pope's earlier tribute, "Still I love the language of his Heart," is unmistakable in Hurd's characterization of the essays: "The sentiments flow from the heart." Johnson's acknowledgment of Cowley's natural, easy, and familiar prose is also variously reexpressed in the growing appreciation of Cowley's intimate, sincere, and graceful manner. Nineteenth-century collections of his prose valued especially the "naturalness," "artlessness," and "freshness" Alexander B. Grosart praises in his 1881 publication of the complete works, the first to reprint the 1656 preface to *Poems* in its entirety. The many editions of his essays further strengthen the preeminence of Cowley as one of England's first and foremost familiar essayists. When the first book-length biographies and studies of his reputation were published in the 1930s, his significance as a poet was for the most part still secondary to his importance as a prose writer. Later-twentieth-century reassessments of his work have begun to shift the emphasis, often stressing the political as well as the personal significance of the prose in relation to both the poetry and the period. The renewed interest in Cowley's poetry, together with a greater appreciation of the classical and contemporary influences in his prose, support Cowley's own sense that he was engaged in a lifelong search, a search in which, looking backward near the end, he maintained, "I was then of the same mind as I am now."

Bibliographies:

Dennis G. Donovan, "Recent Studies in Cowley," *English Literary Renaissance,* 6 (Autumn 1976): 466–475;

M. R. Perkin, *Abraham Cowley: A Bibliography,* Pall Mall Bibliographies, no. 5 (Folkestone, U.K.: Dawson, 1977).

Biographies:

Thomas Sprat, "An Account of the Life and Writings of Mr. Abraham Cowley," in *The Works of Mʳ. Abraham Cowley,* edited by Sprat (London: Printed by John Macocke for Henry Herringman, 1668), sigs. A1ʳ–E4ᵛ; reprinted in *Essays of the Seventeenth Century,* volume 2, edited by J. E. Spingarn (Oxford: Oxford University Press, 1908; Bloomington: Indiana University Press, 1957), pp. 119–146;

Samuel Johnson, "Cowley," in his *Lives of the English Poets,* 3 volumes, edited by George Birkbeck Hill (Oxford: Clarendon Press, 1905), I: 1–69;

Jean Loiseau, *Abraham Cowley: Sa vie, son oeuvre* (Paris: Didier, 1931);

Arthur H. Nethercot, *Abraham Cowley: The Muse's Hannibal* (London: Oxford University Press, 1931; revised edition, New York: Russell & Russell, 1967).

References:

Raymond A. Anselment, *Loyalist Resolve: Patient Fortitude in the English Civil War* (Newark: University of Delaware Press, 1988), pp. 155–184;

Achsah Guibbory, "Imitation and Originality: Cowley and Bacon's Vision of Progress," *Studies in English Literature,* 29 (Winter 1989): 99–120;

Robert B. Hinman, *Abraham Cowley's World of Order* (Cambridge, Mass.: Harvard University Press, 1960);

Hinman, " 'The Pindarique Way': Abraham Cowley's 'Character of His Own Thoughts' in His *Essays,* Particularly 'Of My Self,' " in *Der Englische Essay,* edited by Horst Weber (Darmstadt: Wissenschaftliche Buchgesellschaft, 1975), pp. 82–94;

Richard Foster Jones, *Ancients and Moderns: A Study of the Rise of the Scientific Movement in Seventeenth Century England* (Berkeley & Los Angeles: University of California Press, 1965), pp. 173–176;

Nicholas Jose, *Ideas of the Restoration in English Literature 1660–71* (Cambridge, Mass.: Harvard University Press, 1984), pp. 67–96;

Arno Löffler, " 'A Hard and Nice Subject': Zur Problematik der Selbstdarstellung in Cowleys Essay 'Of My Self,' " *Anglia,* 104 (1986): 349–368;

Jean Loiseau, *Abraham Cowley's Reputation in England* (Paris: Didier, 1931);

Anthony Low, *The Georgic Revolution* (Princeton: Princeton University Press, 1985), pp. 126–131;

H. R. Mead, "Two Issues of Cowley's 'Vision,' " *The Papers of the Bibliographical Society of America,* 45, no. 1 (1951): 77–81;

Arthur H. Nethercot and Jones, "Concerning Cowley's Prose Style," *PMLA,* 46 (September 1941): 962–967;

Ruth Nevo, *The Dial of Virtue: A Study of Poems on Affairs of State in the Seventeenth Century* (Princeton: Princeton University Press, 1963), pp. 119–133;

Michael O'Loughlin, *The Garlands of Repose: The Literary Celebration of Civic and Retired Leisure* (Chicago: University of Chicago Press, 1978);

Alexander Pope, *The First Epistle of the Second Book of Horace, Imitated* (London: Printed for T. Cooper, 1737);

Allan Pritchard, "Marvell's 'The Garden': A Restoration Poem?" *Studies in English Literature,* 23 (Summer 1983): 371–388;

Pritchard, "Six Letters by Cowley," *Review of English Studies,* new series 18 (1967): 253–263;

Maren-Sofie Røstvig, *The Happy Man: Studies in the Metamorphoses of a Classical Ideal, 1600–1700,* volume 1 (Oslo: Norwegian Universities Press, 1962), pp. 15–51;

Thomas Sprat, *History of the Royal Society,* edited by Jackson I. Cope and Harold Whitmore Jones (Saint Louis: Washington University Studies, 1958);

David Underdown, *Royalist Conspiracy in England, 1659–1660* (New Haven: Yale University Press, 1960), pp. 317–319;

Geoffrey Walton, *Metaphysical To Augustan: Studies in Tone and Sensibility in the Seventeenth Century* (London: Bowes & Bowes, 1955), pp. 94–120;

Clarence Webster, *The Great Instauration: Science, Medicine and Reform, 1626–1660* (New York: Holmes & Meier, 1975).

Papers:

The only autograph manuscript of Abraham Cowley's published prose, the essay "The Garden," is in the Donald and Mary Hyde Collection, Four Oaks Farm, Summerville, New Jersey. Peter Beal discusses the nature and location of Cowley manuscripts, both autograph and copies, in his *The Index of English Literary Manuscripts, Volume II 1625–1700, Part I* (New York: Mansell, 1987), pp. 235–265.

John Donne
(1572 – 31 March 1631)

Clayton D. Lein
Purdue University

See also the Donne entry in *DLB 121: Seventeenth-Century British Nondramatic Poets.*

BOOKS: *Pseudo-Martyr. Wherein ovt of Certaine Propositions and Gradations, This Conclusion is euicted. That Those Which Are of the Romane Religion in this Kingdome, may and ought to take the Oath of Allegiance* (London: Printed by William Stansby for Walter Burre, 1610);

An Anatomy of the World. Wherein, by Occasion of the vntimely death of Mistris Elizabeth Drvry the frailty and the decay of this whole world is represented (London: Printed for Samuel Macham, 1611); revised as *The First Anniuersarie. An Anatomie of the World* (London: Printed by M. Bradwood for Samuel Macham, 1612);

Conclaue Ignati: Siue Eivs In Nvperis Inferni Comitiis Inthronisatio (London: Printed for Walter Burre, 1611); translated by Donne as *Ignatius his Conclaue: or His Inthronisation in a late Election in Hell,* anonymous (London: Printed by N. O. for Richard More, 1611);

The Second Anniuersarie. Of the Progres of the Soule (London: Printed by M. Bradwood for Samuel Macham, 1612);

A Sermon upon the XV. Verse of the XX. Chapter of the Booke of Ivdges: Wherein occasion was iustly taken for the Publication of some Reasons, which his Sacred Maiestie had beene pleased to giue, of those Directions for Preachers, which he had formerly sent forth. Preached at the Crosse the 15th. of September. 1622 (London: Printed by William Stansby for Thomas Jones, 1622);

A Sermon vpon the VIII. Verse of the I. Chapter of the Acts of the Apostles. Preach'd To the Honourable Company of the Virginian Plantation. 13°. Nouemb. 1622 (London: Printed by Augustin Matthewes for Thomas Jones, 1622);

Encænia. The Feast of Dedication. Celebrated At Lincolnes Inne, in a Sermon there vpon Ascension day, 1623. At the Dedication of a new Chappell there, Consecrated by the Right Reuerend Father in God, the Bishop of London (London: Printed by Augustine Matthewes for Thomas Jones, 1623);

Three Sermons vpon Speciall Occasions (London: Printed for Thomas Jones, 1624);

Devotions vpon Emergent Occasions, and seuerall steps in my Sicknes: Digested into 1. Meditations vpon our Humane Condition. 2. Expostvlations, and Debatements with God. 3. Prayers, vpon the seuerall Occasions, to him (London: Printed by Augustine Matthewes for Thomas Jones, 1624);

The First Sermon Preached to King Charles, at Saint James: 3°. April. 1625 (London: Printed by Augustine Matthewes for Thomas Jones, 1625);

Fovre Sermons vpon Speciall Occasions. (Viz.) 1. A Sermon preached at Pauls Crosse. 2. To the Honourable, the Virginia Company. 3. At the Consecration of Lincolnes Inne Chappell. 4. The first Sermon preached to K. Charles at Sᵗ Iames, 1625 (London: Printed for Thomas Jones, 1625);

A Sermon, Preached to the Kings Mᵗⁱᵉ· at Whitehall, 24. Febr. 1625 (London: Printed for Thomas Jones, 1626);

Five Sermons vpon Speciall Occasions. (Viz.) 1. A Sermon preached at Pauls Crosse. 2. To the Honorable the Virginia Company. 3. At the Consecration of Lincolnes Inne Chappell. 4. The first Sermon preached to K. Charles at Sᵗ. Iames, 1625. 5. A Sermon preached to his Maiestie at White-hall, 24. Febr. 1625 (London: Printed for Thomas Jones, 1626);

A Sermon of Commemoration of the Lady Dàuers, late Wife of Sʳ. Iohn Dàuers. Preach'd at Chilsey, where she was lately buried. By Iohn Donne D. of Sᵗ. Pauls, Lond. I Iuly 1627. Together with other Commemorations of Her; By her Sonne G. Herbert (London: Printed by John Haviland for Philemon Stephens & Christopher Meredith, 1627);

Deaths Dvell, or, A Consolation to the Soule, against the dying Life, and liuing Death of the Body. Deliuered in a Sermon at White Hall, before the Kings Maiesty, in the beginning of Lent, 1630. By that late learned and Reuerend Diuine, Iohn Donne, Dʳ. in Diuinity,

John Donne; miniature by Isaac Oliver (Collection of Her Majesty the Queen, Windsor Castle)

& Deane of S. Pauls, London. Being his last Sermon, and called by his Maiesties houshold The Doctors Owne Fvnerall Sermon (London: Printed by Thomas Harper for Richard Redmer & Benjamin Fisher, 1632);

Ivvenilia: Or Certaine Paradoxes, and Problemes (London: Printed by E. P. for Henry Seyle, 1633; revised, 1633); enlarged as *Paradoxes, Problems, Essayes, Characters* (London: Printed by Thomas Newcombe for Humphrey Moseley, 1652);

Poems, By J. D. with Elegies on the Authors Death (London: Printed by Miles Flesher for John Marriot, 1633; revised, 1635; revised edition, London: Printed for John Marriot, to be sold by Richard Marriot, 1650);

Six Sermons Upon Severall Occasions, Preached before the King, and elsewhere (London: Printed by the printers to the Universitie of Cambridge, sold by Nicholas Fussell & Humphrey Moseley, 1634);

Sapientia Clamitans, Wisdome Crying out to Sinners to returne from their evill wayes: Contained in Three pious and learned Treatises, by Donne and Thomas Jackson, edited by William Milbourne (London: Printed by John Haviland for Robert Milbourne, 1638); republished as *Wisdome Crying out to Sinners to returne from their evill wayes. Contained in Three pious and learned Treatises* (London: Printed by Marmaduke Parsons for John Stafford, 1639);

LXXX Sermons (London: Printed for Richard Royston & Richard Marriot, 1640);

ΒΙΑΘΑΝΑΤΟΣ. *A Declaration of That Paradoxe, or Thesis, that Selfe-homicide is not so Naturally Sinne, that it may never be otherwise. Wherein The Nature, and the extent of all those Lawes, which seeme to be violated by this Act, are diligently surveyed* (London: Printed by John Dawson, 1647?);

Fifty Sermons, Preached by That Learned and Reverend Divine, John Donne, D^r in Divinity, Late Deane of the Cathedrall Church of S. Pauls London. The Second Volume (London: Printed by James Flesher for Miles Flesher, John Marriot, & Richard Royston, 1649);

Essayes in Divinity; By the late Dr Donne, Dean of S Paul's. Being Several Disquisitions, Interwoven with Meditations and Prayers: Before he entered into Holy Orders. Now made publick by his Son J. D. D^r of the Civil Law (London: Printed by Thomas Maxey for Richard Marriot, 1651);

XXVI. Sermons Preached by That Learned and Reverend Divine John Donne, Doctor in Divinity, Late Dean of the Cathedral Church of St. Pauls, London. The

Third Volume (London: Printed by Thomas Newcombe for James Magnes, 1660).

Editions: *The Works of John Donne, D.D., Dean of Saint Pauls 1621–1631, With a memoir of his life,* 6 volumes, edited by Henry Alford (London: John W. Parker, 1839);

Essays in Divinity, edited Augustus Jessopp (London: Tupling, 1855);

The Life and Letters of John Donne, 2 volumes, edited by Edmund Gosse (London: Heinemann, 1899);

The Poems of John Donne, 2 volumes, edited by Herbert J. C. Grierson (Oxford: Clarendon Press, 1912);

Donne's Sermons: Selected Passages, edited by Logan Pearsall Smith (Oxford: Clarendon Press, 1919);

Devotions upon Emergent Occasions, edited by John Sparrow (Cambridge: Cambridge University Press, 1923);

The Courtier's Library, edited by Evelyn Mary Simpson (London: Nonesuch Press, 1930);

John Donne Dean of St. Paul's, Complete Poetry and Selected Prose, edited by John Hayward (London: Nonesuch Press / New York: Random House, 1949);

Essays in Divinity, edited by Simpson (Oxford: Clarendon Press, 1952);

The Sermons of John Donne, 10 volumes, edited by Simpson and George R. Potter (Berkeley & Los Angeles: University of California Press, 1953–1962);

John Donne: The Anniversaries, edited by Frank Manley (Baltimore: Johns Hopkins University Press, 1963);

John Donne's Sermons on the Psalms and Gospels. With a Selection of Prayers and Meditations, edited by Simpson (Berkeley & Los Angeles: University of California Press, 1963);

The Complete Poetry of John Donne, edited by John T. Shawcross (Garden City, N.Y.: Doubleday, 1967);

John Donne: Selected Prose, edited by Simpson, Helen Gardner, and Timothy Healy (Oxford: Clarendon Press, 1967);

Donne's Prebend Sermons, edited by Janel M. Mueller (Cambridge, Mass.: Harvard University Press, 1971);

Devotions upon Emergent Occasions, edited by Anthony Raspa (Montreal: McGill-Queen's University Press, 1975);

Paradoxes and Problems, edited by Helen Peters (Oxford: Clarendon Press, 1980);

Biathanatos, edited by Ernest W. Sullivan II (Newark: University of Delaware Press, 1984);

Pseudo-Martyr, edited by Raspa (Montreal: McGill-Queen's University Press, 1993).

OTHER: *"Amicissimo & meritissimo BEN: IONSON,"* in *Ben: Ionson his Volpone* (London: Printed for Thomas Thorppe, 1607);

"Incipit Ioannes Donne (Oh to what height will loue of greatnesse driue)," *"In eundem Macaronicon,"* and *"Incipit Ioannes Dones* (Loe her's a Man, worthy indeed to trauell)," in *Coryats Crudities,* by Thomas Coryate (London: Printed by William Stansby, 1611);

"Elegie on the vntimely Death of the incomparable Prince, Henry. By Mr Donne," in Joshua Sylvester's *Lachrymae Lachrymarum,* third edition (London: Printed by Humfrey Lownes, 1613);

"Newes from the very Country," in *A Wife Now the Widow of Sir Thomas Ouerburye. Being A most exquisite and singular Poem of the choice of a Wife. Whereunto Are Added many witty Characters, and conceited Newes, written by himselfe and other learned Gentlemen his friends* (London: Printed for Lawrence Lisle, 1614).

John Donne is now recognized as one of the great originals in the history of English poetry and as an equally accomplished master of English prose. The twentieth century has restored him, in fact, to a place in the literary pantheon much like the one he held in his own time. The enigmatic life of the "Black prince of witts" and his quirky, passionate sensibility have proved as fascinating to men and women today as in his own age. The well-annotated editions of his works produced in the late twentieth century, moreover, have made his writings accessible to a wider readership than ever before.

Donne's prose writings extend over most of his life and, like his poetry, exhibit well-marked phases of development. Yet, had Donne succeeded in his quest for a secular career his status as a poet of the first order might remain unchallenged, but he would, at best, appear as a minor figure among the prose writers of his age. Donne's stature as an artist in prose is directly linked to his transformation into a great preacher whose unique blend of verbal virtuosity, far-ranging learning, emotional and psychological profundity, and imaginative range set him apart from his clerical peers.

Born sometime during the first half of 1572, Donne was the son of John Donne, a successful merchant in the Ironmongers' Company, although the younger Donne suppressed this feature of his heritage. The critical factor, as he saw it, was his birth into a family notable for its passionate attachment to the Catholic faith. Through his mother, Elizabeth Heywood Donne, he was related to Sir Thomas More; one of his uncles was a leader in the Jesuit mission to England in the 1580s. After the death of his father in January 1576, his mother wed John Syminges, a Catholic doctor who became president of the Royal College of Physicians.

Donne apparently received his earliest education from Catholic tutors, and that education may have had much to do with his affection for medieval thinkers and his great familiarity with medieval devotional traditions. He also seems to have taken an interest in medicine, for references to medical practice and theory abound in his writings. In 1584 he proceeded to Oxford with his younger brother, matriculating at Hart Hall, a haven for Catholics. He left, however, without taking a degree: graduation required signing an oath of allegiance to the monarch, an act that would have compromised his Catholicism. After 1591 he was in London: first at Thavies Inn, then at Lincoln's Inn, one of the leading centers for legal training and another popular refuge for Catholics.

These early years are notoriously obscure. Izaak Walton, Donne's friend and first biographer, maintained that Donne went from Oxford to Cambridge; owing to faulty records, the statement cannot be verified, nor can the length of Donne's stay in Cambridge – if he did go there – be determined. Donne was known as a traveler, but his travels (some of them, presumably, undertaken early in his life) are vexingly difficult to date. Donne may have traveled – perhaps even fought – on the Continent in the period preceding his entrance into Thavies Inn. His life at the Inns of Court was interrupted at least twice by participation in military expeditions (one of them celebrated in the early poems "The Storme" and "The Calme," first published in *Poems, By J. D. with Elegies on the Author's Death* [1633]), after each of which he may also have traveled on the Continent.

Donne did not enter Lincoln's Inn to pursue a legal career, although Walton insists that he was a diligent student. For Donne, as for perhaps most of his male contemporaries, the Inns of Court served to provide the final polish for life as a gentleman and for a public career in which knowledge of law would prove useful. Donne, accordingly, spent much of his time at Lincoln's Inn in pursuit of London's material and cultural pleasures. He entered the world of fashion, mastered the arts of am-

orous courtship, joined literary coteries, and spent countless hours in the theater. The change effected in his habits is documented in the two earliest portraits of him. In the first Donne is eighteen, a somber military man; in the second, the well-known Lothian portrait, he is a dandy and a wit, beseeching his mistress (in a Latin tag painted into the picture) to "lighten our darkness" – a brazen parody of a Collect from Evensong.

Donne's early poems are as difficult to date as his activities. Most have been assigned to the years at Lincoln's Inn and those immediately following. Men at the Inns of Court characteristically dabbled in literature, and the generic range of Donne's early poetry testifies to his eager participation in England's literary renaissance: he composed epigrams, elegies, satires, a variety of amorous lyrics known (beginning in the 1635 edition of his *Poems*) as *Songs and Sonets,* some letters in verse, and a brutal mock-epic, *Metempsychosis,* completed in 1601 and first published in the 1633 edition of *Poems.*

These works can be made to appear more original than they are, for the young Donne was not quite the rebel of legend. In composing epigrams, satires, verse letters, and elegies he carried forward the humanist tradition of the Renaissance. In the form and content of his works, Donne may be considered one of the founders of the neoclassical tradition in English verse, and readers of these poems will readily understand why Donne and Ben Jonson became fast friends and why Donne's youthful poems remained Jonson's favorites. The love poems, similarly, borrow material and poetic stances from traditions of erotic verse from classical times through the Renaissance.

What impresses the reader of the youthful works is the vitality of Donne's imitations, and signs of rebelliousness are present everywhere. In satire he imitates Juvenal, Horace, and Persius rather than the writers of medieval complaint whom Edmund Spenser followed. He sides, too, with those who were subverting the conventions that governed Elizabethan poetry. In larger terms, he intrudes himself into the literary avant-garde and leaps to the fore: he refuses to write sonnets; he displays a marked preference for skeptical and naturalistic material and exhibits a passion for subversion equal to Christopher Marlowe's. He follows Marlowe, in fact, in rejecting the Ovid of the *Metamorphoses,* so cherished by Elizabethan poets, imitating instead the rakish and urbane Ovid of the *Amores* and *Ars Amatoria.*

The richest of the early poems, the *Satyres,* repay repeated readings and are irreplaceable for understanding Donne's temperament and evolution. Donne may not have been the first to imitate classical satire, but his five pieces constitute the finest legacy from the outpouring of satiric verse in the 1590s. Behind them lies a bold scorn for shallow materialism and a barely controlled hatred for the hypocrisy of contemporary life, particularly life at court. One senses in these poems, moreover, the interplay between the personalities revealed by the early portraits.

Satyre 3 is one of the outstanding poems of its age. Reviewing the activities and goals of his countrymen, Donne finds his compatriots content with false achievement and characterized by "courage of straw." Nowhere does he find zealous dedication to the only meaningful quest, the quest for truth, which for Donne and his contemporaries is implicitly a quest for religious truth. Within the classical imitation one thus meets a passionate religious spirit. The provocative wit of the *Elegies* and of the Lothian portrait is also present, for he likens love of God's Church to love of various mistresses. But the message of the satire is anything but frivolous: the poem reveals that his Catholicism has been badly shaken by the reading of Protestant material. Unsure at the moment where to place his trust, he is confident that in such times people must "doubt wisely." Although unable to make a final choice, he knows that the task requires "hard knowledge," and he reminds his contemporaries of the urgency of the quest:

> in strange way
> To stand inquiring right, is not to stray;
> To sleepe, or runne wrong, is: On a huge hill,
> Cragged, and steep, Truth stands, and hee that will
> Reach her, about must, and about must goe;
> And what the hills suddennes resists, winne so;
> Yet strive so, that before age, deaths twilight,
> Thy Soule rest, for none can worke in that night.

Donne presents himself, furthermore, as More's spiritual heir: he insists that in the pursuit of truth no one can afford to surrender the conscience to political authority: "Foole and wretch, wilt thou let thy Soule be tyed / To mans lawes, by which she shall not be tryed / At the last day?" Such gestures confirm that Donne's serious nature, though periodically kept under wraps, never disappeared.

The achievement of the *Satyres,* as of the *Songs and Sonets,* rests in the end on a particular habit of mind, a curious mixture of detachment and impassioned engagement. Growing up a Catholic outsider in Protestant England may have produced in Donne an ironic detachment from the world in which most people felt at home, and Donne repeatedly observes his society from unconventional perspectives. His poetry, consequently, seems to inhabit a natural niche in the great age of Elizabethan drama, and Donne (a great "frequenter of Playes," according to a friend) was doubtless stimulated by plays he observed and read. His stances, in fact, resemble nothing so much as the ironic points of view manifest in the plays of Marlowe and of William Shakespeare.

Donne's earliest experiments in prose, the *Paradoxes* and *Problems,* display a like temperament. Written for himself and select friends and never intended for publication (they were published as *Juvenilia* in 1633), they are among his most attractive productions. The editor of the 1980 edition of *Paradoxes and Problems* places the *Paradoxes* in the early 1590s, making them contemporary with the epigrams, *Satyres,* and *Elegies;* the *Problems* are usually assigned to the next decade. Again, Donne's choice of genres confirms his place in the literary avant-garde at the end of the sixteenth century, when the composition of paradoxes and problems became popular in certain circles: Donne appears to have been the first to compose literary problems in English, and others quickly followed.

Although they belong to different periods and have discernible differences, the *Problems* and the *Paradoxes* are generally grouped together because of shared qualities. It is evident, for example, that Donne had systematically studied the prose paradox (a source for the epigrams and *Songs and Sonets,* as well). Donne intends, as did earlier writers in the genre, to shock, mislead, and surprise. As in the early poetry, the reader meets a mind impatient – even contemptuous – of customary thinking, a mind ready and able to promote any proposition to agitate conventional sensibilities ("That all things kill themselves"; "That Nature is our worst Guide"; "Why are the fayrest falsest?"; "Why have Bastards best Fortune?"). His approach owes much to his training in dialectic at Oxford and in argument at the Inns of Court, and there are clear precedents for his practices. Nonetheless, those who study his sources arrive at conclusions parallel to those reached by students of his early poetry: Donne borrows material freely, but he consistently moves beyond his models. Even when he adopts arguments from an earlier master, he complicates the original. He loves the virtuoso performance.

The early prose manifests other features of the early poetry – the flamboyant, libertine wit of the *Elegies,* for example, as well as the stylistic rebelliousness embodied in the epigrams and the *Songs*

All Ryuers, though in their Course they are content to serue publique uses, yett their end ys, to returne into the Sea, from whence they issued. So, though I should haue much Comfort, that this Booke might giue contentment to others, yet my Direct end in ytt was, to make yt a testimony of my gratitude towards yo.r L.p. and an acknowledgement, that those poore sparks of Vnderstandinge or Iudgement w.ch are in mee, were deriued and kindled from yo.w and owe themselues to yo.w. All good that ys in ytt, yo.r L.p may be pleasd to accept as yo.rs; and for the Errors, I cannot despayr of yo.r pardon, since yo.w haue longe since pardond greater faults in mee.

yo.r L.ps

humble and faythfull Seruant

J Donne

Undated letter, written in 1610, from Donne to his former employer, Sir Thomas Egerton. Donne was discharged as Egerton's secretary after eloping in 1601 with Egerton's niece, Ann More (private collection; lent to Pierpont Morgan Library).

and Sonets. The packed conciseness of these pieces, constructed of crisp, staccato phrases and sentences, matches the terse form and chiseled diction of the *Songs and Sonets.* All display Donne's dislike for ornate Elizabethan modes of expression. More important, the pieces bear witness to Donne's seemingly inexhaustible attraction to paradox, particularly rhetorical and philosophical paradox. Many make use of theological and philosophical paradoxes to which he later returns.

Also present, particularly in the *Problems,* is the savage temper of the *Satyres,* which found further ventilation in *Metempsychosis.* This bitter antiepic bears signs of Donne's study of the great skeptics of the ancient world and exposes, at the same time, bitter feelings that he struggled to harness throughout his early period. Particularly pertinent is his hatred for the venality, insincerity, and corruption of life at court. Similar sentiments inform the *Problems* ("Why are Courtiers sooner Atheists then men of other Condition?"; "Why are new Officers least oppressing?"; "Why are Statesmen most Incredible?").

By 1601 Donne had earned a place for himself as one of the angry young men of his generation. He had also achieved notable personal success. Through his participation in the naval expeditions against Spain in the late 1590s he had made the acquaintance of the sons of Sir Thomas Egerton, the lord keeper. Probably due to their influence, Donne became Egerton's secretary about 1597. The arrogant, ambitious Donne was on the fast track to a brilliant career of public service.

Then, in December 1601, he eloped with Ann More, the seventeen-year-old niece of Egerton's late wife. Donne was almost thirty; he should have realized what the consequences would be. But he apparently believed that he could defy social conventions as willfully as literary ones. He severely underestimated the reaction and influence of his wife's father, Sir George More, who was a member of Parliament, Egerton's brother-in-law, and a favorite of the queen. Sir George was apoplectic: Donne had an unsavory reputation; his family was identified with the Catholic underground; and he had obtained More's daughter in an underhanded way. Sir George had Donne and his helpers thrown into jail, and he destroyed Donne's career by forcing Egerton to dismiss him.

Donne was ruined. According to legend, he summed up his situation in the phrase "*John Donne, Anne Donne, Un-done.*" He established the validity of his marriage in court, but through one impulsive act he had lost his position, his social standing, and all reasonable hope for a brilliant career. The severity of the turn of events is captured by a remark he made in 1612: "I died ten years ago." Donne had, moreover, virtually exhausted his inheritance, and Sir George denied Donne his daughter's dowry.

The first dozen or so years following the marriage sorely taxed the spirits of husband and wife. What Walton calls the "remarkable error of his life" closed the doors to virtually every form of public employment, and the couple was forced into exile from London to Pyrford. They survived through the generosity of friends and patrons, who often provided places for them to live. Donne was reduced to the status of a client to any patron willing to pay for his services, a situation galling to one of his independent temperament. He most certainly did not want to accompany Sir Robert Drury to the Continent in 1611 over the protests of his pregnant wife, but he felt obligated to his patron. He had to support not only himself and his wife but also an almost yearly addition to his family (the Donnes had twelve children, including two who were stillborn).

Such conditions made these years the most unstable period of his life, a time of freakish swings of emotion and opinion. Donne may well have calculated the amount of his wife's dowry in venturing upon the marriage, but he also obviously married for love. Exhilaration at the success of his romantic union led to Neoplatonic celebrations of love. Love and marriage also deepened and gentled him. Consequently, to Donne's flagrantly improvident marriage are owed some of the finest lyrics in English on mutuality in love and on the superiority of such love to all other earthly experience.

Donne's letters from this period provide a somber counterpoint to these imaginings, chronicling unrelenting struggles with illness, depression, and the sense of exile. Despair at the state of his fortunes mixed with strong religious feelings and a deep cynicism and intellectual discontent to produce a succession of arresting and disturbing works, among them certain problems, BIAΘANATOΣ (*Biathanatos,* 1647), and the poems known as *Holy Sonnets* (first published in the first edition of *Poems*). Throughout, celebration contends with anxiety, outrage, and insecurity, making this time the most complex period of his life.

Mixed emotions certainly inform the quirkiest of his prose productions, *Catalogus Librorum Aulicorum,* or *The Courtier's Library,* of which Evelyn Mary Simpson dates the initial composition about 1604 or 1605 and which was first published in the 1650 edition of Donne's *Poems.* Donne offers here a mock catalogue of books in imitation of Rabelais's catalogue of the library of Saint Victor; and, like Rabelais's, Donne's work is full of high jinks. Yet, scrutinized closely, Donne's catalogue can be seen to be more resentful, exhibiting some of the same targets and sources as the darker of the problems and *Metempsychosis.* He attacks not simply false learning and abstruse thinkers (esoteric Neoplatonists and cabalists) but also public types of a more disturbing character: pursuivants and state servants, for example, who betray harmless Catholics (Richard Topcliffe, the infamous informer and torturer, is targeted here, as he also is in *Satyre 4*). In Donne's fiction, moreover, the bibliography has been compiled for busy courtiers, who have neither the time nor intelligence necessary to acquire the minimal knowledge to support their pretensions. Donne is as estranged from life at court here as in *Satyre 4,* and that his scorn was directed on occasion at the new king is revealed by such poems as "The Canonization."

At the same time, *The Courtier's Library* bears witness to much recondite reading, and the decade following his marriage was a period of intense research. Donne threw himself into the study of theology and of civil and canon law, probably in preparation for some employment. He seems to have been of service to some friends, and after a few years he was able to establish a residence of his own at Mitcham in Surrey. Circumstantial evidence supports the tradition that by 1606 he had become an assistant to Thomas Morton, who was composing replies to the king's Catholic adversaries, and, perhaps as a result of such employment, Donne reestablished quarters in London. Efforts to secure a public position, however, were to no avail.

Donne's busiest years as a writer, particularly in prose, may have been from 1607 to 1613. Unfortunately, it proves to be as difficult to order the writings of this middle period as it is the earlier writings, and, as before, composition in poetry and prose was carried on simultaneously. Much of the new verse was directed to patrons. Donne's celebratory side found expression, for example, in hyperbolic verses addressed to female acquaintances and patrons, particularly Lucy, Countess of Bedford. Perhaps the finest of these efforts is "The Autumnall," an elaborate verse paradox in the form of an elegy in honor of Magdalen Herbert, mother of the future poet George Herbert.

Biathanatos, Donne's first extended work in prose, was completed in 1607 or 1608. It, too, is an elaborate paradox, an intricate argument of the Scholastic sort but on a forbidden topic as is stated in the subtitle: *A Declaration of that Paradoxe . . . that Selfe-homicide is not so naturally Sinne, that it may never be otherwise.* Once again Donne subjects nigh universally held "verities" to trenchant analysis. The work is vintage Donne, railing against "the tyranny of . . . praeiudice," "weak credulous Men," and "lazy affecters of Ignorance." The author, meanwhile, who commences a thought "So when from those true propositions, which are the eldest Children and issue of our light of Nature, and of our discourse" is the Donne of *Satyre 3,* maintaining the proposition that "though truth and falshood bee / Neare twins, yet truth a little elder is." The discourse must, accordingly, make use of the full testimony of history. Nor does Donne abandon his earlier method for discovering truth. Just as, regarding the *Paradoxes,* he confessed to a friend that "they were made rather to deceave tyme then her daughter truth . . . if they make you to find better reasons against them they do there office . . . they are rather alarums to truth to arme her then enemies," so in *Biathanatos* he says: "because I thought, that as in the Poole of *Bethsaida,* there was no health till the Water was troubled, so the best way to finde the truith in this matter was to debate and vexe it, (for *we must as well dispute De veritate, as pro veritate*) I abstaynd not for feare of misinterpretation, from this vndertaking."

Some regard *Biathanatos* as the natural outcome of Donne's intense studies. The work offers a virtuoso display of learning in history and in civil and canon law but is not limited to such sources. Donne's miscellaneous learning here recalls the strange brew of *Metempsychosis,* its assemblage of blatantly diverse materials documenting Donne's frantic attempt to make sense of wildly differing authorities.

Others view the work as a subterfuge: a deviously crafted, ironic argument devoid of ultimate purpose. If so, it is an ironic argument along the lines of Desiderius Erasmus's *Moriae encomium* (1511; translated as *The Praise of Folie,* 1549), and there seems little point in denying that in *Biathanatos* Donne examined motivations that were tormenting him personally (comparisons have often been made between Donne in this work and Robert Burton in *The Anatomy of Melancholy,* 1621). Donne's scholarship and approach do indicate that the work is not one of "psychological introspection," but to claim (as does Ernest W. Sullivan II) that "neither melancholy nor suicidal tendencies motivated his defence of suicide" is to go too far. The work was hardly an innocent academic exercise; earlier works and letters confirm that suicidal impulses flashed through his mind repeatedly. As early as "The Storme" he suspected a death wish in himself, and the early *Par-*

adox, "That all things kill themselves," contains, in embryo, notions that are advanced with rigor in *Biathanatos.* Donne's letters bear additional witness to conditions that could easily conduce to self-murder, including a fear of insanity ("But, of the diseases of the mind there is no criterion, no canon, no rule, for our taste and apprehension and interpretation should be the judge, and that is the disease itself"). He fell prey to bouts of melancholy ("Everything refreshes, and I wither, and I grow older and not better"). He also confessed to a powerful temptation to suicide. At about the time of the composition of *Biathanatos* he confided to Sir Henry Goodyer, "I have often suspected myself to be overtaken . . . with a desire of the next life." He draws the same link, as R. C. Bald notes, in *Biathanatos:* "I haue often such a sickly inclination." Behind *Biathanatos,* then, is the same acceptance of vagrant impulses of the mind that is discovered in the *Songs and Sonets,* driven here to deeper intellectual purpose. Particularly valuable is Donne's compulsion to trace his disposition to its origins: "I had my first breeding, and conversation with Men of a suppressed and afflicted Religion, accustomed to the despite of death, and hungry of an imagin'd Martyrdome." In the end Donne's refusal to relinquish personal truth leads (as, much later, Sigmund Freud's similar refusal would also lead) to a broader understanding of the human condition: "euen the purest times did cherish in men this desire of Death."

To treat *Biathanatos* with overscholarly detachment or as outrageously flippant robs the work of the very features that make it a remarkable manifestation of Donne's mind. Faced with suicidal temptations and drawn to seductive arguments concerning martyrdom (themes presiding in "The Canonization," as well), Donne confronted the issues squarely, probing into the sources of the temptation and subjecting them to the severest analysis. Nor was it possible to conduct that analysis without awareness of danger. However sincere, an extended defense of suicide was more than simply risky for a man of tainted reputation; and Donne determined to drive the matter to the proof "that this Act may be free, not onely from those enormous degrees of Sinne, but from all." He knew that if the work circulated it could only result in charges of heresy; *Biathanatos* was, nonetheless, a work he had to write. Nor did he compromise the integrity of the effort by destroying it: he refused to burn the manuscript, but only a few friends were permitted to see it. *Biathanatos* thus reaffirms the passionate declaration of *Satyre 3:* "Keepe the'truth which thou hast

found." Donne was by nature (like Michel de Montaigne) a private rather than a public thinker: truths, he found, often could not be voiced in the public arena.

The ruthless self-scrutiny of *Biathanatos* reappears in the tortured *Holy Sonnets,* the majority of which are generally believed to have been written around 1609. Coupled with *Biathanatos,* these celebrated poems further the impression of a man gripped by terrifying thoughts. "May not I accuse, and condemne my selfe to my selfe?" he cried out in *Biathanatos.* In the *Holy Sonnets* he condemns himself before God: "Oh my blacke Soule! . . . Thou'art like a pilgrim, which abroad hath done / Treason"; "Reason your viceroy in mee, mee should defend, / But is captiv'd, and proves weake or untrue." He finds himself desiring God but of the devil's party. He lacks a sense of election: "Oh I shall soone despaire, when I doe see / That thou lov'st mankind well, yet wilt not chuse me, / And Satan hates mee, yet is loth to lose me." The tempestuous emotions lead to a violent quest for resolutions: "Take mee to you, imprison mee, for I / Except you'enthrall mee, never shall be free, / Nor ever chast, except you ravish mee." There are good reasons to see the poems as evidence of a supreme personal struggle, possibly related to attempts to discover a new grounding for his faith — efforts involving a direct confrontation with Calvinist theology.

Pseudo-Martyr, Donne's first published work in prose, must have been composed concurrently with some of the *Holy Sonnets.* Completed late in 1609 and appearing early the following year, it is the least popular of his major writings. Yet the number of surviving copies demonstrates that the work enjoyed wide circulation at the time, and it was undoubtedly responsible for his subsequent advancement. It is designed to persuade English Catholics to subscribe to the Oath of Allegiance established by Parliament in the wake of the Gunpowder Plot and, hence, a defense of royal supremacy against claims of papal supremacy. On the one hand, as Simpson notes, the work follows naturally from *Biathanatos,* whose issues of martyrdom and self-murder are central to *Pseudo-Martyr,* as well; annotations in the two works reveal a reliance on the same notes. On the other hand, the work was a flagrant bid for royal favor: Donne dedicated it to the king, confessed that he hoped the work would attract James's attention, and rushed to present the king with a copy when the work was published. More important, although supporting the king's position, the central argument does not tally well with opinions voiced privately in Donne's letters.

Title page, engraved by Matthaus Merian II, for a posthumous collection of Donne's sermons

Donne's targets in *Pseudo-Martyr* are those within the English Catholic community who were advocating resistance to the oath and promising native Catholics a martyr's crown if resistance resulted in death. To counter such claims – which were being promulgated, in Donne's opinion, chiefly by Jesuits – he advances elaborate arguments contending that the pope possesses no authority over temporal monarchs, and that according to the most reliable authorities within the Catholic tradition itself, death resulting from resistance to a legitimate ruler fails to meet accepted criteria for martyrdom and, hence, can only be regarded as a form of self-murder. To make these points requires almost four hundred pages, and they are pages untouched by the wit that generally enlivens his productions. It won for Donne, however, the royal attention he sought as well as an M.A. from Oxford.

Pseudo-Martyr is pervaded by personal reminiscences, rendering it essential reading for every student of Donne. In no other work can one learn so much about Donne's experiences and feelings as a Catholic. He voices pride in his membership in a family noted for its willingness to sacrifice itself for the highest spiritual causes. He notes his presence at a secret meeting among Jesuits in the Tower of London and his presence at the execution of "Trayterous *Priests,*" events from his youth. But Donne rehearses his past, in part, to trace his painful journey from Catholicism to a Reformed faith: "I had a longer worke to doe than many other men; for I was first to blot out, certaine impressions of the Romane religion, and to wrastle both against the examples and against the reasons, by which some hold was taken; and some anticipations early layde vpon my conscience, both by Persons who by nature had a power and superiority ouer my will, and others who by their learning and good life, seem'd to me iustly to claime an interest for the guiding, and rectifying of mine vnderstanding in these matters."

Pseudo-Martyr thus lays bare some grounds for Donne's defection from the Catholic fold. Whatever his earlier hesitations, by late 1609 Donne was comfortable with the Reformation, convinced that "the Church hath recouered more health in one age, then she had lost in anie two." In the end he had been moved by evidence of grotesque corruptions in practice, scholarship, and doctrine. "Though truth and falshood bee / Neare twins," he had declared in *Satyre 3,* "yet truth a little elder is." Again and again in *Pseudo-Martyr* Donne demonstrates that positions advocated by the pope and his Jesuit defenders derive from late, corrupt doctrines and textual authorities. The brilliance of *Pseudo-Martyr* lies in its masterful deployment of the finest Catholic authorities to overturn the pope's position (a technique he shared with Morton).

What emerges with stark clarity is Donne's disgust with the papacy and the Jesuit order. He is offended by the papacy's imperial pretensions and by its steady aggrandizement of spiritual and temporal powers, a corrupt historical development alarmingly accelerated (in his eyes) by Jesuit polemics. He views with horror the process by which the papacy is placed beyond all limitation. He objects strenuously to the "transcendent Titles" assumed by current leaders in the Catholic church, especially the way in which "they giue all the names of Christ to the Pope." To Donne, "by the magnifying of the Bishoppe of Rome with these Titles, our religion degenerates into superstition." Theologically, Donne is outraged by the way in which allegiance to the pope displaces the experience of Christ's suffering and sacrifice upon the cross, the experience central to the *Holy Sonnets* and to his later theology.

Equally pernicious to Donne was the Jesuit insistence on "blind Obedience" to the pope. Donne viewed this doctrine as a violent perversion of the practices of the primitive church. As early as *Satyre 1* he had worried about sins against one's conscience; here he sees the problem in its severest form: "Nothing in the world is more spiritual and delicate, and tender then the conscience of a man." The Jesuit position can only lead to a wounding of the conscience, since "it is not allowed for a Martyrdome to witnes by our blood . . . except we be ready to seale with our blood contradictorie things, and incompatible for the time past: (since euidently the Popes haue taught contradictorie things) and for the time present, obscure and irreuealed things." *Pseudo-Martyr* produces massive evidence of corrupt authority, evidence that the Jesuit code requires an honorable believer to ignore. The conclusion is obvious: "blind Obedience" leads to further corruption, never to a return to purity.

However dry to twentieth-century readers, *Pseudo-Martyr* addressed writers and issues familiar to Donne's audience. It is impossible not to be impressed by the sweep of his learning; the bristling citations argue that he had indeed, as he claimed, "to the measure of my poore wit and iudgement, suruayed and digested the whole body of Diuinity, controuerted betweene ours and the Romane Church." Striking, too, is Donne's command of the ancient canons of the church and of the writings of the church fathers (a fluency apparent earlier in *Biathanatos*).

Hard on the heels of *Pseudo-Martyr* came *Conclave Ignati,* written in Latin in the latter part of 1610 and ready for purchase by the following February. Donne seems to have followed the work through the press, producing an English version, *Ignatius His Conclave,* shortly thereafter. It was, thus, composed at the same time that Donne made final revisions to *The Courtier's Library.* The works point to some of Donne's Continental sources. A vision of hell with Menippean and Dantean overtones (as was *Satyre 4*), *Ignatius His Conclave* is a reminder that Donne enjoyed Dante, as he did Rabelais, for the Italian poet's robust mixture of political, academic, and ecclesiastical satire, and that his notions of satire were as deeply influenced by late medieval and Renaissance masters as by ancient ones.

Walton's discredited story about the composition of *Pseudo-Martyr* — that it had been written in six weeks at the king's command — may apply instead to *Ignatius His Conclave,* which was clearly written quickly. More echoes have been found to the king's works in *Ignatius His Conclave,* for example, than in comparable works by others writing on the king's behalf. In addition, like *Pseudo-Martyr, Ignatius His Conclave* belongs to the controversy between the king and his Catholic adversaries over the issue of royal supremacy. But if the work had indeed been commanded by James, the king may have been prompted in that direction by Donne's attacks on the Jesuits in *Pseudo-Martyr.* Donne's principal target in *Ignatius His Conclave* was the king's chief opponent, the Jesuit Cardinal Robert Bellarmine.

Ignatius His Conclave gave Donne the opportunity to lash out at two of his favorite bêtes noires — the Jesuit order and life at court; his vision of hell is not of Dantean circles but of chambers within chambers, each of more private access, such as would be found in a Renaissance court. The narrator is swept "in an Extasie" to hell, where he discovers an inner sanctum, a "secret place" reserved by Satan for innovators, all vying for supremacy. Claimants for the post of Lucifer's assistant there include Nicolaus Copernicus, Ignatius of Loyola, Paracelsus, Niccolò Machiavelli, Christopher Columbus, and Philip Neri, the founder of the Oratorians. Each figure advances his claims, and the satire develops through the depiction of Ignatius's increasingly flamboyant and desperate efforts either to diminish others' achievements or to appropriate them for himself or members of his order. As a counterpoint Donne develops a delightful comic portrait of a frightened Satan, himself desperate to keep the monarchy of hell out of Ignatius's ambitious grasp.

Donne reveals considerable knowledge and understanding of Machiavelli, who provides the only serious challenge to Ignatius's aspirations. Donne offers his own translation of a passage from the *Discorsi* (1517), and *Ignatius His Conclave* indicates that unlike most of his contemporaries Donne was aware of Machiavelli's republican streak. *Ignatius His Conclave* is the last great flourish of Donne's interest in the new science. In addition to Copernicus, he refers to Johannes Kepler and to Galileo's *Siderus Nuncius,* which had appeared in Venice only a few months before. Donne's sympathy for much of the new science is evident in the weakness of the satire directed against such figures (Ignatius admits that the opinions of Copernicus "may very well be true"). The notable exception is Paracelsus (whose notions Donne adapted in his poetry), who comes in for abuse for his pompous manner.

The real targets of Donne's satiric anger are Ignatius of Loyola and various members of his order, whom he rightly views as the militant arm of the revolutionary Counter-Reformation. Donne had been building toward a diatribe against them for some time. The Jesuits were associated with satanic designs as early as the *Problem* "Why did the Devill reserve Jesuits for these latter times?" Donne is disgusted by the endless contention fomented by members of this order and by their dedication to violence, which he underscores throughout by reminding readers of Jesuit political assassinations. He is at equal pains to present Jesuits as willful distorters of tradition and truth. To pursue their violent ends, the Jesuits fabulate freely and wrench authorities to their purposes: "therefore they provide, that the *Canons* and *Histories* bee detorted to that opinion." Proud of his order's ingenuity in disposing of inconvenient texts, Ignatius boasts, "For so the truth be lost, it is no matter how." As in *Pseudo-Martyr,* Donne blames the popes and the Jesuits for

destroying the ancient faith. He is especially affronted at the influence of the Jesuits on the Council of Trent, for which he has Ignatius offer an uncharacteristic apology: "I must confesse, that the *fathers* of our *Order,* out of a youthfull fiercenesse, which made them dare and undertake any thing (for our *order* was scarce at yeares at that time) did amisse in inducing the *Councell* of *Trent* to establish certaine *Rules & Definitions,* from which it might not be lawfull to depart: for indeed there is no remedy, but that sometimes wee must depart from them." As in *Pseudo-Martyr* Donne accuses the Jesuits of forcing sincere believers into needless crises of conscience. He likewise attacks the Jesuit doctrine of equivocation, which destroys good-faith bonds of communication in society.

In its attacks on innovation, however, *Ignatius His Conclave* exposes the deep conservatism of Donne's worldview, which insists on the primacy of the authority of the past. The thinking represents Donne's mature stand, for he maintains similar positions in the sermons: God "does not call them from their calling, but he mends them in it. It is not an Innovation: God loves not innovations; Old doctrines, old disciplines, old words and forms of speech in his service, God loves best."

Ignatius His Conclave and *The Courtier's Library* serve as reminders, too, that Donne was a writer of Latin poetry and prose, much of which has not survived. One hears, for instance, of a set of Latin epigrams, now lost. Surviving are a fine Latin epistle to Goodyer, several Latin poems, and an elaborate Ciceronian address to the Convocation of the See of Canterbury, which Donne delivered as dean of St. Paul's in 1626. These works confirm that Donne had received a rigorous education in Latin and that he was conversant with the full range of Latinate styles. (He worries about "barbarisms" in his style in *Ignatius His Conclave* and comments throughout the sermons on the style of the church fathers.) Indeed, until late in his life Donne is often (as evidenced by *Conclave Ignati*) a more accomplished stylist in Latin than English prose. The early works in Latin also show that Donne's attention had been caught by the anti-Ciceronian movement and that he may well have been making a bid in *Conclave Ignati* to be recognized as a master of the Lipsian ("Attic") style. Here, again, he is found in the front lines of stylistic revolutions, if less accomplished in this arena than Francis Bacon.

Nowhere in *Conclave Ignati* or *Ignatius His Conclave* did he reveal his name, but his identity was soon known in court and academic circles, and the work earned, together with *Pseudo-Martyr,* the king's approbation. That favor, however, did not lead to the envisioned reward, for the king decided that Donne should become a clergyman.

A door had opened to Donne's future, but Donne refused to cross the threshold. This was not the first time such a course had been suggested: Morton's chaplain and Walton report independently that Morton had offered Donne employment in the church around 1607. Donne's resistance to this step makes charting his spiritual development difficult, yet much if not all of Donne's early religious poetry appears to follow on the heels of Morton's offer. The *Holy Sonnets,* moreover, seem to reflect a great spiritual crisis; some regard them as a meditative sequence concerning Donne's choice of vocation. Whatever the case, throughout this period Donne's prose as well as his religious poems advance positions central to his later vocation.

Donne fought for a long time against making his now-celebrated choice. Instead, the years following Morton's offer found him searching energetically for a suitable secular position. Nothing bore fruit, and the lack of clearly defined employment frayed Donne's nerves. "Our soul," he wrote to a friend in 1611, "is not sent hither, only to go back again, we have some errand to do here."

Donne was considerably agitated by the soul's pilgrimage through this life, and the soul becomes an increasing preoccupation in the verse preceding his entry into the ministry. Three of his finest poems — the two *Anniversaries,* written and published in 1611 and 1612, respectively, and "Goodfriday, 1613. Riding Westward" — reveal considerable concern over the orientation of his soul at the same time that they manifest a curious mixture of secular and sacred interests.

Subtitled *An Anatomie of the World* and *Of the Progres of the Soule,* respectively, the *Anniversaries* are the great works of Donne's middle period and two of his most eccentric ones. They are occasional in every sense: circumstantially, because the poems are funeral elegies on the death of the daughter of Donne's future patron Sir Robert Drury (and, hence, belong with the many products written by Donne in his quest for patronage). More important, the *Anniversaries* are occasional in the sense evoked by Donne in *Devotions upon Emergent Occasions* (1624): the death of a young woman (whom Donne had never met) offered an occasion to unfold a visionary statement. His imagination was in an unusual state of readiness, and he poured into the poems hard-earned learning and religious experience.

The reference to Dante in *Pseudo-Martyr* and Dantean resonances in *Ignatius His Conclave* are enlightening, for Donne attempts in the *Anniversaries* to express a comprehensive religious vision and to create a poetic space capable, like Dante's, of encompassing both the arena of sin and the sphere of glory and capable, too, of providing scope for the full range of his poetic voice, from satiric diatribe to sacred praise and celebration. As in Dante's works, each structural unit deals with a symbolic region. Unlike Dante, however, Donne refuses to evoke the regions of hell and purgatory. (In *Ignatius His Conclave,* following Reformed controversialists, Donne accused Catholic theologians of basing their notions of hell and purgatory on pagan fictions, refusing to grant them scriptural authority; in "A Litanie" he suppressed the customary references to souls in purgatory.) The symbolic regions of Donne's poems are the world here and hereafter, the worlds of Saint Augustine's *City of God.*

Donne thus takes an innocent virgin's death as an opportunity to analyze the nature of earthly life and to compare the conditions of that life with the nature of the life to come for those able (like her) to wend their way to heaven. The first poem in the two-part movement is "Hamlet," a dark meditation on the world as a region of universal death, decay, and (as in *Satyre 2*) fragmentation, eliciting from Donne the celebrated lament, "'Tis all in peeces, all cohaerence gone." The world is a region where the soul is in prison. And, like Hamlet in despair over the way in which "The dram of [ev'l] / Doth all the noble substance of a doubt / To his own scandal," Donne demands that we recollect how "a small lump of flesh could poison thus" through Original Sin. Behind the sardonic attacks on the world lies deep-seated contempt for the realm of the senses and for human dependence on them. The stance derives from the *contemptus mundi* tradition and is given fresh force through Donne's brilliance.

In Donne's eyes Elizabeth represents powers opposed to those conditions. Her death is more than the loss of a young woman; it represents some form of ultimate loss. But his presentation of Elizabeth confuses readers, for his praise of her and of her effect on the fallen world reaches hyperbolic extremes. Elizabeth's "name defin'd thee [the world], gave thee forme and frame"; she "did inanimate and fill / The world"; "though she could not transubstantiate / All states to gold, yet [she] guilded every state." These seem grotesquely overstated valuations to attach to a not-quite-fifteen-year-old virgin.

Donne is curiously uninterested, moreover, in Elizabeth as an individual; her importance for him

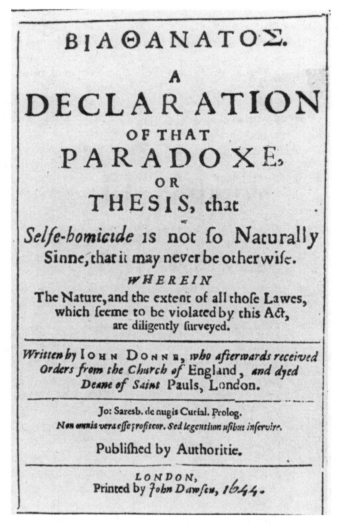

ΒΙΑΘΑΝΑΤΟΣ.

A

DECLARATION

OF THAT

PARADOXE,

OR

THESIS, that

Selfe-homicide is not so Naturally
Sinne, that it may never be otherwise.

WHEREIN

The Nature, and the extent of all those Lawes,
which seeme to be violated by this Act,
are diligently surveyed.

Written by IOHN DONNE, *who afterwards received
Orders from the Church of* England, *and dyed
Deane of Saint* Pauls, London.

Jo: Saresb. de nugis Curial. Prolog.
Non omnia vera esse profiteor. Sed legentium usibus inservire.

Published by Authoritie.

LONDON,
Printed by John Dawson, 1644.

*Title page for Donne's work on suicide. The date of publication has been written in by hand in a blank space left
by the printer, but it is incorrect: although the book was licensed on 20 September 1644, it was not published
until 1647 (Sotheby's auction catalogue, London, 27 September 1988).*

is symbolic. He was obviously hard-pressed to find a symbolic vehicle sufficient to express certain ranges of thinking and feeling. His style of praise is indebted to Italian poets of the early Renaissance, Dante and Petrarch in particular. (Joseph Hall notes in a prefatory poem that Elizabeth is similar to Petrarch's Laura.) At the same time, insofar as the *Anniversaries* are a revolutionary attempt to create a religious poetry embodying "rectified devotion," hence situated between Catholic and Protestant devotional patterns and ideologies, Elizabeth substitutes for the Virgin as an object of meditation and praise, as Donne's various addresses to her as "blessed maid" and "Immortal Mayd" imply. Jonson was offended, contending that the first *Anniversary* was "profane and full of Blasphemies; that he

told Mr. Donne, if it had been written of ye Virgin Marie, it had been something."

The *Anniversaries* clearly represent a strenuous experiment, one leading, as Barbara Kiefer Lewalski argues, to the incarnational theory of good and virtue in individual men and women evidenced in the sermons. The treatment of Elizabeth was also the culmination of repeated attempts in the verse letters to praise ideal women and the power of virtue. Donne's response to Jonson was that he described "the Idea of a Woman," the Platonic perfect form. Lewalski demonstrates how Donne celebrates in Elizabeth the image of God within the rectified human soul.

Donne also conducts, as Lewalski points out, a "metaphysical inquiry into the bases of human worth." Meditation on Elizabeth's "rich," innocent soul provides vital perspectives on the world, and by performing an anatomy on the world's body following her death — which is the world's own death, since she was the world's soul — the poet reveals how poor, crippled, ugly, and lacking in life the world truly is. Through Elizabeth herself, in contrast, Donne attempts to define and celebrate the presence of some cosmic, restorative energy capable of holding universal entropy at bay.

In *The Second Anniversarie* Donne analyzes the nature and fate of Elizabeth's soul. By following her soul's journey to heaven he educates himself and his readers in the "Art of knowing Heaven." As in *Satyre 3,* so in the *Anniversaries* Donne first arms his readers against their enemies then provides them with the knowledge they need. Elizabeth is a proper object of meditation because she is one "to whose person Paradise adhear'd." She is the utter opposite of Ignatius. Where that pride-driven figure fomented tumult and contention, Elizabeth

> made peace, for no peace is like this,
> That beauty'and chastity together kisse:
> Shee did high justice; for shee crucified
> Every first motion of rebellious pride.

Meditation on the fate of Elizabeth's soul, furthermore, allows Donne's readers to liberate themselves from fear of death by recognizing the benefits the soul receives from death. Donne leads his readers, in a formally organized meditation, to understand that they can reach heaven only through death and that, once there, souls abandon lower for higher modes of perfection, exchanging ignorance for knowledge, corrupt for perfect society, accidental for "essential" joys. Recognizing the joyous consequences of Elizabeth's "religious" death (replacing the first poem's emphasis on her "untimely" death), the reader gazes upward and turns from grief to celebration.

Elizabeth also expresses Donne's mature realization that he was not removed from but deeply involved with the rest of humanity. The ironic detachment characterizing his early work shifts in these middle years to an awareness of various forms of involvement and mutually sustaining activity. Donne's relation to Elizabeth is hence central to the spiritual action of the poem. The *Holy Sonnets* reveal how oppressively Donne experienced life in a sinful body ("like an usurpt towne"). Unable in the *Holy Sonnets* to free his soul from its mortal misery or to achieve a vision of God through his own powers, in the *Anniversaries* he experiences the thrilling liberation of the soul in its direct flight to heaven. Through a subtle manipulation

of pronouns, Donne's soul becomes fused with Elizabeth's; by forging a relationship with another soul, Donne frees his own from its customary mortal condition. The subsequent vision of the experience of redeemed souls after death points directly to the sermons, for Elizabeth's experience of growing joy ("This kind of joy doth every day admit / Degrees of grouth, but none of loosing it") belongs to the order of experience Donne will promise his congregations: "For heaven and salvation is not a Creation, but a Multiplication; it begins not when wee dye, but it increases and dilates itself infinitely then."

Into the study of the world and of the "progress" of a virtuous soul Donne inserted observations and autobiographical revelations. As in *Pseudo-Martyr,* he confesses to an unquenchable yearning for life in the next world, a desire that needs to be kept in check: "Thirst for that time, O my insatiate soule, / And serve thy thirst, with Gods safe-sealing Bowle." As in the *Holy Sonnets,* he is still conducting a frantic search for self-understanding and self-worth. "What hope have we to know our selves," he declaims, "when wee / Know not the least things, which for our use bee?" Donne's willingness to pay tribute to Elizabeth's soul becomes the mechanism confirming that he truly possesses a soul of his own: "(For who is sure he hath a soule, unlesse / It see, and Judge, and follow worthinesse, / And by Deedes praise it?)." But in the opening of the second poem the sense, found earlier in *Metempsychosis* and the *Holy Sonnets,* of a desperate quest for salvation in the face of impending disaster also appears: "Yet in this Deluge, grosse and generall, / Thou seest mee strive for life."

Donne is thus not free from anxieties in the *Anniversaries* (the late hymns establish that he was never able to purge himself of uncertainties and personal terrors); by the end of the poetic journey, however, he arrives at a more secure footing. He is "The Trumpet, at whose voice the people came." The self-image reveals that, like the *Holy Sonnets,* the *Anniversaries* were preparatory exercises to his final choice. Donne discovered, for one thing, that he could lay claim to a genuine religious vision and voice. In the writings of 1611–1612 he offered visions of heaven and hell in Dantean and prophetic terms, and the structures and central notions in these writings anticipate gestures, ideas, and structures found in his sermons.

At the same time the *Anniversaries* expose once more Donne's misgivings about involvement with the court and with the system of patronage underlying clerical advancement:

> what station
> Canst thou choose out, free from infection,

That wil nor give thee theirs, nor drinke in thine?
Shalt thou not finde a spungy slack Divine
Drinke and sucke in th'Instructions of Great men,
And for the word of God, vent them agen?
Are there not some Courts, (And then, no things bee
So like as Courts) which, in this let us see,
That wits and tongues of Libellars are weake,
Because they doe more ill, then these can speake?
The poyson'is gone through all.

The lines resonate shrilly when one recalls that Donne was steered toward the ministry by the king and by aristocratic patrons.

Donne's progress to the pulpit was ponderous and erratic, involving titanic struggles of conscience. The *Holy Sonnets* and "La Corona," written after Morton's offer, point to a spiritual paralysis and to Donne's fears about his own salvation, conditions that demanded resolution before he could accept a spiritual vocation.

Delineation of Donne's progress is, however, obscured by the absence of firm dates for many works. It seems that Donne was often divided against himself; he also had to confront unresolved issues stemming from his Catholic past. Anti-Protestant sentiment is still apparent in the final revisions of *The Courtier's Library*. Hence, even as late as 1610 or 1611, although a political conformist and weaned from the full Roman position, Donne may not have known to which ecclesiastical institution to entrust his fate.

Walton asserts that Donne had first surveyed "the Body of Divinity, as it was then controverted betwixt the *Reformed* and the *Roman Church*" as a student at Lincoln's Inn. Walton's testimony must always be handled gingerly, yet certain allusions in Donne's early works make his claim tenable. From roughly 1605 to 1612, however, Donne converted familiarity into an absolute mastery of contemporary divinity. He seems conversant with virtually everything written about and by the Jesuits, and he was reading such works, and works of divinity published on the Continent, promptly upon publication. Sullivan notes that Donne refers in *Biathanatos* to nearly all of the church fathers and that his "theological readings extended far beyond the works of controversialists." Donne's approach, however, was that of a canon lawyer, not yet that of a theologian.

In the same period, perhaps in consequence of Morton's urgings, Donne extended his knowledge of liturgical and devotional traditions. The *Holy Sonnets,* "La Corona," and "A Litanie" bear the impress of the study of Ignatian methods of meditation, of traditions surrounding the rosary, and of various litanies, including those of the medieval writers

Ratpertus and Notker Balbulus, that Donne encountered in a volume published in 1608. Donne had doubtless been familiar with some of these traditions in childhood, but they did not become a major creative source until this time.

Donne had thus acquired much of the requisite learning for his ministry – a detailed knowledge of church history, a solid comprehension of the chief points of controversy between the Roman and Reformed churches, an understanding of liturgical and devotional traditions, and a mastery of controversial technique – long before his final years of preparation, but those years witnessed further developments. Most important were Donne's discovery of a personal spiritual vision, triumphantly affirmed in the *Anniversaries,* and a concomitant acceptance of the English national church as a form of the visible church of Christ. Donne also ardently explored the word of God. He found a crucial passage in John 5:39: "Search the Scriptures, because in them ye hope to have eternall life." To do so, he turned to the biblical languages, studying Hebrew with one of the translators of the new English version of the Bible.

Donne explored the full scope of the Scriptures and various methods of interpreting them. The preliminary results of those studies appear in *Essayes in Divinity* (1651). Donne's son, who supervised the publication of the essays, insisted that they were "printed from an exact Copy, under the Authors own hand: and, that they were the voluntary sacrifices of severall hours, when he had many debates betwixt God and himself, whether he were worthy, and competently learned to enter into Holy Orders." This comment places the work prior to Donne's entry into the ministry in 1615, but *Essayes in Divinity* is as difficult to date as the *Holy Sonnets.* Links abound to other works; especially intriguing are sections showing an intimate connection to passages and themes in the *Anniversaries.* The overall tone convinced Simpson that the essays were composed later than *Ignatius His Conclave;* later scholars (on the basis of citations from the Geneva rather than the King James Bible) contend that the work predates 1611. Although some of its sources were not published until 1609, moreover, Helen Gardner is probably correct in her supposition that *Essayes in Divinity* rests on research conducted prior to 1605 (as do *Biathanatos* and *Pseudo-Martyr*). The prayers, in particular, differ in style from the essays themselves and in biographical content may point to Donne's time at Pyrford or his early years at Mitcham. Hence *Essayes in Divinity* may be a conflation of material written over many years.

The two sections of the work are devoted to meditations on the initial verses of Genesis and Exodus, respectively, and constitute Donne's first theological excursion in prose. He probes the Scriptures with the help of standard commentaries, the church fathers, and a range of esoteric writers. Donne doubtless shared Sir Thomas Browne's sense of the Bible being the most difficult book in his acquaintance, and the heterogeneous sources of the essays reveal his initial responses to difficulties in biblical textuality – specifically, a certain hesitation concerning the appropriate tools for unlocking the meanings of a text. He was drawn, like Browne, to esoteric writers in an attempt to make sense of these early books, and the essays are valuable as proof of Donne's interest throughout his middle years in numerological, cabalistic, and Neoplatonic material, sources that inform *Metempsychosis,* certain poems among the *Songs and Sonets* ("The Primerose" and "The Extasie"), the *Anniversaries,* and the later *Devotions upon Emergent Occasions,* as well.

The essays thus provide useful markers of Donne's concerns. As his theological interests deepen, esoteric sources disappear as principal resources for comprehending biblical texts. Instead, he turns increasingly to the church fathers and to the complex textuality of the Bible itself. Conte Giovanni Pico della Mirandola, for instance, appears repeatedly here but only once in the sermons; contrariwise, Donne refers to Saint Augustine modestly in the essays, but the saint appears in all but 5 of the surviving 160 sermons.

The essays also provide an important marker concerning Donne's abilities in prose. It is not entirely fair to judge a work lacking the author's final revisions; nonetheless, the prose of the essays is awkward, as is the prose in manuscript versions of some early sermons. Donne is not yet comfortable in prose, and in the end the essays are more successful in their design, which manifests the influence of Montaigne, than in their execution. Simpson deems the book the "kindest, the happiest, the least controversial of Donne's prose works." Nor did Donne despise it: he drew on the manuscript for sermons throughout his preaching career.

That Donne found his way to a genuine calling is beyond dispute. No one, however, would now accept Walton's depiction of a sharp Augustinian transformation in 1615, although Donne himself promoted such a view: "I date my life from my Ministery." Scholars judge Donne as less than secure in his calling then, maintaining that the transformation Walton describes did not occur until after the death of Donne's wife in 1617. Of more

significance than Donne's shaky beginnings are further factors behind Donne's reluctance to embrace a public ministry.

Unlike many of his countrymen Donne did not envision theological problems in national terms. From the beginning he sought religious truth amid the contentions produced by the international clash of the Reformation and the Counter-Reformation. Along the way he found much to respect in the writings and activities of each of the warring parties, and much to deplore; perhaps too much of both, for by 1609 he could assign superior authority to none: "You know I never fettered nor imprisoned the word Religion," he confided to his closest friend, Goodyer, never "immuring it in a *Rome,* or a *Wittemberg,* or a *Geneva;* they are all virtuall beams of one Sun." In the essays he maintains, "So Synagogue and Church is the same thing and of the Church, *Roman* and *Reformed,* and all other distinctions of place, Discipline, or Person, but one Church, journying to one *Hierusalem,* and directed by one guide, Christ Jesus." "In all Christian professions," he wrote in an undated letter to Goodyer, probably in May or June 1609, "there is way to salvation." He added significantly, "The channels of Gods mercies run through both fields [Roman and Reformed]; and they are sister teats of his graces, yet both diseased and infected." He was distraught by the ignorance and shameless partisanship displayed by controversialists on all sides. He said in a 1609 letter to Goodyer that a book by a spokesman for the established church "hath refreshed, and given new justice to my ordinary complaint, That the Divines of these times, are become meer Advocates, as though Religion were a temporall inheritance; they plead for it with all sophistications, and illusions, and forgeries."

"Keepe the truth which thou hast found," he had declaimed; yet to profess God's word meant to speak from the pulpit of some established church, and Donne needed to do so without subscribing to ignorant partisanship. Never did he yield his conviction that the Roman church was a true church, although his own archbishop, George Abbot, railed against "that most *Damnable* and *Heretical Doctrine* of the *Church* of *Rome,* the Whore of *Babylon.*" Donne found his way to the national church, consequently, not quickly, but with some originality. In the church defined by Richard Hooker's charitable theology he discovered positions sympathetic to his own, and at the height of his career he would be able to assert confidently that "nearer to [God], and to the institutions of his Christ, can no Church, no not of the *Reformation,* be said to have come, then

Old St. Paul's Church, where Donne served as dean from November 1621 until his death. The church was destroyed in the Great Fire of 1666 and rebuilt by Sir Christopher Wren; it is now St. Paul's Cathedral (detail of an engraving from C. J. Visscher's View of London, *circa 1616).*

ours does." Again and again he manipulated traditions and ideas in ways calculated to defy easy assignment to one of the contesting parties, blending (as in "A Litanie" and the *Anniversaries*) the best of various traditions and permitting them to enrich each other. In shaping such a literary style and concomitant theology, Donne became one of the formative figures in developing the Anglican position as a mean between Reformed and Roman Catholic extremes.

Once committed to the priesthood, Donne blossomed, and the products of his ministry – particularly those of his final decade – possess a power and a spaciousness exceeding those of even his finest earlier achievements. In the prose sermon Donne arrived at the most capacious medium for his learning and ever-agitated imagination, and the words of Scripture freed the full powers of his poetic intelligence. His clerical career made the fullest public use of his training and talents, and the influence of his friends and the king clearly lay behind his meteoric advancement. Shortly after his ordination in January 1615 he became the king's chaplain; the next year he was made divinity reader at Lincoln's Inn; he served as a member of an official diplomatic party to the elector palatine in 1619; in 1621, a mere six years following his entry into the

priesthood, he became dean of St. Paul's. As dean Donne served as a justice of the peace and on many ecclesiastical courts and commissions that made use of his legal training.

Donne also became, like most of the leading clerics of his time, a pluralist. Unlike many of them, however, Donne held his benefices honorably by the standards of the time. He maintained a curate in each of his rural parishes and preached annually to the parishioners. In 1624 he became vicar of St. Dunstan's-in-the-West, not far from Lincoln's Inn in the heart of London's legal quarter, and he neglected no opportunity (so he claims in a letter of 15 January 1631 to Mrs. Ann Cokayne) to preach there. Among his auditors at St. Dunstan's was Walton.

Donne's lengthy preparation is no doubt partly responsible for the overall consistency in form and technique in the printed sermons. Subtle differences can be charted, but from beginning to end his sermons are more alike than not, and excellent sermons survive from every period of his ministry. Some of that uniformity may be owing to the late writing out of the printed sermons. With the notable exception of his final and best-known sermon, which he seems to have written out in advance, it is not known what Donne's sermons were like as he delivered them from the pulpit; he spoke either from memory or from notes, following the considerable preparation that is detailed by Walton in his memorable sketch. As printed, however, the sermons are largely products of the final half-dozen or so years of Donne's life, when his sermon style was fully formed.

His sermons generally shun controversy ("I am not curious in inquiry" is a typical comment). He leads listeners away from, or ignores, abstruse or contested points of theology ("impertinent and inextricable curiosities"), insisting – in a style far from simple – that the Bible delivers plainly all truths necessary for salvation. Donne's instinct was for elucidation, consolation, and celebration, operations leading the heart of the listener (and reader) to a love of God and desire for heaven.

Donne displays great virtuosity in expanding his chosen text into a full discourse. Like Lancelot Andrewes, he focuses on the specific words, generally dividing the text into discrete organizational units that are announced at the outset (and carefully noted in the margins of the original editions). The sermon then develops each of the designated units. He demonstrates considerable flexibility, however, in his methods of division and subdivision. He mastered the principal systems for dividing and developing a text – patristic, Scholastic, and Ramist – and turns to them freely. Donne thus exhibits in his sermons the same formal virtuosity and comprehensive command of form as in the *Satyres,* the *Paradoxes,* the *Songs and Sonets,* and the later *Devotions upon Emergent Occasions.* He does not favor the reductive, moralistic handling of Scripture promoted by Puritan preachers: behind Donne's choice of the established church lay a preference for its veneration of the church fathers and the leading Scholastics, with their attentiveness to the specific language of Scripture.

Donne's towering interest is in biblical language, which he explores with the acumen of a brilliant wordsmith. Indeed, his development as a preacher is linked to his response to biblical language and his deepening awareness of its plenitude: "there is an infinite sweetnesse, and infinite latitude in every Metaphor, in every elegancy of the Scripture." He rejected from the outset restricted treatments of the language (and hence the meanings) of the texts, spurning readings too dependent on a narrow context. Scripture was written, he argued, by the Holy Ghost, and hence must evince the clarity and coherence of God's larger designs. Meaning must not be determined by arbitrarily chosen scraps of Scripture: "GODS *whole Booke,* and not a fewe

mis-understood *Sentences* out of that Booke" should suggest the path of meaning. As a result Donne surveys the specific words of his text in light of the entire Bible. The few isolated words with which he begins branch out associatively to make the reader aware of broad systems of meaning within the Bible, and Donne's careful consideration of the handling of the text by authorities ranging from the church fathers to leading Reformers makes the reader conscious of the Christian community throughout time, not simply the church in the present moment of its existence – an effect extended by Donne's fondness for quoting from the Vulgate, so that the voice of the ancient church may be experienced directly.

The language of the Bible also settled Donne's quest for literary authority. So thoroughly did it gain his admiration that other literary achievements paled in comparison: "whatsoever hath justly delighted any man in any mans writings, is exceeded in the Scriptures"; "*David* is a better *Poet* than *Virgil.*" His sermons sparkle with perceptive comments on literary features of biblical texts. Donne pondered those texts for every manifestation of design and intention, discovering in this way the artistry of the Bible, its metaphoric and rhetorical density, so different from the unadorned style promulgated by Puritan clerics: " The Holy Ghost in penning the Scriptures delights himself, not only with a propriety, but with a delicacy and harmony, and melody of language; with height of Metaphors, and other figures, which may work greater impressions upon the Readers, and not with barbarous, or triviall, or market, or homely language." The poetic textures of the Bible, in turn, released and sanctioned his own poetic energies. His sermons exhibit rich figural and metaphoric play, amplifying and, at times, contextualizing elements of the biblical text itself. Entire sermons are constructed on metaphors derived from the biblical text.

Donne's sermons at St. Paul's on Christmas, Candlemas, and Easter display the full sweep of his commanding poetic style. For Easter Day 1628, for example, Donne chose a text by Saint Paul on the change in sight that will occur at the end of time: "For now we see through a glass darkly, but then face to face." In this text light is nowhere mentioned, however implicit the idea may be. Donne's sermon, however, is a paean to light; it is flooded with scores of references to light, including derivatives such as *enlighten.* In this fashion the sermons become extraordinarily energetic, Donne's language melding with that of the Bible in verbal structures of exceeding complexity. The sermons are as meticulously constructed as his finest poems.

Donne's purpose, however, as Walton understood, was to win people away from sin and place them on the pathway to salvation and a love of God: "a Preacher in earnest; weeping sometimes for his Auditory, sometimes with them: always preaching to himself, like an Angel from a cloud, but in none; carrying some, as St. *Paul* was, to Heaven in holy raptures, and inticing others by a Sacred Art and Courtship to amend their lives." Donne's are thus highly participative sermons, designed to lead his hearers to a direct knowledge of God and to stir them to desire a place in God's kingdom. Meticulous exposition of Scripture is intended to encourage the listener to "draw the Scriptures to thine own heart, and to thine own actions, and thou shalt finde it made for that." By searching the Scriptures the individual discovers the personal relevance of God's word, finds "the *histories* to be *examples* to me, all the *prophecies* to induce a Saviour for *me,* all the *Gospell* to apply Christ Jesus to *me.*"

Donne's early fascination with the anxieties and exaltations of the amorous mind becomes in the sermons a fascination with the burdens and ecstasies of the religious mind; and as in the poetry, his power lies in his extraordinary ability to penetrate and dramatically render the pressures experienced by a particular personality: "I aske not *Mary Magdalen,* whether lightnesse were not a burden; (for sin is certainly, sensibly a burden) But I aske *Susanna* whether even chast beauty were not a burden to her; And I aske *Ioseph* whether personall comelinesse were not a burden to him." Donne can out-Puritan a Puritan, moreover, in devastating analyses of the intricacies of sin: "I throw my selfe downe in my Chamber, and I call in, and invite God, and his Angels thither, and when they are there, I neglect God and his Angels, for the noise of a Flie, for the ratling of a Coach, for the whining of a doore. . . . Sometimes I finde that I had forgot what I was about, but when I began to forget it, I cannot tell. A memory of yesterdays pleasures, a feare of to morrows dangers, a straw under my knee, a noise in mine eare, a light in mine eye, an any thing, a nothing, a fancy, a Chimera in my braine, troubles me in my prayer. So certainely is there nothing, nothing in spirituall things, perfect in this world." The preacher thus serves as the trumpet of God (one of Donne's favorite images) to awaken a consciousness of sin.

But the wake-up call leads to a sweeter music: "there is alwayes roome for *Repentence,* and *Mercie,*" if with sober warnings attached — "but his Judge-

ments and Executions are *certaine,* there is no room for *Presumption* nor *Collusion.*" If Donne analyzes human sinfulness with fervor, he extends considerable comfort in return. John Carey finds Donne to be fixated in the sermons on power; more characteristic is Donne's care to provide comfort for his fellow Christians, for his goal in sermon after sermon is to bring his reader or auditor to an active belief in God's presence, mercy, and ever-active love. Donne's God is not remote, and Donne repeatedly collapses space and categories to bring the human and divine into relationship. His God reaches out to all people: "There is but one; But this one God is such a tree, as hath divers boughs to shadow and refresh thee, divers branches to shed fruit upon thee, divers armes to spread out, and reach, and imbrace thee." Donne's God communicates directly: "God will speak unto me, in that voice, and in that way, which I am most delighted with, and hearken most to." God speaks in Scripture, he affirms, "as that he would be thought by thee to speake singularly to thy soule in particular."

Donne's attractiveness to congregations in his own time was doubtless connected to his rejection of the sterner notions of predestination and to his insistence that Christ's mission was universal: "Christ makes heaven all things to all men, that he might gaine all." "Gods mercy" is always present and "alwaies in season": "The aire is not so full of Moats, of Atomes, as the Church is of Mercies; . . . we cannot speak, we cannot sigh a prayer to God, but that that whole breath and aire is made of mercy." No dimension of space or time shall hinder God in his efforts to reach the soul; he will come to a contrite heart in defiance of all normal rhythms: *"to day if you will heare his voice,* to day he will heare you. . . . He can bring thy Summer out of Winter, though thou have no Spring." Donne is also firmly Christocentric: "Neither does any man know God, except he know him so, as God hath made himselfe known, that is, In Christ." He attempts to bind the listener to Christ: "teach thine own eyes to weep, thine own body to fulfil the sufferings of Christ"; "woe unto that single soul that is not maried to Christ."

Donne is acutely aware of his text and, equally, of his audience; he manipulates both elements to create a characteristic experience. From a sense of limit and immersion in the present, the reader moves through successive patterns of expansion toward a perception of plenitude. All is amplified in an attempt to make the reader feel not the constriction of doctrine but the fullness of God's creation and the reader's creative place within it.

Donne's sermons are ordered emotionally, as well, quite often moving from a negative to a celebratory mood. At the end of a sermon Donne commonly strives to lead his audience out of despair over their sins to a vision and expectation of their final joy and participation in the great community of believers at the end of time: "Joy then, and cheerfulnesse, is *sub praecepto,* it hath the nature of a commandment, and so he departs from a commandment, that departs and abandons himself into an inordinate sadness . . . despair thou not."

Equally spacious is Donne's sermonic style: students of the seventeenth-century sermon draw attention to his unusual stylistic reach. Generally composed in an elevated style, Donne's sermons nevertheless move through broad ranges of diction and tone. Dignified utterance jostles with the pungently colloquial, and common words are thrown together with a stunning array of rarefied terms, characteristically Latin in origin, such as *recidivation, exinanition, levigated,* and *inchoation.* The sermons possess a decided macaronic texture as English vies with Latin, Hebrew, and, on occasion, Greek.

Donne's early prose, like his early poetry, reacted against the copious rhetorical styles favored by Elizabethan writers, which led in prose to the construction of elaborate euphuistic or Ciceronian periods. At that time Donne flirted with the pointed, asymmetrical curt style, a style also favored by Bacon in his early essays and one associated with skeptical thinking. Donne continues to make use of the curt style in the sermons but as a counterfoil. In the sermons he comes to a compromise with Ciceronian style: he builds elaborate sentences but in the meditative, "loose" Senecan style, which seems ideally suited to convey the sense of a mind in motion. Donne's sentences, however, are longer and more rhythmically organized than is customary for that style, so that they recapture something of the harmoniousness and authoritativeness of Ciceronian utterance. Donne's manipulations of the "loose" style, moreover, are subversive. As Joan Webber observes, his sentences seem "shaped for exploration and recollections of known truths, rather than for exposition and persuasion."

In the winter of 1623 Donne fell victim to an outbreak of spotted fever. The instantaneous destruction of his health — "this minute I was well, and am ill, this minute. I am surpriz'd with a sodaine change, & alteration to worse, and can impute it to no cause," he says in *Devotions upon Emergent Occasions* — released the exceptional powers of his imagination to the full, as the combined force of danger and change did throughout his life. He recorded the daily progress of the disease, evincing an acute interest in the medical details. Donne converted the situation into another opportunity for rigorous self-scrutiny, and on recovering from the illness he worked up his notes into *Devotions upon Emergent Occasions,* his best-known work in prose.

The volume is indeed, as Bald avers, "unique in the annals of literature," but it is often misdescribed. Walton was first in this respect; he says that the book is "not unfitly . . . called a *Sacred Picture of Spiritual Extasies,*" suggesting that the volume as it exists is the volume as drafted during Donne's illness. Such is unlikely to be the case. In a letter written before his full recovery he confessed that he was diverting himself while convalescing by putting "the meditations had in my sicknesse, into some such order, as may minister some holy delight." The scattered, incomplete jottings scrawled during the illness were, hence, compacted and shaped by Donne's redoubtable literary talents. Each day's activities are divided into three sections, called meditations, expostulations, and prayers, and various verbal, numerological, and figural structures link the sections in intricate patterns of relationships.

The structural complexities of the devotions are not immediately apparent to modern readers: even the first twentieth-century editor of the work judged it to be a bag of inconsistencies. Students of devotional and meditative traditions, however, have revealed that the work was patterned along well-known lines. Nevertheless, Donne handles meditative form with the same bold originality he displays in composing other works. Behind the devotions, moreover, as behind the *Holy Sonnets* and the *Anniversaries,* lie years of familiarity with meditative and devotional techniques. Many perceive in the devotions a debt to the forms and patterns of Ignatian meditation; others have demonstrated that Ignatian materials provide an inadequate account of many features of Donne's work and that to understand his masterpiece one needs a working knowledge of the larger themes and patterns of the native devotional tradition, of Donne's sermons at large, of the Anglican doctrine of repentance (as espoused by writers such as Hooker), and of Donne's special interest in figural language in the Scriptures and in the writings of the church fathers. Donne drew broadly on these sources to produce a work that surged beyond the customary bounds of a meditative manual.

Readers bewildered by the structural and linguistic virtuosity of the work still find themselves caught up in the riveting drama of Donne's pilgrimage to grace. As in the *Holy Sonnets* Donne is at fever

*Donne in his shroud; effigy at St. Paul's Cathedral, sculpted by
Nicholas Stone in 1631*

pitch and fearful of his fate. The ferocity and immediate consequences of his illness fill him with dread: his quarantined solitude, along with the sickness, assures him that he is in a grievous, sinful condition and estranged from God. He confesses to Prince Charles in the dedication that the sickness was an "Image *of my* Humiliation," a sign of God's anger.

Matters are made more perplexing by his attempts in the expostulations to apply Scripture to his condition. Instead of reassuring messages the scriptural passages offer paradoxical indications of the working of God's will. Donne's pathway to salvation is thus fraught with pitfalls, and the journey is not a straightforward ascent following a fall into sin. There are innumerable backtrackings and backslidings, developments intensified by the cyclical return of the narrative to the meditations, with their relentless focus on the sinfulness and decay of the body.

The larger shaping of Donne's spiritual journey, however, adheres to Christian devotional traditions running from Saint Bernard to John Bun-

yan. Donne gradually discovers in his sickness not simply signs of his sin but also equal evidence of God's concern and mercy. Horror at sin leads to new resolve to abandon its ways and intense desire to live in God's ways. From the initial state of isolation in sin, Donne arrives at last at a perception of the necessary fellowship enjoyed by all humanity: "Perchance he for whom this *Bell* tolls, may be so ill, as that he knowes not it *tolls* for him; And perchance I may thinke my self so much better than I am, as that they who are about mee, and see my state, may have caused it to toll for me, and I know not that. The *Church* is *Catholike, universall,* so are her *Actions; All* that she does, belongs to *all.* When she *baptizes a child,* that action concernes mee . . . who bends not his *ear* to any *bell,* which upon any occasion rings? But who can remove it from that *bell,* which is passing a *peece of himself* out of this *world*? No Man is an *Island,* intire of it selfe; every man is a peece of the *Continent,* a part of the *maine;* if a *Clod* bee washed away by the *Sea, Europe* is the lesse, as well as if a *Promontorie* were, as well as if a *Mannor* of thy *friends,* or of *thine owne* were; Any Mans *death* diminishes *me,* because I am involved in *Mankinde*; And therefore never send to know for whom the *bell* tolls; It tolls for *thee*." This celebrated passage possesses greater power in context by virtue of the painful struggle to its insight. Nor is it the final stage of revelation: understanding of humanity's mutual involvement leads in the end to a perception of the plenitude of the world sustained by God. The journey, spread over twenty-three tripartite units, thus moves (as did the *Anniversaries*) from an intense focus on ruin and decay to a vision of the fullness and glory of God's ways and creation.

Donne expressed a desire to die in the pulpit, and he came close to obtaining his wish. As he lay, weakened from a bout of illness, at his daughter's house in January 1631 he received the customary request to preach before the king on the first Friday of Lent. Donne accepted the request despite his illness and created for the occasion his most notorious sermon, a meditation drawn from a verse from Psalm 68: "*And unto God the Lord belong the issues of death.*" The sermon is a dramatic and rhetorical tour de force, providing irrefutable witness that even at the edge of death Donne's literary skills remained intact. The sermon has a rich polyphonic structure, wherein the central text on death is subdivided and developed through a set of refrains not unlike those in the *Anniversaries,* interwoven with complicating metaphoric structures, some of his own design, some developed from scriptural passages.

Donne's emaciated appearance in the pulpit frightened his friends, but, according to Walton, after an uncertain start he proceeded to deliver one of his most dramatic sermons, in which he urged his audience to weep with him openly while contemplating Christ's Passion. The sermon's delivery exhausted Donne, and he returned to his bedchamber at the deanery. About four weeks later, on 31 March, he died. Walton gives a memorable account of his final days. Donne took solemn leave of his friends, many of whom received a special seal ring. Walton's claim that Donne busied himself with the writing of a hymn has been contested, but Donne had always been stimulated by sickness and the nearness of death, and he may well have toyed with a poem. He also posed for a portrait in a funeral shroud, contemplating that image as he waited to die. It was a characteristic action: throughout his life he had striven to capture his self-image at critical moments – entering Lincoln's Inn, becoming a minister, becoming dean of St. Paul's.

Donne's evolution into a remarkable preacher produced no fissure within his essential sensibility. There had always been present, even under the ban-

tering and licentiousness of the early poetry, a vein of intense seriousness, and, as the *Satyres* bear witness, from the outset Donne's writings reveal an earnest spirit searching for expression. His eccentric journey to the ministry did involve a momentous break with a religious tradition he held in great regard, but in the end one is struck more by profound continuities. The youthful bandying with paradox as a means of subverting tired commonplaces led finally to a rapt fascination with the complex character of God's universe and with the mysterious and paradoxical ways in which God works within it. It hardly seems accidental, moreover, that the poet who could rush through the dodges of a lover's mind would, in the words of an admiring contemporary, Sidney Godolphin, unravel in the pulpit "the thousand mazes of the hearts deceit." Those who appreciate religious discourse soon discover that Donne's sermons, or certain segments of them, can exert as haunting a hold on the imagination as do his secular poems. Readers of the sermons also find that Donne remained a student of love: Walton testifies that Donne wooed his congregations to lead holy lives; his sermons, in Richard E. Hughes's elegant phrase, became "festivals of love." His final sermon drives to an impassioned envisioning of Christ on the cross to force the reader to confront the paradox of an immortal God who elects to die out of love. Donne, the libertine amorist, became a rapt celebrant of the divine lover of humankind.

Letters:

Letters to Severall Persons of Honour, edited by John Donne, Jr. (London: Printed by James Flesher for Richard Marriot, 1651); facsimile edition, with introduction by M. Thomas Hester (Delmar, N.Y.: Scholars' Facsimiles & Reprints, 1977);

A Collection of Letters, Made by Sr Tobie Mathews Kt., edited by John Donne, Jr. (London: Printed for Henry Herringman, 1660);

Letters to Severall Persons of Honour by John Donne, edited by Charles Edmund Merrill, Jr. (New York: Sturgis & Walton, 1910).

Bibliographies:

Geoffrey Keynes, *A Bibliography of Dr. John Donne: Dean of St. Paul's,* fourth edition (Oxford: Clarendon Press, 1973);

John R. Roberts, *John Donne: An Annotated Bibliography of Modern Criticism, 1912–1967* (Columbia: University of Missouri Press, 1973);

Roberts, *John Donne: An Annotated Bibliography of Modern Criticism, 1968–1978* (Columbia: University of Missouri Press, 1982).

Biographies:

Izaak Walton, "The Life And Death Of Dr Donne, Late Deane Of St Pauls London," in Donne's *LXXX Sermons* (London: Printed for Richard Royston & Richard Marriot, 1640); revised and enlarged as *The Life of John Donne, Dr. in Divinity, and Late Dean of Saint Pavls Church London* (London: Printed by J. G. for Richard Marriot, 1658); revised in his *The Lives of Dr John Donne, Sir Henry Wotton, Mr Richard Hooker, Mr George Herbert* (London: Printed by Thomas Newcombe for Richard Marriot, 1670; revised edition, London: Printed by Thomas Roycroft for Richard Marriot , 1675);

Edmund Gosse, *The Life and Letters of John Donne*, 2 volumes (London: Heinemann, 1899);

R. C. Bald, *Donne & the Drurys* (Cambridge: Cambridge University Press, 1959);

Bald, *John Donne: A Life* (New York & Oxford: Clarendon Press, 1970);

Wilbur Applebaum, "Donne's Meeting with Kepler: A Previously Unknown Episode," *Philological Quarterly*, 50 (January 1971): 132–134;

Dennis Flynn, "Donne's Catholicism: I," *Recusant History*, 13 (April 1975): 1–17;

Flynn, "Donne's Catholicism: II," *Recusant History*, 13 (April 1976): 178–195;

Flynn, "Donne and the Ancient Catholic Nobility," *English Literary Renaissance*, 19 (Autumn 1989): 305–323.

References:

Don Cameron Allen, "Dean Donne Sets His Text," *English Literary History*, 10 (September 1943): 208–229;

Judith H. Anderson, "Life Lived and Life Written: Donne's Final Word or Last Character," *Huntington Library Quarterly*, 51 (Autumn 1988): 246–259;

Mary Arshagouni, "The Latin 'Stationes' in John Donne's *Devotions upon Emergent Occasions*," *Modern Philology*, 89 (November 1991): 196–210;

James S. Baumlin, *John Donne and the Rhetorics of Renaissance Discourse* (Columbia: University of Missouri Press, 1991);

John Carey, *John Donne: Life, Mind and Art* (New York: Oxford University Press, 1981);

Gale H. Carrithers, Jr., *Donne at Sermons: A Christian Existential World* (Albany: State University of New York Press, 1972);

John S. Chamberlin, *Increase and Multiply: Arts-of-Discourse Procedure in the Preaching of Donne* (Chapel Hill: University of North Carolina Press, 1976);

David Chanoff, "Donne's Anglicanism," *Recusant History*, 15 (May 1980): 154–167;

Charles Monroe Coffin, *John Donne and the New Philosophy* (New York: Columbia University Press, 1937);

Gerard H. Cox III, "Donne's *Devotions*: A Meditative Sequence on Repentance," *Harvard Theological Review*, 66 (July 1974): 331–351;

Gillian R. Evans, "John Donne and the Augustinian Paradox of Sin," *Review of English Studies*, 33 (February 1982): 1–22;

Peter Amadeus Fiore, ed., *Just So Much Honor: Essays Commemorating the Four-Hundredth Anniversary of the Birth of John Donne* (University Park: Pennsylvania State University Press, 1972);

Dennis Flynn, "Donne's *Ignatius His Conclave* and Other Libels on Robert Cecil," *John Donne Journal*, 6, no. 2 (1987): 163–183;

Flynn, "The Originals of Donne's Overburian Characters," *Bulletin of the New York Public Library*, 77 (Autumn 1973): 63–69;

Kate Gartner Frost, *Holy Delight: Typology, Numerology, and Autobiography in Donne's Devotions upon Emergent Occasions* (Princeton: Princeton University Press, 1990);

Helen Gardner, ed., *John Donne: A Collection of Critical Essays* (Englewood Cliffs, N.J.: Prentice-Hall, 1962);

William Gifford, "John Donne's Sermons on the 'Grand Days,'" *Huntington Library Quarterly*, 29 (May 1966): 235–244;

Gifford, "Time and Place in Donne's Sermons," *PMLA*, 82 (October 1967): 388–398;

Herbert J. C. Grierson, "John Donne and the '*Via Media*,'" *Modern Language Review*, 43 (July 1948): 305–314;

Michael L. Hall, "Searching and Not Finding: The Experience of Donne's *Essays in Divinity*," *Genre*, 14 (Winter 1981): 423–440;

M. Thomas Hester, *Kinde Pitty and Brave Scorne: John Donne's Satyres* (Durham, N.C.: Duke University Press, 1982);

Richard E. Hughes, *The Progress of the Soul: The Interior Career of John Donne* (New York: Morrow, 1968);

Itrat Husain, *The Dogmatic and Mystical Theology of John Donne* (London: S.P.C.K., 1938);

Robert S. Jackson, *John Donne's Christian Vocation* (Evanston, Ill.: Northwestern University Press, 1970);

John Klause, "The Montaigneity of Donne's *Metempsychosis*," in *Renaissance Genres: Essays on Theory, History, and Interpretation,* edited by Barbara Kiefer Lewalski (Cambridge, Mass.: Harvard University Press, 1986), pp. 418–443;

Eugene Korkowski, "Donne's *Ignatius* and Menippean Satire," *Studies in Philology,* 72 (October 1975): 419–438;

Robert Kreuger, "The Publication of John Donne's Sermons," *Review of English Studies,* 15 (May 1964): 151–160;

Clayton D. Lein, "Donne's 'The Storme': The Poem and the Tradition," *English Literary Renaissance,* 4 (Winter 1974): 137–163;

Lein, "Theme and Structure in Donne's *Satyre II,*" *Comparative Literature,* 32 (Spring 1980): 130–150;

J. B. Leishman, *The Monarch of Wit: An Analytical and Comparative Study of the Poetry of John Donne* (London: Hutchinson's University Library, 1951);

Barbara Kiefer Lewalski, *Donne's "Anniversaries" and the Poetry of Praise: The Creation of a Symbolic Mode* (Princeton: Princeton University Press, 1973);

A. E. Malloch, "The Definition of Sin in Donne's *Biathanatos,*" *Modern Language Notes,* 72 (May 1957): 332–335;

Malloch, "John Donne and the Casuists," *Studies in English Literature,* 2 (Winter 1962): 57–76;

Arthur F. Marotti, *John Donne: Coterie Poet* (Madison: University of Wisconsin Press, 1986);

Margaret Maurer, "The Poetical Familiarity of John Donne's Letters," *Genre,* 15 (Spring/Summer 1982): 183–202;

Janel M. Mueller, "Donne's Epic Venture in the *Metempsychosis,*" *Modern Philology,* 70 (November 1972): 109–137;

Mueller, "The Exegesis of Experience: Dean Donne's *Devotions upon Emergent Occasions,*" *Journal of English and Germanic Philology,* 67 (January 1968): 1–19;

William R. Mueller, *John Donne: Preacher* (Princeton: Princeton University Press, 1962);

David Novarr, *The Disinterred Muse: Donne's Texts and Contexts* (Ithaca, N.Y.: Cornell University Press, 1980);

Dennis Quinn, "Donne and the Wane of Wonder," *English Literary History,* 36 (December 1969): 626–647;

Quinn, "Donne's Christian Eloquence," *English Literary History,* 27 (December 1960): 276–297;

Quinn, "John Donne's Principles of Biblical Exegesis," *Journal of English and Germanic Philology,* 61 (April 1962): 313–329;

Mary Paton Ramsay, *Les Doctrines Médiévales chez Donne, le poète métaphysicien de l'Angleterre* (London: Humphrey Milford, 1917);

Anthony Raspa, "Theology and Poetry in Donne's *Conclave,*" *English Literary History,* 32 (December 1965): 478–489;

Raspa, "Time, History and Typology in John Donne's *Pseudo-Martyr,*" *Renaissance and Reformation,* 11 (Spring 1987): 175–183;

John R. Roberts, ed., *Essential Articles for the Study of John Donne's Poetry* (Hamden, Conn.: Archon, 1975);

Murray Roston, *The Soul of Wit: A Study of John Donne* (Oxford: Clarendon Press, 1974);

Lynn Veach Sadler, " 'Meanes Blesse': Donne's *Ignatius His Conclave,*" *CLA Journal,* 23 (June 1980): 438–450;

Winfried Schleiner, *The Imagery of John Donne's Sermons* (Providence, R.I.: Brown University Press, 1970);

Paul R. Sellin, *John Donne and "Calvinist" Views of Grace* (Amsterdam: Free University Press, 1984);

Sellin, *So Doth, So Is Religion: John Donne and Diplomatic Contexts in the Reformed Netherlands, 1619–1620* (Columbia: University of Missouri Press, 1988);

Jeanne M. Shami, "Donne on Discretion," *English Literary History,* 47 (Spring 1980): 48–66;

Shami, "Donne's Protestant Casuistry: Cases of Conscience in the *Sermons,*" *Studies in Philology,* 80 (Winter 1983): 53–66;

I. A. Shapiro, "John Donne's Sermon Notes," *Review of English Studies,* 30 (May 1979): 194; 31 (February 1980): 54–56;

Shapiro, "The Text of Donne's *Letters to Severall Persons,*" *Review of English Studies,* 7 (July 1931): 291–301;

Terry G. Sherwood, *Fulfilling the Circle: A Study of John Donne's Thought* (Toronto & Buffalo, N.Y.: University of Toronto Press, 1984);

Evelyn Mary Simpson, *A Study of the Prose Works of John Donne,* second edition (Oxford: Clarendon Press, 1948; reprinted, 1969);

Thomas O. Sloane, *Donne, Milton, and the End of Humanist Rhetoric* (Berkeley: University of California Press, 1985);

A. J. Smith, ed., *John Donne: Essays in Celebration* (London: Methuen, 1972);

M. Van Wyk Smith, "John Donne's *Metempsychosis*," *Review of English Studies,* 24 (February 1973): 17–25; (May 1973): 141–152;

John Sparrow, "John Donne and Contemporary Preachers," in *Essays & Studies by Members of the English Association,* in volume 16, edited by Grierson (Oxford: Clarendon Press, 1931), pp. 144–178;

Theodore Spencer, ed., *A Garland for John Donne, 1631–1931* (Cambridge, Mass.: Harvard University Press, 1931);

John Stachniewski, "John Donne: The Despair of the 'Holy Sonnets,' " *English Literary History,* 48 (Winter 1981): 677–705;

P. G. Stanwood, "John Donne's Sermon Notes," *Review of English Studies,* 29 (August 1978): 313–320;

Stanwood and Heather Ross Asals, eds., *John Donne and the Theology of Language* (Columbia: University of Missouri Press, 1986);

Arnold Stein, *John Donne's Lyrics: The Eloquence of Action* (Minneapolis: University of Minnesota Press, 1962);

Claude J. Summers and Ted-Larry Pebworth, eds., *The Eagle and the Dove: Reassessing John Donne* (Columbia: University of Missouri Press, 1986);

Edward W. Tayler, *Donne's Idea of a Woman: Structure and Meaning in 'The Anniversaries'* (New York: Columbia University Press, 1991);

Sister M. Geraldine Thompson, " 'Writs Canonicall': The High Word and the Humble in the Sermons of John Donne," in *Familiar Colloquy: Essays Presented to Arthur Edward Barker,* edited by Patricia Bruckmann (Ottawa: Oberon Press, 1978), pp. 55–67;

Herbert H. Umbach, "The Merit of the Metaphysical Style in Donne's Easter Sermons," *English Literary History,* 12 (June 1945): 108–129;

Thomas F. Van Laan, "John Donne's *Devotions* and the Jesuit Spiritual Exercises," *Studies in Philology,* 60 (April 1963): 191–202;

Joan Webber, *Contrary Music: The Prose Style of John Donne* (Madison: University of Wisconsin Press, 1963);

James E. Wellington, "The Litany in Cranmer and Donne," *Studies in Philology,* 68 (April 1971): 177–199.

Papers:

A few letters; some early prose works, including *Biathanatos;* and various sermons by John Donne survive in manuscript and are listed in critical editions and in Peter Beal, *Index to English Literary Manuscripts,* volume 1 (London: Bowker, 1980). *The Variorum Edition of the Poetry of John Donne,* under the editorship of Gary Stringer (forthcoming), promises to provide a complete textual and critical history of Donne's poems.

John Earle

(1600 or 1601 – 17 November 1665)

Bruce McIver

BOOK: *Micro-cosmographie. Or, A Peece of the World discovered; in Essayes and Characters,* anonymous (London: Printed by William Stansby for Edward Blount, 1628; revised and enlarged, London: Printed for Robert Allot, 1629; revised and augmented, London: Printed by R. Allde for Robert Allot, 1633).

Editions: *Microcosmography; or, A Piece of the World Discovered; in Essays and Characters,* edited by Philip Bliss (London: White & Cochrane, 1811);

Micro-Cosmographie; or, A Piece of the World Discovered in Essayes and Characters, edited by Gwendolen Murphy (Waltham Saint Lawrence: Golden Cockerel Press, 1928).

OTHER: Εἰκὼν βασιλικὴ: *Vel Imago regis Caroli,* translated into Latin by Earle (The Hague: Printed by Samuel Broun, 1649; London: Printed by J. Williams & F. Eglesfield, 1649).

John Earle — or Earles, as he signed his name — was an Anglican clergyman who is chiefly known for his *Micro-cosmographie. Or, A Peece of the World discovered; in Essayes and Characters* (1628), an influential book of "characters" — the short, witty descriptions of types of men and women that were popular in the second decade of the seventeenth century. *Micro-cosmographie* is one of the best collections of characters in English.

Earle was born in 1600 or 1601 in York, where his father, Thomas Earles, was registrar to the archbishop's court. In 1618 Earle entered Oxford University as a commoner at Christ Church; he received his B.A. degree in 1619 and was elected probationary fellow at Merton College. He received his M.A. in 1624 and his D.D. in 1640. In 1631 he served as proctor to the university. He was also chaplain to Philip, Earl of Pembroke, who at the time was chancellor of Oxford. In the 1630s Earle was part of the Great Tew Circle, a group of notables including Edward Hyde,

the future Earl of Clarendon; Thomas Hobbes; and Gilbert Sheldon who were invited by Lucius Cary, second Viscount Falkland, to spend time at his estate, Great Tew, in Oxfordshire. In 1641 Earle became tutor to the Prince of Wales, the future Charles II, and he spent sixteen years in exile with the royal family. At the Restoration he was appointed dean of Westminster, rising to become bishop of Worcester in 1662 and bishop of Salisbury in 1663. He died in November 1665 in Oxford, where he had gone with the king during the plague. He is buried near the high altar of Merton College Chapel, where a Latin monument commemorates his achievements.

The character as a literary genre was revived from the ancient Greek and instilled with fresh vigor with the appearance of Isaac Casaubon's Latin translation of the *Characters* (1592) of Theophrastus, Joseph Hall's *Characters of Vertues and Vices* (1608), and John Healey's English translation of Casaubon's translation (1616). There followed an eruption of more than one hundred books of characters; the most popular of them, Sir Thomas Overbury's *A Wife, Now a Widowe* (1614), went through seventeen editions by the end of the century. The character gave form to a new interest in the representation of people in all walks of life. Perhaps because of the accelerated rate of social change during the early seventeenth century, with diverse types of people emerging on the scene, there arose a fascination with the delineation of human personality. Though the genre did not lend itself to the depiction of specific individuals, striking similarities have been found between a few of Earle's characters and his friends. It is, however, for its contribution to the development of English prose as well as to its understanding of human nature that Earle's work is chiefly remembered.

The initial concern of the seventeenth-century character writers was, as in Hall's book, with moral character, with goodness and vice; but that concern shifted to the representation of character for its own sake in the work of Overbury and Earle. While Overbury and his followers stressed cleverness and sometimes employed outrageous comparisons in their characters, Earle mastered the form with brevity of expression and sharpness of wit. Earle's willingness to forgive and reluctance to condemn human folly and vice reflect the measured and well-balanced personality of the author, who was praised by his friends for his attractive and pleasing manners. Hyde said of him: "no man's company was more desired and more loved."

As the title suggests, *Micro-cosmographie* is a description of the "little world" of the human being. The subtitle says that a piece of this world has been discovered, just as pieces of the New World were then being discovered and mapped. There is no logic to the organization of the characters in Earle's book; they simply follow one another as the types occurred to their author. The characters, as Benjamin Boyce says, are "not . . . necessary, numbered bricks in a venerable social arch but merely . . . picturesque and interesting parts of the giddy social scene."

Micro-cosmographie, in the most complete edition (1633), consists of seventy-eight characters; beginning with the tender "A Child" and ending with the stark "A Suspicious or Jealous Man," they represent a diverse range of social and psychological types of men and women. Among Earle's characters of professions and trades are the Student, the Preacher, the Antiquarian, the Fiddler, the Constable, the Attorney, the Cook, and the Baker. His psychological types include the Modest Man, the Discontented Man, the Self-conceited Man, the Indolent Man, the Lascivious Man, the Sordid Man, the Blunt Man, the Drunkard, the Flatterer, the Rash Man, and the Staid Man. The She-Precise Hypocrite and the Handsome Hostess comprise Earle's only characters of women. Finally, his characters include four descriptions that are not of people but of places: Paul's Walk, a Tavern, a Bowle-alley, and a Prison.

There are three characters based on age, five on religion, seven on university life, two on rural life, fifteen on the humble and menial ranks, six on business or professional types, thirty on moral or psychological types, and four on social institutions. Some of the characters may have been based on figures in the plays of William Shakespeare: the Coward on Falstaff, the High Spirited Man on Coriolanus, and the Blunt Man on Kent. The few based on Earle's friends include the Pot Poet, who may represent aspects of the poet Edmund Waller, one of Earle's Great Tew Circle associates. But for

the most part Earle's characters are generalized types that call to the reader's mind many different individuals.

Unlike other character writers, Earle rarely condemns his subjects even when he is most critical of them, and few of their faults escape his eye. His style is witty but subtle; his tone is humorous and nonjudgmental. Rather than satirize, as many of the character writers did, Earle teases and playfully instructs. His Pretender to Learning is one who "might with less labor cure his ignorance, than hide it." Like many of Earle's subjects, the Pretender to Learning is more concerned with how he is perceived than with what he is: "He is tricked out in all the accoutrements of learning. . . . His table is spread wide with some Classic Folio, which is as constant to it as the carpet, and hath laid open in the same page this half year." The Pretender to Learning might well learn his cure from reading his own character; so could the She-Precise Hypocrite, who "is so taken up with faith, shee ha's no roome for Charity, and understands no good Workes, but what are wrought on the Sampler."

Some of Earle's characters investigate not how men and women perceive themselves but how they are perceived. No one wants to befriend the Poor Man, "whom men fall out with before-hand to prevent friendship. . . ." His "services [are] suspected, as handsome sharking, and tricks to get money." The Poor Man differs from "the beggerliest knaves," who "have art not to seem so"; the Poor Man "has not vizard enough to maske his vices, nor ornament enough to set forth his vertues: but both are naked and unhandsome. . . ." Whatever virtues the Poor Man has are rarely perceived; they "lie dead upon his hands, for want of matter to employ them, and at the best are not commended, but pittied, as vertues ill plac't and we say of him, 'Tis an honest man, but 'tis pitty: and yet those that call him so, will trust a knave before him." Earle's Poor Man is "the true speculation of the world, because all men shew to him in their plainest, and worst, as a man they have no plot on, by appearing good to: whereas rich men are entertaind with a more holy-day behaviour, and see onely the best we can dissemble."

Earle's general distrust of tradesmen and shopkeepers is to be expected in a Royalist clergyman, and his portraits of them tend to be the most stereotypical. His Cook is a drunkard, his Baker a heartless cheapskate "who thinks his Bread cast away when it is given to the poore." His Shopkeeper arouses the upper-class suspicion of the rising middle classes: "He is an arrogant commender of his owne things: for whatever he shewe you, is the best in the Towne, though the worst in his shop." The professions of medicine and law are also exposed to Earle's skepticism of human motives: his Surgeon "thinkes the Law against Duels, was made meerly to wound his Vocation," and his Attorney "first racks [his poor country Clients] soundly himself, and then delivers them to the Lawier for execution." Earle's criticisms, however, even of the characters he finds most repugnant, are usually tempered by a forgiving wit and humor.

Human error does not arouse Earle's anger; he is too forgiving a Christian humanist for that. Rather, he seeks to show people their own image; if doing so provides a cure, so much the better, but if it does not, nothing is really lost. Earle was well aware of humanity's unhappy lot, and none of his subjects escape it. Even his most praiseworthy character, the Staid Man, "is confident of nothing in futurity."

Perhaps the character that most resembles Earle himself is his Grave Divine, for whom "divinity is not the beginning, but the end of his studies." For his sermons Earle was praised as "a most eloquent and powerful preacher," but none of them survive. Evelyn said of one of them, "the discourse was so passionate that few could abstaine from teares," and of another, "I hardly in my whole life heard a more excellent discourse." Earle's sermons may have mirrored those of his Grave Divine: "His discourse there [in the Pulpit] is substance, not all Rethorique, and he utters more things then words. His speech is not help'd with inforce'd action, but the matter acts it selfe. Hee shoots all his meditations at one But: and beats upon his Text, not the Cushion, making his hearers, not the Pulpit groane." Earle's Grave Divine, following Hamlet's advice to the players, suits the word to the action and the action to the word. "His tongue preaches at fit times, and his conversation is the every dayes exercise," and "he counts it not profanenesse to bee polisht with humane reading...." This well-rounded clergyman gives offense only to the lawyer, "by whom he is spited for taking up quarrels."

Hyde asserted that Earle "was among [the] few exellent men, who never had, nor ever could have an enimy, but such a one who was an enimy to all learninge and virtue, and therefore would never make himself knowne." Izaak Walton gave Earle the highest praise by comparing him to Richard Hooker, whose *Of the Laws of Ecclesiastical Polity* (1593) Earle translated into Latin (the translation was never published); Walton wrote in *The Life of Mr. Rich. Hooker* (1665) that "since Hooker died, none have lived whom God hath blessed with more innocent wisdom, or sanctified learning, or a more pious, peaceable, primitive temper...." When Earle died in his lodgings at Oxford, one may imagine that he composed himself in the image of his own Grave Divine: "His death is the last Sermon, where in the Pulpit of his Bed, he instructs men to die by his example."

Bibliographies:

Gwendolen Murphy, *A Bibliography of English Character Books, 1608–1700* (Oxford: Bibliographical Society, 1925), pp. 35–46;

Peter Beal, *Index of English Literary Manuscripts,* volume 1 (London: Mansell, 1980), pp. 435–441.

Biography:

J. S. Darwin, "The Life of John Earle," Bachelor of Letters thesis, Oxford University, 1963.

References:

Benjamin Boyce, *The Theophrastan Character in England to 1642* (Cambridge, Mass.: Harvard University Press, 1947);

Bruce McIver, "John Earle: The Unwillingly Willing Author of Microcosmography," *English Studies,* 72, (June 1991): 219–229;

J. W. Smeed, *The Theophrastan Character: The History of a Literary Genre* (Oxford: Clarendon Press, 1985).

Papers:

John Earle materials are concentrated primarily in England at the Bodleian Library, Oxford, and at the British Library. Other holdings are in the United States at the Folger Shakespeare Library, Washington, D.C.; the Henry Huntington Memorial Library and Art Gallery, San Marino, California; Yale University; and Harvard University.

Eikon Basilike
(30 January 1649)

Elizabeth Skerpan
Southwest Texas State University

FIRST PUBLICATION: Εἰκὼν βασιλικὴ: *The Pourtraicture of his Sacred Maiestie in his Solitudes and Sufferings* (London: Printed for Richard Royston, 1648 [1649]).

Edition: *Eikon Basilike: The Portraicture of His Sacred Majesty in His Solitudes,* edited by Philip A. Knachel, Folger Documents of Tudor and Stuart Civilization (Ithaca, N.Y.: Cornell University Press for the Folger Shakespeare Library, 1966).

According to an old joke, Charles I was walking and talking half an hour after his head was cut off. The joke refers to the publication, on the day of Charles's execution, of the "King's Book," Εἰκὼν βασιλικὴ: [*Eikon Basilike*]: *The Pourtraicture of his Sacred Maiestie in his Solitudes and Sufferings* (1649), a work purportedly written by the king himself. Possibly the most successful piece of Royalist propaganda ever produced in England and enormously popular from the day of its publication, the *Eikon Basilike* (the title means "royal image") provoked fierce responses of loyalty or distaste until the early twentieth century. David Hume called it "the best prose composition, which at the time of its publication, was to be found in the English Language"; Thomas Carlyle called it "one of the paltriest pieces of vapid, shovel-hatted, clear-starched immaculate falsity and cant I have ever read." John Milton attacked it in *Eikonoklastes* (1649), and generations of royalists produced many popular editions of it, the last of which appeared in 1904. Today it merits study not only by Milton scholars but also by students of seventeenth-century rhetoric and of the history of the book as a cultural artifact. As much an event as an argument, the *Eikon Basilike* is one of the earliest examples of the power of the mass media.

Over and above its content, much of the initial power of the *Eikon Basilike* derived from the circumstances of its publication and its presumed authorship. From 1642 to 1648 England suffered two civil wars that shifted the balance of political power from the king to Parliament. From June 1646 the king was a prisoner, first of the Scots, then of the Parlia-

ment and the army. By mid November 1648 his captors had concluded that a negotiated peace with Charles would be impossible. On 6 December the parliamentary commander Thomas Pride, in Pride's Purge, ousted from the House of Commons any members likely to have monarchist sympathies, and the Council of Officers began to draft an ordinance for the king's trial. From 20 to 23 January 1649 Charles was tried for treason; found guilty, he was condemned to death. On 30 January he was beheaded on a public scaffold in front of the Banqueting Hall, which had been designed for the recreation of the Stuart monarchs.

The king's trial and execution had no precedent in European history, and the witnesses to the event had been raised on the rhetoric of the divine right of kings, a principle stoutly affirmed by both James I and Charles I. The *Eikon Basilike* thus appeared at a moment when people craved reassurance, when the familiar form of government was gone and no one knew what was to take its place. Although its authorship was questioned from the start, the *Eikon Basilike* presented itself literally as the "King's Book" – a work written by Charles himself, offering reflections and meditations on the events of the recent past. Breaking with long-established practices of royal iconography, the *Eikon Basilike* presents Charles as a sharer in his subjects' pain and offers testimony to his faith in God in language reminiscent of the narratives in the great Protestant propaganda tract of the sixteenth century, John Foxe's *Actes and Monuments of These Latter and Perillous Dayes, Touching Matters of the Church* (1563), known as *Foxe's Book of Martyrs*.

The earliest edition of the *Eikon Basilike* consists of a fold-out frontispiece, title page, table of contents, list of errata, and the text proper. Designed by William Marshall, the frontispiece depicts Charles, dressed in his royal robes, kneeling at a table and looking up at a window on the viewer's right. At his feet lies his crown, labeled "Vanitas" and "splendidam at Gravem" (splendid but heavy). He holds a crown of thorns bearing the words "Gratia" and "asperam at levem" (harsh but light). A

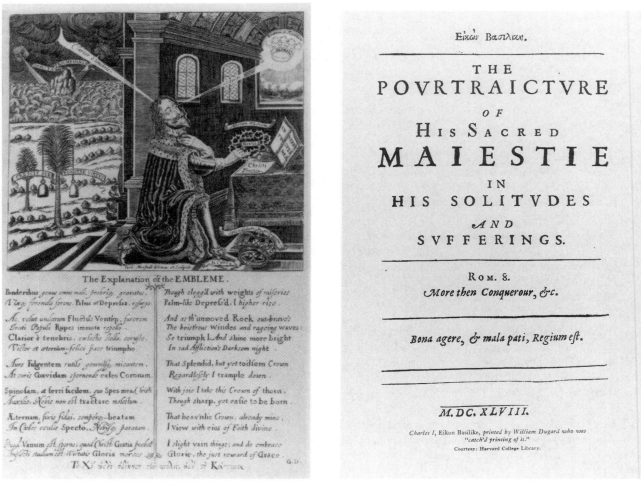

Frontispiece, engraved by William Marshall, and title page for Eikon Basilike

beam of light, labeled "coeli specto" (I contemplate heaven), issues from the king's eyes, directing his gaze to a martyr's crown in the sky. It is identified as "gloria" and "Beatam et Æternam" (blessed and eternal). The king's foot rests on a map marked "Mundi Calco" (I tread upon the world). On the table are a paper bearing the phrase "Christi Tracto" and a book open to a page that reads "verbo tuo spes mea" (in your word [is] my hope). To the left stands a tree with two weights suspended from its branches; its legend reads "crescit sub pondere virtus" (virtue grows under a burden). Behind the tree are waters and a mountain, labeled "immota triumphans" (triumphantly steadfast), and winds blowing to the king the words "clarior é tenebris" (more brightly from the darkness).

The frontispiece instructs readers that the work is the narrative of a Christian martyr purified by his suffering. The book on the table serves two functions: considered in conjunction with the paper labeled "Christi tracto" it suggests the Bible and urges readers to find hope in the Scriptures; as it is turned outward, away from the kneeling figure of Charles and toward the readers, the book may also represent the *Eikon Basilike* itself, offering words of comfort and hope to grieving subjects.

The text of the *Eikon Basilike* is divided into sections. Each of the first twenty-six sections describes, from the king's point of view, a significant moment in the events leading up to the civil wars or in the wars themselves, and each ends with a meditation and prayer on the subject, often echoing one of the penitential psalms. The twenty-seventh section is addressed to the Prince of Wales, and the work closes with the twenty-eighth section, "Meditations upon Death." The tone of the work may be gathered from a passage in chapter 11, "Upon the 19 Propositions first sent to the King; and more afterwards": "Some things here propounded to Me have been offered by Me; Others are easily granted;

King Charles I, the purported author of Eikon Basilike, *during his trial;*
painting by Edward Bower (Royal Academy of Arts, London)

The rest (I think) ought not to be obtruded upon Me, with the point of the Sword; nor urged with the injuries of a War; when I have already declared that I cannot yeild to them, without violating My Conscience; 'tis strange, there can be no method of peace, but by making warre upon My soule.... This Honour they doe Mee, to put Mee on the giving part, which is more princely and divine. They cannot ask more than I can give, may I but reserve to My self the Incommunicable Jewell of my Conscience; and not be forced to part with that, whose losse nothing can repaire or requite." The Charles of the *Eikon Basilike* is, thus, presented as a religious martyr; not politics but conscience determines his actions. His first-person narrative echoes the prison narratives of *Foxe's Book of Martyrs;* Charles becomes merely another Englishman suffering for his faith. He invites not awe but compassion.

The concluding address to the Prince of Wales further strongly distinguishes the *Eikon Basilike* from other Royalist tracts of 1649: it is the only one of these tracts to offer a positive program

for the future. The advice to the prince implicitly responds to all the accusations of Charles's opponents as well as to the reservations against the Stuart monarchy perhaps harbored by some readers of the book. The Prince of Wales should show moderation when he attains the throne, protecting his country's laws and traditions. By urging protection of subjects' religion, property, and liberty, the *Eikon Basilike* invokes the rhetoric of the parliamentary opposition of 1642. In the chaotic atmosphere of 1649, the language of the work assures readers that both their political and their religious aspirations will be served best by a return to monarchy.

The initial success of the *Eikon Basilike* lay in its ability to cast a traumatic and unprecedented event in familiar, and therefore reassuring, terms. The structure and imagery of the work allowed readers to assimilate the king's death into the narrative of almost a century of English political and religious struggle. And, like *Foxe's Book of Martyrs,* the *Eikon Basilike* took on a life of its own. In 1649 alone it went through thirty-five English editions. From the second edition onward, it underwent elaborations that created a powerful mythology around it. The edition printed by William Dugard on 15 March 1649, for example, adds a dedicatory poem, "Upon His Sacred Majesties incomparable EIKON BASILIKE"; four prayers, identified as "A Perfect Copie of Prayers Used By His Majesty in the time of His Sufferings: Delivered to Doctor Juxon, Bishop of London, immediately before His Death"; a letter from the Prince of Wales to his father; the text of remarks the king prepared but never delivered to the High Court of Justice, which sentenced him to death; three accounts of meetings of the king with two of his children while he was awaiting execution; an epitaph, beginning "So fall's that stately Cedar"; and a collection of brief, quotable phrases from the *Eikon Basilike* called "Apophthegmata Aurea," which, like the other additions, was also published separately. Through the additions, more than in the *Eikon Basilike* itself, readers are presented with the figure of Charles the martyr. The personal, familiar tone of the work enables readers to become witnesses to the king's final moments with his family and, in effect, to overhear his most private prayers. Thus, the early editions of the *Eikon Basilike* bring the image of Charles close to the reader, enabling the reader to identify with him and producing far more adulation for the king than did any other Royalist work.

Later editions perpetuated the martyrology with additional epitaphs, illustrations such as portraits of the king's children, and a poem – "Majesty in Misery" – attributed to the king and first added to the *Eikon Basilike* in 1681. There were translations into five languages, including John Earle's Latin version (1649), ordered by Charles II. Works inspired by the *Eikon Basilike* range from a poem explaining the frontispiece and a verse rendering of the text to John Wilson's *Psalterium Carolinum; The Devotions of his Sacred Majestie in his Solitudes and Sufferings, Rendred in Verse; Set to Musick for 3 Voices and an Organ, or Theorbo* (1657). From the Restoration until 1904 dedicated Royalists periodically republished the *Eikon Basilike* as testimony to their belief in the sacred nature of kingship.

From the start the *Eikon Basilike* was the focus of critical controversy. The earliest attack, the anonymous *Eikon Alethine: The Pourtraiture of Truths Most Sacred Majesty Truly Suffering, Though Not Solely*, appeared on 26 August 1649. Milton's *Eikonoklastes* followed on 6 October and was the first to identify one of the king's supposed prayers as a direct plagiarism of Sir Philip Sidney's *Arcadia* (1590). Defenders countered with such works as the anonymous *Eikon Episte: Or, the Faithfull Pourtraicture of a Loyall Subject,* published on 11 September 1649; the anonymous *The Princely Pellican: Royall Resolves Presented in Sundry Choice Observations, Extracted from His Majesties Divine Meditations, With Satisfactory Reasons to the Whole Kingdome, that His Sacred Person was the Onely Author of Them* (1649); and Joseph Jane's *Eikon Aklastos: The Image Unbroaken* (1651), a response to Milton.

The attribution of authorship to the king was generally accepted until 1690. In that year the Whig publisher of an edition of *Eikonoklastes* made public what became known as the Anglesey Memorandum, a copy by William Ashurst of a note written by Arthur Annesley, first Earl of Anglesey, and kept among Annesley's papers until he died in 1686. The note mentioned the contribution of the clergyman John Gauden to the production of the *Eikon Basilike*. From 1690 onward a partisan controversy over authorship occupied all consideration of the *Eikon Basilike,* with Tories defending the king and Whigs upholding Gauden. The debate was settled in 1950 with the publication of Francis Falconer Madan's authoritative bibliography, which argues for dual authorship: according to Madan, Gauden wrote the *Eikon Basilike* based on memoranda written by Charles.

The *Eikon Basilike* contributed its image to subsequent political pamphleteering. During the Restoration, Whig writers borrowed the title for works attacking Charles II and James II. This method of criticism reached its zenith in the *Eikon Basilike Deutera: The Pourtraicture of His Sacred Majesty King Charles II* (1694), a full-fledged parody of the *Eikon Basilike,* complete with a frontispiece echoing those both of the original and of the *Eikon Alethine.* In seventy-seven chapters, the *Eikon Basilike Deutera* copies the method of the original, presenting what purports to be the king's explanation of his own reign. And Tories employed the symbolism of the *Eikon Basilike* in their attacks on Whigs. In the fourth (1704) and subsequent editions of Edward Ward's *The Secret History of the Calves-Head Club* (1703), a clandestine republican club uses the book as part of its scandalous ritual: "After the Repast was over, one of their Elders presented an *Eikon Basilike,* which was with great solemnity Burn'd upon the Table, whilst the Anthems were Singing. After this, another produc'd *Milton's Defensio Populi Anglicani,* upon which all lay'd their Hands, and made a Protestation in form of an Oath, for ever to stand by, and mentain." Especially in Tory writing, defense of the king often included an attack on Milton. Thus, as late as January 1879, an anonymous writer

Engraving showing the execution of Charles I on 30 January 1649

in *Church Quarterly* observed of *Eikonoklastes,* "Every admirer of Milton must regret that he was the author of that work; the errors of argument, the imperfect knowledge which he displays of his subject, the supreme bad taste of insulting the fallen and departed King, have not even the excuse that they are the ill-considered outburst of spontaneous feeling." In the minds of many the *Eikon Basilike* was a sacred text, to be defended against critical examination by even the greatest writers.

In the twentieth century the revival of interest in Milton's prose has prompted significant, if brief, examination of the *Eikon Basilike* by such critics as Thomas N. Corns, Richard Helgerson, Jane Hiles, and David Loewenstein. Critical interest in political iconography and discourse has also led to analysis of the *Eikon Basilike* for its own sake. Nancy Klein Maguire and Lois Potter have situated the *Eikon Basilike* in the context of Royalist drama and poetry, while Elizabeth Skerpan investigates its rhetoric. Unburdened of the need to take sides politically, modern critics have been free to appreciate the work as an artful manipulation of culture, politics, and religion and as an early example of the deliberate use of mass media for popular appeal.

The *Eikon Basilike* is one of the most significant seventeenth-century English prose texts. Artistically, it is greatly surpassed by the polemics of Milton; intellectually, it poses no threat to the works of

Thomas Hobbes. But, measured by its initial reception and its continuing impact on popular political sentiment, the "King's Book" is a key document for understanding early modern language and culture and is a landmark in the history of the relationship between politics and media.

The most important collections of editions of the *Eikon Basilike* are at the British Library; the Bodleian Library, Oxford; and the University Library, Cambridge. Other libraries with significant holdings include those at Harvard University, Yale University, and the University of Illinois.

Bibliographies:

Samuel Keble, *An Account of the Several Impressions, or Editions of King Charles the Martyr's Most Excellent Book, Intituled, Eikon Basilike* (London, 1695);

Edward Almack, *A Bibliography of The King's Book, or Eikon Basilike* (London: Blades, East & Blades, 1896);

Sten Bodvar Liljegren, *Studies in Milton* (Lund, 1918; reprinted, New York: Haskell House, 1967), pp. 91–108;

Francis Falconer Madan, *A New Bibliography of the "Eikon Basilike,"* Oxford Bibliographical Society Publications, new series 3 (Oxford: Oxford University Press for Oxford Bibliographical Society, 1950).

References:

Thomas Carlyle, *Historical Sketches of Notable Persons and Events in the Reigns of James I. and Charles I.,* edited by Alexander Carlyle (London: Chapman & Hall / New York: Scribners, 1898);

Thomas N. Corns, "Imagery in Civil War Polemic: Milton, Overton and the Eikon Basilike," *Milton Quarterly,* 14 (March 1980): 1–6;

Richard Helgerson, "Milton Reads the King's Book: Print, Performance, and the Making of a Bourgeois Idol," *Criticism,* 29 (Winter 1987): 1–25;

Jane Hiles, "Milton's Royalist Reflex: The Failure of Argument and the Role of Dialogics in *Eikonoklastes,*" in *Spokesperson Milton: Voices in Contemporary Criticism,* edited by Charles W. Durham and Kristin Pruitt McColgan (Cranbury, N. J.: Susquehanna University Press, forthcoming 1995);

David Loewenstein, " 'Casting Down Imaginations': Milton as Iconoclast," *Criticism,* 31 (Summer 1989): 253–270;

Nancy Klein Maguire, "The Theatrical Mask/Masque of Politics: The Case of Charles I," *Journal of British Studies,* 28 (January 1989): 1–22;

Lois Potter, *Secret Rites and Secret Writing: Royalist Literature, 1641–1660* (Cambridge: Cambridge University Press, 1989);

Elizabeth Skerpan, *The Rhetoric of Politics in the English Revolution, 1642–1660* (Columbia: University of Missouri Press, 1992);

H. R. Trevor-Roper, "*Eikon Basilike:* The Problem of the King's Book," in his *Historical Essays* (London: Macmillan, 1957), pp. 211–220.

Owen Felltham

(1602? – 23 February 1668)

Frederick Waage
East Tennessee State University

See also the Felltham entry in *DLB 126: Seventeenth-Century British Nondramatic Poets, Second Series.*

BOOKS: *Resolves: Divine, Morall, Politicall* (London: Printed for Henry Seile, 1623); enlarged as *Resolves: A Duple Century one new an other of a second Edition* (London: Printed for Henry Seile, 1628); published as *Resolves, a duple century, ye 3d edition: with a large Alphabeticall Table there-vnto* (London: Printed by Felix Kyngston for Henry Seile, 1628); revised as *Resolves, Divine, Moral, Political: The eight Impression. With New and Severall Other Additions both in Prose, and Verse* (London: Printed by E. Cotes for Anne Seile, 1661);

Three Moneths Observations of the Low-Countries, Especially Holland. Containing a brief Description of the Country, Customes, Religions, Manners, and Dispositions of the People (London: Printed for William Ley, 1648 [pirated edition]); authorized and unabridged edition published as *A brief Character of the Low-Countries under the States. Being three weeks observation of the Vices and Vertues of the Inhabitants* (London: Printed for Henry Seile, 1652); enlarged as *Batavia: Or The Hollander displayed: In Brief Characters & Observations of the People & Country, The Government Of their State and Private Families, Their Virtues and Vices. Also, A Perfect Description of the People & Country of Scotland* (London: Printed for G. Widdowes, 1672).

The place and date of birth of Owen Felltham are uncertain, but he was probably born around 1602 as the second son of Thomas Felltham, a gentleman and landowner in the village of Mutford, Suffolk. It has been surmised that he received his creditable education, including thorough knowledge of Latin and classical literature, from a private tutor.

Felltham first enters the public record with his marriage to Mary Clopton of Melford, Suffolk, in London on 10 October 1621; their daughter Mary was born in August 1622. Barbara E. Bergquist believes that around this time Felltham was a merchant in London.

In the 1661 edition of his *Resolves, Divine, Morall, Politicall,* Felltham says that he wrote what became the first edition of the work when he was eighteen; but this claim may not be accurate, and there is no indication what — if any — interval occurred between the writing and the publication of the first edition in 1623. Other significant events that presumably occurred in the early 1620s were the deaths of Felltham's wife and daughter and the trip to the Netherlands that would result in the publication of his only other book.

The one hundred "resolves" in the 1623 edition are short, aphoristic commentaries on aspects of the three realms delineated by the title: divine, ethical, and political. As Ted-Larry Pebworth says, they concern in equal measure the private and public realms of middle-class English life: "the great squirearchical and merchant classes: in short, the work was for people very much like Felltham himself." The 1623 title page shows the author's handwriting from his heart, under the protective sanction of God and friends; columns and a foundation represent the stage of human life, whereon classical and Christian virtues play out the human condition by their presence or absence.

The notion of acting on the basis of meditated resolutions and the form — short prose pieces evolving associatively from an initial concept — derive from diverse literary traditions. The classical epigram developed, on the one hand, into the "character" and, on the other hand, into the more loosely conceived "meditation"; prototypes of these forms were provided for seventeenth-century English writers by Joseph Hall in his *Characters of Vertues and Vices* (1608) and his *Meditations and Vowes, Divine and Moral* (1606), respectively. The true originator of Felltham's form in the Renaissance was Michel de Montaigne, whose influence is shown in the personal, though not intimate, references in Felltham's pieces. Another tradition, of which too little has been made in regard to Felltham's work, is that of the Christian meditation; Pebworth notes that "The resolve and the vow, its close relative, developed out of the concluding statements of religious meditations, but they soon overshadowed the meditations to which they were attached." Akin to Felltham's resolves are the meditations in John Donne's *Devotions upon Emergent Occasions* (1624), which fuse secular and spiritual concerns. Felltham works toward a similar fusion of his three realms — the divine, the moral, and the political — achieving it most fully in the 1661 edition of the *Resolves*.

The 1623 collection, like its successors, seems to be arranged according to no particular principle — unless it be that of the constantly shifting mind, active in all three realms by turns. The 1623 resolves also vary widely in length. The main question addressed is how to live well as a Christian in this life — not how to be assured of salvation in the next. More specifically, Felltham is concerned with the acceptance of conditions that cannot be changed; he sees the origin of sins — and of their secular equivalents, violations of order — in futile acts of rebellion against what the world has dealt one. The title of Resolve 66, for example, is "Content[ment] Makes [One] Rich."

For the 1628 edition Felltham added a new century of resolves that is longer than the original one, and he placed the new century first. He also added more specific and secular subjects than those treated in the first edition, such as dreams, poetry, and war. Pebworth notes the importance of the name *excogitations* that Felltham gives these pieces: they are workings out by the mind of issues that do not lend themselves to simple resolution. Not only is the style in these new pieces looser and less "Senecan" but they also contain more quotations and topical allusions. Many of them are, as well, less specifically defined, providing the author with a broader field on which to play verbally; for example, Resolve 92 in the original century has the title "Of the Minde of man after the conquest of a strong Temptation"; but, with few exceptions, those of the new century follow the formula "Of Fate," "Of Censure," "Of Scandall," and so on.

The printer of the 1628 volume apologizes for its errata on the basis of the author's "absence," but one cannot know the nature of this absence. It was in this period that Felltham met not only some of the literary celebrities of his time, such as Ben Jonson and Thomas Randolph, but also Barnabas O'Brien, who in 1639 would succeed to his brother's title as earl of Thomond. Around 1628 Felltham became steward of O'Brien's manor in

Title page for the first edition of Owen Felltham's collection of aphorisms

Great Billing, Northamptonshire; he spent the rest of his life in the position, serving Barnabas's son Henry when he succeeded to the title in 1657. During the civil war the manor, although it was in hostile territory, became a favorite Royalist gathering place. The 1661 edition of the *Resolves* celebrates the Restoration.

For the 1661 edition Felltham made radical changes in his original 1623 resolves; he left the century added in the 1628 edition untouched, but because of what he calls their "young weaknesses," the earlier ones were rewritten, omitted, or substituted for throughout, and the revised ones were retitled. For example, the original fifth resolve, "Three things aggravate a Miserie," is omitted in 1661; the fourth, "Of Lyes, and Untruths," is revised and retitled "Of Truth and Lying"; and a new fifth resolve, "Of Preparing Against Death," is inserted. To Pebworth the key change in 1661 is "the expansion of aphorisms into statements that approach conversation." This loosening of style corresponds to a loosening of attitude, a more tolerant humanism. In number 51, "Against Compulsion," Felltham says, "The noblest weapon wherewith Man can conquer, is love"; in number 76, "Of Moderation," he says, "Nothing makes Greatness last, like the Moderate use of Authority"; in number 85, "Of Marriage and Single Life," he says, "A wise wife comprehends both sexes: she is a woman for her body, and she is a man within: for her soul is like her Husbands. . . . It is a Crown of blessings, when in one woman a man findeth both a wife and a friend." The 1661 edition also includes "Lusoria," a collection of Felltham's poems; a series of letters, some addressed to individuals, others to generic ladies; two biblical commentaries; and "Three Weeks Observation of the Low Countries, Especially Holland," a reprint of a work that was first officially published in 1652 as *A brief Character of the Low-Countries under the States.* In this sense the 1661 *Resolves* becomes Felltham's "collected works."

Felltham's only other independently printed work, *A brief Character of the Low-Countries under the States,* exists in diverse manuscript copies dating from the early 1630s. Filled with biting cultural commentary, it was pirated without the author's permission in 1648. Pebworth points out that Felltham had probably refused to print it because of the political amity between England and the Low Countries under the Stuarts, but "in 1652, when war broke out between England and Holland, a good market for anti-Dutch books was created in London."

"Characters" of other countries published in England in the seventeenth century were almost always critical, and Felltham's is no exception; but it excels in its colorful language and focuses on the "moral character" of the Dutch: "They are seldom deceived; for they trust nobody." They are boorish, materialistic, and warlike. Dutch houses reflect the national character: "every door seems studded with diamonds." Felltham observes that "The Soyl is all fat, though wanting the colour to shew it so; for indeed it is the buttock of the World, full of veines and bloud, but no bones in't." Some of his strongest political commentary comes in his condemnation of Dutch democracy, which he sees as subversive of the social order that mirrors the divinely governed world.

Felltham died on 23 February 1668 in the London house of O'Brien's widow. His will reveals more of his true individuality than all of his works; speaking of his tomb he says, "When the Jewell is gone wee use not to be solicitous about the Case." That he then authorizes thirty pounds to pay for the "Case" demonstrates how paradoxical this paragon of moderation could be.

Bibliographies:

Max Donald Cornu, "A Biography and Bibliography of Owen Felltham," Ph.D. dissertation, University of Washington, 1928;

Ted-Larry Pebworth, "An Annotated Bibliography of Owen Felltham," *Bulletin of the New York Public Library,* 79 (Winter 1976): 209–224.

Biographies:

Max Donald Cornu, "A Biography and Bibliography of Owen Felltham," Ph.D. dissertation, University of Washington, 1928;

Barbara E. Bergquist, "Owen Felltham: A Few Biographical Facts," *Notes and Queries,* new series 3 (May–June 1976): 233–235.

References:

Ted-Larry Pebworth, "An Anglican Family Worship Service of the Interregnum: A Canceled Early Text and a New Edition of Owen Felltham's 'A Form of Prayer,'" *English Literary Renaissance,* 16 (Winter 1986): 206–233;

Pebworth, *Owen Felltham* (Boston: Twayne, 1976);

Laurence Stapleton, "The Graces of the Muses: Felltham's *Resolves,*" in his *The Elected Circle: Studies in the Art of Prose* (Princeton: Princeton University Press, 1973), pp. 73–92;

Stanley Stewart, "Authorial Representation in Owen Felltham's *Resolves,*" *Cithara,* 28 (May 1989): 7–33.

Sir Robert Filmer

(circa 1586 – 30 May 1653)

Margaret J. M. Ezell

Texas A&M University

BOOKS: *Of the Blasphemie against the Holy Ghost,* anonymous, sometimes attributed to John Hales (London, 1646);

The Free-holders Grand Inqvest touching Our Soveraigne Lord the King and his Parliament, anonymous (London: Printed for Richard Royston, 1648);

The Anarchy of a Limited or Mixed Monarchy; Or, A Succinct Examination of the Fundamentals of Monarchy, Both in this and other Kingdoms, as Well about the Right of Power in Kings, as of the Originall or Naturall Liberty of the People: A Question Never yet Disputed, though Most Necessary in these Times, anonymous (London: Printed for Richard Royston, 1648);

The Necessity of the Absolute Power of all Kings; and in Particular, of the King of England, as Jean Bodin (London: Printed by Richard Royston, 1648); published, under Filmer's name, as *The Power of Kings, and in Particular of the King of England* (London: Printed by Walter Davis, 1680);

Observations concerning the Originall of Government, upon Mr. Hobs Leviathan, Mr. Milton against Salmasius, H. Grotius De Jure Belli, anonymous (London: Printed for Richard Royston, 1652);

Observations upon Aristotles Politiques, Touching Forms of Government. Together with Directions for Obedience to Governours in Dangerous and Doubtful Times, anonymous (London: Printed for Richard Royston, 1652);

An Advertisemnt to the jury-men of England, touching witches. Together with a Difference between an English and Hebrew Witch, anonymous (London: Printed by I. G. for Richard Royston, 1653);

Quaestio Quodlibetica, or, A discourse whether it may bee lawfull to take use for money, as R. F. (London: Printed by Humphrey Moseley, 1653);

Patriarcha; or, The Natural Power of Kings (London: Printed and sold by Walter Davis, 1680); revised as *Patriarcha; or, The Natural Power of Kings. 2nd edition, Corrected according to the Original Manuscript of the Author,* edited by Edmund Bohun (London: R. Chiswell, Gillyflower, G. Wells, 1685).

Editions: *Patriarcha and Other Political Works of Sir Robert Filmer,* edited by Peter Laslett (Oxford: Blackwell, 1949);

Patriarcha and Other Writings, edited by Johann P. Sommerville (Cambridge: Cambridge University Press, 1991).

OTHER: "In Praise of the Vertuous Wife," in Margaret J. M. Ezell, *The Patriarch's Wife: Literary Evidence and the History of the Family* (Chapel Hill: University of North Carolina Press, 1987), pp. 169–190.

While the life and writings of Sir Robert Filmer may be less familiar to students of seventeenth-century prose than those of his literary and political opponents, his literary career as a defender of absolute monarchy is significant for what it reveals not only about his participation in the political crises of his day but also about authorship during the early seventeenth century. Although he was well known and respected by historians, lawyers, and scholars of his time, his reputation as a polemicist of absolutism, both monarchical and domestic, was largely created by subsequent generations of opponents — in particular by John Locke, whose *Two Treatises of Government* (1690) was written thirty-six years after Filmer's death to refute the political position represented by Filmer's *Patriarcha* (1680). Filmer's analyses of absolute monarchy and its biblical origins form the subject matter of most of his printed texts; less well known but equally important are his manuscript pieces on the politics of the family and the institution of marriage.

Filmer is also an illuminating example of the dynamics of group or coterie manuscript circulation among amateur writers in the early and mid seventeenth century. While he did have several short tracts on political topics published anonymously toward the end of his life, his best-known work, *Patriarcha,* was not published until after his death. Several short pieces that remained in manuscript form until the twentieth century were written

Frontispiece, depicting King Charles II, and title page for Sir Robert Filmer's defense of the Divine Right of Kings
(Bodleian Library)

for circulation among Filmer's friends rather than for publication.

Filmer was born in East Sutton, Kent, around 1586, the eldest of eighteen children of Sir Edward Filmer and Elizabeth Argall Filmer. He matriculated at Trinity College, Cambridge in July 1604; he then studied law at Lincoln's Inn, having gained a special admission in January 1605. He was called to the bar in 1613. On 8 August 1618 he married Anne Heton, the daughter of the former bishop of Ely, Martin Heton, in Saint Leonard's Church, London. (Early biographers gave the year of their marriage as 1610, resulting in the mistaken belief that Filmer wed a child bride.)

The couple resided at the Porter's Lodge in Westminster during the early years of their marriage and had six of their eight children there. In January 1619 Filmer was knighted by James I at Newmarket. On the death of his father in 1639 Fil-

mer returned to the family residence at East Sutton Park and became the titular head of the large Filmer family, which included members residing in America.

During the 1630s and early 1640s Filmer was part of a lively intellectual and literary milieu that included historians, classical scholars, translators, poets, and dramatists. Peter Heylyn, the royal canon of Westminster, remembered Filmer warmly in his *Certamen Epistolare; or, The Latter Combate* (1659): "so affable was his conversation, his discourse so rational, his judgment so exact in most parts of learning and his affections to the Church so exemplary in him, that I never enjoyed a greater felicity in the company of any man living than I did in his." There is a good chance that Filmer met Henry King and Izaak Walton at this time through his relatives in Colchester. In addition to literary figures, during the time Filmer served on the magistrate's bench at Maidstone after 1635 his associates included Sir Edward Dering, Sir Roger Twysden, Sir Thomas Culpepper, and Sir John Marsham, described as an "Egyptologist and chronologer." Filmer and his friends exchanged essays on many topics; the majority of Filmer's writings were intended for this small audience, not for publication.

Filmer appears to have cooperated with the Long Parliament in 1640 and 1641, but the unrest had filtered down to the local level. Complaints were raised about Filmer; in her diary, now lost, Anne Filmer recorded that "one J. B[usher], the only neighbour or tenant that ever my husband had any suit with in all his lifetime . . . did most untruly inform some of the committee that my husband had hid some arms in the parish church." Although Filmer appears to have protested his neutrality, his eldest son, Edward, joined the king's forces in York. Meanwhile, Filmer faced increasing demands for money, arms, and support from the various local parliamentary committees. East Sutton Park was raided several times in 1643; according to a document in the family papers, "In October last [Filmer] was demanded by Sir John Sedley, Sir Humfrye Tufton and Captaine Skinner, what armes, horse, mony or plate he would lend or give to the Parlament. He answered his horse, armes and ammunition was already taken for the Parlament's service, that he had many other goods taken away and his house then set on fire, all without order that he knowes of or cause, but as he informed upon a mistake of his house for Sir Anthony Sentleger's house, who was then with the King." Finally, the aging Filmer, in poor health, was imprisoned for at least eighteen months in Leeds Castle.

During his imprisonment the estate was managed by his wife, who wrote repeatedly to the authorities on her husband's behalf. Filmer appears to have continued writing while in prison; "In Praise of the Vertuous Wife," which was not published until 1987, and the still-unpublished "Touching Marriag and Adultery" appear to date from that period. After his release sometime between 1645 and 1647 Filmer began having his short political treatises published. *The Necessity of the Absolute Power of all Kings* (1648) and *Observations concerning the Originall of Government* (1652) attack the writings of John Milton and Thomas Hobbes. The year before his death Filmer attended the trial of six witches in Maidstone; his final publication during his life, *An Advertisement to the jury-men of England, touching witches. Together with a Difference between an English and Hebrew Witch* (1653), was a criticism of such trials.

Filmer died on 30 May 1653 and was buried in East Sutton Park. His wife died in 1671. Their son Edward was rewarded for his loyalty to the crown; he had been gentleman of the Privy Chamber to Charles I and held the same position under Charles II. When Edward died unmarried the estate passed to Filmer's second son, Robert, who was created baronet in 1674, supposedly in acknowledgment of Filmer's sufferings during the war. The baronetcy continued for nine generations, ending in 1916.

Because of the continuity in the Filmer family's residence at East Sutton Park, historians and critics have had an unusually good opportunity to place Filmer's published work in the context of the preserved family papers. These papers also give insight into the practice of authorship in Filmer's circle and demonstrate the complex bibliographical problems coterie literary production can create. For example, in addition to Filmer's own writings, the papers include several complete manuscripts by his friends, including "A short view of King Henry the Third his Raigne written by Sir Rob. Cotton, 1614" and Ambrose Fisher's play *Pathomachia*. There are also many short manuscripts and fragments with no attributions attached, some in Filmer's hand, some in others'. As James Daly has pointed out, under such conditions the existence of a manuscript in Filmer's handwriting is no guarantee that he was the author. Nor does the publication history of Filmer's works clarify the authorship of these pieces: they were circulated, copied by others, amended or "improved" by the author or his friends, and sometimes replied to long before being printed. Some scholars have argued that *The Freeholders Grand Inquest* (1648) was actually written by the Oxford lawyer Sir Robert Holbourne, while *Of the Blasphemie against the Holy Ghost* (1646), often ascribed to John Hales, is now generally attributed to Filmer.

Dating Filmer's essays is also difficult. The date of composition of *Patriarcha* rests on questions of palaeography in the two manuscript versions and the relationship of its specific textual references to Filmer's other datable writings. Peter Laslett, Filmer's first modern editor, dated the Cambridge manuscript of *Patriarcha* from before the civil war, between 1635 and 1642; this view was challenged by others, who argued on textual grounds that the work was the final expression of his lifelong philosophy and was written during the final stages of the war. Bibliographers now place the writing of the Chicago manuscript before 1631 and support Laslett's dating of the Cambridge manuscript. All of Filmer's works show the intertextual relationship of coterie manuscript pieces; Filmer frequently quotes from his own writings, and he often updated earlier pieces. Because of these practices, Filmer's key ideas are expressed over and over in different formats.

What is clear is that, as the civil war approached, Filmer was actively engaged in analyzing the nature and origin of political authority and what constitutes evidence. His biographers have pointed out that Filmer's views on the nature of patriarchal power were hardly original or extreme for his generation and that most of his texts include summaries of his reading of other writers. When placed in the context of thought before the war — rather than read, as Locke read them, as statements from an apologist for a losing political position — Filmer's views on the nature of monarchical, domestic, and scriptural authority show a scrupulous care in distinguishing the features of each while asserting their structural similarity. Filmer's position on the nature and extent of patriarchal power was never as rigid or as all-encompassing as subsequent generations of commentators made it.

The work for which Filmer became best known, *Patriarcha,* was not published until many years after his death; when it finally appeared in 1680 it was read in an entirely different political context from the one in which it was created. There is some anecdotal evidence that Filmer refused requests by friends to have the piece published during the 1640s: Heylyn recorded that "had he been pleased to have suffered his excellent discourse called Patriarcha to appear in public, it would have given such satisfaction to all our great masters in the schools of polity that all other tractates in that kind had been found unnecessary. But he did not think fit while he was alive to gratify the nation in publishing that excellent piece." Instead, it came out not in the context of the civil war but during the debates leading to the Glorious Revolution, and through its use by commentators it became a document of that political crisis.

Filmer was strongly attacked by Whig writers supporting the Glorious Revolution. Algernon Sidney portrayed him as "a vicious wretch," "a Court flatterer" in the company of "Bawds, Whores, Buffoons, Players, Slaves, and other base people"; Locke described *Patriarcha* as "glib nonsense." Filmer's text became, as Laslett has pointed out, a voice from the past against which liberal writers and thinkers could define themselves.

When read as part of the earlier political crisis, however, as Laslett has observed, *Patriarcha* and Filmer's other political writings are less of an anatomy of a political system than a meditation on the origins of political power. Filmer makes heavy use

of scriptural evidence, based on his belief that the Bible contains the truth about the nature of the world and humanity's role in it. Whether he is analyzing the paternal nature of political authority, the differences between witches in the Scriptures and witches in seventeenth-century England, or the differences between polygamy practiced in the Old Testament and bigamy under English law, Filmer grounds his arguments in biblical precedent. With scrupulous attention to the details of individual cases, he attempts to clarify how modern social institutions such as monarchy, marriage, and usury conform to, even when they may seem to contradict, the paradigm presented in the Scriptures.

For example, in *Patriarcha* and in his manuscript piece on revolt Filmer argues that human society originated in one person — Adam, who was created first and singly. Hobbes's notion of "the Right of Nature," therefore, contradicts the story of the Creation. "The Right of Nature" cannot be "conceived without imagining a Company of men at the very first to have been all Created together without any dependency one of another," Filmer writes in *Observations concerning the Originall of Government,* as if like "Mushrooms (*fungorum more*) they all on a sudden were sprung out of the earth without any obligation one to another . . . the Scripture teaches us otherwise, that all men came by succession, and generation from one man: We must not deny the truth of the History of Creation." Children cannot "consent" to be governed by their parents; it is a natural obligation on both sides, and, he says in *Patriarcha,* "this subordination of children is the foundation of all regal authority, by the ordination of God himself." Through the practice of primogeniture, orderly succession was assured. For Filmer, before the Fall "directive power" would have been sufficient to ensure order; but after the Fall humanity's once-commendable desire for liberty would lead to anarchy if a strong "coercive power," the monarch, were not present to check it.

Though Filmer designates Adam as the original source of political power, he acknowledges that it is only through Eve that there is a body politic. In his manuscript essays "In Praise of the Vertuous Wife," "Touching Marriag and Adultery," and "Theology or Divinity" Filmer discusses the qualities necessary in a "good" wife. While he believes that the Scriptures show that God gave Eve to Adam "as a possession" and that "the prime duty" of the husband is to "teach his wife," Filmer does not, as some interpreters of his published works have thought, view the husband or king's authority to be absolute or a license for despotism: in "Theology or Divinity" he maintains, for example, that a modern husband does not have the authority, as a Roman one did, to "exercise upon [his wife] any corporall restreynt or correction" unless he is a magistrate. This careful distinction between the powers of the private individual from those of the public official is typical of Filmer.

In the modern family, Filmer says, the good wife is expected to play a large role in running the family government through administration of the household and, during times of war, the estate, as well as through her traditional care of the children. Filmer admits that the question of the wife's authority in modern times is perplexing, for it is "not servile, yett intangled with froward accidents." The bad wife is the one who, through ignorance or idleness, does not act as her husband's lieutenant. Bad wives, Filmer maintains, are generally created by poor education or ill-conceived marriage arrangements rather than by any innate flaws in the female nature. In general Filmer displays a more careful and flexible approach to issues of power and authority than do most of his commentators.

Filmer and his writings thus serve as a source of insight about mid-seventeenth-century practices of authorship, about the responses of the gentry to the civil war, and about how texts take on new lives with new generations of readers. Sending the manuscript on revolt to a friend, he wrote: "I presume to send you these ensuing considerations, mine only by abstract from others, wich I hope may fix your yet unsetled judgment in the great cause now disputed (not only with pens but Pistolls)." To subsequent generations the individual became himself an institution, Filmerism, which represented the position that had to be attacked to establish the next great cause.

Biographies:

Peter Laslett, "Sir Robert Filmer: The Man versus the Whig Myth," *William and Mary Quarterly,* third series 5 (October 1948): 523–546;

Bruce Filmer, *Filmer Family Notes* (London: Privately printed, 1984).

References:

James Daly, *Sir Robert Filmer and English Political Thought* (Toronto: University of Toronto Press, 1979);

Margaret J. M. Ezell, "Case Studies: Sir Robert Filmer, Mary More, and Robert Whitehall," in her *The Patriarch's Wife: Literary Evidence and the History of the Family* (Chapel Hill: University of North Carolina Press, 1987), pp. 127–160;

Robert Ford, "The Filmer Manuscripts: A Handlist," *Notes,* 34 (1978): 214–235;

Gordon J. Schochet, *Patriarchalism and Political Thought* (Oxford: Blackwell, 1975);

Schochet, "Sir Robert Filmer: Some New Bibliographical Discoveries," *Library,* fifth series 26 (June 1971): 135–160;

Quentin Skinner, "The Ideological Context of Hobbes's Political Thought," *Historical Journal,* 9 (1966): 286–317;

Johann P. Sommerville, "From Suarez to Filmer: A Reappraisal," *Historical Journal,* 25 (1982): 525–540;

Richard Tuck, "A New Date for Filmer's Patriarcha," *Historical Journal,* 29 (1986): 183–186;

Corinne Comstock Weston, "The Case for Sir Robert Holbourne Reasserted," *History of Political Thought,* 8 (Winter 1987): 435–460.

Papers:

Sir Robert Filmer's papers are held at the Record Office of the Kent County Council, Maidstone; they are referred to as the East Sutton Papers. Several of his essays exist in manuscript in the Harleian Collection in the British Library and the Tanner MSS at the Bodleian Library, Oxford. Peter Laslett owns the manuscripts for "In Praise of the Vertuous Wife" and "Theology or Divinity." The University of Cambridge has the bound presentation copy of the manuscript for *Patriarcha;* the University of Chicago possesses the other manuscript for the work.

Thomas Fuller

(1608 – 16 August 1661)

Florence Sandler
University of Puget Sound

BOOKS: *David's Hainous Sinne, Heartie Repentance, Heavie Punishment* (London: Printed by Thomas Cotes for John Bellamie, 1631);

The Historie of the Holy Warre (Cambridge: Printed by Thomas Buck, 1639);

Ioseph's Partie-Coloured Coat, Containing, a Comment on Part of the II. Chapter of I. Epistle of S. Paul to the Corinthians. Together with Severall Sermons (London: Printed by John Dawson for John Williams, 1640);

The Holy State (Cambridge: Printed by Roger Daniel for John Williams, 1642) – includes *The Profane State*;

A Fast Sermon Preached on Innocents Day (London: Printed by L. N. and R. C. for John Williams, 1642);

A Sermon Preached At The Collegiat Church of S. Peter in Westminster, on the 27. of March, being the day Of His Majesties Inauguration (London: Printed for John Williams, 1643);

A Sermon of Reformation, Preached at the Church of the Savoy, Last Fast Day, July 27, 1643 (London: Printed by T. B. for John Williams, 1643);

Truth Maintained, Or Positions Delivered in a Sermon at the Savoy: Since Traduced For Dangerovs: Now Asserted For Sound and Safe (Oxford [London?], 1643);

Jacobs Vow: A Sermon Preached before His Majesty and the Prince His Highnesse, at St. Maries in Oxford. The Tenth of May, 1644, Being the Day of Publique Fast (Oxford: Printed by Leonard Lichfield, 1644);

Good Thoughts in Bad Times, Consisting of Personall Meditations. Scripture Observations. Historicall Applications. Mixt Contemplations (Exeter: Printed for Thomas Hunt, 1645);

Feare of Losing the Old Light; or, a Sermon Preached in Exeter (London: Printed by T. H. for John Williams, 1646);

Andronicus, or, The Unfortunate Politician. Shewing, Sin: Slowly Punished. Right, Surely Rescued (London,

Printed by W. Wilson for John Williams, 1646);

The Cause and Cure of a Wounded Conscience (London: Printed for John Williams, 1647);

Good Thoughts in Worse Times: Consisting of Personall Meditations. Scripture Observations. Meditations on the Times. Meditations on All Kind of Prayers. Occasionall Meditations (London: Printed by W. W. for John Williams, 1647);

A Sermon of Assurance: Fourteene Yeares Agoe Preached in Cambridge, since in Other Places. Now by the Importunity of Friends Exposed to Publike View (London: Printed by J. D. for John Williams, 1647);

A Sermon of Contentment (London: Printed by J. D. for John Williams, 1648);

The Just Mans Funeral: Lately Delivered in a Sermon at Chelsey, before Several Persons of Honour and Worship (London: Printed by William Bentley for John Williams, 1649);

A Pisgah-Sight of Palestine and the Confines thereof, with the History of the Old and New Testament acted thereon (London: Printed by J. F. for John Williams, 1650);

A Comment on the Eleven First Verses of the Fourth Chapter of S. Matthew's Gospel, Concerning Christs Temptations (London: Printed by Ja: Cottrel for George Eversden, 1652);

Perfection and Peace: Delivered in a Sermon Preached in the Chapel of the Right Worshipful Sir Robert Cook at Drydens (London: Printed by Roger Norton for John Williams, 1653);

The Infants Advocate: Of Circumcision and Baptisme on Jewish Christian Children (London: Printed by R. Norton for J. Williams, 1653);

Two Sermons: The first, Comfort in Calamitie, teaching to Live well. The other, The Grand Assizes, minding to Dye well (London: Printed for G. and H. Eversden, 1654);

A Comment On Ruth (London: Printed for G. and H. Eversden, 1654);

Thomas Fuller; a portrait by Isaac Fuller (Berkeley Castle)

A Triple Reconciler, Stating the Controversies Whether: Ministers have an Exclusive power of Communicants from the Sacrament; Any persons Unordained may lawfully Preach; the Lords Prayer ought not to be used by all Christians (London: Printed by William Bentley for John Williams, 1654);

Life out of Death, a Sermon Preached at Chelsey, on the Recovery of an Honourable Person (London: Printed for John Williams, 1655);

The Church-History of Britain, from the Birth of Jesus Christ untill the Year M. DC. XLVIII. (London: Printed by John Williams, 1655);

A Collection of Sermons: The Best Employment, A Gift for God Alone, The True Penitent, The Best Act of Oblivion, Together with Notes upon Jonah (London: Printed for John Stafford, 1656);

The Best Name on Earth. Together with Severall Other Sermons Preached at S. Brides; and in Other Places (London: Printed by R. D. for John Stafford, 1657);

A Sermon Preached at St. Clement Danes (London: Printed by R. W., 1657);

The Appeal Of Iniured Innocence: Unto The Religious Learned and Ingenuous Reader. In a Controversie betwixt the Animadvertor Dr. Peter Heylyn And The Author Thomas Fuller (London: Printed by W. Godbid, sold by John Williams, 1659);

An Alarum to the Counties of England and Wales, with the Oath, of Abjuration, for Ever to Be Abjur'd. Or, The Sad Malady, and Sole Remedy of England. By a Lover of his Native Countrey, anonymous (London, 1660); reprinted in *A Happy Handfull, Or Green Hopes in the Blade* (London: Printed for John Williams, 1660);

Mixed Contemplations in Better Times (London: Printed by R. D. for John Williams, 1660);

A Panegyrick to His Majesty, On His Happy Return (London: Printed for John Playford, 1660);

Andronicus: A Tragedy. Impieties Long Successe, or Heavens Late Revenge, as Philanax, attributed to

Fuller (London: Printed by Richard Hall, 1661);

The History of the Worthies of England, edited by John Fuller (London: Printed by J.G.W.L. & W. G., 1662).

Editions: *Anglorum Speculum, Or The Worthies of England, in Church and State: Alphabetically Digested into the several Shires and Counties therein contained,* edited by "G. S." (London: Printed for Thomas Passinger, William Thackary, and John Wright, 1684);

Good Thoughts in Bad Times; and Good Thoughts in Worse Times, preface by James Hinton (Oxford: Printed by and for J. Bartlett & for William & Smith, and Baynes, London, 1810);

The History of the Worthies of England, 2 volumes, edited by John Nichols (London: Printed for F. C. & J. Rivington, Payne &c., 1811);

The Cause and Cure of a wounded Conscience; The Second Edition, with corrections and Improvements (London: Printed for C. Brown, 1812);

Selections from the Writings of Fuller and South, with Some Account of the Life and Character of the Former, edited by Arthur Broome (London: J. Newman, 1815);

Good Thoughts in Bad Times: Good Thoughts in Worse Times; Mixt Contemplations in Better Times (London: Pickering, 1830); enlarged as *Good Thoughts in Bad Times, Good Thoughts in Worse Times, Mixt Contemplations in Better Times; To Which Is Added The Cause and Cure of a Wounded Conscience,* preface by Arthur T. Russell (London: Pickering, 1841);

The Holy and Profane States: With Some Account of the Author and His Writings, edited by Alexander Young (Cambridge, Mass.: Hilliard & Brown, 1831; London: Swan Sonnenschein, 1884);

The History of the University of Cambridge from the Conquest to the Year 1634, edited with notes by Marmaduke Prickett and Thomas Wright (Cambridge: Printed at the University Press for J. & J. J. Deighton and T. Stevenson / London: John W. Parker, 1840);

The History of the Holy War (London: Pickering, 1840);

A History of the Worthies of England, 3 volumes, edited by P. Austin Nuttall (London: Thomas Tegg, 1840);

The History of the University of Cambridge, and of Waltham Abbey. With The Appeal of Injured Innocence, edited by James Nichols (London: Thomas Tegg, 1840);

The Holy State, and The Profane State, edited by Nichols (London: Thomas Tegg, 1841);

The Church History of Britain, from the Birth of Jesus Christ until the Year MDCXLVIII, 3 volumes, edited by Nichols (London: Thomas Tegg, 1842);

The Church History of Britain; from the Birth of Jesus Christ until the Year 1648, 6 volumes, edited by J. S. Brewer (Oxford: Oxford University Press, 1845);

Good Thoughts in Bad Times, and Other Papers (Boston: Ticknor & Fields, 1863);

Joseph's Party-Coloured Coat: A Comment on 1 Cor. XI., with several Sermons; and David's Heinous Sin, Hearty Repentance, Heavy Punishment: A Poem, edited by William Nichols (London: William Tegg, 1867);

A Comment on Ruth; and, Notes on Jonah, edited by William Nichols (London: William Tegg, 1868);

Poems and Translations in Verse (Including Fifty-nine Hitherto Unpublished Epigrams) of Thomas Fuller, D.D., and His Much-Wished Form of Prayer, edited by Alexander B. Grosart (Edinburgh: Nisbet, 1868);

A Pisgah Sight of Palestine and the Confines Thereof; with the History of the Old and New Testament Enacted Thereon (London: William Tegg, 1869);

The Collected Sermons of Thomas Fuller, 1631–1659, 2 volumes, edited by John Eglington Bailey, completed by William E. A. Axon (London: Unwin, 1891);

Wise Words and Quaint Conceits of Thomas Fuller, Selected and Arranged, with a Sketch of the Author's life, edited by Augustus Jessopp (Oxford: Clarendon Press, 1892);

The Marvellous Wisdom and Quaint Conceits of Thomas Fuller, D.D., Being "The Holy State" Somewhat Abridged and Set in Order by Adelaide L. J. Gosset. Whereunto is Added "The First Biography" of "The Doctor of Famous Memory" (London: Pickering & Chatto, 1893);

Fuller's Thoughts, edited by Alfred R. Waller (London: Richards, 1902);

Selections; with Essays by Charles Lamb, Leslie Stephen, &c., edited by E. K. Broadus (Oxford: Clarendon Press, 1928);

The Holy State and The Profane State, 2 volumes, edited by Maximilian Graff Walten (New York: Columbia University Press, 1938);

The Worthies of England, edited by John Freeman (London: Allen & Unwin, 1952);

Thoughts and Contemplations: Good Thoughts in Bad Times; Mixt Contemplations in Better Times, edited by James O. Wood (London: S.P.C.K., 1964).

The Savoy Chapel, London, where Fuller preached in 1642–1643

OTHER: *Genethliacum Illustrissimorum Principum Caroli & Mariae,* poem by Fuller (Cambridge, 1631);

Rex Redux, two poems by Fuller (Cambridge, 1633);

Abel Redevivus: Or, The Dead Yet Speaking. The Lives and Deaths of the Moderne Divines, preface and contributions by Fuller (London: Printed by Thomas Brundenell for John Stafford, 1651);

Richard Holdsworth, *The Valley of Vision,* preface by Fuller (London: Printed by M. S., 1651);

"On the Worthy Work of My Respected Friend Ed. Sparke, D.D.," in *Scintillula Altaris,* by Edward Sparke (London: Printed by T. Maxey for Richard Marriot, 1652); republished, with an additional poem, as "On My Worthy Friend Dr. Sparke's Learned Book" (1660);

"An Eccho," in *Ayres and Dialogues,* by Henry Lawes (London: Printed by T. H. for John Playford, 1653);

Ephemeris Parliamentaria, Or, A Faithfull Register of the Transactions in Parliament, edited by Fuller (London: Printed for John Williams & Francis Eglesfield, 1654); republished as *The Sovereigns Prerogative, and The Subjects Priviledge* (London: Printed for Martha Harrison, 1657);

"Life of Mr. Henry Smith," in *Sermons,* by Smith (London: Printed by T. Mabb for John Saywell, 1657);

John Spencer, ed., *KAINA KAI PALAIA, Things New and Old, Or, A Storehouse of Similes, Sentences, Allegories,* excerpts from Fuller's sermons and preface by Fuller (London: Printed by W. Wilson and J. Streater for John Spencer, 1658);

Pulpit Sparks, or Choice Forms of Prayer, By several Reverend and Godly Divines, prayer by Fuller (London: Printed for W. Gilbertson, 1659);

"A Short View and True Character of the Jews," in Flavius Josephus, *The Wonderful, and Most deplorable History of the Latter Times of the Jews,* edited by James Howell (London: John Stafford, 1662);

"Mr. Fuller's Observations of the Shires," Chiefly collected, and now first published, from the manuscripts of Archbishop Sancroft," in *Collectanea Curiosa, or Miscellaneous Tracts, relating to the history and antiquities of England and Ireland,* volume 1, edited by John Gutch (Oxford: Clarendon Press, 1781), pp. 222–226.

Prolific, scholarly, witty, and engaging, Thomas Fuller was a highly acclaimed writer in his own day and enjoyed a remarkable revival in the nineteenth century. A reexamination of Fuller's work in the late twentieth century is likely to start from the ideological construction involved in all his writing – not only his sermons and the essays but also the histories and biographies for which he has been chiefly renowned.

Born in June 1608 in the village of Aldwincle, Northamptonshire, Fuller was the first child of Thomas Fuller, the rector of St. Peter's parish, and Judith Davenant Fuller; he was the cousin of William Davenant, the poet laureate. In 1621 Fuller entered Queen's College, Cambridge, where his uncle John Davenant, the Lady Margaret Professor of Divinity, was president. Receiving his B.A. in 1625 and M.A. in 1628 but failing to receive a fellowship, he entered Sidney Sussex College as a fellow-commoner in 1629.

Fuller's first ecclesiastical appointment came in 1630, when he became curate of St. Bene't's Church, Cambridge. Among the parishioners he buried during the plague winter was Thomas Hobson, the university carrier (haulage and transportation contractor) and the subject of a sonnet by John Milton, who was Fuller's contemporary at Cambridge. In 1631 Fuller was appointed a perpetual prebendary of Salisbury by his uncle, who was then the bishop, and three years later became the vicar of a country parish, Broadwindsor in Dorset. He received his Bachelor of Divinity degree from Cambridge in 1635.

Fuller had shown his literary ambitions during his Cambridge days, when he had contributed Latin verses to an anthology celebrating the birth of the Princess Mary (1631) and had had his didactic poem *David's Hainous Sinne, Heartie Repentance, Heavie Punishment* (1631) published. He would turn out occasional poems and dedicatory verses throughout his life, but verse was not his métier. Increasingly, he was to emerge as the writer of sermons, meditations, histories, essays, and biographies that constructed an ethos for nation and church by presenting a common heritage and the grounds for unity as political and ecclesiastical divisions widened.

His first major work, *The Historie of the Holy Warre* (1639), is a lively and well-informed account of the Crusades that appeared in seven editions through the seventeenth century. Picking up his narrative where Flavius Josephus's *The History of the Jewish War* leaves off – with the Romans' destruction of Jerusalem and the Temple in the first century – Fuller proceeds to the Crusades, summarizing his subject at the end of the fourth book: "Thus

after a hundred ninety and four years ended the Holy War; for continuance the longest, for money spent the costliest, for bloodshed the cruelest, for pretences the most pious, for the true intent the most politic the world ever saw." The fifth book analyzes the political and economic weakness of the Crusades. The futility of the holy war, and the economic and social ruin it occasioned, is presented in the design engraved for the title page by William Marshall, presumably under Fuller's direction: a great procession – kings, knights, prelates, monks, soldiers, and people, ordered in their estates – sets out from Europe for the Temple of the Sepulchre, only to return through a wilderness, decimated and dispersed. The caption above reads, "We went out full, but return empty."

Fuller traveled to London in 1640 as one of the representatives of the diocese of Bristol to the convocation that met along with the Short Parliament. Like his uncle, Fuller belonged to the moderate group in the Church of England that was trying to hold to the terms of the Elizabethan Settlement but was disturbed by the increasing polarization on issues of church government and liturgy between the Laudians and the advocates of the Genevan discipline.

In 1637 Fuller married Eleanor Grove, daughter of Hugh Grove, member of Parliament for Shaftesbury, and already his relation by marriage; she would die in 1641 with the birth of their only child, a son named John. (Her family name was established only in 1918; Fuller must have suppressed the information out of concern for his son's career, since Eleanor was the half-sister of the Royalist hero Capt. Hugh Grove, who was beheaded in 1655 on Oliver Cromwell's orders for his part in the Penruddock uprising at Salisbury.)

Fuller's *The Holy State* (1642), comprising four series of essays on the Holy State and one series (with its own title page) on its opposite, the Profane State, presents the ideal of the unified Church and State, describes the virtues required in those who occupy its various estates and ranks, and illustrates these virtues in the lives of exemplary personalities from ancient history and from recent times. The life of William Cecil, Lord Burghley, for example, illustrates the Wise Statesman; that of William Camden the Good Herald; and those of Saint Augustine and Nicholas Ridley the Good Bishop. Fuller professed to no particular sophistication as an essayist: "For curious method, expect none," he announces in his preface, "Essays for the most part not being placed as at a *Feast*, but placing themselves as at an *Ordinary*." Yet he has devised his own

Waltham Abbey, Essex, where Fuller served as curate from 1649 to 1658

literary form, combining several current genres appropriate for the moralist. He writes in the tradition of the Baconian essay, with its series of maxims and elaborations, but he also borrows from the traditions of the courtesy book, the book of estates, and the Theophrastan book of characters, where he follows especially Joseph Hall's *Characters of Vertues and Vices* (1608). He gives particular prominence to the life, where his closest model is Henry Holland's *Heroologia Anglica* (1620); indeed, Fuller shares many of his English examples with Holland, and Marshall, who was still Fuller's engraver, copied almost all of the portraits of those subjects from Holland's book.

The Holy State represented not only the maturation of Fuller's personal vision of the commonwealth but also the orthodoxy of the Caroline state — fully articulated just at the point of its collapse. As Fuller says in the preface, he had set out on his enterprise in fair weather but had been overtaken by the tempest. The title page shows the monarch as the keystone of the arch spanning the pillars of Church and State, which reach out a hand to each other; these pillars represent Truth and Justice, respectively, and each is founded on its own law: the Church on the two Testaments, the State on its laws

and statutes. Royalism was a position from which Fuller never wavered, though, like his defense of episcopacy, it was moderate in character: the true king, he says "*willingly orders his actions by the Laws of his realm,*" and he praises Charles I for his adherence to legal precedent through the previous decade: "whatsoever the Theories of absolute Monarchy be, our King . . . thinks that his power is more safely lock'd up for him in his Laws then kept in his own will."

Since Fuller is proceeding on the Aristotelian notion that the family is the basis of the state, his first series of essays addresses the roles within the family in liberal, though conventional, terms. The good wife, for example, "*commandeth her husband in any equall matter, by constant obeying him*"; "*She keeps home if she hath not her husbands company, or leave for her patent to go abroad.*" Somewhat incongruously in an early modern work, the family models are likely to be drawn from the heroes of the Bible or the history of the church: the good wife is exemplified by Saint Monica, the good husband by Abraham. Even more surprising in a model delivered to a Protestant society, the type of the virgin woman is not a woman preparing herself for a chaste marriage but "a constant Virgin," learned and pious, represented by

Hildegard von Bingen — not the Hildegard of modern liberation theology but the Hildegard of John Foxe's *Actes and Monuments* (1563), a visionary and prophet who testified to the corruption of the Church of Rome and thus anticipated the church of the Reformation. Fuller, who mistrusts claims for personal visions and miracles in his own day because they are likely to be advanced by the sectaries, on the one hand, or the papists, on the other, is prepared to credit Hildegard's visions and even her miracles; and he defends her right to be a scholar and author, even as he limits those roles: "Let none object that her very writing of fifty eight Homilies on the Gospel is false construction, where the feminine Gender assumes an employment proper to men: for though S. Paul silenceth women for speaking in the Church, I know no Scripture forbids them from writing on Scripture."

For the issues that were to confront the citizen and church member in the wars and struggles of the next two decades, and for the principles by which Fuller would judge his own actions in subsequent years, the most significant section of *The Holy State* is the pair of essays "Of Time-serving" and "Of Moderation," where he wrestles to differentiate the honest from the dishonest mode of each of those practices. While he condemns the kind of timeserving that arises out of ignorance or affectation, he can pardon the kind that arises from human infirmity and approve that which arises "out of Christian discretion." "*He is a good Time-server that in time of persecution neither betrayes Gods cause, nor his own safety,*" he notes, presumably having in mind those who had survived and yet kept their integrity through the persecutions of Christians in the early church or of the Protestants under Mary; the problem would be his own during the Interregnum, when the Westminster Assembly moved against ministers who adhered to the Book of Common Prayer. True moderation he defines as "*not an halting betwixt two opinions, when the through-believing of one of them is necessary to salvation,*" nor "*a lukewarmeness in those things wherein Gods glory is concernd. . . . But it is a mixture of discretion and charity in ones judgement.*" The moderate man distinguishes between things concerning faith and practice that are necessary to salvation from those that are indifferent, holding firmly to the first while exercising discretion and flexibility in the second; he abates any "stiffness of his judgment" out of charity to his neighbors, aiming "at the good of others, and unity of the Church." Such "*moderate men are commonly crush'd betwixt the extreme parties on both sides.*" This treatment they must accept patiently, but they may also hope for a time, "once in an age,"

when moderation is valued, when the moderate man may even find himself courted by each extreme and have the opportunity to "be a Peace-maker betwixt opposite parties." In any case, he has the advantage that "his religion is more constant and durable; being here, *in via,* in his way to Heaven, and jogging on a good Traveller's pace he overtakes and outgoes many violent men, whose over-hot ill-grounded Zeal was quickly tired."

In his life of Ridley, Fuller reproves, among these more violent men, Milton, the anonymous author of a recent pamphlet, *Of Reformation* (1641), which had slandered Ridley and the other two bishops martyred in the days of Queen Mary — heroes from the *Actes and Monuments* familiar to Fuller and his contemporaries from childhood. Showing "an excellent facultie in uncharitable Synecdoches," such authors condemn the person's whole life for one imperfect action. Fuller's own style as a moralist, in *The Holy State* and elsewhere, is not to set the standard at moral perfection and rail at lapses but to ask for charity in judgment and to acknowledge faithfulness and acts of courage shown by fallible humans. Here, too, he is consciously the moderate, apt to cite Paul's injunctions to moderation as his proof texts.

Fuller became preacher at the Savoy Chapel in London in 1642, just as the king and his court left London for Oxford and both cities were fortified for war. Like many in his congregation Fuller was anxious for reconciliation between Parliament and the crown. In early January 1643 he was one of a delegation of six men who made a last-ditch effort for peace by persuading the House of Lords to send them to the king with the so-called Westminster Petition. On their way the group was arrested by Parliamentary soldiers for possession of writings hostile to Parliament and returned to London by order of the Commons. Some months later Fuller could no longer tolerate the increasingly restrictive oaths of loyalty to Parliament or conform to the Westminster Assembly's directives for faith and worship; he preached his final sermon, *A Sermon of Reformation* (1643), criticizing the program of radicalization, and left for the king's court before it was published. At Oxford, too, however, his moderate position was unwelcome.

In late 1643, at the height of the civil war, Fuller became chaplain to the army of Sir Ralph Hopton, one of the most able of the Royalist generals and himself a moderate. During his extensive travels with the army in the West Country Fuller was collecting notes for the books that were to appear as *The Church-History of Britain* (1655) and *The*

*Title page for Fuller's description of the geography and history of
Palestine during biblical times*

History of the Worthies of England (1662); he survived
the siege of Basing House, where, amid the battle,
he made good use of the marquess of Winchester's
excellent library; and he retreated with the Royalist
armies to Exeter in 1644, arriving just after the
queen, fleeing from the Parliamentary armies, had
given birth there and escaped to France. Fuller was
appointed by the king to be chaplain for the new-
born Princess Henrietta; his *Good Thoughts in Bad
Times* (1645), the first book ever published in Exeter, was dedicated to the princess's governess, Mary
Villiers, Lady Dalkeith, who, on the surrender of
the city, disguised herself as a beggar woman and
escaped with the child to France.

 Good Thoughts in Bad Times was the first of
Fuller's three books of meditations. The works are
somewhat similar to John Donne's *Devotions upon
Emergent Occasions* (1624), but they adhere even more
closely, in devotional and literary technique, to the
plainer and more consciously Protestant model of
Hall's *Occasionall Meditations* (1630). *Good Thoughts in
Bad Times* comprises one hundred meditations, each
about a paragraph long and consisting of an observation followed by the application of the observation to the state of sin and the amendment of life.
Meditation VII, for example, begins: "Lord: Before
I commit a sin, it seems to me so shallow that I may
wade through it dry-shod from any guiltiness; but
when I have committed it, it often seems so deep
that I cannot escape without drowning, thus I am always in the extremities: either my sins are so small
that they need not my repentance, or so great that

they cannot obtain thy pardon. Lend me, O Lord, a reed out of thy sanctuary, truly to measure the dimension of my offences. . . . " The meditations are arranged in four series – Personal, Scriptural, Historical, and Mixed – with no particular hierarchy among the categories. Fuller delivers thanks for his escape from the dangers of the war, confesses his shortcomings, provides an exegesis for a scriptural passage, or points out a moral from the history of the Wars of the Roses or the topography of Merioneth.

Good Thoughts in Bad Times went into three editions within a year; *Good Thoughts in Worse Times* appeared in 1647; and the two works were combined into a single volume that ran to another seven editions over the next forty years. In the nineteenth century the Fuller revival produced many editions of the meditations, both academic and popular, on both sides of the Atlantic. Noting that Fuller wrote from his own experience with the army and for a readership of religious men in the army and in towns, such as Exeter, that were under siege, Albert Currier recalls that the Boston publishing house of Ticknor and Fields republished the meditations during the American Civil War "as suitable to our condition as a people at that time and afterwards," and that "they had a wide circulation."

While at Exeter, Fuller worked on his *Andronicus, or, The Unfortunate Politician: Shewing, Sin: Slowly Punished. Right, Surely Rescued* (1646). He had already used the Machiavellian Andronicus Comnenus, a usurper of the throne of Byzantium in the twelfth century, to illustrate the character of the tyrant in the profane state; now he expanded the theme under the inspiration of contemporary events and personalities. The work became immensely popular, especially among the Royalists in England and in exile in Holland, who regarded Oliver Cromwell as the original for Andronicus. (A tragedy in heroic verse, published in 1663 and based on Fuller's text, may have been written by Fuller himself.)

With the Royalist defeat and the surrender of Exeter in 1646, Fuller was free to travel back to London; the articles of the surrender guaranteed that he would not be required to subscribe to the Solemn League and Covenant. Nevertheless, in the years leading up to the regicide he found himself without a living, without a home, and (as he lamented equally) without a library. For a time he stayed with his publisher and friend, John Williams, at the Sign of the Crown (the crown device becomes prominent on the title pages of Fuller's publications from Williams's press in these years); later, as a guest of the Montagus at Boughton House in

Northamptonshire, he wrote *The Cause and Cure of a Wounded Conscience* (1647), a therapy for his own distress and a tract for the times. Cast in dialogue form, the work is tight, direct, and balanced; it shows Fuller as the careful physician of souls in extremis – the other side of the man who usually treated his friends and readers to his tonic wit and his fund of stories. Even in these years Fuller maintained a circle of friends and patrons on both sides of the quarrels in Church and State. Appalled by the execution of Charles I in 1649, he nevertheless remained a friend of Sir John Danvers, one of the judges who condemned the king.

Security in his livelihood and a measure of private peace returned only in 1649, when James Hay, Earl of Carlisle, appointed Fuller to the curacy of Waltham Abbey in Essex. Fuller valued the abbey for its antiquity and for its associations with Foxe, who had resided in the parish, and Hall, who had preceded him in the pulpit. The proximity to London gave him access to his publisher and to the library at Sion College. While remaining a hardworking minister in his parish, he traveled around the country consulting archives, informants, and learned friends in preparation for the three major works he was to write in this last and most productive period of his life: *A Pisgah-Sight of Palestine and the Confines Thereof, with the History of the Old and New Testament Acted Thereon* (1650), *The Church-History of Britain,* and *The History of the Worthies of England.* One of his parishioners, Lionel Cranfield, third Earl of Middlesex, gave him an excellent library that had originally been the property of the first earl, who had been lord treasurer to James I. In 1652 Fuller married Mary Roper, sister of Thomas, Viscount Baltinglass; of the three children of the marriage, only a son, Thomas, survived.

A Pisgah-Sight of Palestine, elaborately printed in 1650 with many maps and illustrations, is now a rare book, having achieved only three editions in the seventeenth century and one since. Though a work of antiquarian scholarship, it responds to the political crises of its time. Fuller intended his work to be a "chorographical description" of the tribal regions of ancient Israel comparable with Camden's description in his *Britannia* (1586) of the tribal areas of Roman Britain. But as he moves geographically from the tribal regions to Jerusalem and focuses on the rebuilding of Jerusalem under Nehemiah after the abolition of the monarchy, the contemporary parallel proves irresistible. Fuller's irritation with the "fantastical" versions of the arrival of the New Jerusalem entertained by the Fifth Monarchists and other sectaries in his day comes through in his

Engraving of Fuller by T. A. Dean, after a portrait by David Loggan

brusque dismissal of Ezekiel's merely "visionary" description of the city, which had no relationship to the Jerusalem that existed in time and space (irregular in shape, built up in increments): Fuller sees such millenial visions as a distraction from the historical task of rebuilding Church and State. But, while impatient with the sectaries and the "new lights," Fuller has come to a more generous understanding of the position of the Jews. In *The Historie of the Holy Warre* he had accepted the traditional Christian notion that God had destroyed Jerusalem and "cast out" the Jews as punishment for the crucifixion of the Messiah; in *A Pisgah-Sight of Palestine* he is coming to the conclusion that, if God has not rejected England, despite the regicide and the dismantling of the church, then God did not reject the Jews. He makes the point explicitly in "A Short View and True History of the Jews," probably written during the years (1655 to 1657) when Manasseh ben Israel was in London negotiating with Oliver Cromwell for the reentry of the Jews into England but published posthumously as a somewhat incongruous addition to James Howell's 1662 edition of Flavius Josephus's *The Wonderful and Most Deplorable History of the Latter Times of the Jews, and of the City of Hierusalem.*

The Church-History of Britain, promised in 1642 in the preface to *The Holy State,* finally appeared in 1655 as a thousand-page narrative of ecclesiastical history from the arrival of Christianity into pagan Britain to Fuller's time, with Fuller's eyewitness account of Archbishop William Laud's last convocation. The work, originally projected to close with the death of James I, ends with a powerful account of the execution of Charles I and his burial in Windsor Chapel that Fuller had received from Charles's cousin, James Stuart, Duke of Richmond, who had accompanied the body to the grave. To *The Church-History of Britain* were appended the substantial "History of the University of Cambridge, since the Conquest," with an engraved plan of the town, and the short "History of Waltham-Abby in Essex."

In the early part of his ecclesiastical history Fuller follows the narrative line of Foxe in the *Actes and Monuments* but adds information and emphases of his own — especially because Foxe's perspective on the English Reformation had unwittingly given support to the Millenialists. Fuller's description is intended to make it clear that Reformation, then or in his own time, is not a final and decisive act but a process. His insistence on seeing the church in a practical and political light led him to employ a familiar, even conversational narrative style that offended some churchmen (William Warburton, the eighteenth-century bishop of Gloucester, among them). The major attack on Fuller's indecorously "merry tales," his scholarship, and his criticism of Laud came in *Examen Historicum* (1659), written by Peter Heylyn, one of the sequestered clergy. Though he had tried to avoid dispute, Fuller replied in *The Appeal of Injured Innocence* (1659), refuting Heylyn's objections one by one with characteristic good humor and an offer of personal reconciliation. ("Why should Peter fall out with Thomas, both being disciples to the same Lord and Master?")

Probably in 1657 Fuller passed the examination by Cromwell's Triers and was allowed to continue to preach. In 1658 he left Waltham, having accepted from George Berkeley the living of Cranford in Middlesex, a smaller parish that gave him better conditions for writing and still provided easy access to London.

With more favorable political circumstances in the early months of 1660 he wrote an anonymous pamphlet, *An Alarum to the Counties of England and Wales,* calling for the election of a free Parliament; it appeared a few days before General George Monck's letter to the same effect. His final book of meditations, *Mixed Contemplations in Better Times* (1660), a plea for moderation on the part of Royalists on the eve of their triumph, is dedicated to Anne, Lady Monck, in appreciation for her support of the Royalist cause. In May he traveled to the Hague with Berkeley, one of the commissioners sent by the House of Lords to accompany Charles II back to England – apparently the only occasion on which Fuller went abroad.

In view of his loyalty to the church during the Protectorate, his political connections, and his literary eminence, Fuller was expected to receive a bishopric in the Restoration church. In the early months of the Restoration he was restored to his stall at Salisbury, received his doctor of divinity degree from Cambridge University by royal mandate, and was appointed chaplain in extraordinary to the king. But in August 1661 he was suddenly struck with fever; he died on the sixteenth and was buried the next day at Cranford.

The History of the Worthies of England, Fuller's most significant contribution to antiquarian scholarship, was published posthumously in 1662 and edited by his son John. The book is a vast encyclopedia, with entries organized by county. (Neither an index nor a table of contents was supplied by the first editor.) In the first chapter Fuller explains his

format as a development of the work of Camden and John Speed: if England is regarded as a kind of large house, they have supplied the account of the rooms, that is, the topographical description of the various counties; Fuller will describe the "furniture," that is, the chief products and commodities, the customs, and the ways of speech. Above all, he supplies lists and often short biographies of the "worthies," and these accounts are arranged according to his idea of the ranking of the estates: "the first quarternion of Persons," including Princes, Saints, Martyrs, and Confessors; then Statesmen, Judges, Soldiers, and Seamen; then Writers in Law, Philology, Divinity, and History; then public benefactors; then the gentry down to the reign of Henry VI and the sheriffs down to the reign of the Stuarts. *The History of the Worthies of England* gives probably the best account of economic activity in the counties in the mid seventeenth century, and it has been valued from the time of its publication as a semantic record and a storehouse of rich biographical information and anecdotes.

Samuel Pepys, who had recorded in his diary his conversations with the man he called "the great Tom Fuller," noted with enthusiasm the first appearance of *The History of the Worthies of England* at the bookseller's; he sat reading it until two o'clock one night, and he spent Easter Day 1664 at home with his wife, both of them reading pleasantly in "Dr. Fuller's book."

In the year of Fuller's death appeared the anonymous *The Life of That Reverend Divine, and Learned Historian, Dr. Thomas Fuller,* still the best source of information about his temperament and habits and the circumstances of his Cranford years. He is described as tall and well built, with a ruddy face and light curly hair, upright and graceful in walking but not at all attentive to his dress; a temperate eater who took little sleep and less exercise; and a man who delighted in his family, his library, and his writing. Even the hostile account given in a 1657 oration by the preacher Robert South gives an engaging picture of Fuller, after the publication of *The Church-History of Britain,* running around London with his big book tucked under one arm and his little wife tucked under the other.

Many of the stories told about Fuller concern his prodigious memory; he is said to have been able to repeat five hundred names after two or three hearings and to recollect all the signs after walking from one side of London to the other. When a committee of sequestrators sitting at Waltham wanted proof of the widely reputed excellence of his memory, Fuller said, "Gentlemen, your worships have thought fit to sequester an honest poor but cavalier parson, my neighbor, from his living, and committed him to prison; he has a great charge of children, and his circumstances are but indifferent; if you please to release him out of prison and restore him to his living, I will never forget the kindness while I live." The jest is said to have persuaded the committee to release and restore the clergyman.

In the politics of his day, Fuller was bound to be seen by some as a timeserver — the criticism of the moderate man that he had anticipated in *The Holy State*. Though he had his hours of heroism during the civil war, he flourished under the Protectorate, when many clergymen had their livings sequestered, and he continued to enjoy significant patronage. (To finance a sumptuous production such as *A Pisgah-Sight of Palestine* he invoked many patrons, sometimes two or three for one engraved page.) Fuller's prose attempts to establish a comfortable society of author and reader. As if in conversation, he is anxious to make distinctions without giving gratuitous offense and to disarm ill will with reasonableness and, especially, with humor. Fuller's witticisms and verbal play indicate good temper and intellectual balance and, thus, a writer who can be enjoyed and also trusted, when other minds in his age have been drawn off into zeal, cynicism, or despair. For Samuel Taylor Coleridge, Fuller was "incomparably the most sensible, the least prejudiced, great man of an age that boasted a galaxy of great men." A more sober assessment is given by Leslie Stephen in his entry on Fuller in the *Dictionary of National Biography* (1889): Fuller's "perfectly genuine moderation enabled him to accommodate himself rather too easily to men of all parties. . . . He steered rather too skilful a course, perhaps, through a revolutionary time; but he really succeeded in avoiding any discreditable concessions, and never disavowed his genuine convictions."

The high point of Fuller's literary revival in the nineteenth century is represented by Coleridge's acclamation, in his notes on the final pages of *The Church-History of Britain,* that "next to Shakespeare," Fuller excited in him "the sense and emotion of the marvellous"; that "wit was the stuff and substance of Fuller's intellect," out of which he shaped the "practical wisdom of his thoughts" and the "beauty and variety" of his truths. Fuller was Robert Southey's "prime favorite author," while Charles Lamb, a great admirer of the "massy reading" afforded by *The History of the Worthies of England,* found Fuller's way of telling a story, "perhaps unequalled" for its "eager liveliness, and the perpetual

running commentary of the narrator happily blended with the narration."

All of Fuller's works were republished in the nineteenth century — mainly to permit enjoyment of his wit and erudition but sometimes also for the sake of the support he could lend to the Broad church movement against the seductions of the Tractarians. (Two significant editions of *The Church-History of Britain* appeared within a decade.) Among his biographers the most eminent is the Manchester antiquary John Eglington Bailey, whose *The Life of Thomas Fuller, D.D.* (1874) includes virtually complete records and bibliography; Bailey also collected and edited Fuller's sermons (1891).

Coleridge's excessive praise for Fuller's wit was bound to lead to disenchantment, especially when the major works were canvassed for anecdotes and epigrams to be collected in anthologies such as Augustus Jessopp's *Wise Words and Quaint Conceits of Thomas Fuller* (1892). Jessopp himself found Fuller lacking in certain intellectual qualities in comparison with some of his contemporaries, pointing out that he had neither the scholastic subtlety nor the mystical intensity of Donne. Jessopp admires Fuller the historian, however, not only for his sound critical instinct and unequaled power of accumulating information but also for his "constructive genius" that "breathes life into the dry bones" and presents the suggestive outline of the growth and life of the people.

Eventually, the fragmentation of Fuller's works produced, in reaction, an attempt to recover the coherence of his viewpoint. The year 1938 saw the publication of Maximilian Graff Walten's definitive annotated edition of *The Holy State and The Profane State* and of Walter Edwards Houghton's extended commentary on the work. (Houghton, giving the most comprehensive treatment of Fuller as a moralist, criticized Fuller's proclivity to conflate prosperity with virtue in a mercantile society.) *The Holy State* is, thus, properly restored to its own time and place. Yet the tendency of Fuller's narrations and maxims, and particularly his meditations, to perpetuate themselves in anthologies testifies to a durable quality in his writing. Much of the attraction comes from the personable voice that, whether in prayer or history or biography, reveals a writer who enjoys his idiom and the articulation of the implications of living in a particular historical moment.

Bibliographies:

The Fuller Collection in the Free Reference Library, King Street, Manchester Public Free Libraries Occasional Lists, no. 2 (Manchester, U.K., 1891);

Strickland Gibson, *A Bibliography of the Works of Thomas Fuller, D.D.,* Oxford Bibliographical Society Proceedings & Papers, volume 4 (Oxford: Printed for the Society at the Oxford University Press, 1936).

Biographies:

The Life of That Reverend Divine, and Learned Historian, Dr. Thomas Fuller (London: Printed for J. W. H. B. and H. M., 1661);

Arthur T. Russell, *Memorials of the Life and Works of Thomas Fuller, D.D.* (London: Pickering, 1844);

Henry Rogers, *An Essay on the Life and Genius of Thomas Fuller, with Selections from His Writings* (London: Longman, Brown, Green & Longmans, 1856);

John Eglington Bailey, *The Life of Thomas Fuller, D.D., with Notices of His Books, His Kinsmen and His Friends* (London: Pickering / Manchester, U.K.: Day, 1874);

Morris Fuller, *The Life, Times and Writings of Thomas Fuller, D.D., the Church Historian,* 2 volumes (London: Hedges, 1884);

Dean Lyman, *The Great Tom Fuller* (Berkeley: University of California Press, 1935);

William Addison, *Worthy Dr. Fuller* (London: Dent, 1951).

References:

James T. Addison, "Thomas Fuller, Historian and Humorist," *Historical Magazine of the Protestant Episcopal Church,* 21 (March 1952): 100–147;

Samuel Taylor Coleridge, *Notes on English Divines,* 2 volumes, edited by Derwent Coleridge (London: Moxon, 1853), I: 127;

Coleridge, *Notes Theological, Political, and Miscellaneous,* edited by Derwent Coleridge (London: Moxon, 1853), p. 101;

Henry J. Cowell, "Thomas Fuller (1608–1661) and Essex," *Essex Review,* 54 (1945): 152–156;

Albert H. Currier, "Thomas Fuller" in his *Biographical and Literary Studies* (Boston & New York: Pilgrim Press, 1915), pp. 209–234;

Maurice Hewlett, "Our Blood and State in 1660," in his *Last Essays* (London: Heinemann / New York: Scribners, 1924), pp. 103–108;

Walter Edwards Houghton, *The Formation of Thomas Fuller's Holy and Profane States* (Cambridge, Mass.: Harvard University Press, 1938);

Charles Lamb, *Complete Works and Letters,* edited by Saxe Commins (New York: Modern Library, 1935), pp. 303–308;

W. B. Patterson, "Thomas Fuller as Royalist Parson during the Interregnum," in *The Church in Town and Countryside,* edited by Derek Baker (Oxford: Blackwell, 1979), pp. 301–314;

Robert B. Resnick, "An Ounce of Mirth: The Function of Thomas Fuller's Wit," *College Language Arts Journal,* 11 (1967): 123–134;

Resnick, "Thomas Fuller: Doctor of the Sugar-Coated Pill," *Lock Haven Review,* 6 (1964): 53–68;

Resnick, "Thomas Fuller's Pulpit Wit," *Xavier University Studies,* 4 (1965): 109–153;

Florence Sandler, "The Temple of Zerubbabel: A Pattern for Reformation in Thomas Fuller's *Pisgah-Sight* and *Church-History of Britain,*" *Studies in the Literary Imagination,* 10 (Fall 1979): 29–42;

Sandler, "Thomas Fuller's *Pisgah-Sight of Palestine* as a Comment on the Politics of Its Time," *Huntington Library Quarterly,* 41 (August 1978): 317–343;

Leslie Stephen, "Thomas Fuller," *Cornhill Magazine,* 25 (January 1872): 28–42;

James O. Wood, "Fuller's Oxford Interlude," *Huntington Library Quarterly,* 17 (May 1954): 185–208;

Lawrence C. Wroth, "Thomas Fuller and His 'Worthies,'" *South Atlantic Quarterly,* 11 (July 1912): 215–223.

Papers:

None of Thomas Fuller's correspondence, nor any manuscript in his own hand, survives.

John Hales

(19 April 1584 – 19 May 1656)

P. G. Stanwood
University of British Columbia

BOOKS: *Oratio Funebris habita in Collegio Mertonensi a J. Halesio quo die Thomae Bodleio funus ducebatur* (Oxford, 1613);

A Sermon Preached at S[t] Maries in Oxford vpon Tvesday in Easter Weeke, 1617. Concerning the Abvses of obscure and difficult places of Holy Scripture, and Remedies against them (Oxford: Printed by John Lichfield & William Wrench, 1617);

A Tract Concerning Schisme and Schismatiqves. Wherein is Briefly Discovered the Originall Causes of All Schisme. Written by a Learned and Judicious Divine, anonymous (Oxford: Printed by L. Lichfield for E. Forrest, 1642);

Golden Remains of the Ever Memorable Mr. John Hales, edited by Peter Gunning (London: Printed for T. Garthwait, 1659; enlarged edition, London: Printed by T. Newcomb for R. Pawlet, 1673);

Sermons Preached at Eton (Oxford, 1660);

Several Tracts (London: Printed for John Blyth, 1677); enlarged as *Several Tracts by the Ever-Memorable Mr. John Hales: To Which Is Added, His Letter to Archbishop Laud, Occasion'd by His Tract of Schism; Never before Published among His Works* (London?, 1716).

Edition: *The Works of the Ever Memorable Mr. John Hales of Eaton,* 3 volumes, edited by David Dalrymple (Glasgow: Foulis, 1765).

Admired for his learning, his wit, and his genial temper, "the ever memorable" John Hales belonged to the philosophic circle of Great Tew. He was the oldest member of that group of thinkers and writers with whom Lucius Cary, second Viscount Falkland, surrounded himself at his country estate near Oxford during the 1630s. Hales's devoted friends, especially Edward Hyde (later earl of Clarendon), William Chillingworth, Sidney Godolphin, Edmund Waller, and Cary, sought out his company and cherished his memory — the inalienable epithet expresses the extraordinary regard in which he was generally held. Hales deeply impressed and profoundly influenced most who knew

him. But little of his work was published in his lifetime. The collected sermons, tracts, and letters represent a meager offering for one so highly honored, yet it is easy to detect in his writing something of the irenic spirit, the tough and determined intellect, and the felicitous style that moved his contemporaries to such lively approbation.

Hales was born in Bath on 19 April 1584; his father, also named John, was steward to a wealthy Somersetshire family. Hales was first educated at the Bath Grammar School, then matriculated on 16 April 1597 as a scholar of Corpus Christi College at Oxford. He was awarded his B.A. degree on 9 July 1603. His learning brought him to the attention of Sir Henry Savile, then warden (president) of Merton College and after 1596 also provost of Eton College, who encouraged him in 1605 to stand for a fellowship of Merton. At the election he was the first to be chosen, probably through Savile's influence; but Anthony à Wood remarks that "he shew'd himself a person of Learning above his age and standing" and that "there was never any one in the then memory of man . . . that ever went beyond him for subtile Disputations in Philosophy, for his eloquent Declamations and Orations; as also for his exact knowledge in the Greek Tongue." The last point no doubt led Savile to employ Hales in his great edition of Saint John Chrysostom's Works (1610–1613); Hales's assistance, according to Clarendon, formed "the greatest Part of the Labour."

Soon after his election as a fellow of Merton, Hales took holy orders; he received an M.A. degree on 20 June 1609. He preached frequently, and in 1612 he became public lecturer in Greek at the university. In 1613 he delivered the funeral sermon for Sir Thomas Bodley, founder of the Bodleian Library; it was published the same year. He was admitted as a fellow of Eton on 24 May 1613, spurning any other kind of preferment that his "Eminency for Learning, and other Abilities," according to Clarendon, might have promised. The only alteration in this retirement among his books and his

John Hales

friends occurred from 1618 to 1619, when he accompanied Sir Dudley Carleton, the ambassador to Holland, as a chaplain. This period coincided with the Synod of Dort, at which Hales was present and from which he wrote a series of cogent letters to Carleton (the first is dated 24 November 1618, the last 7 February 1619) commenting, as Clarendon put it, on the "Ignorance, and Passion, and Animosity, and Injustice" of the consultations of that assembly. There he was led, as he said in his letter to Carleton of 19 January 1619, to "bid John Calvin good-night" as he heard Simon Episcopius, professor of divinity at the University of Leiden, press the Arminian doctrine of grace. But the most lasting effect of the synod on Hales was to encourage his irenicism and nonsectarianism.

Hales returned to Eton in 1619. On 27 June 1639 he was installed in a canonry at Windsor; he was ejected from it by Parliament in 1642. In April 1649, on his refusal to take the "engagement," or oath of allegiance to the Commonwealth, he was

formally dispossessed of his fellowship at Eton. He retired to Richings Lodge near Colnbrook in Buckinghamshire, the residence of Lady Salter, the sister of Brian Duppa, bishop of Salisbury, and was tutor to her son William. He eventually returned to lodgings in Eton, where he died on 19 May 1656.

Hales was known as "a man of infinite reading, and no less ingenuity; free of Discourse, and as communicative of his knowledge as the Coelestial Bodies of their light and influences," according to the usually severe Peter Heylyn. Hales's company was much sought after; in addition to taking part in the conversations at Great Tew he was a regular visitor to the wits of London, for Sir John Suckling gives him a place in his poem "A Session of the Poets," written around 1637. Perhaps Clarendon best describes Hales's character in his account of the origin and consequence of Hales's celebrated *A Tract Concerning Schisme and Schismatiques,* written about 1636 though not published until 1642. This work is an occasional discourse in which Hales urges that "*Schisme* . . . is nothing else but an unnecessary separation of Christians from that part of the visible Church, of which they were once members." The tract reached Archbishop William Laud, who was concerned that church order and discipline might be diminished if Hales's ideas were generally accepted. Clarendon writes that Laud

> sent for Mr. *Hales,* whom, when They had both lived in the University of *Oxford,* He had known well; and told him, that He had in Truth believed him to be long since dead; and chid him very kindly for having never come to him, having been of his old Acquaintance; then asked him, whether He had lately writ a short Discourse of Schism, and whether He was of that Opinion, which that Discourse implied. He told him, that He had, for the Satisfaction of a private Friend (who was not of his Mind) a Year or two before, writ such a small Tract, without any Imagination that it would be communicated; and that He believed it did not contain any Thing, that was not agreeable to the Judgment of the Primitive Fathers; upon which, the Archbishop debated with him upon some Expressions of *Irenaeus,* and the most ancient Fathers; and concluded with saying, that the Time was very apt to set new Doctrines on Foot, of which the Wits of the Age were too susceptible; and that there could not be too much Care taken, to preserve the Peace and Unity of the Church; and from thence asked him of his Condition, and whether He wanted any Thing, and the other answering, that He had enough, and wanted, or desired no Addition, so dismissed him with great Courtesy; and shortly after sent for him again, when there was a Prebendary of *Windsor* fallen, and told him, the King had given him the Preferment, because it lay so convenient to his Fellowship of *Eton;* which (though indeed the most convenient Preferment that could be thought of for him) the Archbishop could not without great Difficulty, persuade him to accept, and He did accept it rather to please Him, than himself; because He really believed He had enough before. He was one of the least Men in the Kingdom; and one of the greatest Scholars in *Europe.*

Hales rather ingenuously wrote "A Letter to Archbishop Laud" (published in 1716) to clarify his attitude and argument: "I am by genius open and uncautelous; and therefore some pardon might be afforded to harmless freedom, and gaiety of spirit, utterly devoid of all distemper and malignity." Hales's wish is for peace and settled authority, and he is happy to reconcile himself with the episcopacy as constituted in the Church of England.

Among the treatises in the posthumously published *Several Tracts* (1677) is "On the Sacrament of the Lord's Supper," addressed to an "enquirer," in which Hales holds that "in the communion there is nothing given but bread and wine." They are signs only, for Christ is not "present" in any sense; the Lord's Supper is a commemoration of the Passion and a testimony to our union with Christ. In "A Tract concerning the Power of the Keys, and Auricular Confession," dated 8 March 1637 and first published in the 1677 volume, Hales writes that the confession of sins is necessary for all Christians but that confession to a priest, while not wrong, is unnecessary; the priest does not hold "the keys" in any special way: "You may as well make your muleteer (if you have one) your confessor, as your parish-priest." The church, Hales continues, has no traditional "notes" or "marks" of word, sacraments, or ministry, for it is made up simply by those who profess faith, with Christ only as the head, no other head being visible: "all these questions concerning the notes, the visibility, the government of the church, if we look upon the substance and nature of the church, they are merely idle and impertinent; if upon the end why learned men do handle them, it is nothing else but faction."

Hales impressed those who knew him with his amiability and his learning; few people of his time received such universal praise. To David Lloyd he was "a person of so large a capacity, so sharp, quick, piercing, and subtile a Wit, of so serene and profound a judgment beyond the ordinary reach . . . that he became the most absolute Master of Polite, Various, and Universal Learning, besides a deep insight into Religion; in search after which he was curious, and of the knowledge of it studious." And yet few highly regarded writers of the early seventeenth century have left such a modest canon: it is difficult to measure his contribution to the Works of Chrysostom, to Chillingworth's *The Religion of Protestants A Safe Way to Salvation* (1638), or to the work and thought of other contemporaries. Among his original works, in addition to the letter to Laud and the tracts, are sixteen elegantly conceived and constructed sermons.

The illustration on the engraved title page of *Golden Remains of the Ever Memorable Mr. John Hales* (1659) refers to a striking passage in Hales's sermon "Of dealing with Erring Christians," on Rom. 14:1: "Him that is weak in the faith receive ye, but not to doubtful disputations." In the passage Hales is decrying the multiplicity of writers and books, the "turning and quoting of sundry Authours," the counting of the number rather than the "weight" of books: "G. Agricola writing *de Animantibus subterraneis,* reports of a certain kind of *Spirits* that converse in *Minerals,* and much infest those that work in them; and the manner of them when they come, is, To seem to busie themselves according to all the custom of workmen; they will dig, and cleanse, and melt, and sever Metalls; yet when they are gone, the workmen do not find that there is any thing done: So fares it with a great part of the multitude, who thrust themselves into the Controversies of the Times; they write Books, move Questions, frame Distinctions, give Solutions, and seem sedulously to do whatsoever the nature of the business requires; yet if any skilful workman in the Lords Mines shall come and examine their work, he shall find them to be but *Spirits in Minerals,* and that with all this labour and stir there is nothing done." The passage exemplifies Hales's detachment, resistance to extremes, incisiveness, and clarity.

The sermon on Luke 18:1, "And he spake a parable unto them, to this end that men ought always to pray, and not to faint," reveals Hales's firm gentleness, peaceableness, and orderly discourse. Hales begins by dividing the text in a way that is typical of much homiletic prose in this period: "My text is like the Temple at Hierusalem, it is the house of prayer, wherein we may learn many special points of the skill and practice of it"; there is the porch, affording meditation before we enter, and the temple itself, wherein we exercise "constant prayer." While Hales is evidently inspired by the "witty" preachers, he lacks the verbal intensity of Lancelot Andrewes or the often dramatic eloquence of John Donne. He refers regularly to the Scriptures, to the church fathers, and to classical authors and ideas; he quotes most frequently — usually in Greek — from Chrysostom, whose works he knew well through his early association with Savile's edition. The effect of the sermon, however, is familiar rather than learned; and the generally uncomplicated syntax is closer to the Restoration style of Isaac Barrow or Robert South than to the preaching of the earlier seventeenth century: "Devotion in ordinary persons is a thing easily raised, and easily allayed. Every strange event, every fear, every little calamity or distress is enough to put us into a strain of religious meditation; but on the contrary side, a small matter doth again as quickly kill it. It seems to be like a quotidian ague, it comes by fits, every day it takes us, and every day it leaves us: or like flax, or straw, or such light and dry stuff, which easily kindles, and as soon goes out. . . ." Prayer is often interrupted, Hales says, because the actions of the world perpetually change, one giving room to another "like unto quarrelsome birds, two of them cannot peaceably dwell in one bush. But prayer hath that property which Aristotle gives unto substance . . . it is at peace, and holds good terms with all our cares of the world. . . . For, saith St. Chrysostom, as they that build houses of clay, must everywhere place studs and pieces of timber and wood so to strengthen the building . . . so all

our cares of this life, which are no better than buildings of dirt and clay, we must strengthen and compact together with frequent and often prayer, as with bonds and props of timber." The studied ease of the discourse, its frequent use of familiar illustrations and moral exempla, its lack of affectation, and its obvious sincerity, moderation, and intelligence convey something of that sensibility so admired by those who knew him, according to Andrew Marvell, as "one of the clearest heads and best prepared breasts in Christendom."

References:

John Aubrey, *Aubrey's Brief Lives,* edited by Oliver Lawson Dick (London: Secker & Warburg, 1950), pp. 117–119;

Paul Avis, *Anglicanism and the Christian Church: Theological Resources in Historical Perspective* (Minneapolis: Fortress Press, 1989), pp. 103–109;

John Butt, "Izaak Walton's Collections for Fulman's Life of John Hales," (July 1934): 267–273;

Pierre Des Maizeaux, *An Historical and Critical Account of the Life and Writings of the Ever-memorable Mr. John Hales . . . Being a Specimen of an Historical and Critical English Dictionary* (London: Printed by R. Robinson, 1719);

James Hinsdale Elson, *John Hales of Eton* (New York: King's Crown Press, 1949);

Peter Heylyn, *Cyprianus Anglicus; or, The History of the Life and Death of . . . William . . . Archbishop of Canterbury* (London, 1668);

Edward Hyde, Earl of Clarendon, *The Life of Edward Earl of Clarendon, Lord High Chancellor of England, and Chancellor of the University of Oxford,* volume 1 (Oxford: Clarendon Printing-House, 1759), pp. 30–59;

David Lloyd, *Memoires of the Lives, Actions, Sufferings, and Deaths of Those Noble, Reverand, and Excellent Personages That Suffered by Death, Sequestration, Decimation or Otherwise for the Protestant Reformation* (London: S. Speed, 1668);

Andrew Marvell, *The Rehearsal Transpos'd; Or, Animadversions Upon a late Book, Intituled, A Preface Shewing What Grounds there are of Fears and Jealousies of Popery* (London: Printed by A. B. for the assigns of John Calvin & Theodore Beza, 1672);

John J. Murray, "John Hales on History," *Huntington Library Quarterly,* 19 (May 1955): 231–243;

Robert Peters, "John Hales and the Synod of Dort," *Studies in Church History,* 7 (1971): 277–288;

Anthony à Wood, *Athenæ Oxonienses,* 2 volumes (London: Printed for Thomas Bennet, 1691, 1692).

Joseph Hall

(1 July 1574 – 8 September 1656)

Ronald Corthell
Kent State University

See also the Hall entry in *DLB 121: Seventeenth-Century British Nondramatic Poets, First Series.*

BOOKS: *Virgidemiarvm, Six Bookes. First Three Bookes, of Tooth-lesse Satyrs. 1. Poeticall. 2. Academicall. 3. Morall* (London: Printed by Thomas Creede for Robert Dexter, 1597; enlarged, 1598);

The Kings Prophecie; or, Weeping Ioy: Expressd in a Poem, to the Honor of Englands Too Great Solemnities (London: Printed by Thomas Creede for S. Waterson, 1603);

Meditations and Vowes Diuine and Morall, Seruing For direction in Christian and Ciuill practice. Diuided into two Bookes (London: Printed by Humphrey Lownes for John Porter, 1605);

Mvndvs Alter Et Idem Siue Terra Australis ante hac semper incognita longis peregrini Academici nuperrime lustrata, anonymous (Frankfurt: Apud haeredes Ascanij de Rinialme [London: Printed by Humphrey Lownes], 1605); translated by John Healey as *The Discovery of A New World or A Description of the South Indies. Hetherto Vnnknowne. By an English Mercury* (London: Printed by Ed. Blount & W. Barrett, 1609?);

Meditations and Vowes Diuine and Morall, Seruing For direction in Christian and Ciuill practice. A Third Century (London: Printed by Humphrey Lownes for John Porter, 1606);

Heaven upon Earth; or, Of True Peace and Tranquillitie of Minde (London: Printed for John Porter, 1606);

The Arte of Divine Meditation: Profitable for all Christians to knowe and practice; Exemplified with a large Meditation of eternall life (London: Printed by Humphrey Lownes for Samuel Macham & Mathew Cooke, 1606);

Holy Observations. Lib. I. Also Some fewe of Davids Psalmes Metaphrased, for a taste of the Rest (London: Printed by Humphrey Lownes for Samuel Macham, 1607);

Characters of Vertues and Vices: In Two Bookes (London: Printed by Melchisedech Bradwood for Eleazar Edgar & Samuel Macham, 1608);

Pharisaisme and Christianity: Compared and Set forth in a Sermon at Pauls Crosse, May 1. 1608, as J. H. (London: Printed by Melchisedech Bradwood for Samuel Macham, 1608);

Epistles, 3 volumes (volumes 1–2, London: Printed by A. Hatfield for Eleazar Edgar & Samuel Macham, 1608; volume 3, London: Printed for Eleazar Edgar & A. Garbrand, 1611);

The Passion-Sermon, Preached at Pavles-Crosse, on Good-Friday, Apr. 14, 1609, as J. H. (London: Printed by H. L. for Eleazar Edgar & Samuel Macham, 1609);

Salomons diuine arts of 1. Ethickes, 2. Politickes, 3. Oeconomickes. That is; the gouernment of 1. Behaviovr, 2. Common-wealth, 3. Familie. Drawne into method, out of his Proverbs & Ecclesiastes. With An open and plaine paraphrase, vpon the Song of Songs (London: Printed by Humphrey Lownes for Eleazar Edgar & Samuel Macham, 1609);

The Peace of Rome. Proclaimed, To All the world, by her famous Cardinall Bellarmine, and the no lesse famous Casuist Navarre. Whereof the one acknowledgeth, and numbers vp aboue three hundred differences of Opinion, maintained in the Popish Church. The other confesses neere threescore differences amongst their owne Doctors in one onely point of their Religion. Gathered faithfully out of their writings in their own words, and diuided into foure Bookes, and those into seuerall Decads. Whereto Is Prefixed A Serious Disswasiue from Poperie, as J. H. (London: Printed for Samuel Macham, 1609);

A Common Apologie of the Chvrch of England: Against the Vniust Challenges of the Ouer Iust Sect, Commonly Called Brownists. Wherein the Grounds and Defence, of the Separation Are Largely Discussed: Occasioned by a Late Pamphlet Published vnder the Name of An Answer to a Censorious Epistle, Which the Reader Shall Find in the Margent (London: Printed for Eleazar Edgar, 1610);

Joseph Hall

Polemices Sacrae Pars Prior Roma Irreconciliabilis: Qua docetur Nullam, Sperari posse, nec debere quidem (vti se nunc res habent) Pontificiorum cum Euangelicis, in causa Religionis, Conciliationem: Cudendamque in solos Pontificios hanc fabam (London: Printed by A. H. for Samuel Macham, 1611);

Contemplations vpon the Principall Passages of the Holy Storie, as J. H. D. D. (London: Printed by Melchisedech Bradwood for Samuel Macham, 1612);

An Holy Panegyrick: A Sermon Preached at Paules Crosse vpon the Anniuersarie Solemnitie of the Happie Inauguration of Our Dread Soueraigne Lord King James, Mar. 24. 1613, as J. H. (London: Printed by John Pindley for Samuel Macham, 1613);

Contemplations vpon the Principal Passages of the Holy Story. The Second Volume: In foure Bookes (London: Printed by H. L. for Samuel Macham, 1614);

A Recollection of such Treatises as haue bene heretofore seuerally published, and are nowe reuised, corrected, augmented. With addition of some others not hitherto extant (London: Printed by Humphrey Lownes

for Arthur Johnson, Samuel Macham & Laurence Lisle, 1615 [1614]);

Contemplations Vpon the principal passages of the Holie Historie. The Third Volume: In Three Books (London: Printed by Humphrey Lownes for Nathanael Butter & William Butler, 1615);

Quo vadis? A Iust Censure of Travell as it is commonly vndertaken by the Gentlemen of our Nation (London: Printed by Edward Griffin for Henry Fetherstone, 1617);

Contemplations vpon the Principall Passages of the Holy Story. The Fovrth Volume: In Three Bookes (London: Printed by Edward Griffin for Henry Fetherstone, 1618);

The Righteous Mammon: An Hospitall Sermon Preach't in the Solemne Assembly of the City on Munday in Easter-Weeke 1618 (London: Printed by E. Griffin for Henry Fetherstone, 1618);

Contemplations, the Fifth Volume (London: Printed by John Haviland for Nathanael Butter, 1620);

The Honor of the Married Clergie, Maintayned against the Malicious Challenges of C. E. Masse-Priest: or, The Apologie Written Some Yeares since for the Marriage of Persons Ecclesiasticall, Made Good against the

Cauils of C. E. Pseudo-Catholik Priest. In Three Books (London: Printed by William Stansby for Henry Fetherstone, 1620);

Contemplations, the Sixth Volume (London: Printed by John Haviland for Nathanael Butter, 1622);

A Sermon preached before his Maiestie at his Court of Thebalds, on Sunday, Sept. 15. 1622. In the ordinary course of attendance (London: Printed by John Haviland for Nathanael Butter, 1622);

The Best Bargaine: A Sermon Preached to the Court at Theobalds, On Sunday, Sept. 21. 1623 (London: Printed by John Haviland for Nathanael Butter, 1623);

Contemplations vpon the Historie of the Old Testament: The Seventh Volume (London: Printed by John Haviland for Nathanael Butter, 1623);

The Great Impostor, Laid open in a Sermon at Grayes Inne, Febr. 2, 1623 (London: Printed by John Haviland for Nathanael Butter, 1623);

Noah's Dove, Bringing an Olive of Peace to the Tossed Arke of Christs Chvrch: A Sermon Preacht in Latine, in the Convocation, Held in Sainte Pavles Chvrch, to the Clergie of England, and Especially That of the Province of Canterbvry, translated by Robert Hall (London: Printed by John Haviland for Hanna Barret, 1624);

The True Peace-Maker: Laid forth in a Sermon before His Majesty at Theobalds, September 19. 1624 (London: Printed by T. Haviland for Nathanael Butter, 1624);

A Sermon Preached at the Reconcilement of the Happily-Restored, and Reedified Chappell of the Right Honourable, the Earl of Exceter, in His House of S. Iohns. On Saint Stephens Day 1623 (London: Printed by Felix Kyngston for George Winder, 1624);

Contemplations vpon the Historicall Part of the Old Testament: The eighth and last volume (London: Printed by M. Flesher for Nathanael Butter, 1626);

A Sermon of Publike Thanksgiving for the wonderfull mitigation of the late Mortalitie; Preacht before his Matie; vpon his gracious command, at his Court of Whitehall, Ian. 29. 1625. and Vpon the same command Published (London: Printed by M. Flesher for Nathanael Butter, 1626);

The Olde Religion: A Treatise, wherein is Laid downe the True State of the Difference betwixt the Reformed, and Romane Church; and the Blame of this Schisme Is Cast vpon the True Avthors. Serving for the Vindication of Our Innocence, for the Setling of Wauering Minds for a Preseruatiue against Popish Insinuations (London: Printed by William Stansby for Nathanael Butter & R. Hawkings, 1628);

One of the Sermons Preacht at Westminster, on the Day of the Publike Fast (April 5, 1628): To the Lords of the High Court of Parliament (London: Printed for Nathanael Butter, 1628);

A Sermon Preached to His Maiestie, on the Sunday before Past (Being March 30) at White-hall in Way of Preparation for That Holy Exercise (London: Printed by M. Flesher for Nathanael Butter, 1628);

An Answer to Pope Vrban His Invrbanity, Expressed In A Breve Sent To Lowis the French King, exasperating him against the Protestants in France. Written in Latine by Ioseph Lord Bishop of Exeter. Translated into English by B. S. (London: Printed by William Jones for Nicolas Bourne, 1629);

The Reconciler: or, An Epistle Pacificatorie of the Seeming Differences of Opinion Concerning the True Being and Visibilitie of the Roman Church. Enlarged with the Addition of Letters of Resolution, for That Purpose, from Some Famous Divines of Our Chvrch (London: Printed for Nathanael Butter, 1629);

The Hypocrite: Set forth in a Sermon at the Covrt; February, 28. 1629. Being the third Sunday in Lent (London: Printed by William Stansby for Nathanael Butter, 1630);

Occasionall Meditations, edited by Robert Hall (London: Printed for Nathanael Butter, 1630); enlarged as *Occasionall Meditations. The Third Edition: With the Addition of 49. Meditations Not Heretofore Published* (London: Printed by William Stansby for Nathanael Butter, 1633);

A Paraphrase vpon the Hard Texts of the New Testament (London: Printed by M. Flesher for Nathanael Butter, 1632);

A Plaine and Familiar Explication (by Way of Paraphrase) of all the hard Texts of the whole Divine Scripture of the Old Testament (London: Printed by M. Flesher for Nathanael Butter, 1633);

Propositiones Catholicae, qvas, ingenvis qvibvscvnqve Christianis, per totvm orbem dispersis, serio pensitandas, supplex offert pius Ecclesias filius (London: Printed by M. Flesher for Nathanael Butter, 1633);

The Works of Joseph Hall, B. of Exeter. With a Table Now Added to the Same (London: Printed by M. Flesher, 1634);

The Second Tome: Containing the Contemplations upon the History of the New Testament, now complete: Together with Divers Treatises not hitherto reduced to the greater Volume: And, Some others never till now published (London: Printed by M. Flesher for Nathanael Butter, 1634);

Αυτοσχεδιασματα: *Vel, Meditatiunculae Subitanae* (London: Printed for Nathanael Butter, 1635);

The Character of Man: Laid forth in a Sermon Preach't at the Court, March 10, 1634 (London: Printed by M. Flesher for Nathanael Butter, 1635);

Henochismus: Sive, Tractus De modo ambulandi cum Deo (London: Printed for Nathanael Butter, 1635);

The Remedy of Prophanesse. Or, Of the true sight and feare of the Almighty. A needful tractate. In two bookes (London: Printed by Thomas Harper for Nathanael Butter, 1637);

A Sermon Preach't in the City of Excester, at the Consecration of a New Buriall-Place, There, on Saint Bartholomew's Day, Aug. 24, 1637 (London: Printed by Thomas Harper for Nathanael Butter, 1637);

Certaine Irrefragable Propositions worthy of Serious Consideration (London: Printed by M. Flesher for Nathanael Butter, 1639);

An Humble Remonstrance To The High Covrt Of Parliament. By A dutifull Sonne of the Chvrch, anonymous (London: Printed for Nathanael Butter, 1640);

Christian Moderation. In Two Books (London: Printed by M. Flesher for Nathanael Butter, 1640);

Episcopacie by Divine Right. Asserted (London: Printed by R. Badger for Nathanael Butter, 1640);

A Defence of the Humble Remonstrance, Against the frivolous and false exceptions of Smectymnvvs. Wherein the Right of Leiturgie and Episcopacie Is Clearly Vindicated from the Vaine Cavils, and Challenges of the Answerers. By the Author of the Said Humble Remonstance, anonymous (London: Printed for Nathanael Butter, 1641);

A Sermon Preach't to His Majesty, at the Court of Whitehall. Aug. 8. (London: Printed by M. Flesher for Nathanael Butter, 1641);

A Short Answer to the Tedious Vindication of Smectymnvvs. By the Author of the Humble Remonstrance, anonymous (London: Printed for Nathanael Butter, 1641);

A Letter Sent to an Honourable Gentleman, in Way of Satisfaction, Concerning Some Slanderous Reports Lately Raised against the Bishops, and the Rest of the Clergie of This Kingdome (London, 1641);

Philadelphvs Vapulans. Theophili Iscani Ad Calumniosam Irenaei Philadelphi Epistolo Responsio (London: Printed by M. Flesher for Nathanael Butter, 1641);

Survey of That Foolish, Seditious, Scandalous, Prophane Libell, The Protestation Protested, anonymous, attributed to Hall (London, 1641);

A Letter Lately sent by A Reverend Bishop from the Tower to A private Friend; and by Him Thought Fit to Be Published, anonymous (London, 1642);

A Modest Confutation of a Slanderous and Scurrilous Libell, Entituled, Animadversions upon the Remonstrants against Smectymnuus, anonymous, attributed to Hall (London, 1642);

A Modest Offer of Some Meet Considerations Tendered to the Learned Prolocutor, and to the Rest of the Assembly of Divines, Met at Westminster. By a True Lover of Truth and Peace, anonymous (Oxford, 1644);

The Devout Soul. Or, Rules of heavenly Devotion. Also The Free Prisoner, Or, The comfort of Restraint (London: Printed by M. Flesher for Nathanael Butter, 1644);

The Lawfvlnes and Vnlawfvlnes of an Oath or Covenant Set downe in Short Propositions Agreeable to the Law of God and Man, and May Serve to Rectifie the Conscience of Any Reasonable Man: Very Fiting for Every Man to Take into Serious Consideration in These Undutifull Times, Whether He Hath Sworne or Not Sworne to Any Late or New Oath or Covenant made by Any Subordinate Authority Whatsoever, anonymous (Oxford [London]: Printed by Leonard Lichfield, 1645);

The Peace-Maker: Laying forth the Right Way of Peace, in Matter of Religion (London: Printed by M. Flesher for Nathanael Butter, 1645);

The Remedy of Discontentment, or A Treatise of Contentation in Whatsoever Condition (London: Printed by M. Flesher for Nathanael Butter, 1645);

The Balme of Gilead: or, Comforts for the Distressed, Both Morall and Divine. Most Fit for These Wofull Times (London: Printed by M. Flesher for Nathanael Butter, 1646);

Christ Mysticall; or The Blessed Union of Christ and His Members. Also, An Holy Rapture: or, A Patheticall Meditation of the Love of Christ. Also, The Christian Laid forth in His Whole Disposition and Carriage (London: Printed by M. Flesher, to be sold by William Hope, Gabriel Beadle & Nathaniel Webbe, 1647);

Satans Fiery Darts Quenched, or, Temptations Repelled. In Three Decades. For the Help, Comfort, and Preservation of Weak Christians in These Dangerous Times of Errour and Seduction (London: Printed by M. Flesher for Nathanael Butter, to be sold by N. Brooks, 1647);

Pax Terris (London, 1648);

Select Thoughts, One Century. Also The Breathings of the Devout Soul (London: Printed by J. L. for Nathaniel Brooks, 1648);

Χειροθεσια. Or, The Apostolique Institvtion of Imposition of Hands, for Confirmation, Revived. By a Lover of Peace, Truth, and Order, anonymous (London: Printed by J. G. for Nathanael Butter, 1649);

Resolutions and Decisions of Divers Practicall Cases of Conscience in Continuall Use amongst Men, Very Necessary for Their Information and Direction, as J. H. (London: Printed by M. Flesher for Nathanael Butter, to be sold by H. Mosley, 1649); enlarged as *Cases of Conscience Practically Received; Containing a Decision of the Principall Cases of Conscience, of Daily Concernment, and Coninual Use amongst Men. Very Necessary for Their Information and Direction in These Evil Times. The Third Edition Much Inlarged* (London: Printed by R. H. & J. G., sold by F. Eglesfield, 1654);

The Revelation Unrevealed. Concerning The Thousand-Yeares Reigne of the Saints with Christ upon Earth. Laying forth the Weak Grounds, and strange Consequences of that plausible, and too-much received Opinion. By an unfained Lover of Truth, Peace, Order, and just Moderation, anonymous (London: Printed by R. L. for J. Bisse, 1650);

Susurrium cum Deo. Soliloquies: or, Holy Self-Conferences of the Devout Soul, upon Sundry Choice Occasions, with Humble Addresses to the Throne of Grace. Together with The Souls Farewell to Earth, and Approaches to Heaven (London: Printed by William Hunt, sold by George Lathum, Jr., 1651);

The Great Mysterie of Godliness, Laid forth by way of affectuous and feeling Meditation. Also, The Invisible World, Discovered to spirituall Eyes, and Reduced to Usefull Meditation. In Three Books (London: Printed by John Place, 1652);

Holy Raptures, or Patheticall Meditations of the Love of Christ. Together with a Treatise of Christ Mysticall. Also the Christian Laid forth in His Whole Disposition & Carriage (London: Printed by E. C. for J. Sweeting, 1652);

The Holy Order or Fraternity of the Mourners of Sion. Whereunto Is Added Songs in the Night, or Cheerefulnesse under Affliction, as J. H. (London: Printed by J. C. for N. Brooke, 1654);

An Apologeticall Letter to a Person of Qvality, Concerning a Scandalous and Malicious Passage, in a Conference Lately Held betwixt an Inquisitor at White-Hall and Mr. Anthony Sadler, Published in His Inquisitio Anglicana. Written by Jo. Hall Bishop of Norwich, in Vindication of Himself (London: Printed for Nathanael Butter, 1655);

The Invisible World, Discovered to Spirituall Eyes, and Reduced to Usefull Meditation. Also, the great Mystery of Godliness, Laid forth by Way of Affectuous and Feeling Meditation, with the Apostolicall Institution of Imposition of Hands, for Confirmation of Children (London: Printed by E. Cotes for John Place, 1659);

A Letter Concerning Christmasse; Sent to a Knight in Suffolke (London: Printed by E. C. for Fran Grove, 1659);

The Shaking of the Olive-Tree: The Remaining Works of That Incomparable Prelate Joseph Hall . . . With Some Specialties of Divine Providence in His Life, Noted by His Own Hand. Together with His Hard Measure, Written also by Himself (London: Printed by J. Cadwell for J. Crooke, 1660);

Divers Treatises, Written upon severall Occasions, by Joseph Hall late Bishop of Norwich: The Third Tome (London: Printed by R. H., J. G. & W. H., 1662);

A Letter Concerning Separation, Written Formerly by æ Reverend Author; and Recommended to All (Especially the Truly Christian and Honest-Minded) Members of the Separation within This Distracted and Divided Kingdom (London: Printed for W. D., 1681).

Editions: *The Works of Joseph Hall, Successively Bishop of Exeter and Norwich, Now First Collected. With Some Account of His Life and Sufferings, Written by Himself,* 10 volumes, edited by Josiah Pratt (London: Printed by C. Whittingham for Williams & Smith, 1808); revised and enlarged, 12 volumes, edited by Peter Hall (Oxford: Talboys, 1837–1839);

The Works of the Right Reverend Joseph Hall, D.D.: A New Edition, Revised and Corrected, with Some Additions, 10 volumes, edited by Philip Wynter (Oxford: Oxford University Press, 1863; New York: AMS Press, 1969);

The Discovery of a New World (Mundus Alter et Idem) Written Originally by Joseph Hall, ca. 1605; Englished by John Healey, ca. 1609, edited by Huntington Brown (Cambridge, Mass.: Harvard University Press, 1937);

Heaven upon Earth, and Characters of Vertues and Vices, edited by Rudolf Kirk (New Brunswick, N. J.: Rutgers University Press, 1948);

The Collected Poems of Joseph Hall, edited by Arnold Davenport (Liverpool: Liverpool University Press, 1949);

Another World and Yet the Same: Bishop Joseph Hall's Mundus Alter et Idem, edited and translated by John Millar Wands (New Haven: Yale University Press, 1981);

Hall and Protestant Meditation in Seventeenth-Century England: A Study with the Texts of The Arte of Divine Meditation *(1606) and* Occasional Meditations *(1633),* edited by Frank Livingstone Huntley (Binghamton, N.Y.: Medieval and Renaissance Texts and Studies, 1981).

OTHER: "To the Praise of the Dead and the Anatomy," in John Donne, *An Anatomy of the World* (London: Printed for Samuel Macham, 1611);

"To the Praise of the Dead and the Anatomy" and "The Harbinger to the Progres," in Donne, *The First Anniuersarie: An Anatomie of the World* (London: Printed by Melchisedech Bradwood for Samuel Macham, 1612).

Joseph Hall produced a substantial body of works that had a significant impact on seventeenth-century English prose. Perhaps best known for his claim to be the "first English satirist," Hall was also an important innovator in prose: he introduced the Theophrastan character sketch and the formal prose epistle into English; he exemplified the fashionable Senecan, or curt, style in these and other works; he wrote what is now regarded as a major devotional treatise, *The Arte of Divine Meditation* (1606); and he experimented in a variety of meditative prose genres. Hall knew, or was known to, major writers: he was attacked in satires by John Marston; he was a close friend of John Donne and wrote poetic prefaces for Donne's *Anniversaries* (1611, 1612); he was attacked by John Milton in a pamphlet war in the 1640s; and he was tended in his later years in Norwich by his friend and physician, Sir Thomas Browne. Hall's long career as a satirist, controversialist, prelate, and devotional writer was closely connected to many of the key developments in the literary and political history of this most eventful period.

Hall rose from humble origins to become a bishop in the national church. He was born on 1 July 1574 at Bristow Park near Ashby de la Zouch, Leicestershire, where his father, John Hall, was the bailiff of Henry Hastings, third Earl of Huntingdon. Like most of his successful contemporaries, Hall advanced by a combination of talent and good connections; but in his autobiography, "Observations of Some Specialties of Divine Providence," published in the posthumous collection *The Shaking of the Olive-Tree* (1660), he singled out, in addition to Providence, his mother as a particularly important force in his development, comparing her influence on him to that of Saint Monica on Saint Augustine. Although one may be tempted to dismiss his claim as autobiographical convention, Winifride Bambridge Hall's Calvinistic piety was part of an environment of Puritanism in Ashby de la Zouch that was politically connected and that had an abiding effect on Hall's spiritual outlook. The earl of Huntingdon had founded the Ashby Grammar School, and he was also among those who established at Cam-

bridge University the Puritan-leaning Emmanuel College to produce a Protestant clergy that was learned in theology. Anthony Gilby, Hall's mother's spiritual counselor, was a Calvinist hard-liner who had gone into exile during the reign of Mary Tudor and who had played a major role in developing the Ashby Grammar School curriculum.

Having been designated early for the ministry, at fifteen Hall entered Emmanuel, where he was tutored by Gilby's son, Nathaniel. He had a brilliant career at the university: he was elected fellow in 1595, and after receiving the M.A. in 1596, he was elected to the university lectureship in rhetoric for two successive terms.

While a fellow of Emmanuel, Hall made literary history with his collection of verse satires *Virgidemiarum, Sixe Bookes* (1597), which gives him a claim (asserted by Hall himself) to be the first English satirist. In a "Post-script" to *Virgidemiarum,* Hall bade farewell to poetry, "having shaked handes with all her retinue," but his literary activities at Cambridge seem to have continued. There is evidence that he was involved in writing the three "Parnassus Plays," which satirized academic life and contemporary literature, and he probably also began his prose satire *Mundus Alter et Idem* (1605).

Hall was ordained on 14 December 1600 and accepted the rectory of Hawstead in Suffolk offered by Sir Robert and Lady Anne Drury; Hall's prefatory poems to Donne's *Anniversaries* eulogize their daughter Elizabeth, who died at age fourteen. It may have been at Hawstead that Hall first met Donne; Donne's sister Anne was married to William Lyly, a friend of Sir Robert's, and they lived in the Drury household from 1598 to 1603. Hall's situation at Hawstead was uneasy; he suspected Lyly of prejudicing Sir Robert against him, and he viewed Lyly's death by the plague as one of the "specialties" performed by Providence in his career. He also felt that he was grossly underpaid by Sir Robert, claiming that he was "forced to write books to buy books." Nevertheless, in 1603 Hall married Elizabeth Winiffe, with whom he would have two daughters and six sons.

Mundus Alter et Idem appeared in 1605; Hall seems to have taken considerable trouble to see the work into print and to conceal his authorship, having the book published surreptitiously in London with a false Frankfurt imprint and a preface by his friend William Knight claiming that Hall opposed publication. (Hall's Latin text was translated into lively English prose by John Healey as *The Discovery of a New World* [1609?]). Although Hall had probably begun it, as Knight says, "for his own training and amusement in a youthful and leisurely academic period," it evidences such detailed knowledge of the Drury home that it is certain that Hall continued to work on it after he left Cambridge. Milton described the book as "the idlest and paltriest Mime that ever mounted upon banke," and his judgment may strike some readers as just. Hall was attempting a work in the vein of Sir Thomas More's *Utopia* (1516) or Desiderius Erasmus's *Moriae encomium* (1511; translated as *The Praise of Folly,* 1549) — a Menippean satire or anatomy (in another passage Milton compares it unfavorably to More's *Utopia*). In Antarctica the Cambridge scholar Mercurius Brittannicus visits the kingdoms of Crapulia (land of gluttons), Viraginia (land of the Amazons), Moronia (land of fools), and Lavernia (land of thieves). A parody of a learned discourse, complete with extensive footnotes and an "Index of Proper Names," it attacks the follies and crimes suggested by the names of the various countries while mocking the genre of travel literature. Although it is difficult to identify in Hall's book the central intellectual or moral pattern that usually underlies a Menippean satire, Hall may have intended an anatomy of flesh and spirit. Crapulia is a reductio ad absurdum of the pursuit of fleshly pleasure; in Viraginia, women, associated with the flesh, rule the men (although Hall, perhaps unwittingly, often seems to undercut the misogynistic premise); in Moronia, which is the opposite of Crapulia and resembles in many particulars the Laputa of Jonathan Swift's *Gulliver's Travels* (1726), the inhabitants misuse reason and pursue various forms of false spirituality; and in Lavernia the consequences of materialism are exposed. The most important section of *Mundus Alter et Idem* is that on Moronia, in which Hall deals with folly in government, philosophy, religion, and morality. At the geographic center of Moronia is the shrine of fortune, where pilgrims are allowed to experience twelve hours of bliss in a drug-induced dream before being unceremoniously returned to reality.

Mundus Alter et Idem appeared just at the time that Hall was establishing himself as a writer of devotional prose with the two volumes of his *Meditations and Vowes Divine and Morall* (1605, 1606) and *The Arte of Divine Meditation.* These works were the first in a series of meditative writings that Hall produced throughout his long life and that perhaps comprise his chief legacy to English literature. The devout humanism and meditative practices of Europe, exemplified in the works of the great spiritual writers of sixteenth-century Spain and seventeenth-century France, have long been held to have influenced the devotional poetry of England in the sev-

enteenth century; more recently scholars have focused on a distinctively Protestant theory and practice of devotion that contributed to a "Protestant poetics" in England. Hall played a key role in this development as both a "theorist" and practitioner of devotion.

His interest in devotional writing may have been sparked by a trip to Europe he took in 1605 with Sir Edmund Bacon, Lady Drury's brother. Hall was fiercely anti-Catholic throughout his life, but he felt equally strongly that Protestantism needed to catch up to the great devotional literature of Catholic Europe. This feeling is discernible in the early sections of *The Arte of Divine Meditation,* where Hall repeatedly presses the urgency of his project of bringing the art of meditation perfected by monks into the lives of active Christians. To accomplish this task he allows for great flexibility in the method of meditation, defining it as "nothing else but a bending of the mind upon some spiritual object, through diverse forms of discourse, until our thoughts come to an issue." While he distinguishes between "extemporal" and "deliberate" meditation, he emphasizes that both aim at "the enkindling of our love of God." *The Arte of Divine Meditation* is chiefly devoted to outlining and illustrating the deliberate type of meditation, since "Of extemporal meditation there may be much use, no rule." Scholars have noted that Hall's Protestant variety of deliberate meditation bears a strong resemblance to the sermon. Deliberate meditation "begins in the understanding, endeth in the affection; begins on earth, ascends to heaven, not suddenly but by certain stairs and degrees till we come to the highest." Differentiating his own method from the "darkness and coincidence" of elaborate scales of meditation used by Continental writers, Hall requires "only a deep and firm consideration of the thing propounded," which is accomplished by running the matter to be meditated through such rhetorical topics of invention as division, definition, cause and effect, and so forth. This "difficult and knotty part of meditation" is followed by the more important stage in which the meditator responds emotionally to the subject: "A man is a man, by his understanding part, but he is a Christian, by his will and affections." Borrowing from the *Scala Meditatoria* of Joannes Maubernus's *Rosetum* (1494), Hall moves the topic through seven degrees of the affections before concluding the exercise with a thanksgiving prayer. He illustrates the method with two complete meditations, "one of eternall life, as the end, the other of Death, as the way."

In the dedication of *The Arte of Divine Meditation* Hall refers to the meditations in *Meditations and*

Vowes Divine and Morall as "those sudden meditations which passed me without rule"; thus, they fall into the category of extemporal meditation. They are the first attempts at a form that Hall would later develop in his *Occasionall Meditations* (1630). In *Meditations and Vowes Divine and Morall* Hall offers brief reflections on commonplace moral topics, moving through the faculties of memory, intellect, and will. Most notable about these brief essays are Hall's clipped Senecan prose style and his presentation of himself in the act of meditating. Instead of placing the reader in the position of the "I" of the meditation, Hall presents his reflections as emphatically *his:* "having after a sort vowed this austere course of judgement and practice to myself, I thought it best to acquaint the world with it that it may either witness my answerable proceeding, or check me in my straying therefrom." Such a relationship between the devout reader and writer contributes to the literary flavor of the work: one is not expected to share uncritically the author's viewpoint but, rather, to "witness" and "check" the author's distinctive shaping of his experience.

A major determinant of that shaping of experience is Hall's style, a particularly severe version of the *stile coupé,* or curt style, that became fashionable in seventeenth-century European prose. Hall's use of this style, which became a trademark – earning him the title of "the English or Christian Seneca" and the scorn of Milton, who derided the manner – derived from his interest in the European revival of Stoicism known as Neostoicism. While at Hawstead, Hall wrote a work of Christian Stoicism, *Heaven upon Earth; or, Of True Peace and Tranquillitie of Minde* (1606). The book went through three English editions between 1606 and 1609 and appears to have contributed significantly to Hall's growing reputation in France and Germany. In the dedication Hall says, "I have undertaken a great taske . . . wherein I have followed Seneca, and gone beyond him; followed him as a Philosopher, gone beyond him as a Christian, as a Divine." An elaborate Ramist chart prefaces the book, and the bifurcated sections of the treatise are mirrored in the balanced, antithetical sentences within them. Throughout the tract Stoic precepts and practices are alternately viewed as admirable and as sadly limited efforts to cope with fundamental human problems: the Stoics diligently sought tranquillity through the exercise of reason; however, "Not *Athens* must teach this lesson, but *Ierusalem.*"

While in London with Sir Robert in 1607, Hall learned of the enthusiastic reception at Prince Henry's court of his *Meditations and Vowes Divine and Morall.* After preaching two sermons before the

prince, Hall was made a chaplain to the court. It was also during this trip that Drury introduced Hall to Baron Edward Denny, who offered Hall the posts of chaplain to his household and rector of the abbey church at Waltham Holy Cross in Essex. Denny was one of the dedicatees of Hall's next literary success, *Characters of Vertues and Vices* (1608).

This book, another of Hall's "firsts," introduced into English the Theophrastan character sketch that became a popular seventeenth-century genre. The 1608 edition consists of nine sketches of virtuous types followed by fifteen portraits of vicious ones; in a collected edition of Hall's works in 1614 two additional "vertues" appear. The work was brilliantly designed to meet with success at the Jacobean court. Hall's prefatory "Premonition, of the Title and Use of Characters" displays his familiarity with the 1592 translation of Theophrastus's *Characters* by Isaac Casaubon, a classical scholar highly regarded by James I. *Characters of Vertues and Vices,* however, like *Heaven upon Earth,* combines classical theory with scriptural models, and also like *Heaven upon Earth* it privileges the scriptural approach. Hall notes that he has followed the path of the ancients, "but with an higher and wider step." This higher way was marked out by Proverbs and Ecclesiastes, biblical works likely to appeal to the king, who styled himself the British Solomon. Hall courted James even more directly with his *Salomons divine arts* (1609), a compilation of "characters" from passages in Proverbs and Ecclesiastes couched in the sententious Proverbial style preferred by James.

Characters of Vertues and Vices and *Salomons divine arts* share a Proverbial, decidedly un-Theophrastan approach to character. Theophrastus opens each of his sketches with the definition of the abstract quality being illustrated, followed by a careful description of specific actions by a person who could be characterized in terms of that quality; the portraits depend on observation, verisimilitude, and clarity for their effect. The scriptural portraits, on the other hand, are frequently vague types, such as the "wicked man," presented in terms of both action and metaphor; the "good wife" of Proverbs and of *Salomons divine arts,* for example, "girdeth her loynes with strength" and "is like the ship of merchants, shee bringeth her food from farre." In Proverbs action is only the tip of the iceberg; the conditions of behavior seem to lie within the heart of the character, not within a set of social or material circumstances. Related to this difference is a difference in tone; where Theophrastus's concentration on externals results in his famous detachment, the Proverbial focus on the state of a character's inner moral being issues in denunciation or praise. Thus the biblical sketches tend to be rhetorical and affective, not representational and ironic as are those of Theophrastus.

Characters of Vertues and Vices incorporates all the features of Proverbial style: figurative description, lack of verisimilitude, overlapping of moral types, and conflation of description and prescription. At the same time Hall calls on the Renaissance literary theory and practice of the "speaking picture": the literary work is to be at once rhetorical and representational. His Ramist habit of mind probably helps to explain the sharp division of sketches into virtues and vices, though his scheme would also have met with the approval of Ben Jonson, who required of the true poet "exact knowledge of all vertues, and their Contraries." Hall seems to have aimed at what Jonson in his *Discoveries* (1640) termed the "feigned commonwealth" of virtues and vices; like Jonson in his *Epigrams* (1616), moreover, Hall makes the most serious claims for a literary form that has come to be seen as minor. Hall was not imitated by the better-known character writers such as Sir Thomas Overbury and John Earle, whose sketches are less pretentious and more entertaining.

Like Hall's other works of this period, *Characters of Vertues and Vices* is done in what would become Hall's signature style, a rather extreme version of the curt style. This style and other so-called anti-Ciceronian prose styles were much studied by literary scholars through the 1960s as signs of shifts from the public, oratorical model of writing represented by Cicero toward a more interiorized, private mode of self-expression, and from a rhetorical to a scientific culture. Hall's comments on prose style reveal his affinity with other writers of the period, such as Sir Francis Bacon, who call for an attention to matter over manner; in *Holy Observations* (1607) Hall writes, "Much ornament is no good sign: painting of the face argues an ill complexion of body, a worse mind." Like many other of these writers, however, Hall paradoxically expresses his preference for matter over manner in a highly wrought, mannered style. But again, Hall's style probably owes more to the Scriptures than it does to Seneca and his imitators, such as Justus Lipsius; his favorite devices — parallelism, parataxis, antithesis, and brevity — are all major features of Proverbs and Ecclesiastes. Furthermore, he employs the style in the service of conventional Christian teaching. The basic building block of Hall's style is the so-called exploded period, a sequence of short clauses connected only by punctuation marks or coordinating conjunctions. Subordinate clauses are used sparingly, and when they do appear they are placed so as to seem detached from the main clause. The first unit of the sentence is sometimes a generalization that is illustrated in succeeding short members by particular instances. On other occasions Hall uses the style to achieve surprise and to force a rereading of the entire sentence to reconstruct its logic, as in the sketch of the "Honest Man": "He would rather want, than borrow, and beg, than not to pay: his faire conditions are without dissembling; and he loves actions above words." Perhaps most distinctive about Hall's style are the brevity and symmetry of grammatical units; his periods are exploded under highly controlled conditions that often evoke euphuism as much as anti-Ciceronianism: the "truly-noble man" "is more carefull to give true honor to his Maker, than to receive civill honor from men." At times the reader will agree with Milton that Hall seems to write his prose by the inch: "More might be said, I deny not, of every Vertue, of every Vice: I desired not to say all, but enough." At his best Hall can deliver the sense of a mind sifting an idea, and in some of the vices he surprises with a final satiric hit: his "distrustful man" "is uncharitable in his censures, unquiet in his feares; bad enough alwaies, but in his owne opinion much worse than he is." A passage from his "Good Magistrate" captures the Proverbial style at its most eloquent: "He is the faithfull Deputy of his Maker, whose obedience is the rule whereby he ruleth; his brest is the Ocean whereinto all the cares of private men empty themselves; which as he receives without complaint and overflowing, so he sends them forth again by a wise conveyance in the streams of justice."

Hall dedicated to Prince Henry the first volume of his three-volume *Epistles* (1608–1611). In the preface he claims that the work introduces "a new fashion of discourse, by epistles; new to our language, usual to others," a familiar form of writing in which "we do but talk with our friends by our pen and express ourselves no whit less easily, somewhat more digestedly." But his letters do not read like one side of a friendly conversation. They need to be seen in light of a rich, though somewhat confusing epistolary tradition that combined classical, medieval, and Renaissance theory and practice. In Seneca's weighty *Epistulae Morales* Hall found authority for the use of the letter as a pretext for moral discourse. Cicero had demonstrated the great range of subject matter and style possible in the epistolary form. Renaissance formularies of letter writing emphasized the close association of letter writing and oratory — an association that continued, if one judges from works such as Angel Day's *The English Secretarie* (1586). Antonio de Guevara's *Epistolas familiares* (1543; translated as *Familiar Epistles,* 1574) and *Golden Epistles* (1575) were particularly impressive examples of the Senecan approach to letter writing. The best known of the Neostoics, Lipsius, had called for a return to a conversational style while arguing for the suitability of the letter to treat a variety of subjects. Hall could also look to the patristic tradition for the epistolary treatise on moral, exegetical, or doctrinal questions; Saint Jerome, in particular, had demonstrated the usefulness of the letter as a method of satire as well as of instruction. Finally, the Pauline writings were particularly brilliant examples of the power of the epistle to convey the character of the writer along with the gravest moral teaching and theological reflection.

Hall's epistles come out of this essayistic or sermonic tradition and have virtually nothing in common with the witty recreations of a Donne or the newsy, familiar communications of James Howell. Even when they do discuss personal matters, they do not do so in an informal way: in the first letter in the collection, written to and attacking a former classmate, Jacob Wadsworth, for converting to Catholicism, Hall reduces Catholic rituals to absurdity. Two-thirds of the letters in the *Epistles* deal with religious topics, such as "the estate of a true, but weak Christian," but there are also discourses on divorce; dueling; Hall's translation of Psalms, which had appeared in 1607; and clerical marriage. There is also a letter to the Separatist leaders John Smith and John Robinson, founders of the Plymouth colony. Among the sprightliest of the epistles is one to Sir Thomas Chaloner that affords a glimpse into the relationship among Hall's literary endeavors, his politics, and his courtship of patrons. One of Hall's newsiest letters, it delivers a "report of some observations in my travel," chief of which are satiric accounts of Catholic hypocrisy and superstition. Hall was amusing Chaloner with a purpose in view, however: Chaloner had been appointed governor to Prince Henry in 1603, had attended Henry at Oxford in 1605, and was made his chamberlain in 1610. When Hall was introduced at court in 1607, negotiations for the marriage of Henry to the Spanish Infanta had been renewed; it is likely that Hall's travelogue was intended to prove instructive both to Chaloner and to his charge. The letter, then, is of a piece with other anti-Romish epistles in the collection: Hall, chaplain to the prince, was using the letters as a means of tightening his relationship to the court circle and of preaching in absentia against the evils of popery. In

the letters to Separatists Hall is less the satirist; alternately conciliatory and accusatory, these letters are what one would expect from Hall as a graduate of the Puritan college of Emmanuel and a rising star in the established church.

As the epistles on Roman Catholicism and Separatism suggest, Hall was becoming active in religious controversy at this time. In writing against these positions, Hall felt that he was constructing a middle way with which most members of the established church could live. Hall could, however, be much harsher with the Separatists than with the Catholics, as is evidenced in his *A Common Apologie of the Church of England: Against the Uniust Challenges of Over Just Sect, Commonly Called Brownists* (1610). His attitude toward Catholicism, on the other hand, was not always one of biting satire; by seventeenth-century standards he was a moderate, and by the time he wrote his most-considered anti-Catholic tract, *The Olde Religion* (1628), he was suspected by some Puritans of Romish sympathizing.

That suspicion needs to be considered in the light of developments in Hall's career and in the growing controversy over church government. King James selected him on three occasions for foreign missions; the most important of these was in 1618, when Hall was appointed as a deputy to the international Synod of Dordrecht in Holland, which had been convened to settle a dispute over Arminianism. Before leaving the synod after two months because of illness, he delivered a sermon on Ecclesiastes, one of James's favorite books, in which he recommended that both sides abandon their hard theological positions and return to Scripture for an answer. That Hall felt that he was playing such a role in his controversial writing is suggested by titles such as "Via Media" (written in 1624 and published in *The Shaking of the Olive-Tree*) and *The Reconciler* (1629), and he was frequently accused of Romanism by the Puritans and of Puritanism by the Laudians.

Hall became bishop of Exeter in 1627. His prospects under the Laudian regime were not initially clear, since, as he wrote in his autobiography, "some that sat at the stern of church had me in great jealousy for too much favor of Puritanism." Hall greatly resented being spied on by Bishop William Laud (who became archbishop of Canterbury in 1633) and even threatened to resign. Nonetheless, Laud had nothing to fear; Hall twice submitted *Episcopacie by Divine Right* (1640), his most important statement in the controversy over church government, to Laud's inspection, and, regardless of his personal feelings about the archbishop, he became

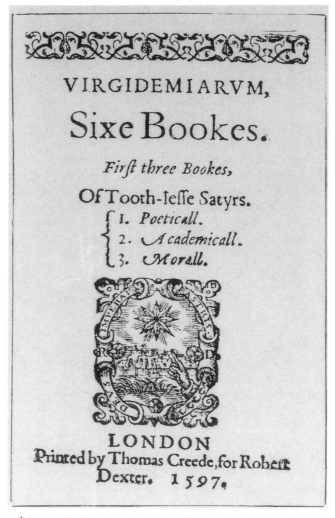

VIRGIDEMIARVM,

Sixe Bookes.

First three Bookes,

Of Tooth-lesse Satyrs.

{ 1. Poeticall.
{ 2. Academicall.
{ 3. Morall.

LONDON

Printed by Thomas Creede, for Robert Dexter. 1597.

Title page for the book that gave Hall a claim to be considered the first English satirist

an important mouthpiece for Laud's extreme views on prelacy. The chain of pamphlets whereby Hall became entangled with Milton in the episcopal controversy began with Hall's *An Humble Remonstrance to the High Court of Parliament. By a dutifull Sonne of the Church* (1640), which argued against the so-called Root and Branch Petition calling for the complete abolition of episcopacy. "Smectymnuus" (a name derived from the initials of five Puritan clergymen) responded to Hall in *An Answer to a Booke Entituled, An Humble Remonstrance* (1641). After an exchange that included Hall's *A Defence of the Humble Remonstrance* (1641), the Smectymnuuans' *A Vindication of the Answer to the Humble Remonstrance* (1641), and Hall's *A Short Answer to the Tedious Vindication of Smectymnuus* (1641), Milton entered the controversy with *Animadversions upon the Remonstrants Defence, against Smectymnuus* (1641). As a controversialist, Hall is remembered primarily as the target of Milton's ad hominem attacks in this work. Milton's attacks were answered in *A Modest Confutation of a Slanderous and Scurrilous Libell* (1642); the authorship of *A Modest Confutation* has never been definitively established, though Milton suspected Hall or one of his sons, as have many scholars of the controversy. Milton countered with *An Apology against a Pamphlet Call'd A Modest Confutation of the Animadversions upon the Remonstrant against Smectymnuus* (1641), which includes well-known autobiographical passages that reply to ad hominem attacks of the confuter. Hall had begun the controversy by appealing, once again, for both sides to show moderation and reasonableness; but as the attacks on him continued, his replies became clogged with erudition and hairsplitting logic. Milton's pamphlets may be vituperative and obscure, but Hall's are boring. Milton portrays Hall as a proud self-dramatizer using his rhetorical skills to advance his career, thus skillfully identifying Hall's early literary persona with the pride and privilege of an episcopal class intent only on preserving its power.

Hall himself thought of his career as one marked by a split, but not of the "Jack Donne / Dr. Donne" variety. A letter to the Drurys, included in the first decade of *Epistles* and written just after his move to Waltham, speaks of a division between his work as a pastor and "a greater work": "It were more ease to me to live secretly hidden in that quiet obscurity, as Saul among the stuff, than to be drawn out into the eye of the world; to act so high a part before a thousand witnesses." As his career advanced and the political climate became more agitated, he would reconceive this division of his work as one between politics and devotion. "As one the sense of whose private affliction is swallowed up of the public," he wrote in *The Devout Soul* (1644), published almost literally in the heat of battle, he decided that "the tears of penitence were more fit to quench the public flame than blood."

Throughout his career as a clergyman Hall insisted that the inner devotional life was the core of religion, and while he was learning the controversialist's trade he was also writing his meditations. *Occasionall Meditations* was described in theory in *The Arte of Divine Meditation,* and it was probably composed over a long period of time that began with the writing of that work. Along with *The Arte of Divine Meditation,* it has been considered an influence on the great religious poets of the century. In *The Arte of Divine Meditation* Hall wrote: "that which we are wont to say of fine wits we may as truly affirm of the Christian heart, that it can make use of anything"; like Duke Senior in William Shakespeare's *As You Like It* (circa 1599–1600), Hall can find "sermons in stones, and good in everything," including well-fleeced sheep, a bladder, a man yawning, a worm, a spider, an arm that has fallen asleep. Hall seems to have intended something like a primer in the art of reading the great "book of creatures": "And if ever these lines shall come to the public view, I desire and charge my reader, whosoever he be, to make me and himself so happy as to take out my lesson and to learn how to read God's great book by mine." Most of the pieces in *Occasionall Meditations* develop in three stages: a careful observation of the "occasion" is followed by an application to the spiritual life of the meditator, which finally issues in a prayer for continued support in the spiritual life. The meditation "Upon the Rain and Waters" illustrates the technique. Hall opens by expressing wonder at the "interchange . . . betwixt union and division" and details the natural processes of evaporation, precipitation, and replenishment that maintain the world's water supply. The application, in this case, works through simple analogy: "So it is or should be with spiritual gifts." After elaborating on the analogy in a bit more detail, the exercise ends with a plea that God "Take back . . . those few drops Thou hast rained upon my soul and return them into that great ocean of the glory of Thine own bounty, from whence they had their beginning." Using this basic pattern, Hall achieves considerable variety through the detail of his observations and the ingenuity of his applications. In some cases the observation seems detached from the application; for example, "Upon Occasion of a Spider in His Window" includes a brilliantly detailed mock-epic description of the spider that works against the earnest analogy to "spiritual freebooters that lie in wait for our souls." Hall also shows flexibility in his use of the tripartite structure; like Psalms, which were an important model for Hall's notion of extemporal meditation, these pieces often move freely between natural and spiritual phenomena.

In addition to his work on the "book of creatures," Hall produced a massive sequence of meditations on the "Book of Scriptures": eight volumes of contemplations on the Old Testament (1612–1626), followed by "The Contemplations upon the History of the New Testament" (1634). In common with many other seventeenth-century Protestants, Hall considered the reading of Scripture an act of meditation; thus, these works join the "private" genre of meditation to the narrative sweep and grandeur of "the Holie Storie." Hall combines highly dramatic incidents from the Bible with his own details of setting, character, and speech to produce in the reader a heartfelt and thoughtful response to the event. Some of the meditations challenge the view that Protestant meditation excludes the imaginative composing of the scene: in his meditation on the cross, for example, Hall says, "Methinks I see and feel, how, having fastened the transverse to the body of that fatal tree, and laid it upon the ground, they racked and strained thy tender and sacred limbs to fit the extent of their fore-appointed measure. . . ." But the chief distinction of the *Contemplations* lies in Hall's psychologizing of scriptural events. The contemplations are more affective than contemplative; in modern terminology, one might say that Hall practices a form of reader response that emphasizes what the scriptural text does to the reader rather than what it means. The "meaning" of the text is to be found in the affective response of the reader/meditator rather than in a clarification of doctrine. Furthermore, Hall frequently composes psychologically compelling portraits of biblical figures. In the meditation "Of Isaac Sacrificed" Hall imagines the thoughts of a weaker heart than Abraham's, given the terrible command; the weaker heart is, of course, the reader's. But he also glimpses the depths of Abraham's psychological suffering when he invents a speech in which Abraham tries to explain the strange command to Isaac. Hall's *Contemplations* is a major work of seventeenth-century devotional literature that affords a valuable insight into Protestant methods of reading the Bible.

Hall's sermons have not been anthologized in modern collections of seventeenth-century prose, but in his own era he was sufficiently noted as a preacher to have been one of the five exemplars included in Abraham Wright's *Five Sermons in Five Several Styles* (1656). He preached frequently at court, and sermons such as "The Beauty and Unitie of the Church," preached at Whitehall, and "Christ and Caesar," preached at Hampton Court, are vigorous statements of Stuart ideology. In the latter Hall turns an admonition – "Let the great *Caesars* of the world then know, that the more subject they are to Christ, the more sure they are of the loyalty of their subjects to them" – into a recommendation of a more activist religious policy in Ireland. At the same time, it must be said that Hall shows consistency when, in another Whitehall sermon titled "The Defeat of Crueltie," he identifies the strength of the nation with its devotional intensity: "What is it that made us so happily successeful in [15]88. beyond all hope, beyond all conceit, but the fervency of our humble devotions?" Hall is a lively preacher who wears his learning lightly. The trademark style is still discernible and, with the frequent shifts to the interrogative and imperative moods, creates a brisk, no-nonsense voice of authority. Hall's sermons are also clearly organized, following either the order of the biblical set text or a logical outline of topics. His wit is aphoristic or proverbial rather than poetic. His language is vivid and stirring, though never deep or disturbing.

Hall suffered for his support of the Stuart absolutism. In 1641 he was impeached by Parliament in July, made bishop of Norwich in November, and charged with high treason and sent to the Tower of London with Laud and eleven other bishops in December. There he wrote "prison works" of the kind usually associated with Puritans, "Some Specialties

of Divine Providence" and *A Letter Lately Sent by a Reverend Bishop from the Tower to a Private Friend* (1642). Hall was released after five months and moved to Norwich. In 1643 he was removed from his bishopric by the Act of Sequestration; in 1648 he was evicted from his house and moved to Higham, where he continued to preach and even to perform ordinations. He describes these hardships in "Hard Measure" (posthumously published in *The Shaking of the Olive-Tree*). He returned to meditative writing and also ventured into casuistry. His wife died in 1652; Hall died on 8 September 1656. It is tempting to see Hall as a figure divided by his Low Church spirituality, on the one hand, and his identification with Stuart absolutism, on the other. By the same token his success as a writer suggests that these two qualities are not necessarily opposed to each other, and the insistence on an active devotional life can also have the side effect of discouraging political activism.

Hall was an innovator in prose style and form, as he was in his verse satires, even if his thought seldom rises above the conventional. His works are interesting for what they reveal about relationships among political, religious, and literary practices of late Tudor and Stuart England. Hall's Senecan style figured in scholarly debates of the 1950s and 1960s on the development of prose style in the seventeenth century, and in the 1960s and 1970s his meditative theory was cited to support opposing views on the question of Catholic versus Protestant influence on devotional poetry of the period. A renewed interest in prose controversy may lead to a reassessment of Hall's writings in this genre, and new historicist work on Stuart court culture provides a context for further study of the *Characters of Vertues and Vices* and the sermons.

Biographies:

John Jones, *Bishop Hall, His Life and Times* (London: Seeley, 1826);

George Lewis, *A Life of Joseph Hall, D.D.* (London: Hodder & Stoughton, 1886);

Tom Fleming Kinlock, *The Life and Works of Joseph Hall, 1574–1656* (London: Staples Press, 1951).

References:

Geoffrey Aggeler, " 'Sparkes of Holy Things': Neostoicism and the English Protestant Conscience," *Renaissance and Reformation/Renaissance et Reforme,* 14 (Summer 1990): 223–240;

R. C. Bald, *Donne and the Drurys* (Cambridge: Cambridge University Press, 1959);

John Booty, "The Arte of Divine Meditation and Anglican Spirituality," in *The Roots of the Modern Christian Tradition,* edited by Rozanne E. Elder (Kalamazoo, Mich.: Cistercian Publications, 1984), pp. 220–228;

Benjamin Boyce, *The Theophrastan Character in England to 1642* (Cambridge, Mass.: Harvard University Press, 1947);

Audrey Chew, "Joseph Hall and John Milton," *Journal of English Literary History,* 17 (December 1950): 274–295;

Chew, "Joseph Hall and Neo-Stoicism," *PMLA,* 65 (December 1950): 1130–1145;

Wendell Clausen, "The Beginnings of English Character-Writing in the Early Seventeenth Century," *Philological Quarterly,* 25 (January 1946): 32–45;

Ronald J. Corthell, "Joseph Hall and Protestant Meditation," *Texas Studies in Literature and Language,* 20 (Fall 1978): 367–385;

Corthell, "Joseph Hall's *Characters of Vertues and Vices:* A 'Novum Repertum,' " *Studies in Philology,* 76 (January 1979): 28–35;

Harold Fisch, "Bishop Hall's Meditations," *Review of English Studies,* 25 (1949): 210–221;

Fisch, "The Limits of Hall's Senecanism," *Proceedings of the Leeds Philosophical Society,* 6 (1950): 453–463;

Frank Livingstone Huntley, *Bishop Joseph Hall 1574–1656: A Biographical and Critical Study* (Cambridge: Brewer, 1979);

U. Milo Kaufmann, The Pilgrim's Progress *and Traditions in Puritan Meditation* (New Haven: Yale University Press, 1966);

Rudolf Kirk, "A Seventeenth-Century Controversy: Extremism vs. Moderation," *Texas Studies in Literature and Language,* 9 (Spring 1967): 5–35;

Thomas Kranidas, "Style and Rectitude in Seventeenth-Century Prose: Hall, Smectymnuus, and Milton," *Huntington Library Quarterly,* 46 (Summer 1983): 237–269;

Claude Lacassagne, "La Satire Religieuse dans *Mundus Alter et Idem* de Joseph Hall," *Recherches Anglaises et Americaines,* 4 (1971): 141–156;

Barbara Kiefer Lewalski, Donne's Anniversaries *and the Poetry of Praise: The Creation of a Symbolic Mode* (Princeton: Princeton University Press, 1973);

Lewalski, *Protestant Poetics and the Seventeenth-Century Religious Lyric* (Princeton: Princeton University Press, 1979);

Louis Martz, *The Poetry of Meditation: A Study in English Religious Literature of the Seventeenth Century,* revised edition (New Haven: Yale University Press, 1962);

Richard McCabe, "The Form and Method of Milton's *Animadversions upon the Remonstrants Defence against Smectymnuus,*" *English Language Notes,* 18 (June 1981): 266–272;

McCabe, *Joseph Hall: A Study in Satire and Meditation* (Oxford: Clarendon Press, 1982);

Gerhard Muller-Schwefe, "Joseph Hall's *Characters of Vertues and Vices:* Notes toward a Revaluation," *Texas Studies in Literature and Language,* 14 (Summer 1972): 235–251;

Philip A. Smith, "Bishop Hall, 'Our English Seneca,' " *PMLA,* 63 (December 1948): 1191–1204;

Gardner Stout, "Sterne's Borrowings from Bishop Hall's *Quo Vadis?,*" *English Language Notes,* 2 (March 1965): 196–200;

Florence S. Teager, "Patronage of Joseph Hall and John Donne," *Philological Quarterly,* 15 (October 1936): 412–413;

Leonard D. Tourney, *Joseph Hall* (Boston: G. K. Hall, 1979);

Tourney, "Joseph Hall and the *Anniversaries,*" *Papers on Language and Literature,* 13 (Winter 1977): 25–34;

John Millar Wands, "The Early Printing History of Joseph Hall's *Mundus Alter et Idem,*" *Publications of the Bibliographical Society of America,* 74, no. 1 (1980): 1–12;

Wands, "The Theory of Climate in the English Renaissance and *Mundus Alter et Idem,*" in *Acta Conventus Neo-Latini Sanctandreani: Proceedings of the Fifth International Congress of Neo-Latin Studies,* edited by D. I. McFarlane (Binghamton, N.Y.: Medieval and Renaissance Texts & Studies, 1982), pp. 519–529;

George Williamson, *The Senecan Amble: A Study in Prose Form from Bacon to Collier* (Chicago: University of Chicago Press, 1951).

Edward, Lord Herbert of Cherbury

(3 March 1582 – 1? August 1648)

Eugene D. Hill
Mount Holyoke College

See also the Herbert of Cherbury entry in *DLB 121: Seventeenth-Century British Nondramatic Poets, First Series.*

BOOKS: *De Veritate Provt Distingvitvr A Revelatione, A Verisimili, A Possibili, Et A Falso* (Paris, 1624; London: Per A. Matthaeum, 1633); third edition, revised and enlarged, with *De Causis Errorum* and *De Religione Laici* (London, 1645); *De Veritate* translated by Meyrick H. Carré as *De Veritate* (Bristol: Published for the University of Bristol by W. Arrowsmith, 1937); *De Religione Laici* edited and translated by Harold R. Hutcheson as *Lord Herbert of Cherbury's De Religione Laici* (New Haven: Yale University Press / London: Oxford University Press, 1944);

De Causis Errorum: Una Cum tractatu de Religione Laici (London, 1645);

The Life and Raigne of King Henry the Eighth. Written By the Right Honourable Edward, Lord Herbert of Cherbury (London: Printed by E. G. for Thomas Whitaker, 1649);

Expeditio In Ream Insulam, Authore Edovardo Domino Herbert (London: Prostant apud Humphredum Moseley, 1656); English version published as *The Expedition to the Isle of Rhé* (London: Printed by Whittingham & Wilkins, 1860);

De Religione Gentilium errorumque apud eos causis (Amsterdam: Printed by John & Peter Blaeu, 1663); translated by W. Lewis as *The Antient Religion of the Gentiles, and Causes of their Errors Consider'd* (London: Printed for John Nutt, 1705);

Occasional Verses of Edward Lord Herbert, Baron of Cherbury and Castle-Island. Deceased in August, 1648 (London: Printed by T. R. for Thomas Dring, 1665);

The Life of Edward Herbert of Cherbury Written by Himself (Strawberry Hill, 1764);

A Dialogue Between a Tutor and his Pupil (London: Printed for W. Bathoe, 1768; New York & London: Garland, 1979).

Editions: "The History of King Henry VIII," in volume 2 of *A Complete History of England,* edited by John Hughes (London: Printed for B. Aylmer, 1706; revised, London: Printed for R. Bonwicke, 1719);

The Life and Reign of King Henry the Eighth (London: Alexander Murray, 1870);

Autobiography of Edward Lord Herbert of Cherbury. The History of England under Henry VIII (London: Alexander Murray, 1872);

The Autobiography of Edward, Lord Herbert of Cherbury, edited, with a continuation of the Life, by Sidney L. Lee (London: Nimmo, 1886; New York: Scribner & Welford, 1886; revised edition, London: Routledge / New York: Dutton, 1906);

The Poems, English & Latin, of Edward, Lord Herbert of Cherbury, edited by G. C. Moore Smith (Oxford: Clarendon Press, 1923);

De Veritate, facsimile edition, edited by Günter Gawlick (Stuttgart-Bad Canstatt: Frommann, 1966);

De Causis Errorum, facsimile edition, edited by Gawlick (Stuttgart-Bad Canstatt: Frommann, 1966);

De Religione Gentilium, facsimile edition, edited by Gawlick (Stuttgart-Bad Canstatt: Frommann, 1967);

A Dialogue between a Tutor and His Pupil, facsimile edition, edited by Gawlick (Stuttgart-Bad Canstatt: Frommann, 1971);

The Life of Edward, First Lord Herbert of Cherbury, edited by J. M. Shuttleworth (London: Oxford University Press, 1976).

Edward, Lord Herbert of Cherbury; portrait attributed to W. Larkin (National Portrait Gallery, London)

OTHER: "Elegy for the Prince," in *Lachrymæ Lachrymarum,* enlarged edition, edited by Josuah Sylvester (London: Printed by H. Lownes, 1613).

Soldier and diplomat, peer, poet, and philosopher, Edward, Lord Herbert of Cherbury, was far more celebrated in his day than his younger brother, the now-familiar devotional poet George Herbert. Whereas the younger brother presented himself as a quiet country parson, the elder boldly developed a creed that carefully evaded, where it did not artfully undermine, the doctrines and practices of revealed religion – Christianity in particular. Herbert's philosophy of religion, embodied in books published during and after his lifetime, informs all his various volumes of history, poems, and autobiography (1764) – the last his most widely appreciated work. He would long

be remembered as a founder of the rationalist view of religion known as deism.

The oldest of seven sons among the ten children of Richard Herbert, Esquire, sheriff of Montgomeryshire, Wales, and Magdalen Newport Herbert, Edward Herbert was born in Eyton-on-Severn, Shropshire, on 3 March 1582. After private studies with tutors in fields that included classics and logic, he matriculated as a gentleman commoner at University College, Oxford, in May 1596. On 28 February 1599 he married his older cousin Mary Herbert, who had to marry someone named Herbert to gain a large inheritance. Herbert and his wife lived with his widowed mother – his father had died in 1596 – and his siblings in Oxford until 1600, when they all moved to London. Among the distinguished visitors Herbert met at his mother's London home were the poet John Donne, the composer William Byrd, and the histo-

189

rian William Camden. Herbert was made a knight of the Order of the Bath by James I in 1603 and became sheriff of Montgomeryshire in 1605.

Herbert traveled to France in 1608 for the first of many visits; his autobiography tells a rich tale of amatory and military adventures. He also served as a gentleman volunteer with the Protestant forces in the Low Countries in 1610 and involved himself in several other campaigns of the decade, always on the Protestant side. In 1619 he was appointed ambassador to France, in which post he encouraged a vigorous anti-Catholic foreign policy. When that position became untenable in 1624, with King James seeking a French princess to marry the prince of Wales, Herbert was eased out of office, probably with the encouragement of the French.

Before leaving Paris, Herbert published his first book, the Latin treatise *De Veritate* (On Truth, 1624; translated, 1937). In his autobiography he reports that he had sought and received "a loud though yet gentle noise from the heavens, for it was like nothing on earth, which did so comfort and cheer me, that I had the sign I demanded, whereupon also I resolved to print the book." It is typical of Herbert interpretation that this report has been variously read as a moment of touching sincerity and as a piece of deadpan mockery of revealed religion.

In *De Veritate* Herbert responds to the skeptical crisis generated by a century of intellectual and military struggles between Protestants and Catholics that was continuing to rage in the Thirty Years' War. In his preface he explains that the "work is published with the aim not of arousing controversy but of closing it, or at any rate, making it unnecessary." He attempts to accomplish this aim by developing a theory of knowledge according to which human beings possess a power of the soul sufficient to embrace what they need to know: by using one's faculties one can arrive at needed truths not merely in simple perception but in ethics and religion. This account may seem to avoid the interesting problems of epistemology, but that is precisely its intention: Herbert's theory of knowledge serves to undergird his concept of natural religion.

Using the faculties, one arrives at universal "Common Notions." The most influential pages of *De Veritate* would be the concluding chapters that expound the Common Notions of religion, which constitute "the perfect sphere of the religion of God." Herbert adds, "If anything is added to it, or taken from it its shape is destroyed, and its perfection ruined." The five notions are: "there is a Supreme God"; he is to be worshiped;

worship consists, above all, in the practice of virtue; "vices and crimes" are to be "expiated by repentance"; and an afterlife exists in which people receive reward or punishment. No Redeemer is mentioned — nor, apparently, in Herbert's opinion, is one needed.

The book concludes with a treatment of revelation, composed with deadpan solemnity. Herbert specifies criteria for evaluating claims to special revelation that would supplement the Common Notions. Typically, he avoids explicit attack on Christianity or any other orthodoxy, but the tendency of the entire book clearly works against allowing any revelation that would ruin the perfect sphere of the Common Notions. The Catholic church was not misreading *De Veritate* when it added the title to its Index of Forbidden Books in 1633. With his first book Herbert had composed the charter of seventeenth-century deism, which the historian Scipion du Pleix defined in 1628 as the religion of "those who indeed believe that there is an eternal divinity. . . . who governs the world, but who cannot savor the mysteries of the Christian religion."

Returning to England after his ambassadorial years, Herbert was heavily in debt from his outlays in Paris — a standard complaint of diplomats in this period. The reward for his services was not swiftly provided. Herbert did become a member of the king's council of war in 1624, in which year he was also admitted to the Irish peerage of Castle Island. Not until 1629 did he become an English baron as Lord Herbert of Cherbury. His efforts to procure favor and support at court led to the first-composed of his English books, in which Herbert, at royal behest, worked up the notes prepared by George Villiers, first Duke of Buckingham, in defense of his disastrous 1627 expedition to relieve the besieged Huguenots on the Isle of Rhé off the western coast of France. *The Expedition to the Isle of Rhé* was presented to King Charles I in 1630, though it was not published until 1656 — and then in a Latin version, *Expeditio in Ream Insulam,* possibly from Herbert's hand; the original English version did not reach print until 1860.

The much-hated Buckingham had been assassinated in 1628, and Charles wanted to have his friend's generalship defended. This was a tall order; Buckingham's bungling of the campaign was widely known. Herbert adopts the tactic of disputing Jacob Isnard's 1629 Latin account of the French victory. He quarrels with "cackling Isnard" on many collateral issues, but as to Buckingham's negligence on central points he offers at best a halfhearted de-

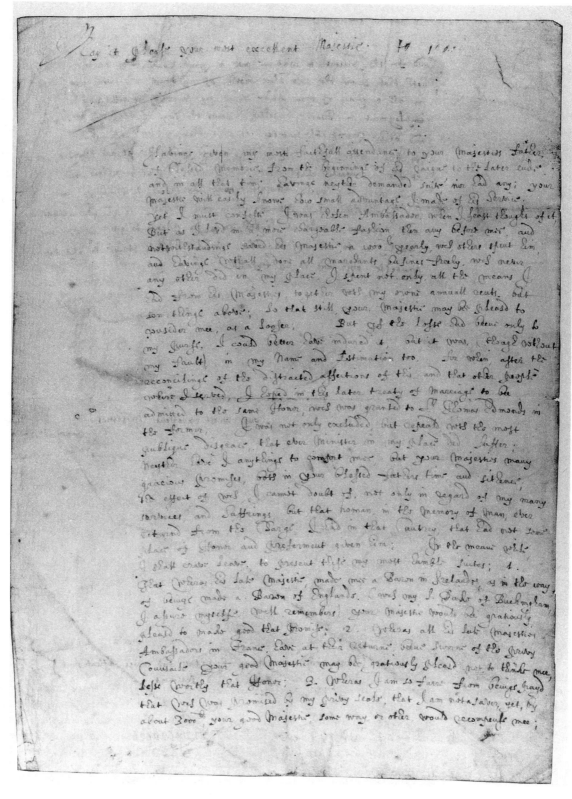

First page of an 8 May 1626 letter from Herbert to King Charles I (private collection; lent to Pierpont Morgan Library)

fense. Buckingham is presented as a stickler for chivalric decorum, which he punctiliously defends at whatever risk to his troops. Herbert's grave mockery produces a marvelous account of the forlorn battle, in which, thanks to their leader, the English were boxed in: "neither on the one side we could conveniently fight nor handsomely retire on the other." Herbert's defense of Buckingham turns on a bitterly whimsical turn of phrase: "if it be granted that the French did triumph over the vanquished, it must not be denied but the English triumphed over the Victory itself." The king's special friend is treated with the same apparent respect but underlying sarcasm accorded special revelation in *De Veritate.*

Herbert, at King Charles's request, began writing *The Life and Raigne of King Henry the Eighth* (1649) in 1632; he had substantially completed it by 1638. The work follows the model of Francis Bacon's *The Historie of the Raigne of King Henry the Seventh* in its "politic" scrutiny of men and motives by a scholar intimately acquainted with the workings of government. Herbert includes many primary documents in this large tome, but what makes *The Life and Raigne of King Henry the Eighth* alive even today is its nuanced portrait of Henry. The first paragraph indicates the complexity of Herbert's viewpoint: "It is not easy to write that prince's history, of whom no one thing may constantly be affirmed." Herbert develops an admiring portrait of the young Henry, and he clearly feels sympathy for the king's efforts to establish a layman's purified religion in place of Roman priestcraft. But, under the influence of Cardinal Thomas Wolsey, Henry is seen as growing increasingly wayward, promoting a personal version of Reformation rather than the generalized deism that Herbert imagines as a live possibility in the early sixteenth century. In the end Henry becomes a monster of self-will, whose reign of terror over England Herbert describes with sly epigrammatic force. The book presents both the tragedy of one man and the tragic failure of the English Reformation. The book ends: "I wish I could leave Henry VIII in his grave." But Herbert knew that the forces of individual self-promotion — as opposed to the irenic Common Notions — raged unabated in the century after Henry's death.

Commentators have not always appreciated the complexity of Herbert's portrait; some have even criticized him for playing the role of apologist for Henry Tudor. But the volume has generally been recognized as a classic work of English history.

The disengagement from sectarian quarrels that one would expect to find in a deist made the revolutionary period a trying one for Herbert; his efforts to avoid overly close commitment to either side in the English civil war earned him the distrust of both. Initially, he stood by King Charles, whom he joined in 1639 on the expedition against the Scots. One moderate remark in the House of Lords that was judged unduly favorable to the king earned Herbert a brief stay in custody in 1642. Soon afterward he pleaded infirmity when asked to raise troops for the king, and he was unwilling to allow a garrison of Royalist troops at Montgomery Castle. Wales was generally Royalist, as were Herbert's near family, including his brother Henry. But when Parliamentary troops arrived at the gates of Montgomery Castle in September 1644, Herbert yielded this strategic position without resistance. The Royalists judged Herbert a traitor, but the Parliamentary forces were happy to provide him with a certificate attesting to his favorable intentions toward them. When he reached London, Herbert was restored to possession of his goods, which had been sequestered as those of a supposed Royalist. From this point Herbert was left in peace, though to this day his conduct at Montgomery Castle earns opprobrious remarks from some historians.

In 1645 a new edition of *De Veritate* appeared that included two supplementary works: *De Causis Errorum* (The Causes of Error) and *De Religione Laici* (A Layman's Religion). The latter text adds to *De Veritate* an explanation of what Herbert takes to be the interested motives, throughout history, of the priestly class. These men, Herbert writes, "conspire everywhere to interpose and to maintain their authority" so that "neither entering nor leaving this world should be quite lawful without their aid." Herbert asks how the layman can "protect himself if every man's individual dogmas about necessary and excellent truth are so proposed as to damn all the rest." The answer, of course, lies in the Common Notions of religion, which are available to all.

Herbert's remaining books, which include his most admired and influential compositions in English, were all published posthumously. Some — *A Dialogue between a Tutor and His Pupil* (1748) in particular — may have been too daring for his contemporaries. Herbert's death would have prevented him from seeing in print *The Life and Raigne of King Henry the Eighth,* which appeared the next year, and also from completing his autobiography. The unsettled state of the country during the civil war also must have played a part in restricting Herbert's access to print.

Herbert's death in August 1648 is described by John Aubrey in his *Brief Lives* (1898). Archbishop

James Ussher, primate of Ireland, visited the dying Herbert, who "would have received the sacrament. He said indifferently of it that *if there was good in anything 'twas in that,* or *if it did no good 'twould do no hurt.* The Primate refused it," and Herbert "then turned his head to the other side, and expired very serenely." Herbert died as he lived, a deist; and he died at peace, though the orthodox claimed that deists would expire in howling terror or be converted at the last moment.

In 1663 Herbert's *De Religione Gentilium* reached print; an English version, *The Antient Religion of the Gentiles,* would appear in 1705. Herbert's prime source for information on pagan religion was Gerard Vossius's massive *De Theologia Gentili* (1641). Vossius seeks to account for the many similarities between pagan mythical theology and the Judeo-Christian Scriptures; he argues, following countless predecessors, that the pagans appropriated and deformed the originals in Scripture. Herbert rejects this interpretation: parallels between pagan and Christian indicate not plagiarism but a common source in the Common Notions. What is reasonable in pagan polytheism derives from human reason; what is unreasonable, from "the crafty Contrivance of the Priests." Herbert's irreverence comes close to the surface when he remarks that "the Matrons of Rome had . . . a most profound Veneration" of the infant Jupiter "greedy after the Breast"; "he was the first God that the Ancients ever adored bawling in a cradle, before he had performed any noble Exploit; for they could not be very fond of such a snivelling Deity." The satiric thrust at Christianity can hardly be mistaken.

In 1665 Herbert's *Occasional Verses* appeared, collecting pieces that G. C. Moore Smith, in his 1923 edition, dates from 1608 to 1644. Moore Smith calls Herbert "a born poet" and goes so far as to assert: "I am inclined to claim that in poetic feeling and art Edward Herbert soars above his brother George." Few readers today are likely to share that inclination, but the intellectual force and musical grace in Edward Herbert's poems deserve recognition. (Herbert was a musician of some competence: a manuscript of pieces for lute that he owned represents a valuable source of French, English, and Italian compositions. A fine recording of pieces from this book by the lutenist Paul O'Dette was issued as a compact disc in 1993.)

Herbert's earliest English poem, "The State progress of Ill," offers a gnarled satire on abuses of political power. It borrows from the style of the early satiric verses of Donne, whose poem "The Progress of

the Soul" is alluded to in the title. More widely admired are Herbert's later poems, especially a sequence in paradoxical praise of a dark beauty. The six lyrics weave together borrowings from the early-seventeenth-century Italian poet Giambattista Marino and from ancient, more philosophically laden, praisers of darkness: passages from the Canticles in the Old Testament, the Greek Anthology, and the dark *Mystical Theology* of the Pseudo-Dionysius. Herbert's sequence proves an elegant confection that is ever threatening to soar into weightless air or collapse into scholarly lumber but ever evading the threat.

The fourth text in the sequence, "Sonnet of Black Beauty," represents Herbert's characteristic voice in lyric, a voice at once dry yet rapturously Platonic in celebration:

> Black beauty, which above that common light,
> Whose Power can no colors here renew
> But those which darkness can again subdue,
> Do'st still remain unvary'd to the sight,
>
> And like an object equal to the view,
> Art neither chang'd with day, nor hid with night;
> When all these colors which the world call bright,
> And which old Poetry doth so pursue,
>
> Are with the night so perished and gone,
> That of their being there remains no mark,
> Thou still abidest so entirely one,
> That we may know thy blackness is a spark
> Of light inaccessible, and alone
> Our darkness which can make us think it dark.

Similar intellectual and musical strengths can be enjoyed in another sequence, Herbert's five poems on Platonic love. The second of the five urges the lady addressed to bestow her favors upon the speaker, rather than upon some unworthy young man. In so arguing, Herbert follows standard Renaissance love lore, though not without some wry sense of his own self-promotion. As so often with Herbert, the verse works not by seduction but by something closer to real persuasion, not least in its summary of what the lovers can expect:

> So that however multipli'd and vast
> Their love increase, they will not think it past
> The bounds of growth, till their exalted fire
> B'ing equally enlarg'd with their desire,
> Transform and fix them to one Star at last.

By far the most admired of Herbert's poems is "An Ode upon a Question moved, Whether Love should continue for ever?" Only since the 1980s, however, has criticism moved from commending the ode to analyzing it in any detail, especially in its connection to Herbert's philosophical views. Answering *quaestiones* is, after all, the task of philosophers, and this carefully moved *demande d'amour* (love question) evokes several of the Common Notions of religion as well as the Neoplatonic love theory that was fashionable in Herbert's time.

The ode clearly follows Donne's brilliant "The Ecstasy" as it explores the supernatural union of the two lovers. But Herbert, ever critical in his philosophical works of any claim to special revelation, as by ecstatic mystical insight, rewrites Donne's poem to separate the lovers' earthly felicity from the ultimate reward of total spiritual union. That paradoxical interanimation, whose alleged attainment on earth constitutes the argument of "The Ecstasy," Herbert reserves for the afterlife. As Melander assures Celinda in stanza 33:

So when from hence we shall be gone,
And be no more, nor you, nor I,
As one another's mystery,
Each shall be both, yet both but one.

The elegant music of Herbert's greatest poem embodies an implicit deist correction of Donne's religious extravagance – metaphysical wit is chastened by the Common Notions.

In 1764 Horace Walpole produced at his Strawberry Hill Press the first edition of Herbert's autobiography, the work by which Herbert would be best known in the nineteenth and twentieth centuries. Walpole, a dedicated compiler of noble folly, found the work an amusing piece of extravagance; in a letter he recounts reading the manuscript to some friends: "we could not get on for laughing and screaming." This generally condescending view of the autobiography has influenced many readers, who join Walpole in failing to recognize the distance the elder author assumes from his youthful self. The autobiography has much been admired, but often for the wrong reasons. Herbert's self-representation is not that of an English Don Quixote pursuing absurdities with sword and phallus.

The autobiography does include some amusingly antic self-revelations: the reckless adulteries, duels, and shenanigans of the young nobleman are as unedifyingly typical as one might wish. But the aged Herbert elegantly counterpoints these events with his later philosophical achievements. The autobiography moves in the opposite direction from the study of Henry VIII: where the royal biography

began with vast promise and ended with willful abuse, the retrospective autobiography opens with fulsomely elaborated self-regard and moves to a more adult concern with common truths. Herbert's version of his experience is a kind of saint's life in reverse: he starts as something special and ends as a representative of, if not the common man, the Common Notions.

Readers of Herbert's autobiography must attend to its parodic inversion of contemporary religious texts. Thus when Herbert boastfully reports that his clothing smelled sweet from sweat, he is offering a wicked parody of the familiar hagiographic assertion that a given saint's body betrayed an odor of sanctity; Herbert finds that sweetness in the natural order of things. Readers less casually snide and more historically alert than Walpole can relish a self-portrait unrivaled for its day in canny self-mockery and implicit self-reduction. Here Herbert, like his younger brother, produces a text that prunes the self of its willful plumage; for Edward Herbert, however, that restored self is not, as it is for George, our Christlikeness but our common humanity as manifested by the Common Notions.

One passage in the autobiography that critics have read with some precision is Herbert's treatment of his celebrated brother: "My brother George was so excellent a scholar, that he was made the public orator of the University in Cambridge; some of whose English works are extant; which, though they be rare in their kind, yet are far short of expressing those perfections he had in the Greek and Latin tongue, and all divine and human literature; his life was most holy and exemplary; insomuch, that about Salisbury, where he lived, beneficed for many years, he was little less than sainted. He was not exempt from passion and choler, being infirmities to which all our race is subject, but that excepted, without reproach in his actions." Careful readers differ in their judgments as to whether this passage offers suitable praise or, as George Held suggests, a "slightly condescending" treatment. Some friction between the two men was inevitable, given the elder brother's delay in disbursing George's family annuity. But the differences between them cry out to be read in less petty terms, and this much-interrogated passage may convey a hint that Lord Herbert's readers should compare two different varieties of "sainted" lives – that of George in his Christian *Temple* (1633) and of Edward in his neopagan religion of reason.

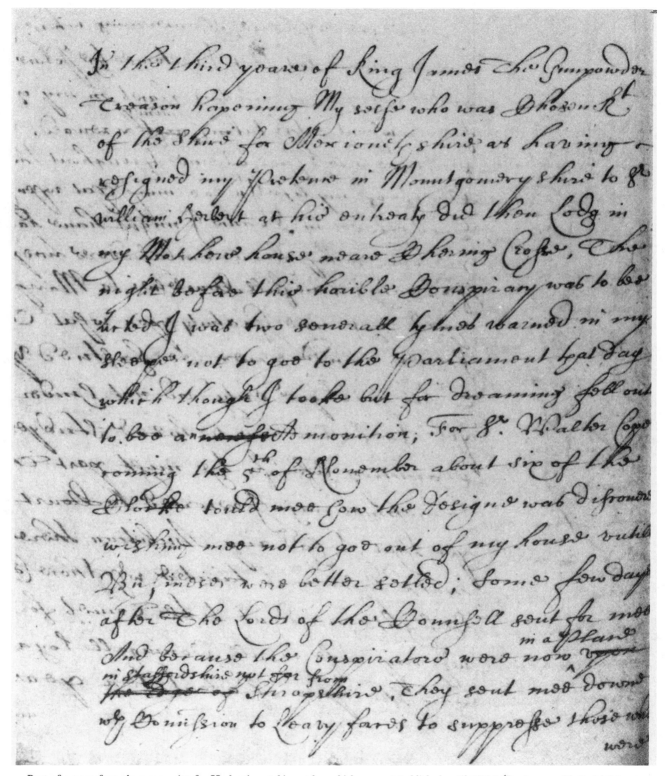

Part of a page from the manuscript for Herbert's autobiography, which was not published until 1764 (Powis mss., National Library of Wales)

In 1768 a London bookseller brought out the last of Herbert's full-length works to reach print, *A Dialogue between a Tutor and His Pupil*. The attribution to Herbert has won general acceptance; the dialogue's anti-Christian edge, though impelling Mario Rossi to doubt Herbert's authorship, is generally taken as evidence that Herbert was writing with no thought of having the work published in his lifetime. The book is a skillful piece of religious polemic; it would be an optimal introduction to Herbert's philosophy of religion.

The book acts out the drama of enlightenment as the sane tutorial voice provides data on the basis of which the Pupil formulates ever more audaciously rationalist judgments of religion and priestcraft. At key moments the Tutor offers clearly inadequate statements of orthodoxy, both testing the youth's analysis by devil's advocacy and tempering the youth's risky enthusiasm with transparently insincere bows to authority. Gradually, the two voices come together in a skeptical view of priestcraft combined with a slyly duplicitous mode of evasive formulation. The Pupil has reached Enlightenment views of religion, sniping at Christianity while defending paganism even more explicitly than Herbert did in *De Religione Gentilium*.

A model of how the work progresses may be found in a discussion the two interlocutors have of the divine command to Abraham to sacrifice his son (Genesis 22). To the Pupil's query as to what "a rational man should do in such a case . . . now," the Tutor argues that "a rational person . . . should believe that this voice came rather from some wicked spirit." Abraham, he adds, must have been "constrained . . . by some irresistible power" to believe the voice to be divine. The Pupil will have none of this: if Abraham was constrained to believe, then the episode was no proper test of his character. The youth argues that the patriarch "might have used other means, than it seems by the text he did, to discover the truth of the voice, and the goodness of the precept, which was represented to him." Thus the story of Abraham and Isaac, rather than a praiseworthy model of faith, becomes an instance of insufficient adherence to reason. The implication is clear: Abraham ought to have followed those Common Notions that are always and everywhere available, separating large ethical notions and nondenominational religious beliefs from the particular and dogmatic demands of obedience. Herbert's analysis would become a familiar one; in his own day it was bold and daring.

Herbert finds a place of honor in every history of deism and rationalist thought. In 1754 John Leland, in his *A View of the Principal Deistical Writers*, rightly called Herbert "the most eminent" of the school. Leland's account of Herbert, though not sympathetic, is basically accurate — more so on crucial points than the work of many later scholars, who seem to have accepted Walpole's disparagement of Herbert as an amusing period eccentric. The standard monograph on Herbert, three massive Italian volumes by Rossi (1947), is written from a viewpoint of considerable distaste for Herbert's skeptical view of religion. Only in recent years, and partly by way of comparative study with the deeply Christian texts of his younger brother, has Edward Herbert begun to receive the detailed and sympathetic literary investigation that his rich books demand and repay.

Letters:

Herbert Correspondence: The Sixteenth and Seventeenth Century Letters of the Herberts of Chirbury, edited by W. J. Smith (Cardiff: University of Wales Press, 1963).

Bibliography:

J. M. Shuttleworth, "Edward, Lord Herbert of Cherbury (1583–1648): A Preliminary, Annotated Checklist of Works by and about Him," *National Library of Wales Journal*, 20 (1977): 151–168.

Biographies:

John Aubrey, *"Brief Lives," Chiefly of Contemporaries*, volume 1, edited by Andrew Clark (Oxford: Clarendon Press, 1898);

Mario M. Rossi, *La vita, le opere, i tempi di Edoardo Herbert di Chirbury*, 3 volumes (Florence: Sansoni, 1947);

John Butler, *Lord Herbert of Chirbury, 1582–1648: An Intellectual Biography* (Lewiston, N.Y.: Edwin Mellen Press, 1990).

References:

R. D. Bedford, *The Defence of Truth: Herbert of Cherbury and the Seventeenth Century* (Manchester: Manchester University Press, 1979);

C. J. Fordyce and T. M. Knox, "The Library of Jesus College, Oxford. With an Appendix on the Books Bequeathed thereto by Lord Herbert of Cherbury," *Proceedings and Papers of the Oxford Bibliographical Society*, 5, part 2 (1937): 53–115;

George Held, "Brother Poets: The Relationship between Edward and George Herbert," in *Like Season'd Timber: New Essays on George Herbert,* edited by Edmund Miller and Robert DiYanni (New York: Peter Lang, 1987), pp. 19–35;

Eugene D. Hill, *Edward, Lord Herbert of Cherbury* (Boston: Twayne, 1987);

John Leland, *A View of the Principal Deistical Writers That Have Appeared in England in the Last and Present Century: With Observations upon Them, and Some Account of the Answers That Have Been Published against Them,* third edition (London: B. Dad, 1754–1756);

Charles Lyttle, "Lord Herbert of Cherbury, Apostle of Ethical Theism," *Church History,* 4 (December 1935): 247–267;

Ronald E. McFarland, "The Rhetoric of Medicine: Lord Herbert's and Thomas Carew's Poems of Green-Sickness," *Journal of the History of Medicine and Allied Sciences,* 30 (July 1975): 250–258;

W. M. Merchant, "Lord Herbert of Cherbury and Seventeenth-Century Historical Writing," *Transactions of the Honourable Society of Cymmrodorion,* Session 1956 (1957): 47–63;

Basil Willey, "Lord Herbert of Cherbury: A Spiritual Quixote of the Seventeenth Century," *Essays & Studies,* 27 (1941): 22–29.

Papers:

The major collection of the papers of Edward, Lord Herbert of Cherbury, formerly at Powis Castle, is now held by the National Library of Wales, Aberystwyth. In addition to the Powis materials, literary autograph manuscripts are in the British Library; the Public Record Office, London; the Bodleian Library, Oxford; and at the Houghton Library, Harvard University. More than nine hundred Greek and Latin volumes owned by Herbert, many annotated, are at Jesus College, Oxford. Herbert's manuscript lute-book is at the Fitzwilliam Museum, Cambridge University.

Thomas Hobbes
(5 April 1588 – 4 December 1679)

Alan T. McKenzie
Purdue University

BOOKS: *De Mirabilibus Pecci* (London, 1636?); republished and translated as *De Mirabilibus Pecci: Being the Wonders of the Peak in Darby-Shire, Commonly called The Devil's Arse of Peak. In English and Latine. The Latine Written by Thomas Hobbes of Malmesbury. The English by a Person of Quality* (London: Printed for William Crooke, 1678);

Elementorum Philosophiae Sectio Tertia De Cive, anonymous (Paris, 1642); revised as *Elementa Philosophica De Cive* (Amsterdam: Elzevir, 1647); translated by Hobbes as *Philosophicall Rudiments Concerning Government and Society. Or, A Dissertation Concerning Man in his severall habitudes and respects, as the Member of a Society, first Secular, and then Sacred* (London: Printed by John Grismond for Richard Royston, 1651);

Humane Nature: Or, The fundamental Elements of Policie (London: Printed by Thomas Newcomb for Francis Bowman, Oxford, 1650);

De Corpore Politico. Or the Elements of Law, Moral & Politick, with Discourses upon several Heads (London: Printed for John Martin and John Ridley, 1650);

Leviathan, Or The Matter, Forme, & Power of a Common-Wealth Ecclesiasticall and Civill (London: Printed for Andrew Crooke, 1651); translated into Latin by Hobbes as *Leviathan, Sive De Materia, Forma, & Potestate Civitatis Ecclesiasticae et Civilis* (Amsterdam: Printed by John Blaev, 1670);

Of Libertie and Necessitie: A Treatise, wherein all Controversie concerning Predestination, Election, Free-will, Grace, Merits, Reprobation, &c. is fully decided and cleared, in answer to a Treatise written by the Bishop of London-derry, on the same subject (London: Printed by William Bentley for Francis Eaglesfield, 1654);

Elementorum Philosophiae Sectio Prima De Corpore (London: Printed for Andrew Crooke, 1655); translated by Hobbes as *Elements of Philosophy, the First Section, Concerning Body. Written in Latine by Thomas Hobbes of Malmesbury. And now translated into English. To which are added Six Lessons to the Professors of Mathematicks of the Institution of Sr. Henry Savile, in the University of Oxford* (London: Printed by Robert & William Leybourn for Andrew Crooke, 1656);

The Questions Concerning Liberty, Necessity, and Chance. Clearly Stated and Debated Between Dr. Bramhall Bishop of Derry, and Thomas Hobbes of Malmesbury (London: Printed for Andrew Crooke, 1656);

Στιγμαι: Αγεωμτριας, Αγροικιας, Αντιπολιτειας, Αμαθειας, *or Markes of the Absurd Geometry Rural Language Scottish Church-Politicks and Barbarisms of John Wallis Professor of Geometry and Doctor of Divinity* (London: Printed for Andrew Crooke, 1657);

Elementorum Philosophiae Sectio Secunda De Homine (London: Printed by T. C. for Andrew Crooke, 1658);

Examinatio & Emendatio Mathematica Hodiernæ. Qualis explicatur in libris Johannis Wallisii Geometriæ Professoris Saviliani in Academia Oxoniensi. Distributa in sex Dialogos (London: Printed for Andrew Crooke, 1660);

Dialogus Physicus, sive De natura Aeris Conjectura sumpta ab Experimentis nuper Londini habitis in Collegio Greshamensi Item De Duplicatione Cubi (London: Printed by J. B. for Andrew Crooke, 1661);

Problemata Physica: De Gravitate. Cap. I. De Æstibus Marinis. Cap. II. De Vacuo. Cap. III. De Calore & Luce. Cap. IV. De Duro & Molli. Cap. V. De Pluvia, Vento, aliisq; Coeli varietatibus. Cap. VI. De Motuum Speciebus. Cap. VII. Adjunctæ sunt etiam Propositiones duæ de Duplicatione Cubi, &

Thomas Hobbes (engraving by William Faithorne)

Dimensione Circuli (London: Printed for Andrew Crooke, 1662); translated anonymously as *Seven Philosophical Problems, and Two Propositions of Geometry. By Thomas Hobbes of Malmesbury. With an Apology for Himself, and his Writings. Dedicated to the King, in the year 1662* (London: Printed for William Crooke, 1682);

Mr. Hobbes Considered in his Loyalty, Religion, Reputation, and Manners. By way of Letter to Dr. Wallis (London: Printed for Andrew Crooke, 1662); republished as *Considerations upon the Reputation, Loyalty, Manners, & Religion, of Thomas Hobbes of Malmsbury. Written by himself, By way of Letter to a Learned Person* (London: Printed for William Crooke, 1680);

De Principiis & Ratiocinatione Geometrarum (London: Printed for Andrew Crooke, 1666);

Quadratura Circuli, Cubatio Sphæræ, Duplicatio Cubi, Breviter demonstrata (London: Printed by John Crooke, Jr., for Andrew Crooke, 1669);

Three Papers Presented to the Royal Society Against Dr. Wallis. Together with Considerations on Dr. Wallis his Answer to them (London: Printed for the Author, 1671);

Rosetum Geometricum. Sive Propositiones Aliquot Frustra antehac tentatæ. Cum Censura brevi Doctrinæ Wallisianæ de Motu (London: Printed by John Crooke, Jr., for William Crooke, 1671); translated by Venterus Mandey as "A Garden of Geometrical Roses; Or Some Propositions Being hitherto Hid, are now made Known," in his *Mellificium Mensionis: or, The Marrow of Measuring. With some Choice Principles and Problems of Geometry conducing thereto. The whole Treatise being comprized in six Books* (London: Printed for the author, sold by Richard Chiswel, Benjamin Clark, and by the author, 1682), pp. 40–107;

Lux Mathematica: Excussa Collisionibus Johannis Wallisii Theol. Doctoris, Geometriæ in celeberrima Academia Oxoniensi Professoris Publici, et Thomæ Hobbesii

Malmsburiensis (London: Printed by John Crooke, Jr., for William Crooke, 1672);

Principia et Problemata Aliquot Geometrica Antè Desperata, Nunc breviter Explicata & Demonstrata (London: Printed by J. C. for William Crooke, 1674); translated by Mandey as "Some Principles and Problems in Geometry Thought formerly Desperate; Now Briefly Explained and Demonstrated," in his *Mellificium Mensionis* (1682), pp. 110–185;

Decameron Physiologicum: Or, Ten Dialogues Of Natural Philosophy (London: Printed by John Crooke, Jr., for William Crooke, 1678);

The History of the Civil Wars of England. From the Year 1640, to 1660, as T. H. (N.p., 1679);

Thomæ Hobbessii Malmesburiensis Vita. Authore Seipso (London, 1679); translated by Benjamin Farrington as "The Autobiography of Thomas Hobbes," in *The Rationalist Annual for the Year 1958* (London: Watts, 1957), pp. 22–31; translated by J. E. Parsons, Jr., and Whitney Blair as "The Life of Thomas Hobbes of Malmesbury," *Interpretation,* 10 (January 1982): 1–7;

The Life of Mr. Thomas Hobbes of Malmesbury. Written by himself In a Latine Poem. And now Translated into English, translated by Richard Blackbourne[?] (London: Printed for A. C., 1680);

Thomæ Hobbes Angli Malmesburiensis Philosophi Vita (London: Printed for William Crooke, 1681);

The Art of Rhetoric, With a Discourse of The Laws of England (London: Printed for William Crooke, 1681);

Tracts of Mr. Thomas Hobbs of Malmsbury. Containing I. Behemoth, the History of the Causes of the Civil Wars of England, from 1640. to 1660. printed from the Author's own Copy: Never printed (but with a thousand faults) before. II. An Answer to Arch-Bishop Bramhall's Book, called the Catching of the Leviathan: *Never printed before. III. An Historical Narration of Heresie, and the Punishment thereof: Corrected by the true Copy. IV. Philosophical Problems, dedicated to the King in 1662. but never printed before* (London: Printed for William Crooke, 1682).

Editions: *Opera Philosophica, Quae Latinè scripsit, Omnia,* 2 volumes (Amsterdam: Printed by John Blaev, 1668);

A Supplement to Mr. Hobbes His Works, Printed by Blaeu at Amsterdam, 1661. Being a third Volume (London: Printed by John Crooke, Jr., for William Crooke, 1675);

The Moral and Political Works of Thomas Hobbes of Malmesbury. Never before collected together. To which is prefixed, The Author's Life, Extracted from That said to be written by Himself, as also from The Supplement to the said Life, by Dr. Blackbourne; and farther illustrated by the Editor, with Historical and Critical Remarks on his Writings and Opinions (London, 1750);

The English Works of Thomas Hobbes of Malmesbury; Now First Collected and Edited, 11 volumes, edited by Sir William Molesworth (London: Bohn, 1839–1845);

Thomæ Hobbes Malmsburiensis Opera Philosophica Quæ Latine Scripsit Omnia in Unum Corpus Nunc Primum Collecta, 5 volumes, edited by Molesworth (London: Bohn, 1839–1845);

The Elements of Law Natural and Politic, edited by Ferdinand Tönnies (London: Simpkin, Marshall, 1889); edited by M. M. Goldsmith (New York: Barnes & Noble, 1969);

Behemoth or The Long Parliament, edited by Tönnies (London: Simpkin, Marshall, 1889); second edition edited by Goldsmith (New York: Barnes & Noble, 1969);

"Answer to Davenant's Preface to *Gondibert*" and "Preface to Homer," in *Critical Essays of the Seventeenth Century,* volume 2, edited by J. E. Spingarn (Oxford: Clarendon Press, 1908), pp. 54–76;

Hobbes's Leviathan, introduction by W. G. Pogson Smith (Oxford: Clarendon Press, 1909);

Leviathan; or, The Matter, Forme and Power of a Commonwealth, Ecclesiasticall and Civil, edited by Michael Oakeshott, Blackwell's Political Texts (Oxford: Blackwell, 1946);

De Cive; or The Citizen, edited by Sterling P. Lamprecht (New York: Appleton-Century-Crofts, 1949);

Leviathan, edited by C. B. Macpherson (London: Pelican, 1968);

A Dialogue between a Philosopher and a Student of the Common Laws of England, edited by Joseph Cropsey (Chicago: University of Chicago Press, 1971);

Man and Citizen, edited by Bernard Gert (Garden City, N.Y.: Doubleday, 1972);

Critique du De Mundo de Thomas White, edited by Jean Jacquot and Harold Whitmore Jones (Paris: Vrin, 1973); translated by Jones as *Thomas White's De Mundo Examined* (London: Bradford University Press, 1976);

Hobbes's Thucydides, edited by Richard Schlatter (New Brunswick, N.J.: Rutgers University Press, 1975);

De Cive, The Latin Version, The Clarendon Edition of the Philosophical Works of Thomas Hobbes, volume 2, edited by Howard Warrender (Oxford: Clarendon Press, 1983);

De Cive, The English Version, The Clarendon Edition of the Philosophical Works of Thomas Hobbes, volume 3, edited by Warrender (Oxford: Clarendon Press, 1983);

The Rhetorics of Thomas Hobbes and Bernard Lamy, edited by John T. Harwood (Carbondale: Southern Illinois University Press, 1986);

Leviathan, edited by Richard Tuck, Cambridge Texts in the History of Political Thought (Cambridge: Cambridge University Press, 1991);

"1668 Appendix to Leviathan," translated, with an introduction and notes, by George Wright, *Interpretation,* 18 (1991): 323–414.

OTHER: *Eight Bookes of the Peloponnesian Warre Written by Thvcydides the sonne of Olorvs. Interpreted with Faith and Diligence Immediately out of the Greeke,* translated by Hobbes (London: Printed for Henry Seile, 1629);

A Briefe of the Art of Rhetorique. Containing in substance all that Aristotle hath written in his Three Bookes of that subject, Except onely what is not applicable to the English Tongue, translated anonymously by Hobbes (London: Printed by Thomas Cotes for Andrew Crooke, 1637);

"Objectiones Tertiæ," in René Descartes, *Meditationes de Prima Philosophia, in qva Dei Existentia, & animæ immortalitas demonstratur* (Paris: Printed for Michael Soli, 1641); translated by William Molyneux as "Objections Made against the Foregoing Meditations," in Descartes, *Six Metaphysical Meditations; Wherein it is Proved That there is a God. And that Mans Mind is really distinct from his Body,* translated by Molyneux (London: Printed by B. G. for Benjamin Tooke, 1680);

Preface to "Ballistica," in Marin Mersenne, *Cogitata Physico Mathematica. In quibus tam naturæ quàm artis effectus admirandi certissimus demonstrationibus explicantur,* 3 volumes (Paris: Printed for Antony Bertier, 1644);

"The Answer of Mr. Hobbs to Sr. William D'Avenant's preface before Gondibert," in D'Avenant, *A Discourse Upon Gondibert, An Heroick Poem, with an Answer to it by Mr. Hobbs* (Paris: Printed for Matthew Guillemot, 1650);

"To the Honourable *Edward Howard,* Esq.; on his intended Impression of his Poem of the British Princes," in Edward Howard, *The Brittish Princes: An Heroick Poem* (London: Printed by T. N. for Henry Herringman, 1669);

The Travels of Ulysses; As they were Related by Himself in Homer's Ninth, Tenth, Eleventh & Twelfth Books of his Odysses to Alcinous King of Phæacia, translated by Hobbes (London: Printed by John Crooke, Jr., for William Crooke, 1673);

Homer's Odysses, translated by Hobbes (London: Printed by John Crooke, Jr., for William Crooke, 1675);

Homer's Iliads in English, translated by Hobbes (London: Printed by John Crooke, Jr., for William Crooke, 1676);

"Considerations touching the facility or Difficulty of the Motions of a Horse on straight lines & Circular," in *A Catalogue of Letters and Other Historical Documents Exhibited in the Library at Welbeck,* compiled by S. Arthur Strong (London: Murray, 1903);

Fulgenzio Micanzio, O.S.M., "Lettere a William Cavendish (1615–1628) nelle versione inglese di Thomas Hobbes," edited by Roberto Ferrini, in *Scrinium historiale,* volume 15 (Rome: Istituto Storico O.S.M., 1987).

Thomas Hobbes lived for ninety-one of the most eventful years in the history of England. Born in the year of England's defeat of the Spanish Armada, he fled to France during the civil war, fled back just before the Restoration, lived through the Great Fire of London and the plague (for both of which the House of Commons tried to hold him partly responsible on account of his supposed atheism), and died in the midst of the "Popish Plot." During many of these years he was contemplating, writing, publishing, or defending influential, sometimes decisive, works in mathematics, optics, aesthetics, history, rhetoric, psychology, and political philosophy. Indeed, he claimed in the "Epistle Dedicatory" to the *Elements of Philosophy* (1656), with typical confidence and vigor, to have founded the latter discipline: "Natural Philosophy is therefore but young; but Civil Philosophy yet much younger, as being no older (I say it provoked, and that my detractors may know how little they have wrought upon me) than my own book *De Cive.*"

Even those who dispute that claim will admit that *Leviathan* (1651), the still-provocative work in which his ideas are spelled out in the most energetic detail, is one of the most important tracts ever written and one of the few masterpieces of political philosophy in the English language. His many and weighty compositions fill sixteen volumes in the standard edition (1839–1845) — eleven in English and five in Latin. They include, in addition to *Levi-*

*Title page, engraved by Thomas Cecil, for Hobbes's translation of
Thucydides' history of the Peloponnesian War*

athan, six other works in political philosophy, ten
polemical pamphlets in mathematics and religion,
and five translations of works of Thucydides, Aristotle, and Homer – the last completed when he was
eighty-six. (A translation of Euripedes' *Medea* into
Latin that he completed at the age of fourteen is
now lost.)

By all accounts an engaging, though studious,
man, Hobbes accumulated a long list of friends, colleagues, patrons, admirers, and enemies. John Aubrey, his first and most vivid biographer, met him
in 1634 and became a lifelong friend and admirer:
"Here was the first place and time that ever I had
the honour to see this worthy, learned man, who
was then pleased to take notice of me. . . ." Aubrey
says that Francis Bacon "loved to converse with"
Hobbes and relied on Hobbes to take dictation and
translate his essays into Latin. Hobbes was also on
intimate terms with such writers and scientists as
William Chillingworth; Abraham Cowley (who celebrated him as the successor to Aristotle and the
rival of Christopher Columbus in a fine Pindaric
ode, "To Mr. Hobs"); Sir William D'Avenant; Sir
Kenelm Digby; William Harvey; Edward, Lord
Herbert of Cherbury; Ben Jonson; and Edmund

Waller. John Dryden was "his great admirer, and
oftentimes ma[de] use of his Doctrine in his Playes,"
Dryden told Aubrey. (Dryden later excepted
Hobbes's translations of the works of Homer from
his admiration.)

Among statesmen, Hobbes knew well the
whole Cavendish family, his patrons for a lifetime, as well as Lucius Cary, second Viscount
Falkland; Edward Hyde, first Earl of Clarendon;
and Sidney Godolphin. He was tutor in mathematics to the Prince of Wales, who recognized,
encouraged, and protected Hobbes when he became Charles II (though he urged Hobbes to be
less controversial). The list of those who objected,
often violently, to one or another of his doctrines
is longer; it includes Clarendon, Robert Boyle,
John Bramhall, Samuel Clarke, Ralph Cudworth,
William Cumberland, John Eachard, John Fell,
Sir Robert Filmer, John Harris, Henry More,
Thomas Tenison, John Wallis, and Seth Ward.
His enemies prevented him from becoming a fellow of the Royal Society – much, Hobbes wrote,
to the discredit and damage of the investigations
of that group; his university posthumously condemned his works as heretical in 1683; and no end

of clergymen and philosophers joined in the hue and cry after *Leviathan*.

One incident that Aubrey recounts has, perhaps, too often been drawn on to explain Hobbes's way of thinking: "He was 40 yeares old before he looked on Geometry; which happened accidentally. Being in a Gentleman's Library, Euclid's Elements lay open, and 'twas the 47 *El. libri* I. [the Pythagorean Theorem]. He read the Proposition. *By G—,* sayd he (he would now and then sweare an emphaticall Oath by way of emphasis) *this is impossible!* So he reads the Demonstration of it, which referred him back to such a Proposition; which proposition he read. That referred him back to another, which he also read. *Et sic deinceps* [and so on] that at last he was demonstratively convinced of that trueth. This made him in love with Geometry." Hobbes became so passionate a mathematician, Aubrey continues, that "he was wont to draw lines on his thigh and on the sheetes, abed. . . ." This incident is frequently seen as an indication of how important mathematical demonstrations were to Hobbes's work, and of how he hungered to carry over the inevitability of mathematical demonstration into his "civill philosophy," little or none of which had been written at the time of this epiphany.

It is noteworthy that this incident took place in a "Gentleman's Library" – probably one in Geneva, though Hobbes made frequent and good use of the fine libraries at the Cavendish estate, Chatsworth, and at Welbeck Abbey, and of many others in several countries. He had access to, and great need of, the libraries of "Gentlemen," who were about the only ones who could afford to buy and shelve large numbers of books in that era. Some gentlemen went so far as to read the books they collected, and a few became patrons of others who would read them and then write books of their own – books dedicated, as Hobbes's always were, to one gentleman or another. While Hobbes was uncommonly fortunate in the gentlemen who encouraged him in his reading and his writing, he well knew that this patronage was not enough, eager though he was to have his works find their way into their libraries and their minds. Aubrey says, "He was much in London till the restauration of his Majesty, having here convenience not only of Bookes, but of learned Conversation. I have heard him say, that at his Lord's house in the Countrey there was a good Library, and bookes enough for him, and that his Lordship stored the Library with what bookes he thought fitt to be bought; but he sayd, the want of learned Conversation was a very great inconvenience, and that though he conceived he could

order his thinking as well perhaps as another man, yet he found a great defect. Methinkes in the country, for want of good conversation, one's Witt growes mouldy." While Chatsworth was better than a university for a man of Hobbes's intellect and temperament, all his life he sought challenging intellects outside stately homes and cloistered colleges. He was wary of the man who read more than he thought or wrote (it seldom occurred to him that a woman might do either): "He was wont to say," according to Aubrey, "that if he had read as much as other men, he should have knowne no more then other men." Some of those other men – notably, Clarendon – claimed that Hobbes would have done better to read more. Hobbes bought few books of his own: "I never sawe," Aubrey says, " . . . above halfe a dozen about him in his chamber. Homer and Virgil were commonly on his Table; sometimes Xenophon, or some probable historie, and Greek Testament, or so."

Paradoxically, the other salient characteristic customarily mentioned in connection with this outspoken, sociable, and well-connected philosopher is his timidity. He commented on it himself at the beginning of an autobiographical poem he wrote in Latin in his eighty-fifth year, insisting, though strict chronology makes it seem unlikely, that his birth on Friday, 5 April 1588, was hastened by his mother hearing of the launching of the Spanish Armada, and that he and fear were twins. There is unquestionably a thread of timidity woven into the texture of Hobbes's life and works.

Little is known about Hobbes's parents, except that his mother's maiden name was Middleton and that his father, also named Thomas, was a quarrelsome and, according to Aubrey, ignorant clergyman who fled his parish of Malmesbury, in Wiltshire, and his family, leaving Thomas and his brother and sister to be brought up by their uncle Francis Hobbes, a generous and successful glover. It is tempting to think that his uncle's trade, which would have required him to deal often and intimately with gentility, taught Hobbes something of that art.

It is certain that Francis Hobbes's success in that trade enabled him to send Thomas to a series of good schools, first at Westport Church in 1592, then at Malmesbury in 1596, and finally to a private school in Westport run by Robert Latimer, where he translated *Medea*. He must have been an apt student, as he proceeded to Magdalen Hall, Oxford, in January 1603. There he mastered the intricacies of the syllogism and the Scholastic method, not without grumbling, and objected to the disputatiousness of the Puritans. According to Aubrey, "He tooke great delight there to goe to the Booke-binders shops, and lye gaping on Mappes." This fascination with maps combines well with his interest in history (he would draw the maps for his translation of Thucydides' history of the Peloponnesian War [1629] himself) and indicates a lifelong concern with representation – and perhaps with motion, which was also to absorb him all his life.

A much better scholar than student, Hobbes did well enough to graduate B.A. on 5 February 1608 and to receive the strong recommendation of the principal as tutor to William Cavendish, soon to become the second earl of Devonshire. This was the first of many gentlemen (three of them Cavendishes) whom he instructed and befriended, and with whom he traveled and lived uncommonly well for a scholar in that or any age. He worked as a tutor until 1640, making three leisurely and luxurious trips to the Continent – from around 1610 to 1613, 1628 to 1631, and 1634 to 1637.

Neither his duties nor his travels kept him from his studies. On the Continent he befriended and impressed Galileo around 1636; Marin Mersenne, a Franciscan who put him in touch with all the latest ideas in Paris, in about 1637; and Pierre Gassendi around 1646. Galileo had drawn everyone's mind to motion; the latest ideas in Paris were primarily those of René Descartes and rationalism; and Gassendi's ideas had largely to do with physiology and sensation.

At home he served as secretary to Bacon in 1623–1624, pursued his studies of psychology and politics, and completed his translation of Thucydides' history of the Peloponnesian War. His translation is something of a classic; it improves considerably in both accuracy and force on its only predecessor, a 1550 translation by Thomas Nicolls based largely on a French intermediary rather than the Greek original from which Hobbes worked. The translation was sufficiently popular to require, and sufficiently important to the translator to receive, three more printings in his lifetime (1634, 1648, and 1676).

Each of these printings, one may assume, was intended primarily for the libraries of gentlemen, those who, though their Greek might be rusty or nonexistent, stood in need of what Hobbes describes, in the dedication to the new earl of Devonshire, as "profitable instruction for noblemen, and such as may come to have the managing of great and weighty actions." Even those readers unlikely to exercise such management might profit from the knowledge of the past presented by the lessons, concocted speeches, and

suggested causes of so politic a historiographer as Thucydides. And the translator must have schooled himself in human nature with this text, as the motives that Thucydides depicted at work in the Athenians – fear, honor, and profit – are those that necessitate the formation of a commonwealth in *Leviathan*. The introductory "Of the Life and History of Thucydides" is, in its attention to history, eloquence, genre, politics, and its own argument, a promising first piece of prose from a scholar who, though forty-one, would be writing for another fifty years.

His work with Thucydides confirmed Hobbes's thoroughgoing humanism – a determination to consider thoughtfully, and to urge others to consider, the wisdom, eloquence, and ethical values of the Greek past. This work also announced and confirmed his strong lifelong preference for the authority and wisdom of a single figure, a king. As he put it in his 1679 autobiography, thinking back to this translation:

> Sed mihi præ reliquis Thucydides placuit.
> Is Democratia ostendit mihi quam sit inepta,
> Et quantum cœtu plus sapit unus homo.

> (But Thucydides delighted me more than the others. He pointed out how inadequate democracy is, and how much wiser one man is than the multitude [translation by J. E. Parsons and Whitney Blair.])

What remained of his time and energy, which must have been considerable, was devoted to developing his systematic philosophical and political system. At some time during this period he consolidated the fascination with motion that was to become central to his philosophy. He says in his autobiography:

> internis nil nisi motus inest.
> Hinc est quod, physicam quisquis vult discere, motus
>   Quid possit, debet perdidicisse prius.
> Ergo materiæ motusque arcana recludo;
> . . . .
> In patriam rursus post menses octo reversus,
>   De connectendis cogito notitiis.
> Motibus a variis feror ad rerum variarum
>   Dissimiles species, materiæque dolos;
> Motusque internos hominum, cordisque latebras:
>   Denique ad imperii justitiæque bona.
> His ego me mersi studiis. . . .

(there is nothing within us except motion. From this circumstance derives the fact that whoever wants to learn physics ought to have learned well beforehand what motion can do. Therefore, I revealed the arcana of matter in motion. . . . Returning to my homeland again after eight months, I thought about weaving together

*Title pages for the first (top left) and revised (top right) editions of Hobbes's first work of political philosophy, written in Latin;
(bottom) "Religion," an illustration for Hobbes's English translation of the work*

my conceptions. I went from the variety of motions to the dissimilar appearances of different things and the deceptions of matter; and to the internal motion of human beings and the hidden fastnesses of the human heart, and at length to the benefits of dominion and justice. And I buried myself in these studies [translation by Parsons and Blair.])

This fascination with motion led Hobbes in some strange directions. There is a preface on ballistics written for Mersenne's *Cogitata Physico Mathematica* (1644–1647) and an unpublished and apparently not very satisfactory manuscript, "Considerations touching the facility or Difficulty of the Motions of a Horse on straight lines & Circular."

As he came to understand motion better, he turned to a systematic and comprehensive project. He proposed to devote one book to the body ("De Corpore"), one to the mind ("De Homine"), and one to the state ("De Cive"). Inklings of this system were circulated widely in manuscripts of his treatise "The Elements of Law Natural and Politique," a tract on citizenship and absolutism that was not published in full until 1889; substantial parts of it appeared in 1650 as *Humane Nature* and *De Corpore Politico. The Elements of Law* is an excellent brief introduction to Hobbes's ideas but not to his method or his manner, which have considerable charms and strength of their own. The ideas alone did not charm many, nor were they intended to, as he himself wrote in *Mr. Hobbes Considered in His Loyalty, Religion, Reputation, and Manners* (1662): "Mr. Hobbes wrote a little treatise in English, wherein he did set forth and demonstrate, that the said power and rights were inseparably annexed to the sovereignty, which sovereignty they did not then deny to be in the King; but it seemes understood not, or would not understand, that inseparability. Of this treatise, though not printed, many gentlemen had copies, which occasioned much talk of the author; and had not his Majesty dissolved the Parliament, it had brought him into danger of his life."

The political ideas in these works were bold; the scholar who produced them was timid; and the times were turbulent. The Puritans were beginning to exercise their power in the Long Parliament, and the Royalists were tense; Parliament attempted to censure Bishop Roger Manwaring for preaching Hobbes's doctrine. In November 1640 Hobbes escaped to Paris, "the first of all that fled," as he said; he would remain there, prudently and productively, though not in the well-

kept manner to which he had been accustomed, for eleven years.

In Paris he kept company with other refugees from the civil war and disputed with Bishop John Bramhall over freedom of the will and with Descartes over the materiality of the mind. He also completed and published *Elementorum Philosophiæ Sectio Tertia De Cive* (1642), which puts forth, with Hobbes's characteristic clarity and vigor, the doctrine that the church must submit to the authority of the crown for the sake of peace. Except for a brief period as tutor to the Prince of Wales in 1646–1647, an illness in 1647 so serious that he took the Anglican sacraments, and a brief but impressive excursion into aesthetics, Hobbes devoted his energies to *Leviathan,* "the manner of writing of which booke (he told me [Aubrey]) was thus. He sayd that he sometimes would sett his thoughts upon researching and contemplating, always with this Rule that he very much and deeply considered one thing at a time (*scilicet,* a weeke or sometimes a fortnight). He walked much and contemplated, and he had in the head of his Staffe a pen and inke-horne, carried always a Note-book in his pocket, and as soon as a notion darted, he presently entred it into his Booke, or els he should perhaps have lost it. He had drawne the Designe of the Booke into Chapters, etc. so he knew whereabout it would come in. Thus that booke was made."

Hobbes's brief, substantial, and uncontroversial contribution to aesthetics is "The Answer of Mr. Hobbes to Sr. Will. D'Avenant's Preface Before *Gondibert,*" published in 1650 in a volume that included that unfinished and unreadable heroic poem. Hobbes is courtly in his consideration of D'Avenant's work and classical in his many examples, as well as in his insistence on meter, decorum, and a rigid hierarchy of genres. It exhibits Hobbes's lifelong fascination with the faculties, which he sees at work here in the making of a poem: "Memory begets Judgement and Fancy: Judgment begets the strength and structure, and Fancy begets the ornaments of a Poem." The text pays special attention to the "celerity" of fancy, without dismissing the discrimination to which it must be subject.

The "Answer" is especially "Hobbesian" in its intriguing division of "Poesy" into three kinds, "Heroique, Scommatique [satiric], and Pastorall," and "mankinde" into three regions, "*Court, City,* and *Country.*" This characteristically schematic classification produces, with a whiff of Euclid, "neither more nor less than six sorts of Poesy" and a handful of intriguing insights. Also Hobbesian (and humanist) is the preference for language that is perspicuous, emanating from a mind that knows well and knows much: "He therefore that undertakes an Heroick Poem, which is to exhibit a venerable & amiable Image of Heroick vertue, must not only be the Poet, to place & connect, but also the Philosopher, to furnish and square his matter, that is, to make both Body and Soul, colour and shadow of his Poem out of his own Store. . . ."

In Paris the French clergy, the English queen, and the pious Scots in exile all professed hostility to Hobbes's supposed irreligion, and the court of the future Charles II expressed dismay at his politics. All of these factors, as well as the manifest dangers of the times and another severe illness, combined with his native timidity to carry Hobbes back to England, where *Leviathan* was published in April or May 1651.

The book that kept Hobbes's mind and body in motion during most of his years in Paris has agitated readers ever since. Whereas classical philosophers and political scientists had hoped to enable humanity to live the good life, Hobbes, who saw deeper into human nature and farther into history, and who worried more about power than justice, would settle for a state that enabled its citizens to live in peace, free from the calamitous civil wars that were ravaging his country as he wrote (and are still ravaging many parts of the world today).

Hobbes begins, as one would expect, with motion; he moves toward stability by way of a social contract. A "faculty psychologist," Hobbes assumes that the mind is divided into separate faculties, or powers, for reasoning, judging, imagining, remembering, and sensing. He explains sensation as "divers motions" in external matter producing various motions in the matter within. Unrelenting in its materialism, this formulation was, and remains, particularly alarming to those who romanticize the creative drive: the motions of the mind subside as the stimulus fades; "IMAGINATION therefore is nothing but *decaying sense*." While the mind may also be put in motion by recalling past sensations, few thinkers have ever wanted their thinking to be considered only the operation of a material substance, whether that substance is called a corpuscle, a muscle, a cell, an atom, beta amyloid protein, or a synapse.

Sensations give rise to a "TRAYNE of Thoughts" or "Mentall Discourse," the province of Hobbes's rationalism and the source of many bothersome complications of the human condition. Mental discourse is inevitably distorted – for example, when it is converted into language so that it can be "shewn"

to others; in this respect Hobbes was an unrelenting nominalist: "For *True* and *False* are attributes of Speech, not of Things. And where Speech is not, there is neither *Truth* nor *Falshood*." The "inconstant signification" of language worried Hobbes all his life, as writer, translator, thinker, and citizen. The deliberate, but needless, complications of metaphor, the distorting and mechanical logic of the Schoolmen, and the devices of the rhetoricians would periodically enrage him.

While language has no certainty of its own, reason is even more suspect, dependent as it is on the passions to put it in motion either toward (desire) or from (aversion) an object – an object that, of course, it can "know" only through sensation. Thus, where true and false are matters of language, good and evil are merely physiological responses to various objects. What is worse, these responses will vary from person to person, and from time to time in the same person.

The passions thus complicate life at the same time that they make it possible by putting the self into motion. They also enliven "wit" (a term, and a faculty, fraught with meaning for Hobbes and his contemporaries) by transferring motion from the mind of the writer to the mind of the reader: "This NATURALL WITTE, consisteth principally in two things; *Celerity of Imagining,* (that is, swift succession of one thought to another;) and *steddy direction* to some approved end" – the idea of motion is implicit in the terms *celerity, swift succession,* and *steddy direction*. But too much motion is bad for the mind, and Hobbes wants wit to be curbed by judgment and discretion. Poems can tolerate more "wit" than can history or logic, but discretion is, for Hobbes, an essential attribute of aesthetics as well as of morals and politics. People need some of the motion imparted by passion, but "to have stronger, and more vehement Passions for any thing, than is ordinarily seen in others, is that which men call MADNESSE."

These troublesome internal motions become much more alarming when beings governed by them come into contact with one another. People driven by sensation and moved by passion compete incessantly for power, the ultimate object of all passions: "So that in the nature of man, we find three principall causes of quarrell, First, Competition; Secondly, Diffidence; Thirdly, Glory." The lives of all people would, thus, be unendingly competitive, insecure, and discontented. The internal motions of the individuals would produce a friction that would be intolerable to Hobbes and, he assumed, to every rational being.

The most infamous formulation in *Leviathan* is that of a purely hypothetical state of nature, or "Naturall Condition of Mankind" – a situation in which there is no government. In that state, people would be "in that condition which is called Warre; and such a warre, as is of every man, against every man." They would have no security, no industry, no culture, no justice or law, "no Knowledge of the face of the Earth; no account of Time; no Arts; no Letters; no Society; and which is worst of all, continuall feare, and danger of violent death; And the life of man, solitary, poore, nasty, brutish, and short." Rather than remain in such a condition, people enter into a social contract wherein each of them transfers all his or her power to a sovereign.

Hobbes pauses frequently in the course of his argument to take his reader with him, to help the reader catch up, and to carry the reader into the continuation of his argument with a clear understanding of where he has been and where he is headed. Motion is, thus, a stylistic entity for Hobbes, a component of his argument as well as a psychological and philosophical concern of his text. Part 2 opens with a succinct restatement of his argument:

> The finall Cause, End, or Designe of men, (who naturally love Liberty, and Dominion over others,) in the introduction of that restraint upon themselves, (in which wee see them live in Common-wealths,) is the foresight of their own preservation, and of a more contented life thereby; that is to say, of getting themselves out from that miserable condition of Warre, which is necessarily consequent (as hath been shewn) to the naturall Passions of men, when there is no visible Power to keep them in awe, and tye them by feare of punishment to the performance of their Covenants, and observation of those Lawes of Nature set down in the fourteenth and fifteenth Chapters.

The sovereign to whom individual humans transfer their power keeps them in awe, holds their passions in check, and, perhaps most astonishing, imparts steady meaning to words. "This is the Generation of that great LEVIATHAN, or rather (to speake more reverently) of that *Mortall God*, to which wee owe under the *Immortall God*, our peace and defence." Hobbes conducts a lengthy, intricate, and detailed analysis of the social contract or covenant that brings this Leviathan – or, as he now calls it, "Common-wealth" – into being, and then spells out the powers that belong to it. Among the powers of the sovereign are judging, punishing, making war, and – one power of which Hobbes had considerable personal knowledge – distributing honors

and benefits. While the sovereign power of a commonwealth may be vested in one person (a monarchy), a group (an aristocracy), or "All that will come together" (a democracy), for reasons of efficiency, consistency, succession, and scriptural authority, all of which are spelled out, as well as reasons of prejudice, prudence, and temperament, all of which are implicit, Hobbes much prefers that the sovereign be a monarch.

Chapter 21 enumerates the obligations (here called "liberties") of the citizens of a commonwealth thus contracted; the chapter scoffs (and Hobbes was a good scoffer) at common definitions of *liberty* and elaborates (he was a great elaborator) various laws and practices. For example, citizens have the liberty to refuse the sovereign's command to kill themselves or others, to resist the power of the sword that the covenant confers on the sovereign, and, most intriguingly and revealingly, not to go to war when the sovereign calls if they are of a timorous nature but to send a substitute. Their obligations to the sovereign last only as long as his power to hold the competitive motions of every citizen in check – a condition not of much comfort to Charles, who was biding his time in Paris while Oliver Cromwell presided over the English Commonwealth.

Part 2 is informed by Hobbes's determination to be fair but thorough (indeed, exhaustive) in his analysis of a commonwealth. It exhibits a distrust of faction and an interest in merchants, commodities, property, currency, and colonies that are a credit to the worldliness of this well-connected scholar. The distrust of common words and public eloquence evident in chapter 25 ("Of Counsell") notwithstanding, the chapter ends with a wonderful figure of motion that combines one of Hobbes's pastimes with one of his prejudices. This figure, in itself, indicates how cogent, practical, vivid, and, indeed, current, his political philosophy can be: "A man that doth his businesse by the help of many and prudent Counsellours, with every one consulting apart in his proper element, does it best, as he that useth able Seconds at Tennis play, placed in their proper stations. He does next best, that useth his own Judgement only; as he that has no Second at all. But he that is carried up and down his businesse in a framed Counsell, which cannot move but by the plurality of consenting opinions, the execution whereof is commonly (out of envy, or interest) retarded by the part dissenting, does it worst of all, and like one that is carried to the ball, though by good Players, yet in a Wheele-barrough, or other frame, heavy of it self, and re-

*Engraved title page for Hobbes's best-known work, written while
he was a refugee in France*

tarded also by the inconcurrent judgements, and endeavours of them that drive it. . . ." An extensive discussion of "civill lawes," heavy with enumerations ("Tenthly . . .") and richly informed by Hobbes's knowledge of language, history, human nature, and Scripture – not to mention an exceedingly civic sense of sin – is full of insights that are common to political philosophy and the other humanities: a sagacious understanding of greed, corruption, power, and partiality are as essential to the historian and the playwright as to the civil philosopher.

Hobbes exhibits that sagacity, that quick, sure movement of the mind toward truth that he values so much, in his shrewd comments on "the absurdity of Dreames," the psychology of laughter, credulity, "Pusillanimity," and the civic uses of "benefits." These and other insights, all vividly expressed and thoughtfully set forth, enliven the progress of the

reader through a dense thicket of psychology, political science, philosophy, and speculation.

Parts 3 and 4, "Of a Christian Common-Wealth" and "Of the Kingdome of Darknesse," are given over to equally detailed consideration of their subjects. Only since the 1960s, with the work of J. G. A. Pocock and David Johnston, perhaps under the impetus of Howard Warrender and F. C. Hood, have these two sections received the attention of critics; it is not clear that they ever received that of readers, except those who made their careers in the church. The treatment of Scripture and religion in these two parts is not orthodox enough to satisfy that sort of reader or analytical enough to attract another. The eloquence and the argument here are inferior to that of parts 1 and 2.

From the start *Leviathan* has had enemies who have objected to its materialism, its rationalism, its nominalism, or its skepticism (the book is prickly with broadsides and asides that denigrate the politics of the Athenians, the conclusions of the School-men, the language of the universities, and the beliefs of the church — there is a whole chapter on the emptiness of religious language). Some who do not fall into any of these groups continue to be offended by Hobbes's low opinion of most of his fellow human beings, as when he refers to "the more ignorant sort, (that is to say, the most part, or generality of the people)." Others do not like the ideas that justice emerges from the social contract rather than from a loftier or deeper source; that good and evil are relative; that truth is merely logical consistency; that sin is only the violation of civil law; or that thought is only a motion of matter.

Yet, because it was bold, rigorous, and accessible, *Leviathan* went through three editions, two of them pirated, or perhaps surreptitious, before it was suppressed. The church and the universities fulminated against the man and his works so long and so loudly that Hobbes became a bogeyman whom no Renaissance gentleman would have allowed into his library and no modern reader would recognize from his publications.

Hobbes was rescued — or, rather, appropriated — by the nineteenth-century utilitarians, especially Jeremy Bentham, Henry Hallam, James and John Stuart Mill, John Austin, George Grote, and Sir William Molesworth, who edited sixteen volumes of his works (1839–1845) — still the only complete edition. He was rescued from his rescuers by the explanations of Croom Robertson and the scholarship of Ferdinand Tönnies, who delivered him into the busy and skilled hands of other editors and scholars.

Twentieth-century critics have emphasized — one might say exaggerated — the bourgeois aspects of *Leviathan* (C. B. Macpherson), reclaimed Hobbes for philosophy by connecting him to traditions of will and artifice (Michael Oakeshott), or accused him of writing literature instead of philosophy (Charles Cantalupo). Others have convicted *Leviathan* of liberalism (Leo Strauss, Richard Tuck) or seen it as essentially a religious (Hood) or a populist (Johnston) tract. Still others have tried to restore Hobbes to the Renaissance (Miriam M. Reik) or promote him into an Augustan (James). *Leviathan* has, in other words, continued to put the minds, and the writing implements, of readers into motion and seems destined to continue to do so.

Hobbes was never to return to the Continent, though his books and his reputation flourished more there than at home. When *Leviathan* was banned in England, Hobbes translated it into Latin and had it published in 1670 in Holland — a country that had more freedom of the press than England and more presses than gentlemen or libraries. The book became so scarce in England that Samuel Pepys had to pay three times the original price for a secondhand copy in 1688.

In 1663 Hobbes resumed his customary and fairly undemanding position of intellectual retainer to the Cavendishes but took up residence in London. There he added the role of controversialist to those of scholar and courtier in a series of pamphlets that are less edifying now than they were then. Hobbes was a better controversialist than mathematician and more quarrelsome than theological. Whatever his genuine religious views, and whether out of prudence, devotion, or a willingness to annoy his detractors, he made it a point to be seen regularly at church. He seems to have conducted his life, if not his disputes, with charity — more charity than his opponents, even those who wore clerical robes, allowed him.

Through the good offices of his many gentlemen friends and of Aubrey he was restored to the good graces of Charles II, who ordered him to publish nothing more on religion or politics. The king gave him an annual pension of one hundred pounds at a time when a schoolmaster was lucky to make twenty pounds per year. It does not seem to have been paid with much regularity.

Around 1660 Hobbes had written a historical dialogue recounting the machinations of the Long Parliament and returning, not completely disinterestedly, to a consideration of heresy and the limitations to which persecutions for it were subject. Prudence and power prevented the publication of this work, *Behemoth,* until 1679, when it appeared in corrupted form as *The History of the Civil Wars of England;* an improved version was published in 1682 in *Tracts of Mr. Thomas Hobbs.* Hobbes's original manuscript was edited by Tönnies and published under the title *Behemoth* in 1889. In the 1670s he continued his mathematical disputes and composed "A Dialogue between a Phylosopher and a Student of the Common-Laws of England" (1681).

Though he had been a somewhat sickly youth, Hobbes enjoyed a vigorous middle and old age by living temperately and keeping out of the care of doctors, though his hand had shaken with palsy since about 1650. He walked regularly and briskly, played tennis at the age of seventy-five, sang, and smoked a pipe.

His mind, like his body, was in motion until the end of his life. He composed two Latin autobiographies (1679, 1681) when he was in his mid eighties, both much less colorful than Aubrey's biography or, indeed, than his life itself, and then turned to translations of the *Odyssey* (1673, 1675) and the *Iliad* (1676). The preface to the latter emphasizes and exhibits wit and discretion and enumerates seven "Vertues of an Heroique Poem": choice of words, construction, contrivance, "Elevation of the Fancie," impartiality of the poet, clarity, and amplitude. Most of his own works written over the previous forty years exhibit all but the fifth of these virtues. His final work was *Decameron Physiologicum: Or, Ten Dialogues of Natural Philosophy* (1678); the most remarkable thing about this work is the age of its author.

On 4 December 1679 the mind and body of Thomas Hobbes came finally to rest, the result of old age and a wintry move from one of the Cavendishes' stately homes, Chatsworth, to the other, Hardwick Hall. He was buried near the latter, in the chancel at Hault Hucknall Church in Derbyshire. Sir Robert Southwell wrote to James, first Duke of Ormond, on 16 December that "Mr. Hobbes is lately dead, in all the forms of a very good christian"; Anthony à Wood thought that "on his death bed he should say that he was 91 yeares finding out a hole to go out of this world, and at length found it." While he posited that life in the state of nature would be solitary, poor, nasty, brutish, and short, he himself lived one that was eminently sociable, commodious, cultured, civilized, and long.

Letters:

Ferdinand Tönnies, "Siebzehn Briefe des Thomas Hobbes an Samuel Sorbière nebst Briefen Sorbières, Mersenne's u. Aa.," *Archiv für Geschichte der Philosophie,* 3, no. 1 (1890): 58–71, 192–232;

Historical Manuscripts Commission, *13th Report, Appendix Part Two: The Manuscripts of His Grace the Duke of Portland, Preserved at Welbeck Abbey,* volume 2 (London: Her Majesty's Stationers, 1893), pp. 124–130;

Tönnies, "Hobbes-Analekten I & II," *Archiv für Geschichte der Philosophie,* 17, no. 3 (1904): 291–317; 19, no. 2 (1906): 153–175;

Historical Manuscripts Commission, *Report on Manuscripts in Various Collections,* volume 7 (London: His Majesty's Stationers, 1914), p. 401;

Harcourt Brown, "The Mersenne Correspondence: A Lost Letter by Thomas Hobbes," *Isis,* 34 (Autumn 1943): 311–312;

I. Bernard Cohen, "A Lost Letter from Hobbes to Mersenne Found," *Harvard Library Bulletin,* 1 (Winter 1947): 112–113;

G. R. De Beer, "Some Letters of Thomas Hobbes," *Notes and Records of the Royal Society,* 7 (April 1950): 195–206;

The Correspondence, 2 volumes, edited by Noel Malcolm, The Clarendon Edition of the Works of Thomas Hobbes, volumes 6–7 (Oxford: Clarendon Press / New York: Oxford University Press, 1994).

Bibliographies:

Hugh Macdonald and Mary Hargreaves, *Thomas Hobbes: A Bibliography* (London: Bibliographical Society, 1952);

Charles H. Hinnant, *Thomas Hobbes: A Reference Guide* (Boston: G. K. Hall, 1980);

William Sacksteder, *Hobbes Studies (1879–1979): A Bibliography* (Bowling Green, Ohio: Philosophy Documentation Center, 1982).

Biographies:

Richard Blackbourne, *Vitae Hobbianae Auctarium,* in Hobbes's *Thomæ Hobbes Angli Malmesburiensis Philosophi Vita* (London: Printed for William Crooke, 1681);

Anthony à Wood, "Thomas Hobbes," in his *Athenæ Oxonienses,* 2 volumes (London: Printed by Thomas Bennet, 1692), II: 477–483;

John Aubrey, "Thomas Hobbes," in *Letters written by Eminent Persons in the Seventeenth and Eighteenth Centuries,* 2 volumes (London: Longman, Hurst, Rees, Orme & Brown, 1813), II: 593–637; republished in *Aubrey's Brief Lives,* edited by Oliver Lawson Dick (London: Secker & Warburg, 1950), pp. 147–159;

Aubrey, "*Brief Lives,*" in *Chiefly of Contemporaries,* 2 volumes, edited by Andrew Clark (Oxford: Clarendon Press, 1898), I: 16–20, 321–403;

Arnold Rogow, *Thomas Hobbes* (New York: Norton, 1986).

References:

Terence Ball, "Hobbes' Linguistic Turn," *Polity,* 17 (Summer 1985): 739–760;

Deborah Baumgold, *Hobbes's Political Thought* (Cambridge: Cambridge University Press, 1988);

John Bowle, *Hobbes and His Critics: A Study in Seventeenth Century Constitutionalism* (New York: Oxford University Press, 1952);

Frithiof Brandt, *Thomas Hobbes' Mechanical Conception of Nature,* translated by Vaughan Maxwell and Annie I. Fausbøoll (Copenhagen: Levin & Munksgaard, 1921);

K. C. Brown, ed., *Hobbes Studies* (Cambridge, Mass.: Harvard University Press, 1965);

Charles Cantalupo, *A Literary "Leviathan": Thomas Hobbes's Masterpiece of Language* (Lewisburg, Pa.: Bucknell University Press, 1991);

Peter Caws, ed., *The Causes of Quarrel: Essays on Peace, War, and Thomas Hobbes* (Boston: Beacon, 1989);

Eldon J. Eisenach, *Two Worlds of Liberalism: Religion and Politics in Hobbes, Locke, and Mill* (Chicago: University of Chicago Press, 1981);

David P. Gauthier, *The Logic of the Leviathan* (Oxford: Clarendon Press, 1969);

M. M. Goldsmith, *Hobbes's Science of Politics* (New York: Columbia University Press, 1966);

Jean Hampton, *Hobbes and the Social Contract Tradition* (Cambridge: Cambridge University Press, 1986);

Charles Hinnant, *Thomas Hobbes,* Twayne's English Authors Series, no. 215 (Boston: G. K. Hall, 1977);

F. C. Hood, *The Divine Politics of Thomas Hobbes: An Interpretation of Leviathan* (Oxford: Clarendon Press, 1964);

David G. James, *The Life of Reason: Hobbes, Locke, Bolingbroke* (London: Longmans, Green, 1949);

David Johnston, *The Rhetoric of "Leviathan": Thomas Hobbes and the Politics of Cultural Transformation* (Princeton: Princeton University Press, 1986);

John Laird, *Hobbes* (London: Benn, 1934);

C. B. Macpherson, *The Political Theory of Possessive Individualism: Hobbes to Locke* (Oxford: Clarendon Press, 1954);

F. S. McNeilly, *The Anatomy of Leviathan* (London: Macmillan, 1968);

Samuel I. Mintz, *The Hunting of Leviathan: Seventeenth-Century Reactions to the Materialism and Moral Philosophy of Thomas Hobbes* (Cambridge: Cambridge University Press, 1962);

Michael Oakeshott, *Hobbes on Civil Association* (Berkeley & Los Angeles: University of California Press, 1975);

Walter J. Ong, S.J., "Hobbes and Talon's Ramist Rhetoric in English," *Transactions of the Cambridge Bibliographical Society,* 1, part 3 (1951): 260–269;

Richard Peters, *Hobbes* (Harmondsworth: Penguin, 1956);

J. G. A. Pocock, "Time, History, and Eschatology in the Thought of Thomas Hobbes," in his *Politics, Language, and Time* (New York: Atheneum, 1973), pp. 148–201;

Raymond Polin, *Hobbes, Dieu, et les hommes* (Paris: Presses Universitaires de France, 1981);

David D. Raphael, *Hobbes: Morals and Politics* (London: Allen & Unwin, 1977);

Miriam M. Reik, *The Golden Lands of Thomas Hobbes* (Detroit: Wayne State University Press, 1977);

George Croom Robertson, *Hobbes* (London & Edinburgh: Blackwood, 1886);

G. A. J. Rogers and Alan Ryan, eds., *Perspectives on Thomas Hobbes* (Oxford: Oxford University Press, 1988);

Ralph Ross, Herbert W. Schneider, and Theodore Waldman, eds., *Thomas Hobbes in His Time* (Minneapolis: University of Minnesota Press, 1974);

Steven Shapin and Simon Schaffer, *Leviathan and the Air-Pump: Hobbes, Boyle, and the Experimental Life* (Princeton: Princeton University Press, 1985);

Richard Sherlock, "The Theology of *Leviathan:* Hobbes on Religion," *Interpretation,* 10 (January 1982): 43–60;

Tom Sorell, *Hobbes* (London: Routledge & Kegan Paul, 1986);

Sorell, ed., *The Cambridge Companion to Hobbes* (Cambridge: Cambridge University Press, forthcoming 1996);

Sir Robert Southwell, "Letters of Sir Robert Southwell to James, 1st Duke of Ormond, 1677–1686," in *Calendar of the Manuscripts of the Marquess of Ormonde, K. P. Preserved at Kilkenny Castle,* new series 4, edited by the Historical Manuscripts Commission (London: HMSO, 1906), pp. 374–398;

Thomas A. Spragens, Jr., *The Politics of Motion: The World of Thomas Hobbes* (Lexington: University of Kentucky Press, 1973);

Patricia Springborg, "Hobbes, Heresy, and the *Historia Ecclesiastica,*" *Journal of the History of Ideas,* 55 (1994): 553–571;

Leslie Stephen, *Hobbes,* English Men of Letters (London: Macmillan, 1904);

Leo Strauss, *The Political Philosophy of Hobbes: Its Basis and Genesis* (Oxford: Clarendon Press, 1936);

A. E. Taylor, "The Ethical Doctrine of Hobbes," *Philosophy,* 13 (October 1938): 406–424; reprinted in Brown, ed., *Hobbes Studies* (1965), pp. 35–56;

Clarence D. Thorpe, *The Aesthetic Theory of Thomas Hobbes* (Ann Arbor: University of Michigan Press, 1940);

Ferdinand Tönnies, *Hobbes Leben und Lehre* (Stuttgart: Frommann, 1896);

Richard Tuck, *Hobbes,* Past Masters Series (Oxford: Oxford University Press, 1989);

Howard Warrender, *The Political Philosophy of Hobbes: His Theory of Obligation* (Oxford: Clarendon Press, 1957);

J. W. N. Watkins, *Hobbes's System of Ideas: A Study in the Political Significance of Philosophical Theories,* second edition (London: Hutchinson, 1973);

Basil Willey, *The English Moralists* (New York: Norton, 1964);

Willey, *The Seventeenth Century Background: Studies in the Thought of the Age in Relation to Poetry and Religion* (New York: Columbia University Press, 1934);

Sheldon S. Wolin, *Hobbes and the Epic Tradition of Political Theory* (Los Angeles: William Andrews Clark Memorial Library, 1970);

Anthony à Wood, *The Life and Times of Anthony Wood, Antiquary, of Oxford, 1632–1695, Described by Himself,* volume 2, edited by Andrew Clark (Oxford: Printed for the Oxford Historical Society at the Clarendon Press, 1892), pp. 471–472;

Yves Charles Zarka, ed., *Thomas Hobbes: Philosophie première, théorie de la science et politique* (Paris: Presses Universitaires de France, 1990).

Papers:

Most of Thomas Hobbes's surviving papers are in the Chatsworth Collection of the duke of Devonshire. There are manuscript (not holograph) copies of *The Elements of Law* at Hardwick Hall and the British Library. The elegant manuscript (again, not holograph) copy of *Leviathan* that Hobbes presented to Charles II is in the British Library, MS Egerton 1910. See also Jean Jacquot, "Notes on an Unpublished Work of Thomas Hobbes," *Notes and Records of the Royal Society,* 9 (1951–1952): 188–195, for a manuscript in the Bibliothèque Nationale. There are some manuscript letters in the Chatsworth Collection of the duke of Devonshire, in the British Library (Harleian MSS. 6, 796; Additional MSS. 28,927); and among the Rawlinson MSS. in the Bodleian Library, Oxford (C. 232, D. 1104).

James Howell
(1594? – November 1666)

Renée Pigeon
California State University, San Bernardino

BOOKS: Δενδρολογία. *Dodona's Grove, or, The Vocall Forest*, as J. H. esquire (London: By T. B. for H. Moseley, 1640);

Instructions for Forreine Travell (London: Printed by T. B. for Humphrey Moseley, 1642); revised as *Instructions and Directions for Forren Travell* (London: Printed by W. W. for Humphrey Moseley, 1650);

The Vote, or, A poeme royall presented to His Majestie for a new-yeares-gift, by way of discourse 'twixt the poet and his muse (London: Printed by T. Badger for Humphrey Moseley, 1642);

Parables, Reflecting Upon the Times, anonymous (Paris [i.e., London], 1643);

The Trve Informer, Who, in the following Discovrs, or Colloqvy, Discovereth unto the World the chief causes of the sad Distempers in Great Brittany and Ireland (Oxford: Printed by Leonard Lichfield, 1643);

A Discourse or Parly, continued betwixt Partricius and Peregrine (upon their landing in France) touching the Civill Wars of England and Ireland (London, 1643);

The Preheminence and Pedigree of Parlement. Whereunto Is Added, a Vindication of Some Passages Reflecting upon Him, in a Booke Called the Popish Royall Favorite, Penn'd and Published by Master Prynne, Page 42. Wherein He Stiles Him, No Friend to Parliaments, and a Malignant. Together, with a Cleering of Some Occurrences in Spaine, at His Majesties Being There, Cited by the Said Master Prynne out of The Vocall Forest (London: Printed by Richard Heron, 1644);

England's Teares, for the Present Wars, Which for the Nature of the Quarrell, the Quality of Strength, the Diversity of Battailes, Skirmiges, Encounters, and Sieges, (Happened in So Short a Compass of Time,) Cannot Be Parallelld by Any Precedent Age (London: Printed by Richard Heron, 1644);

Mercurius Hibernicus: Or, A Discourse of the Late Insurrection in Ireland, Displaying, 1 The True Causes of It (till Now Not So Fully Discovered.) 2 The Course That Was Taken to Suppresse It. 3 The Reasons That Drew on a Cessation of Arms, and Other Com-

pliances Since. As also Touching Those Auxiliaries, Which Are Transported Thence to Serve in the Present Warre (Bristol, 1644);

Epistolæ Ho-Elianæ. Familiar Letters Domestic and Forren; Divided into Six Sections, Partly Historical, Politicall, Philosophicall, Upon Emergent Occasions, as J. H. (London: Printed for Humphrey Moseley, 1645; revised and enlarged, London: Printed by W. H. for Humphrey Moseley, 1650; revised and enlarged again, London: Printed for Humphrey Moseley, 1655);

Lustra Ludovici: or the Life of the late Victorious King of France, Lewis XIII. (and of his Cardinall de Richelieu.) Divided into Seven Lustres (London: Printed for Humphrey Moseley, 1646);

A New Volume of Letters Partly, Philosophicall, Politicall, Historicall (London: Printed by T. W. for Humphrey Moseley, 1647);

A Letter to the Earle of Pembrooke Concerning the Times, and the sad condition both of Prince and People (London, 1647 [i.e., 1648]);

Down-right Dealing, or The Despised Protestant Speaking Plain English to the Kings Most Excellent Majesty, the Honourable Houses of Parliament, the City of London, the Army, and All Other Peace-Desiring Commons, as J. H. an impartiall observer (London, 1647);

The Instrvments of a King: Or, A Short Discovrse of the Sword. The Scepter. The Crowne (London, 1648);

A Venice Looking-Glasse: Or, A Letter Written very lately from London to Rome, by a Venetian Clarissimo to Cardinal Barberino, Protector of the English Nation, Touching These Present Distempers. Wherein, as in a True Mirrour, England May Behold Her Owne Spots, Wherein She May See, and Fore-See, Her Follies Pass'd, Her Present Danger, and Future Destruction. Faithfully rendred out of the Italian into English (London, 1648);

Bella Scot-Anglica: A Briefe of all the Battells, and Martial Encounters which have happened 'twixt England and Scotland from all times to this present. Whereunto Is Annexed a Corollary, Declaring the Causes Whereby

214

Engraving from Londinopolis *(1657)*

the Scot Is Come of Late Years to Be So Hightned in
His Spirits, anonymous (London, 1648);

A Winter Dreame (London, 1649);

*A Trance. Or, Newes from Hell, Brought fresh to Towne
By Mercurius Acheronticus* (London, 1649);

*An Inquisition after Blood To the Parliament in statu quo
nunc, and to the Army Regnant; or Any Other
Whether Royallist, Presbyterian, Independent or Lev-
eller, Whom It May Concern* (London, 1649);

Δενδρολογία. *Dodona's Grove, Or the Vocall Forest.
Second Part* (London: Printed by W. H. for
Humphrey Moseley, 1650);

*S.P.Q.V. A Survey of the Signorie of Venice, of Her Ad-
mired Policy, and Method of Government, &c.*
(London: Printed for Richard Lowndes,
1651);

*The Vision Or a Dialog between the Soul and Bodie. Fan-
cied in a Morning-dream* (London: Printed for
William Hope, 1651);

A German Diet: Or, the Ballance of Europe (London:
Printed for Humphrey Moseley, 1653);

*Ah, ha; tumulus, thalamus: Two counter-poems, the First,
an Elegy upon Edward Late Earl of Dorset; the Second, an Epithalamium to the Lord M. of Dorchester*
(London: Printed for H. Moseley, 1653);

*Some of Mr. Howell's Minor Works Reflecting Upon the
Times Upon Emergent Occasions* (London, 1654);

*Som Sober Inspections Made into the Carriage and Consults
of the Late-long Parlement, whereby Ocasion is Taken
to Speak of Parlements in Former Times, and of
Magna Charta, with Som Reflexes upon Government
in General* (London: Printed by E. C. for
Henry Seile, 1655);

Londinopolis; an Historical Discourse; or, Perlustration of the city of London, the Imperial Chamber, and Chief Emporium of Great Britain: Whereunto Is Added Another of the City of Westminster, with the Courts of Justice, Antiquities, and New Buildings Thereunto Belonging (London: Printed by J. Streater for Henry Twitford, George Sawbridge & John Place, 1657);

A Discours of the Empire, And of the Election of a King of the Romans, the Greatest Business of Christendom Now in Agitation, as also of the Colledg of Electors, Their Particular Interests, and Who Is Most Likely to Be the Next Emperour (London: Printed by F. L. for Charles Webb, 1658);

A Particular Vocabulary or Nomenclature in English, Italian, French, and Spanish: of the proper Terms belonging to several Arts and Sciences, to Recreations, to common Professions and Callings both Liberal and Mechankik, &c. (London: Printed by Thomas Leach, 1659); republished as *Lexicon Tetraglotton an English-French-Italian-Spanish Dictionary: Whereunto Is Adjoined a Large Nomenclature of the Proper Terms (in All the Four) Belonging to Several Arts and Sciences, to Recreations, to Professions Both Liberal and Mechanick, &c. Divided to Fiftie Two Sections* (London: Printed by J. G. for Cornelius Bee, 1660);

A Brief Admonition of Some of the Inconveniences of All the Three Most Famous Governments Known to the World: With Their Comparisons Together, anonymous (London, 1659);

Englands Alarm, The State-Maladies, and Cure: A Memento to the Soldiers, and A Parallel of Egypts Plagues with Englands Sinnes: To Which Is Added, A Perpetual Almanack, as J. H., a lover of Englands peace (London, 1659);

θηρολγία: *The Parley of Beasts; Or, Morphandra Queen of the Inchanted Iland: Wherein Men Were Found, Who Being Transmuted to Beasts, though Proffer'd to Be Dis-inchanted, and to Become Men Again; Yet, in Regard of the Crying Sins, and Rebellious Humors of the Times, They Prefer the Life of a Brute Animal before That of a Rational Creture: Which Fancy Consists of Various Philosophicall Discourses, Both Morall, Metaphysicall, Historicall, and Naturall, Touching the Declinings of the World, and Late Depravation of Human Nature; with Reflexes upon the Present State of Most Countries in Christendom. Divided into a XI Sections* (London: Printed by W. Wilson for William Palmer, 1660);

A Late Letter From the Citty of Florence, Written by Signor Fabrico Pisani a Counsellor of the Rota Touching these present Distempers of England (London, 1660);

A cordial for the cavaliers (London: Henry Marsh, 1661);

Som Sober Inspections Made Into those Ingredients That went to the Composition of A late Cordial, call'd A Cordial For the Cavaliers. For the Satisfaction of Som Who Mis-apprehended the Author (London: Printed for Henry Brome, 1661);

Divers Historicall Discourses Of the late Popular Insurrections in Great Britain, and Ireland, Tending all, to the asserting of Truth, in Vindication of their Majesties, Newly Retreev'd, Collected, and Publish'd, edited by Richard Royston (London: Printed by J. Grismond, 1661);

A New English Grammar Prescribing as certain Rules as the Language will bear, for Forreners to learn English . . . Also Another Grammar of the Spanish or Castilian Tung, with Som Special Remarks upon the Portugues Dialect, . . . A Discours or Dialog Containing a Perambulation of Spain and Portugall (London: Printed for T. Williams, Henry Brome & Henry Marsh, 1662);

A Brief Account of the Royal Matches or Matrimonial Alliances Which the Kings of England Have Made from Time to Time since the year 800, to this Present 1662, anonymous (London: Printed by J. G. for Henry Brome, 1662);

Poems On several Choice and Various Subjects, Occasionally Composed By an Eminent Author, edited by Payne Fisher (London: Printed by J. Cottrell, sold by Samuel Speed, 1663);

Προεδρια-Βασιλικὴ: *A Discourse Concerning the Precedency of Kings: Wherein the Reasons and Arguments of the Three Greatest Monarks of Christendom, Who Claim a Several Right Therunto, Are Faithfully Collected, and Rendered. Wherby Occasion Is Taken to Make Great Britain Better Understood Then Some Forren Authors (either out of Ignorance or Interest) Have Represented Her in Order to This Particular. Whereunto Is also Adjoynd a Distinct Treatise of Ambassadors, &c..* (London: Printed by J. Cottrel for Sam Speed, 1664);

A Discours of Dunkirk, with som Reflexes Upon the late Surrender Therof, &c. In Answer to Some Things That Have Bin Obtruded Lately, and Printed Both Abroad and at Home, to the Prejudice of England in This Great Action (London: Printed by J. C. for Samuel Speed, 1664).

Editions: *Epistolæ Ho-Elianae: The Familiar Letters of James Howell, Historiographer Royal to Charles II,* edited by Joseph Jacobs (London: Nutt, 1890);

Epistolæ Ho-Elianæ: The Familiar Letters of James Howell, 2 volumes, edited by W. H. Bennett (London: Stott, 1890);

Instructions for Forreine Travell, 1642; Collated with the Second Edition of 1650, edited by Edward Arber (London: Constable, 1895);

Familiar Letters; or, Epistolæ Ho-Elianæ, 3 volumes, edited by Oliver Smeaton (London: Dent, 1903);

Epistolae Ho-Elianae: The Familiar Letters of James Howell, 4 volumes, introduction by Agnes Repplier (Boston & New York: Houghton, Mifflin, 1907).

OTHER: Ferrante Pallavacino, *St. Paul Late Progres Upon Earth, About a Divorce 'twixt Christ and the Church of Rome,* translated by Howell (London: Printed by Richard Heron for Matthew Wal, 1644);

Randle Cotgrave and Robert Sherwood, *A French-English Dictionary Compil'd by Mr. Randle Cotgrave: With Another in English and French. Whereunto Are Newly Added the Animadversions and Supplements, &c. of James Howell Esquire* (London: Printed by W. H. for Octavian Pulleyn, 1650);

Alessandro Giraffi, *An Exact Historie of the Late Revolutions in Naples And of their Monstrous Successes, Not to be paralleled by any Antient or Modern History,* 2 volumes, translated by Howell (volume 1, London: Printed for R. Lowndes, 1650; volume 2, London: Printed by A. M. for Abel Roper, 1652);

Agustín de Hierro, *The Process and Pleadings In the Court of Spain, upon the death of Anthonie Ascham, Resident for the Parliament of England, and of John Baptista Riva, his Interpretor,* translated by Howell (London: Printed by William Du Gard, 1651);

Cottoni Posthuma: Divers Choice Pieces Of That Renowned Antiquary Sir Robert Cotton, edited by Howell (London: Printed by Francis Leach for Henry Seile, 1651);

Flavius Josephus, *The Wonderful and Most Deplorable History of the latter Times of the Jews, and of the City of Hierusalem,* translated by Howell (London: Printed for John Stafford & Humphrey Moseley, 1652);

The Nuptialls of Peleus and Thetis consisting of a Mask and a Comedy, attributed to Francesco Butl or Diamante Galrielli, translated by Howell (London: Printed for Henry Herringman, 1654);

Scipio Mazzella, *Parthenopeia, or the History of the Most Noble and Renowned Kingdom of Naples,* translated and augmented by Howell (London: Printed by Humphrey Moseley, 1654);

Finetti Philoxenis: Som Choice Observations of Sr John Finett, Knight and Master of Ceremonies to the two last Kings, Touching the Reception and Precedence . . . of Forren Ambassadors in England, edited by Howell (London: Printed by T. R. for H. Twyford & G. Bedell, 1656);

Παροιμιογραθια: *Proverbs, Or, Old Sayed Saws & Adages, in English (or the Saxon Toung) Italian, French and Spanish Whereunto the British, for Their Great Antiquity, and Weight Are Added,* compiled by Howell (London: Printed by J. G., 1659);

Jules Mazarin, *The last will and testament of the late renowned Cardinal Mazarini, deceased February 27, 1660 together with some historical remarques of his life,* translation attributed to Howell (London: Printed by Peter Lillicrap for William Gilbertson, 1663);

János Nadányi, *Florus Hungaricus, or, The History of Hungaria and Transylvania, deduced from the original of that nation, and their settling in Europe in the Year of our Lord 461, to this dangerous and suspectful period of the kingdome by the present Turkish invasion, anno 1664,* translated by Howell (London: Printed by W. G. for N. Brook, 1664).

James Howell's reputation rests primarily on *Epistolæ Ho-Elianæ. Familiar Letters Domestic and Forren* (1645), which provides an intimate view of contemporary events and in which Howell discourses on a variety of topics. A contemporary, Payne Fisher, wrote in the preface to Howell's *Poems on several Choice and Various Subjects* (1663) that the letters "teacheth a new way of Epistolizing; and that *Familiar Letters* may not only consist of words, and a bombast of compliments, but that they are capable of the highest speculations and solidest kind of knowledge." Howell himself describes them as "those rambling Letters of mine, which indeed are nought else than a Legend of the cumbersome Life and various Fortunes of a cadet." Although he is remembered for *Epistolæ Ho-Elianæ,* Howell was a prolific author who composed prose allegories, political pamphlets, histories, lexicographic works, and a smattering of poetry, in addition to translating French, Italian, and Latin works – an impressive output, especially when one considers that his writing career did not begin until he was more than forty years old.

Born in Abernant, Carmarthenshire, Wales, probably in 1594, Howell was the son of Thomas Howell, a curate. In a letter to his father (included in *Epistolæ Ho-Elianæ*) he praises the "most indulgent and costly care you have been pleased (in so extraordinary a manner) to have had of my breeding (though but one child of fifteen) by placing me in a choice methodical school (so far distant from your dwelling) under a learned (though lashing) master; and by transplanting me thence to Oxford, to be graduated; and so holding me still up by the chin until I could swim without bladders." The "choice methodical school" was Hereford Grammar School; Howell entered Jesus College, Oxford, on 16 June 1610 and was graduated with the Bachelor of Arts degree on 17 December 1613. His letters do not address his school or university experiences, but he always speaks of Oxford with great respect and affection as his "mother."

After leaving Oxford, Howell became steward of a glass factory owned by Sir Robert Mansell, who was related to his Oxford tutor, Francis Mansell. In 1617 he was sent abroad to procure materials and artisans for the factory. He traveled through Holland, France, Spain, and Italy, a grand tour recounted in the first section of *Epistolæ Ho-Elianæ;* his assignment seems to have been relatively elastic, allowing him to combine edification and commerce. Having completed his commission for the glass factory, he continued his travels in Italy, returning home in the winter of 1620. He had contracted a severe illness, which was treated by William Harvey, discoverer of the circulation of the blood.

Howell was employed as a tutor to the two sons of Sir Thomas Savage during 1621; he declined to accompany the young men on their own grand tour of the Continent, however, fearing the potential embarrassment of Roman Catholic pupils accompanied by a Protestant tutor. Instead, he joined Richard Altham, son of Sir James, Baron Altham, on a brief excursion through the Netherlands and France.

When Howell returned to England in 1622 he was named envoy to the court of Spain by a group of London merchants whose vessel, the *Vineyard,* had been seized by Sardinia, a Spanish possession; the ambassador to Spain, John Digby, first Earl of Bristol, had suggested the appointment of a special agent to negotiate the return of the *Vineyard* and her valuable cargo. This assignment resulted in Howell being present when Charles, Prince of Wales, and George Villiers, first Duke of Buckingham, arrived incognito in 1623 on the abortive expedition to court the Spanish Infanta that is described by Howell in *Epistolæ Ho-Elianæ:* "The great business of the match was tending to a period, the articles reflecting both upon Church and State being capitulated and interchangeably accorded to both sides, and there wanted nothing to consummate all things, when, to

the wonderment of the world the Prince and the Marquis of Buckingham arrived at this court on Friday last upon the close of evening. They alighted at my Lord of Bristol's house, and the Marquis (Mr Thomas Smith) came in first with a portmanteau under his arm, then (Mr John Smith) the Prince was sent for, who stayed a while the other side of the street in the dark." The royal attempt at matchmaking forestalled Howell's negotiations, but he made the acquaintance of many important courtiers, including Endymion Porter and Sir Kenelm Digby, the cousin of the earl of Bristol.

Returning to London in 1624, Howell applied for various positions, but the death of King James in 1625 increased the power of Buckingham, who objected to Howell on the basis of his association with the Digbys. He acted as tutor in Spanish to Jane Paulet, the marchioness of Winchester; in 1626 he was appointed secretary to Emanuel, Lord Scrope, Lord President of the North; and in 1627 he was elected to Parliament for Richmond, Yorkshire.

His next significant appointment, in 1632, was accompanying Robert Sidney, second Earl of Leicester, to Denmark on a twofold mission: to offer condolences to the Danish king on the death of his mother, the queen dowager (the mother-in-law of James I and grandmother of Charles I), and to claim a share of her estate. Howell notes in *Epistolæ Ho-Elianæ* that she "died worth near two millions of dollars, so that she was reputed the richest queen of Christendom." Howell was chosen to deliver the formal Latin oration: "we made a comely gallant show . . . when we went to Court, for we were near upon a hundred all of one piece in mourning. It pleas'd my Lord to make me the Orator, and so I made a long Latin speech, *alta voce,* to the King in Latin, of the occasion of this Embassy, and tending to the praise of the deceased Queen. . . . "

Howell's source of employment for the next ten years has been the subject of speculation; the best evidence leads to the conclusion reached by Joseph Jacobs: that "during . . . 1632–42 Howell was nothing more or less than a Royalist spy." His literary career began during this period with the publication in 1640 of Δενδρολογία [Dendrologia], *Dodona's Grove, or, The Vocall Forest,* an allegory in which historical and contemporary figures are represented as trees. The allegorical method Howell employed became increasingly popular as a means of evading censorship during the civil war and the Interregnum.

The year 1642 saw the publication of Howell's *Instructions for Forreine Travell,* a brief compendium of advice to first-time travelers. Howell praises travel as providing an excellent education: "And indeed this is the prime use of Peregrination, which therefore may be not improperly called a moving Academy, or the true Peripatetique School." *Instructions for Forreine Travell* appeared in a second edition in 1650 with an appendix, "for Travelling into Turkey and the Levant parts" – an addition not based, as was the rest of the book, on Howell's personal experiences.

On 30 August 1642 Howell was appointed a clerk of the council, making him next in line for a vacant post; in November he was arrested – possibly for debt, but more likely because his political activities over the previous years had gained him enemies among the Parliamentarians. In *Epistolæ Ho-Elianæ* he provides a lively description of his arrest: "I was lately come to London upon some occasions of mine own . . . but one morning betimes there rush'd into my chamber five Armed Men, with Swords, Pistols, and Bills, and told me they had a warrant from the Parliament for me: I desir'd to see their Warrant, they deny'd it: I desir'd to see the date of it, they deny'd it: I desir'd to see my name in the Warrant, they deny'd all. At last one of them pull'd a greasy Paper out of his Pocket, and shew'd me only three or four Names subscrib'd, and no more; So they rush'd presently into my Closet and seiz'd on all my Papers and Letters, and anything that was Manuscript; and many printed Books they took also, and hurl'd all into a great hair Trunk, which they carry'd away with them." Howell describes how he remained under guard in his chambers until evening, when he appeared before the Committee for Examination; a report was made to Parliament that nothing offensive was found among his papers, but he was committed to the Fleet Prison. There he supported himself by his extensive literary output; William Harley Vann remarks that "it was because of his imprisonment that Howell's literary career had its real beginning. . . . stern necessity now forced upon him a career as a man of letters."

In 1643 Howell returned to political allegory with *Parables, Reflecting upon the Times,* published anonymously and inscribed "printed at Paris." *Parables* comprises twelve allegories, such as "Parliament of Stars," "the great Counsel of Birds," and "Parliament of Flowers," each of which is followed by a moral. In the dedication Howell accounts for his use of allegory: "amongst many other Barbarisms which like an impetuous torrent have lately rush'd in upon us, the interception and opening of letters is none of the least . . . the thought itself cannot say 'tis free, much less the tongue, or pen. Which makes

me impart unto you the traverses of these turbulent times, under the following fables." Howell followed the *Parables* with several political pamphlets: *The True Informer* (1643); a sequel to that work, *A Discourse or Parly, Continued betwixt Partricius and Peregrine* (1643); *England's Teares* (1644); and *Mercurius Hibernicus* (1644). In a pamphlet, *The Popish Royall Favourite* (1643), William Prynne attacked Howell as "no friend to Parliament and a malignant now in custody"; Howell defended himself in *The Preheminence and Pedigree of Parlement. Whereunto Is Added, a Vindication of Some Passages Reflecting upon him, in a Book called the Popish Royall Favorite* (1644). Prynne relented to some extent, calling Howell a "most learned gentleman" in his *A Moderate Apology against a Pretended Calumny* (1646).

Epistolæ Ho-Elianæ appeared in 1645. The letters are undated and are divided into six sections, beginning with Howell's first visit to Europe and ending with several letters written during his imprisonment. In 1647 *A New Volume of Letters, Partly, Philosophicall, Politicall, Historicall* was published; a second edition of *Epistolæ Ho-Elianæ* appeared in 1650, incorporating letters dated from 1646 to 1649; and a third edition in 1655 included additional letters. These subsequent volumes differ from the first edition of *Epistolæ Ho-Elianæ* in that Howell's letters tend to become more belletristic and self-consciously literary; as Vann notes, "comparatively few are anything like real letters."

Whether any of the letters in *Epistolæ Ho-Elianæ* are "real" – that is, actually written as letters – has been the subject of detailed debate. The dates appended to the letters in the second and subsequent editions are often inaccurate or impossible, and few originals of Howell's letters have been discovered in the archives of their addressees. Vann speculates that Howell created the "letters" from his notebooks and diary rather than reproducing actual letters. David Manuszak has argued that Howell's letters are similar to the "model letters" in guidebooks that were popular in the seventeenth century but are distinguished from the latter by the "aura of the authentic" given them by the use of actual rather than generic addressees such as "To a Lady": "whether real, imaginative, or both, the letters in *Epistolæ Ho-Elianæ* through their specific addressees give the reader the sense and illusion of being privy to genuine human communication."

Howell's style in *Epistolæ Ho-Elianæ* has been praised for its clarity and liveliness. The first letter in the second and subsequent editions compares letters with orations and establishes Howell's criteria for good epistolary style: "the one should be attired like a woman, the other like a man. The latter of the two is allowed large side robes, as long periods, parentheses, similes, examples, and other parts of rhetorical flourishes: but a letter or epistle should be short-coated, and closely couched. . . . Indeed we should write as we speak, and that's a true familiar letter which expresseth one's mind, as if he were discoursing with the party to whom he writes in succinct and short terms." David Lawrence Cole finds Howell a "praiseworthy champion of modern trends in prose, marking a transition from the elegant patterns of Ciceronian rhetoric to the brevity and simplicity of the plain style."

Critics have typically read *Epistolæ Ho-Elianæ* in the context of its genre — letter collection or essay — and this reading has led to Howell being considered primarily as a forerunner of eighteenth-century epistolary novelists or essayists. Offering a corrective to the tendency to focus on the literary aspects of Howell's letters, Annabel Patterson has returned to the first edition of 1645, in which she finds a distinctive structure that becomes subsumed in the later, augmented editions. Patterson contends that *Epistolæ Ho-Elianæ* can be read as "topical, royalist statement." The division of the first edition into six sections is not random but a purposeful structuring meant to alert the perceptive reader to the covert message of the text. Each section opens with a letter to Howell's father, "marking both a stage in Howell's travels and a new phase in the political history of his day. It gradually becomes clear that the emphasis on travel (the formal excuse for correspondence) is really a further excuse, for the introduction of Europe as the scene and cause, ultimately, of the English civil war."

During his remaining years of imprisonment in the Fleet, Howell produced a variety of works, including a sequel to *Dodona's Grove* (1650) and two political tracts that employ the convention of the dream vision, *A Winter Dreame* (1649) and *A Trance. Or, Newes from Hell* (1649). His historical works from this period include *Lustra Ludovici* (1646), a history of Louis XIII and Cardinal Richelieu dedicated to Prince Charles; and a translation from the Italian of Alessandro Giraffi's *An Exact Historie of the Late Revolutions in Naples* (1650), an account of tax riots.

In 1651 Howell was released from prison; Jacobs notes that "how, where and from what he lived" after his release is unclear. During the Interregnum he produced historical works, translations, and a last allegory, θηρολγία: *The Parley of Beasts* (1660). At the restoration of Charles II, Howell joined other claimants in appealing to the new monarch for a position, and in 1661 he was appointed historiographer royal.

Following this appointment, he entered into a brief pamphlet skirmish with Sir Roger L'Estrange. L'Estrange objected to the broadside *A Cordial for the Cavaliers* (1661), in which Howell counseled patience to those Royalists who had not yet seen a tangible reward from the restoration of the monarchy. L'Estrange responded in *A Caveat to the Cavaliers* (1661), which elicited Howell's *Som Sober Inspections Made into those Ingredients That Went to the Composition of a Late Cordial, Call'd A Cordial for the Cavaliers. For the Satisfaction of Som Who Mis-apprehended the Author* (1661). L'Estrange fired the final salvo with his *A Modest Plea both for the Caveat, and the Author of it* (1661), which listed passages from Howell's earlier works in an attempt to prove that Howell had supported Oliver Cromwell and Parliament.

Howell's other works during this final period of his life include *Divers Historicall Discourses of the Late Popular Insurrections in Great Britain, and Ireland* (1661), a collection of his pamphlets; *A New English Grammar* (1662), intended for the new queen, the Portuguese Catherine of Braganza; a collected edition of his poems (1663); translations of the will of Cardinal Jules Mazarin (1663) and of a history of Hungary (1664); and his final original work Προ∈δρία-Βασιλικὴ: *A Discourse Concerning the Precedency of Kings* (1664), in which Howell attempts to establish the ancient traditions of the English monarchy by comparing it to the French and Spanish.

Howell's long and adventurous life came to an end at his lodgings in Holborn in November 1666. He had never married, commenting in *Epistolæ Ho-Elianæ* that "had I been dispos'd to have married for wealth without affection, or for affection without wealth, I would have been in bonds before now; but I did never cast my eyes upon any yet, that I thought I was born for, where both these concurr'd. . . . But to come to the point of Wiving, I would have you know, that I have, tho' never marry'd, divers children already, some French, some Latin, one Italian, and many English; and tho' they be but poor brats of the brain, yet they are legitimate, and Apollo himself vouchsafed to cooperate in their production." Howell's will distributed his estate to his siblings and nephews, leaving "thirty pounds in a white bag which is designed for a tomb wherein I desire my executor to be very careful"; he was buried in the Temple Church.

Howell's work has not received sustained attention from scholars; this neglect may, in part, be due to what Patterson refers to as "the elusive place that letters (as epistles) have always had in letters (as literature)." His allegorical works hold a minor place in the history of prose fiction generally and, more specifically, of seventeenth-century political allegories. *The Parley of Beasts* may have been known to Jonathan Swift and may have influenced his *Gulliver's Travels* (1726); Howell's works were also known to Daniel Defoe. During his lifetime *Epistolæ Ho-Elianæ* probably inspired collections of letters by Thomas Forde (1661) and Robert Loveday (1662); the edition of John Donne's letters published by Donne's son (1651) and the familiar letters of Margaret Cavendish, Duchess of Newcastle (1664), are also indebted to Howell's model. Vann credits Howell with influencing the development of the essay, noting that he "prepared the way for [Richard] Steele and [Joseph] Addison in the eighteenth century." Manuszak argues that Howell "appears to have been one of the first English letter writers to realize that a possible step from a group of individual narrative units, each discrete and separate, was to narrative units strung together. In this respect *Epistolæ Ho-Elianæ* is a forerunner of the epistolary novel." Patterson's analysis of *Epistolæ Ho-Elianæ* in her *Censorship and Interpretation* (1984) suggests the possibility of a new focus on Howell's work and its implications, emphasizing its historical context. Though most of Howell's long list of works will undoubtedly remain unfamiliar and generally unread, *Epistolæ Ho-Elianæ* has secured his place in literary history; its "true familiar letters" written in "short and succinct terms" continue to enlighten and entertain.

Bibliography:
William Harley Vann, *Notes on the Writings of James Howell* (Waco, Texas: Baylor University, 1924).

References:
Douglas Bush, *English Literature in the Earlier Seventeenth Century 1600–1660* (Oxford: Oxford University Press, 1945), pp. 195–197, 554–555;

David Lawrence Cole, "James Howell and the Speech of the Commonwealth: Seventeenth-Century Prose Style in Transition," Ph.D. dissertation, Texas Tech University, 1974;

V. M. Hirst, "The Authenticity of James Howell's Familiar Letters," *Modern Language Review,* 54 (October 1959): 558–561;

David Manuszak, "Beyond the Guidebooks: The Freeing of the Familiar Letter in James Howell's *Epistolae Ho-Elianae,*" *Cahiers Elisabethains,* 24 (October 1983): 47–59;

Annabel Patterson, *Censorship and Interpretation: The Conditions of Writing and Reading in Early Modern England* (Madison: University of Wisconsin Press, 1984), pp. 210–218;

Peter K. Shea, "James Howell on Translation," *Notes and Queries,* 23 (December 1976): 550–552;

A. W. Ward and A. R. Waller, *The Cambridge History of English Literature,* volume 7 (Cambridge: Cambridge University Press, 1911), pp. 196–201.

James VI of Scotland, I of England

(19 June 1566 – 27 March 1625)

Catherine C. Gannon
California State University, San Bernardino

BOOKS: *The Essayes of a Prentise, in the Divine Art of Poesie* (Edinburgh: Printed by Thomas Vautroullier, 1584);

Ane fruitfull Meditatioun contening ane plane and facill expositioun of ye 7.8.9 and 10 versis of the 20 chap. of the Reuelatioun in forme of ane sermon, edited by Patrick Galloway (Edinburgh: Printed by H. Charteris, 1588);

Ane Meditatioun vpon the xxv., xxvi., xxvii., xxviii., and xxix. verses of the xv. chapt. of the first buke of the Chronicles of the Kingis, edited by Galloway (Edinburgh: Printed by H. Charteris, 1589);

His Maiesties Poeticall Exercises at vacant houres (Edinburgh: Printed by Robert Walde-graue, 1591);

Daemonologie, in Forme of a Dialogue, Diuided into three Bookes (Edinburgh: Printed by Robert Walde-graue, 1597);

The Trve Lawe of free Monarchies: or The Reciprock and Mutuall Dvtie Betwixt a free King, and his naturall Subiectes (Edinburgh: Printed by Robert Walde-graue, 1598);

ΒΑΣΙΛΙΚΟΝ ΔΩΡΟΝ. *Deuided into three books* (Edinburgh: Printed by Robert Walde-graue, 1599); revised as ΒΑΣΙΛΙΚΟΝ ΔΩΡΟΝ. *Or His Maiesties Instrvctions to His Dearest Sonne, Henry the Prince* (Edinburgh: Printed by Robert Walde-graue, 1603);

A Covnter-blaste to Tobacco, anonymous (London: Printed by Robert Barker, 1604);

Triplici nodo, triplex cuneus. Or, An apologie for the oath of allegiance, against the two breves of Pope Pavlvs Ovintvs, and the late letter of Cardinal Bellarmine to G. Blackwel, the Arch-priest (London: Printed by Robert Barker, 1607; enlarged, 1607);

Declaration dv Serenissime Roy Iacqves I. Roy de la Grand' Bretaigne France et Irlande, Defenseur de la Foy. Pour le droit des rois & independance de leurs Couronnes, contre la Harangve de L'Illustrissime Cardinal du Perron prononcée en la chambre du tiers Estat le XV. de Ianuier 1615, Pierre du Moulin (London: Printed by John Bill, 1615); translated by Richard Betts as *A Remonstrance of the Most Gratiovs King James I. King of Great Brittaine, France, and Ireland, Defender of the Faith, &c. for the Right of Kings, and the independence of their Crownes. Against an Oration of the Most Illustrious Card. of Perron, pronounced in the Chamber of the third Estate. Ian. 15. 1615. Translated out of his Maiesties French copie* (Cambridge: Printed by Cantrell Legge, printer to the University of Cambridge, 1616);

The Workes of the most high and mightie Prince, James, by the grace of God, King of Great Britaine, France and Ireland, defender of the faith, &c. Pvblished by James, bishop of Winton, and deane of His Maiesties chappel royall (London: Printed by Robert Barker & John Bill, 1616; reprinted, Hildesheim & New York: Olms, 1971);

A Meditation vpon The Lords Prayer, Written By The Kings Maiestie, For the benefit of all his subjects, especially of such as follow the Court. Ioh. 16.23. (London: Printed by Bonham Norton & John Bill, 1619);

A Meditation Vpon The 27, 28, 29, Verses of the XXVII. Chapter Of S^t. Matthew. Or a paterne for a Kings inauguration (London: Printed by John Bill, 1620);

The Poems of James VI of Scotland, 2 volumes, edited by James Craigie (Edinburgh: Printed for the Scottish Text Society by W. Blackwood, 1955, 1958);

New Poems of James I of England, from a Hitherto Unpublished manuscript (Add. 24195) in the British Museum, edited by Allan F. Westcott (New York: Columbia University Press, 1911; reprinted, New York: AMS Press, 1966).

Editions: *The Political Works of James I, Reprinted from the Edition of 1616,* edited by Charles Howard McIlwain (Cambridge, Mass.: Harvard University Press, 1918; New York: Russell & Russell, 1965);

The Basilicon Doron of King James VI, 2 volumes, edited by James Craigie (Edinburgh & London:

James I of England; portrait attributed to Jan de Critz (National Maritime Museum, Greenwich)

Printed for the Scottish Text Society by W. Blackwood & Sons, 1944, 1950);

Minor Prose Works of King James VI and I, edited by Craigie and A. Law (Edinburgh: Scottish Text Society, 1982).

OTHER: *The Psalmes of King David, Translated by King James* (Oxford: Printed by William Turner, 1631).

The regard in which King James I is held as a writer has flourished or foundered in tandem with his historical reputation. His position in the ranks of British literature's secondary figures, however, is secure. In publications on topics from political theory and practice to the condemnation of tobacco, James's prose is distinguished by systematic argument, memorable phrasing, homey wit, and vivid imagery. His poetry, although uneven, displays considerable skill — especially when his mature work, unpublished until the twentieth century, is included. The King James Version of the Bible (1611) was produced under his aegis, and he encouraged and patronized other writ-

ers, both Scottish and English. As G. P. V. Akrigg points out in *Letters of King James VI & I* (1984), "a king who could address a courtier as 'my little pork' and a Secretary of State as 'my little beagle' or 'my little wiffe-waffe,' and who could warn a son in quest of a wife to think 'as well upon the business of Christendom as upon the codpiece point" does not deserve the Goddess Dullness's "commendation" in Alexander Pope's *The Dunciad* (1728).

The only son of Mary, Queen of Scots, James embodied his country's hope that the House of Stuart would follow the House of Tudor on the English throne. Mary had returned to Scotland in 1561, after thirteen years in France; her reign as queen consort to Francis II had been ended by her husband's early death in 1560. While Mary was abroad, the Scottish Reformation had left Scotland's politics controlled by nobles closely allied with the ministers of the kirk. In 1565, despite protests from Queen Elizabeth I of England and opposition from the Scottish Protestant lords, Mary wed her cousin Henry Stuart (or Stewart), Lord Darnley, who, like Mary, was descended from Margaret Tudor, Henry

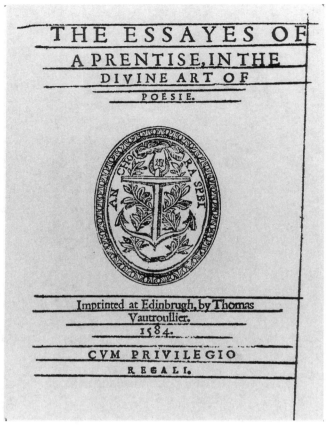

*Title page for a volume of James's poems. The book includes the
first critical treatise on Scottish poetry.*

VIII's sister. Darnley proved to be debauched, arrogant, and treacherous, participating in the murder of Mary's Italian secretary, David Rizzio, less than nine months after the marriage and six months into the queen's pregnancy.

Mary's assurances to Darnley that the child, born on 19 June 1566 in Edinburgh Castle, was his son are evidence both of the suspicion of illegitimacy under which the prince was born and of the ruinous state of the couple's marriage. In December Charles James, Prince and Stewart of Scotland, Duke of Rothesay, Earl of Carrick, Lord of the Isles, Baron of Renfew, was baptized in a Catholic ceremony. His godparents, represented by proxy, were Queen Elizabeth and the king of France. Darnley was strangled about two months after his son's baptism. Mary placed her son in the custody of John Lennox, first Earl of Mar, at Stirling Castle; a month later she was abducted by James Hepburn, fourth Earl of Bothwell, a principal in Darnley's murder; she and Bothwell were married on 15 May 1567. Captured by rebellious Protestant lords at Carberry Hill on 15 June, Mary was forced to abdicate, conveying the crown to James and appointing her half brother, James Stuart (or Stewart), first Earl of Murray (or Moray), as regent. On 29 July 1567 the baby became King James VI of Scotland.

The government appointed the poet and humanist George Buchanan and Peter Young, a scholar who had studied in Geneva, to supervise the king's education. At a young age James could translate the Bible extempore from Latin into French and then into English. Young and Buchanan amassed a considerable library for the king: the collection included maxims and moral tales, such as Plutarch's apothegms and Aesop's fables, sources for the aphorisms the king would write; European histories; treatises on government; theological works and writings by the Protestant Reformers; and books on mathematics, logic, and natural history. The bulk of the collection was in Latin; but it also included many French volumes, including poetry from Mary's library. When James wrote verses in his teens, he would model his work on the classics and on French rather than English poetry. Through Young, the king received a thorough grounding in Calvinistic theology and acquired a zest for debating theological questions. His skill as a debater is apparent in his prose, where the systematic marshaling of ideas is a distinguishing trait.

Mary's reign had awakened old feuds and created new dissension among the nobles. Her escape from prison and flight to England in 1568 was followed by civil war, which touched the king directly in 1571 when his grandfather Matthew Stuart (or Stewart), fourth Earl of Lennox, who had been regent since 1570, was brought wounded into the castle, where he died the same day.

James Douglas, fourth Earl of Morton, who had been instrumental in Mary's deposition, was selected as regent in 1572. He was a stern authority but one with a grasp of the nation's problems. In March 1578 Morton's power was eclipsed when John Stuart (or Stewart), fourth Earl of Atholl, and Colin Campbell, sixth Earl of Argyll, persuaded James to control his own kingdom. The young John Erskine, second Earl of Mar, wrested the king's guardianship from his uncle, Alexander Erskine, who had become guardian after his brother's death, and restored Morton to power.

In 1579 the earliest of a series of male favorites, Esmé Stuart (or Stewart), Seigneur d'Aubigny, came to Scotland. First cousin to James's father, the French courtier charmed the young, ungainly king. His rise to power was instantaneous: he was created earl and then duke of Lennox and admitted to the king's council; the degree to which the influence was explicitly sexual is debated by historians. James Craigie, in his edition of the king's poems, speculates that the relationship was a catalyst for James's literary ambitions and influenced him to cultivate a circle of poets at court that included Alexander Montgomerie, John Stewart, William Fowler, Alexander Hume, and Robert Hudson. James set Fowler and Hudson to translating Continental poetry, and Montgomerie helped the king revise his own verse, which was first published in *The Essayes of a Prentise* (1584). The essay "Reulis and Cautelis," included in the volume, although derivative in its pronouncements, is the first critical treatise on Scottish poetry. The only other volume of James's poetry published during his lifetime was *His Majesty's Poeticall Exercises* (1591); it includes his poem on the battle of Lepanto, which was translated into French by Guillaume de Salluste Du Bartas and disseminated on the Continent.

In June 1581 Morton was executed for taking part in Darnley's murder. The king remained under Lennox's influence for about a year longer, but after the 1582 Ruthven Raid, in which the king was forcibly restrained by a group of nobles led by William Ruthven, fourth Lord of Ruthven and first Earl of Gowrie, Lennox was ordered to leave the country. In a poetic lament for him James figures Esmé as a resplendent phoenix, flown to France to escape attack. The king's post-Ruthven chancellor, James Stewart, Earl of Arran, was similarly removed from office in 1585 by a show of force orchestrated by Queen Elizabeth.

From England, where she was being held prisoner by Elizabeth, Mary proposed to James a plan for shared power between mother and son; she pointed out that the Catholic states, by refusing to recognize James as king of Scotland, might ultimately foil his claim to the English crown. James, however, evolved an alternative policy: disregarding the mother he had never known and reaching accord with Elizabeth. After his mother's execution on 8 February 1587, James sent a note of strong protest but took no other action.

In 1589 James married Anne of Denmark in Oslo. Three of the couple's seven children survived infancy: Prince Henry, Princess Elizabeth, and Prince Charles.

James experienced periodic attempts to seize his person; the most persistent of these threats involved Francis Stewart Hepburn, fifth Earl of Bothwell, who was accused in 1590 of consulting two North Berwick witches about the date of the king's death and of paying them to create storms during James's voyage home from Denmark. On 27 December 1592 he and about forty other nobles attempted to capture Holyrood Palace, where the king and queen were in residence. James's book *Daemonologie* (1597) resonates with the incidents surrounding Bothwell, but Maurice Lee, Jr. sees James's insistence in the work on the reality of witchcraft and Satan not as superstition but as political tenets underlying divine right: the authority of the king derives from that of God, and the existence of the devil underscores the existence of God. The vitality and vividness of the short three-part dialogue are its literary attractions.

The later years of James's Scottish reign were preoccupied principally with the imposition of law and order, relations between the state and the kirk, and the question of the English succession. The kirk, with Andrew Melville as a principal spokesman, claimed the power to direct secular rulers. James struggled to subject the kirk to the control of bishops, a contest he ultimately won, and to counter objections to the doctrine of indefeasible hereditary right. These issues helped shape the king's two best-known works on the subject of kingship, *The True Lawe of free Monarchies* (1598) and Βασιλικον δωρον (*Basilikon Doron* [Royal Gift], 1599). The first of these pithy, well-written pieces treats the theoretical

James's queen, Anne of Denmark, whom he married in 1589; oil painting by Paul van Somers (Collection of Her Majesty the Queen)

basis of kingship; the second deals with government in practice, or what James called "kingcraft."

In 1601 Robert Cecil, Queen Elizabeth's chief minister, entered into a secret correspondence with James to smooth the succession. Cecil and his cohorts did not educate their future king about the issues he would face in his new country; this omission may have been a ploy to enhance the king's dependence on them. They succeeded in undermining potential political rivals, such as Sir Walter Ralegh. Elizabeth died on 24 March 1603, and James crossed into England with a relatively small agenda, much of it related to Scotland: he saw the union of Scotland and England as his major task; he would also end England's war with Spain and work at sustaining peace for all of Europe.

When he was crowned James I of England at Westminster in July, the new king felt that he had entered the promised land, partly because of the contrast between England's prosperity and Scotland's poverty. His journey south had been marked by evident public jubilation and lavish private entertainment, but it was easy to misinterpret both: joy over a peaceful succes-

sion was not the same as endorsement of the monarch and his policies, and private wealth belied the empty treasury James had inherited. Perhaps because he had so little else to give, James was lavish with titles, knighting more men in four months than Elizabeth had created during a forty-five-year reign. He appointed fellow countrymen to posts close to his person, especially the Bedchamber, fueling an impression of a "foreign" king, with a broad Scots accent, in a court monopolized by "barbarians" controlling patronage and politics.

The new king brought with him a deserved reputation for learning. Within days of Queen Elizabeth's death *Basilikon Doron* was published in its first public edition. Presented as instructions to Prince Henry on the duties of a king, the book comprises three parts: "Of a King's Christian Duty Towards God," "Of a King's Duty in His Office," and "Of a King's Behavior in Indifferent Things." In contrast to the 1599 Scottish edition, of which only seven copies were distributed to James's most trusted servants, this version put between thirteen thousand and sixteen thousand copies into circula-

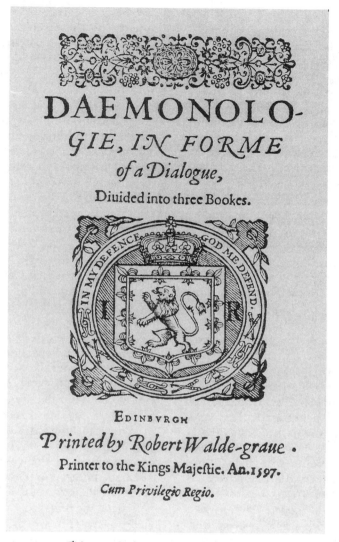

DAEMONOLO-
GIE, IN FORME
of a Dialogue,
Diuided into three Bookes.

EDINBVRGH
Printed by Robert Walde-graue.
Printer to the Kings Majestie. An. 1597.
Cum Privilegio Regio.

Title page for James's treatise on witchcraft

tion. It was soon translated into most of the languages of western Europe and was central to the many collections of King James's table talk and apothegms that were published throughout the seventeenth century. The 1603 edition was revised in part to add an air of learning through references to the classics, and in part for reasons of state. The generally didactic tone is enlivened by quaint phrasing with an abundance of pungent, quotable passages, such as "Make not a fool of yourself in . . . wearing long hair or nails, which are but excrements of nature." James writes of his hopes, hatreds, and frustrations: "The merchants think the whole commonweal ordained for making them up; and accounting it for their lawful gain and trade, to enrich themselves upon the loss of all the rest of the people, they transport from us things necessary;

bringing back sometimes unnecessary things, and at other times nothing at all. They buy for us the worst wares, and sell them at the dearest prices."

Leading Puritans petitioned James to reform the Church of England; in response the king called a conference at Hampton Court in 1604. Although James sided with the established church, the Puritans gained his support on the necessity of a preaching ministry and for curbing abuses such as pluralism and absenteeism. James's religious and political views converged: he opposed a presbyterian system because it challenged kingly authority. For individuals, however, James distinguished between private beliefs and public foment: on the one hand, he would not "compel men's consciences"; on the other, he moved against fanaticism, extremism, and proselytizing.

The Authorized Version of the Bible (1611) arose out of this conference. The so-called King James Bible was technically a revision of the eighteenth edition (1602) of the Bishops' Bible, first published in 1568 — not a new translation but a culminating synthesis of the preceding century's English versions. It was, for its time, highly accurate, and it was stylistically beautiful because it was designed for public reading and because of the influence of the king's literary reputation. Although substantiating its impact is difficult because some of its most widely used phrases appear in earlier translations, the Authorized Version remained preeminent for more than 250 years.

In 1604 James's vituperative condemnation of smoking, *A Counter-Blaste to Tobacco,* was published anonymously. In this short piece, he disparages the "precious stink" on medical, moral, and social grounds. He ends by describing it as "A custome loathsome to the eye, hatefull to the Nose, harmefull to the braine, dangerous to the Lungs, and in the blacke stinking fume thereof, nearest resembling the horrible Stygian smoke of the pit that is bottomlesse."

After the failure of the Catholic-backed attempt to blow up the king and Parliament on 5 November 1605 in the Gunpowder Plot, which James claimed that he alone had penetrated, the king's fears of assassination led to the passage of a law requiring an oath of allegiance. Pope Paul V's breve of 22 September 1606 commanded English Catholics not to take the oath; a second breve reiterated the command. James's *Triplici Nodo, Triplex Cuneus. Or, An Apologie for the Oath of Allegiance* (1607) was a rebuttal alleging that the oath was a civil matter. After Cardinal Robert Bellarmine counterattacked, James added to a second edition of the work "A Premonition to All Most Mightie Monarchies" to show all European princes that the papacy menaced the rights they claimed as sovereign rulers. The controversy continued as the oath became a European as well as an English issue.

Masques, performed as least annually from the staging of Ben Jonson's *The Masque of Blackness* in January 1605 until the end of James's reign, were the quintessential courtly extravagances. These elaborate allegorical entertainments relied as much, if not more, on the sumptuous costumes, illusionistic scenery, and stage contrivances of Inigo Jones as they did on the words — although Jonson transformed his materials into fables of royal divinity. Many leading personalities of the court, including the queen, took part; the king did not, but he was the focal point of the performance: he was the

audience. Although other dramatists, notably William Shakespeare, worked in companies patronized by royalty, these self-congratulatory masques became the genre most intimately associated with James and his court.

James's lack of interest in public display was only one of the contrasts between his style and Elizabeth's. Her progresses and court were central to national life; James was less businesslike, devoting himself to hunting and delegating much to officials such as Cecil. He did, however, appropriate to himself foreign and religious policy. The English Parliament, more independent than the Scottish, viewed the king's reasoning about his prerogatives as "misinformed." The House of Commons was able to bypass the king by its right to vote supplies, and its desire to aid Protestants abroad ran counter to James's vision of a European peace achieved through the agency of Catholic Spain. Furthermore, the union of Scotland and England had no appeal to the Commons, and Cecil's attempt to secure an annual royal income through the Great Contract of 1610 was also rejected. The king's efforts to generate funds by extraparliamentary methods, such as creating the order of baronets, were unpopular and, ultimately, insufficient. Tensions, consequently, increased between the king and his parliaments.

In 1612 James lost his son Henry, the Prince of Wales, to typhoid; Cecil, whom he had created first Earl of Salisbury in 1605, died as well. The consequences of Princess Elizabeth's marriage in 1613 to the Elector Palatine, Frederick V, would form the background of James's troubled foreign policy for the remainder of his reign. His daughter's wedding was, however, one of the most popular and spectacular celebrations of the time.

After Salisbury died James planned to train Robert Carr to replace him as secretary of state, even though the young Scottish favorite had, until then, been unconnected with the government. In September 1613 Sir Thomas Overbury, whose ambitions allied him with the favorite, was found dead in the Tower. In December, shortly after Carr was created earl of Somerset, he married Frances Howard, the former countess of Essex, who had been freed from her marriage by a declaration of nullity after long and titillating proceedings. In a new wave of scandal the couple were found guilty in 1616 of poisoning Overbury and were imprisoned in the Tower (they were pardoned but were not released until 1622). As one favorite was descending, another, George Villiers, who was made earl of Buckingham in 1617 and marquess in 1618, was emerging. James's new protégé inflicted still more damage

Page from the manuscript for Basilikon Doron, *the book of instructions on a monarch's duties that James wrote for his son Prince Henry (British Library)*

*Title page, engraved by Renold Elstrack, for the collected edition of
James's prose works*

on the monarchy in the realm of public perception: Buckingham was known for his impromptu capers at masques; he was the king's "sweet Steenie," and James was his "dear dad and husband."

In the spring of 1619 James fell ill; Anne had recently died. In that same year the most intractable foreign-affairs crisis ever to confront James arose when his son-in-law, Frederick, making a show of consulting James, accepted the Bohemian crown without waiting for his advice. The problem James faced after Frederick's decision was insoluble, because he could neither control his son-in-law nor abandon him. Although England had no national interest in Bohemia, James's daughter was a potential heir to the English throne.

The politics of the collapsing Holy Roman Empire led James to believe that Spain could control its Austrian cousins and the Catholic party in the empire. This misconception had been actively promoted by the Spanish ambassador, Don Diego Sarmiento de Acuña, Conde de Gondomar, since his arrival in England in 1613. James's execution of Ralegh in 1618 to appease Spain was a political error because it was seen as a concession to the unpopular Gondomar.

A marriage between Philip II's daughter, the Infanta Maria, and Prince Charles was intended to provide a tacit Spanish pledge that there would be no ideological war. Unfortunately for James, the Spanish marriage was like the Anglo-Scottish union: almost no one supported it. Gondomar promoted the match as a chance for England's reconversion to Catholicism and as a guarantee of England's neutrality in case of renewed war between Spain and Holland. When Charles and Buckingham failed to conclude a marriage treaty after six months in Madrid in 1623, both returned advocating war with Spain. Acting contrary to James's policy, the politically unreliable Buckingham (who was made a duke that year) theatrically denounced the Spaniards before Parliament, asserting that they had never planned to help Frederick regain the Lower Palatinate. The two houses petitioned the king to end all treaties with Spain and offered war assistance. While James lived, there was no war; but after his death on 27 March 1625 his peacekeeping efforts disintegrated.

Formerly vilified as a principal cause of the civil war, James's religious and foreign policies, stance on legal and constitutional issues, and relations with Parliament are receiving favorable reconsideration. According to Lee in *Great Britain's Solomon* (1990), the "dark and undeserved shadow over James's reputation" has been cast because in the last three years of his reign he "was a man floundering in the net of circumstance, trying vainly to make the strategy and tactics to which he had committed himself work."

James was unusual among monarchs: a litterateur who was recognized as such by most of his contemporaries. Although some of James's positions, such as his advocacy of divine right, are now seen as misguided, he was both a disciplined controversialist and a prose stylist with a flair for images and proverbs. Many of his well-turned phrases were extracted from his speeches and writings and continued to be popular long after his death. He was an author who, at his best, combined originality with clarity — no mean accomplishment for a literary man and almost without precedent for a king.

Letters:
Letters of the Kings of England, 2 volumes, edited by James Orchard Halliwell (London: Colburn, 1848);
The Letters of Queen Elizabeth and King James VI of Scotland, edited by John Bruce (London: Camden Society, 1849; New York: AMS Press, 1968);
Correspondence of King James VI of Scotland with Sir Robert Cecil and Others in England, edited by Bruce (Westminster: Camden Society, 1861; New York: AMS Press, 1968);
Calendar of the State Papers Relating to Scotland and Mary, Queen of Scots, 1547–1603, 13 volumes (Edinburgh: H.M. General Register House, 1898–1969);
Letters of King James VI & I, edited by G. V. P. Akrigg (Berkeley, Los Angeles & London: University of California Press, 1984).

Biographies:
David Harris Willson, *King James VI and I* (London: Cape, 1956);

Gordon Donaldson, *Scotland: James V to James VII* (Edinburgh & London: Oliver & Boyd, 1965);
Caroline Bingham, *The Making of a King: The Early Years of James VI and I* (London: Collins, 1968);
Antonia Fraser, *King James VI of Scotland I of England* (New York: Knopf, 1975);
Bingham, *James VI of Scotland* (London: Weidenfeld & Nicolson, 1979);
Bingham, *James I of England* (London: Weidenfeld & Nicolson, 1981).

References:
G. P. V. Akrigg, *Jacobean Pageant; or, The Court of King James I* (London: Hamilton, 1962);
Akrigg, "The Literary Achievement of King James I," *University of Toronto Quarterly,* 44 (Winter 1975): 115–129;
David Bergeron, *Royal Family, Royal Lovers* (Columbia & London: University of Missouri Press, 1991);
Jonathan Goldberg, *James I and the Politics of Literature: Jonson, Shakespeare, Donne, and Their Contemporaries* (Baltimore & London: Johns Hopkins University Press, 1983);
Maurice Lee, Jr., *Government by the Pen: Scotland under James VI and I* (Urbana: University of Illinois Press, 1980);
Lee, *Great Britain's Solomon: James VI and I in His Three Kingdoms* (Urbana: University of Illinois Press, 1990);
David Mathew, *James I* (London: Eyre & Spottiswoode, 1967);
William McElwee, *The Wisest Fool in Christendom: The Reign of King James I and VI* (New York: Harcourt, Brace, 1958);
John Nichols, *The Progresses, Processions, and Magnificent Festivities of King James the First,* 4 volumes (London: J. B. Nichols, 1828);
Linda Levy Peck, ed., *The Mental World of the Jacobean Court* (Cambridge & New York: Cambridge University Press, 1971);
Helena Shire, *Song, Dance, and Poetry of the Court of Scotland under James VI* (London: Cambridge University Press, 1969);
C. J. Sisson, "King James the First of England as Poet and Political Writer," in *Seventeenth Century Studies, Presented to Sir Herbert Grierson* (Oxford: Clarendon Press, 1938), pp. 47–63.

Papers:
Letters and papers of James I are in the Public Record Office and the British Library in London and the National Library of Scotland and the Scottish Record Office in Edinburgh.

John Milton

(9 December 1608 – 8? November 1674)

Keith W. F. Stavely

See also the Milton entry in *DLB 131: Seventeenth-Century British Nondramatic Poets, Third Series.*

SELECTED BOOKS: *A Maske Presented at Ludlow Castle, 1634: On Michaelmas night, before the Right Honorable, Iohn Earle of Bridgewater, Vicount Brackly, Lord Præsident of Wales, And one of His Maiesties most honorable Privie Counsell* [*Comus*] (London: Printed for Humphrey Robinson, 1637);

Epitaphivm Damonis. Argvmentvm (London: Printed by Augustine Mathewes?, 1640?);

Of Reformation Touching Chvrch-Discipline in England: And the Cavses that hitherto have hindered It. Two Bookes, Written to a Freind (London: Printed for Thomas Underhill, 1641);

Of Prelatical Episcopacy, and Whether it may be deduc'd from the Apostolical times by vertue of those Testimonies which are alledg'd to that purpose in some late Treatises: One whereof goes under the Name of Iames' Arch-Bishop of Armagh (London: Printed by R. O. & G. D. for Thomas Underhill, 1641);

Animadversions upon The Remonstrants Defence, against Smectymnuus (London: Printed for Thomas Underhill, 1641);

The Reason of Church-governement Urg'd against Prelaty by Mr. John Milton. In Two Books (London: Printed by E. G. for John Rothwell, 1641 [i.e., 1642]);

An Apology Against a Pamphlet Call'd A Modest Confutation of the Animadversions upon the Remonstrant against Smectymnuus (London: Printed by E. G. for John Rothwell, 1642);

The Doctrine and Discipline of Divorce: Restor'd to the Good of Both Sexes, From the bondage of Canon Law, and other mistakes, to Christian Freedom, guided by the Rule of Charity. Wherein also many places of Scripture, have recover'd their long-lost meaning: Seasonable to be now thought on in the Reformation intended (London: Printed by Thomas Payne & Matthew Simmons, 1643); revised and enlarged as *The Doctrine & Discipline of Divorce: Restor'd to the good of both Sexes, From the*

bondage of Canon Law, and other mistakes, to the true meaning of Scripture in the Law and Gospel compar'd. Wherin also are set down the bad consequences of abolishing or condemning of Sin, that which the Law of God allowes, and Christ Abolisht Not. Now the second time revis'd and much augmented, In Two Books: To the Parlament of England with the Assembly*, as J. M. (London, 1644);

Of Education. To Master Samuel Hartlib (London: Printed for Thomas Johnson, 1644);

Areopagitica; a Speech of Mr. John Milton for the Liberty of Vnlicenc'd Printing, To the Parlament of England (London, 1644);

Tetrachordon: Expositions upon The foure chief places in Scripture, which treat of Mariage, or nullities in Mariage. On Gen. 1. 27. 28. compar'd and explain'd by Gen. 2. 18.23.24. Deut. 24. 1. 2. Matth. 5. 31. 32. with Matth. 19. from the 3^d. v. to the 11th. 1 Cor. 7 from the 10th to the 16th. Wherin the Doctrine and Discipline of Divorce, as was lately Publish'd, is confirm'd by explanation of Scripture, by Testimony of ancient Fathers, of Civill Lawes in the Primitive Church, of famousest Reformed Divines, And lastly, by an intended Act of the Parlament and Church of England in the last yeare of Edward the Sixth, as J. M. (London: Printed by Thomas Payne & Matthew Simmons, 1645);

Colasterion: A Reply to a Nameles Answer against The Doctrine and Discipline of Divorce. Wherein The Trivial Author of that Answer is Discover'd, the Licenser conferr'd with, and the Opinion which they traduce defended, as J. M. (London: Printed by Matthew Simmons, 1645);

Poems of Mr. John Milton, Both English and Latin, Compos'd at several times. Printed by his true Copies. The Songs were set in Musick by Mr. Henry Lawes (London: Printed by Ruth Raworth for Humphrey Moseley, 1645);

The Tenure of Kings and Magistrates: Proving, That it is Lawfull, and hath been held so through all Ages, for any, who have the Power, to call to account a Tyrant, or wicked King, and after due conviction, to depose, and put him to death; if the ordinary Magistrate have neglected, or deny'd to doe It. And that they, who of

John Milton; pastel by William Faithorne, circa 1670 (Princeton University Library)

late, so much blame Deposing, are the Men that did it themselves, as J. M. (London: Printed by Matthew Simmons, 1649); enlarged as *The Tenure of Kings and Magistrates: Proving, That it is Lawfull, and hath been held so through all Ages, for any, who have the Power, to call to account a Tyrant, or wicked King, and after due conviction, to depose, and put him to death; if the ordinary Magistrate have neglected, or deny'd to doe It. And that they, who of late, so much blame Deposing, are the Men that did it themselves. Published now the second time with some additions, and many Testimonies also added out of the Best & learnedest among Protestant Divines asserting the position of this book* (London: Printed by Matthew Simmons, 1650);

'ΕΙΚΟΝΟΚΛΑ'ΣΤΗΣ. *In Answer To a book Intitl'd* E'ΙΚΩ'Ν ΒΑΣΙΛΙΚH̀, *the Portrature of his Sacred Majesty in his Solitude and Sufferings,* as J. M. (London: Printed by Matthew Simmons, 1649; revised and enlarged edition, London:

Printed by T. N., sold by Thomas Brewster & Gregory Moule, 1650);

Joannis Miltoni Angli pro Populo Anglicano Defensio contra Claudii Anonymi, aliàs Salmasii, Defensionem Regiam (London: Printed by William Dugard, 1651; revised edition, London: Printed by Thomas Newcomb, 1658);

Joannis Miltoni Angli pro Populo Anglicano Defensio Secunda. Contra infamem libellum anonymum cui titulus, Regii sanguinis clamor ad Cœlum adversus parricidas Anglicanos (London: Printed by Thomas Newcomb, 1654);

Joannis Miltoni Angli pro Se Defensio contra Alexandrum Morum Ecclesiasten, Libelli famosi, cui titulus, Regii sanguinis clamor ad Cœlum adversùs Parricidas Anglicanos, authorem Rectè Dictum (London: Printed by Thomas Newcomb, 1655);

A Treatise of Civil Power in Ecclesiastical causes: Shewing That it is not lawfull for any power on earth to com-

pell in matters of Religion, as J. M. (London: Printed by Thomas Newcomb, 1659);

Considerations Touching The likeliest means to remove Hirelings out of the church. Wherein is also discourc'd Of Tithes, Church-fees, Church-revenues; And whether any maintenance of ministers can be settl'd by law, as J. M. (London: Printed by Thomas Newcomb, 1659);

The Readie & Easie Way to Establish a Free Commonwealth, and The Excellence therof Compar'd with The inconveniences and dangers of readmitting kingship in this nation (London: Printed by Thomas Newcomb, sold by Livewell Chapman, 1660; revised and enlarged edition, London: Printed for the author, 1660);

Brief Notes Upon a late Sermon, Titl'd, The Fear of God and the King; Preachd, and since Publishd, By Matthew Griffith, D. D. And Chaplain to the late King. Wherin many Notorious Wrestings of Scripture, and other Falsities are observed by J. M. (London, 1660);

Paradise lost. A Poem Written in Ten Books (London: Printed & sold by Peter Parker, Robert Boulter & Matthias Walker, 1667); revised and enlarged as *Paradise Lost. A Poem in Twelve Books. The Author John Milton. The Second Edition Revised and Augmented by the same Author* (London: Printed by Samuel Simmons, 1674);

Accedence Commenc't Grammar, Supply'd with sufficient Rules, For the use of such as, Younger or Elder, are desirous, without more trouble then needs, to attain the Latin Tongue; the elder sort especially, with little teaching, and their own industry (London: Printed by Samuel Simmons, 1669);

The History of Britain, That part especially now call'd England. From the first Traditional Beginning, continu'd to the Norman Conquest. Collected out of the antientest and best Authors thereof (London: Printed by J. M. for James Allestry, 1670);

Paradise Regain'd. A Poem. In IV Books. To which is added Samson Agonistes (London: Printed by J. M. for John Starkey, 1671);

Joannis Miltoni Angli, Artis Logicæ Plenior Institutio, ad Petri Rami Methodum concinnata, Adjecta est Praxis Annalytica & Petri Rami vita (London: Printed for Spencer Hickman, 1672);

Of True Religion, Hæresie, Schism, Toleration, And what best means may be us'd against the growth of Popery, as J. M. (London, 1673);

Joannis Miltonii Angli, Epistolarum Familiarium Liber Unus: Quibus Accesserunt, Ejusdem, jam olim in Collegio Adolescentis, Prolusiones Quædam Oratoriae (London: Printed for Brabazon Aylmer, 1674);

A Declaration, or Letters Patents of the Election of this present King of Poland John the Third, Elected on the 22d of May last past, Anno Dom. 1674. Containing the Reasons of this Election, the great Vertues and Merits of the said Serene Elect, His eminent Services in War, especially in his last great Victory against the Turks and Tartars, whereof many Particulars are here related, not published Before. Now faithfully translated from the Latin Copy (London: Printed for Brabazon Aylmer, 1674);

Literæ Pseudo-Senatús Anglicani, Cromwellii, Reliquorumque Perduellium nomine ac jussu conscriptæ (Amsterdam: Printed by Peter & John Blaeu, 1676); translated by Edward Phillips, with omissions and additions, as *Letters of State, Written by Mr. John Milton, To most of the Sovereign Princes and Republicks of Europe. From the Year 1649. Till the Year 1659. To which is added, an Account of his Life. Together with Several of His Poems; And a Catalogue of his Works, never before Printed* (London, 1694);

Mr John Miltons Character of the Long Parliament and Assembly of Divines. In MDCXLI. Omitted in his other Works, and never before Printed, And very seasonable for these times (London: Printed for Henry Brome, 1681);

A Brief History of Moscovia: And Of other less-known Countries lying eastward of Russia as far as Cathay. Gather'd from the Writings of several Eye-Witnesses (London: Printed by M. Flesher for Brabazon Aylmer, 1682);

A Complete Collection of the Historical, Political, and Miscellaneous Works of John Milton, Both English and Latin; with som Papers never before Publish'd. To which is Prefix'd the Life of the Author, 3 volumes, edited by John Toland (Amsterdam [i.e., London], 1698);

A Complete Collection of the Historical, Political, and Miscellaneous Works of John Milton: Correctly Printed from the Original Editions. With an Historical and Critical Account of the Life and Writings of the Author; Containing Several Original Papers of His, Never before Published, 2 volumes, edited by Thomas Birch (London: Printed for A. Millar, 1738); revised as *The Works of John Milton, Historical, Political, and Miscellaneous. Now more correctly printed from the Originals, than in any former Edition, and many passages restored, which have been hitherto omitted. To which is prefixed, An Account of his Life and Writings*, 2 volumes, edited by Birch and Richard Baron (London: Printed for A. Millar, 1753);

Joannis Miltoni Angli De Doctrina Christiana libri duo posthumi, edited and translated by Charles R.

Sumner (Cambridge: Printed at the Cambridge University Press by John Smith, Printer to the University, 1825);

A Common-place Book of John Milton, and a Latin Essay and Latin Verses Presumed To Be by Milton, edited by A. J. Horwood, Camden Society Publications, new series 16 (Westminster: Printed for the Camden Society, 1876; revised, 1877);

A Common-Place Book of John Milton. Reproduced by the Autotype Process from the Original Manuscript in the Possession of Sir Frederick J. U. Graham. . . . With an Introduction by A. J. Horwood (London: Privately printed at the Chiswick Press, 1876);

The Works of John Milton, 18 volumes in 21, edited by Frank Allen Patterson (New York: Columbia University Press, 1931–1938).

Editions: *The Poetical Works of Mr. John Milton. Containing Paradise Lost, Paradise Regain'd, Sampson Agonistes, and His Poems on Several Occasions. Together with Explanatory Notes on Each Book of the Paradise Lost and a Table Never before Printed,* with notes to *Paradise Lost* by David Hume (London: Printed for Jacob Tonson, 1695);

*The Works of M*ʳ*. John Milton* (London, 1697);

The Prose Works of John Milton: With a Life of the Author, 7 volumes, edited by Charles Symmons (London: J. Johnson, 1806);

The Prose Works of John Milton: Containing His Principal Political and Ecclesiastical Pieces, with New Translations, and an Introduction, 2 volumes, edited by George Burnett (London: Printed for J. Miller, 1809);

A Selection from the English Prose Works of John Milton, 2 volumes, edited by Francis Jenks (Boston: Bowles & Dearborn, 1826);

The Prose Works of John Milton; with an Introductory Review, edited by Robert Fletcher (London: Westley & Davis, 1833);

The Prose Works of John Milton: With a Biographical Introduction, 2 volumes, edited by Rufus Wilmot Griswold (Philadelphia: Hooker, 1845);

The Prose Works of John Milton, 5 volumes, edited by J. A. St. John and Charles Sumner (London: Bohn, 1848–1853);

The Works of John Milton, in Verse and Prose, Printed from the Original Editions, with a Life of the Author, 8 volumes, edited by John Mitford (London: Pickering / Boston: Little & Brown, 1851);

Milton's Prose, edited by Malcolm W. Wallace (London: Oxford University Press, 1925);

Areopagitica and Other Prose Works (London: Dent, 1927; New York: Dutton, 1927);

The Student's Milton, Being the Complete Poems of John Milton, with the Greater Part of His Prose Works, *Now Printed in One Volume, Together with New Translations into English of His Italian, Latin and Greek Poems,* edited by Frank Allen Patterson (New York: Crofts, 1930; revised, 1933);

John Milton: Prose Selections, edited by Merritt Y. Hughes (New York: Odyssey Press, 1947);

Complete Prose Works of John Milton, 8 volumes in 10, edited by Don M. Wolfe and others (New Haven: Yale University Press, 1953–1982);

Complete Poems and Major Prose, edited by Hughes (New York: Odyssey Press, 1957);

Milton's Prose Writings, edited by K. M. Burton (London: Dent / New York: Dutton, 1958);

The Prose of John Milton, edited by J. Max Patrick and others (Garden City, N.Y.: Doubleday, 1967);

Selected Prose edited by C. A. Patrides (Harmondsworth, U.K.: Penguin, 1974; Columbia: University of Missouri Press, 1985).

OTHER: "A Postscript," in *An Answer to a Booke Entitvled, An Humble Remonstrance,* by Stephen Marshall, Edmund Calamy, Thomas Young, Matthew Newcomen, and William Spurstow, as Smectymnuus (London, 1641), pp. 85–94;

The Ivdgement of Martin Bucer, Concerning Divorce. Writt'n to Edward the sixt, in his second Book of the Kingdom of Christ. And Now Englisht. Wherin a late Book restoring the Doctrine and Discipline of Divorce, is heer confirm'd and justify'd by the authoritie of Martin Bucer. To the Parlament of England, translated by Milton (London: Printed by Matthew Simmons, 1644);

"Observations upon the Articles of Peace with the Irish Rebels, on the Letter of Ormond to Col. Jones, and the Representation of the Presbytery at Belfast," in *Articles of Peace, Made and Concluded with the Irish Rebels, and Papists, by James Earle of Ormond, for and in behalfe of the late King, and by vertue of his Autoritie. Also a Letter sent by Ormond to Col. Jones, Governour of Dublin, with his Answer thereunto. And a Representation of the Scotch Presbytery at Belfast in Ireland. Upon all which are added Observations* (London: Printed by Matthew Simmons, 1649), pp. 43–64;

T. B., *The Cabinet-Council: Containing the Cheif* [sic] *Arts of Empire, And Mysteries of State; Discabineted In Political and Polemical Aphorisms, grounded on Authority, and Experience; And illustrated with the choicest Examples and Historical Observations. By the Ever-renowned Knight, Sir Walter Raleigh, Published by John Milton, Esq.,* edited by Milton (London: Printed by Thomas Newcomb for Thomas Johnson, 1658).

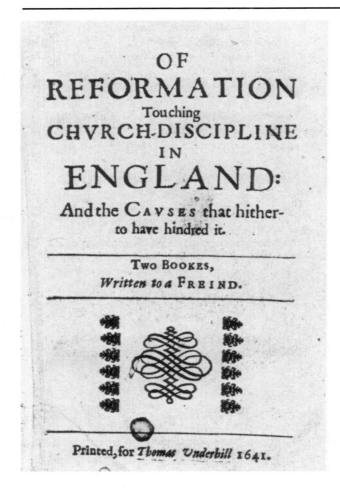

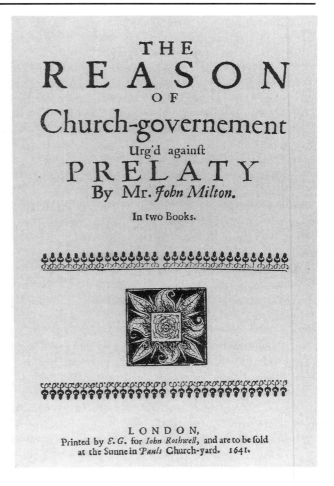

Two of Milton's contributions to the 1641–1642 pamphlet war between the Presbyterians and the Episcopalians. Milton advocated the Presbyterian position.

John Milton's claim to continued recollection rests primarily, of course, on his preeminence as a poet. In 1642 he said that he had been forced by a sense of political duty to interrupt his efforts to become "a Poet soaring in the high region of his fancies." He had instead to linger "here below in the cool element of prose," where he had the use of his "left hand" only. In terms of his ultimate creative ambitions, poetry was to prose as heaven was to earth. But Milton's own early assessment of the discursive media competing for his energies should not be taken at face value. His earthly commitments were strong enough to keep him "here below in the cool element of prose" for nearly two decades, until the demise of the English Revolution in 1660. Even then Milton did not fall entirely silent as a prose writer: in the 1670s he published two works of political commentary.

Milton's renewed involvement in political discourse a decade after the Restoration was based on a judgment that it had again become possible to gain a hearing for his most cherished convictions. In this respect his final prose works anticipate a central feature of the posthumous publication history of all his prose: there has been an interest in the prose for its own sake mostly when the political situation has made it seem relevant again. This pattern has prevailed from the first publication of the *Character of the Long Parliament* in 1681, through the publication or translation of many of his pamphlets during the American and French revolutions, all the way to the twentieth century, in which, in the aftermath of the 1960s, there has been a marked increase in the number of academic books and articles about Milton's prose. It should come as no surprise that the author of *Paradise Lost* (1667) should have poured forth sufficient vitality of thought and expression from his "left hand" alone to command attention at most of the moments of high political passion and resolve in modern Anglo-American and Western history.

Milton was born in London on 9 December 1608, the second of the three children of John and Sara Jeffrey Milton who would survive into adulthood. His father's father was Richard Milton, an Oxfordshire yeoman who had been excommunicated from the Church of England in 1582 for his persistent allegiance to Roman Catholicism. Around this time, Richard Milton had come upon his son reading an English Bible. This adherent of the old "true religion" was not about to countenance the observance of the new "heretical" religion of the Reformation by his own son and heir. In the quarrel that thereupon erupted, the son was disinherited.

The man who was to become the poet's father proceeded to London, where he gradually made his way as a scrivener, a profession that included lending money, copying documents, and providing other financial, clerical, and legal services. He also gained a considerable reputation as a musician and composer. Around the turn of the seventeenth century, John Milton married and occupied the premises in All Hallows parish in which his illustrious namesake was to be born.

Most of the households in this neighborhood were inhabited by industrious merchants and entrepreneurs and their dependents, the sort of people who had begun in the 1560s, under clerical leadership, to demand the elimination from the Church of England of all traces of Roman Catholic hierarchalism and ceremonialism. Derisively named "Puritans" by their ecclesiastical opponents, these were people among whom one might well expect to find a man who had been disinherited by a Catholic father for reading the Bible. And indeed, during Milton's childhood the Puritan minister of All Hallows did stress from the pulpit continuous reading of the Bible and other tenets of Puritan ideology.

John Milton, Sr., devoted "ceaselesse diligence and care," as well as a great deal of money, to the education of his eldest son, expecting that at the end of the process would emerge a clergyman of the same stripe as his own minister. Lessons were given at home by a tutor, the Scottish Presbyterian Thomas Young, another Puritan influence. By the age of twelve Milton had developed "so keen an appetite" for intellectual pursuits that he was apt to stay awake studying until midnight. It was probably around this time that he was sent to St. Paul's School. This institution was a product of sixteenth-century humanism, a movement that, in its criticisms of the papacy and aversion to medieval Scholastic theology, anticipated many of the central features of Protestantism. In the early seventeenth century the curriculum at St. Paul's continued to be grounded in humanist admiration for the cultures of ancient Greece and Rome.

By 1625 Milton was ready for higher education. There was, no doubt, little hesitation about sending him to Cambridge, which had been a major center of the Puritan movement for two generations, and he matriculated there on 9 April. As part of his course of study at Cambridge, Milton composed his *Prolusiones* in Latin prose. From these exercises, which were not published until 1674, it is clear that by the time his formal education was completed Milton had thoroughly mastered the methods and patterns of classical rhetoric.

After taking his M.A. on 3 July 1632, Milton decided not to proceed directly to ordination for the ministry but to devote himself to private study at his parents' homes in London from 1632 to 1635 and in Horton, Buckinghamshire, from 1635 to 1638. During this period of contemplation his hesitations about the ministry were exacerbated by two factors: the beginnings of fulfillment of his long-harbored poetic ambitions with the successful performance of his masque *Comus* in 1634 (published, 1637) and the closing down of safe havens for clergymen of Puritan inclinations after the installation of William Laud as archbishop of Canterbury in 1633. Laud was determined that the Puritan clergy would either cease evading the established forms and ceremonies of the Church of England or cease functioning as its priests. His policies propelled many Puritans across the Atlantic to New England, and they also helped to propel Milton into redefinition of his life's work. At some point during the 1630s Milton came to view himself as a minister of an unconventional sort, one whose care of Christian souls would be exercised through writing poetry.

In April 1638 Milton went on a tour of the Continent, where he met such leading intellectual figures as Hugo Grotius, Galileo, and Giovanni Battista Manso, the onetime patron of the Italian epic poet Torquato Tasso. In Florence, Milton was welcomed as a participant in the private academies that constituted the core of the city's intellectual life and that were a legacy of the Florentine humanist Renaissance. In John Calvin's Geneva, the center and symbol of European Protestantism, he frequented the house of the leading theologian, Giovanni Diodati, the uncle of his closest friend, Charles Diodati.

Milton had planned to visit Sicily and Greece as well, but while in Naples he learned of "the sad tidings of civil war from England." A conflict over church government was brewing in Scotland. Scotland had a long tradition of presbyterian church government, a system in which the only ecclesiastical authority higher than that of the local parish minister, or presbyter, was that exercised by groups of such presbyters. Beginning in 1637, Charles I had sought to impose on the land of his birth an episcopalian church government similar to that which Archbishop Laud was endeavoring to impose in England, in which local ministers functioned in strict subordination to bishops. By late 1638 it was clear that war was about to break out over the issue.

This was the phase of the struggle of which Milton probably received news in Naples. He later claimed that he immediately decided to change his travel plans and return home, "for I thought it base that I should travel abroad at my ease for the cultivation of my mind, while my fellow-citizens at home were fighting for liberty." This version of what transpired is open to question, since approximately six months elapsed between the time Milton heard of the troubles and his arrival back in England. During those months of northward journeying he continued to cultivate his mind in the centers of Continental learning and piety. On the other hand, it is not implausible to suppose that the news Milton heard in Naples stirred up tensions between a desire to continue to ready himself for ultimate creative fulfillment and a sense of immediate duty. He manifested his inability to resolve these tensions by reversing the direction of his journey of inner cultivation so that he was moving toward, not away from, the sites of Puritan and English values and struggles.

Arriving in England in July 1639, Milton established himself in London and began giving lessons to his two young nephews, the sons of his sister, Anne. Meanwhile, the disenchantment of major portions of the English public with the rule of Charles and Archbishop Laud continued to intensify. In 1640 financial pressures forced Charles to call Parliament into session for the first time in eleven years, and from November onward this body, known to history as the Long Parliament, proceeded to seek redress of grievances on many fronts. In regard to the Church of England, within six weeks, its resolve strengthened by the multitude of anti-Laudian pamphlets that were being circulated with the collapse of the apparatus of censorship, the House of Commons had voted to abolish Archbishop Laud's policies of liturgical ceremonialism and episcopal power.

It remained unclear whether the episcopal hierarchy was to be eliminated or merely reformed.

The moderate Episcopalian, Bishop Joseph Hall, argued that the office of bishop was grounded in succession from the Apostles and that established liturgical practices were also amply justified. The most ambitious reply to Hall, *An Answer to a Booke Entituled, An Humble Remonstrance* (1641), was written under the pseudonym Smectymnuus by Milton's old tutor, Young, with the assistance of four other ministers of presbyterian sympathies. Young and his colleagues maintained that in the early church the terms *bishop* and *presbyter* had been synonymous and that the sorts of liturgical practices required in the Laudian church should be, at most, optional. Appended to this presbyterian tract was a nine-page postscript now thought to have been written by Milton.

In the pamphlets that Milton began to produce at this time he generally exploited, among sixteenth- and seventeenth-century discursive traditions, the conventions of both "Ciceronian" and "loose" Senecan prose. Ciceronian syntax usually builds through subordinate clauses to climactic resolutions. It gives the impression of careful planning and organization, and, as its being named for a Roman statesman implies, it is well suited to the affirmation of public dignity and order, which is how it was used by its most notable English practitioner, Richard Hooker. Loose syntax, most artfully displayed in English in the writings of Sir Thomas Browne, strives for an impression of greater spontaneity through such devices as the "trailing effect," in which a clause is generated not by the main idea of the clause preceding it but by its last word only — as though the act of placing that word on the page had, at that very moment, associatively conjured up the fresh thought expressed in the trailing clause. Such a syntax is suited to convey the sort of energetic private inquisitiveness that a "Ciceronian" public order may tend to ignore or repress.

Characteristically, Milton writes a Ciceronian suspended sentence, to which, at the moment of its resolution, he loosely attaches a trailing clause that itself generates a series of suspended clauses building toward another resolution and climax; or, in some cases, the progress of the subordinate clauses toward resolution is interrupted by a proliferation of second-order subordinate clauses with their own second-order resolutions. Sometimes the result is nothing but long-winded manipulation, but at its best Milton's style projects an image of a public realm in constant process of renewal and recreation.

In his first pamphlet, *Of Reformation,* published in May 1641, Milton assumes the truth of the Presbyterian view of church government and devotes

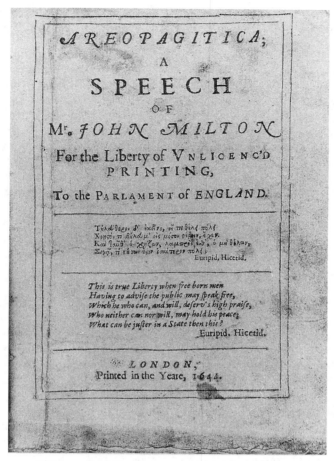

Title page for Milton's argument for freedom of the press

his energies to presenting the standard scenarios of Puritan apocalypticism. This set of attitudes, given wide currency by the immensely popular *Actes and Monuments* (1563) of John Foxe, used the prophecies of the Book of Revelation as keys to the interpretation of Christian history, identifying the period of papal dominance as the reign of Antichrist. As the struggle within the English church between Puritan and anti-Puritan had persisted, the denunciations of established authority as Antichristian had begun to be directed more at the immediately oppressive English prelacy than at the more distant Roman papacy. To say that the bishops of the state church are Antichristian, as Milton does in *Of Reformation,* is obviously, in the circumstances of 1641, to rule out every option but the radical one of the total abolition of episcopacy. Moreover, where earlier, more cautious writers had recommended to people confronted with Antichristian tyranny a posture of reliance on the leadership of truly Christian leaders in church and state, Milton takes more seriously the core Protestant principle of the priesthood of all be-

lievers, stressing the indispensable role of lay agency and initiative as against deference to established authority, however worthy.

Milton's second pamphlet, *Of Prelatical Episcopacy,* appeared one or two months after *Of Reformation.* Defenders of episcopacy were relying on the writings of the post-Apostolic early church leaders, the "fathers." Milton insists that such patristic evidence is not only unreliable but also superfluous and even impious when set against the absolute authority of the Bible, which clearly makes no distinction between bishops and other ministers.

At this point Milton intervened directly in the controversy between his former tutor and the other Presbyterian ministers, on the one hand, and Bishop Hall, on the other. It seemed to him that his Presbyterian friends, while easily having the best of the argument on substantive grounds, were losing out rhetorically by ignoring Hall's pose of continuously condescending urbanity. He therefore produced a fiercely satiric attack on Hall titled *Animadversions upon the Remonstrants Defence, against*

Smectymnuus (1641). Scholars have placed this pamphlet in a tradition of rough Puritan handling of bishops that goes back to the "Martin Marprelate" tracts of the 1590s.

Six or seven months later, in early 1642, Milton brought out another antiepiscopal pamphlet, *The Reason of Church-Governement*. This work includes one of the best-known passages in all of his prose: an account of his reasons for choosing not to become a clergyman, his motives for engaging in pamphleteering, and his poetic aspirations. This self-portrait is not as digressive as it may at first seem. The pamphlet's other feature of particular interest is its continued urging of the right of the average Protestant layperson to participate fully in the life of the church. Indeed, Milton now speaks in favor of tolerating the sectarian groups that, with the collapse of episcopal authority, were beginning to proliferate and that were already being viewed as heretical by the Presbyterians with whom he had thus far been allied. With this emphasis in mind, one can see the autobiographical passage as the tract's most developed celebration of lay dignity, a testimonial to the virtually unbounded capabilities of the regenerate Protestant once the episcopal shackles have been thrown off.

In his fifth and final antiprelatical pamphlet Milton was again entangled with Bishop Hall. Hall had published a reply to Milton's *Animadversions,* in response to which Milton brought out in April 1642 *An Apology against a Pamphlet Call'd A Modest Confutation of the Animadversions upon the Remonstrant against Smectymnuus*. This tract amplifies the self-portrait presented in *The Reason of Church-Governement* and offers biblical and classical justification for the vehemence of the satiric procedures in *Animadversions*.

About a month after the publication of the *Apology,* at a time when the Parliamentary and Royalist forces were maneuvering for position in the impending civil war, Milton married Mary Powell, the eldest daughter of an Oxfordshire gentry family that was in debt to Milton's father. The Powells were also Royalists, and one month after Milton returned to London with his new wife, she left him to go back to her family home in what was to be Royalist territory. For three years she would refuse to be reunited with her husband.

This calamity was the precipitating cause of Milton's next pamphlet, *The Doctrine and Discipline of Divorce,* published in August 1643. Here he advocates what was, at the time, an extremely radical idea: divorce for reasons of incompatibility of temperament. The biggest problem in constructing an argument in support of this position was that Jesus

had seemed to prohibit divorce for any reason other than adultery. Milton was forced into ingenious maneuvers in scriptural interpretation: marriage had originally been instituted as a remedy for loneliness; Eve had been created and given to Adam as a source of full human companionship; sexual congress and procreation had been left as merely secondary purposes; under Old Testament Law, divorce had been permitted for "uncleanness," which, Milton claims, referred to the failure to fulfill this primary marital end of fullness of companionship. Since the New Testament is more charitable to legitimate human needs than the Old, Jesus's comments on divorce could not have been meant to overturn the Old Testament's concession to the human propensity to err. Instead, he was only rebuking the Pharisees, who had been abusing the Mosaic permission of divorce by granting it for frivolous reasons.

In February 1644 Milton published an expanded second edition of *The Doctrine and Discipline of Divorce* in which he availed himself of an analogy that apologists for the parliamentary struggle against the king had begun to use. They were likening Parliament's withdrawal of allegiance to the king, on the grounds that he had failed to perform his part in his implicit contract with the nation, to the right of a husband or wife to divorce if the other party to the marriage fails, by committing adultery, to perform her or his part in the marital contract. In the preface to the revised edition Milton stands this analogy on its head: if the nation may, in effect, divorce itself from an unfit monarch, as it was now doing, so may a man or woman be divorced from an unfit, incompatible wife or husband.

Milton's own fresh experience of marital travail is not far below the surface of this tissue of fine-spun reasoning. Although he is consistent enough to recognize that his proposed reform must apply to women as well as men, his portrayals of domestic unhappiness invariably show an idealistic husband whose quest for companionship is being frustrated by a grossly unfit wife. Such an emphasis has lent credibility to the views of those who regard Milton as a proponent of the subordination of women. The issue is complex, but the most thorough investigation to date of Milton's thinking on gender relations (by James Grantham Turner) shows that both of the traditions within which he was working, Protestantism and Renaissance humanism, were riddled with ambiguity and contradiction. Both insisted that women were inferior to men but then acknowledged that they ought to be treated as virtual equals. In Milton's writings such contradictions are intensified.

Milton's advocacy of divorce reform is one of the turning points in his intellectual development. His search for a remedy for his marital situation led him into a line of thought that identified him in the eyes of his former Presbyterian allies as heretical, for his public rhetorical response to his private crisis occurred just at the moment that a great divide was opening up in the antiepiscopal and anti-Royalist coalition between Presbyterians and moderates, on the one hand, and "Independents" and radicals, on the other. The primary aims of the former were to replace an Episcopalian national church with a Presbyterian one, under which a code of orthodoxy would be even more stringently enforced, and to prosecute the war against the king in such a way that the structure of traditional authority would remain in place. Many of those in the more radical group were inclined to wage the war against the king in the most vigorous fashion, to reduce to a minimum all authority in the church beyond the local level, and to tolerate and even welcome the flood of intellectual experimentation that the revolutionary crisis had let loose.

The moderates were quick to impute to the radicals all the worst irregularities – especially sexual ones – that had allegedly befouled that great cautionary precedent in the annals of Protestant extremism, the commune briefly established in the German city of Münster in the 1530s in the wake of the Lutheran Reformation. Milton's ideas on divorce were at once perceived within these ready-made categories: he was accused of advocating "divorce at pleasure." None of his subsequent efforts to demonstrate the unimpeachable Protestant sobriety of his position were of any avail against these stereotyped accusations. Milton learned that one of the leading lights of the Reformation, Martin Bucer, had written a treatise on divorce arguing a position quite similar to his own. He rushed his translation of Bucer's work into print in August 1644 with a preface triumphantly demanding that his detractors cease and desist from their wild charges of novelty and lewdness. He had his answer a week later, when a Presbyterian divine declared that Milton's "wicked book" on divorce was "deserving to be burnt."

Milton returned to the fray in March 1645 with *Tetrachordon*. Here he associates his argument more integrally with the Parliamentary case against the king. Parliament's spokesmen had begun to argue that all government was grounded in the "secondary law of nature," which God had framed after the Fall to facilitate the continuance of human life. Under this law, kingship would be a valid form of government as long as it fostered a modicum of civilized existence; once it ceased to do so, the same law provided equal warrant for the overthrow of kingship and its replacement with something better. Milton proceeds to argue that marriage is also a manifestation of the secondary law of nature. When marriage fails to serve its purpose of counteracting the Fall, divorce is the secondary law of nature's secondary remedy.

Simultaneously with *Tetrachordon* appeared *Colasterion*, which was occasioned by the only published reply to *The Doctrine and Discipline of Divorce*. *Colasterion* consists principally of ridicule of the humble social origins of Milton's opponent. It thus forms part of what has been called "Milton's quest for respectability" in response to heresy baiting. But he remained a notorious figure. Those, such as Daniel Featley in Κατα-βαπτισται χατ'απτυστοι: *The Dippers Dipt* (1644), who were appalled at the direction in which the nation seemed to be heading would continue to list "a Tractate of Divorce, in which the bonds of matrimony are let loose to inordinate lust" among the books freely circulating that were espousing "many . . . most damnable doctrines, tending to carnall liberty . . . and a *medley* and *hodg-podge* of all Religions."

Featley does not mention anything by Milton as promoting a medley and hodgepodge of all religions; that honor he bestows on *The Bloudy Tenent of Persecution* (1644), by Roger Williams. But he might have accused Milton of malfeasance in this regard as well. Only two of the pleas for toleration and liberty of conscience produced by the radical faction within the parliamentary and Puritan coalition were destined for lasting fame and influence: Williams's *Bloudy Tenent* and *Areopagitica; a Speech of Mr. John Milton for the Liberty of Unlicenc'd Printing, To the Parliament of England* published in November 1644. *Areopagitica* is not a component of a quest for respectability on Milton's part; it is, rather, an embrace of that very culture of emergent disrespectability in which he stood accused of participating.

The immediate issue to which Milton was responding was Parliament's Licensing Ordinance of June 1643. This legislation required, as had the Stuart regime's Star Chamber Decree of 1637, that no book or pamphlet be published without official approval. It amounted to an attempt on the part of the evolving revolutionary state apparatus to regain some sort of control over the nation's intellectual and cultural life, the traditional institutions and means of such control having disappeared in 1641 along with the other organs of the Stuart and episcopal regime. Like many others, Milton had not al-

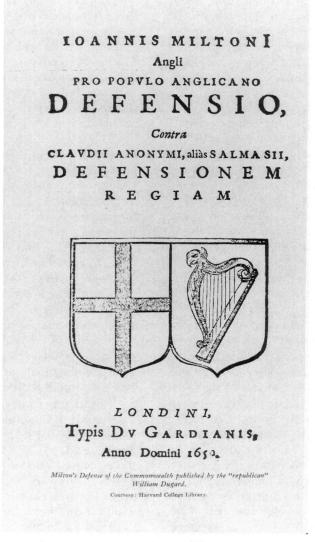

IOANNIS MILTONI
Angli
PRO POPVLO ANGLICANO
DEFENSIO,
Contra
CLAVDII ANONYMI, aliàs SALMASII,
DEFENSIONEM
REGIAM

LONDINI,
Typis DV GARDIANIS,
Anno Domini 1650.

Milton's Defense of the Commonwealth published by the "republican"
William Dugard.
Courtesy: Harvard College Library.

Title page for Milton's defense of the Commonwealth

lowed the Licensing Ordinance to influence his conduct, not bothering to obtain the stipulated approval for *The Doctrine and Discipline of Divorce.* Now he chose to defy the ordinance more flamboyantly: not only did he have his arguments against it published without permission but he also, by the way in which he constructed the title, made his responsibility for this insubordinate gesture an integral part of the gesture itself.

Milton offers many arguments against prepublication censorship; the final and most important one is that censorship impedes the progress of truth. For centuries truth had been conceived of as something settled, a body of interrelated dogmas that, once properly apprehended, was no more capable of alteration than was the immutable God whose manifestation it was. Milton did not invent the alternative conception of truth he brings forward in *Areopagitica;* it had been gaining ground in radical Protestant circles for some time. But his is the most forceful exposition to that point of the idea that truth is not a thing at all but a process — that very process of untrammeled inquiry and debate that had been taking place since the rule of bishops and absolutist courtiers had been overthrown. Parliament should not fear and repress but should encourage and embrace, as the happiest of the many happy results of its policies, this splendid emergence of empowerment and articulation. Truth would be revealed in ever greater fullness only if such collective intellectual energy were permitted to be freely manifested in perpetuity.

By 1644 Milton had been tutoring his nephews for more than four years. An acquaintance who was devoted to educational reform urged him to make public his thoughts on this question. The result was *Of Education,* published in June 1644. In a well-known phrase that reflects the heady optimism of those early days of the revolution, Milton says that the purpose of education is "to repair the ruins of our first parents." Grounding his ideas in positive recollections of St. Paul's and negative ones of Cambridge, as well as in his own teaching practices, Milton proposes that the Scholastic abstractions that continue to dominate university education be replaced by a course of study in which students attain to knowledge of the abstract by way of the concrete and of the complex by way of the simple. The Fall is to be reversed by a curriculum based on a sense of reality.

For almost four years after the publication of his final divorce tracts in the spring of 1645 Milton wrote no more prose pamphlets. Sometime that year a reconciliation with his wife was effected. In 1646 Mary Powell Milton gave birth to a daughter, Anne, and in 1648 to a second daughter, Mary. At some point in the 1640s Milton began to have trouble with his eyesight. He probably began composing *The History of Britain, That Part Especially Now Call'd England. From the First Traditional Beginning, Continu'd to the Norman Conquest. Collected out of the Antientist and Best Authors Thereof* (1670) during these years and perhaps completed his grammar and logic textbooks and *A Brief History of Moscovia* (1682).

This period of renewed mental cultivation on Milton's part was also a period of dramatic developments in the political realm: the formation, at the instigation of the Independent and radical forces led by Oliver Cromwell, of an army that would fight the war more energetically; its victory over the Royalist forces; the deterioration of relations between the army and Parliament, along with efforts by the defeated king to turn these quarrels among his enemies to his own advantage; the king's resumption of the war and his immediate defeat. In the autumn and winter of 1648–1649 Parliament was purged by the army of its conservative and Presbyterian members. Charles was tried and, on 30 January 1649, put to death as a tyrant.

Within two weeks of the regicide, Milton was in print with *The Tenure of Kings and Magistrates,* written in rejoinder to the multitude of sermons and pamphlets by the Presbyterians denouncing the proceedings against the king. The presbyterians maintained that the army's coup d'état was illegal; the Bible and Protestant political thought commanded

obedience to lawful authority. With the same emphasis on the inherent prerogatives of the ordinary person that had characterized his prose from the beginning, Milton responds with the contractual arguments he had used in his divorce pamphlets: the subject's allegiance to the king is conditional on the king's ruling justly; a failure to rule justly leaves the subject with the right conferred by his native human dignity to seek redress consistent with that dignity; if the injustice has been so flagrant as to amount to tyranny, he is justified in punishing the tyrant.

Milton also devotes himself to demonstrating that the Presbyterians' present position is opposed to their past actions: in their previous exhortations to resist the king, they had begun the process of punishing him that the army and High Court of Justice are only bringing to a logical conclusion. *The Tenure of Kings and Magistrates,* however, leaves the impression not of triumphant counterattack but of frustrated defense. The same charges of traitorous inconsistency are leveled again and again, suggesting that Milton senses that his trenchant reasoning and biting eloquence have not laid the opposition of the Presbyterians decisively to rest and betraying an uneasy awareness on Milton's part that the actions of the army and radical Independents had little support in the nation at large.

A month after the publication of *The Tenure of Kings and Magistrates* Milton accepted an offer from the Council of State of the new English republic to be its secretary for foreign languages. His primary task would be composing and translating diplomatic correspondence, but he would also function as a propagandist for the government. He was at once ordered to begin working at the latter aspect of his new job: Charles I's representative in Ireland had concluded a treaty with the Irish Catholics and was negotiating with the Ulster Presbyterians, and there was a real danger that a potent Royalist coalition, devoted to placing the slain monarch's son, Prince Charles, on the throne of England, would be formed. Milton's endeavor to defuse this threat, "Observations on the Articles of Peace," was in print by mid May. His primary rhetorical strategy was to stress the Royalists' open alliance with Irish Catholics.

Milton's next official rhetorical chore immediately awaited him. Within days of the regicide there had appeared a book entitled Εικων βασιλικη [*Eikon Basilike*]: *The Pourtraicture of His Sacred Maiestie in His Solitudes and Sufferings.* This work proved to be the most spectacularly successful piece of propaganda of the seventeenth century. In every respect *Eikon Basilike* was masterfully calculated to play on traditional veneration for the monarch as a sanctified, quasi-divine figure and to stir up fears of the incalculable consequences that would be visited on the nation if substantial atonement – such as the acceptance of the martyred king's son as his successor – were not soon forthcoming.

Milton's answer, ʼEIKONOKΛAʼΣTHΣ [*Eikonoklastes*], was published in October 1649, but the battle was already over. *Eikonoklastes* is, indeed, devastatingly iconoclastic, demonstrating that *Eikon Basilike* is as deceptive a piece of sentimentality and theatricality as the verses, plays, and masques that were so central a feature of court life during Charles's reign. It was a hollow victory, however. In the context established by the posture of paternal magnanimity taken by *Eikon Basilike,* any vigorous refutation was bound to seem cruel – an impression Milton exacerbated by writing in tones of haughty contempt. In the second edition, published in 1650, this hauteur is combined with abuse of the English people for their foolishly fond reception of *Eikon Basilike*. Like the attacks on the presbyterians in *The Tenure of Kings and Magistrates,* the repetitiousness of this litany of denunciation testifies only to the writer's sense of political weakness, his inability to reduce the forces arrayed against him to manageable proportions.

The Commonwealth regime faced rhetorical assault in 1649 from yet another quarter. The eminent scholar Claudius Salmasius had been commissioned by Prince Charles to write something that would discredit the regicides in the court of educated European public opinion. The resulting Latin treatise, *Defensio Regia, pro Carolo I* (The Defense of King Charles I), was in print by November 1649. The Council of State delegated to its secretary for foreign languages the task of composing a reply. To Milton this was the opportunity of a lifetime. He had dedicated himself to learning, eloquent discourse, and the fight for liberty; he had hoped that the eloquent discourse would primarily take the form of poetry, but the exigencies of the fight for liberty seemed to be dictating otherwise. Here, at least, was a chance both to strike a blow for liberty and, given the stature of his opponent, attain the sort of intellectual fulfillment and glory to which he had always aspired. Despite a warning from his doctors that the effort of producing such a work would result in total blindness, he at once accepted the challenge.

Salmasius sets forth the familiar Royalist claim that a king is the father of his people and holds his office by divine right. The killing of a king, therefore, combines the worst of crimes: sacrilege and parricide. Salmasius also stresses that the regicide had been carried out by a small group of army officers and fanatics, with virtually no support from the nation as a whole. Milton's Latin answer, *Joannis Miltoni Angli pro Populo Anglicano Defensio contra Claudii Anonyomi, aliàs Salmasii, Defensionem Regiam* (The Defense of the People of England, by John Milton, Englishman, against the Defense of the King by Claudius Anonymous, Alias Salmasius), was published in February 1651. It repeats the arguments of *The Tenure of Kings and Magistrates* about the conditional nature of all government, and it also makes use of the sort of ridicule that Milton had employed ten years before against Bishop Hall and that was a common feature of seventeenth-century polemics. To the charge of oligarchy Milton offers the response to which he would thenceforth stubbornly cling: that in politics the key categories are not majorities and minorities but virtue and merit; if it is only a minority that is prepared to act decisively on behalf of true political principles, so be it.

Milton's rhetorical victory over Salmasius was more complete than he had dared to hope. Throughout 1651 there were reports that his *Defensio* was being eagerly read and admired everywhere on the Continent. He had scored a smashing success not only for the Commonwealth but also for himself personally. Not until the summer of 1652 did there appear a Royalist reply of sufficient force to necessitate a rebuttal: the anonymously published *Regii Sanguinis Clamor ad Cœlum adversus Parricidas Anglicanos* (The Cry of the King's Blood to Heaven, against the English Parricides). Responding to Milton's ridicule of Salmasius, the work revives the heresy-mongering of the divorce controversy: small wonder, it said, that a demonic enemy of the family was also the foe of divinely constituted government.

Milton did not reply until May 1654. In *Joannis Miltoni Angli pro Populo Anglicano Defensio Secunda* (The Second Defense of the People of England, by John Milton, Englishman) he propounds once again the cases for regicide and rule by a meritocratic elite, offers an elegantly crafted autobiography, and vilifies the author of *Regii Sanguinis Clamor ad Cœlum adversus Parricidas Anglicanos,* whom he had come erroneously to believe was Alexander More, a Continental clergyman and professor. *Defensio Secunda* also includes panegyrics to Cromwell and other leaders of the revolution, not all of whom were in accord with one another by this time. It closes with a plea for liberty of conscience addressed to Cromwell, who the year before had dis-

Bust of Milton, circa 1654 (Christ's College, Cambridge)

solved the Commonwealth and established the quasi-monarchical Protectorate, and with advice for the entire nation to the effect that the fight for liberty will have been in vain if it is not henceforth accompanied by a recognition that liberty and a wholehearted commitment to virtue are one and the same thing. It has been argued that the defenses, especially the *Defensio Secunda,* should be regarded as the fulfillment in prose of Milton's epic ambitions, a narrative on the grand scale of a nation's unfinished struggle to transform itself.

But what had begun as high drama or epic, with national destinies and major intellectual reputations at stake, was about to conclude as farce. Milton had chosen to have the *Defensio Secunda* published exactly as he had written it, in spite of having received, in advance of publication, credible information that More had not written *Regii Sanguinis*

Clamor ad Cœlum adversus Parricidas Anglicanos. In October 1654 More published a vindication of himself, protesting his innocence of the authorship of the earlier work, but Milton refused to budge. In August 1655 he brought out *Joannis Miltoni pro Se Defensio contra Alexandrum Morum Ecclesiasten, Libelli Famosi, cui Titulus, Regii Sanguinis Clamor ad Cœlum adversùs Parricidas Anglicanos, Authorem Rectè Dictum* (The Defense of Himself by John Milton, Englishman, against the Clergyman Alexander More, Who Is Rightly Called the Author of an Infamous Libel Entitled The Cry of the King's Blood to Heaven, against the English Parricides), offering the lamest of justifications for continuing to regard More as the author of *Regii Sanguinis Clamor ad Cœlum adversus Parricidas Anglicanos* and reiterating his indictment of More's character.

In March 1651 Milton's wife had given birth to a son, John. In February 1652 the predictions of ·

Milton's doctors about the consequences of his writing the first *Defensio* had been borne out: Milton had become entirely blind. In May a daughter, Deborah, had been born; three days later, Mary Powell Milton had died, and shortly thereafter the fifteen-month-old John Milton, Jr., was also dead.

In spite of his blindness, Milton continued until 1659 as secretary for foreign languages. By the sort of irony in which victorious revolutionaries almost inevitably become entangled, the author of *Areopagitica* was called on to be the government's licenser of printed materials. In 1651 he had approved the publication of the Racovian Catechism, the testament of faith of the Socinians of Poland, in which the Trinity was denied and other heresies were affirmed. From 1652 onward, others, Andrew Marvell and John Dryden among them, were employed alongside Milton.

Beginning in 1655, Milton had more leisure for the cultivation of his mind; he may have begun composing *Paradise Lost* at this time. Most scholars believe that he also began work in the mid 1650s on *De Doctrina Christiana* (Of Christian Doctrine), a Latin treatise in which he attempts to reconstruct Christian theology from the ground up. This work indicates Milton's agreement with the anti-Trinitarian heresy that he had permitted to be disseminated in the Racovian Catechism, and it indicates as well that he had become heterodox on other points. The manuscript for the work was lost at Milton's death and not recovered until the early nineteenth century. It was first published in 1825 and is now regarded as an aid to the understanding of Milton's major poems.

On 12 November 1656 Milton married Katherine Woodcock. Eleven months later a daughter, Katherine, was born. In February and March 1658, respectively, Milton's wife and baby daughter both died.

This abrupt termination of Milton's attempt to reconstitute his domestic life was followed in September 1658 by the first of the series of events that would lead to the unraveling of his political life: the death of Cromwell, who had been named Lord Protector of England in 1654. Cromwell had become king in all but name, and his rule had gravitated in a conservative direction, to the increasing dissatisfaction of many of those who had been associated with him in the days of the regicide and the Commonwealth. With his death, restraints on the open expression of these conflicts were removed, and within two years the monarchy would be restored.

Questions relating to the church had in the meantime come to the fore. In spite of objections propounded by Milton and other radicals, neither the Commonwealth nor the Protectorate governments had based their ecclesiastical policies on an unqualified affirmation of liberty of conscience. In 1654 procedures had been established for examining the credentials of candidates for the ministry and dismissing scandalous or incompetent incumbents. No provision was made for an official confession of faith, but clergymen were to continue to be paid by the state.

From Milton's point of view, it was bad enough that the concept of an established church had not been renounced. But matters had been made even worse by another recent development: a conference of leading Independent clergymen had drafted a confession of faith, the Savoy Declaration. The very existence of such a document, however tolerant, was objectionable to Milton: it could easily be used as a test of orthodoxy, inhibiting the free flow of speculation and discourse that Milton had commended in *Areopagitica* and in which he was probably engaged at the moment, if he was in fact working on *De Doctrina Christiana*.

In an effort to avert these dangers, in February 1659 Milton addressed to Parliament *A Treatise of Civil Power in Ecclesiastical Causes*, his first prose pamphlet in English in nine years. Writing in a relatively plain style, he offers a succinct argument for the separation of church and state. First, the Protestant faith is based on the Bible as understood by each individual believer. The only genuine faith is an inwardly persuaded, conscientious faith. No external power, therefore, can legitimately compel anyone to believe in any particular set of dogmas or form of worship. All church society is voluntary, and all church discipline is spiritual only. A wayward member of a particular church can be excommunicated but cannot be fined or imprisoned.

Moreover, state coercion in religion violates the essential nature of the New Testament. The difference between the New and Old Testament dispensations is precisely that Christ set regenerate believers free from the external ecclesiastical apparatus of the Old Testament, as well as from many other aspects of external authority. External law in matters of religion – set forms, places, times, and creeds – no longer applies. And if people are not now required to obey what God himself had once commanded, they certainly do not have to obey what mere human beings have later invented.

In August 1659 Milton dealt with the related question of the payment of clergy in *Considerations Touching the Likeliest Means to Remove Hirelings out of the Church*. The primary form of clerical maintenance in the Church of England was tithes, the requirement that parishioners yield up one-tenth of their incomes and resources for the support of parish priests. Demands for the reform or elimination of this practice had formed part of the debate about the church throughout the two decades of the revolution; in 1659 the issue continued to be energetically discussed, with radicals – including the Quakers, who had emerged in the 1650s as the distillation of everything that had been appalling conservatives since the early 1640s – arguing and petitioning once again for the abolition of tithes.

To Milton, tithes were profoundly incompatible with the essential nature of the Christian religion. Christ having abolished all aspects of the Old Testament state church, there was no further justification for a clerical caste in the pay of the state. What qualifies any given believer to preach and teach is not an education at one of the established universities but the inward prompting of the Holy Spirit. The requisite linguistic, theological, and historical knowledge can be obtained at relatively little expense by private study. The financial support of such an inspired minister can only come from the freely given contributions of those to whom he ministers, not from taxation. Moreover, such ministers should also be capable, like the Apostles, of pursuing some practical trade or craft, thus breaking the spiritually dangerous link between economic interest and ministerial practice.

Considerations Touching the Likeliest Means to Remove Hirelings out of the Church was addressed to a different Parliament than *A Treatise of Civil Power in Ecclesiastical Causes* had been, for during the intervening six months the conflict between conservatives and radicals had come to a head. In April the radicals in the army and Parliament had dissolved the conservative Parliament sitting at the time of *A Treatise of Civil Power in Ecclesiastical Causes*. They had then proceeded not only to depose Richard Cromwell, the son whom Oliver Cromwell had chosen to succeed him as lord protector, but also to bring the Protectorate to an end and recall the Parliament known as the Rump, which in 1649, after the ejection of the recalcitrant majority of the members of the Long Parliament, had carried out the trial and execution of Charles I. It was to the Rump that Milton offered his thoughts on questions of ecclesiastical economics.

But the Rump proved incapable of developing a stable ruling coalition. The dilemma remained the same as it had been all along: putting into practice the central republican principle of consent of the governed would mean the end of the republican re-

gime. Various constitutional schemes were floated; most involved withholding the franchise from the great majority of the nation, which would, if given the opportunity, vote to bring back the monarchy.

By October the army and the Rump were at loggerheads as significant elements in the army began to suspect that the Rump was no longer fully committed to what was then being called "the good old cause." In the middle of the month the army forced the Rump to bring its deliberations to an end, and the nation was left without a legislative body. The situation had become desperate indeed if the few remaining radicals could no longer agree among themselves. Among the voices immediately contributing to the search for a way out of the impasse was that of Milton. On 20 October he dictated the brief "A Letter to a Friend, Concerning the Ruptures of the Commonwealth," condemning the army's coup and proposing that the crisis be resolved by the establishment of a senate based on two fundamental points: religious liberty for all conscientious Protestants and the denial of sovereignty to any "single person." The army would appoint the members of the senate, including as many members of the Rump as would agree to these two points. In stunning testimony to Milton's awareness that there was no hope of obtaining the consent of the governed for his or any other republican constitution, he proposed that senate membership be lifelong (he did not specify how a deceased senator was to be replaced). As a safeguard against the danger of oligarchy manifestly inherent in this scheme, he suggested a more consensually based system of county government.

"A Letter to a Friend" was not published during Milton's lifetime (it first appeared in a collection of his works edited by John Toland in 1698) and is of interest primarily because it contains the gist of the proposals that were more fully presented a few months later in his final, quixotically courageous pamphlet, *The Readie & Easie Way to Establish a Free Commonwealth* (1660). The hopeless circumstances in which this work was published were primarily the result of the intervention of George Monck, the commander of the army in Scotland. Certain that the current situation of naked military rule was untenable, Monck brought pressure to bear for the renewed sitting of the Rump. In this move he was seconded by various other forces, particularly the City of London, where demands for a newly elected Parliament were also beginning to be heard. In the midst of these agitations of November and December, Milton composed "Proposalls of Certaine Expedients for the Preventing of a Civill War Now

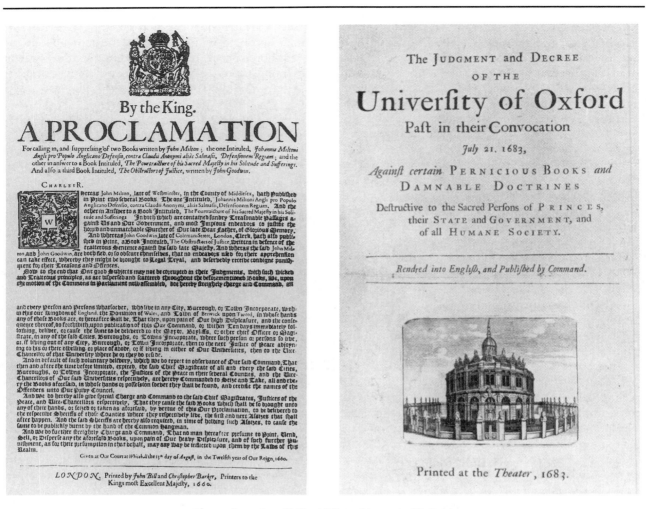

Two condemnations of Milton's Eikonoklastes *and* Defensio

Feared, & the Settling of a Firme Government," essentially another manuscript draft for what was to become *The Readie & Easie Way to Establish a Free Commonwealth,* adding ideas for legal and educational reform on the local level. This work was also not published in Milton's lifetime (it first appeared in volume eighteen of *The Works of John Milton,* 1931–1938).

The Rump was restored in late December, but it immediately had to cope with two ominous developments: Monck's decision, unbidden by it, to march his army from Scotland to London; and demands for new parliamentary elections that were increasing daily in volume and intensity from all over England. By early February 1660 Monck and his army were in London. A few days later Monck sent the Rump an ultimatum demanding that it make itself a more genuinely representative body by holding elections to fill its vacant seats, many of which had remained empty since the expulsion in 1648 of the members opposed to any proceedings against Charles I.

This demand amounted to a declaration on Monck's part that he wanted the monarchy restored. The Rump made one last show of resistance, drawing up restrictions on who was eligible to run for office that would have ensured that no supporters of a restoration would have become members. Monck thereupon forced the readmission of enough of the presbyterian members who had been expelled in 1648 to constitute a majority of the body. Parliament thus became a reasonable facsimile of the pre-1649 Long Parliament, which had never wanted to do away with the monarchy in the first place. The restrictive qualifications on candidacy for a new Parliament were at once abolished, and preparations began to be made to hold elections for a Parliament that would have the nation's mandate to invite Prince Charles to occupy the throne as Charles II.

The Readie & Easie Way to Establish a Free Commonwealth was published in two editions. The first was written during the brief interval in February when the Rump had promulgated its restrictive electoral qualifications. Thus, the way was apparently "readie and easie" for the implementation of the scheme Milton had concocted the previous autumn. Reconstituted by the elections that were about to take place, the Rump could simply establish itself as Milton's perpetual senate. By the time the tract was published, however, the situation had completely changed, as Milton acknowledges in a prefatory paragraph. With a majority of Parliament hostile to the republican enterprise, the restoration of monarchy was inevitable; the idea of a ready and easy stabilizing of republican rule had become unrealistic, as Milton must have realized on some level.

Indeed, he almost certainly realized it while he was composing the pamphlet, before events had turned decisively in the direction of a restoration. *The Readie & Easie Way to Establish a Free Commonwealth* alternates between ostentatiously calm descriptions of its proposed constitutional settlement and sprawling passages of prophetic denunciation of the popular clamor for monarchy. It is the passages of prophetic rage that have the last word. As in *The Tenure of Kings and Magistrates* and *Eikonoklastes,* the reader is left with the impression that the forces hell-bent on a restoration are too strong to be held in check, despite the strenuous efforts of the most distinguished rhetorical champion of English republicanism. Milton brings his part in the fight for liberty to conclusion and climax by representing himself as going down fighting for liberty.

He had not quite finished fighting for it, however. It was probably a few days after the first edition of *The Readie & Easie Way to Establish a Free Commonwealth* was published that he drafted a letter to General Monck, "The Present Means, and Brief Delineation of a Free Comonwealth," (first published in the 1698 collection), suggesting a procedure for organizing the forthcoming elections so as to guarantee a republican result. His suggestions were ignored, and by the latter part of March 1660 the elections were in progress. Also by this time the writing and dissemination of arguments against monarchy had become dangerous. The bookseller of the first edition of *The Readie & Easie Way to Establish a Free Commonwealth* was arrested on 27 March. Milton nevertheless published a revised and expanded second edition, perhaps in an attempt, which he had to have realized was doomed, to influence the outcome of the elections. The tone and structure of the first edition are retained and intensified. Milton speaks as an even more impassioned biblical prophet, crying woe upon a backsliding, degenerate nation that is refusing to listen.

There was one additional minor episode in Milton's revolutionary prose career, *Brief Notes upon a Late Sermon, Titl'd, The Fear of God and the King* published sometime before 20 April 1660 in reply to a prematurely exultant welcoming of the Restoration by an Episcopalian divine. Milton desperately proposes that if a king cannot be avoided, let it be General Monck himself.

But the king who was not to be avoided would be Charles II. The proud defender of regicide had good reason to fear retribution at the hands of the new government, and he went into hiding. The recently passed Act of Indemnity and Oblivion granted pardon for actions committed during the previous twenty years that the restored monarchy regarded as crimes, but some were excepted from its provisions: along with those directly involved in the regicide, twenty additional men would be singled out as meriting punishment.

In June 1660, as the identity of the twenty marked men was being debated, Parliament issued an order for the arrest of Milton and the public burning of *Eikonoklastes* and the first *Defensio.* Milton's name was brought up as the twentieth and last man on the list, but nobody seconded the motion, and the list was completed with another name. It is thought that among those interceding on Milton's behalf was Marvell, his former colleague in the work of the office of the secretary for foreign languages and at this time a member of Parliament. Milton came out of hiding, and within a few months, probably in November 1660, the order for his arrest was carried out. He petitioned for pardon under the Act of Indemnity and Oblivion; the petition was granted, and in mid December he was released. One hostile member of Parliament remarked in the course of the proceedings that, as far as he was concerned, Milton deserved hanging.

The remainder of Milton's life was, for the most part, lived out of the public eye. On 24 February 1663 he married his third wife, Elizabeth Minshull. There was apparently bad feeling between Milton and his new wife, on the one hand, and at least some of his daughters, on the other.

Apart from such domestic difficulties, Milton could devote himself to the private cultivation of his mind. The exact periods of composition of those of his works that remained to be created and published remain uncertain, but he did not confine himself to poetry. *Paradise Lost* was published in 1667, *Paradise Regain'd* and *Samson Agonistes* together in 1671. He may have continued working on *De Doctrina Christiana,* and he almost certainly made final changes in *The History of Britain,* which he had begun in the 1640s and which was published in 1670. This chronicle of the rise and fall of chieftains and kings is probably intended as covert commentary on the failure of the revolution, as the narrative points toward the Norman Conquest as a national punishment analogous to the Restoration.

In the last years of his life and first few years after his death several of Milton's old manuscripts were published: in 1669 *Accedence Commenc't Grammar,* a textbook probably written in the 1640s when he was teaching his nephews; in 1672 the *Artis Logicæ Plenior* (Art of Logic), another textbook from the same period; in 1674 the Cambridge school exercises, the *Prolusiones,* in a volume of his letters; in 1681 the *Character of the Long Parliament,* an indictment of the conservative forces in the revolutionary coalition that was intended to be inserted in *The History of Britain* and is believed to have been composed in the late 1640s; and in 1682 *A Brief History of Moscovia,* a geographical and historical survey probably also written in the 1640s for pedagogical purposes.

Milton wrote two additional prose works during his last years. In 1673 he brought out a pamphlet, *Of True Religion, Hæresie, Schism, Toleration, and What Best Means May Be Us'd against the Growth of Popery,* on the issue that had always most centrally concerned him: liberty of conscience. In 1672 Charles II had attempted to grant to Roman Catholics, and incidentally to former Puritans as well, some relief from the coercive Restoration ecclesiastical settlement. But a "no Popery" agitation had immediately erupted, and during its meeting of February and March 1673 Parliament annulled Charles's proclamation. Parliament also proceeded, however, to debate a bill that would have significantly widened liberty of conscience for the former Puritans, who were known by this time as Nonconformists. *Of True Religion* was Milton's attempt to influence this legislative situation. It repeats the arguments from *A Treatise of Civil Power,* stressing, in view of the widespread hostility to Roman Catholicism, the argument that liberty of conscience is virtually the defining characteristic of Protestantism. Milton also hoped to convince Parliament to alter the bill so that toleration would be more widely extended, even to those who denied the Trinity. Finally, *A Declaration, or Letters Patents of the Election of This Present King of Poland John the Third* (1674) was perhaps intended, by its portrayal of an elected as opposed to a hereditary monarch, as another piece of oblique political commentary.

Milton's prose is not Milton's poetry. On the other hand, Milton's poetry would not have been what it became without Milton's prose, and scholars are no longer inclined to dismiss the prose as a subtraction from a larger body of poetry that might have been. With the preference since the 1970s for a more historically informed literary criticism there has been increasing fascination with the idea that a figure long accounted England's second-greatest poet (after William Shakespeare) placed himself, during the prime of his life, near the center of a series of historical events that played an important part in the emergence of the modern world. Milton's prose writings are intensely interesting because the English Revolution is intensely interesting.

Such an approach has consequences for perceptions of Milton's poetry as well. Between 1641 and 1660 Milton developed a set of political principles and commitments. He also came to appreciate the unfolding, dynamic nature of history in general and to understand the history of his own time in particular as a major turning point. What he had distilled from his political and historical experience he poured into the major poems that he wrote after gaining this experience. Especially in *Paradise Lost* he mobilized all the resources of ancient Western wisdom to meditate more effectively on the overall course of human historical development as it had unfolded into, and would continue to unfold into, the modern world. A faith in humanity's power to shape its own historical destiny has never been more movingly portrayed than in the concluding lines of *Paradise Lost.* There, in spite of a record of failure and defeat that would extend from the Fall to the calamitous events of 1660 and beyond, the representatives of the human race set forth into a world that continues to lie all before them, open to their initiatives and efforts.

In November 1674 John Milton died of the gout, from which he had been suffering for several years. As a poet he had achieved all that he had hoped to achieve, and more. As a prose writer, his best epitaph is perhaps the closing words of one of his last pamphlets: "I in the mean while have borne my witnes not out of season to the church and to my countrey."

Bibliographies:

David Harrison Stevens, *Reference Guide to Milton: from 1800 to the Present Day* (Chicago: University of Chicago Press, 1930);

Calvin Huckabay, *John Milton: An Annotated Bibliography, 1929–1968* (Pittsburgh: Duquesne University Press, 1969);

John T. Shawcross, *Milton: The Critical Heritage* (London: Routledge: 1970);

Shawcross, *Milton, 1732–1801: The Critical Heritage* (London: Routledge, 1972);

James Holly Hanford and William A. McQueen, *Milton,* second edition (Arlington Heights, Ill.: AHM, 1979);

Shawcross, *Milton: A Bibliography for the Years 1624–1700* (Binghamton, N.Y.: Medieval & Renaissance Texts & Studies, 1984);

C. A. Patrides, *An Annotated Critical Bibliography of John Milton* (Brighton, U.K.: Harvester, 1987);

P. J. Klemp, *The Essential Milton: An Annotated Bibliography of Major Modern Studies* (Boston: G. K. Hall, 1989).

Biographies:

David Masson, *The Life of John Milton: Narrated in Connexion with the Political, Ecclesiastical, and Literary History of His Time,* 7 volumes (Cambridge & London: Macmillan, 1859–1894);

Helen Darbishire, ed., *Early Lives of Milton* (London: Constable, 1932);

J. Milton French, *The Life Records of John Milton,* 5 volumes (New Brunswick, N.J.: Rutgers University Press, 1949–1958);

William R. Parker, *Milton: A Biography,* 2 volumes (Oxford: Oxford University Press, 1968);

A. N. Wilson, *The Life of John Milton* (Oxford: Oxford University Press, 1983);

John T. Shawcross, *John Milton: The Self and the World* (Lexington: University Press of Kentucky, 1993).

References:

David Aers and Gunther Kress, "Historical Process, Individuals and Communities in Milton's *Areopagitica,*" in *Literature, Language and Society in England, 1580–1680,* by Aers, Kress, and Bob Hodge (Totowa, N.J.: Barnes & Noble, 1981), pp. 152–183;

Raymond A. Anselment, *"Betwixt Jest and Earnest": Marprelate, Milton, Marvell, Swift and the Decorum of Religious Ridicule* (Toronto: University of Toronto Press, 1979), pp. 61–93;

Arthur E. Barker, *Milton and the Puritan Dilemma, 1641–1660* (Toronto: University of Toronto Press, 1942);

Joan S. Bennett, *Reviving Liberty: Radical Christian Humanism in Milton's Great Poems* (Cambridge, Mass.: Harvard University Press, 1989);

Bruce Boehrer, "Elementary Structures of Kingship: Milton, Regicide, and the Family," *Milton Studies,* 23 (1987): 97–117;

Thomas N. Corns, *The Development of Milton's Prose Style* (Oxford: Oxford University Press, 1982);

Corns, *Uncloistered Virtue: English Political Literature, 1640–1660* (Oxford: Oxford University Press, 1992), pp. 11–63, 194–220, 269–293;

Zera S. Fink, "The Development of Milton's Political Thought," *PMLA,* 57 (September 1942): 705–736;

Stanley E. Fish, "Driving from the Letter: Truth and Indeterminacy in Milton's *Areopagitica,*" in *Re-membering Milton: Essays on the Texts and Traditions,* edited by Mary Nyquist and Margaret W. Ferguson (London: Methuen, 1987), pp. 234–254;

Fish, "Reasons that Imply Themselves: Image, Argument, and the Reader in Milton's *Reason of Church Government,*" in his *Self-Consuming Artifacts: The Experience of Seventeenth-Century Literature* (Berkeley: University of California Press, 1972), pp. 265–302;

Michael Fixler, *Milton and the Kingdoms of God* (Evanston, Ill.: Northwestern University Press, 1964);

Kevin Gilmartin, "History and Reform in Milton's *Readie and Easie Way,*" *Milton Studies,* 24 (1988): 17–41;

Donald L. Guss, "Enlightenment as Process: Milton and Habermas," *PMLA,* 106 (October 1991): 1156–1169;

Gary D. Hamilton, "Milton and the Anti-Rump Tracts: On Revising *The Readie and Easie Way,*" *Renaissance Papers,* 36 (1989): 101–117;

K. G. Hamilton, "The Structure of Milton's Prose," in *Language and Style in Milton: A Symposium in Honor of the Tercentenary of Paradise Lost,* edited by Ronald D. Emma and John T. Shawcross (New York: Ungar, 1967), pp. 304–332;

Charles Hatten, "The Politics of Marital Reform and the Rationalization of Romance in *The Doctrine and Discipline of Divorce,*" *Milton Studies,* 27 (1991): 95–113;

Richard Helgerson, "Milton Reads the King's Book: Print, Performance, and the Making of a Bourgeois Idol," *Criticism,* 29 (Winter 1987): 1–25;

Christopher Hill, *Milton and the English Revolution* (New York: Viking, 1978);

James Holstun, ed., *Pamphlet Wars: Prose in the English Revolution* (London: Cass, 1992);

Holstun, *A Rational Millennium: Puritan Utopias of Seventeenth-Century England and America* (Oxford: Oxford University Press, 1987);

John Illo, "Areopagiticas Mythic and Real," *Prose Studies,* 11 (May 1988): 3–23;

Christopher Kendrick, *Milton: A Study in Ideology and Form* (London: Methuen, 1986);

Barbara K. Lewalski, "Milton: Political Beliefs and Polemical Methods, 1659–60," *PMLA,* 74 (June 1959): 191–202;

Michael Lieb and John T. Shawcross, eds., *Achievements of the Left Hand: Essays on the Prose of John Milton* (Amherst: University of Massachusetts Press, 1974);

Henry S. Limouze, "Joseph Hall and the Prose Style of John Milton," *Milton Studies,* 15 (1981): 121–141;

Limouze, "The Surest Suppressing: Writer and Censor in Milton's *Areopagitica,*" *Centennial Review,* 24 (Winter 1980): 103–117;

David Loewenstein, *Milton and the Drama of History: Historical Vision, Iconoclasm, and the Literary Imagination* (Cambridge: Cambridge University Press, 1990);

Loewenstein and James Grantham Turner, eds., *Politics, Poetics, and Hermeneutics in Milton's Prose* (Cambridge: Cambridge University Press, 1990);

Elizabeth M. Magnus, "Originality and Plagiarism in *Areopagitica and Eikonoklastes,*" *English Literary Renaissance,* 21 (Winter 1991): 87–101;

Annabel Patterson, "The Civic Hero in Milton's Prose," *Milton Studies,* 8 (1975): 71–101;

John M. Perlette, "Milton, Ascham, and the Rhetoric of the Divorce Controversy," *Milton Studies,* 10 (1977): 195–215;

Jason P. Rosenblatt, "Milton's Chief Rabbi," *Milton Studies,* 24 (1988): 43–71;

Irene Samuel, "Milton on the Province of Rhetoric," *Milton Studies,* 10 (1977): 177–193;

Ernest Sirluck, "Milton's Political Thought: The First Cycle," *Modern Philology,* 61 (1964): 209–224;

Elizabeth Skerpan, *The Rhetoric of Politics in the English Revolution, 1642–1660* (Columbia: University of Missouri Press, 1992);

Harry R. Smallenburg, "Contiguities and Moving Limbs: Style as Argument in *Areopagitica,*" *Milton Studies,* 9 (1976): 169–184;

Keith W. Stavely, *The Politics of Milton's Prose Style* (New Haven: Yale University Press, 1975);

Paul Stevens, "Discontinuities in Milton's Early Public Self-Representation," *Huntington Library Quarterly,* 51 (Autumn 1988): 261–280;

Turner, *One Flesh: Paradisal Marriage and Sexual Relations in the Age of Milton* (Oxford: Oxford University Press, 1987);

John A. Via, "Milton's Antiprelatical Tracts: The Poet Speaks in Prose," *Milton Studies,* 5 (1973): 87–127;

Michael Wilding, "Milton's *Areopagitica:* Liberty for the Sects," *Prose Studies,* 9 (September 1986): 7–38;

Don M. Wolfe, *Milton in the Puritan Revolution* (New York & London: Nelson, 1941).

Papers:

Milton materials are scattered around the world, but most of the important collections of manuscripts and early printed editions are in Britain and the United States. In Britain, the important depositories are the British Library in London, the Bodleian Library in Oxford, and the Trinity College Library in Cambridge. In the United States the important depositories are the New York Public Library, the Folger Shakespeare Library, the Henry E. Huntington Library, the Yale University Libraries, the University of Kentucky Libraries, the Columbia University Library, the Union Theological Seminary Library, the University of Illinois Library, and the Princeton University Library.

Sir Thomas Overbury

(circa 18 June 1581 – 15 September 1613)

Charles A. S. Ernst
Hilbert College

BOOKS: *A Wife, Now A Widowe* (London: Printed for Laurence L'isle, 1614); enlarged as *A Wife Now The Widdow Of Sir Thomas Overburye. Being A most exquisite and singular Poem of the choice of a Wife. Whereunto Are Added many witty Characters, and conceited Newes, written by himselfe and other learned Gentlemen his friends* (London: Printed for Lawrence Lisle, 1614); enlarged as *A Wife. Now The Widdow Of Sir Tho: Overburye. Being a most exquisite and singular Poem of the choice of a Wife. Whereunto Are Added many witty Characters, and conceited Newes, written by himselfe and other learned Gentlemen his friends. The third Impression; With addition of sundry other new Characters* (London: Printed by Edward Griffin for Lawrence Lisle, 1614); enlarged as *A Wife. Now The Widdow of Sir Tho: Overburye. Being a most exquisite and singular Poem of the choice of a Wife. Whereunto Are Added many witty Characters, and conceited Newes, written by himselfe and other learned Gentlemen his friends. The fourth Impression, enlarged with more Characters, than any of the former Editions* (London: Printed by G. Eld for Lawrence Lisle, 1614; enlarged, London: Printed by T. C. for Laurence Lisle, 1614); enlarged as *New and Choise Characters, of severall Authors: Together with that exquisite and unmatcht Poeme, The Wife, Written by Syr Thomas Overburie. With the former Characters and conceited Newes, All in one volume. With many other things added to this sixt Impression* (London: Printed by Thomas Creede for Laurence Lisle, 1615); revised and enlarged as *Sir Thomas Overburie His Wife, With New Elegies upon his (now knowne) untimely death. Whereunto are annexed, new Newes and Characters, written by himselfe and other learned Gentlemen. Editio Septima* (London: Printed by Edward Griffin for Laurence L'isle, 1616); enlarged as *Sir Thomas Overburie. His Wife. With New Elegies upon his (now knowne) Untimely Death. Whereunto are annexed, new Newes and Characters, written by himselfe and other learned Gentlemen. The Eight Impression* (London: Printed by Edward Griffin for Laurence L'isle, 1616); enlarged as *S*^{ir} *Thomas Overbury His Wife. With Addition Of many new Elegies upon his untimely and much lamented death. As Also New Newes, and divers more Characters, (never before annexed) written by himselfe and other learned Gentlemen. The ninth impression augmented* (London: Printed by Edward Griffin for Laurence L'isle, 1616); enlarged as *Sir Thomas Overbury His Wife. With Additions Of New Characters, and many other Wittie Conceits never before Printed. The eleventh Impression* (London: Printed for Laurence Lisle, 1622); republished as *The Illustrious Wife: Viz. That Excellent Poem, Sir Thomas Overburie's Wife. Illustrated By Giles Oldisworth, Nephew to the same Sir T. O. Prov. 31. 12. She will do him good and not evil, all the daies of her life* (London, 1673); republished as *The Wife, A Poem. Express'd in a Compleat Wife. With An Elegy on the Untimely Death of the Author, Poyson'd in the Tower, &c. By Sir Thomas Overbury. The 17th edition* (London: Printed by H. Hills, 1709);

The First And Second part of The Remedy of Love: Written by Sir Thomas Overbury Knight (London: Printed by Nicholas Okes for John Wels, 1620);

Sir Thomas Overbury His Observations In His Travailes Upon The State Of The Xvii. Provinces As They Stood Anno Dom. 1609. The Treatie of Peace being then on foote ([London]: Printed by B. Alsop for J. Parker, 1626); republished as *Observations Upon the Provinces United. And On The State Of France. Written by S*^{r} *Thomas Overbury* (London: Printed by T. Maxey for R. Marriot, 1651).

Editions: *The Miscellaneous Works In Verse and Prose of Sir Thomas Overbury, Knt. With Memoirs of his Life. The Tenth Edition* (London: Printed for J. Bouquet, 1753);

The Miscellaneous Works In Prose and Verse Of Sir Thomas Overbury, Knt. Now First Collected. Edited

Sir Thomas Overbury; portrait by Cornelius Janssen van Ceulen
(Bodleian Library, Oxford)

With Notes, And A Biographical Account Of The Author, By Edward F. Rimbault, LL.D., Etc. Etc., Library of Old Authors (London: John Russell Smith, 1856);

The Overburian Characters To which is added A Wife, edited by Wilfred James Paylor, Percy Reprints, no. 13 (Oxford: Blackwell, 1936; New York: AMS Press, 1977);

Characters or witty descriptions of the properties of Sundry Persons. Drawn from the pen of Sir Thomas Overbury (Chicago: Frumious Press, 1967);

The "Conceited Newes" Of Sir Thomas Overbury And His Friends: A Facsimile Reproduction Of The Ninth Impression Of 1616 Of Sir Thomas Overbury His Wife. With a Commentary And Textual Notes On The "Newes," edited by James E. Savage (Gainesville, Fla.: Scholars' Facsimiles & Reprints, 1968);

Sir Thomas Overbury: His Observations In His Travailes, The English Experience: Its Record in Early Printed Books Published in Facsimile, no. 154 (Amsterdam: Theatrum Orbis Terrarum / New York: Da Capo Press, 1969).

OTHER: "Crumbs Fall'n From King James' Table," in *The Prince's Cabala: Or Mysteries of State. Written by King James the First, and some Noblemen in his Reign, and in Queen Elizabeth's. With Isocrates' Discourse To A Prince, On Kingly Government. Translated from the Greek* (London: Printed for R. Smith & G. Strahan, 1715).

Writer, careerist, and political adviser, Sir Thomas Overbury is a minor literary figure associated with the vogue of seventeenth-century English character-writing, a prose form similar to the essay but loosely modeled on the short sketches of character types, such as "The Garrulous Man" and "The Coward," composed by the ancient Greek writer Theophrastus. From 1614 to 1664 Overbury's posthumous character book *A Wife Now a Widowe,* comprising poems, characters, and "conceited *Newes,*" was reprinted more frequently than other character books, including Joseph Hall's pioneering *Characters of Vertues and Vices* (1608) and John Earle's popular *Micro-cosmographie* (1628). Overbury's writings were inextricably linked to his murder in the

Two of the conspirators in the murder of Overbury: Robert and Frances Carr, Earl and Countess of Somerset; portraits by unknown artists (National Portrait Gallery, London)

Tower of London: unflagging public interest in his death by slow poisoning made the publication of his characters a bookseller's dream. Many of the more than eighty Overburian characters appearing in successive publications were written by "*other* learned Gentlemen his friends," including the playwright John Webster, who wrote thirty-two characters, and the playwright and pamphleteer Thomas Dekker, who contributed six prison characters; perhaps eleven or fewer of the sketches in the first edition were Overbury's. Yet his literary influence on character-writing cannot be measured solely by this slim output. The association of his name with character books ensured that such pieces would attract readers and encourage other writers to create sketches. Overbury's literary example in the sketches he did compose – and his contributors' work – set the pattern for contemporary writers. The Overburian sketches extended the range of depicted character types to include moral, social, and occupational categories and established a standard for witty expression that influenced later character-writers. The commercial success of Overbury's character book, however, owes as much to the sensational circumstances of his death as to the literary merits

of the sketches and the public's growing interest in the seventeenth-century English prose character.

Although the family home was at Bourton-on-the-Hill, Gloucestershire, the eldest surviving son of Nicholas and Mary Overbury was born in the home of his maternal grandfather, Giles Palmer, at Compton-Scorpion in the parish of Ilmington, Warwickshire, and was baptized at Barton-on-the-Heath on 18 June 1581. Overbury had an older sister, Frances; three younger sisters, Mary, Meriall, and Margaret; and two brothers, Giles and Walter, who – like their father and eldest brother – would eventually be knighted.

Overbury matriculated as a gentleman-commoner in Queen's College, Oxford, on 27 February 1595. He graduated with a Bachelor of Arts degree in 1598 and entered the Middle Temple, where university preparation in philosophy and logic were joined to legal studies. In 1601 he traveled to Edinburgh, where he met the person on whom his political success and ultimate fate would depend: Robert Carr, page to Sir George Home, Earl of Dunbar.

Eager for advancement Overbury gained employment in London with Sir Robert Cecil, the secretary of state; but four years after James I's corona-

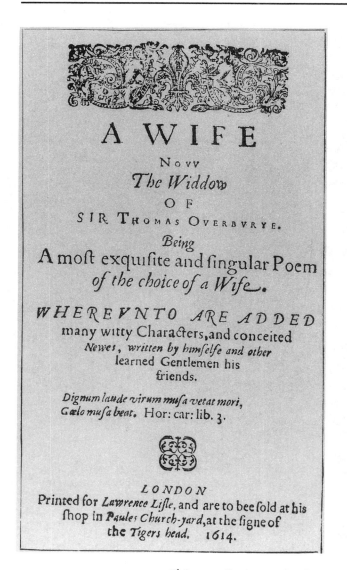

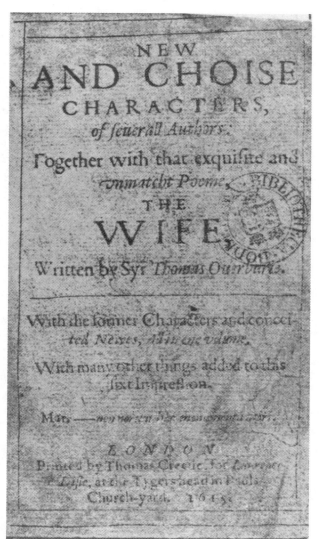

Title pages for the second and sixth editions of Overbury's character book

tion in 1603 Carr's political value as the king's favorite became evident. Carr lacked education and training in diplomatic affairs and increasingly relied on Overbury for advice — so much so that James's queen, Anne of Denmark, called Overbury Carr's governor. Her attitude toward her husband's attachment to attractive young men is shown in Overbury's "Crumbs Fall'n From King James's Table," written at court but not published until 1715 in *The Prince's Cabala:* he quotes James as observing that "The Queen was angry with me for receiving many men whome she had discountenanced, when indeed all their fault was, love to me...." Overbury's portrait by Cornelius Janssen van Ceulen reveals a lean, handsome face somewhat resembling that of his greater literary

contemporary John Donne, and Carr was similarly striking. Since James was attached to Carr, Carr and Overbury became a formidable "power" couple at court.

Carr was knighted on 23 or 24 December 1607 and, either at that time or shortly afterward, appointed gentleman of the bed chamber. Through Carr's influence Overbury received his knighthood on 19 June 1608 at Greenwich, and Overbury's father became a judge in Wales. When further advancement did not materialize, Overbury traveled to the Low Countries and France in 1609 and wrote *Sir Thomas Overbury His Observations in His Travailes upon the State of the Xvii. Provinces as They Stood Anno Dom. 1609.* Unlike Owen Felltham's *A Brief Character of the Low-Countries under the States* (1652) — a witty extension of character-writing that profiled countries as "types" – Overbury made little attempt to infuse his work with the far-fetched and clever comparisons or conceited wit that would make the Overburian characters distinctive. An exercise in self-fashioning, the book is less remarkable for displaying Overbury's grasp of the two countries' governments, military strength, economy, geography, and people than for advertising to the English court his diplomatic mettle. That this text would only appear in print in 1626 to promote the sale of books by a man whose murder had made him a household name is an irony of Overbury's political and literary career.

Overbury's other texts were written at court. Aside from collecting King James's "crumbs," Overbury may have composed between 1605 and 1610 – as a parlor game with other courtiers – examples of "conceited *Newes.*" Samples by several hands offering aphoristic comments on court and country, nation and city, bedchamber and chimney corner, appear in Overbury's character book, including his own "Newes from Court." James E. Savage observes that the "carefully wrought beginnings and endings, uniform images, self-conscious use of the conceit, and, in general, an approach scornful or ironic" suggest kinship with character-writing, which may also have emerged as a pastime at court, given the influence of Isaac Casaubon's editions of Theophrastan sketches (1592, 1599, 1612) and Ben Jonson's character descriptions in *Every Man out of His Humor* (1600) and *Cynthia's Revels* (1601), followed by the 1608 publication of Hall's character book.

Appreciating Overbury's literary gifts, Jonson read Overbury's poem "A Wife," elaborating a wife's ideal character in forty-seven stanzas, to Sir Philip Sidney's daughter, Elizabeth Manners, Countess of Rutland, who praised the line, "He comes too *neere,* that comes *to be denide.*" In a conversation in January 1619 recorded by William Drummond of Hawthornden, Jonson acknowledged that "Overbury was first his friend, then turn'd his mortall enimie" when Jonson "discorded with Overburie" over the latter's intent to court Lady Rutland through Jonson's reading.

Carr had the king's ear, but Overbury had Carr's. Thus when Carr became Viscount Rochester on 25 March 1611, Overbury's influence soared. After the death on 24 May 1612 of Cecil, who had become the earl of Salisbury on 4 May 1605, the king assumed Cecil's secretarial duties with Rochester's and Overbury's assistance. Unofficially, Overbury became an undersecretary of state, writing reports and advising James, through Rochester, in support of a pro-

Protestant foreign policy. From this powerful vantage point Overbury fell victim to court intrigue.

The cause of Overbury's downfall was Frances Howard, Countess of Essex. Disenchanted with her husband, Robert Devereux, third Earl of Essex, she turned from dalliance with the king's son, Henry, Prince of Wales, to become Rochester's mistress. The liaison was initially encouraged by Overbury, who was, nevertheless, wary of the Howard family's pro-Catholic sympathies. In 1612, when the annulment of her marriage to Essex made remarriage to Rochester possible, Overbury opposed Rochester's contemplated union with a woman of such low character. Overbury's "A Wife," employed to flatter Lady Rutland, was available to remind Rochester of virtues lacking in Lady Essex. Another Overburian poem, *The Remedy of Love* (1620), paraphrasing Ovid, may have furnished additional arguments: it offers practical advice on how to fall out of love.

Literary persuasion could not compete with Lady Essex's charms, and it was decided to silence Overbury by removing him from court. He was offered an embassy to help establish an English protectorate in northern Russia against Poland and Sweden; but Rochester encouraged Overbury to refuse the ambassadorship, and James had Overbury arrested on 21 April 1613.

Mistakenly imagining that he had Rochester's support, Overbury languished in the Tower for nearly five months while Lady Essex and accomplices tried repeatedly to poison him. On 15 September 1613 he finally succumbed. Lady Essex married Rochester, who by this time had become earl of Somerset, on 26 December. The plot was discovered, and the sensational trials of 1615, known as the Great Oyer of Poisoning, led to the hanging of several accomplices: Anne Turner; the apothecary James Franklin; Sir Gervase Elwes, the lieutenant of the Tower; and his underkeeper Richard Weston. Somerset and his wife were sentenced to death, remanded to the Tower, released in 1622, and confined to Oxford quarters until Somerset received a full pardon on 7 October 1624. The scandalous events were retold in works such as *The Bloody downfall of Adultery, Murder, Ambition* (1615) that attracted readers for decades.

When Overbury died, his literary life began. "A Wife," rechristened *A Wife, Now a Widowe,* was published in 1614. To meet public demand for Overburian material, the bookseller Lawrence Lisle ballasted later printings with characters and other texts by Overbury and his friends. By 1622 the eleventh impression included elegies on the death of

Engraving of Overbury by Renold Elstrack

Overbury by Daniel Tuvill and others; memorial verses for Lord William Hayward, Baron of Effingham, and Lady Rutland; more than eighty characters, including sketches attributed to Overbury, Webster, Dekker, Donne ("The true Character of a Dunce"), John Cocke (or Cooke), and Sir Henry Wotton (the versified "Character Of a happie life"); "conceited *Newes*," by Overbury and others; courtly *"Edicts"* for *"Eutopia,"* by Lady Frances Southwell; an essay on valor ascribed to Donne; a series of humorous paradoxes; and light material in prose and verse on mountebanks.

Thomas Fuller declared in his *The History of the Worthies of England* (1662) that Overbury was "the first writer of characters of our nation, so far as I have observed," a comment repeated in Anthony à Wood's *Athenæ Oxonienses* (1691): "Which Characters, as 'tis observed, were the first that were written and published in *England*." Whether or not Overbury composed characters before Hall did, Hall's were the first to appear in print, while

Overbury's character book was the first to involve a collective effort by several character-writers.

The Overburian range is considerable: moral characters ("A good Woman," "A very Woman," "Her next part") reinforcing Overbury's "A Wife" are accompanied by social, professional, and national types ("A Roaring Boy," "A meere Common Lawyer," and "A Welchman," respectively); a character of place ("A Prison"); controversial pieces ("A Puritane," "A Jesuite"), prefiguring polemic characters of civil war years; and a concept character ("What a Character is").

Departing from Theophrastus, whose sketches first defined in plain style a dominant trait subsequently actualized in typical speech and behavior, Overburian character-writing begins by defining with clever conceits and wordplay the character itself: "An ordinarie Widdow" "Is like the Heralds Hearse-cloth; shee serves to many funerals, with a very little altering the colour"; "A covetous man" "would love honour and adore God if there were an L. more in his name.... " Such material is elaborated through witty accumulations of discrete details that gain coherence by their relation to the illustrated type. Although Theophrastus ends with the last detail, Overburians often close epigrammatically or project the character's future: "In briefe, these *Chamber-maydes* are like Lotteryes: you may drawe twenty, ere one worth any thing" ("A Chamber-Mayde"); "He is now at an end, for hee hath had the wolfe of vaineglory, which he fed untill himselfe became the food" ("A golden Asse"). The most widely quoted character, the anonymous "What a Character is," combines drawing, music, and charactery to exemplify the speaking picture so described:

> ... it is a picture ... quaintlie drawne in various collours, all of them heightned by one shadowing. It is a quicke and soft touch of many strings, all shutting up in one musicall close: It is wits descant on any plaine song.

When a rival character-writer, John Stephens, assailed actors in "A common Player" in his *Satyrical Essayes Characters and Others* (1615), Webster defended them in "An excellent Actor" in the sixth impression of the Overbury volume (titled *New and Choise Characters, of Severall Authors,* 1615) and ridiculed "the imitating Characterist," causing Stephens to retaliate in *Essayes and Characters* (1615). Yet unlike character books by Stephens, Nicholas Breton, Francis Lenton, and Richard Brathwait, only Earle's *Micro-cosmographie* matched the Overburian collection in popularity.

Joshua Poole's *English Parnassus* (1657) is the first known school text to include passages by the Overburians and Earle as composition models; Ralph Johnson, using Overbury, Hall, and Earle, codified character-writing in *The Scholar's Guide* (1665). When fascination with type charactery in witty prose subsided, Henry Gally acknowledged, in the first extended essay on character-writing (1725), the growing preference for depicting, in simpler style, individuals over types; he also criticized Overbury's wit, yet he praised "A fayre and happy Milke-mayd."

Twentieth-century interest in Overbury and his collaborators is indebted to W. J. Paylor's Overburian edition (1936), the bibliography of characters by Chester Noyes Greenough and J. Milton French (1947), and genre studies by Benjamin Boyce (1947) and J. W. Smeed (1985). If English prose characters broadened their appeal through being associated with Overbury's name, that appeal has, conversely, preserved Overbury's reputation as an influential contribu-

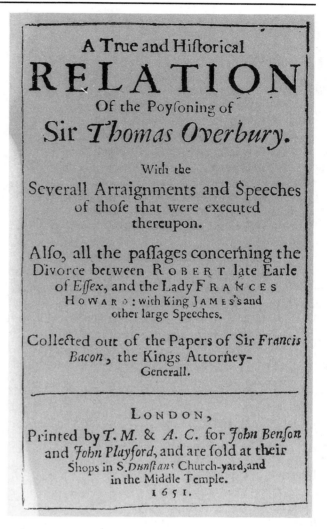

Title page for one of the many accounts of the Overbury murder

tor to one of the seventeenth century's most significant character books.

Bibliographies:

Gwendolen Murphy, ed., *A Bibliography of English Character-Books, 1608–1700* (London: Oxford University Press, 1925);

W. J. Paylor, "The Editions of the 'Overburian' Characters," *Library,* fourth series 17 (June 1936–March 1937): 340–348;

Chester Noyes Greenough and J. Milton French, comps. and eds., *A Bibliography of the Theophrastan Character in English with Several Portrait Characters,* Harvard Studies in Comparative Literature, 18 (Cambridge, Mass.: Harvard University Press / London: Geoffrey Cumberlege, Oxford University Press, 1947; republished, Westport, Conn.: Greenwood Press, 1970).

Biographies:

Andrew Amos, *The Great Oyer of Poisoning: The Trial of the Earl of Somerset for the Poisoning of Sir Thomas Overbury in the Tower of London, and Various Matters Connected Therewith, from Contemporary MSS* (London: Bentley, 1846);

Philip Hamilton Gibbs, *King's Favourite: The Love Story of Robert Carr and Lady Essex* (Philadelphia: Lippincott, n.d.; republished, Philadelphia: Jacobs, 1908; London: Hutchinson, 1909);

Charles Edward Gough, *The Life and Characters of Sir Thomas Overbury* (Norwich, 1909);

Charles Whibley, *Essays in Biography* (London: Constable, 1913);

Edward Abbott Parry, *The Overbury Mystery: A Chronicle of Fact and Drama of the Law* (London: Unwin / New York: Scribners, 1925); republished, New York: Blom, 1972);

William L. McElwee, *The Murder of Sir Thomas Overbury* (London: Faber & Faber, 1952);

Alfred S. Reid, ed., Sir Thomas Overbury's Vision *(1616) by Richard Niccols and Other English Sources of Nathaniel Hawthorne's* The Scarlet Letter (Gainesville, Fla.: Scholars' Facsimiles & Reprints, 1957);

Miriam Allen DeFord, *The Overbury Affair: The Murder Trial That Rocked the Court of King James I* (Philadelphia: Chilton, 1960);

Beatrice White, *Cast of Ravens: The Strange Case of Sir Thomas Overbury* (New York: George Braziller, 1965);

Edward LeComte, *The Notorious Lady Essex* (New York: Dial, 1969);

Chester Dunning, "The Fall of Sir Thomas Overbury and the Embassy to Russia in 1613," *Sixteenth-Century Journal,* 22 (Winter 1991): 695–704.

References:

Richard Aldington, "Introduction," in *A Book of "Characters" from Theophrastus: Joseph Hall, Sir Thomas Overbury, Nicholas Breton, John Earle, Thomas Fuller, and Other English Authors; Jean de La Bruyère, Vauvenargues, and Other French Authors,* compiled and translated by Aldington (London: Routledge / New York: Dutton, 1924), pp. 1–26;

Edward Chauncey Baldwin, "The Relation of the English 'Character' to Its Greek Prototype," *PMLA,* 18 (1903): 412–423;

Baldwin, "The Relation of the Seventeenth Century Character to the Periodical Essay," *PMLA,* 19 (1904): 75–114;

Baron A. F. Bourgeois, "John Webster a Contributor to Sir Thomas Overbury's 'Characters,' " *Notes and Queries,* eleventh series 10 (4 July 1914): 3–6; (11 July 1914): 23–24;

Bourgeois, "John Webster and 'Overbury's Characters,' " *Notes and Queries,* eleventh series 12 (9 October 1915): 282–283;

Benjamin Boyce, *The Theophrastan Character in England to 1642* (Cambridge, Mass.: Harvard University Press, 1947; London: Cass / New York: Humanities Press, 1967);

Wendell Clausen, "The Beginnings of English Character-Writing in the Early Seventeenth Century," *Philological Quarterly,* 25 (January 1946): 32–45;

W. P. Courtney, "Verses Prefixed to Sir Thomas Overbury's 'Wife,' " *Notes and Queries,* fourth series 4 (6 November 1869): 386–387;

R. W. Dent, "Characters," in *John Webster's Borrowing* (Berkeley & Los Angeles: University of California Press, 1960), pp. 279–288;

Charles A. S. Ernst, "Contextualizing the Character: Generic Studies of Text and Canon, Rhetoric, Style, and Quantitative Analysis in the Seventeenth-Century English Prose Character," Ph.D. dissertation, University of Pennsylvania, 1988;

Dennis Flynn, "The Originals of Donne's Overburian Characters," *Bulletin of the New York Public Library,* 77 (Autumn 1973): 63–69;

Charles R. Forker, *Skull Beneath the Skin: The Achievement of John Webster* (Carbondale & Edwardsville: Southern Illinois University Press, 1986), pp. 120–134;

Forker, " 'Wit's Descant on Any Plain Song': The Prose Characters of John Webster," *Modern Language Quarterly,* 30 (March 1969): 33–52;

Henry Gally, *The Moral Characters of Theophrastus. Translated from The Greek, with Notes. To which is prefix'd A Critical Essay On Characteristic-Writings* (London: Printed for John Hooke, 1725); republished as *A Critical Essay on Characteristic-Writings from his Translation of* The Moral Characters of Theophrastus *(1725),* edited by Alexander H. Chorney, Augustan Reprint Society, no. 33 (Los Angeles: William Andrews Clark Memorial Library, University of California Press, 1952);

G. S. Gordon, "Theophrastus and His Imitators," in *English Literature and the Classics,* edited by Gordon (Oxford: Clarendon Press, 1912), pp. 49–86;

C. R. H., "Where Did Sir Thomas Overbury Write 'The Wife?,'" *Notes and Queries,* third series 8 (4 November 1865): 365–366;

G. B. Harrison, ed., "Notes of Conversations with Ben Jonson Made by William Drummond of Hawthornden, January 1619," in *Discoveries, 1641; Conversations With William Drummond of Hawthornden, 1619,* by Ben Jonson, edited by Harrison, Elizabethan and Jacobean Quartos (New York: Barnes & Noble, 1966), pp. 1–28;

W. Carew Hazlitt, "Sir Thomas Overbury's 'Wife': Collation of an Early MS," *Notes and Queries,* fourth series 2 (7 November 1868): 434–435;

Irmgard von Ingersleben, *Das Elizabethische Ideal der Ehefrau bei Overbury (1613)* (Cöthen: Schulze, 1921);

Hobart Sidney Jarrett, "The Character-Writers and Seventeenth-Century Society: 1608–1658," Ph.D. dissertation, Syracuse University, 1955;

Karl Lichtenberg, *Der Einfluss des Theophrast auf die englischen Character-Writers des 17. Jahrhunderts* (Weimar, 1921);

John Leon Lievsay, "The 'D. T.' Poems in Overbury's *A Wife,*" *Modern Language Notes,* 63 (March 1948): 177–180;

C. F. Main, "Wotton's 'The Character of a Happy Life,'" *Library,* fifth series 10 (December 1955): 270–274;

J. C. Maxwell, "A Dramatic Echo of an Overburian Character," *Notes and Queries,* 192 (28 June 1947): 277;

Gwendolen Murphy, "Introduction: Development of the Character," in *A Cabinet of Characters,* edited by Murphy (London: Humphrey Milford, Oxford University Press, 1925), pp. v–xxxvi;

Wilhelm Papenheim, *Die Charakterschilderungen im "Tatler," "Spectator" und "Guardian": Ihr Verhältnis zu Theophrast, La Bruyère und den englischen Character-Writers des 17. Jahrhunderts, Beiträge zur englischen Philologie,* 15, edited by Max Förster (Leipzig: Tauchnitz, 1930);

W. J. Paylor, "Thomas Dekker and the 'Overburian' Characters," *Modern Language Review,* 31 (April 1936): 155–160;

Ted-Larry Pebworth, "New Light on Sir Henry Wotton's 'The Character of a Happy Life,'" *Library,* 33 (September 1978): 223–226;

Forrest G. Robinson, "Picturæ Loquentes: The English Character-Writers," in his *The Shape of Things Known: Sidney's* Apology *in Its Philosophical Tradition* (Cambridge, Mass.: Harvard University Press, 1972), pp. 206–214;

Paul James Schumacher, "Virtue and Vice: A Study of the Characters of Hall, the Overburians, and Earle," Ph.D. dissertation, Saint Louis University, 1968;

Evelyn M. Simpson, "John Donne and Sir Thomas Overbury's 'Characters,'" *Modern Language Review,* 18 (October 1923): 410–415;

J. W. Smeed, *The Theophrastan "Character": The History of a Literary Genre* (Oxford & New York: Clarendon Press, 1985);

Frances E. M. Swallow, "Theophrastus and the English Theophrastans: A Comparative Study in Greek and English 'Charactery,'" Ph.D. dissertation, Cornell University, 1941;

H. Dugdale Sykes, "Was Webster a Contributor to 'Overbury's Characters'?," *Notes and Queries,* eleventh series 11 (24 April 1915): 313–315; (1 May 1915): 335–337; (8 May 1915): 355–357; (15 May 1915): 374–375;

Sykes, "Webster and Sir Thomas Overbury," *Notes and Queries,* eleventh series 8 (20 September 1913): 221–223; (27 September 1913): 244–245; (4 October 1913): 263–265; (11 October 1913): 282–283; (18 October 1913): 304–305;

Elbert N. S. Thompson, "Character Books," in his *Literary Bypaths of the Renaissance* (New Haven: Yale University Press / London: Humphrey Milford, Oxford University Press, 1924), pp. 1–27;

Charles Whibley, "Characters," *Blackwood's Magazine,* 185 (June 1909): 757–769;

George Williamson, *The Senecan Amble: A Study in Prose Form From Bacon to Collier* (Chicago: University of Chicago Press / London: Faber & Faber, 1951; republished, Chicago: University of Chicago Press, 1966).

Papers:

Manuscripts for Sir Thomas Overbury's *Observations in his Travailes Upon the State of the Xvii. Provinces* are in the British Museum and Lambeth Palace. The British Museum also preserves Overbury's correspondence to Somerset and others in several manuscripts; Overbury's epitaph; and a manuscript for "Crumbs Fall'n From King James' Table," purportedly copied from an original in Overbury's hand. Manuscripts treating details of Overbury's murder and the subsequent legal proceedings are at the British Library; the Bodleian Library, Oxford; the Cambridge University Library; Lambeth Palace; and the Public Record Office, London.

Henry Peacham
(1578 – 1644?)

Alan R. Young
Acadia University

BOOKS: *The Art of Drawing with the Pen, and Limming in Water Colours* (London: Printed by Richard Braddock for William Jones, 1606); enlarged as *Graphice or The most Auncient and Excellent Art of Drawing and Limming, Disposed into Three Bookes* (London: Printed by W. S. for John Browne, 1612); also published as *The Gentleman's Exercise. Or An Exquisite Practise, as well for drawing all manner of Beasts in their true Portraittures: as also the making of all kinds of colours, to be used in Lymning, Painting, Tricking, and Blason of Coates, and Armes, with diuers others most delightfull and pleasurable obseruations, for all yong gentlemen and others. As also seruing for the necessarie vse and generall benefite of diuers tradesmen and artificers, as namly painters, ioyners, freemasons, cutters and caruers &c. for the further gracing, beautifying, and garnishing of all their absolute and worthie peeces* (London: Printed for John Browne, 1612);

The More the Merrier. Containing: Threescore and Odde Headlesse Epigrams (London: Printed by J. Windet for G. Chorleton & T. Man, 1608);

Minerva Britanna Or A Garden Of Heroical Deuises, furnished, and adorned with Emblemes and Impresa's of sundry natures, Newly devised, moralized, and published (London: Printed by W. Dight, 1612);

The Period of Mourning. Disposed into six Visions. In Memorie of the Late Prince. Together with Nuptiall Hymnes, in Honour of this Happy Marriage betweene the great Prince, Frederick Count Palatine of the Rhene, and the Most Excellent . . . Elizabeth onely Daughter to our Soueraigne, His Maiestie. Also the manner of the celebration of the marriage at White-Hall, on the 14. of February, being Sunday, and S^t. Valentines Day (London: Printed by T. Snodham for John Helme, 1613);

Prince Henrie Revived. Or A Poeme Upon the Birth, and in Honor of the Hopefull Yong Prince Henrie Frederick, First Sonne and Heire Apparent to the Most Excellent Princes, Frederick Count Palatine of the Rhine, and the Mirrour of Ladies, Princesse Elizabeth, His Wife, Only Daughter to Our Soueraigne Iames King of Great Brittaine, &c. (London: Printed by W. Stansby for John Helme, 1615);

A Most True Relation of the Affaires of Cleve and Gvlick, As also Of all what hath passed this last summer, since the most Excellent and Victorious Prince, Mavrice of Nassav, tooke the field with his Armie, encamping before Rees in Cleueland: and the losse of Wesel, taken in by the Marques Spinola: Vnto the breaking vp of our Armie in the beginning of December last past. 1614. With the Articles of the Peace, propounded at Santen (London: Printed by W. Stansby for John Helme, 1615);

Thalia's Banqvet: Furnished with an Hundred and Odde Dishes of Newly Deuised Epigrammes, Whereunto (Beside Many Worthy Friends) Are Inuited All That Loue in Offensiue Mirth, and the Muses (London: Printed by N. Okes for Francis Constable, 1620);

The Compleat Gentleman Fashoning him absolute in the most necessary & commendable Qualities concerning Minde or Bodie that may be required in a Noble Gentleman (London: Printed for Francis Constable, 1622; enlarged, 1627; enlarged again, 1634);

An Aprill Shower Shed in Abundance of Teares, for the Death and Incomparable Losse, of . . . Richard Sackvile, Baron of Bvckhvrst, and Earle of Dorset (London: Printed by E. Allde, 1624);

Thestylis Atrata: Or A Funeral Elegie upon the Death of the Right Honourable, Most Religious and Noble Lady, Frances, Late Countesses of Warwick, Who Departed This Life at Her House in Hackney neere unto London, in the Moneth of June Last Past. 1634 (London: Printed by J. Haviland for Francis Constable, 1634);

Coach and Sedan, Pleasantly Disputing for Place and Precedence, the Brewers-Cart Being Moderator (London: Printed by Robert Raworth for John Crowch, to be sold by E. Paxton, 1636);

The Valley of Varietie: Or, Discourse fitting for the Times, Containing Very Learned and Rare Passages out of Antiquity, Philosophy, and History. Collected for the

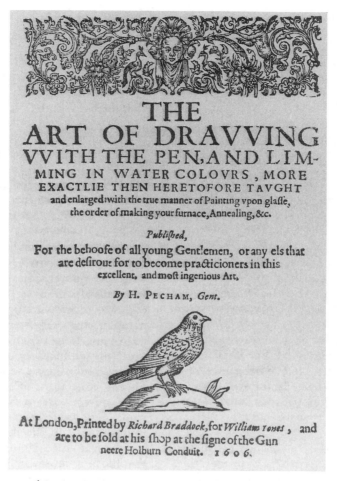

THE
ART OF DRAVVING
VVITH THE PEN, AND LIM-
MING IN WATER COLOVRS, MORE
EXACTLIE THEN HERETOFORE TAVGHT
and enlarged: with the true manner of Painting vpon glaſſe,
the order of making your furnace, Annealing, &c.

Publiſhed,
For the behoofe of all young Gentlemen, or any els that
are deſirour for to become practicioners in this
excellent, and moſt ingenious Art,

By H. PECHAM, *Gent.*

At London, Printed by *Richard Braddock,* for *William Iones,* and
are to be ſold at his ſhop at the ſigne of the Gun
neere Holburn Conduit. 1 6 0 6.

Title page for Henry Peacham's treatise on the graphic arts

Use of All Ingenious Spirits, and True Lovers of Learning (London: Printed by M. Parsons for James Becket, 1638);

The Truth of Our Times: Revealed out of One Mans Experience, by Way of Essay (London: Printed by N. Okes for James Becket, 1638);

A Merry Discourse of Meum, and Tuum, or, Mine and Thine, Two Crosse Brothers, That Make Strife and Debate Wheresoever They Come; with Their Descent, Parentage, and Late Progresse in Divers Parts of England (London: Printed by the assigns of T. Purfoot for J. Clark, 1639);

The Duty of All True Subiects to Their King: As also to Their Native Countrey, in Time of Extremity and Danger. With Some Memorable Examples of the Miserable Ends of Perfidious Traytors. In Two Bookes (London: Printed by E. Purslowe for Henry Seyle, 1639);

The Worth of a Peny: Or, A Caution to Keep Money. With the Causes of the Scarcity and Misery of the Want Hereof in These Hard and Mercilesse Times. As also, *How to Save It in Our Diet, Apparell, Recreations, &c. And also, What Honest Courses Men in Want May Take to Live,* as H. P. master of arts (London, 1641; revised and enlarged edition, London: Printed by S. Griffin for William Lee, 1664);

A Dialogue between the Crosse in Cheap, and Charing Crosse. Comforting Each Other, as Fearing Their Fall in These Uncertaine Times, as Ryhen Pameach (London, 1641);

The Art of Living in London; or, A Caution how Gentlemen, Countreymen and Strangers, drawn by occasion of businesse, should dispose of themselves in the thriftiest way, not onely in the Citie, but in all other populous places, as H. P. (London, 1642);

A Paradox, in the Praise of a Dunce, to Smectymnuus (London: Printed for Thomas Paybody, 1642);

Square-Caps Turned into Round-Heads: or The Bishops Vindication, and the Brownists Conviction. Being a Dialogue between Time, and Opinion: Shewing the

Folly of the One, and the Worthinesse of the Other, as H. P. (London: Printed for J. Gyles & G. Lindsey, 1642);

Emblemata Varia, edited by Alan R. Young (Ilkley & London: Scolar Press, 1976).

Editions: *Peacham's Compleat Gentleman, 1634,* edited by G. S. Gordon (Oxford: Clarendon Press, 1906);

Coach and Sedan; Reprinted from the Edition of 1636, edited by Hugh Macdonald (London: Frederick Etchells & Hugh Macdonald, 1925);

The Truth of Our Times, by Henry Peacham. Reproduced in Facsimile from the Edition of 1638, edited by Robert Ralston Cawley (New York: Published for the Facsimile Text Society by Columbia University Press, 1942);

The Complete Gentleman, The Truth of Our Times, and The Art of Living in London, edited by Virgil B. Heltzel (Ithaca, N.Y.: Published for the Folger Shakespeare Library by Cornell University Press, 1962);

Minerva Britanna, 1612 (Leeds: Scolar Press, 1966);

The Compleat Gentleman. London 1622, The English Experience, no. 59 (Amsterdam: Theatrum Orbis Terrarum / New York: Da Capo Press, 1968);

Minerva Britanna, edited by John Horden, English Emblem Books, no. 5 (Menston: Scolar Press, 1969);

The Art of Drawing with the Pen. 1606, The English Experience, no. 230 (Amsterdam: Theatrum Orbis Terrarum / New York: Da Capo Press, 1970);

Minerva Britanna. London 1612, The English Experience, no. 407 (Amsterdam: Theatrum Orbis Terrarum / New York: Da Capo Press, 1971);

A Most True Relation of the Affaires of Cleue and Gulick, The English Experience, no. 549 (Amsterdam: Theatrum Orbis Terrarum / New York: Da Capo Press, 1973).

OTHER: "Ad Robertum Doulandum," in Robert Dowland, *A Musical Banquet* (London: Printed by T. Snodham for T. Adams, 1610);

"Upon the Authour and his most commendable and necessary work," in Arthur Standish, *The Commons Complaint* (London: Printed by William Stansby, 1611);

"Memoriae Sacrum," "To the famous Traveller" and "In the Utopian tongue," in Thomas Coryate, *Coryats Crudities* (London: Printed by William Stansby, 1611);

"Graenwich," verses for etching by Wenceslaus Hollar (1637);

"Seleucus and Son," verses for etching by Hollar (1637);

"Richard II. Virgin and Child," verses for etching by Hollar (1639);

"En Surculus Arbor," verses for etching by Hollar (1641);

"The World is Ruled and Governed by Opinion," verses for etching by Hollar (1641 or 1642);

"Royal Exchange," verses for etching by Hollar (1644).

Henry Peacham proudly declared in his *Graphice* (1612): "By profession I am a Scholler." For Peacham the term *Scholler* seems to have meant someone dedicated to a wide range of scholarly pursuits, including poetry, history, cosmography, painting, music, mathematics, heraldry, and numismatics. Matching this diversity was Peacham's multiplicity of activities as teacher, graphic artist, writer, composer, social critic, antiquarian, war correspondent, and observant traveler. Part of the fascination of his writings is that they reflect these many interests. Those works considered today as of most importance are his two treatises on the graphic arts, his emblem books (four manuscript, one printed), his essays and pamphlets on topical issues, his two collections of epigrams, and, above all, the best-known work of courtesy literature of the period, *The Compleat Gentleman* (1622). An important minor figure in the history of English literature, Peacham is also a familiar name to historians of the graphic arts, music, education, and social history.

Peacham was the son of the clergyman-author of the important rhetorical treatise *The Garden of Eloquence* (1577). His father, also named Henry Peacham, was the minister at North Mymms, Hertfordshire, where his wife, Anne Fairclough Peacham, bore five children; Henry, born in 1578, was the second. Peacham went to school nearby and, later, in London. In 1592 he entered Trinity College, Cambridge, receiving his B.A. in 1595 and his M.A. three years later. In 1597 he carved his name and age on an interior stone window ledge of the church in South Leverton, Lincolnshire, where his father held a second living; the effects of this act of vandalism have survived to this day. He seems to have traveled for some years in pursuit of his developing antiquarian interests; on the evidence of his reference in *The Compleat Gentleman* to "mine owne Master, *Horatio Vecchi* of *Modena,*" he may have gone to Italy to study music.

By the early 1600s, however, he was forced to seek a livelihood. In *The Truth of Our Times* (1638) he looks back on this period in his life and, quoting the Twenty-seventh Psalm, remarks: *"When my Father and Mother forsooke me, thou oh Lord tookest me up:*

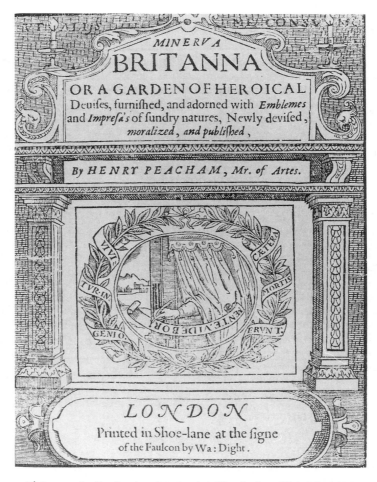

Title page for Peacham's only printed emblem book, published in 1612

which freely I confesse, I may say my selfe, being left young to the wide world to seek my fortune." As the primary means of supporting himself Peacham made the familiar choice of the needy scholar – teaching. His first post was at the free grammar school in Kimbolton, Huntingdonshire, and it was there that he began to write. He would intermittently hold other teaching posts, but, as an epigram in *Thalia's Banquet* (1620) makes clear, teaching was a necessity rather than a vocation:

Windham I love thee, and I love thy soile,
Yet ever loath'd that never ceasing toile
Of thy faire Schoole, which while that it was free,
My selfe the Maister lost my libertie.

Peacham was teaching in Kimbolton in 1603 when King James VI of Scotland, following the death of Queen Elizabeth, traveled to London to be crowned James I of England. On the way James passed through Huntingdon, which is eight miles

from Kimbolton, and Peacham presented the new king with some of his emblems. It is likely that on the same occasion Peacham's one extant musical composition, "King James his quier," was performed. In hope, no doubt, of some kind of preferment, Peacham shortly thereafter composed two emblem books based on James's Βασιλικον δωρον (*Basilikon Doron,* 1599), a treatise that the king had written for his son, Prince Henry. Peacham dedicated one of the manuscripts to James and the other to Henry, though neither may actually have been presented to the intended recipient.

While at Kimbolton, Peacham published the first of his two treatises on the graphic arts. *The Art of Drawing with the Pen, and Limming in Water Colours* (1606) was written, according to its title page, "For the behoofe of all young Gentlemen, or any else that are desirous for to become practicioners in this excellent, and most ingenious Art." More particularly, as he explains later, it was composed for the "benefit of many young Gentlemen, who were my

Schollers for the Latine and Greek tongues" (presumably those at Kimbolton). Such a purpose reveals Peacham's deliberate challenge to the general absence of the visual arts from grammar-school curricula and the belief, in spite of the precepts of earlier humanist thinkers and educators such as Baldassare Castiglione, Sir Thomas Elyot, and Richard Mulcaster, that drawing and painting were not suitable activities for a gentleman. In *The Compleat Gentleman* Peacham would recall how his own interest in drawing had been harshly discouraged when he was a schoolboy:

> Painting is a quality I love (I confesse) and admire in others, because ever naturally from a child, I have beene addicted to the practise hereof; yet when I was young, I have beene cruelly beaten by ill and ignorant schoolemasters, when I have been taking, in white and blacke, the countenance of someone or other (which I could do at thirteene and fourteene yeares of age) . . . yet could they never beat it out of me. I remember one Master I had (and yet living not farre from *S. Albanes*) took me one time drawing out with my pen that pearetree and boyes throwing at it, at the end of the Latine Grammar: which he perceiving, in a rage strooke mee with the great end of the rodde, and rent my paper, swearing it was the onely way to teach mee to robbe Orchards; beside, that I was placed with him to bee made a scholler and not a painter, which I was very likely to doe.

It was with a hint of defiance and challenge, then, that Peacham published his first book, since, as he explains in the preface, it includes directions "in respect of their brevity & plainnesse, fit for the capacitie of the young learner, for whom they were first and principally intended."

In writing such a treatise Peacham was following in the footsteps of Nicholas Hilliard, whose "A Treatise Concerning the Art of Limning" (circa 1597–1603) had been circulated in manuscript, and Paolo Lomazzo, whose *Trattato dell'arte della Pittura* (1584) had been translated into English by Richard Haydocke in 1598. Peacham's work broadly follows the arrangement of Hilliard's, and the first of its three books begins with a chapter that defines painting in a partial paraphrase of the opening of Lomazzo's first chapter. Peacham's second chapter, which is somewhat similar to a section in Lomazzo's work, gives a condensed history of the great painters from classical times, through Michelangelo and Albrecht Dürer, to his contemporaries Hilliard and Isaac Oliver. Succeeding chapters deal with the dangers of misusing the visual arts for satire, pornography, and representations of the Godhead, and with all the basic practicalities, in order of increasing difficulty, that the student needs to know. The brevity of the discussions, which are interspersed with jokes and stories, suggests that the teacher Peacham well understood the way to hold a student's attention. Books 2 and 3 are more technical, providing recipes for making colors and discussions of gilding, of making inks of different colors, and of the art of creating stained glass.

It was perhaps Peacham's hope of gaining royal patronage that caused him to move to London and then to Westminster in about 1607. In 1610 he completed another, longer emblem book (this one in color) based on *Basilikon Doron;* it was presented to the prince and was followed by Peacham's one printed emblem book, *Minerva Britanna* (1612), also dedicated to Henry.

Whether by 1610 or so Peacham had obtained a place in Henry's court at St. James's Palace and Richmond is not known, but in *Minerva Britanna* he expresses his gratitude for Henry's "gratious favor" and "*Princely* and *Generous* inclination"; and two years later, in *Graphice,* he mentions having frequently drawn the portrait of his majesty while the latter was "sitting at dinner, or talking with some of his followers." At about this time Peacham got to know John Dowland, one of the most important early-seventeenth-century composers, together with such key figures at Henry's court as the architect and scenic designer Inigo Jones; Edward Wright, keeper of the prince's library; Robert Peake, a painter; and Adam Newton, the prince's secretary and former tutor.

In 1612 Peacham published a greatly enlarged version of *The Art of Drawing* under the title *Graphice or The most Auncient and Excellent Art of Drawing and Limming.* This version, which also appeared the same year under the title *The Gentleman's Exercise,* is so changed, however, that it should properly be considered a separate work. As Roy Strong points out, some of the new material probably reflects Peacham's contact with the St. James's court and his exposure to pictures and works of art he had not known six years before. According to the title page of *The Gentleman's Exercise,* the work is now intended not only for young gentlemen but for "divers Trades-men and Artificers, as namly Painters, Ioyners, Free-masons, Cutters and all their absolute and worthie peeces. . . ." Book 1 of the new work incorporates the whole of *The Art of Drawing,* with the exception of some of the lighter anecdotal material, and several additions. In book 2 Peacham makes available for the first time in English material from Cesare Ripa's *Iconologia* (1593), the first illustrated edition of which had appeared in 1603, with a sec-

Frontispiece for Peacham's A Most True Relation of the Affaires of
Cleve and Gulick

ond illustrated edition in 1611. Ripa's extremely influential book, which had already been made use of by Ben Jonson and Inigo Jones, sets down the actions, gestures, and attributes appropriate to the depiction of such qualities as Eternity, Piety, Time, and Matrimony. Peacham, though without following Ripa's alphabetical arrangement or acknowledging his source, offers in book 2 a lengthy selection of topics based on Ripa's book. Because *Graphice* (or *The Gentleman's Exercise*) was one of Peacham's most widely read works, with further editions in 1634 and 1661, his role in acquainting English readers with Ripa may have been considerable. Book 3 consists of a manual of blazonry. Treatises on the topic had already been published in England by such authors as Gerard Legh, John Guillim, John Ferne,

and Edmund Bolton; and Peacham largely presents a restatement of the basic facts in a form appropriate to his intended readership. Striking, however, is Peacham's use of dialogue form, a favored technique of earlier humanists and one to which he would return in later works.

On the sudden death late in 1612 of the prince, an ambitious young man who had attempted to create a courtly academy around himself that had attracted poets, painters, and musicians, Peacham found himself once more without a focus for his talents. A year or so after the dissolution of Henry's remarkable household Peacham began a period of traveling in Europe – principally in France, Germany, and the Low Countries – visiting ancient buildings, exploring libraries, learning Dutch, meeting well-known artists, and observing educational methods. Before he left England he had completed *The More the Merrier* (1608), his first collection of epigrams; "The Period of Mourning" (1613), his contribution to the spate of elegies published at Prince Henry's death; and "Nuptiall Hymnes" (1613), four poems in honor of the marriage in 1613 of Princess Elizabeth and Frederick, the Count Palatine.

During travels in Europe, Peacham spent some time in the household of the lord governor of Utrecht, Sir John Ogle, to whom, Peacham explains in *The Compleat Gentleman,* "resorted many great Schollers and Captaines." Ogle, who came from Pinchbeck, not far from Leverton, made his household a kind of academy; there Peacham completed *Prince Henrie Revived* (1615), a poem in honor of the birth in 1614 of Prince Henry Frederick, the son of Princess Elizabeth and the Count Palatine. There is evidence that in setting off for Europe, Peacham may have planned to seek the patronage of Princess Elizabeth, but the wars then raging on the Continent prevented him from reaching her. Peacham came in close contact with the fighting while with Colonel Ogle's regiment, and he composed an account of his experiences that was published on his return to England under the title *A Most True Relation of the Affaires of Cleve and Gulick* (1615).

He returned to teaching, taking a job at the free grammar school in Wymondham, Norfolk. Judging from the various dedications in his next publication, the collection of epigrams *Thalia's Banquet,* Peacham made many friends in Norfolk; among those he met was the son of Thomas Howard, fourteenth Earl of Arundel, the five-year-old William Howard, to whom he would dedicate *The Compleat Gentleman.* In 1620 or 1621 Peacham returned to London and took a teaching post at St. Martin-in-the-Fields; but in 1622 he gave his address as Hoxton, a village just north of the city. Ever in search of a patron, Peacham appears at this time to have sought favor from Sir Julius Caesar, to whom he presented a manuscript emblem book, "Emblemata Varia." Peacham may also have found favor with Richard Sackville, third Earl of Dorset, at about this time.

In 1622 Peacham published his most important work, *The Compleat Gentleman.* Originally intended, as Peacham explains, "for the private use of a Noble young Gentleman my friend" (William Howard), the scope of the work is considerable. First, it offers an outline of the ideal pattern of education and training for the "gentleman," by that time a vague term that could apply not only to one of aristocratic birth but also to anyone who possessed appropriate qualities of character and habits of mind. Successive chapters deal with the importance of learning; the duties of teachers, parents, and students; and what studies are most appropriate, including both music and painting.

Sackville's death in 1624 appears to have forced Peacham to return to Lincolnshire and more years of schoolmastering at Heighington. In 1627 he published a second edition of *The Compleat Gentleman* with some added material, including a chapter on fishing – the first occasion on which that activity had been included in a treatise on the education of a nobleman or gentleman. A third edition appeared in 1634 with more additional material, including a new chapter, "Of Antiquities," dealing with sculpture, inscriptions, and coins. The attention given to ancient sculpture probably mirrors a passion of the earl of Arundel, who had initiated excavations in Rome and had exhibited his acquisitions in the galleries and gardens of Arundel House. (Today many of Arundel's treasures can be found among the holdings of the Ashmolean Museum in Oxford.)

The same year as the third edition of *The Compleat Gentleman* Peacham also published *Thestylis Atrata,* an elegy on the death of Frances Rich, Countess of Warwick, from whom, according to the "Epistle to the Reader," he had received "many favors." In the "Epistle" Peacham talks of still "being employed in a toilsome calling," but in 1635 he left Heighington and returned to London. In the remaining years of his life he rapidly produced a series of writings, as if making up for the paucity of new work during his ten years in Lincolnshire. His lighthearted and amusing dialogue *Coach and Sedan* (1636) assesses the relative merits of the available forms of London transportation, including the Thames waterboat, the cart, and one's own two legs. The issue was a topical one, since the press and noise of coaches in the city streets had led to a restraining order against them in January 1636. *The Truth of Our Times,* published in 1638, is a collection of fourteen essays expressing Peacham's thoughts about a variety of subjects, together with incidental autobiographical information having to do with his failure to receive patronage; his decision to give up "those vanities" of poetry, painting, and music; his disenchantment with teaching; and his being exercised in another "Calling," the exact nature of which he does not reveal. In 1638 appeared *The Valley of Varietie,* a compendium of exempla, anecdotes, and information designed to provide conversationalists and writers with useful material. *The Worth of a Peny: Or, A Caution to Keep Money* (1641) is an exhortation to thrift and an analysis of poverty, which he

Title page for Peacham's courtesy book

saw as chiefly resulting from the control of vast wealth by a few powerful men who, unlike their feudal predecessors, felt no responsibility to assist those in need. There were at least eight more editions of this work before the century came to a close. In *The Worth of a Peny* Peacham adopts his familiar role of teacher and guide; he repeats this stance in *The Art of Living in London* (1642), which offers practical advice to those whose business might bring them among the many dangers, temptations, and distractions of London.

At this time Peacham was, of course, a witness to the conflict between king and Parliament and the related events leading up to the civil war, and like hordes of other pamphleteers he participated in the religious and political struggles that were as heated in the print medium as they would become on the battlefields. In *The Duty of All True Subjects to Their King* (1639) Peacham, a man of moderate Royalist and Church of England sympathies, staunchly defends king and church against the Puritan and Parliamentary reformers. *A Dialogue between the Crosse in Cheap, and Charing Crosse* (1641) is a four-page dialogue between two London landmarks that had become the focus for Puritan hostility and iconoclasm. Peacham tried to make fun of what he considered irrational extremism, but within a few months an angry mob attacked the cross in Cheapside (Charing Cross was already in ruins), and in 1643 Parliament ordered it to be razed. *A Paradox, in the Praise of a Dunce, to Smectymnuus* (1642) was Peacham's contribution to the pamphlet war set off in 1640 by Joseph Hall, who, at the suggestion of Archbishop William Laud, had published a defense of episcopacy; the controversy is remembered today largely because of John Milton's involvement on the Puritan side. In his work Peacham takes to the middle ground, pointing out that the problems of the established church were in part of its own making. *Square-Caps Turned into Round-Heads* (1642) is far less compromising; Peacham identifies himself with Bishop Hall concerning the crucial matters of liturgy and church government and defends (probably with certain accusations made by Milton in mind) the good works that various bishops had engaged in down through the centuries.

In 1642 King Charles I raised his standard at Nottingham, beginning the civil war. As London became the center of Parliamentary activities, many with Royalist sympathies left the city. Peacham may have followed suit, or he may already have moved to Chelsea by this time. It is known that by 1637 Peacham had formed an association with the Bohemian artist Wenceslaus Hollar, one of the finest engravers of the period, who had been brought to England by the earl of Arundel in 1636. Peacham and Hollar produced eight works together between 1637 and 1644, Peacham supplying poems to accompany Hollar's etchings. Arundel had fled England in 1642; Hollar left in 1644, and perhaps Peacham went too. Whether Peacham was ever ordained and, if he was, whether he held a church living have never been conclusively ascertained, and because of a comment in *The Truth of Our Times* it was once thought that he had never married. He not only married, however, but he had two daughters: Sara, baptized on 27 April 1612, and Elizabeth, baptized on 13 November 1623. He may even have married twice: there is a document that concerns a Henry Peacham's intentions to marry a sixty-year-old widow, Anne Emmerson, in November 1636, and the details indicate that this Peacham and the writer were one and the same.

While the main features of Peacham's biography are fairly clear, the date and circumstances of his death remain a mystery. Scholars have suggested that in old age he was reduced to poverty and turned to hack writing as a means of subsistence; the possible marriage to the dowager Anne Emmerson, however, suggests otherwise. Also, the marriage document refers to Peacham as a "Clarke" living in Chelsea, suggesting that he had given up teaching, had been ordained, and had taken a living in Chelsea; this may be the new "Calling" to which he refers in *The Truth of Our Times*. In any case, the last concrete evidence of his existence consists of the two poems in Latin and English that he wrote to accompany Hollar's 1644 etching of the Royal Exchange.

Whatever the explanation for Peacham's silence after 1644, his works were not forgotten, and he was warmly remembered for the rest of the century and through that which followed — chiefly as the author of *The Compleat Gentleman, The Gentleman's Exercise,* and *The Worth of a Peny.* Essentially a conservative thinker, Peacham strikes one as an eloquent spokesman for much that was conventional and commonplace in late-Renaissance thought; but

his particular concerns as an educator, his entertaining and often anecdotal style, and above all his somewhat unconventional championship of music and painting make his voice stand out. At the same time, for students of literature, music, art, and social history, Peacham offers an important — sometimes unique — source of knowledge and understanding of early-seventeenth-century English culture.

References:

Michael Bath, *Speaking Pictures: English Emblem Books and Renaissance Culture* (London: Longman, 1994), pp. 90–110;

John Besly, "Malone's Own Notes in Copies of Peacham's Various Publications," *Notes and Queries,* first series 11 (24 March 1855): 218;

Robert R. Cawley, *Henry Peacham: His Contribution to English Poetry* (University Park: Pennsylvania State University Press, 1971);

Edmund K. Chambers, "The First Illustration to 'Shakespeare,' " *Library,* fourth series 5 (March 1925): 326–330;

James D. Clarke, "Henry Peacham's *Minerva Britanna* (1612): A Bibliographical Description and Analysis," M.A. thesis, University of Leeds, 1977;

Rosemary Freeman, *English Emblem Books* (London: Chatto & Windus, 1948), pp. 68–82;

Ruth Kelso, *The Doctrine of the English Gentleman in the Sixteenth Century* (Urbana: University of Illinois Press, 1929);

Harold P. Levitt, "The Political Writings of Henry Peacham," Ph.D. dissertation, New York University, 1968;

F. J. Levy, "Henry Peacham and the Art of Drawing," *Journal of the Warburg and Courtauld Institute,* 37 (1974): 174–190;

John L. Livesay, *Stefano Guazzo and the English Renaissance* (Chapel Hill: University of North Carolina Press, 1961), pp. 244–247;

R. E. R. Madelaine, "*The Duchess of Malfi* and Two Emblems in Whitney and Peacham," *Notes and Queries,* 29 (April 1982): 146–147;

John E. Mason, *Gentlefolk in the Making: Studies in the History of English Courtesy Literature and Related Topics from 1531 to 1774* (Philadelphia: University of Pennsylvania Press, 1935);

Edith Annette Palmer, "George Puttenham and Henry Peacham: Copia and Decorum in Sixteenth Century Literature," M.A. thesis, London University, 1969;

Margaret C. Pitman, "The Epigrams of Henry Peacham and Henry Parrot," *Modern Language Review,* 29 (April 1934): 129–136;

Pitman, "Summaries of Theses: No. CXVI: Studies in the Works of Henry Peacham," *Bulletin of the Institute of Historical Research,* 11 (1933): 189–192;

Edward F. Rimbault, "Autobiographical Notices of Henry Peacham," *Notes and Queries,* third series 12 (21 September 1867): 221–222;

S. Schuman, "Two Notes upon Emblems and the English Renaissance Drama," *Notes and Queries,* 18 (January 1971): 28–29;

D. T. Starnes, "Elyot's 'Governour' and Peacham's 'Compleat Gentleman,' " *Modern Language Review,* 22 (1927): 319–322;

Roy Strong, *Henry, Prince of Wales and England's Lost Renaissance* (London: Thames & Hudson, 1986);

E. N. S. Thompson, *Literary By Paths of the Renaissance* (New Haven: Yale University Press, 1924);

Mason Tung, "From Heraldry to Emblem: A Study of Peacham's Use of Heraldic Arms in *Minerva Britanna,*" *Word and Image,* 3 (January–March 1987): 86–94;

Tung, "From Impresa to Emblem: Peacham's Use of Typotius' *Symbola* and Other Impresa Collections in *Minerva Britanna,*" *Emblematica,* 3 (Spring 1988): 79–119;

Tung, "From Mirror to Emblem: A Study of Peacham's Use of *Mikrokosmos* in *Minerva Britanna,*" *Word and Image,* 5 (October–December 1989): 326–332;

Tung, "From Natural History to Emblem: A Study of Peacham's Use of Camerarius's *Symbola et Emblemata,*" *Emblematica,* 1 (Spring 1986): 53–76;

Tung, "From Personifications to Emblems: A Study of Peacham's Use of Ripa's *Iconologia* in *Minerva Britanna,*" in *The English Emblem and the Continental Tradition,* edited by Peter M. Daly (New York: AMS Press, 1988), pp. 109–150;

Tung, "A List of Flora and Fauna in Peacham's *Minerva Britanna* and Alciati's *Emblemata* Together with Possible Models in Contemporary Illustrations," *Emblematica,* 1 (Fall 1986): 345–357;

Tung, "A Reference Index to Peacham's Manuscript Emblem Books and *Minerva Britanna,*" *Emblematica,* 6 (Spring 1992): 104–146;

Tung, "A Serial List of Aesopic Fables in Alciati's *Emblemata,* Whitney's *A Choice of Emblemes* and Peacham's *Minerva Britanna,*" *Emblematica,* 4 (Fall 1989): 315–329;

Elkin C. Wilson, *Prince Henry and English Literature* (Ithaca, N.Y.: Cornell University Press, 1946);

John Dover Wilson, "*Titus Andronicus* on the Stage in 1595," *Shakespeare Survey,* 1 (1948): 17–22;

Alan R. Young, "A Biographical Note on Henry Peacham," *Notes and Queries,* new series 24 (June 1977): 214–217;

Young, "The Emblems of Henry Peacham," in *The European Emblem: Towards an Index Emblematicus,* edited by Daly (Waterloo: Wilfred Laurier University Press, 1980), pp. 83–108;

Young, *Henry Peacham* (Boston: Twayne, 1979);

Young, "Henry Peacham, Author of *The Garden of Eloquence* (1577)," *Notes and Queries,* new series 24 (December 1977): 503–507;

Young, "Henry Peacham, Ben Jonson, and the Cult of Elizabeth-Oriana," *Music and Letters,* 60 (July 1979): 305–311;

Young, "Henry Peacham, Ripa's *Iconologia,* and Vasari's *Lives,*" *Renaissance and Reformation,* new series 9, no. 3 (1985): 177–188;

Young, "Henry Peacham's First Emblem Book: MS. Rawlinson poetry 146," *Bodleian Library Record,* 10 (December 1979): 86–97.

Papers:

Henry Peacham's drawing of a scene from William Shakespeare's *Titus Andronicus* is in the possession of the marquess of Bath at Longleat, Harley Papers, volume 1, fol. 159; the manuscript for the madrigal "King James his quier" is in the British Library, MS Harleian 6855, Art. 13; the manuscript emblem book "ΒΑΣΙΛΙΚΟΝ ΔΩΡΟΔ In Heroica Emblemata" is in the Bodleian Library, Oxford, MS Rawlinson poetry 146; the manuscript emblem book "ΒΑΣΙΛΙΚΟΝ ΔΩΡΟΔ ΕΙΣ ΤΑ ΕΜΒΛΗΜΑΤΑ ΒΑΛΙΛΚΑ" is in the British Library, MS Harleian 6855, Art. 13; the manuscript emblem book "ΒΑΣΙΛΙΚΟΝ ΔΩΡΟΔ in BASILICA EMBLEMATA" is in the British Library, MS Royal 12A LXVI; the frontispiece portrait of Prince Henry in watercolors for James Cleland's "Le Pourtraict de Monseigneur le Prince," dated 1612, is in the British Library, MS Royal 16E XXXVIII; and the manuscript "Emblemata Varia" is in the Folger Shakespeare Library, Washington, D.C., MS V. b. 45.

Samuel Purchas

(1577? – September 1626)

Craig M. Rustici
Hofstra University

BOOKS: *Purchas his pilgrimage. Or, Relations of the world and religions observed in all ages and places discouered, from the creation vnto this present* (London: Printed by William Stansby for Henry Fetherstone, 1613; enlarged, 1614; enlarged again, 1617; enlarged again, 1626);

Purchas his pilgrim. Microcosmvs, or, The Historie of Man. Relating the Wonders of his Generation, Vanities in his Degeneration, Necessity of his Regeneration, Meditated on the words of David. Psalm 39.5. Verily, every man at his best state is altogether Vanitie. Selah (London: Printed by William Stansby for Henry Fetherstone, 1619);

The king's towre and triumphant arch of London. A sermon (London: Printed by William Stansby for Henry Fetherstone, 1623);

Hakluytus posthumus, or Purchas his pilgrimes, contayning a history of the world in sea voyages and lande travells, by Englishmen and others, 4 volumes (London: Printed by William Stansby for Henry Fetherstone, 1625).

Editions: *The Strange Adventures of Andrew Battell of Leigh, in Angola and the Adjoining Regions, Reprinted from "Purchas His Pilgrimes,"* edited by E. G. Ravenstein, Works Issued by the Hakluyt Society, second series, no. 6 (London: Printed for the Hakluyt Society, 1901; reprinted, Nendeln, Liechtenstein: Kraus Reprint, 1967);

Hakluytus Posthumus, or Purchas His Pilgrimes: Contayning a History of the World in Sea Voyages and Lande Travells by Englishmen and Others, 20 volumes (Glasgow: MacLehose, 1905–1907).

Samuel Purchas, a vigorous self-promoter, was well aware of the significance of his publications. He described history and geography as "the two Eyes with which wee see the World," and in the preface to his *Hakluytus Posthumus, or Purchas His Pilgrimes* (1625) he promised a grand vision: "Here therefore the various Nations, Persons, Shapes, Colours, Habits, Rites, Religions. . . . Languages, Letters, Arts, Merchandises, Wares, and other remarkeable Varieties of Men and humane Affaires are by Eye-witnesses related more amply and certainly then any Collector ever hath done, or perhaps without these helpes could doe." Indeed, although by his own admission Purchas never traveled more than two hundred miles from his birthplace, he assembled a collection of travel narratives more than twice as large as *The Principall Navigations, Voiages, Traffiques and Discoveries of the English Nation* (1598–1600), which his predecessor Richard Hakluyt had compiled. Moreover, his publications included narratives of great literary interest, such as William Strachey's account of the wreck of the *Sea Venture* – a source for William Shakespeare's *The Tempest* (1611) – and a description of Xanadu that inspired Samuel Taylor Coleridge's *Kubla Khan* (1816).

Purchas was the son of George Purchas of Thaxted, Essex. The date of Purchas's birth is uncertain: a marriage document stating that he was "about 27" in 1601 contradicts baptismal records, the title page of *Hakluytus Posthumus,* and a remark in the body of that work, all of which point to a 1577 birth. He took the degree of M.A. at St. John's College, Cambridge, in 1600. In 1601, while a curate of Furleigh in Essex, he married a servant in the parson's household, Jane Lease of Westhall Suffolk. They had a son, Samuel, who assisted his father in his editorial labors, and two daughters, Martha and Mary. From 1604 to 1613, when he published his first book, Purchas served as vicar of Eastwood in Essex.

As the titles of Purchas's works imply, he chose pilgrimage as a unifying theme; he retained the sensibility of a clergyman even as he assembled geographical texts. For him humanity's pilgrimage began with the expulsion from Eden, and Christ's Incarnation represented a pilgrimage from heaven to earth and back again. In *Hakluytus Posthumus* he describes pilgrimage as an essential human enterprise: "And thus is Mans whole life a Pilgrimage, either from God as Cains, or from himselfe as Abels. . . . " The alliteration on *Purchas* and various forms of the word *pilgrim* in the titles of his three major works also points to the dominant feature of Purchas's literary style: the elaborate play with the sound of words that is evident, for example, in a passage from *Purchas his Pilgrim:* "But these *Idle bellies* are also *Idoll bellies* Canonized, Deified of the most, *whose God is their belly,* as the jealous god himselfe hath complayned: wee are all belly, we are *Sonnes of Belial* (Belly-all) indeed." Such passages have prompted the critic George Bruner Parks to describe Purchas's style uncharitably as "a vapid and tasteless euphuism of a sophomoric sort."

The vicariate at Eastwood placed Purchas only two miles from the thriving port of Leigh on the Thames and in contact with well-traveled seamen. There Purchas met, for example, Andrew Battell, an adventurer who had traveled in Angola and who brought with him to Leigh an African boy who claimed to have been abducted by a gorilla. Conversations with Battell may have fueled Purchas's interest in foreign cultures and certainly provided material for his first published work, *Purchas His Pilgrimage* (1613). According to Purchas, in this historical and geographic survey of religious practices and beliefs, he brought "Religion from Paradise to the Ark, and thence follow[ed] her round about the World." He cites seven hundred authors, and as he enlarged the work in subsequent editions that number grew to thirteen hundred. He examines the religions of Asia, Africa, the Middle East, and the Americas and devotes special attention to the history of the Jewish people both before and after the Diaspora. Purchas's discussion of the Americas includes accounts of Martin Frobisher's voyages, of Hernán Cortés's conquest of Mexico, and of English plantations in Virginia.

Purchas His Pilgrimage was a great success. John Selden endorsed the work by contributing an epigram to the first edition, and according to Purchas, King James I claimed to have read the text through seven times. In 1614 George Abbot, the archbishop of Canterbury, to whom Purchas dedicated the work and who had himself written a geography text, *A Briefe Description of the Whole Worlde* (1599), named Purchas his personal chaplain. In the same year John King, the bishop of London, helped Purchas secure the rectorate of St. Martin's, Ludgate. In 1615 he was incorporated B.D. of Oxford.

Publication of *Purchas His Pilgrimage* also initiated Purchas's relationship with Hakluyt. In the first edition Purchas acknowledged his debt to Hakluyt's *Principall Navigations,* and Hakluyt provided manuscripts that Purchas used in the expanded second edition of *Purchas His Pilgrimage,* published in 1614. Although Purchas appeared disappointed with the assistance that Hakluyt provided during the preparation of a third edition (1617), in that text he began campaigning for access to Hakluyt's manuscripts, as he wished that "some Juno Lucina would help to bring forth the Posthumus issue of his Voyages not yet published" and thus create a final testimony to Hakluyt's great labors.

In 1618 Purchas's brother and brother-in-law died, burdening him not only emotionally but also financially as he tried to provide for their families. A year later Purchas's mother and daughter Mary died. To assign a broader significance to these events, Purchas associated them with the death of Queen Anne in 1619 and returned to notes he had prepared for a Lenten sermon years earlier. With his typical commitment to comprehensiveness and fascination with historically and culturally distant peoples, he elaborated his meditation on the scriptural aphorism "Verily, every man at his best state is altogether Vanitie" (Ps. 39:5) into *Purchas His Pilgrim. Microcosmus, or, The Historie of Man (1619)* — eighty-six chapters in more than eight hundred pages on the physical, psychological, and spiritual frailty of human beings and societies. He mocked even the worldly accomplishments that he would celebrate in *Hakluytus Posthumus,* observing that the bold mottoes of Europeans' westward enterprise, *Plus ultra* (there is more beyond) and *Non suffict Orbis* (the world is not enough), "could not bee sufficient in the greatest Monarch, against these least and basest" of fevers and illnesses. Purchas stocked these reflections with references to *Purchas His Pilgrimage* and ultimately designated this somber meditation a "Pilgrimage of Vanitie."

By August 1621 Purchas was thoroughly engaged in bringing forth Hakluyt's "Posthumus Issue." By 1622 he had secured access to East India Company records and was spending his summers at the College at Chelsea (later Chelsea Hospital) preparing *Hakluytus Posthumus* for the press. In 1623 he published *The King's Towre and Triumphant Arch of London,* based on a sermon that he had preached a year earlier at Paul's Cross to commemorate King James's escape from the Gunpowder Plot. Even in these reflections on 2 Sam. 22:51 ("He is the towre of salvation for his king") he found occasion to praise the navigations and worldwide trade of London merchants and seamen.

In *Hakluytus Posthumus, or Purchas His Pilgrimes* Purchas returns to the theme of pilgrimage — but this time in a quite different mood, as he assembles "a world of Pilgrimes . . . each of which presents one or other countrey; and all, the rarities and varieties of all." As the title implies, Purchas built on the

Engraved title page for Samuel Purchas's updating and enlargement of Richard Hakluyt's collection of travel narratives and printed title page for the first part

PVRCHAS
HIS
PILGRIMES.
IN FIVE BOOKES.

The firſt, Contayning the Voyages and Peregrinations made *by ancient Kings, Patriarkes,* Apoſtles, *Philoſophers, and* others, to and thorow the remoter parts of the knowne World: *Enquiries alſo of Languages and Religions, eſpecially of the* moderne diuerſified Profeſſions of CHRISTIANITIE.

The ſecond, *A Deſcription of all the Circum-Nauigations* of the GLOBE.

The third, Nauigations and Voyages of *Engliſh-men,* alongſt the Coaſts of Africa, *to the Cape of* Good Hope, *and from thence to the* Red Sea, the Abaſſine, *Arabian,* Perſian, *Indian,* Shoares, Continents, and Ilands.

The fourth, Engliſh *Voyages beyond the* Eaſt Indies, *to the Ilands of* Iapan, *China, Cauchinchina,* the *Philippinæ* with others, and the *Indian* Nauigations further proſecuted: Their iuſt Commerce, nobly vindicated againſt *Turkiſh* Treacherie; victoriouſly defended againſt *Portugall* Hoſtilitie; *gloriouſly aduanced againſt* Mooriſh and Ethnike *Perſidie;* hopefully recouering from *Dutch* Malignitie; iuſtly maintayned *againſt ignorant and malicious Calumnie.*

The fifth, Nauigations, Voyages, Traffiques, Diſcoueries, of the *Engliſh* Nation *in the* Eaſterne parts of the World: continuing the Engliſh-Indian *occurrents,* and contayning the *Engliſh* Affaires with the *Great* Samorine, in the *Perſian* and *Arabian* Gulfes, and in other places of the Continent, and Ilands of and beyond the *Indies:* the Portugall Attempts, and *Dutch* Diſaſters, diuers Sea-fights *with both; and many other remarkable* RELATIONS.

The Firſt Part.

Vnus Deus, Vna Veritas.

LONDON
Printed by *William Stansby* for *Henrie Fetherſtone,* and are to be ſold at his ſhop in *Pauls* Church-yard at the ſigne of the Roſe.
1 6 2 5.

Jodocus Hondius's map of England, reproduced by Purchas in part 4 of Hakluytus Posthumus

foundation of Hakluyt's publications and manuscripts. In the published text he carefully marks Hakluyt's contributions with an *H,* and Parks has estimated that about 40 percent of the material in *Hakluytus Posthumus* had been collected by Hakluyt; the vast majority of the Hakluyt material – more than 80 percent – had never before been published. But Purchas does not merely update the work of his predecessor; he expands the scope of the project, adding discussions of ancient travel and more narratives from non-English authors. Purchas divides *Hakluytus Posthumus* into two parts and imposes a rough geographical organization on the work: the first part concerns regions known to ancient Europeans: Africa, India, and the Middle East; the second part concerns regions that Europeans had discovered since antiquity: Tartary, Japan, China, Korea, the Philippines, the Americas, and the Arctic. Certain topics, such as circumnavigations, the search for a northwest passage, and England's war with Spain, are given special attention.

Even within this broader outline, Purchas retains Hakluyt's nationalistic concern with promoting English commerce and colonization. He argues that natural law sanctions and encourages international trade and that navigation could unite peoples whom "Rites, Languages, Customes and Countries" had separated. Most likely with England's Spanish Catholic rivals in mind, he condemns the recent "perverse conversions in America" and the invoking of religion to justify conquest. In contrast, he defends the English colonization of Virginia as the possession of vacant land and conveniently, but inaccurately, characterizes the Native Americans in Virginia not as inhabitants but as vagabonds who hold "no settled possession" and "range rather than inhabite." The information that Purchas offered could both ease the consciences of English expansionists and better equip them for their undertaking. Consequently, he contends in the pages of *Hakluytus Posthumus* that "All Nations dance in this Round to doe the English service, . . . to perfect the English, at lest the knowledge of the World to the English."

Although the ambition of Purchas's project readily impresses a reader, it also contributes to the work's greatest shortcoming. Sir William Foster has estimated that accounts of expeditions undertaken after the publication of Hakluyt's *Principall Navigations* would have comprised a work as long as

Hakluyt's; Purchas's decision to broaden the scope of the project and to include previously published materials necessitated that, as Purchas put it, "these vast Volumes are contracted, and Epitomised, that the nicer Reader might not be cloyed." Whereas an eighteenth-century essay attributed to the philosopher John Locke complains that Purchas was not a sufficiently selective editor, modern readers have regretted that some of the sections that Purchas trimmed from his sources have been lost forever. Moreover, modern scholars, including E. G. Ravenstein, who have studied closely particular sections of Purchas's work have found apparent editorial errors such as contradictions between accounts of Battell's adventures in *Purchas His Pilgrimage* and in *Hakluytus Posthumus.*

While Purchas's work does not satisfy the standards of modern editorial practice, it did please much of its original audience. A year after its publication the East India Company rewarded Purchas with a gift of one hundred pounds. The reception of his new text apparently encouraged Purchas to bring out a fourth, enlarged edition of *Purchas His Pilgrimage* in 1626. He had characterized a posthumous enlarged edition of Hakluyt's *Principall Navigations* as a "testimony" to the author's "pains"; the 1626 edition of *Purchas His Pilgrimage* had to perform a like function for Purchas, who died in September of that year. In 1657 a "Samuel Purchas A.M." published *Spiritual Honey from Natural Hives; or, Meditations and Observations on the Natural History and Habits of Bees;* scholars believe the author was Purchas's son and consider the fourth edition of *Purchas His Pilgrimage* the elder Purchas's last publication.

By the end of his career Purchas had secured a high reputation among his contemporaries; Anthony à Wood reports in his *Athenae Oxonienses* (1691, 1692) that some in Purchas's seventeenth-century audience acclaimed him as "our English Ptolemy." Today the assessment of Purchas's eighteenth-century critic (Locke?) remains valid: despite his failings, Purchas was "the next great English collector of travels after Hackluyt," and he "preserved many considerable voyages which might otherwise have perished."

References:

Philip L. Barnour, "Samuel Purchas; The Indefatigable Encyclopedist Who Lacked Good Judgment," in *Essays in Early Virginia Literature Honoring Richard Beale Davis,* edited by J. A. Leo Lemay (New York: Franklin, 1977), pp. 35–52;

Sir William Foster, "Samuel Purchas," in *Richard Hakluyt and His Successors: A Volume Issued to Commemorate the Centenary of the Hakluyt Society,* edited by Edward Lynam (London: Hakluyt Society, 1946; reprinted, Nendeln, Liechtenstein: Kraus Reprint, 1967), pp. 47–61;

Walter L. Heilbronner, "The Earliest Printed Account of the Death of Pocahontas," *Virginia Magazine of History and Biography,* 66 (July 1958): 272–277;

John Locke (attributed), "A Catalogue and Character of Most Books of Voyages and Travels," in *The Works of John Locke: New Edition, Corrected,* 10 volumes (London: Printed for Thomas Tegg, 1823), X: 513–564;

John Parker, "Samuel Purchas, Spokesman for Empire," in *Theatrum Orbis Librorum: Liber Amicorum Presented to Nico Israel on the Occasion of His Seventieth Birthday,* edited by Ton Croiset van Uchelen, Koert van der Horst, and Gunter Schilder (Utrecht: HES, 1989), pp. 47–56;

George Bruner Parks, *Richard Hakluyt and the English Voyages,* second edition (New York: Ungar, 1961);

Dirk Passman, "Purchas and Swift; Where Horses Talk and Eagles Carry Men," *Notes and Queries,* 31 (September 1984): 390–391;

D. S. Proudfoot and D. Deslandres, "Samuel Purchas and the Date of Milton's *Muscovia,*" *Philological Quarterly,* 64 (Spring 1985): 260–265;

John T. Shawcross, "The Bee-Simile Once More," *Milton Quarterly,* 15 (May 1981): 44–47;

Andrew A. Tadie, "Hakluyt's and Purchas's Use of the Latin Version of Mandeville's Travels," in *Acta Conventus NeoLatini Turonensis,* edited by Jean-Claude Margolin (Paris: Vrin, 1980), pp. 537–545;

E. G. R. Taylor, *Late Tudor and Early Stuart Geography 1583–1650* (London: Methuen, 1934);

Nai Tung Ting, "From Shangtu to Xanadu," *Studies in Romanticism,* 23 (Summer 1984): 205–222;

Anthony à Wood, *Athenae Oxonienses: An Exact History of All the Writers and Bishops Who Have Had Their Education in the Most Antient and Famous University of Oxford from the Fifteenth Year of King Henry the Seventh A.D. 1500, to the End of the Year 1690 . . . To Which Are Added, the Fasti or Annals of the Said University, for the Same Time,* 2 volumes (London: Printed for Thomas Bennet, 1691, 1692).

Alexander Ross

(1 January 1591 – 25 February 1654)

John R. Glenn

BOOKS: *Rerum Iudaicarum Memorabiliorum ab Exitu ex Ægypto ad Ultimum usque Hierosolymitanum, Excidium, Liber Primus* (London: Printed by Edward Griffin for Francis Constable, 1617);

Rerum Iudaicarum Memorabiliorum ab Exitu ex Ægypto ad Ultimumusque Hierosololymitanum, Excidium, Liber Secundus (London: Printed by Edward Griffin for Francis Constable, 1617);

Rerum Iudaicarum Memorabilium ab Exitu ex Ægypto ad Ultimum usque Hierosolymitanum, Excidium, Liber Tertius (London: Printed by Edward Griffin for Francis Constable, 1619);

The First Booke of Questions and Answers upon Genesis. Containing Those Questions That Are Most Eminent and Pertinent upon the Six First Chapters (London: Printed by Nicholas Okes for Francis Constable, 1620);

The Second Booke of Questions and Answers upon Genesis . . . from the Sixt to the Fiveteenth Chapter (London: Printed by John Legatt for Francis Constable, 1622);

An Exposition on the Fovrteene First Chapters of Genesis, by Way of Question and Answere (London: B. Alsop & T. Fawcet for Anthony Upphill, 1626);

Κουρευs αποξυροs, *id est, Tonsor ad Cutem Rasus* (London: Printed by Miles Fletcher for Nathaniel Butter, 1627);

Three Decads of Diuine Meditations. Whereof Each One Containeth Three Parts. 1. A History. 2. An Allegory. 3. A Prayer, with a Commendation of the Private Countrey Life (London: Printed by A.M. for Francis Constable, 1630);

Rerum Iudaicarum Memorabiliorum, ab Exitu ex Ægypto ad Ultimum usque Hierosolymitanum Excidium. Liber Quartus (Totam Josuæ Historiam Continens — Paraphrasis Psalmi CIV.) (London: Printed by Thomas Harper for the author, 1632);

Commentvm de Terrae Motv Circulari: Duobus Libris Refutatum. Quorum Prior Lansbergi, Posterior Carpentari, Argumenta vel Nugamenta Potius Refellit (London: Printed by Thomas Harper, 1634);

Virgilius Evangelisans. Sive Historia Domini & Salvatoris Nostri Iesu Christi, Virgilianis Verbis & Versibus Descripta (London: Printed by John Legate for Richard Thrale, 1634);

Virgilii Evangelisantis Christiados Libri XIII. In Quibus Omnia Quae de Domino Nostro Iesu Christo in Utroque Testamento, vel Dicta vel Praedicta Sunt, Altisona Divina Maronis Tuba Suavissime Decantantur (London: Printed by John Legate for Richard Thrale, 1638);

Gods House, Or The Hovse Of Prayer, Vindicated from prophanenesse and Sacriledge. Delivered in a Sermon the 24. day of February, Anno 1641, in Southampton (London, 1642);

Gods House Made a Den of Theeves. Delivered in a Second Sermon in Southampton (London, 1642);

Mel Heliconium: or, Poeticall Honey, gathered out of the weeds of Parnassus. The First Book (London: Printed by L. N. and J. F. for William Leak, 1642);

Medicus Medicatus: or the Physicians Religion Cured, by a Lenative or Gentle Potion: with Some Animadversions upon Sir Kenelme Digbie's Observations on Religio Medici (London: Printed by James Young for Charles Green, 1645);

The Philosophicall Touch-Stone: or Observations upon Sir Kenelm Digbie's Discourses of the Nature of Bodies, and of the Reasonable Soule. In which His Erroneous Paradoxes Are Refuted, the Truth, and Aristotelian Philosophy Vindicated, the Immortality of Mans Soule Briefly, but Sufficiently Proved. And the Weak Fortifications of a Late Amsterdam Ingeneer, Patronizing the Soules Mortality, Briefly Slighted (London: Printed for James Young, sold by Charles Green, 1645);

A Centurie of Divine Meditations upon Predestination, and Its Adjuncts (London: Printed by James Young, 1646);

The New Planet No Planet: or, the Earth No Wandring Star: Except in the Wandring Heads of Galileans. Here out of the Principles of Divinity, Philosophy, Astronomy, Reason, and Sense, the Earth's Immobility Is Asserted; the True Sense of Scripture in This Point, Cleared; the Fathers and Philosophers Vindicated; Divers Theologicall and Philosophicall Points Handled, and Copernicus His Opinion, as Erroneous,

Frontispiece and title page for the enlarged edition of Alexander Ross's mythography

Ridiculous, and Impious, Fully Refuted. By Alexander Rosse. In Answer to a Discourse, That the Earth May Be a Planet (London: Printed by J. Young for Mercy Meighen & Gabriel Bedell, 1646);

The Picture of the Conscience Drawne to the Life, by the Pencell of Divine Truth. Wherein Are Set out 1. Its Nature. 2. Infirmities. 3. Remedies. 4. Its Duties. Consisting First in the Truths to Be Believed. 2. The Vertues to Be Practised. 3. The Vices to Bee Avoyded. 4. The Heresies to Bee Rejected. All Seasonable for These Distracted Times (London: Printed by Thomas Badger for M.M. & Gabriel Bedell, 1646);

Gnomologicon Poëticum: Hoc Est, Sententiæ Veterum Poëtarum Insigniores, in Ordinem Alphabeticum Digestae (London: Printed by Thomas Brüdenelli for John. Marshal, 1647);

Mystagogvs Poeticvs, or The Muses Interpreter: Explaining the Historicall Mysteries, and Mysticall Histories of the Ancient Greek and Latine Poets (London: Printed for Richard Whitaker, 1647; enlarged edition, London: Printed by T. W. for Thomas Whitaker, 1648; enlarged again, London: Printed by S. G. for Joshua Kirton, 1653);

Isogoge Grammatica, in Gratiam Illorum Qui Nolunt Memoriam Multis & Longis Regulis Gravari, Concinnata (London: Printed by William Dugard for Joshua Kirton, 1648);

Enchiridion Duplex: Oratorium: nempe, et Poeticum Hoc ab Alexandro Rossaeo Illud a Theodorico Morello Concinnatum (London: Printed by William Du-gard for Andrew Crooke, 1650);

The Marrow of Historie, or an Epitome of All Historical Passages From All Creation, to the End of the Last Macedonian War. First Set out at Large by Sir Walter Rawleigh, and Now Abbreviated, edited by Ross (London: Printed by W. Dugard for John Stephenson, 1650);

Som Animadversions and Observations upon Sr Walter Raleigh's Historie of the World. Wherein His Mistakes Are Noted, and Som Doubtful Passages Cleered (London: Printed by William Dugard for Richard Royston, 1650?);

Arcana Microcosmi: or The Hid Secrets of Man's Body Disclosed: First in an Anatomical Duel between Aristotle and Galen, about the Parts Thereof; Secondly, by a Discovery of the Strange and Marvellous Diseases, Symptomes, and Accidents of Mans Body. With a Refutation of Doctor Browns Vulgar Errors (London: Printed by Thomas Newcomb for George Latham, 1651); enlarged as *Arcana Microcosmi: or, The Hid Secrets of Man's Body Discovered, in an Anatomical Duel between Aristotle and Galen Concerning the Parts Thereof. As also, by a Discovery of the Strange and Marveilous Diseases, Symptomes & Accidents of Man's Body. With a Refutation of Doctor Brown's Vulgar Errors, the Lord Bacon's Natural History, and Doctor Harvy's Book, De Generatione, Comenius, and Others* (London: Printed by Thomas Newcombe for John Clark, 1652);

The History of the World: The Second Part in Six Books Being a Continuation of the Most Famous History of Sir Walter Raleigh, Knight: Beginning Where He Left; viz. at the End of the Macedonian Kingdom, and Deduced to These Later-Times: that is, From the Year of the World 3806. or, 160 Years before Christ, till the End of the Year 1640 after Christ. . . . Together with a Chronology of Those Times, &c., and an Alphabeticall Table by the Author (London: Printed for John Saywell, 1652);

Leviathan Drawn out with a Hook: or Animadversions upon Mr Hobbs His Leviathan. Together with Some Animadversions upon Sr Walter Raleigh's History of the World (London: Printed by Thomas Newcomb for Richard Royston, 1653);

Πανσεβεια: *or, a View of All Religions in the World: with the Several Church-Governments, from the Creation, to these Times. Together with a Discovery of All Known Heresies, in all Ages and Places, throughout Asia, Africa, America, and Europe* (London: Printed by James Young for John Saywell, 1653; enlarged edition, London: Printed by T. C. for John Saywell, 1655);

Virgilius Triumphans, in Tres Libros Dispartitus Quibus Ostenditur, Quantum Mantuanus Olor Plumarum Candore, & Cantus Suavitate Alios Omnes Cygnos Superavit. Una cum Psychomachia Virgiliana, edited by George Ross (Rotterdam: Printed by Arnoldus Leer, 1661).

Edition: *A Critical Edition of Alexander Ross's 1647 Mystagogus Poeticus, or the Muses Interpreter,* edited by John R. Glenn, The Renaissance Imagination, volume 31 (New York & London: Garland, 1987).

OTHER: "Echo Nobilissimi Authoris Opera Reddita Visibilis," in *Papa Perstrictus (Echo)*

Ictus, by Edward Benlowes (London: Printed by James Young, 1645);

Francis Quarles, *Solomons Recantation, Entituled Ecclesiastes, Paraphrased* (London: Printed by M. F. for Richard Royston, 1645), Latin and English verses by Ross; English verses republished in *Argalus and Parthenia,* by Quarles (London: Printed by W. W. for H. Moseley, 1656);

Theologicall Miscellanies of Doctor David Pareus, translated by Ross (London: Printed by James Young for Steven Bowtell, 1645);

Titus Maccius Plautus, *Colloquia Plautina Viginti, ex Totidem M. Plauti Comoediis Excerpta,* edited by Ross (London: Printed by James Young, 1646);

"A Needfull Caveat or Admonition for Them who Desire to Know What Use May Be Made of, or if There Be Danger in Reading the Alcoran," in *The Alcoran of Mahomet, Translated out of Arabique into French; by the Sieur Du Ryer . . . And Newly Englished For the Satisfaction of All that Desire to Look into the Turkish Vanities* (London, 1649);

François de la Mothe le Vayer, *Of Liberty and Servitude,* translated by John Evelyn, Latin verses by Ross (London: Printed for M. Meighen & G. Bedell, 1649);

"Epigramma in Politam hanc Translationem Anglican Trium D. Helmontii Tractatuum, a Domino Gualt. Charletonio, M.D. Clarissimo Emissam," in *A Ternary of Paradoxes,* by J. B. van Helmont, translated by Walter Charleton (London: Printed by James Flesher for William Lee, 1650);

Johann Wolleb, *The Abridgement of Christian Divinity . . . By John Wollebius, . . . Translated into English, and in Some Obscure Places Cleared and Enlarged,* edited and translated by Ross (London: Printed by T. Mab and A. Coles for John Saywell, 1650);

John Hewes, *Florilogium Phrasicon. Or a Survey of the Latine Tongue . . . Collected by John Huise . . . Now Inlarged with a Thousand Phrases,* enlarged by Ross (London: Printed by R.N. for W. Garret, 1650);

"In Nobilissimi Ducis et Amici Intimi Henrici Oxindeni Armig. Iobum Triumphantem Alexandri Rossaei Exastichon," in *Iobus Triumphans,* by Henry Oxinden (London, 1652);

Benlowes, "Praelibatio ad Theophilae Amoris Hostiam: Quae Unica Cantio," translated into Latin by Ross, in *Theophila, or Loves Sacrifice,* by Benlowes (London: Printed by R.N. for H. Seile & H. Moseley, 1652).

Alexander Ross — schoolmaster, scholar and author, Anglican priest, Royalist, and defender of tradition and the "ancient wisdom" in a time of political, religious and intellectual change — is of interest today partly because of the sheer bulk and variety of his writings (some thirty-seven books, extant in nearly one hundred editions), partly because he took sides in some key controversies of his day, and partly because enough is known about his life to piece together a reasonably full picture of an individual who left his mark on an age long past.

Little is known of Ross's origins other than that he was born in Aberdeen, Scotland, on 1 January 1591, that he had two younger brothers, and that his father died about 1641. Between 1606 and 1615 he studied at Marischal College, University of Aberdeen, emerging with a master of arts degree (a four-year, first degree in Scotland).

After leaving the university Ross joined the exodus of Scots seeking opportunity in the more prosperous England of King James I. He evidently had influential friends in England: in April 1616 he was appointed master of the "Free Grammar School" in Southampton on the recommendation of Edward Seymour, Earl of Hertford. In 1619 he was ordained an Anglican priest and licensed to preach; by 1620 he was "Preacher at Saint Maries neer Southampton, and One of his Maiesties Chaplaines." He resigned his teaching position that year after a complaint that he was often absent and left his pupils to a less qualified substitute. Ross's chaplaincy "in ordinary" was an honorary post, but it does indicate that he had connections in the court of King James and, later, in that of Charles I.

During his tenure as schoolmaster Ross produced his earliest writings, three books of "Jewish Histories" titled *Rerum Iudaicarum Memorabiliorum* and published in London in 1617 and 1619. These, with a fourth book written about 1623 but not printed until 1632, tell in Latin verse the biblical story of the Israelites from Joseph to the death of Joshua. In 1620 and 1622 Ross published two volumes of questions and answers on the book of Genesis; they were collected in one volume in 1626. Catechistic in concept and method, these works amount to an elementary textbook and commentary on the Creation of the universe and humanity.

In the late 1620s Ross began involving himself in controversies seemingly outside the scope of a provincial clergyman. His Κουρευς αποξυρος [*Koureus Apoxuros*], id est, *Tonsor ad Cutem Rasus* (The

Barber Shaved to the Skin, 1627) is a competent and biting response to an unidentified work by an Ingolstadt Jesuit who denied the legitimacy of the English church and monarchy. Unhindered by his status, Ross undertakes a thorough defense of the church under the Tudors and Stuarts.

Ross's clerical career was not meteoric. Not until 1628 did he become rector of All Saints Parish in Southampton. In 1634, probably recommended by his patron William Laud, archbishop of Canterbury, he became vicar of Carisbrooke Parish on the nearby Isle of Wight. Ross visited the island frequently; but for the most part he remained in Southampton, leaving the pastoral duties at Carisbrooke to a curate.

In 1634 appeared the first of Ross's two books directed against the "new astronomy," *Commentum de Terrae Motu Circulari* (Comment on the Rotation of the Earth). Dedicated to Archbishop Laud, the book specifically targets writings by Philip Lansberg and Nathanael Carpenter but is also a broad refutation of the post-Copernican astronomy that undermined the Aristotelian-Ptolemaic worldview favored by the church. Ross, with his faith in the received authority of Scripture, the church fathers, and the Greek and Roman poets and philosophers, was unsuited by education or temperament to understand the new theories scientifically. To him, denying that the Earth was the unmoving center of God's physical universe was not a matter of science but of perverse, foolish unbelief.

While in Southampton, Ross produced two Virgilian centos, "patchwork" poems made up of lines from the works of Virgil, who was for Ross the "King of Poets." *Virgilius Evangelisans* (Virgil the Evangelist, 1634) uses Virgil's words to relate the Christian Gospel. In 1637 this concept was worked out on a more impressive scale as *Virgilii Evangelisantis Christiados* (The "Christiad" of the Evangelist Virgil). The epic of more than ten thousand Virgilian hexameters traces the "types" of Christ in the Old Testament and his role in Scripture through the Last Judgment. *Virgilii Evangelisantis Christiados* is rich in allusions to England's growing unrest and concludes with an appeal for peace and unity among Christians.

In 1640 Ross's *Commentum de Terrae Motu Circulari* (1634) was criticized by John Wilkins in *A Discourse concerning a New World & Another Planet*. Ross countered with a book whose title makes his position clear: *The New Planet No Planet: or, the Earth No Wandring Star: Except in the Wandring Heads of Galileans. Here out of the Principles of Divinity, Philosophy, Astronomy, Reason, and Sense, the Earth's Immobility is Asserted . . . and Copernicus His Opinion, as Erroneous, Ridiculous and Impious, Fully Refuted.* The work was written immediately after the appearance of that of Wilkins, but, due to the political and religious turmoil that would lead to civil war in 1642, it was not published until 1646.

The late 1630s and early 1640s ended Ross's comfortable life in Southampton. Even before the town declared for the Parliament, the anticlerical Puritans gave little peace to the orthodox Ross, who was an outspoken supporter of Charles I and Archbishop Laud. After 1640, with the summoning of the Long Parliament and the impeachment and imprisonment of Laud, Ross was powerless against increasing sectarian abuse. In 1641 he married Barbara Bowerman of the Isle of Wight in Carisbrooke Church; she apparently died shortly after the marriage. In early 1642 Ross left Southampton after delivering and publishing two highly provocative sermons: *Gods House, or the House of Prayer,* delivered on 24 February, defends the Book of Common Prayer and accuses his critics of sacrilege. The reaction was strong, and three weeks later he delivered his bridge-burning sermon, *Gods House Made a Den of Theeves,* in which he vowed to "serve these theeves as Christ did, scourge them out of the Temple with the whip of Gods word."

Nothing is known of Ross's whereabouts immediately following his hasty departure from Southampton in the spring of 1642, a few months before the outbreak of war; in all likelihood he was in discreet seclusion, perhaps staying with a friend or patron. In March 1645 he was in London, writing, operating a boarding school in his house, tutoring his young friend Thomas Denne of Wenderton, and corresponding with Denne's guardian, Henry Oxinden of Barham, Kent. The Ross-Oxinden correspondence, which ends with Denne's death in 1648, shows that Ross was highly regarded in London for his learning and judgment. He earned the respect of literary figures of compatible belief such as the emblematist Francis Quarles; the poet Edward Benlowes; and the diarist John Evelyn, who listed Ross among the most "Famous and Illustrius Persons" of his time.

Ross received a stipend as rector of All Saints until 1646; to help support himself he produced a steady stream of hastily prepared publications. His schoolbooks include two collections of sententiae from the ancient poets, *Colloquia Plautina* (1646) and *Gnomologicon Poëticum* (1647); *Isagoge Grammatica* (1648), a Latin grammar in verse; and two adaptations of other authors' works, *Enchiridion Duplex* (1650), based on Theodoricus Morellus's *Enchiridion ad Verborum Copiam* (1525), and *Florilogium Phrasicon*

(1650), which enlarged on John Hewes's 1633 work of the same title.

In 1647 Ross produced the successful *Mystagogus Poeticus, or The Muses Interpreter,* England's first handbook or encyclopedia of classical myth that merits comparison with the scholarly sixteenth-century mythographies compiled on the Continent by Lilius Gregorius Gyraldus, Vincenzo Cartari, and Natalis Comes. *Mystagogus Poeticus* began life as *Mel Heliconium, or Poeticall Honey,* a partially finished myth handbook that had been written in the 1630s and hastily published in 1642 as "The First Part." To transform the slight *Mel Heliconium* into the substantial *Mystagogus Poeticus,* Ross removed the verse "meditations" and added fifty-one mythological entries, expanding the alphabetical coverage from the *Gs,* where *Mel Heliconium* stops, to the *Vs* (*Vulcan*). Each of the ninety-nine entries in *Mystagogus Poeticus* includes a short introduction to the ancient god, hero, or monster, followed by a longer section that interprets the myth in historical, physical, moral, or Christian terms.

Mystagogus Poeticus was well received, and Ross immediately expanded it for a second edition (1648); the book was enlarged again in 1653 and reprinted in 1664, 1672, and 1675. While *Mystagogus Poeticus* is squarely in the ancient mythographical tradition, as revived in the Renaissance by Giovanni Boccaccio's *Genealogiae Deorum Gentilium* (Genealogies of the Pagan Gods, 1351–1360), and draws heavily on the sixteenth-century Continental mythographers, it is distinctively English in its ethical and Christian emphasis: the tortured Prometheus, for example, becomes "our blessed Saviour . . . nailed to the Crosse upon mount Calvarie, where his heart was divided by a launce, onely for the love that he bore to man." How seriously Ross and his readers took such inventions is unclear, but *Mystagogus Poeticus,* though intended as a schoolbook, was probably read as much for pleasure as for instruction. Its interpretations are a vivid illustration of the allegorical and metaphoric turn of mind still prevalent in the mid seventeenth century.

Although nominally rector of All Saints until 1647, Ross could not air his religious views from a London pulpit. Still, he managed to express them, with due caution, in nearly every book he produced. In 1645 Ross published *Theologicall Miscellanies, of Doctor David Pareus,* his translation of Latin tracts by a Heidelberg theologian. *A Centurie of Divine Meditations upon Predestination, and Its Adjuncts* (1646) consists of one hundred prose meditations on predestination (which Ross calls a "comfortable" doctrine) and sixteen on divine justice. The *Picture of the Conscience Drawne to the Life, by the Pencell of Divine Truth* (1646) is a revealing guide to what Ross considered the practical basics of true Christian belief and conduct in a time of religious division. *The Abridgement of Christian Divinitie* (1650) is a heavily annotated translation of Johann Wolleb's popular theological guidebook, *Compendium Theologiae Christianae* (1642).

Given Ross's conservatism, it is somewhat surprising that he was responsible for the first English version of the Koran, *The Alcoran of Mahomet, Translated out of Arabique into French; by the Sieur Du Ryer . . . And Newly Englished, for the Satisfaction of All that Desire to Look into the Turkish Vanities* (1649). Whether he did the actual translation from André du Ryer's French version is not known, but he did write the appended essay, "A Needfull Caveat or Admonition," a disclaimer anticipating the criticism he received for promulgating a "heathenish" work. Ross argues that Christians have a duty to become familiar with other religions to strengthen and defend their own faith; at the same time, he notes that Christians could learn much from the "Turks" about "devotion, piety, and works of mercy."

To avoid provoking the new political powers and the Presbyterian and independent sects that replaced the established church, Ross turned his critical instincts against safer targets – Roman Catholic sympathizers as well as anyone who showed disrespect for the traditional wisdom handed down from the ancients. The result is several seemingly gratuitous "refutations" of the ideas of individuals who are held in considerable esteem today, including Sir Thomas Browne, Sir Kenelm Digby, Francis Bacon, William Harvey, and Thomas Hobbes. In his *Medicus Medicatus: or The Physicians Religion Cured* (1645) Ross exposes the Catholic tendencies in Browne's *Religio Medici* (1642), adding a critique of Digby's *Observations upon Religio Medici* (1645). In the same year he published *The Philosophicall Touch-stone: or Observations upon Sir Kenelm Digbie's Discourses of the Nature of Bodies, and of the Reasonable Soule,* attacking Digby's differences with Aristotle as vigorously as his Catholicism.

In Ross's battles with the "new science," there is often less than meets the eye. In *Arcana Microcosmi* (Secrets of the Microcosm, 1651), which pits Aristotle (favored) against Galen in a verbal duel on anatomy, Ross also defends the "ancient wisdom" against Browne's *Pseudodoxia Epidemica* (1646), which exposes as "Vulgar Errors" certain universally accepted "facts" of nature received from the ancients; to Browne's debunking of the idea that "the Elephant hath no joynts," for example, Ross counters that the ancients meant simply that the beast's joints are "not so easily flexible as those of other animals." The second edition of *Arcana Microcosmi* (1652) also briefly attacks Bacon and Harvey. Ross's "refutation" of Bacon consists of quibbling over some highly questionable assertions in Bacon's little-read *Sylva Sylvarum* (1626) – such as that "the French-Pox is begot by eating of mans flesh." Although notorious as a critic of Harvey, Ross never brings up Harvey's theory of the circulation of the blood but takes issue with his less important non-Aristotelian theories on sexual reproduction.

Ross's *Leviathan Drawn out with a Hook: or, Animadversions upon Mr. Hobbs His Leviathan* (1653) is perhaps the first major exposé of the atheistic implications of Hobbes's *Leviathan* (1651). Although Ross was ill equipped to follow Hobbes's disciplined and original thought, he is most effective in pointing out Hobbes's contradictions of the ancients and of church fathers and the heretical and atheistic tendencies of Hobbes's skepticism.

In the early 1650s Ross based several books on Sir Walter Ralegh's *History of the World* (1614), finding congenial its view of history as a series of tragedies intended by God to warn humanity away from sin. *Som Animadversions and Observations upon Sr Walter Raleigh's Historie of the World* (1650?), a small book of "corrections," was followed by *The Marrow of Historie* (1650), an epitome of Ralegh's work for busy readers. More ambitious and original is Ross's *The History of the World: The Second Part in Six Books Being a Continuation of the Most Famous History of Sir Walter Raleigh, Knight* (1652). Less digressive than Ralegh, Ross takes the reader rapidly through eighteen hundred years of world history, ending with the calling of the Long Parliament in November 1640 – beyond which he dared not go. Compiled from hundreds of ancient and modern sources, the work provides useful insight into seventeenth-century perceptions of comparatively recent historical events. In this respect, Ross's work may be more useful to students of the seventeenth century than Ralegh's superior one.

Ross apparently lived in London, teaching and writing, until mid 1651, when he retired to Bramshill, the northeast Hampshire mansion of his longtime friend and patron, Sir Andrew Henley. His last book to be published in his lifetime is by far his most ambitious and popular work: Πανσεβεια [*Pansebeia*]: *or, A View of All Religions in the World: With the Several Church-Governments, from the Creation, to These Times* (1653); it was enlarged just before Ross's death for the second edition (1655). *Pansebeia* uses Ross's schoolbook question-and-answer format to reveal the beliefs and practices of "all religions" in all times and places. Out of fifteen books, twelve deal with the most familiar religions – Christianity in its various forms, Judaism, Islam, and the cults of ancient Greece and Rome. The religions of more-remote areas, including those of Persia, Egypt, China, Japan, the Philippine Islands, Sumatra, and "the Northern Countries neere the Pole," are discussed cursorily, with Ross supplying whatever details he could find in a broad array of secondary sources. The 1655 and later editions include a candid discussion of the "Sects of this age," including the Anabaptists, Muggletonians, Quakers, and Ranters in England. Ross's scorn for the sectarians, who to him were no better than heathens, is explicit; yet, having accommodated himself over the years to religious and political reality, he grants that a state might tolerate a variety of religions "in privat," although a single established church is preferable for preserving order. In his sixties Ross can even admit that all human institutions are imperfect and that the differences between Presbyterianism and "Episcopacy" are not worth fighting over.

Ross continued writing vigorously and occasionally visiting London until he fell ill and died at Bramshill on 25 February 1654. He was buried in nearby Eversley Church, where two monuments to him exist. For an immigrant scholar who placed his hopes in an eclipsed church and monarchy, he left a sizable fortune, with substantial sums to the son and four daughters of his brother George as well as legacies to benefit the poor in Southampton and Aberdeen and educational institutions, including Marischal College, the Southampton Grammar School, and the university libraries of Oxford and Cambridge. His testament also orders the publication of his "sermons and manuscripts." Two new posthumous works were eventually published, but not until 1661, following the restoration of Charles II. Published in a single volume by George Ross in Rotterdam, they are tributes to Virgil, whose poetry was Ross's lifelong passion. "Virgilius Triumphans," written around 1650–1651, is a piece of literary criticism setting passages of Virgil against parallel passages from other Latin poets and finding Virgil superior to all; "Psychomachia Virgiliana," written in 1649, is Ross's final Virgilian cento, depicting a battle of the virtues and vices inspired by the *Psychomachia* of Prudentius.

At least since Samuel Butler's well-known dart at him in *Hudibras* (1663–1678) – "There was an an-

cient sage Philosopher, / That had read Alexander Ross over" – Ross has been viewed as an anachronism, a medieval polymath in a century of emerging empirical science and skepticism. Whether this is a balanced view is a matter of perspective. Ross readily admitted to living in the past, and yet his many books, all expressing the same conservative outlook, found a ready market among contemporary readers. Perhaps Ross was less anachronistic than his age was diverse. In any case, his ubiquitous writings merit being consulted more often as a "corrective" background for students of the period. Ross's works are particularly valuable sources for the history of science (astronomy, anatomy, natural history), late-Reformation theology, the development of comparative religion, the survival of the classical tradition (especially mythology and the cult of Virgil), the metaphoric mindset of the age, and social and religious aspects of the English civil war.

Letters:

The Oxinden and Peyton Letters, 1642–1670: Being the Correspondence of Henry Oxinden of Barham, Sir Thomas Peyton of Knowlton, and Their Circle, edited by Dorothy Gardner (London: Sheldon, 1937).

Reference:

C. P. Corney, "Alexander Ross (1590–1654): A Biographical and Critical Study," B. Litt. thesis, Oxford University (Jesus College), 1954.

Papers:

The manuscript for Alexander Ross's "The First Centurie of Divine, Naturall and Morall Exercises on Genesis Containing a 100. Choise Questions with Their Solutions upon the First 14 Chapters of the Sayd Booke," written in 1638 – the unpublished expansion of Ross's earlier commentaries on Genesis, which includes the text of the epitaph on Ross's monument in Eversley Church, Hampshire – is in the University of Cambridge Library, MS. Ll. v. 19. (f). Holograph notebooks are in the British Library, MS. Sloane 965, and in the Cambridge University Library: MS. Dd. 6. 69. (H); MS. Dd. 9. 63. (C); and MS. Dd. 12. 38. (G). Many records pertaining to Ross are in the City of Southampton's Civic Records Office. Ross's correspondence with Henry Oxinden is in the British Library: Add. MSS. 28,001–28,010, 54,332; Ross's testament is in the Public Records Office, London.

Richard Sibbes
(1577 – 5 July 1635)

Janice Knight
University of Chicago

BOOKS: *The Saints Cordials. As They Were Delivered in Svndry Sermons upon Speciall Occasions, in the Citie of London, and Else-where. Published for the Churches Good* (London: Printed by Miles Flesher for Robert Dawlman, 1629); enlarged as *The Saints Cordialls; Delivered in Svndry Sermons at Graies-Inne, and in the Citie of London. Whereunto Is Now Added, The Saints Safety in Evill Times, Preached in Cambridge upon Speciall Occasions* (London: Printed by M. F. for H. Overton, 1637); republished as *The Saints Cordialls, Wherein We Have Particularly Handled, The Saints Safety and Hiding-Place. The Saints Assurance. Christs Sufferings for Mans Sin. The Saints Refreshing. Salvation Applyed. The Churches Visitation. Christ Is Best. The Life of Faith. The Art of Self-Judging and Humbling. The Difficulty of Salvation. The Danger of Back-sliding. The Ungodlies Misery, with Other Material Things. Delivered in Sundry Sermons, at Graies-Inne, in the City of London, and at Cambridge* (London: Printed by M. S. for Henry Cripps, 1658);

The Bruised Reede and Smoaking Flax. Some Sermons Contracted out of the 12 of Matth. 20 (London: Printed for Robert Dawlman, 1630);

The Saints Safetie in Euill Times. Delivered at St. Maries in Cambridge the Fift of November, upon Occasion of the Powder-Plot. Whereunto Is Annexed a Passion-sermon, Preached at Mercers Chappel London upon Good-Friday. As also The Happiness of Enjoying Christ Laid Open at the Funerall of Mr. Sherland Late Recorder of Northampton. Together with the Most Vertuous Life and Heavenly End of That Religious Gentleman (London: Printed by Miles Flesher for Robert Dawlman, 1633 [i.e., 1634]);

The Churches Visitation: Discovering the Many Difficulties and Tryalls of Gods Saints on Earth: Shewing Wherein the Fountaine of Their Happinesse Consists: Arming Christians How to Doe, and Suffer for Christ; and Directing How to Commit Themselves, and All Their Wayes to God in Holinesse Here, and Happinesse Hereafter. Preached in Sundry Sermons at Grayes-Inne, London, as R. S. (London: Printed by Miles Flesher for Robert Dawlman, 1634);

The Sovles Conflict with It Selfe, and Victory over It Selfe. A Treatise of the Inward Disquietments of Distressed Spirits, with Comfortable Remedies to Establish Them (London: Printed by Miles Flesher for Robert Dawlman, 1635);

Two Sermons Vpon The First words of Christs last Sermon Iohn XIIII.I. Being also the last Sermons of Richard Sibbs D.D. Preached to the honourable society of Grayes Inne, Iune the 21. and 29. 1635. Who the next Lords day following, died, and rested from all his labours (London: Printed by Thomas Harper for Lawrence Chapman, 1636);

The Spirituall-Man's Aime. Guiding a Christian in his Affections & Actions, through the sundry passages of this life. So that Gods glory and his owne Salvation may be the maine and of all, edited by Thomas Goodwin and Philip Nye (London: Printed by Edward Griffin for John Rothwell, 1637);

A Fountain Sealed; or, The Duty of the Sealed to the Spirit, and the Works of the Spirit in Sealing. Wherein Many Things Are Handled about the Holy Spirit, and Grieving Of It: As also of Assurance and Sealing What It Is, the Priviledges and Degrees of It, with the Signes to Discerne, and Meanes to Preserve It. Being the Substance of Divers Sermons Preached at Grayes Inne, edited by Goodwin and Nye (London: Printed by Thomas Harper for Lawrence Chapman, 1637);

The Christian Portion, Wherein Is Unfolded the Unsearchable Riches He Hath by His Interest in Christ, edited by Goodwin and Nye (London: Printed by John Norton for John Rothwell, 1637; enlarged, 1638);

Divine Meditations and Holy Contemplations (London: Printed by Thomas Cotes for John Crooke & Richard Sergier, 1638; Philadelphia: Lang & Ustick, 1795);

Light From Heaven, Discovering The Fountaine Opened. Angels Acclamations. Churches Riches. Rich Povertie. In foure Treatises, edited by John Sedgwick (London: Printed by E. Purslow for Nicholas Bourne & Rapha Harford, 1638);

The Riches of Mercie. In Two Treatises; 1. Lydia's Conversion. 2. A Rescue from Death (London: Printed by John Dawson for F. Eglesfield, 1638);

Yea and Amen: or, Pretious Promises, and Priviledges. Spiritually Unfolded in Their Nature and Vse. Driving at the Assurance and Establishing of Weak Believers, edited by Goodwin and Nye (London: Printed by R. Bishop for Robert Dawlman, to be sold by Humphrey Moseley, 1638);

The Spirituall Jubilie in Two Sermons (London: Printed by Edward Purslow for Nicholas Bourne, 1638);

The Brides Longing for Her Bride-groomes Second Coming. A Sermon Preached at the Funerall of Sir Thomas Crew (London: Printed by Edward Purslow for Rapha Harford, 1638);

A Glance of Heaven. Or, A Pretious Taste of a Glorious Feast. Wherein Thou Mayst Taste and See Those Things Which God Hath Prepared for Them That Love Him, edited by Lazarus Seaman (London: Printed by E. Griffin for John Rothwell, to be sold by Henry Overton, 1638);

The Saints Comforts. Being the Substance of Diverse Sermons Preached on, Psal. 130. the Beginning. The Saints Happinesse, on Psal. 73.28. The Rich Pearle; on Math. 13, 45, 46. The Successe of the Gospelle, on, Luk. 7, 34, 35. Maries Choyce, on Luk. 10. 38, 39, 40 (London: Printed by Thomas Cotes, to be sold by Peter Cole, 1638);

A Miracle of Miracles; or, Christ in Our Nature. Wherein Is Contained the Wonderfull Conception, Birth, and Life of Christ, Who in the Fulnesse of Time Became Man to Satisfie Divine Justice and to Make Reconciliation between God and Man. Preached to the Honourable Society of Grayes Inne (London: Printed by W. H. for John Rothwell, 1638);

The Saints Priviledge; or, A Christians Constant Advocate: Containing a Short, but Most Sweet Direction for Every True Christian to Walke Comfortably through This Valley of Teares (London: Printed by George Miller for George Edwards, 1639);

The Christians End. Or, The Sweet Soveraignty of Christ, over His Members in Life and Death. Wherein Is Contained the Whole Scope of the Godly Mans Life, with Divers Rules, Motives and Incouragements, to Live and Die to Iesus Christ. Being the Substance of Five Sermons Preached to the Honorable Society of Grayes Inne (London: Printed by Thomas Harper for Lawrence Chapman, 1639);

Richard Sibbes

Christs Exaltation Purchast by Humiliation. Wherein You May See Mercy and Misery Meete Together, edited by Goodwin and Nye (London: Printed by Thomas Cotes, to be sold by John Bartlet, 1639);

The Returning Backslider, or, A Commentarie upon the Whole XIIII. Chapter of the Prophecy of the Prophet Moses. Wherein Is Shewed the Large Extent of Gods Free Mercy, Even unto the Most Miserable Forlorne and Wretched Sinners That May Be, upon Their Humiliation and Repentance (London: Printed by George Miller for George Edwards, 1639);

Beames of Divine Light, Breaking Forth from severall Places of Holy Scripture, as They Were Learnedly Opened, in XXI. Sermons. The III First Being the Fore-going Sermons to That Treatise Called the Bruised-Reed, Preached on the Precedent Words, edited by Sedgwick and Arthur Jackson (London: Printed by George Miller for Nicholas Bourne & Rapha Harford, 1639);

The Excellencie of the Gospell above the Law. Wherein the Liberty of the Sonnes of God Is Shewed. With the Image of Their Graces Here, and Glory Hereafter, edited by Goodwin and Nye (London: Printed by Thomas Cotes, to be sold by John Bartlet, 1639);

A Breathing after God, or A Christians Desire of Gods Presence (London: Printed by John Dawson for Ralph Mabb, to be sold by Thomas Slater, 1639);

An Exposition of the Third Chapter of the Epistle of St. Paul to the Philippians: Also, Two Sermons of Christian Watchfulnesse. The First upon Luke 12.37. The Second upon Revel. 16.15. An Exposition of Part of the Second Chapter of the Epistle to the Philipp. A Sermon upon Mal. 4.2.3. (London: Printed by Thomas Cotes for Peter Cole, 1639);

Bowels Opened, Or, A Discovery Of The Neere and deere Love, Vnion and Communion betwixt Christ and the Church, and consequently betwixt Him and every beleeving soule. Delivered in divers Sermons on the fourth fifth and sixt chapter of the Canticles, edited by Goodwin and Nye (London: Printed by George Miller for George Edwards, 1639);

The Spiritvall Favorite At The Throne of Grace (London: Printed by Thomas Paine for Ralph Mabb, 1640);

Evangelicall Sacrifices. In XIX. Sermons. 1. Thankfull Commemorations for Gods Mercy in Our Great Deliverance from the Papists Powder Plot. 2. The Successefull Seeker. 3. Faith Triumphant. 4. Speciall Preparations to Fit Us for Our Latter End in Foure Funerall Sermons. 5. The Faithfull Covenanter. 6. The Demand of a Good Conscience. 7. The Sword of the Wicked, edited by Sedgwick and Jackson (London: Printed by T. Badger & Edward Purslow for Nicholas Bourne & Rapha Harford, 1640);

A Consolatory Letter to an Afflicted Conscience, full of pious admonitions and divine instructions (London, 1641);

The Glorious Feast of the Gospel. Or, Christ's Gracious Invitation and Royall Entertainment of Believers. Wherein amongst Other Things These Comfortable Doctrines Are Spiritually Handled: viz. 1. The Marriage Feast between Christ and His Church. 2. The Vaile of Ignorance and Unbeliefe Removed. 3. Christs Conquest over Death. 4. The Wiping Away of Teares from the Faces of Gods People. 5. The Taking Away of Their Reproaches. 6. The Precious Promises of God, and Their Certaine Performance. 7. The Divine Authority of the Holy Scriptures. 8. The Duty and Comfort of Waiting upon God. Delivered in Divers Sermons upon Isai. 25. Chap. 6, 7, 8, 9 Verses, edited by Jackson, James Nalton, and William Taylor (London: Printed by John Rothwell, 1650);

A Heavenly Conference Between Christ And Mary After His Resurrection. Wherein, The intimate familiarity, and near relation between Christ and a Beleever is discovered (London: Printed by S. G. for John Rothwell, 1654);

A Learned Commentary, or Exposition, upon the First Chapter of the Second Epistle of S. Paul to the Corinthians; Being the Substance of Many Sermons, edited by Thomas Manton (London: Printed by J. L. for S. G., 1655);

Antidotum contra Naufragium Fidei & bonæ conscientiæ (London, 1657);

The Complete Works of Richard Sibbes, D.D., Master of Catherine Hall, Cambridge; Preacher of Gray's Inn, London, 7 volumes, edited, with memoir of Sibbes, by Alexander Balloch Grosart (Edinburgh: Nichol, 1862–1864) — includes "Dr. Sibbs, his Life," by Zachary Catlin.

OTHER: Henry Scudder, *A Key of Heaven,* preface by Sibbes (London, 1620);

Ezekiel Culverwell, *A Treatise of Faith. Wherein Is Declared How a Man May Live by Faith, and Finde Releefe in All His Necessities,* second edition, epistle to the reader by Sibbes (London: Printed by John Dawson for William Shefford, 1623);

Thomas Gataker, *Christian Constancy Crowned by Christ. A Funerall Sermon on Apocalypse ii. 10. Preached at the Buriall of M. W. Winter,* edited by Sibbes (London, 1624);

John Preston, *The New Covenant, or the Saint's Portion,* edited by Sibbes and John Davenport (London: Printed by J. D. for Nicholas Bourne, 1629);

Preston, *The Breast-Plate of Faith and Love. A Treatise, Wherein the Ground and Exercise of Faith and Love . . . Is Explained,* edited by Sibbes and Davenport (London: Printed by W. J. for Nicholas Bourne, 1630);

John Ball, *A Treatise of Faith. Divided into Two Parts: The First Shewing the Nature, the Second, the Life of Faith,* preface by Sibbes (London: Printed by George Miller for Edward Brewster, 1632);

Richard Capel, *Tentations, Their Nature, Danger, Cure,* preface by Sibbes (London: Printed by R. B., 1633);

Culverwell, *Time Well Spent in Sacred Meditations, Divine Observations, Heavenly Exhortations,* dedicatory epistle by Sibbes (London: Printed by Miles Flesher for H. Skelton, 1634);

Paul Baynes, *An Entire Commentary upon the Whole Epistle of the Apostle Paul to the Ephesians. Wherein the Text Is Learnedly and Fruitfully Opened, with a Logicall Analysis, Spirituall and Holy Observations, Confutation of Arianisme and Popery and Sound Edification for the Diligent Reader,* preface by Sibbes

(London: Printed by Miles Flesher for R. Milbourne & John Bartlet, 1643).

Richard Sibbes (he also spelled his name Sibbs and Sibs) was one of the most important Puritan preachers of the seventeenth century. Equal in influence to such prominent divines as William Perkins and William Ames, Sibbes articulated the mystical element within Puritan faith and practice. Emphasizing the love of God, the communion of saints, and the possibility of a millennial kingdom on earth, Sibbes preached a doctrine that sustained Puritan dissidents in a time of High Church persecutions and provided a basis for the "saints' revolution" during the English civil war.

Sibbes was born in Tostock, Suffolk, in 1577 to the wheelwright Paul Sibs and Johan (or Joanna) Sibs. He received his early education at the grammar school of Bury St. Edmunds. With the support of local ministers and gentry, Sibbes was sent to St. John's College, Cambridge, in 1595, where he received his B.A. in 1599, M.A. in 1602, B.D. in 1610, and D.D. in 1627. In 1610 he became the first preacher to hold the influential lectureship at Holy Trinity, Cambridge, a post that later would be held by John Preston and then Thomas Goodwin before it was returned to Sibbes in 1634. In 1615, it appears, Sibbes was suspended from Holy Trinity for nonconformity, but through the influence of powerful friends he was appointed lecturer at Gray's Inn in 1617. One of the most prestigious posts in London, Gray's Inn provided the forum from which Sibbes addressed powerful lawyers, future leaders of the Long Parliament, and leading intellectuals of his day. George Herbert, Francis Bacon, Jeremy Taylor, and John Milton, along with the Veres, Grevilles, Cromwells, and Drakes, may have been among Sibbes's auditors there.

Of his preaching contemporaries, Sibbes counted as intimates Laurence Chaderton, Arthur Hildersam, John Dod, William Gouge, Philip Nye, Jeremiah Burroughs, and Simeon Ashe. Among his patrons were the earls of Pembroke; the Veres; Robert Rich, second Earl of Warwick; William Fiennes, first Viscount Saye and Sele; Sir Henry Yelverton; Robert Greville, second Baron of Brooke; and, briefly, King James I's favorite, George Villiers, first Duke of Buckingham. Finally, Sibbes was instrumental in the spiritual development of a host of younger preachers: Preston, Gouge, John Cotton, John Davenport, John Norton, and Thomas Goodwin credit Sibbes as a spiritual mentor. These names constitute a roll call of the most influential Puritan leaders of the prewar years, including many of those destined to dominate at Westminster.

Indeed, Sibbes's popularity and prestige became such that when other Puritan preachers were being ousted from their posts, he was receiving calls to more pulpits than he could accept. In 1626, through the maneuvering of Buckingham, Preston, and Goodwin, Sibbes was offered the mastership of St. Catherine's College in Cambridge. When Sibbes was appointed, St. Catherine's was in decay, neither a Puritan stronghold nor a prestigious college. Under his leadership, however, it soon joined Emmanuel as a favored training ground for sons of the Puritan gentry. In 1627 Archbishop James Ussher, another great friend and patron, offered Sibbes the position of provost of Trinity College, Dublin, but he declined it. At the time of his death, when other Puritans had been deprived of even the most obscure lectureships, Sibbes held three of the most coveted posts in England: he had served nine years as master of St. Catherine's, twenty years as lecturer at Gray's, and had commanded the pulpit at Trinity for more than seven years. These offices placed him among the most visible and the most influential Puritan preachers of his day.

Sibbes's career is an example of success based on moderation. Privileging the doctrine of the spirit over the letter of conformity, he kept his pulpit while continuing to preach a spiritist brand of Puritanism. In part, he evaded the disciplining arm of the churchmen precisely by preaching the importance of religious affections and leaving aside ecclesiastical reform for a more propitious moment. Like every Puritan, Sibbes objected to what he saw as corrupted church rituals, but he was willing to compromise outwardly on issues of conformity for the sake of a continued ministry and the preservation of his congregation. He followed the advice he gave his flock in *The Soule's Conflict with It Selfe, and Victory over It Selfe* (1635) to keep secret counsel on such matters: "Christians should be as minerals, rich in the depth of the earth." In this way Sibbes retained his pulpit and his power throughout a period of general persecution of Puritan preachers.

Sibbes was a convert of the "holy Dr. [Paul] Baynes," a contemporary of Perkins who eschewed Perkins's covenantal doctrine in favor of a theology based on God's unconditional and loving prevenience (the grace that precedes all human initiative), and he proved a worthy successor to Baynes's gentle and affective pastoral style. Known as the "sweet dropper" and as "honey-mouthed," Sibbes was considered the most effective converting preacher of his day. Giles Firmin claimed that the hardened sinner "would not hear Dr. Sibbes, for fear he should convert him." In his preface to Sibbes's *Bowels Opened* (1639) Dod describes the sermons as so "full of heavenly treasure" that weak Christians would find "their temptations answered, their fainting spirits revived, their understandings enlightened, and their graces confirmed." Richard Baxter testified in his *Reliquiæ Baxterianæ* (1696) that Sibbes's *The Bruised Reede and Smoaking Flax* (1630) "opened more the love of God" and provided "a livelier apprehension of the mystery of redemption" than all the other books he had read.

Sibbes preached a mystical brand of piety that contrasts and supplements the more austere and legalistic tenets of such Puritan divines as Perkins and Ames: the sovereignty of God, the sinfulness of humankind, the centrality of a contractual covenant in the operations of salvation, and the importance of human cooperation in preparing the heart for redemption are usually regarded as central features of Puritan faith. Sibbes, along with the moderate Puritans who congregated around him, emphasized, instead, the benevolence of God and a view of sinners less as depraved than as weak and foolish. He presented redemption in terms of a free testament rather than a conditional covenant, and, while he urged the penitent to meditate and pray, he preferred to describe sinners as wholly passive in the reception of grace. Though some scholars have claimed that Sibbes was a "preparationist," stressing human agency in cleansing and preparing the soul for salvation, a careful review of his sermons reveals him to be a classic Augustinian in his view of sin as a privation of good and his emphasis on God's complete prevenience in dealing with humankind.

The majority of Sibbes's extant sermons were published posthumously, edited by such friends and admirers as Goodwin and Nye. Only two volumes of collected sermons were published with Sibbes's approval: *The Bruised Reede and Smoaking Flax* and *The Soules Conflict with It Selfe, and Victory over It Selfe*. In *The Bruised Reede and the Smoaking Flax*, his best-known book, Sibbes declares that his primary intention is to comfort weak souls with the assurance that God "will not quench the smoking wick or flax." The message of this sermon series is repeated throughout Sibbes's corpus: "there are heights, and depths, and breadths of mercy in [God] above all the depths of our sin and mercy." Human beings need not fear God nor their own weakness, for "we are saved by a way of love, that love might be kindled by this way in us to God again."

Given this emphasis on divine intercession, it is surprising that scholars such as Perry Miller, R. T. Kendall, and Norman Petit have claimed that Sibbes was a covenant theologian, emphasizing Christian duties over divine prevenience. One explanation for the variety of interpretations of Sibbes's theology is selective reading: while the vast majority of Sibbes's sermons, including *The Bruised Reede and Smoaking Flax,* articulate the dominant theme of divine intercession, some occasional sermons, such as "Lydia's Conversion" (1638) and "The Faithful Covenanter" (1640), do consider the place of human agency in salvation. These utterances must be considered, however, in the context of Sibbes's entire corpus. As did all ministers of the day, Sibbes conceived his sermons less as individual "works" than as parts of the larger project of unfolding the mysteries of Scripture and explaining the work of redemption. Since the sermons most often rehearse the same biblical texts and teach the same theological truths, emphasizing differences between individual sermons tends to produce partial or distorted readings of Sibbes's theology.

With respect to God's nature, Sibbes emphasized mercy and benevolence over the attributes of divine power or sovereignty. In *The Excellencie of the Gospell above the Law* (1639), for example, Sibbes considers the question "what attribute shines most, and is most glorious" in God's nature. He devotes page after page to elaborating the answer: "Oh it is mercy and free grace." He preaches that "the name of God" itself is "Mercy . . . it is the name whereby he will be known." Sibbes's sermons unfold as a series of encounters between the human and the divine – encounters emphasizing the nearness and intimacy of that relationship. The chief biblical sources to which Sibbes returns again and again are those that domesticate the human/divine relationship – Canticles, the Gospel of John, and the Epistles of Paul. In *A Glance of Heaven. Or, A Pretious Taste of a Glorious Feast* (1638) he draws God down from heaven by converting metaphors of kingship into ones of kinship: "Then as God's goodness is great and fit, so it is near us. It is not a goodness afar off, but God follows us with his goodness in whatsoever condition we be. He applies himself to us, and he hath taken upon him near relations, that he might be near us in goodness. He is a father, and everywhere to maintain us. He is a husband, and everywhere to help. He is a friend, and everywhere to comfort and counsel. So his love it is a near love. Therefore he hath taken upon him the nearest relations, that we may never want God and the testimonies of his love." In *The Bruised Reede and Smoaking*

Flax Sibbes encourages his auditors by urging them to "consider the comfortable relations [Christ] hath taken upon him of husband, shepherd, brother." Divine benevolence is reflected even in the extrascriptural designations Sibbes attributes to Christ: "his borrowed names from the mildest creatures, as lamb, hen, &c., which shew his tender care."

Accordingly, Sibbes describes God's dealings with human beings in terms of an unconditional gift or testament rather than the conditional covenant usually associated with Puritan theodicy. In "the sweet combination" of human and divine actions, God is the principal agent: "God stirs us to do all that we do. We see, but he opens our eyes to see; we hear, but he opens our ears; we believe, but he opens our hearts to believe." In *A Learned Commentary, or Exposition, upon the First Chapter of the Second Epistle of S. Paul to the Corinthians* (1655) Sibbes counters Arminian assertions of human agency by answering the question, "Doth God's Spirit do all, and we do nothing?" with the assertion that "we do all subordinately; we move as we are moved; we see as we are enlightened; we hear as we are made to hear; we are wise as far as he makes us wise. We do, but it is he that makes us do." Sibbes is here adopting a position some critics identify with high Calvinism, rejecting the notion of faith as either a condition or antecedent of justification.

Sibbes fills his sermons with a poetry insisting on human passivity and divine intercession: "The soul is a chamber, and the bed; and, as it were the cabinet for God himself, and Christ to rest in only." In the second edition of *The Saints Cordials* (1658) he balances the creature's emptiness against God's fullness. God's free mercy is frequently described as an oil "above all liquors," an "oil of mercy" to be "put in broken vessels" of the heart. Sibbes counsels his auditors to "bring 'empty vessels' now, and we shall have oil enough." "God calls, and we answer." God's action is always primary: "Faith is nothing else but a spiritual echo, returning that voice back again, which God first speaks to the soul." In his assault on Arminian tendencies both without and within the Puritan movement Sibbes calls on the authority of Scripture to counter assertions of human agency in the process of salvation. In *The Excellencie of the Gospell above the Law* he argues that Scripture is filled not with verbs of action but with passive constructions: "therefore it is here in the passive term, 'We are changed from glory to glory, as by the Spirit of the Lord.' So in the chain of salvation you have passive words in them all." As might be expected, Sibbes understood sin as a privation of holiness rather than as active malignancy: the Fall resulted in God's withdrawal of human ability to will the good. In *A Fountain Sealed* (1637) Sibbes explains that originally "there was planted in man by nature a desire of holiness, and a desire of happiness." But as a result of Adam's rebellion, "the desire of happiness is left still in us, but for holiness, which is the perfection of the image of God in us, is both lost, and the desire of it extinguished." Only freely bestowed grace can restore this desire.

In keeping with this view, Sibbes spends relatively little energy considering the effects of the Fall or calculating the sinner's loss of faculties. Rather than a vile hypocrite, the creature is often cast as a willful or foolish child, already eager to return to God. For Sibbes, human insufficiencies are always made good by God, who uses them as opportunities to draw his creatures near. Like the Creator in George Herbert's poem "The Pulley" (1633), the God of *The Bruised Reede and Smoaking Flax* "suffers the soul to tire and beat itself, that, finding no rest in itself, it might seek him"; according to Sibbes, "God will have us rest sweetly in his bosom." In a poetic language again reminiscent of (or perhaps influencing) that of Herbert, Sibbes describes God as the faithful gardener who "pruneth his trees in fittest time," the physician who cures us with bitter medicine, the musician who tunes our breast to make us fit instruments for his praise.

Because he regarded despair as the greatest sin, Sibbes almost always coaxes rather than threatens his auditors. This technique is clear, for example, in several imagined dialogues with "bruised" Christians who would withdraw from God out of conviction of their unworthiness. In *The Soules Conflict with It Selfe, and Victory over It Selfe* Sibbes reassures reluctant members of his flock with the same patience he extols in the Saviour:

> *Obj:* But I have often relapsed and fallen into the same sin again and again.
> *Ans:* If Christ will have us pardon our brother seventy-seven times, can we think that he will enjoin us more than he will be ready to do himself. . . . Where the work of grace is begun, sin loses strength by every new fall. . . . That should not drive us from God, which God would have us make use of to fly the rather to him.

These interchanges between preacher and self-doubting questioners are reminiscent of the loving exchange between the reluctant guest and the welcoming Christ of Herbert's "Love III" (1633). Evident in this passage is not merely Sibbes's faith in the goodness of his "sinful" auditor but also his willingness to take on the sorrows of his fellows in a personal way. Sibbes converts parishioners' doubts into his own and then assuages them. Always Sibbes works the transformation of the "I" into "we," which is the essence of fellow feeling. Throughout his sermons Sibbes emphasizes the communion of saints as the fruit of regeneration. Just as God loves his creature, the preacher loves his auditor, and the saints are to love one another.

Sibbes was an extremely effective evangelist; his success was due in no small measure to the beauty and power of a prose that often seems akin to poetry. His writing is notable for its lyricism, poetic imagery, and acoustic design. While Sibbes may be classed, moreover, with the Puritan plain-stylists who eschewed ornate language in favor of homey metaphors, he did not adhere to the austere formal organization stipulated in what is often taken to be the handbook of Puritan sermonic theory, Perkins's "The Arte of Prophesying" (1617). Sibbes rejects Perkins's tripartite structure of doctrine, explication, and application; lyrical, incantatory, threading thoughts together on a chain of repeated words, his sermons privilege affect over logic, rhetoric over reason, association over argument, sensibility over meaning – and, sometimes, sound over sense. Most often they unfold by the organic ordering of associational logic – that is, by pursuing the ways in which biblical texts allude to and clarify each other.

In *Light from Heaven, Discovering the Fountaine Opened* (1638) Sibbes recurs to metaphors of discovery rather than exhortation to describe the office of the ministry: preachers bring forth what is hidden; they "lay open the unsearchable riches" and "unfold the hidden mysteries of Christ," the incarnated Word. They are miners who "dig deep, and find out the treasure"; friends who "lay open the tapestry, the rich treasure of God's mercies"; servants who open "the box of sweet ointment, that the savour of it may be in the church, and spread far." It is not difficult to see how such a position would dictate a sermon form that would be associative and allusive rather than linear and plotted. Beginning with an assumption akin to Herbert's understanding of Scripture as a "box where sweets compacted lie," Sibbes dilates on the wonders of that sacred sweetness. In his sermons he opens biblical texts word by word, meditates on single phrases and tropes, collates similar texts, and stresses exegesis over applications.

An entire sermon, for example, may focus on the many meanings of a single word such as *behold*. In "A Description of Christ," Sibbes begins with Matthew 12:18: "Behold my servant whom I have chosen." Ranging over such diverse scriptural texts as the Gospels, Hebrews, and Revelation to collate and multiply the significance of this seemingly inconsequential form of address, Sibbes asserts that "in all the evangelists you have this word often repeated, and the prophets likewise when they speak of Christ; there is no prophecy almost but there is this word 'Behold.' " By its repetition, *behold* is drained of literal content; the word becomes, instead, something of a spiritual mantra. Sibbes concludes his long meditation with the declaration: " 'behold,' it is a word of wonderment, and, indeed, in Christ there are a world of wonders, everything is wonderful in him. Things new and wonderful, and things rare, and things that are great, that transcend our capacity, are wonderful, that stop our understanding that it cannot go through them. . . . Now whatsoever may make wonderment is in Jesus Christ, whose name is Wonderful . . . therefore the prophet saith, 'Behold.' " By verbal association *behold* becomes identified with the wonder of Christ himself, becomes a blank counter that can be transformed into an acoustical conduit to Christ. The incantatory mode so often deployed by Sibbes insists on a transcendent meaning that exceeds rational argumentation but is accessible to the regenerate senses of the saint who has "ears to hear." This sermonic style, which shares much with the poetry of Herbert and the music of Canticles, offered an alternative literary model to that of Perkins. Together with Sibbes's theology of divine love, this lyrical literary mode marks a distinctive pietistic style within Puritanism that might be identified as "Sibbesian."

Sibbes was not only a successful evangelist but also a highly visible and effective political advocate. Sibbes furthered the Puritan cause by several means besides his influential pulpit at Gray's Inn. As master of St. Catherine's he (along with Preston, as master of Emmanuel) helped shape a generation of Puritan scholars. Moreover, he was active in collecting and bringing to press important sermons of other Puritan activists; for instance, he and John Davenport collected and published Preston's extant sermons after Preston's death in 1628.

The Puritans were disappointed in the failure of King James I to support the Protestant cause in the Palatinate. The Puritans regarded the war as an attempt by the Antichrist to destroy God's Church; failure to enter the fray seemed a capitulation to Satan that risked the destruction of England itself. Sibbes spoke for his generation in his lament: "How little support hath the church and cause of Christ at this day! how strong a conspiracy is against it!" In sermons such as *The Soules Conflict* and *The Bruised*

Reede and Smoaking Flax he warned that "the spirit of antichrist is now lifted up" and that "the church of God now abroad . . . is in combustion." Counseling auditors to go "to Bohemia, go to the Palatinate, and see what God hath done there," he urged that "judgments of God abroad" were "fair warning" to English "saints" to contend for the faith or risk God's abandonment.

Sibbes focused intensely on the Christian duty to work for the world church. In *The Churches Visitation* (1634) he demands that English "saints" look beyond their own borders to consider the state of the church universal, arguing that "God hath but one true church in the whole world, which spreads itself into divers nations and countries upon the face of the earth." In his commentary on Corinthians he offers a distressing description of the troubled congregations in the Palatinate and Bohemia to awaken English "saints" to their broader responsibilities: "And surely there is not a heart that was ever touched with the Spirit of God, but when he hears of any calamity of the church, whether it be in the Palatinate, in France, in the Low countries, or in any country in the world, if he hears that the church hath a blow, it strikes to the heart of any man that hath the Spirit of God in them, by a sympathetical suffering." Intonations of doom, however, were insufficient responses to a crisis of international – indeed, in Sibbes's opinion, of cosmic – proportions. Sibbes urged the "saints" to be zealous in praying for the church. Union in prayer was Sibbes's irenic version of a holy war: "Everyone, the poorest man, may contend with his prayers. . . . Everyone may help forward the kingdom of Christ; he may help forward Jerusalem and pull down Jericho; everyone that hath a fervent devotion to prayer."

Prayer was not the only requirement of the "saints," however. In 1627 Sibbes joined with Davenport, Gouge, and Thomas Taylor to organize a collection for Protestants suffering "the furie of the merciless papists in the Upper Palatinate." They issued a circular letter to "all godly persons . . . as fellowe feelings members of the same body of Jesus Christ," urging contribution of funds from the private sector "till some publique means (which hereafter may be hoped) may be raised for their reliefe."

Advancing the Kingdom also meant reform of the churches at home. For Sibbes, not violence but "preaching, and writing, and such good means" were "the way to hinder popery from prevailing." Reform would come about in "one main way, the planting of an able ministry; for this painted harlot, she cannot endure the breath of the ministry." From 1626 to 1633 Sibbes, Davenport, and ten others formed the Corporation of Feoffees to plant such ministries. From 1627 to 1631 Sibbes served as president of the group, which met as often as twice a week to plan its strategy for reform. By 1633 the feoffees had engrossed advowsons, impropriate tithes, and schools in some twenty-six parishes; they also controlled the prized St. Antholin Lectures, which High Churchmen fearfully looked on as a "seminary" where, "bringing up youth as they please," the anti-Laudians would "after six yeares . . . disperse them in the Country." William Laud, the archbishop of Canterbury, accused the feoffees of finding "a cunning way, under a glorious pretense, to overthrow the Church Government, by getting into their power more dependency of the clergy, than the King, and all the Peers, and all the Bishops in all the kingdom had."

In 1633 the feoffees were called before the Star Chamber to answer for these subversive activities; the corporation was dissolved, and hopes for pacific reform were ended. Sibbes never preached violence; in the last years of his life, the darkest days of Laud's regime for the Puritans, he continued to preach a doctrine of the pure community of saints. He reminded his auditors that suffering for God's Church was a privilege and that the persecuted were "as the three children in the fiery furnace" witnessing for the truth of the gospel. His teachings were heeded by a generation of Puritan revolutionaries.

Sibbes died on 5 July 1635. He had witnessed the rise of Puritanism and contributed powerfully to the religious and political sentiments that flowered in the civil war. He was revered by Puritans in Old and New England alike. Though not a Puritan, Izaak Walton nevertheless expressed the conviction of a host of Puritan pietists in his set of verses on Sibbes: "Of this blest man let this just praise be given, / Heaven was in him before he was in heaven."

Biographies:

Samuel Clarke, *A Generall Martyrologie, Containing a Collection of All the Greatest Persecutions Which Have Befallen the Church of Christ from the Creation to Our Present Times. Whereunto Are Added, the Lives of Sundry Modern Divines* (London: Printed by A. M. for Thomas Underhill & John Rothwell, 1651);

Thomas Fuller, *The History of the Worthies of England,* edited by John Fuller (London: Printed by J.G.W.L. & W. G., 1662);

J. E. B. Mayor, "Materials for a Life of Richard Sibbes," *Antiquarian Communications,* 1 (1856);

William Haller, *The Rise of Puritanism* (New York: Columbia University Press, 1938).

References:

Bert Affleck, "The Theology of Richard Sibbes, 1577–1635," Ph.D. dissertation, Drew University, 1969;

Isabel Calder, *Activities of the Puritan Faction of the Church of England 1633–1635* (London: SPCK, 1957);

J. T. Cliffe, *The Puritan Gentry: The Great Puritan Families of Early Stuart England* (London: Routledge & Kegan Paul, 1984);

Andrew Delbanco, *The Puritan Ordeal* (Cambridge, Mass.: Harvard University Press, 1989);

Mark E. Dever, "Moderation and Deprivation: A Reappraisal of Richard Sibbes," *Journal of Ecclesiastical History,* 43 (July 1992): 396–413;

R. T. Kendall, *Calvin and English Calvinism to 1649* (Oxford: Oxford University Press, 1979);

Janice Knight, *Orthodoxies in Massachusetts: Rereading American Puritanism* (Cambridge, Mass.: Harvard University Press, 1994);

John R. Knott, Jr., *The Sword of the Spirit: Puritan Responses to the Bible* (Chicago: University of Chicago Press, 1971);

James Fulton Maclear, " 'The Heart of New England Rent': The Mystical Element in Early Puritan History," *Mississippi Historical Review,* 42 (1955): 621–652;

Perry Miller, "The Marrow of Puritan Divinity," in his *Errand into the Wilderness* (Cambridge, Mass.: Harvard University Press, 1956), pp. 48–98;

Geoffrey Nuttall, *The Holy Spirit in Puritan Faith and Experience* (Oxford: Blackwell, 1946);

Norman Pettit, *The Heart Prepared: Grace and Conversion in Puritan Spiritual Life* (New Haven: Yale University Press, 1966);

Sidney Rooy, *The Theology of Missions in the Puritan Tradition* (Grand Rapids: Eerdmans, 1965);

Michael Schuldiner, *Gifts and Works: The Post-Conversion Paradigm and Spiritual Controversy in Seventeenth-Century Massachusetts* (Macon, Ga.: Mercer University Press, 1991);

Harold P. Shelley, "Richard Sibbes: Early Stuart Preacher of Piety," Ph.D. dissertation, Temple University, 1972;

Richard Strier, *Love Known: Theology and Experience in George Herbert's Poetry* (Chicago: University of Chicago Press, 1983).

Jeremy Taylor

(circa 1613 – 13 August 1667)

Edmund Miller
C. W. Post Campus, Long Island University

BOOKS: *A Sermon Preached in Saint Maries Church in Oxford. Vpon the Anniversary of the Gunpowder-Treason* (Oxford: Printed by Leonard Litchfield, Printer to the University, 1638);

Of the Sacred Order, and Offices of Episcopacy, by Divine Institution, Apostolicall Tradition, & Catholike practice. Together With their titles of Honour, Secular employment, manner of election, delegation of their power, and other appendant questions, asserted against the Aerians, and Acephali, new and old (Oxford: Printed by Leonard Litchfield, Printer to the University, 1642);

The Psalter of David with Titles and Collects according to the matter of each Psalme, anonymous (Oxford: Printed by Leonard Litchfield, Printer to the University, 1644);

A Discourse concerning Prayer Ex tempore, or, By pretence of the Spirit. In Iustification of Authorized and Set-formes of Lyturgie, anonymous (N.p. [Oxford], 1646); enlarged as *An Apology for Authorised and Set Forms of Liturgie: against The Pretense of The Spirit. 1. For ex tempore Prayer, And 2. Formes of Private composition* (London: Printed for Richard Royston, 1649);

A new and easie Institution of Grammar. In Which the Labor of many yeares, usually spent in learning the Latine Tongue, is shortned and made easie, by Taylor and William Wyatt (London: Printed by John Young for Richard Royston, 1647);

Θεολογια Ἐκλεκτικὴ: *A Discourse of The Liberty of Prophesying. Shewing the Unreasonableness of prescribing to other mens Faith, and the Iniquity of persecuting differing opinions* (London: Printed for Richard Royston, 1647);

The Great Exemplar of Sanctity and Holy Life according to the Christian Institution. Described In the History of the Life and Death of the ever Blessed Jesus Christ the Saviour of the World. With Considerations and Discourses upon several Parts of the Story, and Prayers fitted to the several Mysteries. In Three Parts (London: Printed by Roger Norton for Francis Ash, 1649);

The Rvle and Exercises of Holy Living. In which are described The Means and Instruments of obtaining every Vertue, and the Remedies against every Vice, and Considerations serving to the resisting all temptations. Together with Prayers containing the whole duty of A Christian, and the parts of Devotion fitted to all Occasions, and furnish'd for all Necessities (London: Printed for Richard Royston, 1650);

A Funerall Sermon, Preached At the Obsequies of the Right Honble and most vertuous Lady, the Lady Frances Countesse of Carbery: Who deceased October the 9th. 1650. at Her House Golden Grove in Caermarthenshire (London: Printed by James Flesher for Richard Royston, 1650);

Clerus Domini: or, A Discourse of the Divine Institution, Necessity, Sacrednesse, and Separation of the Office Ministerial. Together with the Nature and Manner of its Power and Operation (London: Printed by James Flesher for Richard Royston, 1651);

XXVIII Sermons Preached at Golden Grove; Being for the Summer half-year, Beginning on Whit-Sunday, And ending on the XXV. Sunday after Trinity. Together with A Discourse of the Divine Institution, Necessity, Sacredness, and Separation of the Office Ministeriall (London: Printed by R. N. for Richard Royston, 1651);

The Rvle and Exercises of Holy Dying. In which are described The Means and Instruments of preparing our selves, and others respectively, for a blessed Death: and the remedies against the evils and temptations proper to the state of Sicknesse. Together with Prayers and Acts of Vertue to be used by sick and dying persons, or by others standing in their Attendance. To which are added. Rules for the visitation of the Sick, and offices proper to that Ministery (London: Printed for Richard Royston, 1651);

A Short Catechism for The Institution of Young Persons in the Christian Religion. To which is added, an Explication of the Apostolical Creed, Easie and useful for these Times. Composed for the use of the Schools in South-Wales, anonymous (London:

Printed by James Flesher for Richard Royston, 1652);

A Discourse of Baptisme, Its Institution, and Efficacy upon all Believers. Together with a Consideration of the Practice of the Church in Baptizing Infants of Beleeving Parents (London: Printed by James Flesher for Richard Royston, 1652);

XXV Sermons Preached at Golden-Grove: Being for the Winter half-year, Beginning on Advent-Sunday, untill Whit-Sunday (London: Printed by Elizabeth Cotes for Richard Royston, 1653);

Ἐνιαυτὸς: *A Covrse of Sermons for All the Sundais Of the Year; Fitted to the great Necessities, and for the supplying the Wants of Preaching in many parts of this Nation. Together with A Discourse of the Divine Institution, Necessity, Sacredness, and Separation of the Office Ministeriall,* 2 volumes (London:

Printed for Richard Royston, 1653, 1655; enlarged edition, London: Printed by E. Taylor for Richard Royston, 1668);

The Real Presence and Spirituall of Christ in the Blessed Sacrament Proved Against the Doctrine of Transubstantiation (London: Printed by James Flesher for Richard Royston, 1654);

The Golden Grove, or, A Manuall of Daily Prayers and Letanies Fitted to the dayes of the Week. Containing a short summary of What is to be Believed, Practised, Desired. Also Festival Hymns, According to the manner of The Ancient Church. Composed for the Use of the Devout, especially of Younger Persons; By the Author of the The Great Exemplar (London: Printed by James Flesher for Richard Royston, 1655); enlarged by the addition of *A Guide to the Penitent,* by Brian Duppa, as *A Choice Manual, Con-*

taining *What is to be Believed, Practised, and Desired or Praied for; the Praiers being fitted to the several daies of the Week. Also Festival Hymns, According to The manner of the ancient Church* (London: Printed by James Flesher for Richard Royston, 1664);

Unum Necessarium. Or, The Doctrine and Practice of Repentance. Describing The Necessities of a Strict, a Holy, and a Christian Life. And Rescued from Popular Errors (London: Printed by James Flesher for Richard Royston, 1655);

A further Explication of The Doctrine of Originall Sin (London: Printed by James Flesher for Richard Royston, 1656);

An Answer to a Letter Written by R. R. the Ld Bishop of Rochester. Concerning The Chapter of Original Sin, In the Unum Necessarium (London: Printed by Elizabeth Cotes for Roger Royston, 1656);

Deus Justificatus; or, A Vindication of the glory of the Divine Attributes in the Question of Original Sin. Against the Presbyterian Way of Understanding it (London: Printed by Roger Norton for Richard Royston, 1656);

Σύμβολον Ἠθικοπολεμικὸν *or A Collection of Polemical and Moral Discourses* (London: Printed for Richard Royston, 1657); enlarged as Σύμβολον Θεολογικὸν: *Or A Collection of Polemicall Discourses Wherein the Church of England. In its worst As well as more Flourishing Condition, is defended in many material Points, against the Attempts of the Papists on one hand, and the Fanaticks on the other. Together with Some Additional Pieces addressed to the Promotion of Practicall Religion and Daily Devotion* (London: Printed by Roger Norton for Richard Royston, 1674) — includes *The Real Presence*;

A Discourse of the Nature, Offices, and Measures of Friendship, with Rules of Conducting It. Written in answer to a Letter from the most ingenious and vertuous M.K.P. (London: Printed for Richard Royston, 1657); revised as *The Measures and Offices of Friendship: With Rules of Conducting it. To which are added, Two Letters written to persons newly changed in their Religion* (London: Printed by J. G. for Richard Royston, 1657); revised and enlarged as *Opuscula: The Measures of Friendship. With Additional Tracts. To which is now Added, His Moral Demonstration, proving that the Religion of Jesus Christ is from God. Never before Printed in the Volume* (London: Printed for Richard Royston, 1678);

A Collection of Offices or Forms of Prayer Publick and Private. Fitted To the needs of all Christian Assemblies In cases Ordinary and Extraordinary. Taken out of the Scriptures and the ancient Liturgies of several Churches, Especially the Greek (London: Printed by James Flesher for Richard Royston, 1658);

A Sermon Preached at the Funerall of that worthy Knight Sr. George Dalston of Dalston in Cumberland, September 28. 1657, anonymous (London: John Martin, James Allestre & Thomas Dicas, 1658);

Ductor Dubitantium, or The Rule of Conscience In all her generall measures; Serving as a great Instrument for the determination of Cases of Conscience. In Four Books, 4 volumes (London: Printed by James Flesher for Richard Royston, 1660);

The Worthy Communicant or A Discourse of the Nature, Effects, and Blessings consequent to the worthy receiving of the Lords Supper And of all the duties required in order to a worthy preparation: Together With the Cases of Conscience occuring in the duty of him that Ministers and of him that Communicates. To which are added Devotions fitted to every part of the Ministration (London: Printed by Roger Norton for John Martin, James Allestre & Thomas Dicas, 1660);

A Sermon Preached at the Consecration of two Archbishops and ten Bishops, in the Cathedral Church of St. Patrick in Dublin, January 27. 1660 (Dublin: Printed by William Bladen for John North, 1661);

A Sermon Preached At the opening of the Parliament of Ireland, May 8. 1661. Before the right Honourable the Lords Justices, and the Lords Spiritual and Temporal and the Commons (London: Printed by James Flesher for Richard Royston, 1661);

Rules and Advices To the Clergy Of the Diocese of Down and Connor: For their Deportment in their Personal and Publick Capacities. Given by the Bishop at the Visitation, at Lisnegarvey (Dublin: Printed by John Crooke, 1661);

Via Intelligentæ. A Sermom [sic] *Preached to the University of Dublin: Shewing by what means the Scholars shall become most Learned and Most Usefull. Published at their desire* (London: Printed for Richard Royston, 1662);

The Righteousness Evangelicall Describ'd. The Christians Conquest Over the Body of Sin: Fides Formata, or Faith working by Love. In Three Sermons Preach'd at Christ-Church, Dublin (Dublin: Printed by John Crooke for Samuel Dancer, 1663);

A Sermon Preached in Christ-Church, Dublin: at the Funeral of The most Reverend Father in God, John, Late Lord Arch-bishop of Armagh, and Primate of all Ireland: with A succinct Narrative of his whole Life (Dublin: Printed by John Crook, to be sold by Samuel Dancer, 1663);

Χρισιζ Τελειωτικη. *A Discourse of Confirmation. For the use of the Clergy and Instruction of the People of Ireland* (Dublin: Printed by John Crooke, to be sold by Samuel Dancer, 1663);

'Εβδομὰζ 'Εμβολιμαῖοζ: *A Supplement to the* 'Ενιαυτὸζ, *Or Course of Sermons for the whole year: Being Seven Sermons Explaining the Nature of Faith, and Obedience; in relation to God and the Ecclesiastical and Secular Powers respectively. All that have been Preached and Published (since the Restauration) By the Right Reverend Father in God, Jeremy, Lord Bishop of Down and Connor. To which is adjoyned, His Advice to the Clergy of his Diocese* (London: Printed for Richard Royston, 1663);

A Dissuasive from Popery To the People of Ireland (Dublin: Printed by John Crooke, to be sold by Samuel Dancer, 1664; enlarged edition, London: Printed by Elizabeth Tyler for Richard Royston, 1668);

Δεκὰζ 'Εμβολιμαῖοζ, *a Supplement to the* 'Ενιαυτὸζ, *Or Course of Sermons for the whole year: Being Ten Sermons Explaining the Nature of Faith, and Obedience, in relation to God, and the Ecclesiastical and Secular Powers respectively. All that have been Preached and Published (since the Restauration) By the Right Reverend Father in God Jeremy Lord Bishop of Down and Connor. With His Advice to the Clergy of his Diocess* (London: Printed for Richard Royston, 1667);

The Second Part of the Dissuasive from Popery: In Vindication of the First Part, And Further Reproof and Conviction of the Roman Errors (London: Printed for Richard Royston, 1667);

XXVII Sermons Preached at Golden Grove; Being for the Summer half-year, Beginning on Whit-Svnday And ending on the XXV. Sunday after Trinity (London: Printed by Elizabeth Tyler for Richard Royston, 1668);

Christ's Yoke an Easy Yoke, and yet the Gate to Heaven a Strait Gate. In two excellent Sermons, Well worthy of the serious perusal of the strictest Professors (London: Printed for F. Smith, 1675);

On the Reverence Due to the Altar: Now First Printed from the Original Manuscript, edited by John Barrow (Oxford & London: John Henry Parker, 1848).

Editions: *The Whole Works of Jeremy Taylor, with a Life of the Author, and a Critical Examination of His Writings,* 15 volumes, edited by Reginald Heber (London: Ogle, Duncan, 1822); revised and corrected by Charles Page Eden and Alexander Taylor as *The Whole Works of the Right Rev. Jeremy Taylor,* 10 volumes (London: Long-

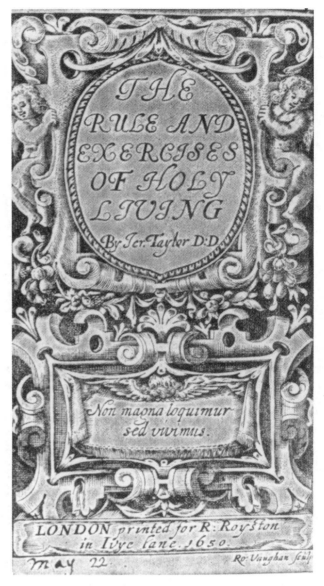

Title page for the first of the devotional works on which Taylor's reputation principally rests

man, Brown, Green & Longmans, 1847–1854);

The Poems and Verse-Translations of the Right Rev. Jeremy Taylor, edited by Alexander B. Grosart (London: Privately printed, 1870);

The Measures and Offices of Friendship (1662), introduction by Travis Du Priest (Delmar, N.Y.: Scholars' Facsimiles and Reprints, 1984).

During the English civil war the Episcopalian theologian Jeremy Taylor earned wide respect for the power and eloquence of his preaching and devotional writing. His theological writings were more controversial, and he gained a certain opprobrium – even from his own party, on some occasions – for being too tolerant. While his theological works are now studied only by specialists, and his sermons, despite the acknowledged effectiveness of the prose style, are seldom looked at even by rhetoricians, he remains a living writer in his devotional works. In *The Rule and Exercises of Holy Living* (1650) and *The Rule and Exercises of Holy Dying* (1651) he still strikes a chord of sympathy with the devout for his meditation on the human condition, and in these works the effectiveness of his loose prose style still stirs the admiration of students of rhetoric. Indeed, Ralph Waldo Emerson called him the "Shakespeare of English Divines."

The third son of Nathaniel and Mary Dean Taylor, Taylor was born in Cambridge; he was baptized at Trinity Church on 15 August 1613. Although his father was a barber, the Taylors had a long connection with learning and the church: Taylor's father and grandfather were churchwardens, and the sixteenth-century Protestant martyr Rowland Taylor was a member of the family. Taylor credited his father with providing his early education, which in those days would have consisted primarily of classical languages and religious knowledge.

Taylor entered Caius College, Cambridge, in 1626 (his age as given in the enrollment documents is somewhat older than it would have been if he had been baptized in infancy). He became a Perse scholar and, after receiving his B.A. in 1631, a Perse fellow. He entered holy orders and was admitted as an M.A. at Cambridge in 1634 and at Oxford in 1635. When he substituted for a friend as lecturer in divinity at St. Paul's Cathedral in London, his preaching attracted general admiration. Among those impressed was William Laud, archbishop of Canterbury, who in 1638 recommended Taylor for several fellowships at Oxford and appointed him his personal chaplain and one of the royal chaplains.

On 5 November 1638 Taylor preached a political sermon on the Gunpowder Plot of 1605 in which he characterized recusancy (adherence to pre-Reformation Christianity) as treason. In light of Taylor's later reputation as a moderate, the tradition arose that he came to regret the harshness of this indictment of Roman Catholicism. At any rate, during the next few years he maintained a low profile, attending to the needs of his parishioners at his living of Uppingham, Rutlandshire, where he became rector in 1638. He married one of those parishioners, Phoebe Langsdale, on 27 May 1639. In addition to children who died young, the couple had a daughter, Mary, who would marry Francis March, archbishop of Dublin.

In 1642 the presentation of the manuscript for *Of the Sacred Order, and Offices of Episcopacy, by Divine Institution, Apostolicall Tradition, & Catholike Practice* to King Charles I brought a royal mandate naming Taylor doctor of divinity at Oxford University. But this royal favor was a mixed blessing. After open warfare broke out between Parliament and the king, Taylor's living was sequestered by the Parliamentary forces. He sought shelter with the royal army, only to find himself taken prisoner for a brief period.

After the king was executed in 1649 and the government of Lord Protector Oliver Cromwell was installed in 1653, Taylor participated in the founding of a school at Newton Hall in Wales; he also served as chaplain to Richard Vaughan, Earl of Carbery, at the earl's estate, Golden Grove. The relative leisure afforded by these two occupations allowed Taylor to complete other literary works, and he became a member of the literary salon of the poet Katherine (Fowler) Philips. Philips – or the "Matchless Orinda," as she was called – was to inspire Taylor's *A Discourse of the Nature, Offices, and Measures of Friendship* (1657).

An impassioned plea for freedom of conscience, Θεολογια Ἐκλεκτικη: *A Discourse of the Liberty of Prophesying* (1647) was the first major work Taylor produced at Golden Grove. It is an important document in the history of the growth of religious toleration. Taylor shows himself to be more tolerant of dissenting views in religion than most of his contemporaries, of whatever political camp or religious sect; but he champions toleration by the device of narrowly defining heresy, which everyone at this period agreed should not be tolerated. He says that there are many degrees of religious error, that only those that undermine fundamental Christian principles are heretical, and that the appropriate response to heresy is excommunication, not censorship. This is essentially the state of affairs in the Western world in the twentieth century, when even the Vatican's *Index Librorum Prohibitorum* has been discontinued. The expression of religious error other than heresy should be tolerated, Taylor suggests, as a natural consequence of fallen human nature. Most of his contemporaries would have defined as heretical any deviation from their own views on religious theology or religious discipline. As a result of his definition, Taylor – unlike John Milton in his similar work, *Areopagitica* (1644) – was willing to tolerate even the publication of works of Roman Catholic theology. But Taylor held that the

Chap. 1. *The Introduction to holy life.*   3

1. Therefore, although it cannot be en-joyn'd, that the greatest part of our time be spent in the direct actions of devotion and religion, yet it will become, not only a duty, but also a great providence to lay aside for the services of God, and the businesses of the Spirit as much as we can : because *God re-wards our minutes with long and eternal happiness ; and the greater portion of our time we give to God, the more we treasure up for our selves ; and No man is a better Merchant then he that layes out his time up-on God, and his money upon the Poor.*

2. Only it becomes us to remember and to adore Gods goodness for it, that God hath not only permitted us to serve the necessities of our nature, but hath made them to be-come parts of our duty; that if we by direct-ing these actions to the glory of God intend them as instruments to continue our persons in his service, he by adopting them into reli-gion may turne our nature into grace, and accept our natural a-ctions, as actions of religion God is pleased to esteem it for a part of his service, if we eat or drink; so it be done temperately, and as may best preserve our health, that our health may enable our services towards him : And there is no one minute of our lives (after we are come to the use of reason) but we are, or may be doing the work of God, even then when we most of all serve our selves.

3. To which if we adde, that in these and all other actions of our lives we alwaies stand before God, acting, and speaking, and think-

B 2   ing

Page from the fifth edition of The Rule and Exercises of Holy Living *(1656), with corrections in Taylor's hand (King's College, Cambridge)* practice of Roman Catholicism in England as an underground religion constituted sedition, and he maintains in *The Liberty of Prophesying,* as he had in the Gunpowder Plot sermon, that the state has a right to prohibit treason and the solicitation to it.

The Liberty of Prophesying provided intellectual validation for Cromwell's policy of toleration, a policy that Queen Elizabeth I had practiced in the previous century but for which her predecessors Henry VIII and Mary I and her successors James I and Charles I were not temperamentally equipped. Such a policy of containment and license, rather than of exclusion and repression, might have prevented the religious warfare that characterized the period.

Taylor's views might be considered self-serving, since at the time he wrote the work his party had been supplanted and he had been deprived of his right to preach. But his approach was so dispassionately legalistic that he ran the risk of appearing to his own followers to have no views at all, as when, in a long digression on the "error" of the Anabaptists, he seemed to many readers to suggest that the orthodox practice of infant baptism cannot be supported either by Scripture or by tradition. Expanding this discussion extensively in the version of *The Liberty of Prophesying* included in Συμβολον Ἠθικοπολεμικὸν or *A Collection of Polemical and Moral Discourses* (1657) to show his familiarity with learned commentary on the matter, Taylor was still unwilling to brand the Anabaptist view as heretical. Taylor's approach allowed those who wished to stifle religious dissent to adopt a broad definition of heresy and then apply to it his equation of heresy with treason.

While at Golden Grove, Taylor also composed the devotional works on which his enduring fame is based. Disavowing casuistry, Taylor continued a medieval tradition in *The Great Exemplar of Sanctity and Holy Life According to the Christian Institution* (1649), a life of Jesus written as an aid to devotion. He presents Jesus as a model for the behavior of ordinary people, a model that is easier to follow than the model of sin. In this and his other devotional works Taylor was influenced by the systematic meditative practices of Saint Francis de Sales, bishop of Geneva.

The Rule and Exercises of Holy Living describes the way to lead a good life as constantly remembering one's heavenly calling while exercising an earthly calling. It is a carefully crafted work that uses meditative techniques to guide the sinner to repentance: "True repentance must reduce to act all its holy purpose, and enter into and run through the state of holy living which is contrary to that state of darkness in which in times past we walked."

Taylor's wife died in 1651. He did not directly comment on this event in any of his works, but in that same year he wrote *The Rule and Exercises of Holy Dying.* Because descriptions of grief so strongly characterize *Holy Dying,* personal sorrow for his wife and for his patron Frances (Altham) Vaughan, Countess of Carbery, who died in 1650, has been attributed to Taylor as a motivation for writing the work. Gerard H. Cox III, however, has pointed out that the work is actually far less comforting to the bereaved than is *Holy Living. Holy Dying* describes sickness as a blessing because it teaches mortification of the flesh, a necessary preparation for the ultimate loss of control of the body in death. The work's rejection of the concept of deathbed conversion as contrary to God's mandate to lead a good life has come to be a distinctively Anglican doctrine, at odds both with the Roman Catholic sacrament of Last Rites and with the Calvinist doctrine of predestination, which teaches that righteous behavior does not guarantee salvation. Cox points out that Taylor's strong rejection of deathbed conversion would provide little solace for most people.

On the other hand, the eloquence of *Holy Dying* is undeniable. Taylor's great strength is in finding a metaphor or extended allegory that gives new life to a commonplace understanding. For example, on the troubles of the rich, Taylor says: "God in mercy hath mingled wormwood with their wine, and so restrained the drunkenness and follies of prosperity." The doubleness of *drunkenness* and *follies* simply gives rhetorical weight to the phrasing, but the specificity of *wine* and especially of the striking *wormwood* brings the idea to life with familiar images. When analyzed, however, the passage is just a restatement of the cliché "Into each life some rain must fall." An effective use of cliché for shock effect is this admonition to accept God's grace: "Lie thou down gently, and suffer the hand of God to do what He please, that at least thou mayest swallow an advantage which the care and severe mercies of God force down thy throat." Sometimes Taylor uses a fullness of phrasing and a familiarity of images to seductive effect. He says that "acts of a holy religion and peaceable conscience," for example, "make us to live even beyond our funerals, embalmed in the spices and odours of a good name, and entombed in the grave of the holy Jesus, where we shall be dressed for a blessed resurrection to the state of angels and beatified spirits." The doubles *religion* and *conscience, spices* and *odours,* and *angels* and *spirit* are, essentially, filler: while in each case there is a differ-

Taylor with members of the family of Richard Vaughan, Earl of Carbery, at the earl's estate, Golden Grove, illustration from the fifteenth edition of Taylor's The Rule and Exercises of Holy Dying *(1690)*

ence in meaning, either meaning would have sufficed to illustrate the point at hand. The unnecessary fullness is, however, all in the interests of ease of understanding. Taylor does not obfuscate with his extra verbiage; he always presents one point at a time without any rhetorical delays or interrupting qualifications. This expository style is solidly in the tradition of the Roman playwright and Stoic philosopher Seneca. At his best, as he often is in *Holy Dying,* Taylor observes normal word order, presents his points clearly but with an engaging redundance, and emphasizes the deep truths that abide in conventional ideas through striking application of familiar images: "neighbours shall say, 'he died a rich man'; and yet his wealth will not profit him in the grave, but hugely swell the sad accounts of doomsday." The end of such a passage resonates with the cumulative effect of technically irrelevant descriptive words: *hugely* personalizes by pressing too hard to control the reader's attitude; *sad* domesticates the scene at Judgment Day by directing attention to the sinner, not Saint Peter. The familiar image of the account book of Doomsday is made newly vivid as the list of the good works and bad deeds of life come to seem like the inventory of a great estate or even the comprehensive census of the Domesday Book (1086).

Taylor produced several works that were conceived as substitutes for the Book of Common Prayer, which was banned at this time by Cromwell's government. *The Golden Grove* (1655) is a manual of private devotion and, accordingly, ought not to have given any offense. But some impolitic observations in the preface led to Taylor's imprisonment. It would, perhaps, have passed to say that his book was necessitated by the "sad declension of religion," but to claim that "never did the excellency of episcopal government appear so demonstrably and conspicuously as now" and that "the people are fallen under the harrows and saws of impertinent and ignorant preachers" was going too far.

In addition to prose devotions, *The Golden Grove* includes some two dozen Festival Hymns. Never regarded as Taylor's happiest effort, this collection must, however, be seen as ceremonial verse — public prayer poetry — not as lyric expression of private sentiments. The conventional end rhymes and the insistent end-stopping should be taken not as evidence of poetic inexperience but as aids to recital by a congregation in unison. The imagery of these poems, on the other hand, is better than it has been given credit for being and sometimes brings a new vividness to the familiar religious occasion or idea, as in the image of Pentecost blowing on embers to rekindle a fire or the description of prayer as an attempt to "pant towards" God to "Unclay" the "wearied spirit."

A Collection of Offices or Forms of Prayer Publick and Private (1658) more daringly reconstitutes a full liturgy – the first time since the Reformation that the scriptural passages had been rendered anew in English; other liturgies were redactions and revisions of the collect of Thomas Cranmer, the sixteenth-century archbishop of Canterbury. The publication in *A Collection of Offices* of an illustration of Jesus at prayer, which was interpreted as diminishing the Godhead of Christ, led to another term of imprisonment for Taylor.

Unum Necessarium (1655) is not a devotional but a theological work. Perhaps as a palliative to the despair he must have found among his fellow Episcopalians during this period, Taylor emphasizes the need for human effort in spiritual matters to such an extent that he was accused of Pelagianism, the heresy of believing that good works are sufficient for achieving salvation. His slighting of the need for divine grace was offensive to all religious parties of the time.

By 1655 Taylor had married Joanna Bridges, an heiress. In 1656 and 1657 two young sons by his first wife died. Taylor worked out his grief by completing what he believed would be his major contribution to systematic theology, *Ductor Dubitantium, or The Rule of Conscience in All Her Generall Measures* (1660). *Ductor Dubitantium* (Guide among Doubtful Things) is a work of moral theology, arguing that conscience teaches natural law and helps bring the understanding that Christ's teaching is the perfection of natural law; since human law derives its authority from divine law, it is to be obeyed by the directive of conscience. Taylor, however, rejects the conventional understanding of the "consent of nations" (what all civilized societies do) as providing insight into the content of natural law, making the commonsensical point that there is no agreement among nations on moral matters: "For there are not many propositions in all which nature can teach; and we should know but a very few things if we did not go to school to God, to tutors, to experience, and to necessity. This pretence would not only establish purgatory, but the worship of images, and the multitude of gods, and idololatrical services, and very many superstitions, and trifling observances, and confidences in dreams, and the sacrifice of beasts, and many things more than can well become or combine with Christianity. When not only some nations but all agree in a proposition, it is a good corroborative, a good second to our persua-

sions, but not a principal. . . ." *Of the Laws of Ecclesiastical Polity* (1594–1662), by Richard Hooker, remains the standard work on natural law for Anglicans, but Taylor's *Ductor Dubitantium* is still valuable to theologians for its extensive presentation of cases of conscience.

In addition to writing and performing his duties at Newton Hall and Golden Grove, Taylor continued to preach to the underground Episcopalian communion both in Wales and in London, where the diarist John Evelyn, who became a close friend, was a member of his illegal congregation. In his preaching Taylor did not emphasize the explication of scriptural texts or other theological matters; indeed, he was not an intellectual preacher at all but, instead, used a relaxed style to show the importance of familiar ethical values. While not without learned allusions, his sermons make their points primarily through metaphor, not syllogisms or appeals to authority. His metaphors – which are often elaborated into conceits – are particularly characterized by nature imagery: "The dream of the yolk of an egg importeth gold, saith Artemidorus; and they that use to remember such fantastic idols are afraid to lose a friend when they dream their teeth shake, when naturally it will rather signify a scurvy." What could be more reassuringly familiar than the image of the patient in a fever with his teeth chattering? The reference to Artemidorus indicates that Taylor is conversant with the classics, but the nononsense, forward-moving prose and the common-sense illustration conspire to undermine the classical authority completely.

In 1658 Edward, Viscount Conway, established Taylor as lecturer for a congregation of Episcopalian diehards at Lisburn, Antrim, Ireland. Although a safe conduct from the doctrinally tolerant Cromwell enabled him to take up his duties, Taylor was soon embroiled in a controversy and was charged with heresy in 1659 for using the outlawed sign of the cross in the administration of baptism. The outcome of the case is obscure.

The peaceful restoration of the monarchy occurred the following year, and in the same year *Ductor Dubitantium* was at last published with a dedication to King Charles II. As probably the most eloquent of the Episcopalian clergy during the Interregnum, Taylor was, in January 1661, among the first to be advanced to the episcopate. But his see of Down and Connor in Ireland embroiled him in intractable antagonisms, for the Protestant population did not welcome a restoration of episcopal rule. During the Interregnum their Presbyterian clergy had been replaced by Cromwell's supporters, and

Letter from Taylor to a friend, the diarist John Evelyn (Pierpont Morgan Library, MA 3383) the Restoration simply made things worse by leaving their clergy disenfranchised and imposing an alien form of church discipline as well. Taylor found it hard to exercise his announced principles of toleration in the face of such opposition and of a charge of heresy based on a much narrower definition than the one he advocated. He asked to be translated to another see, preferably in England; instead, in June 1661 he was given Dromore as an additional Irish diocese. Taylor's inability to find common ground with the Presbyterians of his diocese left them to organize an independent church, which still exists.

Furthermore, Protestantism was confined to the middle classes in Ireland; thus, Taylor also had to contend with the Roman Catholicism of the vast majority of the population. A *Dissuasive from Popery to the People of Ireland* (1664; enlarged, 1668) was his unsuccessful approach to this problem. While the work is a clear and full presentation of the conventional Protestant objections to Catholicism, Taylor was so oblivious to the cultural gulf between the native population of Ireland and the Protestant establishment that he blithely criticizes the Catholic church for conducting services in Latin, a language no longer understood by most people, without acknowledging that the Church of Ireland was doing much the same thing in relation to the Irish by conducting services in English.

On 13 August 1667 Taylor died of a fever contracted while visiting the sick. His second wife seems to have survived him until at least 1679. Joanna, the one child of this marriage to reach adulthood, inherited her mother's estates and married Edward Harrison, a member of Parliament for Ireland.

James Roy King has suggested that the great variations in the style and intellectual quality of Taylor's prose are the consequence of a consistent methodology. Taylor adopts so wholeheartedly the popular loose Senecan method of composition that anacoluthon, the sudden abandonment of one grammatical structure for another, seems to characterize his whole output. When he is impassioned, he invents metaphors that carry the reader (or, in the case of the sermons, the hearer) beyond the conventions of logic and coherence; but when he is less engaged by his subject the metaphors are less brilliant and, consequently, fail to compensate for the changes of focus, which then reveal themselves as, at best, a self-indulgent mannerism and, at worst, an obstacle to sequential argument. Nevertheless, on the whole Taylor's style is the basis of his abiding greatness because of its subtle responsiveness to content. Although his devotions still have the power

to move, readers of the late twentieth century will regard his disputations as mere casuistry.

Letters:

H. J. Lawlor, "Two Letters of Jeremy Taylor," *Church of Ireland Gazette,* 43 (1901): 482–483;

William Proctor Williams, "Eight Unpublished Letters of Jeremy Taylor," *Anglican Theological Review,* 58 (1976): 179–193.

Bibliographies:

Robert Gathorne-Hardy and William Proctor Williams, *A Bibliography of the Writings of Jeremy Taylor to 1700 with a Selection of Tayloriana* (De Kalb: Northern Illinois University Press, 1971);

Williams, *Jeremy Taylor, 1700–1976: An Annotated Checklist* (New York: Garland, 1979).

Biographies:

Reginald Heber, *The Life of Jeremy Taylor,* 2 volumes (London: James Duncan and R. Priestley, 1824; Hartford, Conn.: F. J. Huntington, 1832);

"Comments on the Biography of Jeremy Taylor," *Gentleman's Magazine,* 53 (April 1855): 376–380;

Charles James Stranks, *The Life and Writings of Jeremy Taylor* (London: Society for the Promotion of Christian Knowledge, 1952).

References:

Sister M. Salome Antoine, *The Rhetoric of Jeremy Taylor's Prose Ornament of the Sunday Sermons* (Washington, D.C.: Catholic University of America, 1946);

John Woolman Brush, *"The Liberty of Prophesying,"* *Crozer Quarterly,* 25 (1948): 216–223;

Gerard H. Cox III, "A Re-Evaluation of Jeremy Taylor's *Holy Living* and *Holy Dying,*" *Neuphilologische Mitteilungen,* 73, no. 4 (1972): 836–848;

Elfreda T. Dubois, "Saint Francis de Sales and Jeremy Taylor: *Introduction à la vie dévote* and *Holy Living:* A Comparison," *History of European Ideas,* 2, no. 1 (1981): 49–63;

Paul Elman, "The Fame of Jeremy Taylor," *Anglican Theological Review,* 44 (1962): 389–403;

Elman, "Jeremy Taylor and the Fall of Man," *Modern Language Quarterly,* 14 (June 1953): 139–148;

Percy Thomas Fenn, Jr., "The Latitudinarians and Toleration," *Washington University Studies,* 13 (1925–1926): 181–245;

Robert Gathorne-Hardy, "Jeremy Taylor and Hatton's *Psalter of David,*" *Times Literary Supplement,* 18 February 1955, p. 112;

Harry Glicksman, "The Figurative Quality in Jeremy Taylor's *Holy Dying,*" *Sewanee Review,* 30 (October 1922): 488–494;

Robert Hoopes, "Voluntarism in Jeremy Taylor and the Platonic Tradition," *Huntington Library Quarterly,* 13 (August 1950): 341–354;

D. S. Hopkirk, "A Seventeenth-Century Classic: Jeremy Taylor's *The Liberty of Prophesying,*" *Reformed Theological Review,* 14 (1955): 81–89;

Frank Livingstone Huntley, *Jeremy Taylor and the Great Rebellion: A Study of His Mind and Temper in Controversy* (Ann Arbor: University of Michigan Press, 1970);

James Roy King, "Certain Aspects of Jeremy Taylor's Prose Style," *English Studies,* 37 (1956): 197–210;

King, *Studies in Six Seventeenth-Century Writers* (Athens: Ohio University Press, 1966);

Elizabeth M. MacKenzie, "Golden Grove," *Times Literary Supplement,* 20 November 1937, p. 891;

Daniel Merriman, "Jeremy Taylor and Religious Liberty in the English Church," *Proceedings of the American Antiquarian Society,* 17 (April 1905): 93–124;

Byron Nelson, " 'Our Brother Is Not Dead': Theme, Imagery, and Use of Liturgy in the Funeral Sermons of John Donne and Jeremy Taylor," *West Virginia Philological Papers,* 25 (1979): 12–20;

Robert Nossen, "Jeremy Taylor: Seventeenth-Century Theologian," *Anglican Theological Review,* 42 (1960): 28–39;

Raymond A. Peterson, "Jeremy Taylor on Conscience and Law," *Anglican Theological Review,* 48 (1966): 243–263;

Peterson, "Jeremy Taylor's Theology of Public Worship," *Anglican Theological Review,* 46 (1964): 204–216;

Paul G. Stanwood, "Stobaeus and Classical Borrowing in the Renaissance with Special Reference to Richard Hooker and Jeremy Taylor," *Neophilologus,* 59 (January 1975): 141–146;

Truman Guy Steffan, "Jeremy Taylor's Criticism of Abstract Speculation," *Studies in English,* 20 (1940): 96–108;

Jeanne K. Welcher, "John Evelyn to Jeremy Taylor," *Notes and Queries,* 214 (October 1969): 375;

Margaret L. Wiley, "Jeremy Taylor, the Sceptic as Churchman," *Western Humanities Review,* 4 (Winter 1949–1950): 3–17;

William Proctor Williams, "The First Edition of *Holy Living:* An Episode in the Seventeenth-Century Book Trade," *Library,* 28 (June 1973): 99–107;

Williams, "Jeremy Taylor's Other Style," *Kansas Quarterly,* 7 (Fall 1975): 91–96.

Papers:

The only work of Jeremy Taylor's that survives in manuscript is *On the Reverence Due to the Altar,* which is at Queen's College, Oxford, part of MS 217. At least seventy-seven manuscript letters of Taylor's survive, not all of which have been published; they are widely dispersed, and no library has a substantial number. The Fitzwilliam Museum, Cambridge University; the British Library; the Bodleian Library, Oxford University; Northern Illinois University; Princeton University; Harvard University; and Yale University have groups of letters. Smaller numbers, mostly individual letters, are held by the Historical Society of Pennsylvania, the Pierpont Morgan Library, the Maine Historical Society, the Buffalo and Erie County Public Library, Dromore Cathedral, Haverford College, the Scottish Record Office, the Hyde Collection (a private collection in Somerville, New Jersey), the Warwickshire Public Records Office, and Belvoir Castle. Still other letters are in private hands.

Izaak Walton

(September? 1593 – 15 December 1683)

Clayton D. Lein
Purdue University

BOOKS: *The Compleat Angler, or the Contemplative Man's Recreation. Being a Discourse of Fish and Fishing, Not unworthy the perusal of most Anglers* (London: Printed by T. Maxey for Richard Marriot, 1653); revised as *The Compleat Angler, or the Contemplative Man's Recreation. Being a Discourse of Rivers, and Fish-Ponds, and Fish, and Fishing. Not unworthy of the perusal of most Anglers* (London: Printed by T. Maxey for Richard Marriot, 1655); revised as *The Compleat Angler, or the Contemplative Man's Recreation. Being a Discourse of Rivers, Fish-Ponds, Fish and Fishing. To which Is added The Laws of Angling: with a new Table of the Particulars in this Book* (London: Printed by J. G. for Richard Marriot, 1661); revised in *The Universal Angler, Made so, by Three Books of Fishing. The First Written by Mr. Izaak Walton; The Second by Charles Cotton, Esq; The Third by Col. Robert Venables. All which may be bound together, or sold each of them severally* (London: Printed for Richard Marriot, 1676);

The Life of John Donne, Dr. in Divinity, and Late Dean of Saint Pavls Church London (London: Printed by J. G. for Richard Marriot, 1658) — revised from "The Life and Death of Dr Donne, Late Deane of St Pauls London," in *LXXX Sermons preached by that learned and reverend divine, Iohn Donne, D^r in Divinity, Late Deane of the Cathedrall Church of S. Pauls London* (London: Printed for Richard Royston & Richard Marriot, 1640);

The Life of Mr. Rich. Hooker, The Author of those Learned Books of the Laws of Ecclesiastical Polity (London: Printed by J. G. for Richard Marriot, 1665); revised in *The Works of Mr. Richard Hooker* (London: Printed by Thomas Newcomb for Andrew Crooke, 1666);

The Life of Mr. George Herbert (London: Printed by Thomas Newcomb for Richard Marriot, 1670); revised in *The Temple. Sacred Poems and Private Ejaculations*, by Herbert, tenth edition (London: Printed by W. Godbid for R. S. & John Williams, 1674);

The Lives of D^r· John Donne, Sir Henry Wotton, M^r· Richard Hooker, M^r· George Herbert. To which are added some Letters written by Mr. George Herbert, at his being in Cambridge: With others to his Mother, the Lady Magdalen Herbert, written by John Donne, afterwards Dean of St. Pauls (London: Printed by Thomas Newcomb for Richard Marriot, 1670; revised edition, London: Printed by Thomas Roycroft for Richard Marriot, 1675) — life of Wotton revised from "The Life of Sir Henry Wotton," in *Reliquiae Wottonianae*, edited by Walton (London: Printed by Thomas Maxey for Richard Marriot, 1651; revised edition, London: Printed by T. Roycroft for Richard Marriot, 1672);

The Life of Dr. Sanderson, Late Bishop of Lincoln. To which is added, some Short Tracts or Cases of Conscience, written by the said Bishop (London: Printed for Richard Marriot, 1678); revised in *XXXV Sermons*, by Robert Sanderson, seventh edition (London: Printed for Benjamin Tooke, 1681);

Love and Truth: in two modest and peaceable letters, concerning the distempers of the present times. Written from a quiet and conformable Citizen of London, to two busie and factious Shopkeepers in Coventry, anonymous (London: Printed by M. C. for Henry Brome, 1680).

Editions: *The Lives of Dr. John Donne; Sir Henry Wotton; Mr. Richard Hooker; Mr. George Herbert; and Dr. Robert Sanderson. By Isaac Walton. With Notes, and the Life of the Author*, edited by Thomas Zouch (York: Printed by Wilson, Spence & Mawman, 1796);

The Complete Angler, or The Contemplative Man's Recreation; Being a Discourse of Rivers, Fish-Ponds, Fish and Fishing, Written by Izaak Walton, and Instructions How to Angle for a Trout or Grayling in a Clear Stream, by Charles Cotton, 2 volumes, ed-

Portrait by Jacob Huysmans (National Gallery, London)

ited by Sir Harris Nicolas (London: Pickering, 1836);

The Complete Angler; or, The Contemplative Man's Recreation, by Isaac Walton. And Instructions How to Angle for a Trout or Grayling in a Clear Stream, by Charles Cotton. With Copious Notes, for the Most Part Original, a Bibliographical Preface, Giving an Account of Fishing and Fishing-Books, from the Earliest Antiquity to the Time of Walton, and a Notice of Cotton and His Writings, by the American Editor. To Which Is Added an Appendix, Including Illustrative Ballads, Music, Papers on American Fishing, and the Most Complete Catalogue of Books on Angling, etc., Ever Printed, edited by George Washington Bethune (New York & London: Wiley & Putnam, 1847);

Waltoniana: Inedited Remains in Verse and Prose of Izaak Walton, edited by Richard Herne Shepherd (London: Pickering, 1878);

The Compleat Angler, or The Contemplative Man's Recreation Being a Discourse of Rivers Fish-Ponds Fish and Fishing Written Izaak Walton, and Instructions How to Angle for a Trout or Grayling in a Clear Stream by Charles Cotton, 2 volumes, edited by R. B. Marston (London: Sampson Low, Marston, Searle & Rivington, 1888);

The Compleat Angler, or The Contemplative Man's Recreation, Being a Discourse of Rivers, Fish Ponds, Fish & Fishing, Written by Izaak Walton, and Instructions How to Angle for a Trout or Grayling in a Clear Stream, by Charles Cotton, 2 volumes, edited by George A. B. Dewar (London: Freemantle, 1902);

The Lives of John Donne, Sir Henry Wotton, Richard Hooker, George Herbert and Robert Sanderson, edited by George Saintsbury (London & New York: Oxford University Press, 1927);

The Compleat Walton, edited by Geoffrey Keynes (London: Nonesuch Press, 1929);

The Lives of John Donne, Sir Henry Wotton, Richard Hooker, George Herbert & Robert Sanderson, edited by S. B. Carter (London: Falcon Educational Books, 1951);

The Compleat Angler 1653–1676, edited by Jonquil Bevan (Oxford: Clarendon Press, 1983).

OTHER: "An Elegie upon D$^{r.}$ Donne," in *Poems, By J. D. with Elegies on the Authors Death* (London: Printed by M. F. for John Marriot, 1633; revised, 1635);

"To my ingenious Friend Mr. Brome, on his various and excellent Poems: An humble Eglog. Daman and Dorus. Written the 29. of May, 1660," in *Songs And Other Poems,* by Alexander Brome (London: Printed for Henry Brome, 1661);

Thealma and Clearchus, a Pastoral History, in smooth and easie Verse. Written long since, By John Chalkhill, Esq; an Acquaintant and Friend of Edmund Spencer, preface by Walton (London: Printed for Benjamin Tooke, 1683).

George Saintsbury once observed that few authors have acquired fame through such different volumes as Izaak Walton's *The Compleat Angler* (1653) and *The Lives of Dr. John Donne, Sir Henry Wotton, Mr. Richard Hooker, Mr. George Herbert* (1670). Walton, one hastens to add, did not anticipate a career as a man of letters. Any account of his life must, accordingly, trace both his evolution into a writer and the influences and experiences that led to such diverse masterpieces.

Walton's fascination with nature, which receives exuberant expression throughout *The Compleat Angler,* may, perhaps, be attributed in part to a childhood spent in the Midlands. The youngest of three children, he was christened on 21 September 1593 in Stafford, to which his father, Gervase, a "tippler" (pub keeper), had migrated a short time before. His father died when Walton was three. In 1598 his mother, Anne, married an innkeeper who later became a burgess of the town. Hence, Walton presumably spent his childhood in Stafford, where his only formal education seems to have been instruction in Latin at the Edward VI Grammar School. That education was sufficient to enable Walton to read simple Latin prose, but Latin composition, or versification of any complexity, would confuse him throughout his life.

He was apprenticed to Thomas Grinsell, a member of the Ironmongers' Company, who had married Walton's sister around 1605. Grinsell established himself as a successful cloth merchant in the parish of St. Dunstan's-in-the-West, London. Walton became a freeman of the Ironmongers' Company on 12 November 1618. From that point he, too, prospered in the cloth trade at various locations on Fleet Street and on Chancery Lane, first (apparently) as a seamster, later as a draper, and finally as a merchant.

Somehow Walton acquired a taste for poetry, in which he would dabble all his life, and that appetite was undoubtedly fed handsomely by the offerings of the prominent booksellers in his parish. By 1613 he had become sufficiently accomplished for a friend, "S. P.," to allude to his poetic abilities in verses prefixed to "The Love of Amos and Laura" in a volume published by Grinsell's neighbor Richard Hawkins. Walton had thus demonstrated literary proclivities by the age of twenty. His earliest mentor may have been Michael Drayton, whom he designates his "honest old friend" in *The Compleat Angler.* Drayton lived near Stafford during Walton's childhood and later had lodgings not far from Walton's store on Fleet Street. Walton may have sought him out to advance such interests; he may also have sought out Ben Jonson and some of Jonson's "sons," whom he also knew.

John Donne, the dean of St. Paul's, became Walton's pastor at St. Dunstan's in 1624. Walton claimed to be his "Convert," so Donne must have played some vital role in his development. Sir Henry Wotton and Henry King were both Donne's intimates, and Donne may have provided introductions to them for Walton. Both men regarded Walton as Donne's friend, and King, in a well-known letter, would place Walton at Donne's deathbed. Evidence increasingly suggests that Walton was a closer acquaintance of Donne's than some critics allow.

After Donne and his circle, the crucial association in Walton's early life derives from his marriage in 1626 to Rachel Floud, who was descended on her mother's side from the family of Archbishop Thomas Cranmer. Since her uncle, William Cranmer, was also in the cloth trade, Walton's association with the family probably began as a trade connection. William Cranmer, Rachel's mother, and Rachel's widowed aunt, Dorothy Field, had all received part of their education from the theologian Richard Hooker, to whom their brother George Cranmer had been quite close. Through them Walton gleaned detailed, if not entirely reliable, information about Hooker.

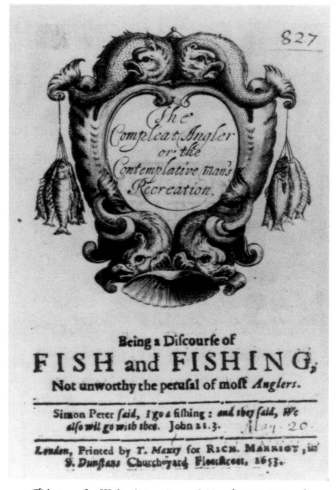

Title page for Walton's treatise on fishing (British Library)

Although Walton's interest in literature can be traced back to his youth, his emergence as a literary figure was decidedly delayed. That career is irrevocably linked to Donne and Donne's circle of friends; neither *The Compleat Angler* nor Walton's early biographies are conceivable apart from that group. Walton's first publication was an elegy on the death of Donne, which appeared in 1633 in the first edition of Donne's poems. For the edition of Donne's poems that appeared in 1635 he revised his elegy, composed a poem on Donne's portrait, and edited a series of Donne's letters. These projects concerning Donne led to Walton's association with the publisher John Marriot, whose son Richard became his lifelong friend, patron, and publisher.

In the 1630s Walton's friendship with Wotton, the provost of Eton, deepened considerably, and about the middle of that decade Wotton told Walton of his intention to write a biography of Donne for an edition of Donne's sermons. Walton,

who had delved into Donne's biography previously, undertook additional research on Wotton's behalf. Walton's visits to Eton, one of which he recounts in *The Compleat Angler,* thus probably had as much to do with biography as with angling. Wotton probably became Walton's mentor in both pursuits. In various libraries at Eton, Walton may have made his acquaintance with several historical sources to which he later refers but that do not appear to have formed part of his personal library.

Walton reached the office of senior warden of the yeomanry in 1638, but, although he was nominated repeatedly thereafter for the livery, he was consistently passed over. Wotton died in December 1639; when it was discovered that he had failed to produce a biography of Donne, Richard Marriot decided to rush ahead with the edition anyway. Marriot's impatience was, in part, fueled by John Donne, Jr.'s attempts to gain control of his father's work. Donne's son's actions persuaded a reluctant

Walton to pick up the task the provost had left unfinished. Walton reviewed the notes he had compiled for Sir Henry and completed the biography on 15 February 1640; it was published in *LXXX Sermons Preached by that Learned and Reverend Divine, John Donne* (1640). Walton was thus shoved into the literary limelight against his wishes but to immediate acclaim. His effort was riddled with errors, yet his narrative was based on the personal testimony of many people who were well acquainted with Donne, and he had at his disposal records that have long since been lost. This material allowed him to chart the fundamental sequences of Donne's life and to preserve priceless details. He recognized the problems with his work, furthermore, and labored to rectify them in subsequent revisions. Whatever the biography's flaws, Donne's mature personality is captured memorably in Walton's pages, and Walton's Augustinian narrative of Donne's evolution is one of the shapeliest biographies of its time. It was justly admired by Walton's contemporaries, among them Thomas Fuller, John Hales, and Charles I.

Walton happened upon literary success just as his business career was waning. In February 1640 he was elected to the vestry, but the outbreak of civil war shattered the parish community. The Parliamentary party gained control of Walton's company, bringing his business career to an end. The same period witnessed the breakup of his family. His wife died in 1640; in 1641 William Cranmer transported his family abroad; and in 1642 Walton lost his seventh and only remaining child by Rachel. Walton may have fled from London at the end of 1643, but he was back at St. Dunstan's in early 1644.

From 1644 until 1647 Walton's movements are obscure, but he had not (as often reported) retired to Staffordshire. If he bore arms, nothing is known of it; but he was associated with many Royalists, and he refers obliquely to "losses." He appears to have been absent from London for most of 1644, but he was regularly in the vicinity of the city thereafter, performing services for kinsmen, friends, and fellow Royalists.

Some of Walton's travel in this period was probably devoted to investigations into the life and work of Wotton, and it seems likely that Walton was at Oxford, as well as at Eton, in the early years of the decade. Walton credits his friend George Morley, who became a canon of Christ Church College in 1642 and whom he had known since 1630, with having introduced him to the theologians William Chillingworth, Henry Hammond, and Robert

Sanderson. These meetings must have taken place in the late 1630s or early 1640s, possibly at Oxford; but Morley and his associates were members of the circle of Lucius Cary, second Viscount Falkland, at Great Tew, near Oxford, so Walton may have met these figures there. Hales was another member of that circle.

In 1647 Walton married Anne Ken, a lawyer's daughter, at St. James Clerkenwell. Clerkenwell became the Waltons' chief residence, and their three children were all baptized there; two, Isaac and Ann, would survive their parents. Around 1653 Walton retired to Staffordshire, migrating between there and London during the remainder of the Interregnum.

Between his second marriage and his retirement Walton grew close to a wide range of figures within Royalist literary and religious circles. King, for example, spoke warmly of "the constant experience of [Walton's] Love, even in the worst of the late sad times." When King joined Hales about 1650 at the house of Dame Ann Salter, the sister of Brian Duppa, bishop of Salisbury, Walton was naturally drawn into deeper friendship with Duppa as well as with Hales. Walton's friendships with Archbishop James Ussher and Thomas Morton, bishop of Durham, also most likely date from this period. The circles, of course, were intricately interconnected, and there seems little doubt that Walton was highly regarded in all of them. This regard partially accounts for Walton's celebrated exploit in 1651, when he transported part of the Garter Regalia lost by Charles I at Worcester from Staffordshire to the Tower of London. Walton is unlikely to have been entrusted with such a task had he not been well known to Royalists about London.

Walton's publications in the 1650s comprise three major works: "The Life of Sir Henry Wotton," published in *Reliquiae Wottonianae* in 1651; *The Compleat Angler,* published in 1653 and revised in 1655; and a major rewriting of the life of Donne, published in book form in 1658. These works are so tightly interrelated that it is impossible to unravel their precise geneses. Walton may have determined to revise the life of Donne shortly after its initial publication; he clearly collected material for such a revision throughout the 1640s, obtaining information from Arthur Woodnoth prior to 1645 and from Bishop Morton prior to 1648. Richard Marriot, meanwhile, engaged Walton to edit the works of Wotton, as well. New evidence suggests that Walton may have commenced work on that project as early as 1640, and the chief materials for that edition had been collected by 1648. *The Compleat Angler*

Walton's friend Charles Cotton, who wrote the sequel to The Compleat Angler;
portrait by Sir Peter Lely (from Izaak Walton, The Compleat Angler, *edited
by Richard Le Gallienne, 1897)*

was clearly an outgrowth of Walton's work on Sir Henry, who, Walton says, had entertained such a project for himself. Walton's life of Wotton assures the reader that he was regularly at Eton to consult Wotton's manuscripts and to confer with Wotton's colleagues. Certain references in *The Compleat Angler* have led to speculation that Walton may have used Hales's library there, a resource that was lost to him after Hales was expelled from his fellowship in 1649.

Walton was, then, engaged throughout the 1640s in three projects involving Sir Henry in one way or another. Interrelationships abound in the final productions. The life of Wotton, the most secular and urbane of Walton's biographies (although it makes much of Wotton's becoming a deacon), is composed in the fashion of Plutarch's parallel lives, with strong echoes to the life of Donne – a relation-

ship that is strengthened in successive revisions. *The Compleat Angler,* meanwhile, acts as a supplement to the life of Wotton: Sir Henry appears in it in less formal, more convivial terms than in the official biography. The three works also serve as Royalist tracts. The life of Wotton is the portrait of a resourceful royal servant; *The Compleat Angler* is a subtle work, directed not simply to aspiring anglers but also to dispersed Royalists: several of the sequestered Anglican clergy, among them Gilbert Sheldon, are mentioned indirectly in the 1655 edition; and the revised life of Donne is a powerful portrait of a restless soul bent to its proper spiritual calling by kingly insistence and, concurrently, an affirmation of the supremacy of the old established church. Walton's political leanings are thus much in evidence in these works.

Morley's return from exile in 1660 as the agent of Lord Chancellor Edward Hyde, first Earl of Clarendon, drew Walton into new spheres of activity. Walton had returned to London by May 1660, at which time he wrote an eclogue on the king's return. Shortly thereafter Morley was made dean of Christ Church College, and in the autumn of that year Walton was acting there on Morley's behalf. When Morley became bishop of Worcester later in 1660, Walton became his steward. Walton's second wife died in Worcester in April 1662 and was buried in the cathedral.

In 1662 Morley became bishop of Winchester. Walton lived thereafter in the bishop's establishments for at least the next twelve years. His personal ties to Morley and Sheldon led to new friendships with the Restoration bishops, among them Humphrey Henchman, Seth Ward, and Thomas Barlow, and he was well known to other leaders in the ecclesiastical establishment. Anthony à Wood's assertion that Walton was "much beloved" by many in these circles is fully borne out by the evidence.

Work for Morley did not inhibit Walton's literary activity. The third edition of *The Compleat Angler,* published in 1661, was the first version to include the Laws of Angling. The following year Archbishop Sheldon proposed that Walton undertake a biography of Hooker, whom the Restoration bishops were eager to appropriate as their champion. At first that task had fallen to John Gauden, the bishop of Exeter, whose first complete edition of Hooker's *The Laws of Ecclesiastical Polity* (1662) included his life of the author. Walton was offended by the biography, which was grossly inaccurate in its details. Sheldon and his associates were offended by the edition itself, for Gauden had published sections disclosing that Hooker was not in full accord with their positions. Sheldon, eager to correct both embarrassments, commissioned Walton to address them. For his labors Walton received a lease on lucrative property in Paternoster Row.

Walton's life of Hooker is incomparably superior to Gauden's, and it was his best-researched biography to that point. It is his first "life-and-times" biography, and his talent for historical summary is displayed to advantage. Walton's relation to the Cranmer family also permitted him to deliver a better picture of Hooker as an individual. Had Walton not been persuaded to compose this life, it is unlikely that many of his details would have survived. Walton similarly provided a more informed account of Hooker's academic and ecclesiastical career than that supplied by Gauden; in this effort, undoubtedly under the sponsorship of Sheldon and

Morley, he was much aided by Oxford antiquaries. Yet, if Walton could rely on privileged information, he was too prone to trust gossip, and he seriously maligned the family of Hooker's wife. His account of the genesis of *The Laws of Ecclesiastical Polity* is likewise incorrect, although his denial of the authenticity of the final books was unquestionably to the liking of Sheldon and his friends. Walton was doubtless guided by their opinions and did not possess the requisite skills to challenge their authority. In the life of Hooker, as in his other biographies, then, Walton's approach committed him to notable errors. *The Life of Mr. Rich. Hooker* appeared in 1665, about which time Walton's daughter married Dr. William Hawkins, a prebendary of Winchester Cathedral.

For Walton and his friends, the period from 1665 to 1670 was marked by disaster. Marriot lost badly in the Great Fire of London and was compelled to relocate his business. Clarendon's fall from power in 1667 also brought Morley and Sheldon into disgrace, pushing Walton and Morley into retreat at Farnham Castle in Surrey, where Walton became better acquainted with figures in that region, particularly Samuel Woodforde, who later supplied prefatory verses for two of his lives.

The startling result of this retirement was Walton's *The Life of Mr. George Herbert* and the collected edition of his first four biographies, both of which appeared in 1670. The life of Herbert, like all of Walton's works, had a long genesis. Walton's professional interest in Herbert dated back to the 1640s, and his works throughout the 1650s all manifest that interest. Walton had seen Herbert at least once: at the funeral in 1627 of the poet's mother, Magdalen, at which Donne had preached. He knew, therefore, of Donne's association with Herbert's family, and he most likely began to gather information about the Herberts in anticipation of a revision of his biography of Donne.

Walton, then, may have been planning the life of Herbert since 1658, being forced to abandon the project by the events of the Restoration and by his commissioned work on the life of Hooker. The delay turned out to be fortunate, for the collected lives benefited greatly from the machinery devised to assist Walton with the Hooker project. In the Restoration bishops Walton enjoyed, in effect, a living biographical college, and he used them heavily for his final biographies. Bishops John Hacket, Henchman, and King, for example, had known Herbert. Walton also had access to clerics such as Robert Creighton, bishop of Bath and Wells; Edmund Duncon; and James Duport. The bishops may also

Walton in 1675; drawing by Edmund Ashfield (from Peter Oliver, A New Chronicle of The Compleat Angler, *1936*)

have supported Walton in archival research, for the biography of 1670 bears evidence of fresh investigations in the archives of both universities. Nearing eighty, Walton found his artistic powers at their peak. *The Life of Mr. George Herbert* is the most subtly crafted of his biographies, an elegantly patterned hagiographic narrative celebrating the beauty of holiness in an Anglican saint and, hence, an implicit defense of the party in disfavor. It likewise served as propaganda for the Sheldonian project of encouraging sons of the upper classes to enter orders. The collected lives featured a dedication generously attributing the excellences of the biographies to Morley's benevolent influence over a forty-year period.

Publication of *The Lives of Dr. John Donne, Sir Henry Wotton, Mr. Richard Hooker, Mr. George Herbert* secured Walton's place as England's premier biographer. He seems not to have contemplated a new project right away, spending his time instead with friends – notably with Charles Cotton, whose celebrated fishing house at the edge of the Dove, built by Cotton to commemorate their friendship, bears an arch piece containing their interwoven initials and the date 1674. Walton also visited Oxford repeatedly in this period. His son Isaac received his B.A. from Christ Church in 1672, and Isaac's presence at Oxford brought Walton into increasing contact with various figures there, chief among them Wood and William Fulman.

In 1672 Walton brought out a further edition of Wotton's works, with an improved biographical narrative. In 1673 he undertook research for a life of Hales to be written by Fulman. He made alterations in *The Life of Mr. George Herbert* for its inclusion in an edition of Herbert's *The Temple* in 1674. In 1675 he published a revised edition of the collected lives, boasting new celebratory verses by

James Duport and Cotton. The following year saw the publication of *The Universal Angler,* which included the final version of Walton's *The Compleat Angler;* the sequel by Cotton, "The Complete Angler, Being Instructions How to Angle for a Trout or Grayling in a Clear Stream"; and a third work on fishing by Col. Robert Venables. Cotton and Duport additionally supplied fresh verses for Walton's portion of the book.

Walton was bringing his literary career to an elegant close by putting his works into the best shape possible. For the 1675 edition of the lives, for example, he reviewed all his notes and incorporated material he had previously left out, including the date of the completion of his first biography and the now notorious description of Donne's vision of his wife with a stillborn child. Other additions demonstrate that Walton had also undertaken further research. He aimed to perfect these biographies (by his lights) in every respect. He particularly wanted to perfect them stylistically. He may have worked on the final versions of *The Compleat Angler* and of the lives simultaneously, which may account for their striking coherence of style and perspective. Walton by this period viewed his writing canonically, and he made subtle adjustments in phrasing to bring his works closer together — a process that had been underway for some time. Walton's biographical subjects, for example, increasingly manifest aspects of Piscator, his spokesman in *The Compleat Angler.* Walton's efforts to polish his narratives thus led to a certain flattening of effect.

Walton's labors in revision apparently revived his creative energies, for he must have begun work on *The Life of Dr. Sanderson* by 1676. He may have considered composing the biography of a member of the Restoration episcopate for some time: after all, he had written lives of a worldly deacon, a saintly poet-priest in a country cure, a metropolitan preacher, and a celebrated theologian; it remained to write an account of a bishop. Sanderson was a natural choice: Walton had known him personally, and he was the dearly admired friend of Sheldon and Morley, both of whom offered Walton personal testimony and doubtless afforded him introductions to assist him in documentary research. The result, published in 1678, is in many ways Walton's most professional biography. Neither the wittiest nor the most elegant, it is, on the other hand, the best researched of Walton's lives. Regarding Sanderson's torturous theology, Walton received help from Bishop Thomas Barlow as well as from Dr. Thomas Pierce, theologians he had known for some time. They led him astray, however, and Walton's account of Sanderson's works, like his account of Hooker's, is flawed. Nevertheless, *The Life of Dr. Sanderson* is one of the great achievements of seventeenth-century biography. Even the Oxford antiquary Wood could not better its research.

It is not known when Walton left Morley's service, but it does not seem to have been prior to 1674. Following the appearance of *The Life of Dr. Sanderson,* however, Walton spent more and more time in Hampshire. His literary activities continued unabated; he clearly could not tolerate idleness. He composed a tract against nonconformity in the form of a letter, dated 12 September 1679, publishing it the following year, with another letter dated 18 February 1667/1668, as *Love and Truth.* The tract appeared anonymously, but scholars have established that Walton was the author. Walton adopts here the pose of a "Quiet and Conformable Citizen of London" addressing it to "Factious Shopkeepers" in Coventry, a notorious nonconformist haven. That same year he sent a celebrated letter to John Aubrey, sharing Morley's reminiscences about Jonson and disclosing the otherwise unknown fact that he, too, had known the great poet. During the last year of his life Walton published *Thealma and Clearchus* (1683), a "pastoral history" for which he supplied a preface. Once attributed to Walton himself, the work is, in fact, by John Chalkhill, a kinsman of Walton's second wife, other verses by whom had appeared in *The Compleat Angler.* The preface is dated 7 May 1678, which seems to indicate that Walton had prepared the edition for the press while putting the final touches on *The Life of Dr. Sanderson.* It is not known what delayed the publication.

Walton also continued to pursue his biographical interests. When *The Life of Dr. Sanderson* was republished by Benjamin Tooke in 1681 in Sanderson's *XXXV Sermons,* it included revisions. There is also new evidence that during his final years Walton commenced work on a biography of Archbishop Sheldon. No one had yet seen fit to preserve his memory, and Walton, perpetually stirred by neglect, took up the task but did not live to bring the project to conclusion.

Walton's publications assure his readers that even toward the close of his life he was regularly in London, and he was obviously often with Morley, for two of Walton's surviving letters are dated from Farnham Castle in 1678 and 1683. But Walton spent more and more time in these years with his daughter and her husband at Winchester and at Droxford, Hawkins's country cure, and men and women from these communities are noticed in his will. The tradition that Walton was living with his

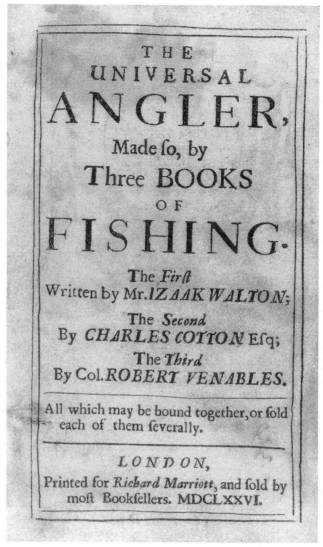

THE
UNIVERSAL
ANGLER,
Made ſo, by
Three BOOKS
OF
FISHING.
The *Firſt*
Written by Mr. *IZAAK WALTON*;
The *Second*
By *CHARLES COTTON* Eſq;
The *Third*
By Col. *ROBERT VENABLES.*

All which may be bound together, or ſold
each of them ſeverally.

LONDON,
Printed for *Richard Marriott*, and ſold by
moſt Bookſellers. MDCLXXVI.

Title page for the volume that includes Walton's final version of The
Compleat Angler

daughter and son-in-law at the end of his life is quite likely true, for cathedral records include notices of Hawkins's enlargement of his premises in 1682, presumably to accommodate Walton; and in his will, which Walton began on 9 August 1683, in his "neintyeth yeare of age," he describes himself as "of Winchester." He died four months later, on 21 December, and was buried in Prior Silkstede's Chapel in Winchester Cathedral. Silkstede had been a great lay benefactor of the cathedral, and Walton wished to be remembered in similar terms: the final decades of his life had been devoted to constant service on behalf of the church he held dear.

Two portraits of Walton survive, and they complement each other well. Both were made in the closing years of his life. The larger of the two, by Jacob Huysmans, now in the National Gallery, is a portrait in oils showing Walton with gloves and sword; it presents the merchant and country gentleman known to dignitaries. The second portrait, a head and shoulders in colored chalk by Edmund Ashfield, displays Walton in plain old-fashioned clothing and with penetrating eyes, the man cherished as a companion.

The Compleat Angler, a guide to freshwater fishing in dialogue form, has proved to be Walton's work of broadest enduring fame. Walton apparently began to fish seriously about 1630, and he was partly inspired to compose his masterpiece because he found no useful, comprehensive guides to the art

315

of angling in English. Walton was a master of older methods of angling, to such an extent that his method and information were derided by some, such as Richard Franck, even in his own time, and by many others since. Walton's scientific interests and his flair for writing about nature have, however, been deftly defended; and some fishermen, most notably the expert angler R. B. Marston, have borne witness to the enduring value of Walton's details.

The Compleat Angler, moreover, is anything but the customary manual. It is, instead, an exceedingly artful book, a fine example of seventeenth-century *genera mixta,* fusing the practical treatise with literary and contemplative material drawn from the various traditions of the georgic, the pastoral, the pastoral drama, the spiritual autobiography, the philosophical dialogue, and tracts for the times. It is (as the title page professes) a volume for the contemplative man, and it is packed with a surprising range of observations. It is also a work of recreation, of "innocent Mirth" for those able to afford it ("if they be not needy"), offering a handy anthology of poems for enjoyment and many songs, including a composition by Henry Lawes printed to be sung around a table. Walton's brotherhood of anglers, furthermore, behaves remarkably like a spiritual community, manifesting patterns of conversion and communion and devoted to the practice of charity, much like the communities of primitive Christians to which Walton makes repeated reference. The text was also politically motivated. The pun between *angler* and *Anglican,* often noted, transformed Walton's seemingly realistic narrative into a subtle allegory and celebration of the "culture of sequestered royalism," identifying the community of anglers as the ultimately superior community, one that, by example, repudiates the society of intolerant, contentious sectaries currently in control of the nation's urban life. By contrast, the society of anglers ("quiet men") is a community of peaceful habits, good cheer, toleration, wide aesthetic inclinations, and deference to authority, enjoying a profound linkage to meaningful ancient traditions (and actively preserving such traditions) and demonstrating a deep and harmonious connection to nature. One sentence may indicate how deftly Walton interweaves these narrative elements into a seamless structure: anglers exhibit, says Piscator, "that simplicity that was usually found in the Primitive Christians, who were (as most Anglers are) quiet men, and followed peace: men that were too wise to sell their consciences to buy riches for vexation." In his successive revisions Walton principally expanded the practical and technical dimen-

sions of the work, a development commonly deplored but that fulfills the promise of the title. His revisions continued to strengthen the meditative and literary dimensions of the work, as well. The resulting compound is utterly idiosyncratic.

Walton's larger importance for English literature lies in his evolution into the first biographer of undeniable stature in English letters. His initial biography filled a mere seventeen folio pages in a large volume of sermons. His final biography was a free-standing work of nearly three hundred pages, with a few tracts appended by way of supplement. That development reflects the career of biography itself, for the greater dignity accorded the free-standing work reflects the mounting importance accorded the genre during the seventeenth century. The publication of the collected lives in 1670 was a sign of Walton's mature reputation, and the publication and republication of that volume did much to advance claims for the artistry and integrity of life writing.

An allusion to Plutarch's *Life of Pompey* in Walton's first biography suggests that some study of the Greek biographer (perhaps under Wotton's tutelage) may have preceded his own work as a biographer. That influence may also account for Walton's conservative theory of biography. Life writing, he maintained, was chiefly commemorative — "an honour due to the dead, and a generous debt due to those that shall live, and succeed us." Such a view did not lead one to cultivate dates and documents, and Walton's fledgling effort displays surprisingly few of the former. The discipline of rendering life histories, however, and the abundance of materials made available to him by his unique connections gradually led Walton to pioneering efforts in the techniques of modern biography: consultation of primary sources and public records, and the citation of a profusion of dates established by such public and private documents. All of these Walton introduced into biographical narrative, and his final efforts reveal extensive use of ecclesiastical, university, and private archives. More noteworthy is Walton's elaborate use of his subjects' correspondence, accounts books, autobiographical statements embedded in prefaces to their works, and (more problematic) their poetry. Walton has been accused of misusing subjective works to establish a life record, and such, on occasion, may be the case, although Walton's responsiveness to such material led to heightened awareness on his part with respect to the inner conflicts and dilemmas of his subjects and strengthened his ability to render their personalities dramatically. Whatever his errors, he was

Inscription by Walton to Mrs. Dorothy Wallop in a copy of The Universal Angler. The inscription is dated 19 December 1678 from Farnham Castle, where Walton was living with George Morley, the bishop of Winchester (Pierpont Morgan Library, PML 6572)

THE CONTENTS.

Page from Walton's copy of Richard Sanderson's sermons, with notes by Walton. His biography of Sanderson was published in 1678 (Maggs Bros. catalogue no. 643, 1937).

ahead of his time in recognizing the significance of such material for biography.

If a pioneer in modern methods, however, Walton falls short of modern scruples. Like virtually all of his contemporaries, Walton wrote his biographies in relation to a preconceived thesis, deeply influenced by his personal knowledge of his subjects. The impressive unity of tone and effect in his biographies is one reward of that approach. To advance his governing paradigm, however, Walton was not above tampering with the evidence – suppressing dates here and there, inventing others, conflating documents, altering texts. Nor did he subject his evidence to the severe tests demanded by modern scholarship. Walton, by nature, trusted authority, particularly clerical authority, and an unusual number of such men were to be found among his informants. Only rarely did he test their anecdotes against documentary evidence, and when he became aware of discrepancies he inclined to trust the anecdote, especially if it corroborated the conception to which he was committed. Walton, in addition, lacked the training for professional research, which would have led him to complicating material and might have provided him with a more skeptical temperament. Yet, for all these flaws, Walton manages to capture fundamental features of his biographical subjects: if he is not wholly right about them, he is exactly right about certain features of their lives.

Walton is redeemed from his transgressions by his artistry. He perpetually deprecated his talent, yet he is an eminent (if labored) stylist in biography, the worthy predecessor of Samuel Johnson, who thoroughly enjoyed his contributions. Walton is a master of structure, which he controls obsessively, as well as of the individual touch; he is ever alert to the implications of the facts he reports, and he coordinates and shapes them meticulously. Walton likewise displays an enviable ability to fashion brisk historical summaries, an ability especially evident in the lives of Wotton, Hooker, and Sanderson. Like James Boswell, moreover, Walton has an insatiable appetite for the telling anecdote, which he renders with dramatic flair and often with sly wit. Walton's love of anecdote reveals a benign delight in human inconsistencies and failures, and his zeal to share such material rescues his biographies from otherwise constricting paradigms and raises them far above the innumerable tedious commemorative biographies written by his contemporaries. In this, as so much else, he looks forward to the future.

Walton is, in sum, a most curious writer. He professes to be "artlesse," claiming merely to be a medium wielding a pen "guided by the hand of Truth." In reality he is an intensely calculating writer, who perfected his various narratives through elaborate, painstaking revisions. He wrote no works of pure literature apart from a few poems (some of the unattributed poems in *The Compleat Angler* may be by Walton); but he succeeded, through craft and imaginative reach, in raising works of utilitarian concern and of historical cast to the realm of literature, and his achievements gained the approval of an impressive number of his more learned contemporaries. He himself viewed his artistic evolution with perpetual wonder and constantly awarded credit to others for his achievement. He died widely admired as much for his person as for his works, leaving behind irreplaceable accounts of eminent personalities of his age and, in William Hazlitt's judgment, the finest pastoral in the language. He would unquestionably be confounded by his subsequent reputation.

Bibliographies:

Peter Oliver, *A New Chronicle of The Compleat Angler* (New York: Paisley / London: Williams & Norgate, 1936);

Bernard S. Horne, *The Compleat Angler 1653–1967: A New Bibliography* (Pittsburgh: University of Pittsburgh Press, 1970).

Biographies:

Anthony à Wood, *Athenæ Oxonienses: A New Edition, with Additions, and a Continuation by Philip Bliss,* 4 volumes (London: Printed for F. C. & J. Rivington, 1813–1820), I: 693–700;

Arthur M. Coon, "The Life of Izaak Walton," Ph.D. dissertation, Cornell University, 1938;

Clayton D. Lein, *Izaak Walton: Angler and Biographer* (forthcoming).

References:

Judith H. Anderson, *Biographical Truth: The Representation of Historical Persons in Tudor-Stuart Writing* (New Haven: Yale University Press, 1984);

John Beresford, "Two Portraits: Izaak Walton (?) and Charles Cotton (?), by Edmund Ashfield," *Notes and Queries,* thirteenth series, 1 (15 September 1923): 203–207; (29 September 1923): 243–245;

Jonquil Bevan and I. A. Shapiro, "Donne and the Walton Forgeries: A Correspondence," *Library,* sixth series, 4 (September 1982): 329–339;

Bevan, "Henry Valentine, John Donne and Izaak Walton," *Review of English Studies,* 40 (May 1989): 179–201;

Bevan, "Izaak Walton and His Publisher," *Library,* fifth series, 32 (December 1977): 344–359;

Bevan, "Izaak Walton's Collections for Fulman's Life of John Hales: The Walker Part," *Bodleian Library Record,* 13 (April 1989): 160–171;

Bevan, *Izaak Walton's The Compleat Angler: The Art of Recreation* (New York: St. Martin's Press, 1988);

Bevan, "Some Books from Izaak Walton's Library," *Library,* sixth series, 2 (September 1980): 259–263;

Tucker Brooke, "The Lambert Walton-Cotton Collection," *Yale University Library Gazette,* 17 (April 1943): 61–65;

John Butt, *Biography in the Hands of Walton, Johnson, and Boswell* (Los Angeles: University of California Press, 1966);

Butt, "Izaak Walton as Biographer," in his *Pope, Dickens and Others* (Edinburgh: Edinburgh University Press, 1969), pp. 39–59;

Butt, "Izaak Walton's Collections for Fulman's Life of John Hales," *Modern Language Review,* 29 (July 1934): 267–273;

Butt, "Izaak Walton's Methods in Biography," *Essays and Studies,* 19 (1933): 67–84;

Jean-François Camé and Charles F. Sadowski, "Attitudes Towards Money in Izaak Walton's *The Complete Angler,*" *Cahiers Elisabéthains,* 9 (April 1976): 41–54;

Arthur M. Coon, "The Family of Izaak Walton," *Times Literary Supplement,* 15 May 1937, p. 380;

Coon, "Izaak Walton and Edmund Carew," *Notes and Queries,* 178 (27 April 1940): 298;

Coon, "Izaak Walton, *Prochein Amy,*" *Modern Language Notes,* 54 (December 1939): 589–592;

Coon, "Izaak Walton's Birthday," *Notes and Queries,* 176 (17 June 1939): 424;

Coon, "Izaak Walton's Mother," *Times Literary Supplement,* 25 December 1937, p. 980;

Coon, "Izaak Walton's Occupation and Residence," *Notes and Queries,* 176 (18 February 1939): 110–112;

Coon, "Izaak Walton's Second Marriage," *Notes and Queries,* 176 (29 April 1939): 299;

John R. Cooper, *The Art of The Compleat Angler* (Durham, N.C.: Duke University Press, 1968);

Francisque Costa, "The Ashmolean Museum and *The Angler,*" *Caliban,* 5 (January 1968): 31–34;

Costa, *L'Oeuvre d'Izaak Walton (1593–1683)* (Paris: Didier, 1973);

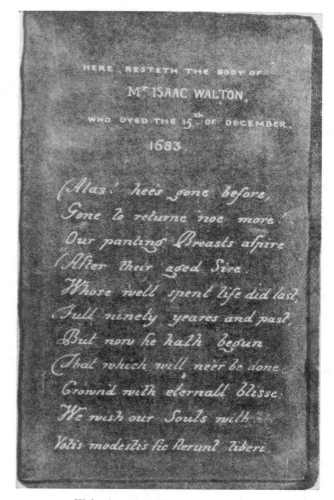

Walton's tomb in Winchester Cathedral

P. J. Croft, "Izaak Walton's John Chalkhill," *Times Literary Supplement,* 27 June 1958, p. 365;

Richard B. Croft, *Izaak Walton and the River Lee* (Ware: Privately printed, 1907);

Austin Dobson, "On Certain Quotations in Walton's 'Angler,' " in his *Miscellanies,* volume 2 (New York: Dodd, Mead, 1901), pp. 157–169;

Simone Dorangeon, "De Phineas Fletcher à Izaak Walton: Quelques Notes Sur la Transmission du Symbolisme Piscatorial," *Bulletin de la Société d'Etudes Anglo-Américaines des XVIIᵉ et XVIIIᵉ Siècles,* 7 (1978): 63–74;

William H. Epstein, *Recognizing Biography* (Philadelphia: University of Pennsylvania Press, 1987);

Richard E. Fehner, "Izaak Walton's *Life of Sir Henry Wotton,* 1651, 1654, 1670, 1672, 1675: A Study of Sources, Revisions, and Chronology," Ph.D. dissertation, University of Minnesota, 1961;

W. Courthope Forman, "In the Canon's Garden," *Cornhill Magazine,* third series, 53 (July–December 1922): 68–70;

Richard Franck, *Northern Memoirs, Calculated for the Meridian of Scotland* (London: H. Mortlock, 1694);

Helen Gardner, "Dean Donne's Monument in St. Paul's," in *Evidence in Literary Scholarship: Essays in Memory of James Marshall Osborn,* edited by René Wellek and Alvaro Ribeiro (Oxford: Clarendon Press, 1979), pp. 29–44;

Marcus Selden Goldman, "Izaak Walton and *The Arte of Angling,* 1577," in *Studies in Honor of T. W. Baldwin,* edited by Don Cameron Allen (Urbana: University of Illinois Press, 1958), pp. 185–204;

Irvine Gray, "An Unknown Record of Izaak Walton," *Country Life,* 30 August 1973, pp. 546–547;

B. D. Greenslade, "*The Compleat Angler* and the Sequestered Clergy," *Review of English Studies,* 5 (October 1954): 361–366;

Jim Hayes, "Izaak Walton's Secret Stream," *Outdoor Life,* 127 (February 1961): 42–43, 96–98;

William Hazlitt, "On John Buncle," in *The Complete Works of William Hazlitt,* 21 volumes, edited by P. P. Howe (London & Toronto: Dent, 1930–1934), IV: 51–57;

F. G. P. Kellendonk, "Izaak Walton and Sir Henry Wotton's Panegyrick of King Charles," *Neophilologus,* 61 (April 1977): 316–320;

Lionel Lambert, *Izaak Walton and the Royal Deanery of Stafford* (Stafford: Mort, 1926);

Clayton D. Lein, "Art and Structure in Walton's *Life of Mr. George Herbert,*" *University of Toronto Quarterly,* 46 (Winter 1976/1977): 162–176;

James Russell Lowell, "Walton," in *The Complete Writings of James Russell Lowell,* 16 volumes (Cambridge, Mass.: Riverside Press, 1904), VIII: 71–112;

W. Gerald Marshall, "Time in Walton's *Lives,*" *Studies in English Literature,* 32 (Summer 1992): 429–442;

R. B. Marston, *Walton and Some Earlier Writers on Fish and Fishing* (London: Stock, 1894);

Anna K. Nardo, " 'A recreation of a recreation': Reading *The Compleat Angler,*" *South Atlantic Quarterly,* 79 (Summer 1980): 302–311;

David Novarr, "Izaak Walton, Bishop Morley, and *Love and Truth,*" *Review of English Studies,* 2 (January 1951): 30–39;

Novarr, *The Making of Walton's Lives* (Ithaca, N.Y.: Cornell University Press, 1958);

H. J. Oliver, "The Composition and Revisions of 'The Compleat Angler,' " *Modern Language Review,* 42 (July 1947): 295–313;

Oliver, "Izaak Walton as Author of *Love and Truth* and *Thealma and Clearchus,*" *Review of English Studies,* 25 (January 1949): 24–37;

Oliver, "Izaak Walton's Prose Style," *Review of English Studies,* 21 (October 1945): 280–288;

Clement Price, "Izaak Walton," *Times Literary Supplement,* 14 August 1919, p. 437;

David Hill Radcliffe, " 'Study to be Quiet': Genre and Politics in Izaak Walton's *Compleat Angler,*" *English Literary Renaissance,* 22 (Winter 1992): 95–111;

Michael P. Rewa, *Reborn as Meaning: Panegyrical Biography from Isocrates to Walton* (Washington, D.C.: University Press of America, 1983);

Herbert Rothschild, Jr., "The 'Higher Hand' in Walton's 'Life of John Donne,' " *Notes and Queries,* 25 (December 1978): 506–508;

Luigi Sampietro, *La Scuola Del Cuore* (Bologna: Pàtron Editore, 1978);

I. A. Shapiro, "Donne and Walton Forgeries," *Library,* sixth series, 3 (September 1981): 232;

C. J. Sisson, *The Judicious Marriage of Mr. Hooker and the Birth of The Laws of Ecclesiastical Polity* (Cambridge: Cambridge University Press, 1940; New York: Octagon, 1974);

Donald A. Stauffer, *English Biography before 1700* (Cambridge, Mass.: Harvard University Press, 1930);

John Vaughan, "Izaak Walton at Droxford," in his *The Wild-Flowers of Selborne and Other Papers* (London: John Lane, 1906), pp. 157–171;

Vaughan, "The Plant-Lore of 'The Compleat Angler,' " *Scribner's Magazine,* 70 (July–December 1921): 720–728;

Vaughan, "Where Izaak Walton Died," *Cornhill Magazine,* third series, 47 (July–December 1919): 595–607;

Richard Wendorf, *The Elements of Life* (Oxford: Clarendon Press, 1990);

Steven N. Zwicker, *Lines of Authority: Politics and English Literary Culture, 1649–1689* (Ithaca, N.Y. & London: Cornell University Press, 1993).

Papers:

The few documents in Izaak Walton's hand that survive are in widely scattered locations, including the British Library and the Public Record Office in London, the Bodleian Library and Corpus Christi College Library in Oxford, and the Harvard University Library.

Checklist of Further Readings

Adolph, Robert. *The Rise of Modern Prose Style*. Cambridge, Mass.: MIT Press, 1968.

Aers, David, Bob Hodge, and Gunther Kress. *Literature, Language and Society in England 1580–1680*. Dublin: Gill & Macmillan / Totowa, N.J.: Barnes & Noble, 1981.

Allen, Don Cameron. *Doubt's Boundless Sea: Skepticism and Faith in the Renaissance*. Baltimore: Johns Hopkins University Press, 1964.

Allen. "Style and Certitude," *English Literary History*, 15 (September 1948): 167–175.

Ashley, Maurice. *England in the Seventeenth Century*, revised edition. New York: Barnes & Noble, 1980.

Ashton, Robert. *The City and the Court, 1603–1643*. Cambridge: Cambridge University Press, 1979.

Aubrey, John. *Aubrey's Brief Lives*, edited by Oliver Lawson Dick, third edition, revised. Ann Arbor: University of Michigan Press, 1957; London: Secker & Warburg, 1958.

Baker, Herschel C. *The Wars of Truth: Studies in the Decay of Christian Humanism in the Earlier Seventeenth Century*. Cambridge, Mass.: Harvard University Press, 1952.

Bennett, H. S. *English Books & Readers, 1603 to 1640: Being a Study of the History of the Book Trade in the Reigns of James I and Charles I*. Cambridge: Cambridge University Press, 1970.

Bethell, Samuel Leslie. *The Cultural Revolution of the 17th Century*. London: Dobson, 1951.

Binns, James W. *Intellectual Culture in Elizabethan and Jacobean England: The Latin Writings of the Age*. Leeds: Francis Cairns, 1990.

Bottrall, Margaret. *Every Man a Phoenix: Studies in Seventeenth-Century Autobiography*. London: Murray, 1958.

Boyce, Benjamin. *The Polemic Character, 1640–1661: A Chapter in English Literary History*. Lincoln: University of Nebraska Press, 1955.

Boyce. *The Theophrastan Character in England to 1642*. Cambridge, Mass.: Harvard University Press, 1947.

Briggs, Julia. *This Stage-Play World: English Literature and Its Background, 1580–1625*. Oxford & New York: Oxford University Press, 1983.

Bush, Douglas. *English Literature in the Earlier Seventeenth Century 1600–1660*, second edition, revised. Oxford: Clarendon Press, 1962.

Cain, T. G. S., and Ken Robinson, eds. *"Into Another Mould": Change and Continuity in English Culture, 1625–1700*. London & New York: Routledge, 1992.

Carlton, Charles. *Charles I, the Personal Monarch*. London & Boston: Routledge & Kegan Paul, 1983.

Chamberlain, John. *The Letters of John Chamberlain,* 2 volumes, edited by Norman Egbert McClure. Philadelphia: American Philosophical Society, 1939.

Colie, Rosalie L. *Paradoxia Epidemica: The Renaissance Tradition of Paradox.* Princeton: Princeton University Press, 1966.

Colie. *The Resources of Kind: Genre-Theory in the Renaissance,* edited by Barbara Kiefer Lewalski. Berkeley: University of California Press, 1973.

Collinson, Patrick. *The Religion of Protestants: The Church in English Society, 1559–1625.* Oxford: Clarendon Press, 1982.

Corns, Thomas. *Uncloistered Virtue: English Political Literature, 1640–1660.* Oxford: Clarendon Press, 1992.

Cressy, David. *Literacy and the Social Order: Reading and Writing in Tudor and Stuart England.* Cambridge: Cambridge University Press, 1980.

Croll, Morris W. *Attic and Baroque Prose Style: The Anti-Ciceronian Movement,* edited by J. Max Patrick and others. Princeton: Princeton University Press, 1969.

Cruttwell, Patrick. *The Shakespearean Moment and Its Place in the Poetry of the 17th Century.* London: Chatto & Windus, 1954; New York: Columbia University Press, 1955.

Curtis, M. H. *Oxford and Cambridge in Transition, 1558–1642: An Essay on Changing Relations between the English Universities and English Society.* Oxford: Clarendon Press, 1959.

Davies, Horton. *Like Angels from a Cloud: The English Metaphysical Preachers, 1588–1645.* San Marino, Cal.: Huntington Library, 1986.

Davies. *Worship and Theology in England,* 5 volumes. Princeton: Princeton University Press, 1961–1975.

Delany, Paul. *British Autobiography in the Seventeenth Century.* New York: Columbia University Press, 1969; London: Routledge & Kegan Paul, 1969.

Donker, Marjorie, and George M. Muldrow. *Dictionary of Literary-Rhetorical Conventions of the English Renaissance.* Westport, Conn. & London: Greenwood Press, 1982.

Ebner, Dean. *Autobiography in Seventeenth-Century England: Theology and the Self.* The Hague: Mouton, 1971.

Ezell, Margaret J. M. *The Patriarch's Wife: Literary Evidence and the History of the Family.* Chapel Hill: University of North Carolina Press, 1987.

Fish, Stanley E. *Self-Consuming Artifacts: The Experience of Seventeenth-Century Literature.* Berkeley: University of California Press, 1972.

Fish, ed. *Seventeenth-Century Prose: Modern Essays in Criticism.* New York: Oxford University Press, 1971.

Fowler, Alastair. *A History of English Literature.* Cambridge, Mass.: Harvard University Press, 1987.

Fraser, Russell A. *The War against Poetry.* Princeton: Princeton University Press, 1970.

Freeman, Rosemary. *English Emblem Books.* London: Chatto & Windus, 1948.

Goldberg, Jonathan. *James I and the Politics of Literature: Jonson, Shakespeare, Donne, and Their Contemporaries.* Baltimore: Johns Hopkins University Press, 1983.

Gordon, D. J. *The Renaissance Imagination: Essays and Lectures,* edited by Stephen Orgel. Berkeley: University of California Press, 1975.

Gordon, Ian A. *The Movement of English Prose.* London: Longmans, 1966; Bloomington: Indiana University Press, 1966.

Grant, Patrick. *The Transformation of Sin: Studies in Donne, Herbert, Vaughan and Traherne.* Montreal: McGill-Queen's University Press / Amherst: University of Massachusetts Press, 1974.

Grierson, H. J. C. *Cross Currents in English Literature of the XVIIth Century: or, The World, the Flesh & the Spirit, Their Actions and Reactions.* London: Chatto & Windus, 1929.

Guibbory, Achsah. *The Map of Time: Seventeenth-Century English Literature and Ideas of Pattern in History.* Urbana: University of Illinois Press, 1986.

Halewood, William H. *The Poetry of Grace: Reformation Themes and Structures in English Seventeenth-Century Poetry.* New Haven: Yale University Press, 1970.

Haller, William. *The Rise of Puritanism.* New York: Columbia University Press, 1938.

Harris, Victor. *All Coherence Gone.* Chicago: University of Chicago Press, 1949.

Haselkorn, Anne M., and Betty S. Travitsky, eds. *The Renaissance Englishwoman in Print: Counterbalancing the Canon.* Amherst: University of Massachusetts Press, 1990.

Haydn, Hiram C. *The Counter-Renaissance.* New York: Scribners, 1950.

Healy, Thomas, and Jonathan Sawday. *Literature and the English Civil War.* Cambridge: Cambridge University Press, 1990.

Helgerson, Richard. *Forms of Nationhood: The Elizabethan Writing of England.* Chicago: University of Chicago Press, 1992.

Hill, Christopher. *Puritans and Revolution: Studies in Interpretation of the English Revolution of the 17th Century,* edited by Donald Pennington and Keith Thomas. Oxford: Clarendon Press, 1978.

Hill. *Society and Puritanism in Pre-Revolutionary England.* London: Secker & Warburg, 1964.

Hirst, Derek. *Authority and Conflict: England, 1603–1658.* Cambridge, Mass.: Harvard University Press, 1986.

Holden, William P. *Anti-Puritan Satire, 1572–1642.* New Haven: Yale University Press, 1954.

Howell, Wilbur Samuel. *Logic and Rhetoric in England, 1500–1700.* Princeton: Princeton University Press, 1956.

Kahn, Victoria. *Rhetoric, Prudence, and Skepticism in the Renaissance.* Ithaca, N.Y.: Cornell University Press, 1985.

Kendall, R. T. *Calvin and English Calvinism to 1649.* Oxford: Oxford University Press, 1980.

King, James Roy. *Studies in Six 17th century writers.* Athens: Ohio University Press, 1966.

Knights, L. C. *Drama and Society in the Age of Jonson.* London: Chatto & Windus, 1937.

Knights. *Public Voices: Literature and Politics with Special Reference to the Seventeenth Century.* Towata, N.J.: Rowman & Littlefield, 1972.

Kranidas, Thomas. "Style and Rectitude in Seventeenth-Century Prose: Hall, Smectymnuus, and Milton," *Huntington Library Quarterly,* 46 (Summer 1983): 237–269.

Lamont, William M. *Godly Rule: Politics and Religion, 1603–60.* London: Macmillan / New York: St. Martin's Press, 1969.

Laslett, Peter. *The World We Have Lost: Further Explored,* third edition. London: Methuen, 1984.

Lee, Maurice Jr. *Great Britain's Solomon: James VI and I in His Three Kingdoms.* Urbana: University of Illinois Press, 1990.

Lewalski, Barbara Kiefer. *Protestant Poetics and the Seventeenth-Century Religious Lyric.* Princeton: Princeton University Press, 1979.

Lewalski. *Writing Women in Jacobean England.* Cambridge, Mass.: Harvard University Press, 1993.

Lewalski, ed. *Renaissance Genres: Essays on Theory, History, and Interpretation.* Cambridge, Mass.: Harvard University Press, 1986.

Lievsay, John L., ed. *The Seventeenth-Century Resolve: A Historical Anthology of a Literary Form.* Lexington: University of Kentucky Press, 1980.

Little, David. *Religion, Order, and Law: A Study in Pre-Revolutionary England.* New York: Harper & Row, 1969.

Lovejoy, Arthur O. *The Great Chain of Being: A Study of the History of an Idea.* Cambridge, Mass.: Harvard University Press, 1936.

Low, Anthony. *Love's Architecture: Devotional Modes in Seventeenth-Century English Poetry.* New York: New York University Press, 1978.

Lyons, Bridget Gellert. *Voices of Melancholy: Studies in Literary Treatments of Melancholy in Renaissance England.* London: Routledge & Kegan Paul, 1971.

Mahood, Molly M. *Poetry and Humanism.* London: Cape, 1950.

Manley, Lawrence. *Convention, 1500–1750.* Cambridge, Mass.: Harvard University Press, 1980.

Martz, Louis L. *The Poetry of Meditation: A Study in English Religious Literature of the Seventeenth Century,* second edition. New Haven: Yale University Press, 1962.

Mazzeo, Joseph A. *Renaissance and Revolution: Backgrounds to Seventeenth-Century Literature.* New York: Pantheon, 1967.

Mazzeo. *Renaissance and Seventeenth-Century Studies.* New York: Columbia University Press, 1964.

Mazzeo. "Seventeenth-Century English Prose Style: The Quest for a Natural Style," *Mosaic,* 6 (Spring 1973): 107–144.

McCanles, Michael. *Dialectical Criticism and Renaissance Literature.* Berkeley: University of California Press, 1975.

Mendelson, Sara Heller. *The Mental World of Stuart Women: Three Studies.* Amherst: University of Massachusetts Press, 1987.

Miner, Earl, ed. *Seventeenth-Century Imagery: Essays on Uses of Figurative Language from Donne to Farquhar.* Berkeley: University of California Press, 1971.

Mitchell, W. Fraser. *English Pulpit Oratory from Andrewes to Tillotson: A Study of Its Literary Aspects.* London: S.P.C.K., 1932.

Mulder, John R. *The Temple of the Mind: Education and Literary Taste in Seventeenth-Century England.* New York: Pegasus, 1969.

Nardo, Anna K. *The Ludic Self in Seventeenth-Century English Literature.* Albany: State University of New York Press, 1991.

Nevo, Ruth. *The Dial of Virtue: A Study of Poems on Affairs of State in the Seventeenth Century.* Princeton: Princeton University Press, 1963.

Nicolson, Marjorie Hope. *The Breaking of the Circle: Studies in the Effect of the "New Science" upon Seventeenth-Century Poetry,* revised edition. New York: Columbia University Press, 1962.

Owens, W. R., ed. *Seventeenth-Century England: A Changing Culture,* 3 volumes. London: Ward Lock Educational, in association with the Open University Press, 1980.

Parry, Graham. *The Seventeenth Century: The Intellectual and Cultural Context of English Literature, 1603–1700.* London & New York: Longman, 1989.

Patrides, C. A., ed. *The Cambridge Platonists.* Cambridge: Cambridge University Press, 1969.

Patrides and Raymond B. Waddington, eds. *The Age of Milton: Backgrounds to Seventeenth-Century Literature.* Manchester: Manchester University Press / Totowa, N.J.: Barnes & Noble, 1980.

Patterson, Annabel. *Censorship and Interpretation: The Conditions of Writing and Reading in Early Modern England.* Madison: University of Wisconsin Press, 1984.

Pebworth, Ted-Larry. "Not Being, But Passing: Defining the Early English Essay," *Studies in the Literary Imagination,* 10 (Fall 1977): 17–27.

Pocock, J. G. A. *The Ancient Constitution and the Feudal Law: A Study of English Historical Thought in the Seventeenth Century,* revised edition. Cambridge: Cambridge University Press, 1967.

Pooley, Roger. *English Prose of the Seventeenth Century 1590–1700.* London & New York: Longman, 1992.

Potter, Lois. *Secret Rites and Secret Writing: Royalist Literature 1641–1660.* Cambridge: Cambridge University Press, 1990.

Praz, Mario. *Studies in Seventeenth-Century Imagery,* 2 volumes, second edition, enlarged. Rome: Edizioni di storia e letterature, 1964, 1974.

Ricks, Christopher, ed. *English Poetry and Prose, 1540–1674.* London: Barrie & Jenkins, 1970.

Rivers, Isabel. *Classical and Christian Ideas in English Renaissance Poetry: A Students' Guide.* London & Boston: Allen & Unwin, 1979.

Ross, Malcolm M. *Poetry and Dogma: The Transfiguration of Eucharist Symbols in Seventeenth Century English Poetry.* New Brunswick, N.J.: Rutgers University Press, 1954.

Røstvig, Maren-Sofie. *The Happy Man: Studies in the Metamorphoses of a Classical Ideal,* 2 volumes, revised edition. Oslo: Norwegian Universities Press, 1962, 1971.

Russell, Conrad. *The Causes of the English Civil War.* Oxford: Clarendon Press, 1990.

Russell. *The Crisis of Parliaments: English History 1509–1660.* London & New York: Oxford University Press, 1971.

Salmon, Vivian. "Early Seventeenth-Century Punctuation as a Guide to Sentence Structure," *Review of English Studies,* 13 (November 1962): 347–360.

Salzman, Paul. *English Prose Fiction, 1558–1700: A Critical History.* Oxford: Clarendon Press, 1985.

Salzman, ed. *An Anthology of Seventeenth-Century Fiction.* Oxford University Press, 1991.

Sasek, Lawrence. *The Literary Temper of the English Puritans.* Baton Rouge: Louisiana State University Press, 1961.

Sharp, Robert L. *From Donne to Dryden: The Revolt against Metaphysical Poetry.* Chapel Hill: University of North Carolina Press, 1940.

Sharpe, Kevin. *Criticism and Compliment: The Politics of Literature in the England of Charles I.* Cambridge: Cambridge University Press, 1987.

Sharpe. *The Personal Rule of Charles I.* New Haven & London: Yale University Press, 1992.

Sharpe and Steven N. Zwicker, eds. *Politics of Discourse: The Literature and History of Seventeenth-Century England.* Berkeley: University of California Press, 1987.

Shawcross, John T. *Intentionality and the New Traditionalism: Some Liminal Means to Literary Revisionism.* University Park: Pennsylvania State University Press, 1991.

Shuger, Debora K. *Sacred Rhetoric: The Christian Grand Style in the English Renaissance.* Princeton: Princeton University Press, 1988.

Skerpan, Elizabeth. *The Rhetoric of Politics in the English Revolution, 1642–1660.* Columbia: University of Missouri Press, 1992.

Slater, Miriam. *Family Life in the Seventeenth Century: The Verneys of Claydon House.* London: Routledge & Kegan Paul, 1984.

Smith, A. J. *Metaphysical Wit.* Cambridge & New York: Cambridge University Press, 1991.

Smith, Nigel. *Perfection Proclaimed: Language and Literature in English Radical Religion 1640–1660.* Oxford: Clarendon Press, 1989.

Sommerville, J. P. *Politics and Ideology in England, 1603–1640.* London & New York: Longman, 1986.

Spingarn, J. E., ed. *Critical Essays of the Seventeenth Century,* 3 volumes. Bloomington: Indiana University Press, 1957.

Spufford, Margaret. *Contrasting Communities: English Villagers in the Sixteenth and Seventeenth Centuries.* Cambridge: Cambridge University Press, 1974.

Spufford. *Small Books and Pleasant Histories: Popular Fiction and Its Readership in Seventeenth-Century England.* Cambridge: Cambridge University Press, 1981; Athens: University of Georgia Press, 1982.

Stanwood, P. G. *The Sempiternal Season: Studies in Seventeenth-Century Devotional Writing.* New York, San Francisco & Bern: Peter Lang, 1992.

Stapleton, Lawrence. *The Elected Circle: Studies in the Art of Prose.* Princeton: Princeton University Press, 1973.

Stauffer, Donald A. *English Biography before 1700.* Cambridge, Mass.: Harvard University Press, 1930.

Steadman, John M. *The Hill and the Labyrinth: Discourse and Certitude in Milton and His Near-Contemporaries.* Berkeley, Los Angeles & London: University of California Press, 1984.

Stedmond, J. M. "English Prose of the Seventeenth-Century," *Dalhousie Review,* 30 (1950): 269–278.

Stewart, Stanley. *The Enclosed Garden: The Tradition and the Image in Seventeenth-Century Poetry.* Madison: University of Wisconsin Press, 1966.

Stone, Lawrence. *The Causes of the English Revolution, 1529–1642.* New York: Harper & Row, 1972.

Stone. *The Crisis of the Aristocracy, 1558–1641.* Oxford: Clarendon Press, 1965.

Stone. *The Family, Sex and Marriage in England, 1500–1800.* New York: Harper & Row, 1977.

Stranks, Charles J. *Anglican Devotion: Studies in the Spiritual Life of the Church of England between the Reformation and the Oxford Movement.* London: SCM Press, 1961.

Summers, Claude, and Pebworth, eds. *"The Muses Common-Weale": Poetry and Politics in the Seventeenth Century.* Columbia: University of Missouri Press, 1988.

Swardson, Harold Roland. *Poetry and the Fountain of Light: Observations on the Conflict between Christian and Classical Traditions in Seventeenth-Century Poetry.* Columbia: University of Missouri Press, 1962; London: Allen & Unwin, 1962.

Tayler, Edward William. *Nature and Art in Renaissance Literature.* New York: Columbia University Press, 1964.

Thirsk, Joan. *Economic Policy and Projects: The Development of a Consumer Society in Early Modern England.* Oxford: Clarendon Press, 1978.

Thomas, P. W. "Two Cultures? Court and Country under Charles I," in *The Origins of the English Civil War,* edited by Russell. New York: Barnes & Noble, 1973, pp. 168–193.

Thompson, Elbert N. S. *The Seventeenth-Century English Essay.* University of Iowa Studies: Humanistic Studies, volume 3, no. 3. Iowa City: University of Iowa, 1926.

Turner, James Grantham. *One Flesh: Paradisal Marriage and Sexual Relations in the Age of Milton.* Oxford: Clarendon Press, 1987.

Turner. *The Politics of Landscape: Rural Scenery and Society in English Poetry. 1630–1660.* Cambridge, Mass.: Harvard University Press, 1979.

Tyacke, Nicholas. *Anti-Calvinists: The Rise of English Arminianism c. 1590–1640.* Oxford: Clarendon Press, 1987.

Tyacke. "Puritanism, Arminianism and Counter-Revolution," in *The Origins of the English Civil War,* edited by Russell. New York: Barnes & Noble, 1973, pp. 119–143.

Vickers, Brian. *Classical Rhetoric in English Poetry.* London: Macmillan / New York: St. Martin's Press, 1970.

Walzer, Michael. *The Revolution of the Saints: A Study in the Origin of Radical Politics.* Cambridge, Mass.: Harvard University Press, 1965; London: Weidenfeld & Nicolson, 1966.

Watkins, Owen C. *The Puritan Experience: Studies in Spiritual Autobiography.* New York: Schocken, 1972; London: Routledge & Kegan Paul, 1972.

Webber, Joan. *The Eloguent "I": Style and Self in Seventeenth-Century Prose.* Madison: University of Wisconsin Press, 1968.

Wedgwood, C. V. *Poetry and Politics under the Stuarts.* Cambridge: Cambridge University Press, 1960.

Wedgwood. *Seventeenth-Century English Literature,* second edition. London: Oxford University Press, 1950.

White, Helen C. *The Metaphysical Poets: A Study in Religious Experience.* New York: Macmillan, 1936.

Wilding, Michael. *Dragon's Teeth: Literature in the English Revolution.* Oxford: Clarendon Press, 1987.

Willey, Basil. *The Seventeenth-Century Background: Studies in the Thought of the Age in Relation to Poetry and Religion.* London: Chatto & Windus, 1934.

Williamson, George. *The Senecan Amble: A Study in Prose Form from Bacon to Collier.* Chicago: University of Chicago Press, 1951; London: Faber & Faber, 1951.

Wilson, F. P. *Elizabethan and Jacobean.* Oxford: Clarendon Press, 1945.

Wilson. *Seventeenth Century Prose: Five Lectures.* Berkeley: University of California Press, 1960.

Wilson, Katharina M., and Frank J. Warnke, eds. *Women Writers of the Seventeenth Century.* Athens: University of Georgia Press, 1989.

Wood, Anthony à. *Athenæ Oxonienses . . . A New Edition, with Additions, and a Continuation by Philip Bliss,* 4 volumes. London: Printed for F. C. & J. Rivington [etc.], 1813–1820.

Wormald, B. H. G. *Clarendon: Politics, History & Religion, 1640–1660.* Cambridge: Cambridge University Press, 1951.

Contributors

Katherine Acheson ....*University of Toronto*
Raymond A. Anselment ....*University of Connecticut*
Moira P. Baker ....*Radford University*
John Channing Briggs ....*University of California, Riverside*
Ronald Corthell ....*Kent State University*
Barbara Hart Dixon ....*Purdue University*
Charles A. S. Ernst ....*Hilbert College*
Margaret J. M. Ezell ....*Texas A&M University*
Catherine C. Gannon ....*California State University, San Bernardino*
John R. Glenn ....*Tampa, Florida*
Eugene D. Hill ....*Mount Holyoke College*
Janice Knight ....*University of Chicago*
Clayton D. Lein ....*Purdue University*
Anthony Low ....*New York University*
Bruce McIver .... *Santa Barbara, California*
Alan T. McKenzie ....*Purdue University*
Edmund Miller.............................*C. W. Post Campus, Long Island University*
Trevor A. Owen ....*Potomac State College of West Virginia University*
Renée Pigeon......................................*California State University, San Bernardino*
Michael W. Price ....*Purdue University*
Craig M. Rustici ....*Hofstra University*
Florence Sandler ....*University of Puget Sound*
Sharon Cadman Seelig ....*Smith College*
Elizabeth Skerpan....................................*Southwest Texas State University*
P. G. Stanwood...*University of British Columbia*
Keith W. F. Stavely..*Cambridge, Massachusetts*
Frederick Waage ....*East Tennessee State University*
Alan R. Young ....*Acadia University*

Cumulative Index

Dictionary of Literary Biography, Volumes 1-151
Dictionary of Literary Biography Yearbook, 1980-1993
Dictionary of Literary Biography Documentary Series, Volumes 1-12

Cumulative Index

DLB before number: *Dictionary of Literary Biography,* Volumes 1-151
Y before number: *Dictionary of Literary Biography Yearbook,* 1980-1993
DS before number: *Dictionary of Literary Biography Documentary Series,* Volumes 1-12

A

Abbey Press DLB-49

The Abbey Theatre and Irish Drama,
   1900-1945 ....DLB-10

Abbot, Willis J. 1863-1934 ....DLB-29

Abbott, Jacob 1803-1879 ....DLB-1

Abbott, Lee K. 1947- DLB-130

Abbott, Lyman 1835-1922 ....DLB-79

Abbott, Robert S. 1868-1940 ....DLB-29, 91

Abelard, Peter circa 1079-1142 .....DLB-115

Abelard-Schuman DLB-46

Abell, Arunah S. 1806-1888 ....DLB-43

Abercrombie, Lascelles 1881-1938 ...DLB-19

Aberdeen University Press
   Limited DLB-106

Abish, Walter 1931- DLB-130

Ablesimov, Aleksandr Onisimovich
   1742-1783 ....DLB-150

Abrahams, Peter 1919- DLB-117

Abrams, M. H. 1912- DLB-67

Abrogans circa 790-800 ....DLB-148

Abse, Dannie 1923- DLB-27

Academy Chicago Publishers DLB-46

Accrocca, Elio Filippo 1923- DLB-128

Ace Books DLB-46

Achebe, Chinua 1930- DLB-117

Achtenberg, Herbert 1938- DLB-124

Ackerman, Diane 1948- DLB-120

Acorn, Milton 1923-1986 ....DLB-53

Acosta, Oscar Zeta 1935?- DLB-82

Actors Theatre of Louisville DLB-7

Adair, James 1709?-1783? DLB-30

Adam, Graeme Mercer 1839-1912 ...DLB-99

Adame, Leonard 1947- DLB-82

Adamic, Louis 1898-1951 ....DLB-9

Adams, Alice 1926- Y-86

Adams, Brooks 1848-1927 ....DLB-47

Adams, Charles Francis, Jr.
   1835-1915 ....DLB-47

Adams, Douglas 1952- Y-83

Adams, Franklin P. 1881-1960 .....DLB-29

Adams, Henry 1838-1918 ......DLB-12, 47

Adams, Herbert Baxter 1850-1901 ...DLB-47

Adams, J. S. and C.
   [publishing house] DLB-49

Adams, James Truslow 1878-1949 ...DLB-17

Adams, John 1735-1826 ....DLB-31

Adams, John Quincy 1767-1848 .....DLB-37

Adams, Léonie 1899-1988 ....DLB-48

Adams, Levi 1802-1832 ....DLB-99

Adams, Samuel 1722-1803 ......DLB-31, 43

Adams, Thomas
   1582 or 1583-1652 ....DLB-151

Adams, William Taylor 1822-1897 ..DLB-42

Adamson, Sir John 1867-1950 ......DLB-98

Adcock, Arthur St. John
   1864-1930 ....DLB-135

Adcock, Betty 1938- DLB-105

Adcock, Betty, Certain Gifts DLB-105

Adcock, Fleur 1934- DLB-40

Addison, Joseph 1672-1719 ....DLB-101

Ade, George 1866-1944 ....DLB-11, 25

Adeler, Max (see Clark, Charles Heber)

Adonias Filho 1915-1990 ....DLB-145

Advance Publishing Company DLB-49

AE 1867-1935 ....DLB-19

Ælfric circa 955-circa 1010 ....DLB-146

Aesthetic Poetry (1873), by
   Walter Pater DLB-35

After Dinner Opera Company Y-92

Afro-American Literary Critics:
   An Introduction DLB-33

Agassiz, Jean Louis Rodolphe
   1807-1873 ....DLB-1

Agee, James 1909-1955 ....DLB-2, 26

The Agee Legacy: A Conference at
   the University of Tennessee
   at Knoxville Y-89

Aguilera Malta, Demetrio
   1909-1981 ....DLB-145

Ai 1947- DLB-120

Aichinger, Ilse 1921- DLB-85

Aidoo, Ama Ata 1942- DLB-117

Aiken, Conrad 1889-1973 ....DLB-9, 45, 102

Aikin, Lucy 1781-1864 ....DLB-144

Ainsworth, William Harrison
   1805-1882 ....DLB-21

Aitken, George A. 1860-1917 ......DLB-149

Aitken, Robert [publishing house] ...DLB-49

Akenside, Mark 1721-1770 ....DLB-109

Akins, Zoë 1886-1958 ....DLB-26

Alabaster, William 1568-1640 ......DLB-132

Alain-Fournier 1886-1914 ....DLB-65

Alarcón, Francisco X. 1954- DLB-122

Alba, Nanina 1915-1968 ....DLB-41

Albee, Edward 1928- DLB-7

Albert the Great circa 1200-1280 ...DLB-115

Alberti, Rafael 1902- DLB-108

Alcott, Amos Bronson 1799-1888 .....DLB-1

Alcott, Louisa May
   1832-1888 ....DLB-1, 42, 79

Alcott, William Andrus 1798-1859 ....DLB-1

Alcuin circa 732-804 ....DLB-148

Alden, Henry Mills 1836-1919 ......DLB-79

Alden, Isabella 1841-1930 ....DLB-42

Alden, John B. [publishing house] DLB-49

Alden, Beardsley and Company DLB-49

Aldington, Richard
   1892-1962 ....DLB-20, 36, 100, 149

Aldis, Dorothy 1896-1966 ....DLB-22

Aldiss, Brian W. 1925- DLB-14

I

J

Q

S

T

Y

Z

Cumulative Index

ISBN 0-8103-5712-7

(Continued from front endsheets)

Documentary Series